Sir John Lavery

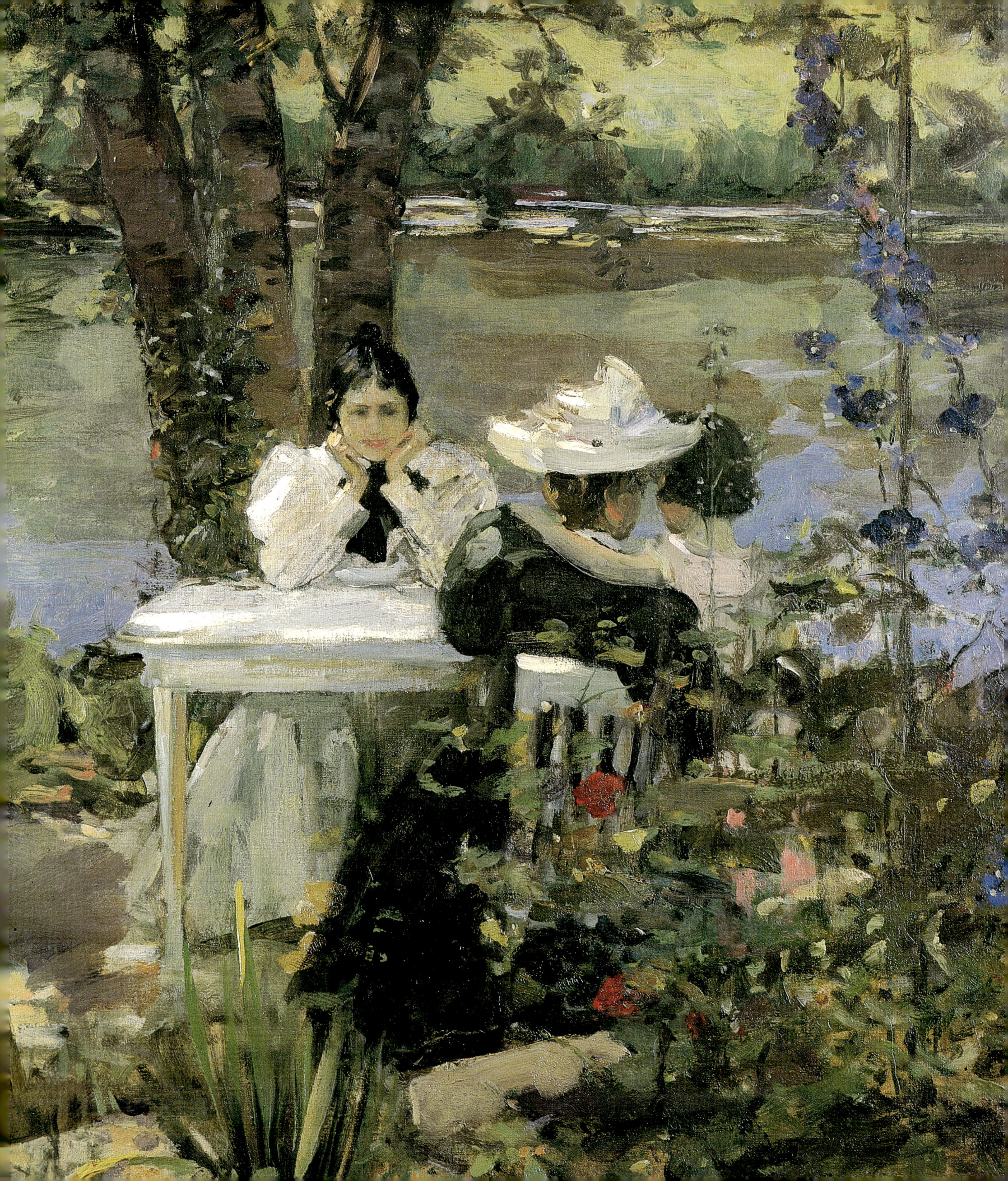

Sir John Lavery

KENNETH McCONKEY

CANONGATE PRESS EDINBURGH

In memory of Elizabeth McConkey and Irwin Thompson Wilson

First published in Great Britain in 1993 by
Canongate Press Ltd, 14 Frederick Street, Edinburgh

ISBN 0 86241 440 7

The publisher acknowledges subsidy from the Scottish Arts Council towards the publication of this volume

British Library Cataloguing in Publication Data
A catalogue record for this book is available on request from the British Library

Design: Caroline Johnston
Typeset in Monophoto Garamond by Servis Filmsetting Ltd, Manchester
Printed and bound in Singapore by Toppan Pte

frontispiece:
A Garden in France, 1898 (detail)
(private collection, courtesy Pyms Gallery, London)

Contents

Acknowledgements

This monograph on the work of Sir John Lavery was conceived in 1985 in the wake of a major exhibition on the artist's work, jointly mounted by the Fine Art Society and the Ulster Museum, Belfast. With the enormous advantage of having selected and catalogued that exhibition behind me, the task of providing a new biography and appraisal of Lavery's career as a painter seemed simple. It was only, however, as a result of the public consciousness-raising for which the exhibition was responsible, that I was able to hear of many other works which had not been available to me at the time of the selection. Even to this day, the possibility of new discovery remains rich. As the final revised manuscript goes to press, I have for instance been given the opportunity to study around fifty newly discovered letters in a private collection in Ireland. Two weeks prior to completion, a research trip to Scotland revealed four important works which had never been seen before. Between 1985 and 1993, many 'new' works have appeared in the salerooms or in dealers' galleries. Previously unlocated private collections have come to light and the search for documented but 'lost' works continues. Now in 1993 I have the edge-pieces and main motifs of a jig-saw which, as yet remains incomplete.

Lavery was enormously prolific. Lady Sempill, the painter's granddaughter, an unfailing supporter of this project, tells me that he painted virtually every day of his life even into his old age. Her recollections and those of the late Alice Gwynn, the artist's step-daughter, have been an invaluable starting point. I have profitted from reading the notes of the late Stuart Chant-Sempill, a friend affectionately remembered. The Hon. Frances Russell, Ian Chant-Sempill, and Nicola Strauss have all contributed their enthusiasm for their great-grandfather's work.

I am grateful to the late Mrs Claire Downing, granddaughter of Lavery's cousin Kate, with whom constant contact was maintained during the last forty years of the painter's life. The late Mrs Fairfax-Cholmeley gave me detailed information concerning her sister, Katherine Fitz Gerald, Lavery's last secretary, and access to the collections of her daughters, Katherine, Elizabeth and Geraldine. Many other private collectors whose parents and grandparents were painted by Lavery have supplied information. In this context I am particularly grateful to Lady Polwarth and Sheriff Harold Ford. Numerous more recent Lavery collectors have given me access to their pictures—many of them wishing to remain anonymous.

I am specially indebted to the staffs of the Ulster Museum and the Fine Art Society for giving me the opportunity of staging the exhibition in 1984. Edward Hickey, Brian Kennedy and Anne Stewart in Belfast and Andrew McIntosh Patrick and Peyton Skipwith in London worked tirelessly on behalf of the show and have maintained their interest in the Lavery monograph. To these should be added the staff of the National Gallery of Ireland, which hosted its final venue. Numerous other curators in Great Britain and Ireland have given generously of their time in unearthing Lavery paintings at my request. Some, like Martin Hopkinson of the Hunterian Art Gallery and Edward Morris of the Walker Art Gallery have brought obscure but important references to my attention. In this respect my thanks are also due to the staffs of the Tate Gallery Archive, Trinity College Library, Dublin, Glasgow University Library, the Mitchell Library, Glasgow, the National Library of Scotland, Edinburgh, Belfast City Reference Library and Record Office and the Linenhall Library, Belfast.

Janet Green, Susan Kent and Susie Pollen of Sotheby's, Rachel Hidderley and Jonathon Horwich of Christie's and James James-Crook of Phillips have given me privileged access to pictures passing through the salerooms. Roger Billcliffe, Laurence Black, James Gorry, Richard Green, Irving Grose, William R. Hardie, Alan and Mary Hobart, Edward King, Amanda Kavanagh, Barclay Lennie, Andrew McIntosh Patrick, Ewan Mundy, Caroline Simon, Ailsa Tanner and Peyton Skipwith have all brought pictures to my attention. Many others have written to me in recent years making me aware of paintings in their possession. In the majority of cases they do not wish to be named, but have graciously permitted their pictures to be reproduced.

There have been two principal areas of scholarly endeavour which, in recent years have had a significant impact upon my research on Lavery. In 1968, with William Buchanan's exhibition, 'The Glasgow Boys', attention began to be focussed upon the work of west of Scotland painters who were early exponents of an Impressionistic style. Other shows involving works by Lavery followed and in 1971 a small retrospective was staged by Spink and Son, London. In 1983 the Glasgow period was further examined in a thesis by David Scruton which resulted in an exhibition, 'John Lavery, the early career, 1880—1895', staged at the Crawford Art Centre, University of St Andrews. Throughout these years Lavery has been represented in many surveys of British painting, especially those devoted to the Glasgow School. His place in the School was considered by Roger Billcliffe in *The Glasgow Boys* (1985). and in Scottish painting generally in Duncan MacMillan's *Scottish Art 1460—1990* (1990). All of these accounts take Lavery to the point when, in 1896 he moved to London.

A second area of interest lies in Ireland, where, following Hugh Lane's epoch-making exhibition of Irish Art at the Guildhall in 1904, Lavery began to rediscover his Irish roots. In this he was aided by his Irish-American wife, Hazel, herself the object of recent research in a thesis by Sinead Nic Cumhaill at the National University, Dublin. Lavery's years as a student in France have been studied in the context of other Irish expatriates by Julian Campbell in a thesis submitted at Trinity College, Dublin in 1980 and in an exhibition of the work of 'Irish Impressionists' in 1984.

None of these, however, has considered the full range of Lavery's work. In isolated articles I have tackled his portraiture and his Grez and Tangier periods. An inveterate traveller and sightseer he is, at times, difficult to keep up with, and in many cases, evidence of his visit to a particular location exists only in surviving paintings. Feeling lame-footed at the time of the Ulster Museum exhibition in 1984, I declared that, aesthetic questions apart, the intense energy expended in Lavery's long career leaves those who try to track his movements, exhausted. Recharged, however, by the sight of over one hundred works, hung with great sensitivity by Anne Stewart, I launched into the present study.

In addition to those scholars, curators, dealers and collectors who have generously given access to unique information and untraced pictures, I am extremely grateful to an anonymous sponsor who came forward at a late stage in its preparation to support this book. I have been assisted in transferring the manuscript to disc by Dawn Fozzard and Carol Kingston. My brother George carried out invaluable research for me in Ireland—in this he has shown more potential as an historian that I ever could as an engineer. At the raw stage, however, when Lavery was too complicated for me to unravel, my wife Annette transformed reams of pencilled scribble into typescript.

Kenneth McConkey
April 1993

Introduction

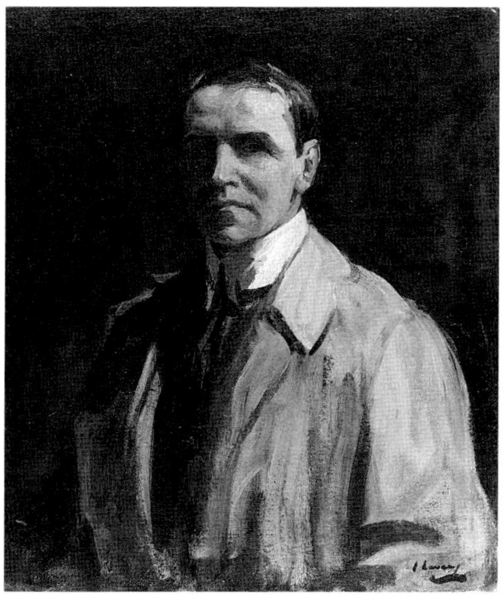

Self-Portrait, *c.*1905, 30 × 25
(private collection)

One of the minor legacies of the Victorian era is contained in the lives of its artists. At the turn of the century, major publications of the 'Life and Works' type set out to record the glowing careers of painters such as Millais, Leighton, Burne-Jones and Whistler. These two-volume tomes combine the desire for an accurate record with a sympathetic response to a reputation commonly acknowledged. The descent into hagiography seems, at times, appropriate—in citing major works, a language of celebration evolved. Aesthetic education and the notation of facts were tempered with hero-worship.

The generation which followed these eminent Victorians missed out on hagiography. Born in the 1850s and 1860s, it was too old to die ingloriously in the trenches and, living on into the inter-war period, its leaders, Clausen, Forbes, Steer, La Thangue, Sickert, Guthrie and Lavery were eclipsed by the fast-flowing mainstream of European modernism. By the time they were ripe for celebration, the world had moved on. They supported one another in these years—Clausen writing about La Thangue after his death and Lavery delivering the oration at the Sir James Guthrie Memorial Exhibition in 1932. However, the Edwardian era, viewed through a gauze of mustard gas and shelled copses, seemed further removed from the present of the 1930s than the deep mythical past of the middle ages. Lavery's world in particular, filled with social butterflies, and guided by rococo notions of beauty, seemed dated in this more egalitarian age. In writing his *Life of a Painter*, published in 1940, he made undeclared assumptions about what he thought his reader might wish to read. With no advocate, he inclined to present himself as an anti-hero; as someone whose life consisted of a series of fortuitous accidents and amusing events, set against great historical moments to which his contribution was merely that of artist-reporter. In his early eighties, vague about dates and sequences, he substituted a series of anecdotes in place of chronology. He was unsystematic and inaccurate and behaved as if the thing which gave him celebrity—his painting—was only of peripheral interest. This layer of confusion adds to the difficulties of a modern appraisal.

During his lifetime, Lavery was feted by others. He was the subject of many critical reviews in the press and catalogues of his solo exhibitions were introduced by such eminent supporters as R. B. Cunninghame Graham and Winston Churchill. In 1911 a monograph, *John Lavery and his Work*, making use of the new possibility of accurate colour reproduction, was published by Walter Shaw Sparrow. The value of this work lies in its rich Edwardian prose and in the lists of exhibited works which form its appendices. It is, however, as thoroughly of its time as *The Life of a Painter*.

Even today there are circumstances which make the publication of a monograph problematic—combining as it does, a modern appraisal of the work with an updated and, hopefully, more accurate biography. Lavery's work as a

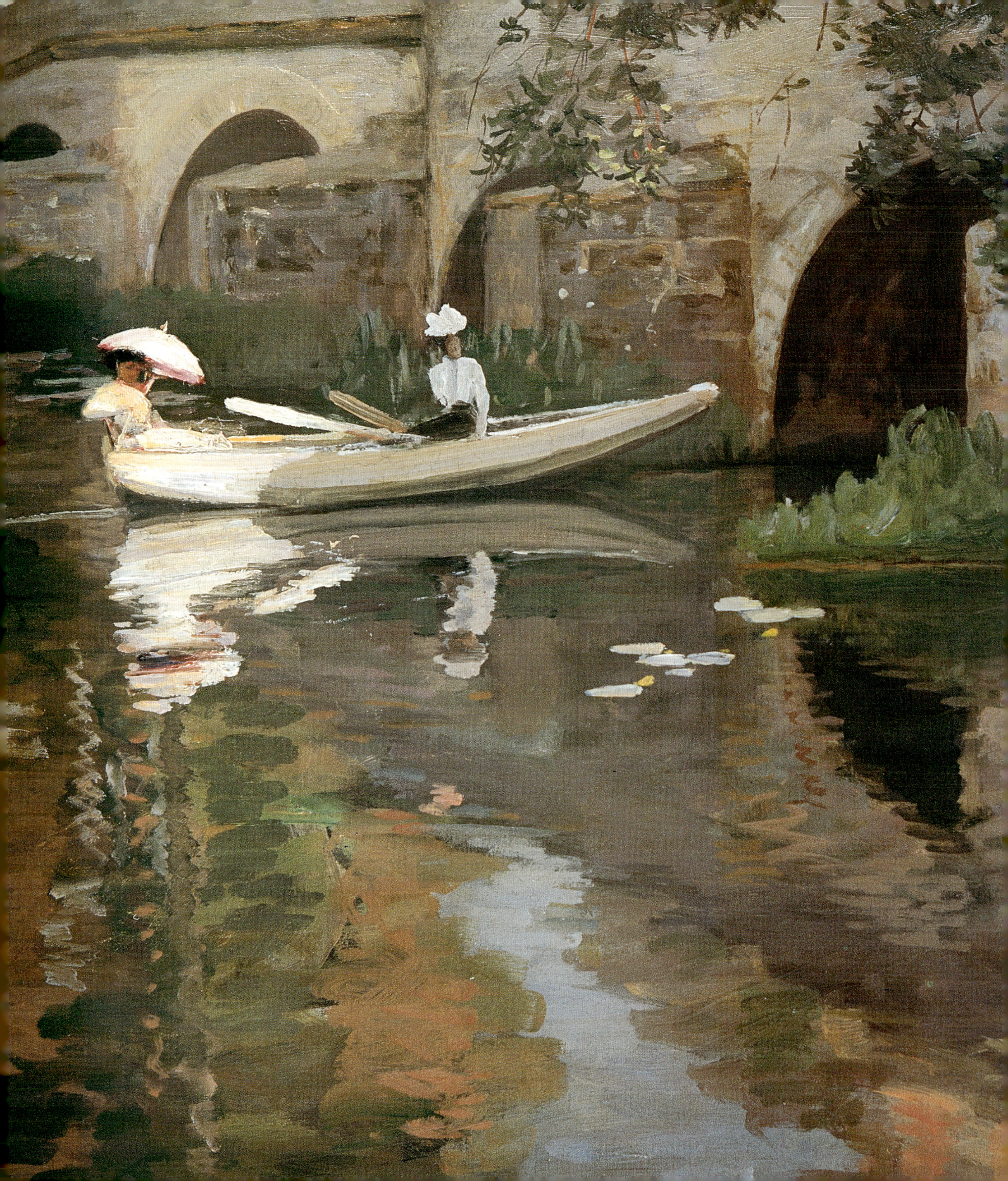

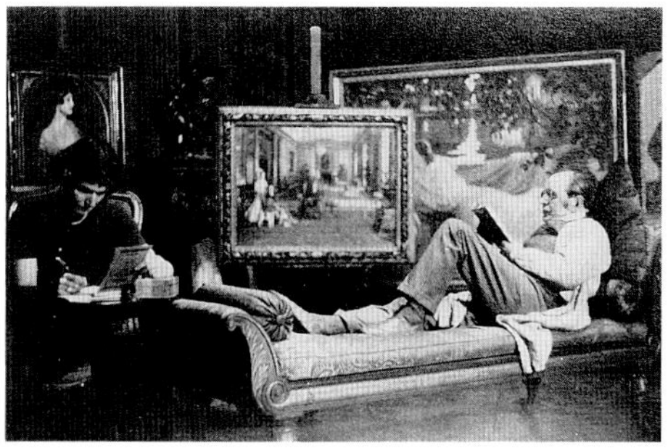

Sir John Lavery at Cromwell Place with Alice McEnery, *c.*1935

portrait painter, for instance, was contiguous with that of the mainstream of Edwardian portraiture in its reassessment of the great traditions of Van Dyck, Velasquez, Reynolds and Gainsborough. We have to accept that the day-to-day currency of contemporary criticism in the Edwardian era can be only partially understood and the impulses and motivations to which the paintings bear witness can never be completely reconstructed. In a real sense, Shaw Sparrow and Lavery himself, for all their deficiencies are more authentic witnesses.

There are also difficulties which are unique to our own age. Art history places less emphasis upon the monograph than it used to. The traditional skills involved in noting stylistic development and charting patterns of influence are challenged by attacks upon the integrity and singularity of the artist/author. Today the history of art is less of a spectacle of universally applauded masters, and painters like Lavery disappear into their time. In an earlier study of Edwardian portraiture, I stressed the significance of the broad phenomenon submerging central figures like Lavery in favour of the study of patterns of patronage, taste and fashion. His isolation here presupposes the claim for a value greater than that of many of his fellow portraitists.

In any case, classifying Lavery as an Edwardian portraitist is a huge over-simplification. His career began in the 1880s in Glasgow where *The Tennis Party* (see Plate 45) was rightly regarded by his fellow artists as a work fit to claim international attention. At the International Exhibition in Glasgow in 1888 Lavery was given the first of a number of commissions as a reporter of events and it was this which led him into portraiture. Throughout the rest of his career, however, portraits occupied only a small part of his production. There was nevertheless, an unbroken continuity between the on-the-spot sketcher and the manager of well-organised studio sittings. Lavery believed simply that the artist should be able to paint anything, anywhere. No challenge, in these terms, was too great. This visual reporter's instinct led him into some extraordinary situations. The risks to life and limb as well as to the success of the picture were part of the process. As a whole, the Lavery *oeuvre* is one of astonishing variety. Its range and richness challenges the historian with many kinds of specialism. On the whole, painters today do not set out to carry this kind of report. Few could, or would wish to lay claim to Lavery's ambition. Attitudes to the medium have changed.

Nevertheless, the past is now perceived as being as potentially rich and confusing as the present. The simplified relay-race of the great moderns is increasingly discredited. In this sense, a monograph upon a less well-known painter of the period of Van Gogh and Picasso can only add to the growing literature which will permit tomorrow's polymath art historian to plot a wholescale revision of the period covered by Lavery's life. For the historian, interested more generally in the period, in the events and personalities, there is the exciting possibility that that which he or she has tried to imagine, was witnessed by a painter.

Opposite
The Bridge at Grez, *c.*1900 (detail)
(The Ulster Museum, Belfast)

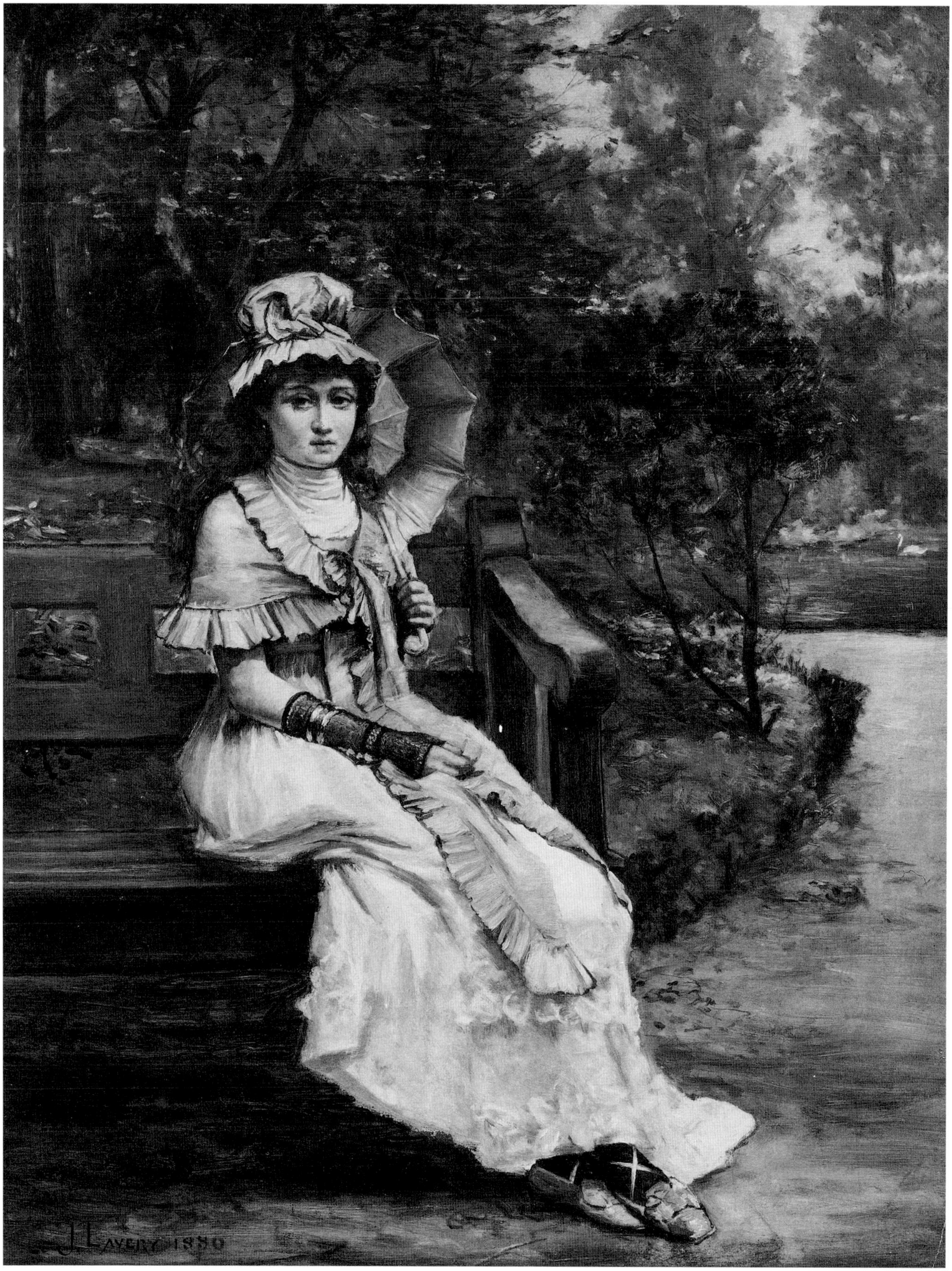

7 *Her First Disappointment*, 1880,
32 × 25 (private collection)

1 'The Back of the Wood'

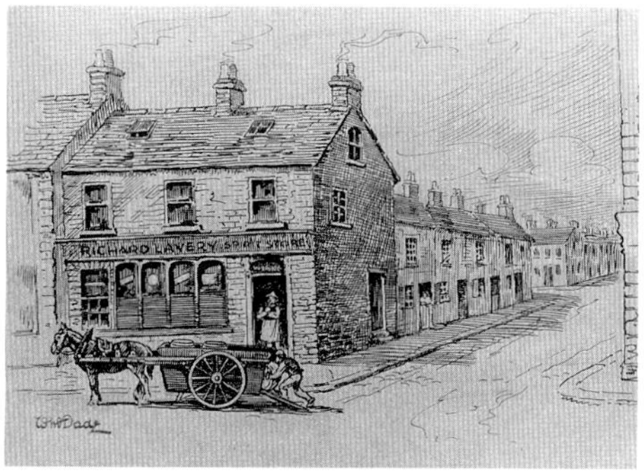

1 The Lavery public house in North Queen's Street 8 × 11 (illus. W. Dade)

In his autobiography, published shortly before his death at the beginning of 1941, John Lavery emphasised the thoughts and feelings of an orphaned child in mid-century Ulster. Although vaguely conscious of sectarian divisions—he recalled the terror of protestant 'Lambeg' drummers on the twelfth of July—the noise of Irish history passed him by. Belfast, his birthplace, was a growing industrial centre, a linen town poised for the rapid expansion which was to occur with the development of the ship-building industry. His family, like many, had recently moved into the city. For more than a century Laverys had been known on the southern shores of Lough Neagh in the lower reaches of the river Bann.[1] Henry Lavery, the painter's father, was the youngest of four sons. After his marriage to Mary Donnelly, a native of Armagh, he was unwilling to remain on the land and moved to Belfast to set up shop as a publican in the catholic enclave of North Queen's Street. The humble two-storey public house was almost facing St Patrick's Church where John Lavery was christened by Father George Conway on 26 March 1856. 'To save explanations when asked', Lavery, in later years gave his birthday as St Patrick's Day.[2]

His upbringing was marked with tragedy. Although there is evidence Lavery's father was reasonably well off at the time of his birth, during the next three years the wine and spirit trade in North Queen's Street failed.[3] Henry Lavery booked passage to New York, hoping for better times. When established in the new world, he intended to send for his wife and children. He set sail from Liverpool on the clipper, *Pomona* on 27 April 1859 as one of 372 passengers. Almost immediately the ship was thrown off course by gales in the Irish Sea and, on 29 April, it foundered on a well-charted sand bank nine miles from the coast of Wexford.[4] After twelve hours of pumping, the ship broke up and 386 lives were lost, including that of Henry Lavery. Of the twenty-three survivors, the majority were crewmen who swiftly dispersed upon reaching the shore. *The Times*, amidst allegations of drunkenness and negligence, called for an admiralty inquiry.[5] Sometime later, Henry Lavery's body was washed ashore and was identified by Edward Byrne, his brother's brother-in-law. Within three months of this tragic event, for reasons unknown to the painter, his mother also died, leaving him, his elder brother Henry, and his sister Jane, orphaned. The children were split up amongst other members of the family, and John Lavery was consigned to his uncle and aunt, Edward and Rose Lavery; his elder brother Henry went to aunt Rose's father and Jane to Richard Lavery, another uncle who was also a publican.[6] The painter recalled that his uncle Edward was a genial farmer whose 'mouth broke into a smile at the slightest provocation'.[7] His aunt, the daughter of a doctor, was acutely conscious of her social position and wore 'the most striking crinolines' and drove 'the smartest jaunting car in the region'.[8] The farm which was now his home, bore the prosaic title, 'The Back of the Wood', despite the fact that contemporary photographs show it to be a substantial Georgian or Regency house. Aunt Rose took early steps to change the name to 'Train View' when railways were laid in the area.

Lavery remembered little of his early days except random incidents which indicate that his childhood was not one of particular discomfort. The farmhands made much of him as 'the poor wee orphan', he attended the local protestant school and he passed his summers roaming the woods around Moira and '. . . lying on the ground looking up through the leaves and drinking in the wondrous colours'.[9] Then, inexplicably, at the age of ten, he was dispatched to the home of a rich cousin of Rose Lavery's who owned a pawn shop at Saltcoats in Ayrshire. The young Lavery accepted his new surroundings with equanimity and enjoyed the local amusements like the travelling theatres. He was at first infatuated by an itinerant actress and then, at the age of thirteen, by a 'loose' blonde-haired girl called Mary Ann. He helped his brother Henry to desert from the naval training ship to which he had been sent by aunt Rose's father and, eventually following his brother's example, at the age of fifteen, he ran away to Glasgow. At first he took lodgings, but when his money ran out, he slept rough on Glasgow Green. Half starved he was returned to Saltcoats and later sent back to 'Train View'. Two further years of rural existence followed.

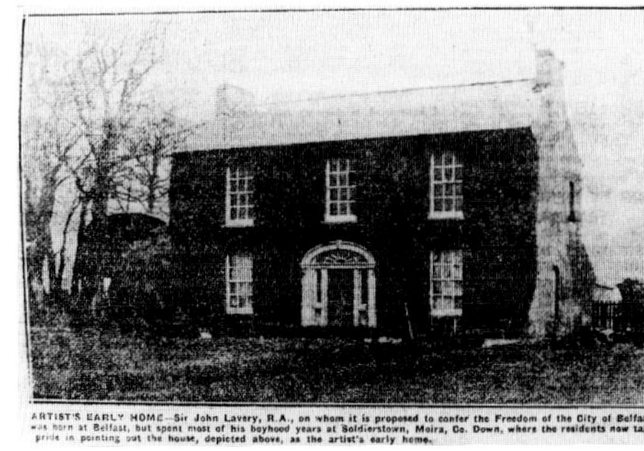

2 'The Back of the Wood', Moira, Co. Down, *c.*1930 (source unknown)

Walter Shaw Sparrow, stressing the birthright of painters like Millet, marvelled at the fact that this return to a rural heritage had so little effect upon Lavery.[10] It did however introduce him to a local grocer who was idolised for his drawing skills, but this was not to be a significant encounter. Being anxious to make his fortune Lavery eventually succeeded in persuading his uncle Edward that a good job as a clerk in the Mineral Department of the Glasgow and South Western Railway awaited him if only he could return to the city of his adoption. At length, Edward Lavery invested £5 in his errant nephew and sent him off to the packet boat bound for Ardrossan. After feasting and taking his Belfast cousins to the theatre and other entertainments, John Lavery found himself back in Glasgow with the princely sum of two shillings and sixpence! He did obtain a job as a railway clerk, but he stuck this hum-drum existence for only a month. There followed a position as a pawn-broker's assistant at Hamilton, from which he was dismissed for failing to appear for work one Monday morning. He then returned to Glasgow penniless, where he ended up in a doss-house amongst navvy-types of all ages: 'The only light came from the fire, and in distant corners I could discern shadowy forms sprawling on the floor seeking rest, while an extra loud snore would occasionally eclipse the conversation round the fire. The squalor was sickening . . .'[11]

To extricate himself from the horror of the doss-house, he briefly considered joining the army, but was disqualified on account of his age.[12] When he heard of these misadventures, Lavery's uncle demanded his return to Saltcoats and at this point, restored to a stable environment, the boy began to take a serious interest in drawing. He gained proficiency in copying from engravings, then answered an advertisement in *The Glasgow Herald* for an apprentice retoucher to the photographer, MacNair. He succeeded in obtaining the post. A three-year contract was drawn up for £10, £15 and £20 per annum, with his living expenses

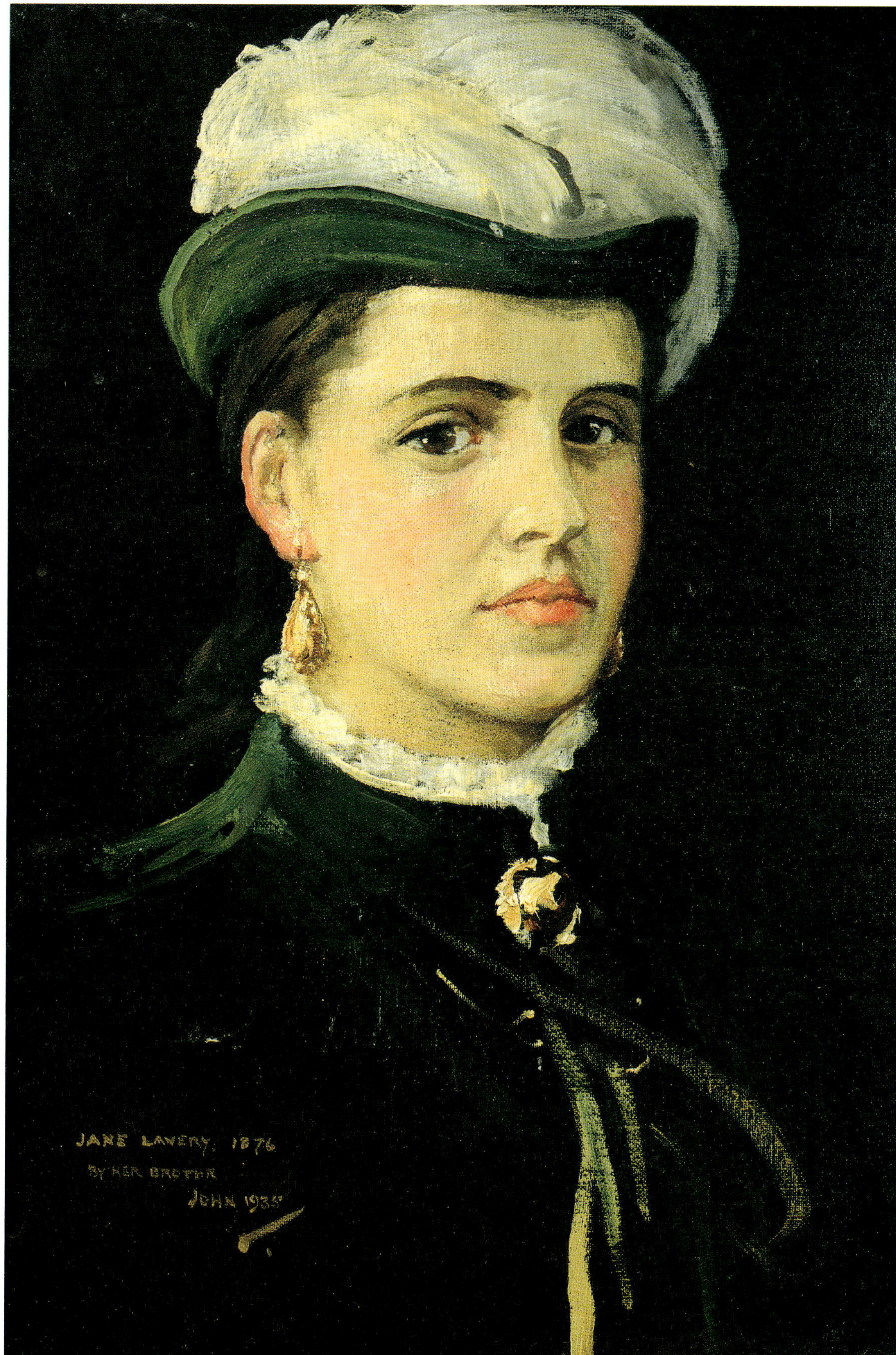

4 *Jane Lavery, a posthumous portrait*, 1935,
20 × 14 (photo, Christies)

being further subsidised by his uncle. Lavery had great admiration for his employer's ability, particularly as a flesh painter. MacNair, a 'tall, thin, nervous, refined' character had a reputation for hand-tinting the cuts and bruises of those who were involved in Glasgow brawls.[13] Lavery's new job gave him the financial security to register at the Haldane Academy of Art in Glasgow. As the predecessor of the Glasgow School of Art, it adopted the teaching programme devised by the National Art Training School at South Kensington. Accordingly, Lavery first practised drawing straight lines and curves and then graduated to copying parts of the human face. As he told Shaw Sparrow, 'Most other students made either designs for fabrics or mechanical drawings but I was privileged, having explained that I wished to become a portrait painter.'[14]

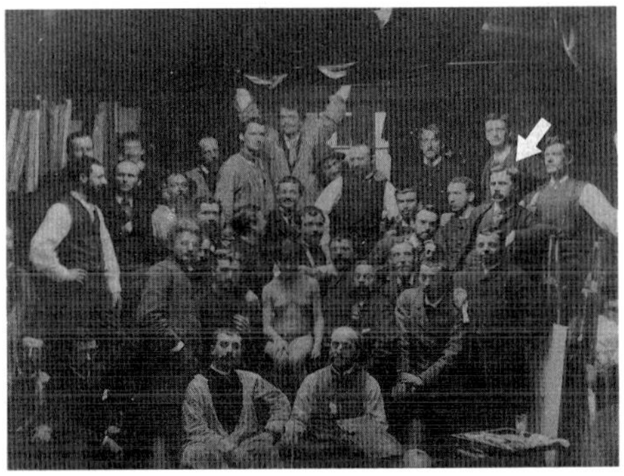

3 The Haldane Academy, *c.*1879, Lavery is arrowed centre right (source unknown)

In his second year, Lavery was able to increase his periods of tuition attending early morning classes as well as evening classes. It was then that he bought his first paintbox, containing only raw umber and flake white. When he had satisfactorily completed a tone study using these two colours, he was allowed to extend his palette.[15]

Lavery records early romantic adventures during these years whilst underlining the fact that he did not allow them to stand in the way of the single-minded pursuit of his new profession. The ruthless commitment which now emerged led him into some regrettable situations, the most tragic of which concerned his sister, Jane. When he was established with a small flat, Jane came to live with him and to act as his housekeeper. Being engrossed with his studies at the Haldane Academy and being at MacNair's from 7 a.m. each morning until late in the evenings, he became oblivious to her and was never able to give her enough money to sustain the household. When he was at work she formed a liaison with a pawnbroker's assistant who absconded to America after he realised that Jane was pregnant. Lavery then insisted that she should follow her lover and that when she had tracked him down, they should be married. Shortly after, she set sail for New York and did succeed in locating and marrying the father of her unborn child and within several months all three returned to Glasgow. They set up home, but with a second baby on the way, it was evident that the marriage was not going to work. Lavery, to his shame in later years, was impervious to his sister's plight and when, late one evening she waited for him at the studio door, he refused to take her in. Two days later she threw herself from Stockwell Bridge into the Clyde. He was devastated by the horror of this event and by the sight of his only sister 'young and beautiful with the strange serenity of death'.[16] However his strong instinct for self-preservation led him to repress his grief and disown all connections with the tragedy. As an old man, he wrote, 'I knew I was wrong and tried to ease my conscience by going to confession, but the knowledge of my miserable want of courage and affection haunted me for years—and haunts me even as I write these lines.'[17] At the end of his life he painted a portrait of Jane 'in memoriam' from a photograph of 1876 and this was used as the first illustration in *The Life of a Painter*.[18]

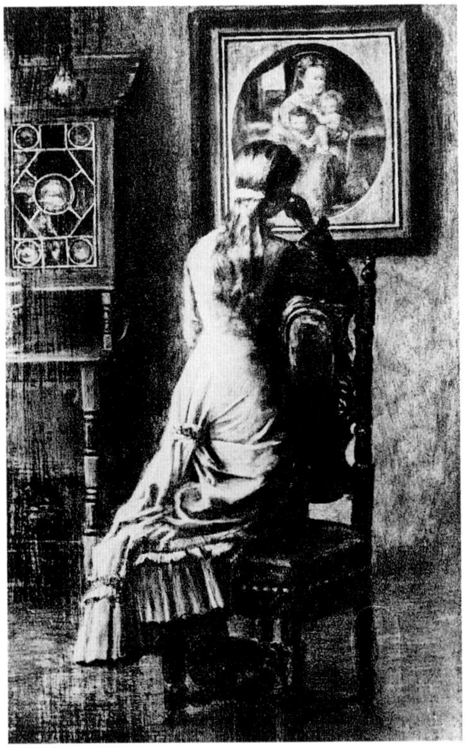

5 *Pious Reflections*, *c.*1879 (present whereabouts unknown)

In this year Lavery produced his first painting, a watercolour version of Henry Wallis's *Death of Chatterton.* This was copied from a popular engraving and he proudly recalled that it was raffled in a local public house. He then spent a year on a

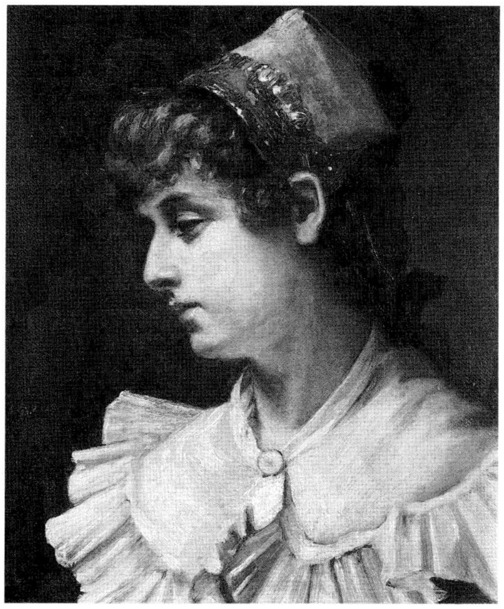

6 *Gretchen of Heidelberg*, 1879, 12 × 10 (present whereabouts unknown, photo, Christies)

picture entitled,—*'Tis better to have loved and lost, than never to have loved at all*, the model for which was a showroom girl from MacNair's called Georgina.[19] This ill-fated effort was rejected at the Royal Academy, rejected at the Glasgow Institute and eventually perished in a studio fire around 1880. A stippled watercolour, it was inspired by the work of John Everett Millais, although the features of the model apparently recalled Frederic Leighton's heroines.

Lavery was now a skilled retoucher, having completed his apprenticeship. He took a job with another photographer on a year's contract for £150. When this came up for renewal, around 1879, and although offered a substantial increase, Lavery decided to set himself up as a painter. He found a patron in an ancient, but alas unidentified, Papal Count, whose one demand from the portrait Lavery was to paint, was that his signet ring be prominently displayed.[20] This gentleman took him to London where he registered at Heatherley's School of Art, with the possible intention of going on to the Royal Academy Schools.

In 1880, Lavery made his debut as an exhibitor at the Glasgow Institute of Fine Arts with a picture of the back view of a girl, possibly Georgina, kneeling on a high-backed Jacobean chair in front of an oval picture of the Madonna and Child. He entitled the work appropriately, *Pious Reflections* (Plate 5). The artist later suggested that this was probably painted from a photograph.[21] Utilising studies from Heatherley's of a girl in quaker costume and a young man dressed as a cavalier, he went on to produce *The Courtship of Julian Peveril*. This untraced painting encapsulated the painter's admiration for the work of Duncan MacKellar, a costume-piece genre specialist. His *Health to the King*, depicting a boozy cavalier was just the sort of work that brought commercial success. It inspired the opportunism of *The Courtship of Julian Peveril*, with the predictable result of an immediate purchase when it was exhibited at the Royal Scottish Academy in 1881. Despite this success, Lavery regarded his winter at Heatherley's as 'the loneliest year I have ever spent in my life'.[22] Daily he commuted from cheap lodgings at Dalston and seems not to have spoken to anyone.

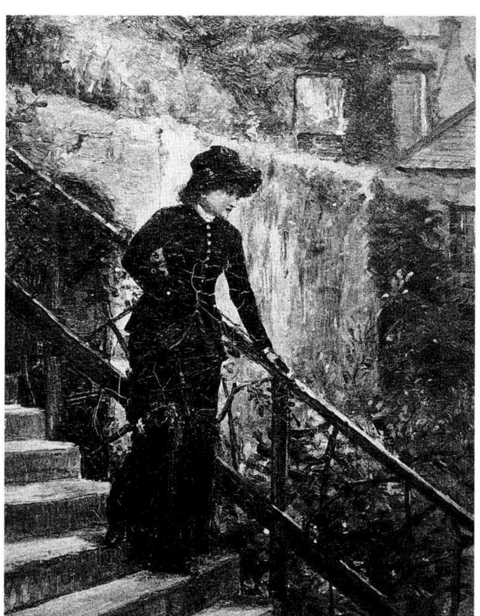

8 *Waiting*, 1881, 8 × 6 (Renfrew Museums and Galleries)

Throughout this time, he continued to work for the select few Glasgow and Paisley patrons. Terence Stevenson, the Glasgow photographer, purchased a group of pictures including two landscapes, a painting entitled *Gretchen of Heidelberg* (Plate 6) and another called *Her First Disappointment* (Plate 7).[23] This was a picture of the well-known skipping-rope dancer, Connie Gilchrist posing forlornly in a park. John Eadie purchased *Waiting* (Plate 8), a small painting exhibited at Paisley Art Institute in 1881, another but more competent blighted-love subject.[24] A further untraced exploration of the theme was a picture of Tennyson's *Mariana*, shown at the Glasgow Institute of Fine Arts in 1881.[25] At the same time, Lavery produced a number of variations on the Faust and Marguerite legend one of which, *Faust* (Plate 9) Mr Eadie bought.[26] He also explored eighteenth-century genre with *Monsieur Le Troubadour* (Plate 10), a composition containing a guitarist dressed in a pale blue velvet coat and knee breeches, laboriously strumming in front of a tapestry backdrop. This picture was exhibited at the Royal Hibernian Academy in 1882.

It follows a visit to Ireland which the painter had made two years earlier at the invitation of a naval captain called Beddoes. He had asked Lavery to give him painting lessons at his house at Belmullet, County Mayo. Lavery recounts the frightful journey, jolting thirty or forty miles in a jaunting car. When he arrived at Beddoes' house, it seemed like 'the acme of comfort' after such a harrowing trip. Painting in the open air, he instantly recognized the poverty of the Irish peasants. On one occasion he met a 'tall, upright, emaciated' woman, on a lonely highroad, who could not comprehend his attempts to induce her to pose on the spot: 'I went on working and she seemed hypnotized. Feeling a bit nervous I signed to her in a friendly way to come and look. She did not move, she remained rooted to the ground. Finishing off I gave her a two-shilling piece . . . she kept turning the money over in her hands as if it were a foreign coin—as in point of fact it was to her . . .'[27]

One of the results of the visit to Ireland was shown at the Paisley Institute in 1881, but it and Lavery's other work in Ireland remain untraced.[28] The heterogeneous character of his early efforts illustrate Lavery's search for successful formulae and his anxiety to demonstrate his ability to handle a variety of genres including landscape, portraiture and still-life. Convinced of the need for public exposure, he showed as many as seventeen pictures in the early Eighties at the Paisley Institute. A more selective approach was adopted for Glasgow and Edinburgh. He was prepared to exploit potentially disastrous events to further his career, as when after a studio-fire had destroyed his early works, he collected £300 insurance money to finance Heatherley's and his first forays in Paris. Although he neglected to mention the discussions which must have taken place in London and Glasgow studios, it was inevitable that for him and his circle, Paris was emerging as the art students' mecca. Later hailed as 'the capital of art', it became the goal of his ambitions in 1881.[29] In November of that year, he set off, taking with him one suitcase and a lunatic!

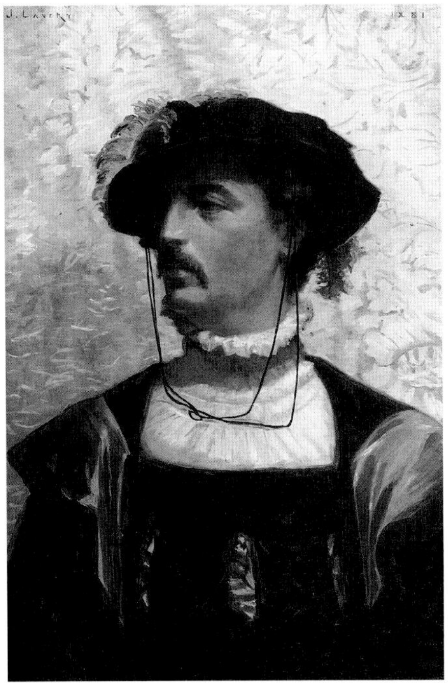

9 *Faust*, *c.*1881, size unknown (present whereabouts unknown, photo, Sotheby's)

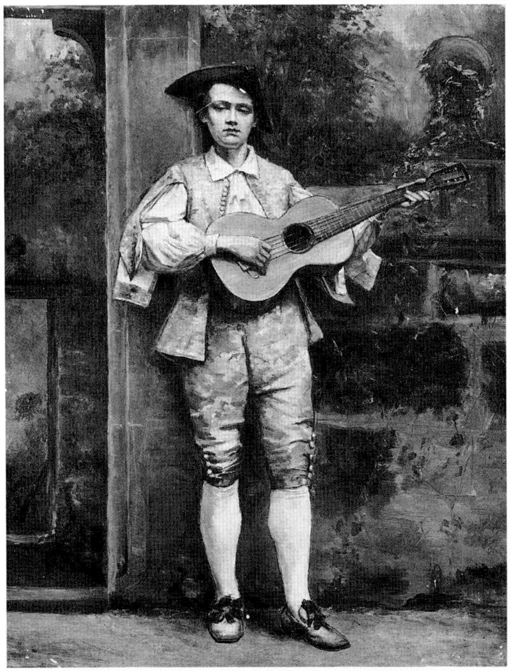

10 *Monsieur Le Troubadour*, *c.*1881, 18 × 14 (Gorry Gallery, Dublin)

2 The Capital of Art

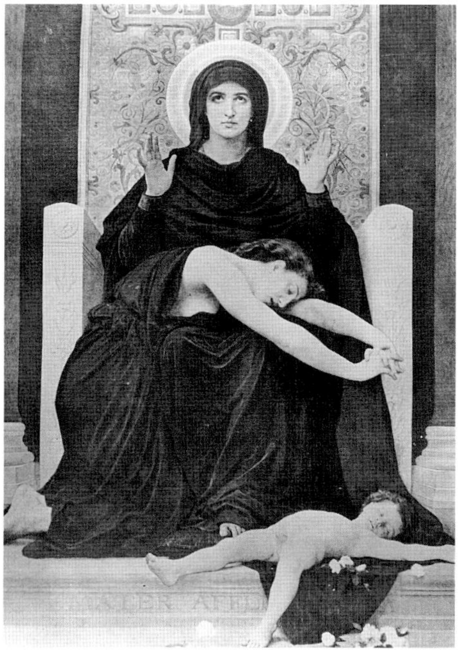

11 William Adolphe Bouguereau, *Vierge Consolatrix*, 1875 (Musée de Strasbourg)

Lavery's journey to Paris was not uncomplicated.[1] He had been taking French lessons from an expatriate named Gravet, who lived in Glasgow with his Irish wife. Gradually, poor Gravet lost his reason and upon hearing that Lavery was bound for Paris, his father-in-law asked the painter to deliver him to the asylum at Charenton.[2] Lavery confessed to losing his charge in the London underground and on the packet boat before he finally got to Paris, where they were met by Gravet's brother. After his installation at Charenton, Lavery continued to visit him on Sundays until his death some months later.

Lavery immediately registered for instruction at the atelier Julian, a popular studio among the British and American art student population. His favourite French picture at the time was William Adolphe Bouguereau's *Vierge Consolatrix* (Plate 11) and it happened that Bouguereau was one of the *chefs d'atelier* at Julian's.[3] At this point in his career, Bouguereau was at the height of his prestige. He already enjoyed much official patronage and had two pictures in the Musée du Luxembourg before the purchase of *Vierge Consolatrix* in 1877. The sanitised asceticism which brought Bouguereau great commercial success could just have easily have been at the root of the young Lavery's admiration. There is no doubt that this lion of officially accepted painting contributed greatly to the popularity of the school.[4] He had the reputation, however, of being a merciless critic, savagely attacking the well-intentioned but pedestrian efforts of foreign students. Shirley Fox records his withering comments upon the work of a typical English suppliant who may well have already passed through British art education with some success.[5] His exacting standards were confirmed by Lavery when in later years he told Shaw Sparrow, 'Though I work as hard as any of the others, my drawing was poor and neither Bouguereau nor Fleury ever gave me much praise. *Pas mal* or *pas trop mal* was about the most I got for encouragement. I discovered that what I thought were my strong points counted for little and that I had yet to understand what drawing really meant.'[6]

The artist here, was probably referring to his ability, or the lack of it, to manipulate light and shade in the conventional sense. As an Ingrist draughtsman, Bouguereau and the other French instructors would have placed greater emphasis upon visual accuracy conveyed in a contour line. Accordingly, Lavery was enjoined to study Holbein in order to acquire linear discipline.[7] The seriousness of his resolve to take up these notions is conveyed in *Her Portrait* (Plate 12), one of the few surviving Lavery drawings of the period. Technically a *fusain*, this finished charcoal study of a young woman inspecting a picture owes a great deal to the draughtsmanship of artists like Leon Lhermitte, a regular exhibitor at Glasgow Institute exhibitions. An original promoter of the Dudley Gallery 'Black and White' exhibitions in London in the 1870s, Lhermitte may well have proposed the institute's own 'Black and White' exhibitions of the early Eighties. Lavery was substantially represented at these shows in 1881 and 1882, but sadly most of his works have disappeared.[8] Their titles, however, illustrate the general shift of emphasis from costume-pieces to modern life themes like *Her Portrait* (Plate 12).[9]

The careful gradation of tone in this drawing is noteworthy. It seems as if, by using the textured 'Ingres' paper, the artist has set down a uniform mid-tone from which the light areas are erased and upon which the darks are more firmly established. A face-value reading suggests that the composition of the work may derive from Fantin-Latour, and the subject-matter derives generally from French genre painting.[10] Following these precedents, there might be a market for *fusains* of modern life.

Bouguereau's linearism, for all the struggle it brought, left little trace in Lavery's art, apart from the confident penmanship that supports his oil sketches later in the decade. To some extent, he could not afford academicism for its own sake. It was necessary to constantly exploit his studies to commercial ends. This was undoubtedly the reason why he registered at Colarossi's studio to work in the evenings from the costumed model. Jacomb Hood later recalled, 'I used to meet him [Lavery] at a studio kept by a retired model named Colarossi, where you could pay by the week and there were models, nude and in costume. Many of us used to work there in the afternoon from the costume model, among our number being Lavery, who was in the habit of faking backgrounds to his costume studies and making them into pictures which were bought by some dealer in Glasgow.'[11]

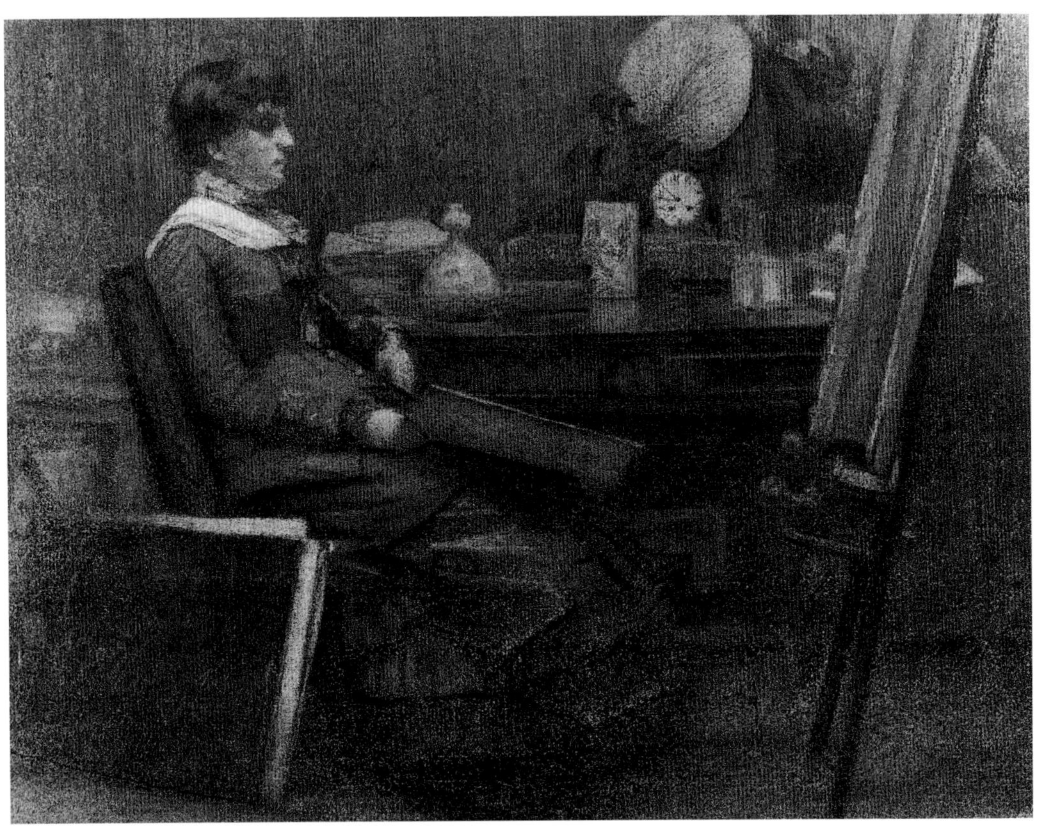

12 *Her Portrait*, *c.* 1882, $10\frac{1}{4} \times 13$, black chalk on paper (Glasgow Art Gallery and Museum)

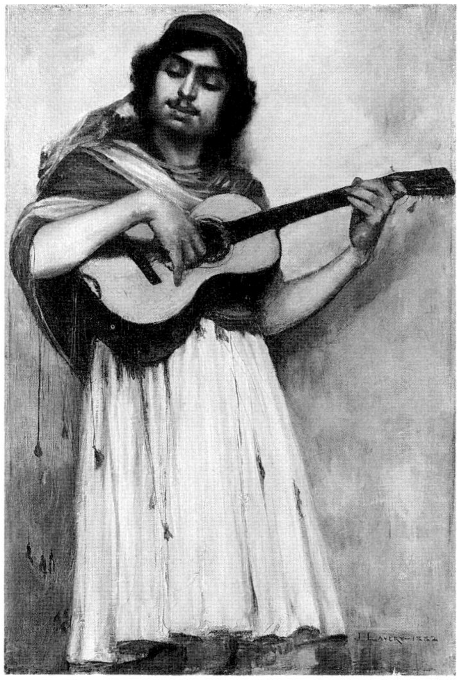

13 *Young Arab Playing a Guitar*, 1882, 21 × 14 (private collection, photo, The Fine Art Society)

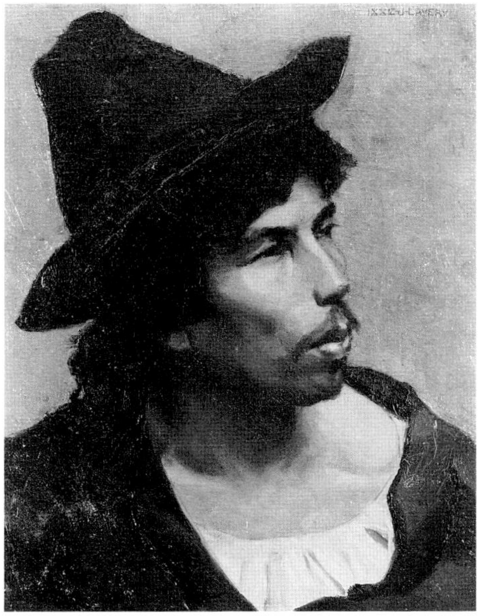

14 *Head of a Brigand*, *c.*1882. 13 × 10 (present whereabouts unknown, photo, Sotheby's)

Lavery was therefore busily adapting his Paris studies into saleable products. Since Colarossi's frequently employed Moorish or middle eastern models, it is likely that the picture of 1882, *Young Arab Playing a Guitar* (Plate 13) represents one of these.[12] It may also be that *Head of a Brigand* comes from the same source.[13] Apart from his lost charcoal, *A Little Arab*, these works must be Lavery's principal early contributions to the current vogue for Orientalist painting.[14]

The Arab guitarist makes a startling comparison with the admittedly more ambitious, earlier *Troubadour* (Plate 10) of 1881. Immediately a new confidence in the manipulation of materials is evident. Although the poses are similar, the instrument is held with greater delicacy in the second picture. The young Arab's face is treated with greater concentration, perhaps betraying an awareness of the work of the great Salon painter, Jean Leon Gérôme, although few conscientious Orientalists would have given their models Spanish guitars to strum.

As a study, however, *Young Arab Playing a Guitar* (Plate 13) exemplifies the painter's sureness in the handling of paint. Thereafter, his work began to lose its timidity and the pace in the development of competence accelerates. Lavery found himself in an intensely stimulating atmosphere. Paris, with its salons, ateliers and artistic *mêlée* greatly expanded the range of possibilities.

It would be impossible now to fully assess the impact of so important an event as the Salon of 1882, but it is clear that Lavery swiftly began to identify with the new phalanx of British and American artists who were currently achieving success.[15] Wintering at the Hotel de Saxe in the Rue Jacob, he must have picked up the atelier *patois* of the Quartier Latin. Amongst the first people he met upon arrival were William Kennedy, Alexander Roche and Thomas Millie Dow and he immediately felt at home in this Scots expatriate community. His board and lodging cost a mere forty francs a month and he and his fellow students met regularly at a little café near the Musée du Luxembourg. Their discussions ranged widely over the whole field of modern art as exemplified in the Salon and Lavery must have quickly begun to realise the naivety of his admiration for Bouguereau. Quoting the recollections of Alexander Roche, Shaw Sparrow tells us that at these café conversations, '. . . ardour and tobacco burned freely before the shrines of Puvis de Chavannes and Jules Bastien-Lepage. Between these extremes the talk went to and fro on summer evenings, but, as a rule, the favourite topics were Bastien-Lepage and *plein-air*.'[16]

In 1882, both of these artists were substantially represented at the Salon. Puvis' large painting of classicised semi-nude maidens and children, *Doux Pays* was awarded a coveted *medaille d'honneur*, while Bastien-Lepage exhibited a controversial life-sized rendering of an old woodcutter and child, entitled *Le Père Jacques*. The choice that young would-be artists faced, was to follow either the naturalist or the idealist tendency—or endeavour to reconcile them. Of the two, Bastien-Lepage probably seemed the most impressive on account of his ability to render natural detail and individual character with almost photographic precision. Hailed by Zola as a naturalist, he was regarded as superior to the Impressionists in that he knew how to 'realise' his impressions.[17] Bastien's appeal, over that of Puvis, was partly because he was near to the young generation in age, being, for instance, a mere eight years older than Lavery. He had risen to fame in the Salons of the late 1870s and had courted notoriety with his controversial picture of *Joan of Arc Listening to the Voices* (see Plate 30), shown in 1880.[18] At the same time as provoking heated debate, in the Paris of the Third Republic, Bastien-Lepage established the basis of his reputation with British artists by holding a small influential retrospective at the Grosvenor Gallery in 1880. Thereafter, he visited London regularly and his work was frequently seen in exhibitions in Britain, including the Glasgow Institute. One picture which Lavery saw, though he mis-ascribed it to Bastien's pupil, Marie Bashkirtseff, was *Pas Mèche*, a painting exhibited both in Paris and London in the spring and early summer of 1882.[19] Had he lingered in London, while returning to Glasgow during that summer, Lavery would have had the chance to study *Pauvre Fauvette*, *La Petite Coquette* and *Le Mendiant*.[20]

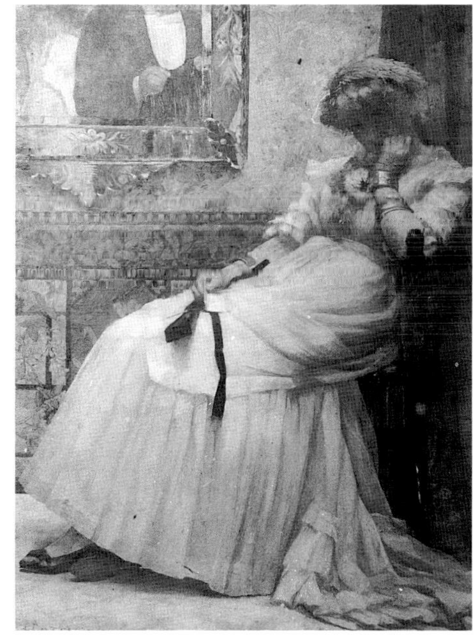

15 *After the Dance*, 1883, 34 × 44 (private collection, photo, Ian Kilpatrick)

These became seminal works, universally approved by Lavery's Scottish contemporaries and widely discussed. Although he was more of a listener at these conversations, the effect of the new influence was overwhelming. 'When I saw Bastien's work', he later confessed, 'it took away my breath.'[21] It was only however, when he had established his own rural base, that Lavery was to truly exploit the innovations of Bastien-Lepage.

The other controversial picture which Lavery recalled from these years was Manet's *Bar at the Folies Bergère*, although in old age he mis-dated the year of its appearance at the Salon.[22] Shaw Sparrow disowned the influence of Manet upon Lavery's early work,[23] but it is likely that the memory of Manet's *Bar* . . . conditioned at least one important work shown at the Glasgow Institute in 1883. *After the Dance* (Plate 15) makes use of an ornate background mirror to expand and extend the action of the picture.[24] A girl with her dance booking-card on her lap, stares out at the spectator, while reflected in the mirror, like the customer at the *Bar* . . . her father or an aged lover approaches holding a cloak. Lavery leaves the identity of this figure deliberately ambiguous, and there is no doubt that, had the painting been shown in Paris, the alluring shadowy face of the girl, coupled with the reflected male would have been given a Zolaesque reading. If he was not directly emulating Manet in the technique of *After the Dance* (Plate 15), the picture does reveal Lavery's awareness of the work of painters of contemporary society such as Tissot and Gervex. In 1879, for instance, Gervex portrayed the tension of a blighted relationship in his celebrated *Retour du Bal*. The sophisticated Salon finish of such a work, rather than Manet's sketchiness, is likely to have appealed to the young Lavery.

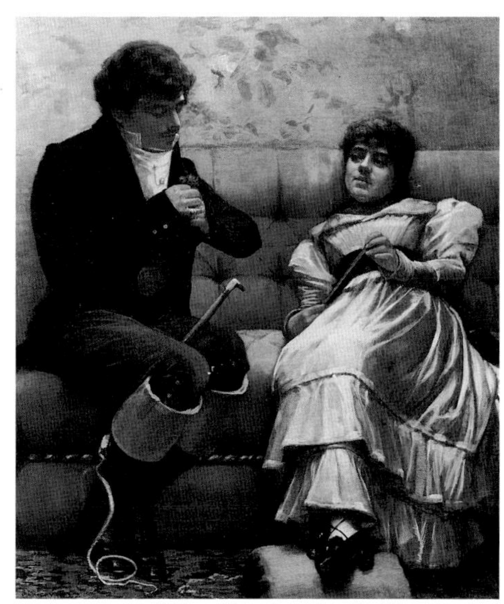

16 *A Conquest*, 1882, $23\frac{7}{8} \times 19\frac{7}{8}$ (Glasgow Art Gallery and Museum)

If the sentiment of *After the Dance* was modern French, *A Heart for a Rose*, shown at the Glasgow Institute in 1883, and probably now known as *A Conquest* (Plate 16) is decidedly British.[25] This picture is an essay in the manner of the popular Victorian Academy exhibitor, Marcus Stone. In the late Seventies, Stone had established a reputation for the depiction of Regency love affairs, a formula sometimes adopted by successful London Scots painters like Pettie and Orchardson. In borrowing this type of subject, Lavery obviously was hoping for commercial success.

Saleability would have been uppermost in Lavery's exhibition strategy as he financed his return trips from Glasgow to Paris. He was anxious to demonstrate his command of classical subject-matter at the institute in 1883 with an untraced classical work entitled *Lamia*. This was accompanied by a quotation by Keats in the institute catalogue:

> She saw the young Corinthian Lycias,
> Charioting foremost in the envious race
> Like a young Jove, with calm uneagre face
> And fell into a swooning love of him.[26]

Without seeing this picture, we can infer the crib from the great Victorian classicists, Sir Frederic Leighton and Edward Poynter.[27]

The final picture shown in Glasgow in 1883 was a painting of a model in a studio, entitled, *Between the Sittings* (Plate 17).[28] It shows the now familiar model for *A Conquest* (Plate 16), with the picture itself resting against the wall in the background. Divested of studio props, this painting reveals a more natural Lavery, but this is not to suggest that it did not have its own specialist market. It is easy to think of the painter turning to such diversions in a mood of relaxation and his personal preference for this kind of intimist theme remained long after the grand artifice of his early attempts at literature and history had vanished.

By the time these paintings were exhibited at the Glasgow Institute, Lavery had returned to Paris for a further winter. It is likely that the more spartan interior, *A Quiet Day in the Studio* (Plate 18) was painted there.[29] In this, a black-haired model warms her ankles by a blazing fire. Little effort has been made to self-consciously arrange this interior and it is devoid of studio props. Large canvases are stacked in

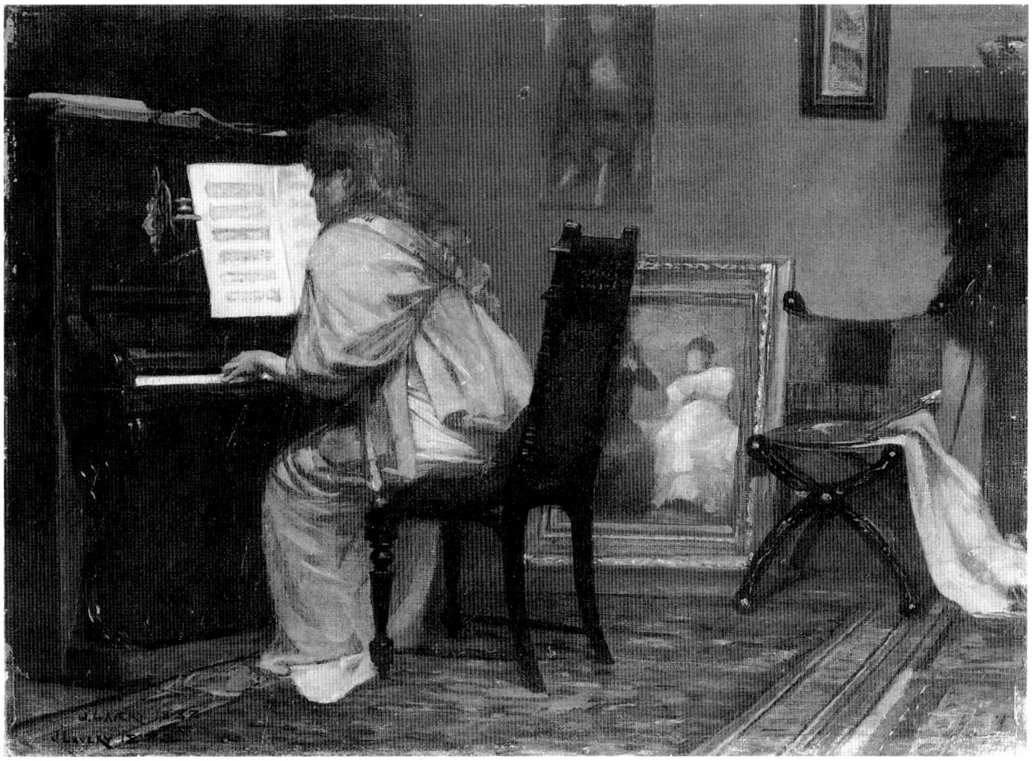

17 *Between the Sittings*, *c.*1882, size unknown (photo, Sotheby's)

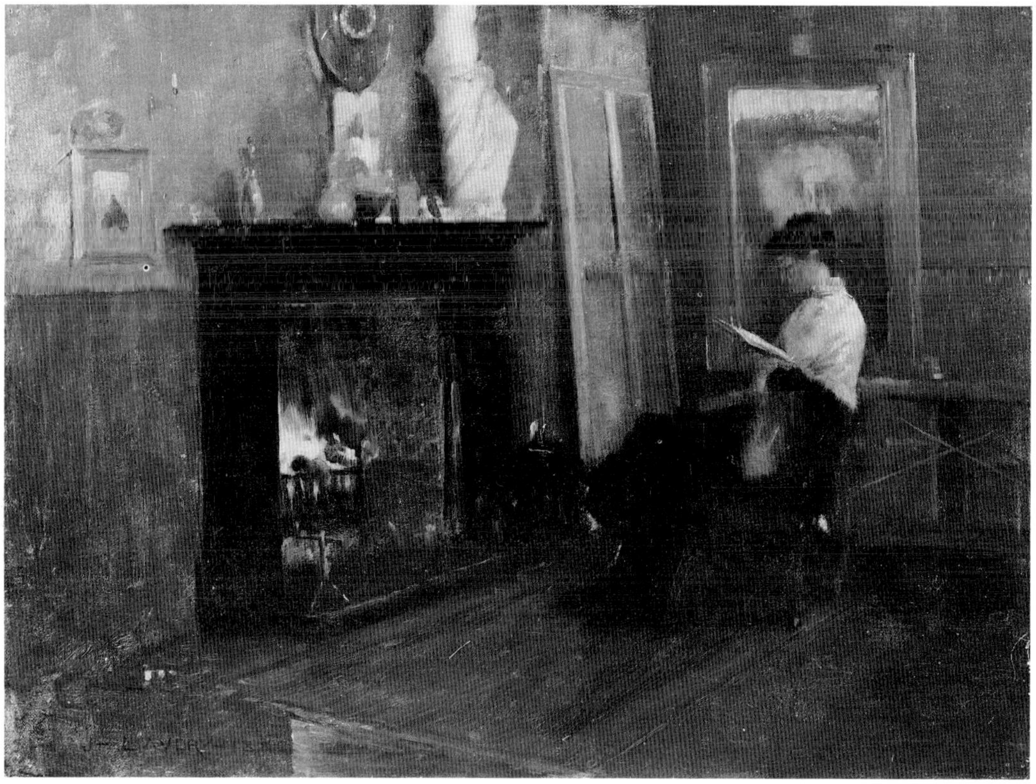

18 *A Quiet Day in the Studio*, 1883, 16½ × 20½ (Glasgow Art Gallery and Museum)

the background and a quarter-sized cast of the *Venus de Milo* sits upon the mantelpiece. Strict tonal control supports the mood of calm concentration and it may well be that Lavery was helped to achieve this effect by his first encounter with the work of Whistler.[30]

The lightness of touch which characterises *A Quiet Day* . . . provides the atmospheric quality of *Portrait of a Woman* (Plate 19), a depiction of the same model.[31] Placing the head and shoulders in *contre-jour* or against the light, Lavery set himself the difficult task of recording subtle gradations of tone. The manner of applying the paint to the surface, in choppy square-shaped brushstrokes, typifies the atelier Julian followers of Bastien-Lepage. D. S. MacColl would have described it as a classic example of, 'one of the popular school methods of painting . . . traced back to a caricature of the mannerisms of Bastien-Lepage. In its extreme form this painting may be recognised by a swaggering way of painting across forms, by a choppy rendering of planes and by attention to values at the expense of colour.'[32]

Lavery did not forsake this newly discovered method until he had evolved his own substitute. His decision at the outset of his second sojourn in Paris not to draw all day in the studio, but to spend his afternoons in out-door sketching, may, in some respects, imply a recognition of the fact that in the opinion of his compatriot, George Moore, the great studio of Julian was '. . . a sphinx, and all the poor folk who go there for artistic education are devoured'.[33] Lavery's determination to master the techniques of painting *en plein-air* took him out of Paris, beyond the *banelieu* to St Cloud and Nogent-sur-Marne. There he painted

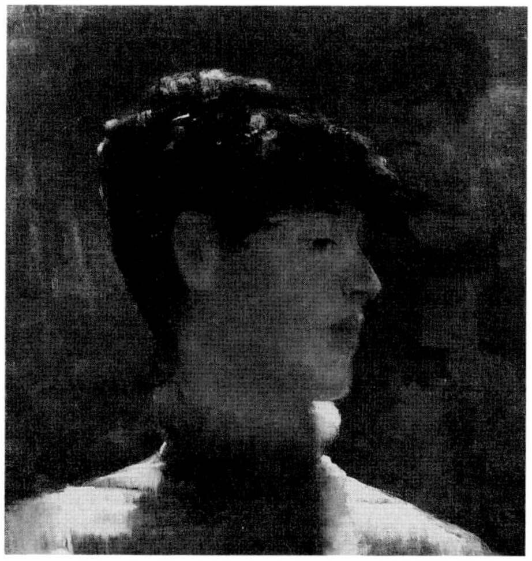

19 *Portrait of a Woman*, 1883, 18 × 18 (Andrew McIntosh Patrick Esq.)

Les Deux Pêcheurs, which was dispatched to the Salon of 1883 and to his amazement, hung in a good position and was purchased by the father of the sculptor Saint-Marceaux.[34] We can only speculate upon this important work which was never reproduced and is now untraced. Shaw Sparrow, probably recounting information supplied by the painter, tells that Lavery produced this picture without much forethought, in contrast to his literary subject pictures. 'Nature' as he metaphorically put it, 'had got into his work unperceived and sent a ripple of her wind over the painted water and through the painted sky.'[35] *La Pêcheuse*, painted at roughly the same time may give approximation of the appearance of Lavery's first Salon success.[36] Rich foreground foliage in a dappled effect creates a textural contrast to the still and silent river.

The appreciation of nature in Lavery's work during the winter of 1882–3 was to some extent an after-effect of the experience of the Salon of 1882. In this crucially significant exhibition, not only were Puvis and Bastien in evidence, but Lavery also had the opportunity to admire some of the work of English-speaking contemporaries who were already gaining success. Among these were Lowell Birge Harrison, John Singer Sargent, Welden Hawkins and Frank O'Meara. But the most important member of the group to whom the praise of critics was unanimously directed was William Stott of Oldham, a painter whose rustic naturalism was overlaid with a limpid sense of poetry. He seemed to have reconciled the conflicting claims of Bastien-Lepage and Puvis de Chavannes and to have done so in evocations of a rural arcadia that was actually only about fifty miles from Paris. His *La Baignade* (*Bathing*) and *Le Passeur* (*The Ferry*, Plate 21) exemplified the new meaning of the concept of 'sentiment'. The banal Victorian portrayal of emotion through literature and costumes could now be discarded for a larger more abstract and intuitive response to the cues provided by nature itself. Having discovered this at Nogent-sur-Marne, Lavery was ready for the experience of Grez-sur-Loing.

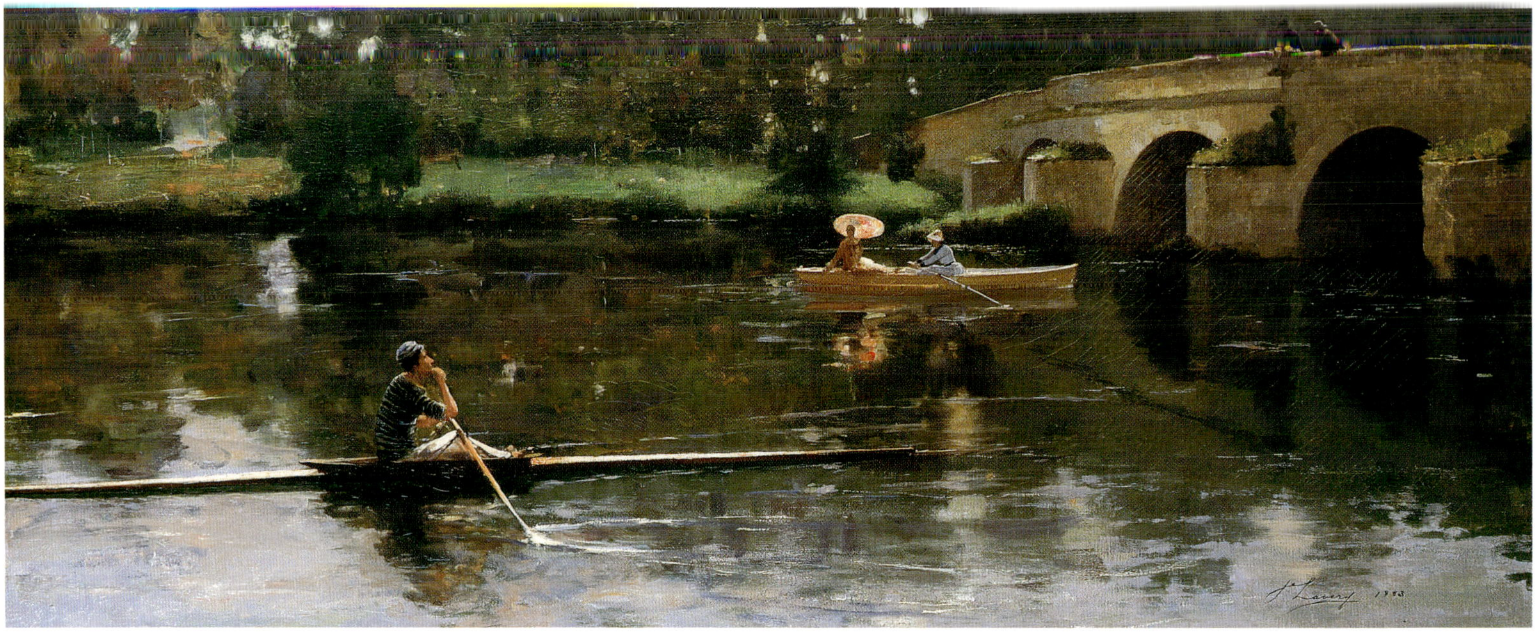

24 *The Bridge At Grez*, 1883, 30 × 72
(private collection, photo, Fine Art Society)

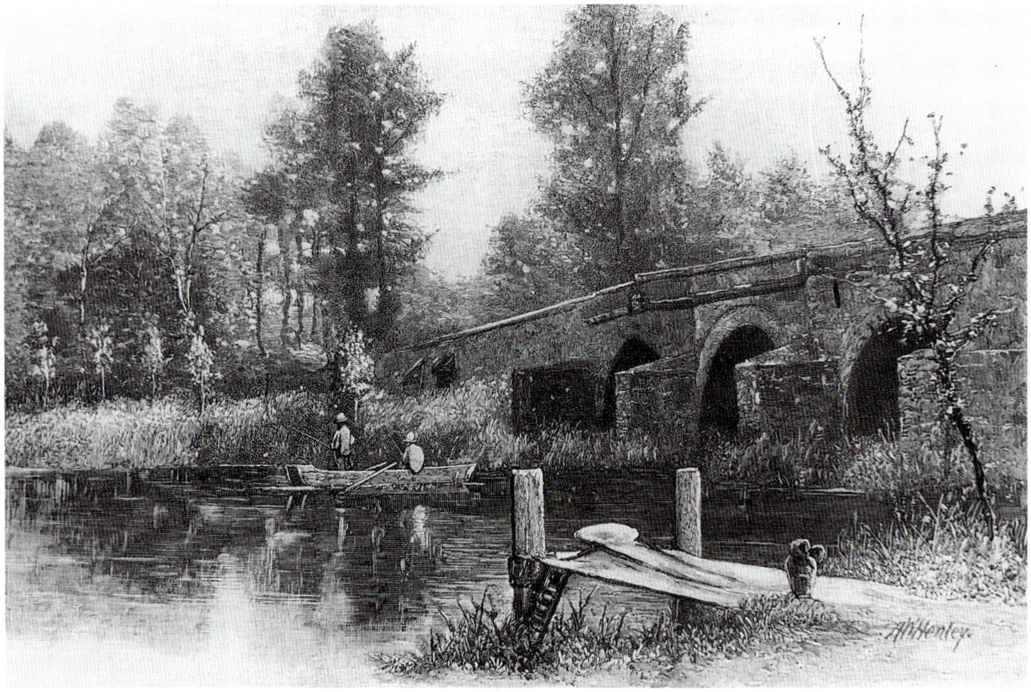

20 A. W. Henley, *The Bridge at Grez*, engraving, *c.*1884, size unknown
(present whereabouts unknown)

3 'A Chronicle of Friendships'

Looking back upon his youth, in his eightieth year, Lavery felt that his 'happiest days in France were passed in the colony outside Paris at Gres-sur-Loinge [sic].'[1] Although Corot had painted there in the 1860s and Jacob Maris had worked nearby at Montigny in 1870, the ancient village of Grez to the south of Fontainebleau did not spawn an artist community until around 1875.[2] Finding that Barbizon, the home of J-F. Millet was already a tourist attraction, a group of students from the atelier of Carolus Duran moved to the village. These new inhabitants, most of whom were British, American or Scandinavian, attested to the attractiveness of the setting. Will H. Low, one of the Americans, who later set down his memoirs in a book entitled *A Chronicle of Friendships*, described it as a place of 'obvious picturesqueness'.[3] Its most distinguished early visitor, Robert Louis Stevenson recorded its charm in a richly poetic manner. Its sounds and scents evoked a magic world: 'Out of unknown thickets comes forth the soft, secret, aromatic odour of the woods . . . as though court ladies, who had known these paths in ages long gone by, still walked in summer evenings, and shed, from their fine brocades, a breath of musk and bergamot upon the woodland winds.'[4]

None of its painters quite shared Stevenson's vision of court ladies, although, in his earliest picture of the bridge at Grez, Lavery's compatriot, Frank O'Meara came close to the ambiance of bygone trysts and autumnal sorrows.[5] A sense of reverie, of sensual delight, permeates the work of the Grez adherents. The bucolic encounter with nature liberated the young painter from the dry routines of the atelier. Obeying Stevenson, the student might hasten to Fontainebleau and, 'address himself to the spirit of the place . . . he will learn more from sketching than from studies, although both are necessary . . . and while he stupefies himself with the mechanical side of his trade, let him walk in the great air, and be a servant of mirth, and not pick and botanize, but wait upon the moods of nature. So will he learn—or learn not to forget—the poetry of life and earth, which, when he has acquired his track, will save him from joyless reproduction.'[6]

In 1884, when these words were published, Stevenson had good evidence for his elegaic reading of artists' responses to this very specific environment. The roll-call of painters who worked at Grez in the final quarter of the nineteenth century is long and impressive.[7] It is important to further define the common characteristics which this ambiance seemed to impart to its inhabitants. A tonal palette which admitted bright notes of pure colour, a willingness to alter handling to suggest different fields of focus, a close observation of detail, particularly in the foreground of a picture, rendered, in Stevenson's words, with 'prae-Raphaelite [sic] minuteness', separated *plein-air* technique from that of the Impressionists. William Stott of Oldham and the American, Alexander Harrison were the most celebrated young lions of the village just before Lavery's arrival—to such an extent that the art student debate tended to be projected in terms of 'the all important question, "does Stott influence Alexander Harrison or is Alexander Harrison influenced by Stott?"'[8] Both painters were lavishly praised at the Paris Salon of 1882, Harrison for *Castles in Spain* and Stott for *Bathing* and *The Ferry* (Plate 21). The poetic quality of Stott's pictures 'surprised and charmed' French critics; they were struck by the 'rare and captivating delicacy of his work'.[9] To the young Lavery, the well-felt evening light of *The Ferry* conveyed much more than the crude stagecraft of costume-pieces manufactured for the market. However, only after he had 'added several inches to his stature' with the Salon success of *Les Deux Pecheurs* and *La Rentrée des Chèvres*, did he take himself to the resort which had had such a remarkable effect upon Stott.[10]

In the summer of 1883 Lavery was thrown in the midst of a group of diverse personalities. One in particular, Louis Welden Hawkins, greatly impressed him for his roguish ability to exploit the artificial pathos of his work. He had painted two sad-looking peasant lovers in a graveyard and, on the advice of a friend, retitled the completed picture, *Les Orphelins* (Plate 22).[11] With this he quickly achieved celebrity, but found that popular approval was difficult to sustain. He was therefore obliged to dress up as a rich collector and visit the Paris dealers asking for his own latest work. He then rushed back to Grez to receive news of the renewed interest.[12]

Lavery's closest friend at Grez-sur-Loing was, however, Frank O'Meara, an Irishman, three years older than he, and, in the opinion of Will Low, 'a pure type of Celt', full of the 'capricious moodiness of his race'.[13] Dreams and reveries alternating with bouts of truculence did not deter Lavery who recognised in O'Meara's work a sensitivity to tonal pitch which conferred upon him the role of mentor. He was a Grez inhabitant of long standing, and pictures like *The Widow* (Plate 23) and *Evening in the Gatinais* carried the distillation of qualities associated with the village. Lavery knew both of these pictures, and in later years seems to have acted informally as O'Meara's agent in Glasgow, providing a vital conduit between his work and west of Scotland collectors.[14]

For all the vaporous sentiment of Grez painting, the artist community was, at

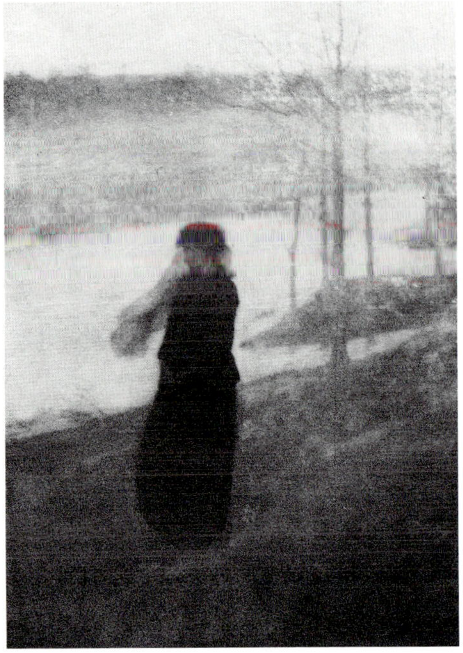

23 Frank O'Meara, *The Widow*, 1882, 59 × 39½, (Hugh Lane Municipal Art Gallery, Dublin)

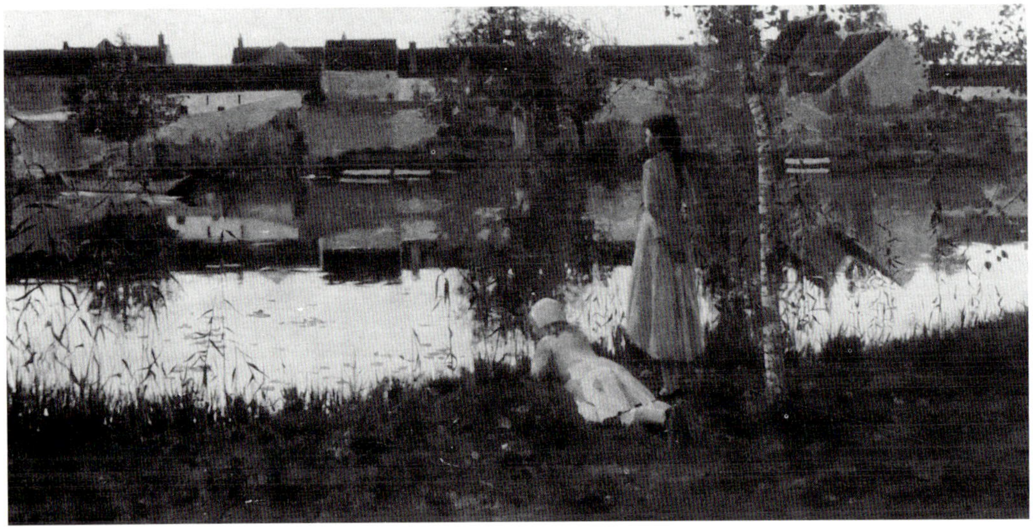

21 William Stott of Oldham, *Le Passeur (The Ferry)*, 1882, 43 × 84¼ (private collection)

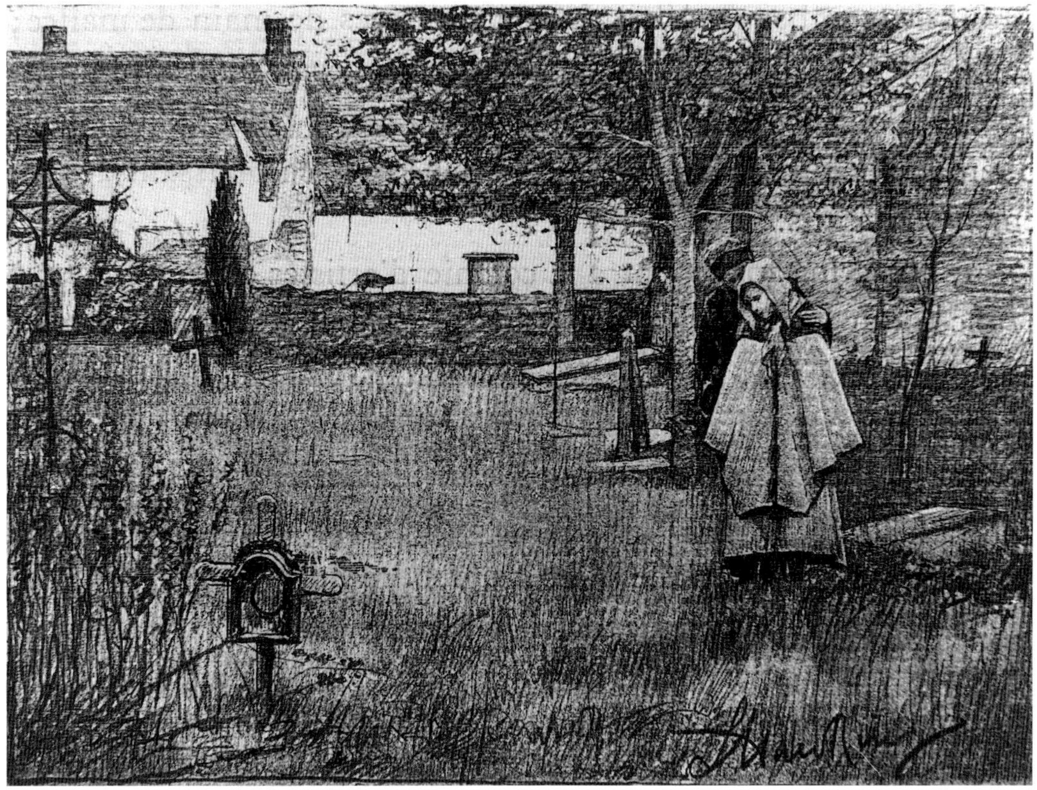

22 Louis Welden Hawkins, *Les Orphelins*, 1881, size unknown (present whereabouts unknown)

times merry and boisterous. Although there were arguments, squabbles and ritual dippings, for the most part the atmosphere in Chevillon's Inn, where the English-speaking painters lodged, was one of good-natured fun. Will Low recalled that 'behind the Inn, in a long garden stretching to the river, the table was spread, and here a score or more would be seated for the mid-day meal, in the lightest of costumes, fresh from a dip in the river.' The mood of relaxation, which could have led to a sense of *laisser aller*, in Lavery's case was a stimulus to creativity. For the first time he was untroubled by the need to make ends meet. 'My pension cost me five francs a day', he later recounted, 'and I could run up to Paris every now and again, untroubled by thoughts of tomorrow, which had been serious enough until that time.'[15] During his two periods at Grez in 1883 and 1884, he produced an impressive volume of work which included two major exhibition-pieces, a group of medium-sized pictures and a number of smaller sketches. All were the by-product of *plein-air* study and it is difficult to underestimate their significance.

The Bridge at Grez (Plate 24), painted on his first visit to the village declares new ambitions. In later years the painter recollected it as '. . . a river picture with a man in a skiff kissing his hand to a pair of happy girls in a distant boat. I called it *A Passing Salute* until I discovered that another painter had used this title for a kindred subject; then my work became *The Bridge at Gres* [sic].'[16] Few 'kindred subjects' can have been as authentic as this. Lavery's new sophistication in the management of space and scaling, his handling of figures and his sensitivity to prevailing atmospherics, were all apparent. When the picture was shown at the end of 1883 at the Paisley Art Institute, along with pre-Paris potboilers, the

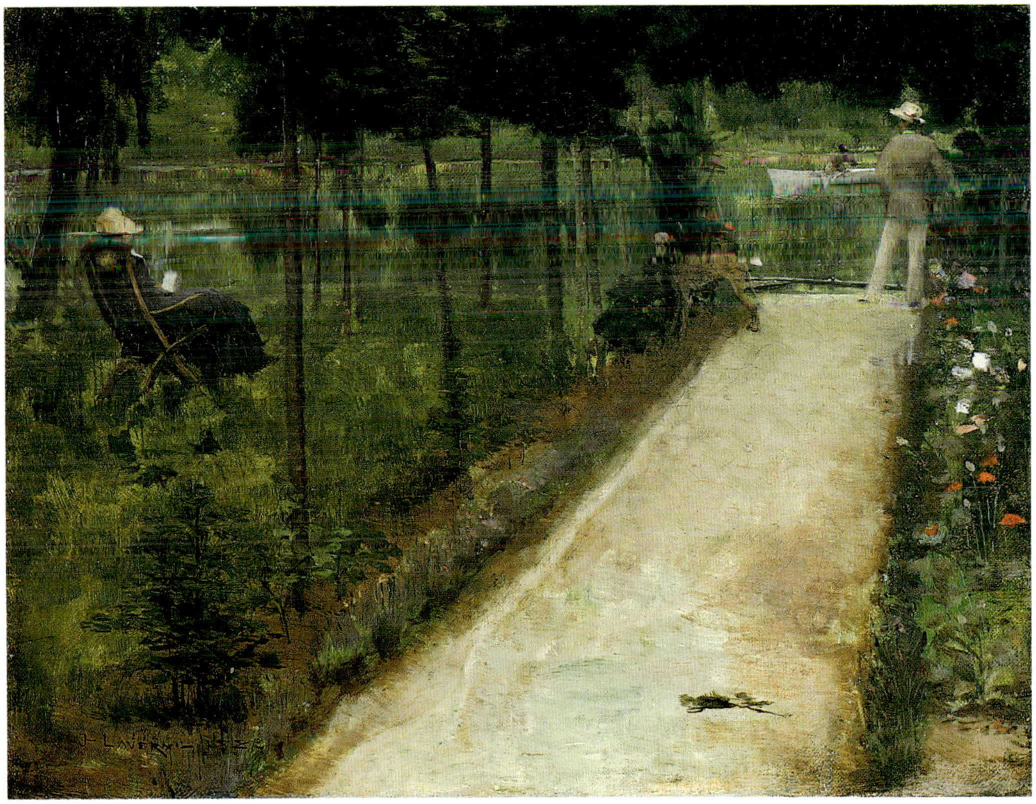

25 *A Grey Summer's Day, Grez*, 1883, $7\frac{1}{2} \times 9\frac{1}{2}$ (Andrew McIntosh Patrick)

evidence of the impressive change now taking place in Lavery's work must have been obvious to all. Thereafter the picture was shown in Edinburgh in 1884; it reappeared at the Exposition Universelle in Paris in 1889, went on to the Royal Academy and, belatedly was exhibited in Glasgow.[17] When it came to rest at the Glasgow Institute of Fine Arts, a newspaper critic commented upon its 'subdued colour harmonies' and 'avoidance of distracting detail' and concluded that it 'might easily pass for a French Salon picture'.[18] The memory of the painting elicited a colourful panegyric from the English critic, Gleeson White, who declared that, 'those who know the original, with its wonderful reach of water under the trees, flecked by rays of sunlight trickling here and there through the branches, will readily admit that few more delightful impressions of summer in the open air have ever hung on the Academy walls.'[19]

By the time these words were penned, the context of Impressionism had become firmly established in the minds of writers on art. It was not inconceivable that later critics might view *The Bridge at Grez* (Plate 24) through spectacles tinted by Monet's riverscapes. However, in 1883, it is doubtful whether Lavery would have had anything other than the most general awareness of Impressionism, filtered through the broader category of *plein-air* painting. He did not record visits to the galleries of Georges Petit and Durand-Ruel, where Impressionist canvases might be found. At the same time references to Bastien-Lepage are plentiful. *The Bridge at Grez* does, nevertheless, significantly differ from Bastien's usual mode of conception. Lavery proposes a social relationship between men and women in a particular setting, rather than heroically placing a single figure in the foreground.

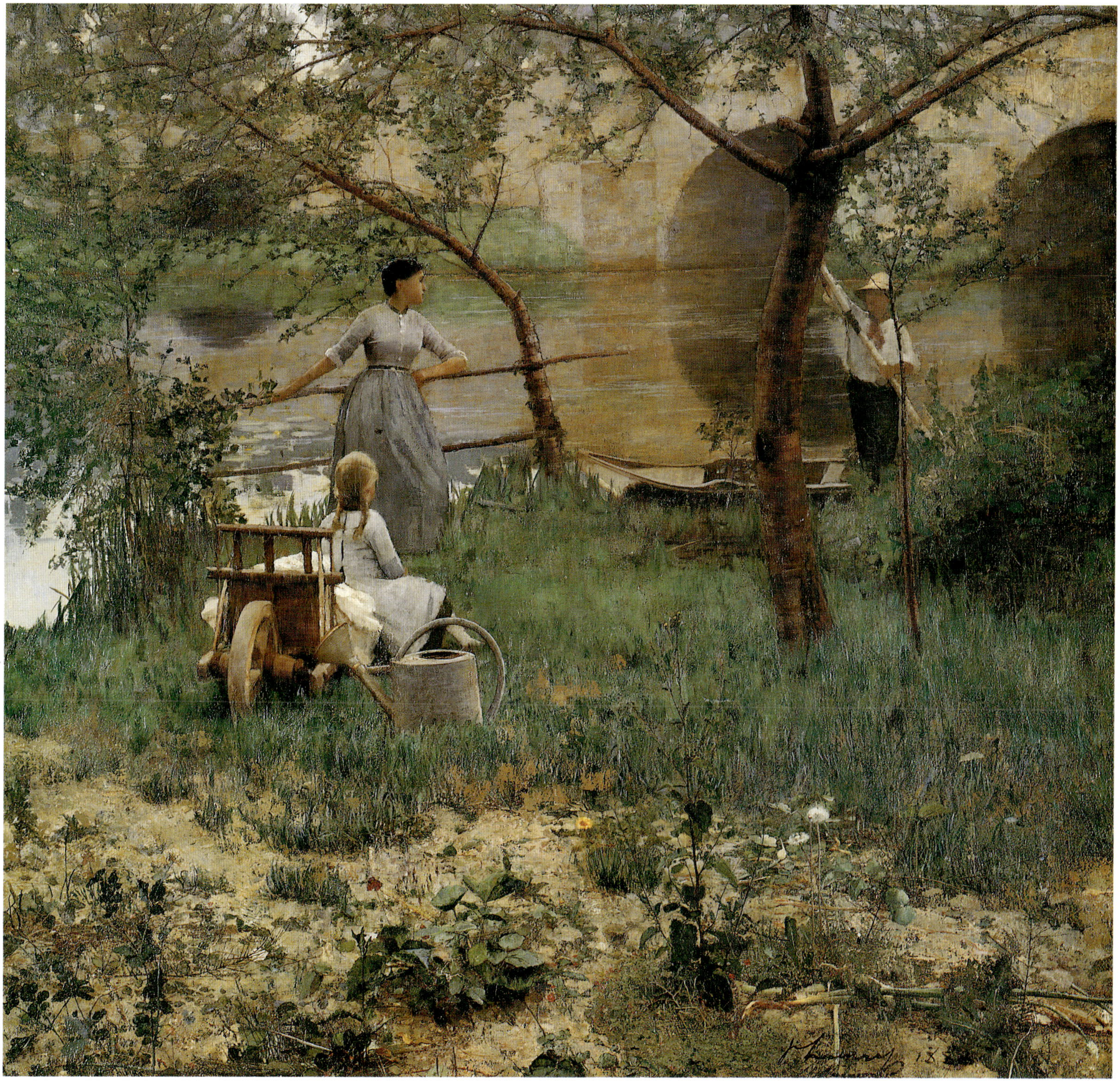

27 *On The Loing: An Afternoon Chat (Under the Cherry Tree)*, 1884, 59½ × 59¼
(The Ulster Museum, Belfast)

The panoramic format of the painting was derived by turning a standard-sized full-length portrait canvas on its side—as Stott and O'Meara had done for comparable works. Lavery's palette is richer than theirs, providing surface *éclat* in the striped shirt of the male oarsman and the brilliant parasol of the woman who attracts his attention. Such liaisons undoubtedly formed sub-plots within the Grez community. On more than one occasion the painter turned his attention to the female members of the artist group.

Despite its sympathetic ambiance, *The Bridge at Grez* failed to find an immediate purchaser and waited until 1898 before it passed to the Carnegie Institute, Pittsburgh, at the first of the institute's international exhibitions, at which Lavery was a member of the jury. Recalling the picture's fame in the United States, the painter remembered the compliment paid to him by a hapless American art dealer, who, desperate to ingratiate himself, declared, 'I think, sir, you are the best-known British painter whose work has reached the States. There sure is no picture more talked about than the beautiful Irish girl's portrait, *Bridget Gray*.'[20]

The tranquil mood of these exchanges on the river Loing is further distilled in one of Lavery's most accomplished small canvases, *A Grey Summer's Day, Grez* (Plate 25).[21] This small painting seems to sum up the enchanted world he had entered. A man in a straw hat with his back to the spectator gazes at the still water. Nearby a woman sits reading in a campaign chair, also with her back to the viewer. The motif of the distant rowing boat suggests a leisurely passing of time, and only the greyhound, alert and attentive, looks down the path and is aware of the approaching spectator. There could be no more concise expression of a timeless summer.

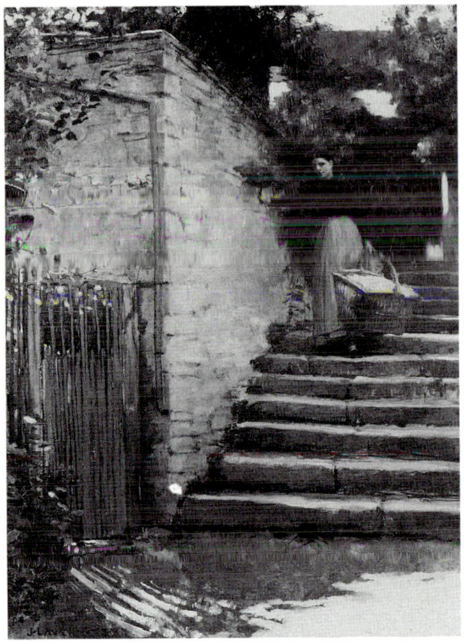

26 *La Laveuse (The Laundress)*, 1883, 25 × 17 (private collection)

Both of these canvases portray middle class leisure activities rather than dealing with aspects of the rural economy. Although he might occasionally treat peasant subject matter, Lavery was not to be typecast with the more mechanical followers of Bastien-Lepage. The artist colony, by the very fact that it contained a floating population created its own society within the rural community. This did not hinder the painter when he came to attend to the picturesqueness of the village, and finding local models to pose in their native habitat—as his colleagues had done and were continuing to do. A canvas, probably painted at Grez, entitled *La Laveuse* (*The Laundress*, Plate 26) exemplifies the continuity of this trend. It is difficult not to see this as a remaking of the earlier untraced costume-piece which he was still trying to sell, *Ye Maid was in the Garden hanging out the Clothes*.[22] We can infer that the false archaising of such a picture was rendered truly old-fashioned by this new treatment of a contemporary French laundress. The activity of going to the communal wash-house or to the river's edge, carrying a huge flat-topped wicker basket remained a consistent feature of village life which had been treated by Jean-François Millet and Leon Lhermitte. Lavery's intention, in contrast to these venerated masters seems to be one of simple objectivity.

It was probably the desire to identify with a particular set of visual sources which prompted Lavery to return to the theme of the laundress in 1884. During the spring months he embarked upon a large composition, the principal motif of which was a washerwoman by the river, conversing with a passing boatman. In front of her, closer to the spectator, a girl sits on a barrow containing a large

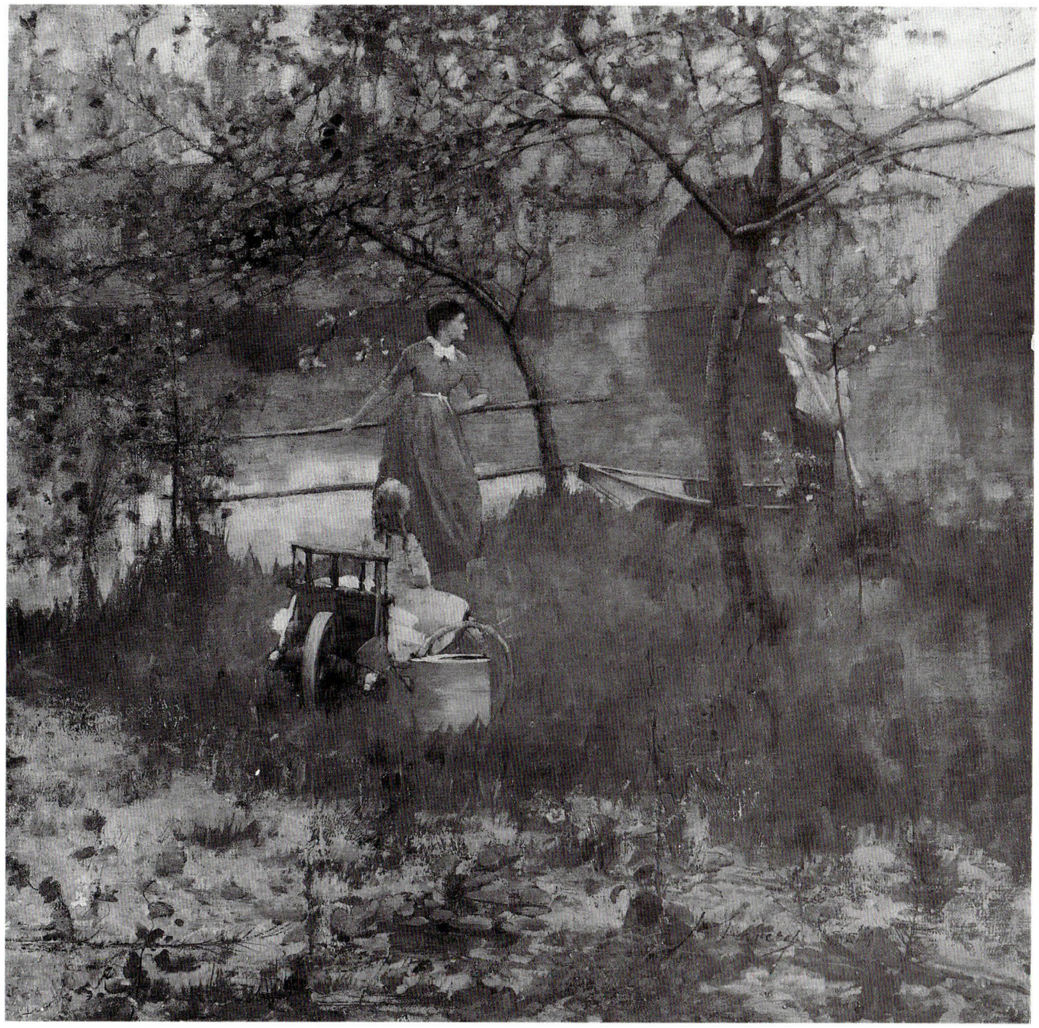

28 *The Bridge at Grez*, 1884, 31 × 31 (private collection, photo, Spink and Son)

bundle of washing. The painting could almost illustrate Stevenson's lines which refer to the village women of Grez who 'wash and wash all day among the fish and waterlilies. It seem as if linen washed there should be specially cool and sweet.'[23] Even here with village characters, Lavery, rather than representing labour, selects a moment of respite. When shown at the Glasgow Institute in 1885, it bore the title, *On the Loing: An Afternoon Chat* (Plate 27).[24]

This large work is almost a thesis statement of Lavery's new *plein-air* style.[25] It was planned upon a smaller canvas of the same format. Initially Lavery took in a wider view of the riverside, giving correspondingly less detail. The figures of the washerwoman and what may be her daughter have been drawn with the point of a sable brush, before being blocked in in solid slabs of opaque pigment, in the manner of the ateliers. Partly because the painter was not elaborating details of foliage, the spatial relationships in this smaller version seem clearer than those of the exhibited work. In the large version, Lavery worked up the foreground with heavy encrustations of paint. The impasto almost creates a foliage proscenium beyond which the actors take their poses. The middle ground figures and objects are shown in more generalised square brush strokes—particularly evident in the treatment of the watering can, habitually used by washerwomen to keep the washing damp in the hot sun. The backdrop, showing a portion of the bridge, is thinly brushed, with minimal detail. These alterations of handling produce an almost stereoscopic effect, analogous to the concept of a 'depth of field' in photography. As stylistic features they have become more marked than, for instance, O'Meara's *Towards the Night and Winter*, a companion Grez picture at the same Glasgow exhibition. While O'Meara softens the effect of his foreground, Lavery accentuates his. With his particular past experience, Lavery would, more than his contemporaries, have understood the processes, effects and possibilities of contemporary photography, yet no evidence of his use of the medium in relation to the sequence of Grez pictures has survived.

The most important model for his composition was Bastien-Lepage's *Joan of Arc Listening to the Voices* (Plate 30), the large Salon picture of 1880, which also treated a garden setting.[26] The greater density of undergrowth, almost pressing in upon the figure of Joan of Arc separates the two works. Lavery was not tackling a supremely nationalist icon—didactic purpose was confined to the visual learning associated with the creation of a convincing naturalistic effect.

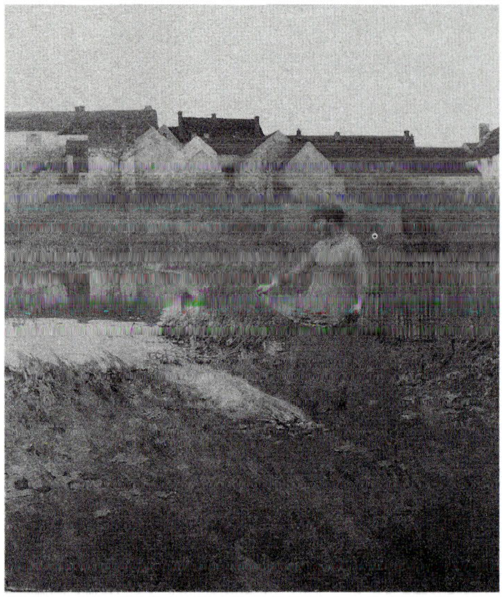

29 Frank O'Meara, *Towards the Night and Winter*, 1885, 59 × 50 (Hugh Lane Municipal Gallery of Modern Art, Dublin)

Lavery deployed similar compositional devices in *Return from Market* (Plate 31).[27] In this instance the surface of the river is viewed from a high bank and foreground recession upon its surface is conveyed by successive clusters of lily-pads. Moving into the riverside shadows, the two women in the punt, or 'shallop', are seen in *contre-jour*, against the bright daylight reflections of the mid-stream. Lavery impressively manipulates a series of diagonals to create a striking visual effect.[28]

Several Grez pictures reveal Lavery's flair for dramatic composition. On the whole his Grez contemporaries preferred to establish their location in the use of strongly stated friezes of buildings upon which their peasant figures are superimposed. This is the case with William Kennedy's *Mademoiselle Cunegonde* and *Spring*, the first of which was painted at Grez in 1884. The closest point of comparison to these works is Lavery's *Sewing in the Shade* (Plate 32), a genre picture, possibly exhibited as *The Two Friends*, and which has an obvious affinity with *Return from Market* (see Plate 31).[29] Tight control in the composition is supported by the most subtle colour harmonies. Yet here, as in *On the Loing: An Afternoon Chat* (see Plate 27), the emphasis is upon social exchange, upon confidences traded by the side of the pale shimmering reaches of the river Loing. Foreground foliage and framing tree-trunk help to contain a mood of intimacy.

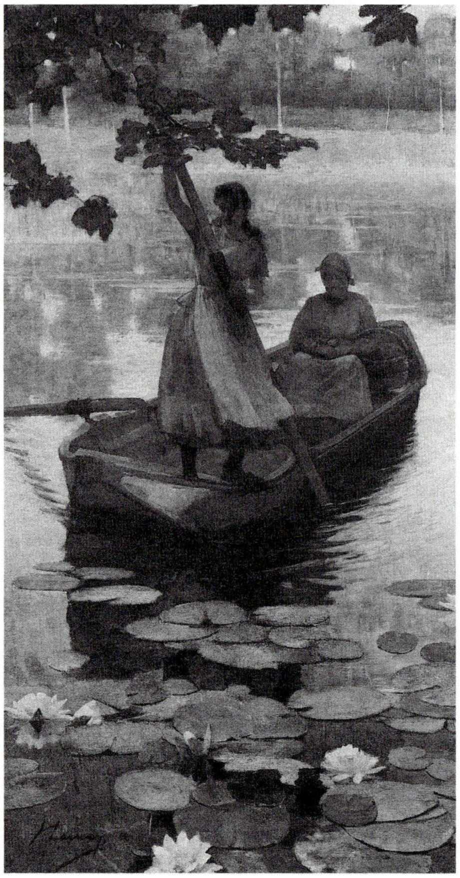

31 *Return from Market*, 1884, $46\frac{3}{4} \times 24\frac{1}{2}$ (private collection)

Artists of the Grez community, Lavery included, consistently presented the peasant women of the village in attitudes of repose. There was little sense of stern social realism, of searching out unremitting toil for brutal portrayal. The comings and goings of the sleepy village were part of the slow pageant which alien artists observed from a distance for a brief period. Lavery was the only painter at Grez to pull back and attempt to visually characterise the relationship between villagers and their artist guests. It became the subject of one of his most interesting canvases. In *On the Bridge at Grez* (Plate 33) an artist, possibly Frank O'Meara, his day's work done, rests against the parapet of the bridge, eyeing two women from the village who are leaning over to talk to an unseen boatman passing under it.[30]

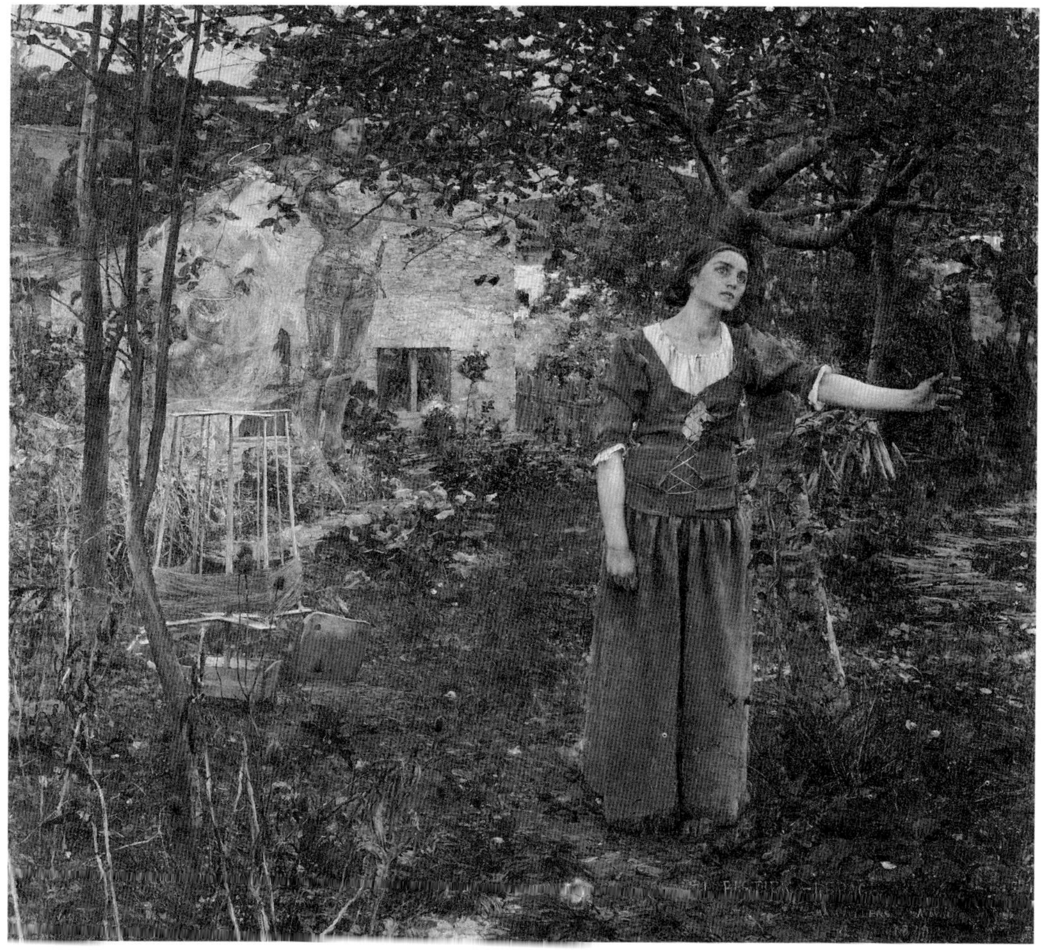

30 Jules Bastien-Lepage, *Joan of Arc Listening to the Voices*, 1880, 100 × 110 (Metropolitan Museum, New York, gift of Erwin Davis 1889)

The woman on the extreme left wears a white scarf similar to that worn by the laundress in the small version of *On the Loing*... In this instance Lavery discovered major preoccupations which were to remain with him throughout his career. Firstly, the motif of the female figure gazing off towards some distant vista, was one which may have struck him in the poetic handling of E. L. Adan's *Soir d'Automne*, shown at the influential Salon of 1882. The subject was revisited often in later years. Secondly, at Grez, Lavery, more than his fellows, studied other artists at work and made this a source of subject-matter.

His preoccupation in this respect, began with a study in concentration, *Painting on a Summer's Day* (Plate 34), executed in the previous year. This young woman artist was to be the prototype for many other images of painters at work. Inscribed 'sketch for a large picture', this could be the first thought for a large lost oil entitled *A Pupil of Mine*.[31] The subject was resumed on two further occasions in 1884 when Lavery painted *The Principal Street at Gretz* [sic] (Plate 35) a small picture of a male colleague, probably William Mouat Loudan, busily engaged upon a large open air study.[32] A further example from 1884, showing a female artist at work, is *A Day in Midsummer*.[33] Although, in this instance, the young woman is apparently alone, one of the legs of another easel in the foreground indicates the presence of at least one other artist offstage.

The artist colony, as well as the Grez peasantry, provided Lavery with an ample

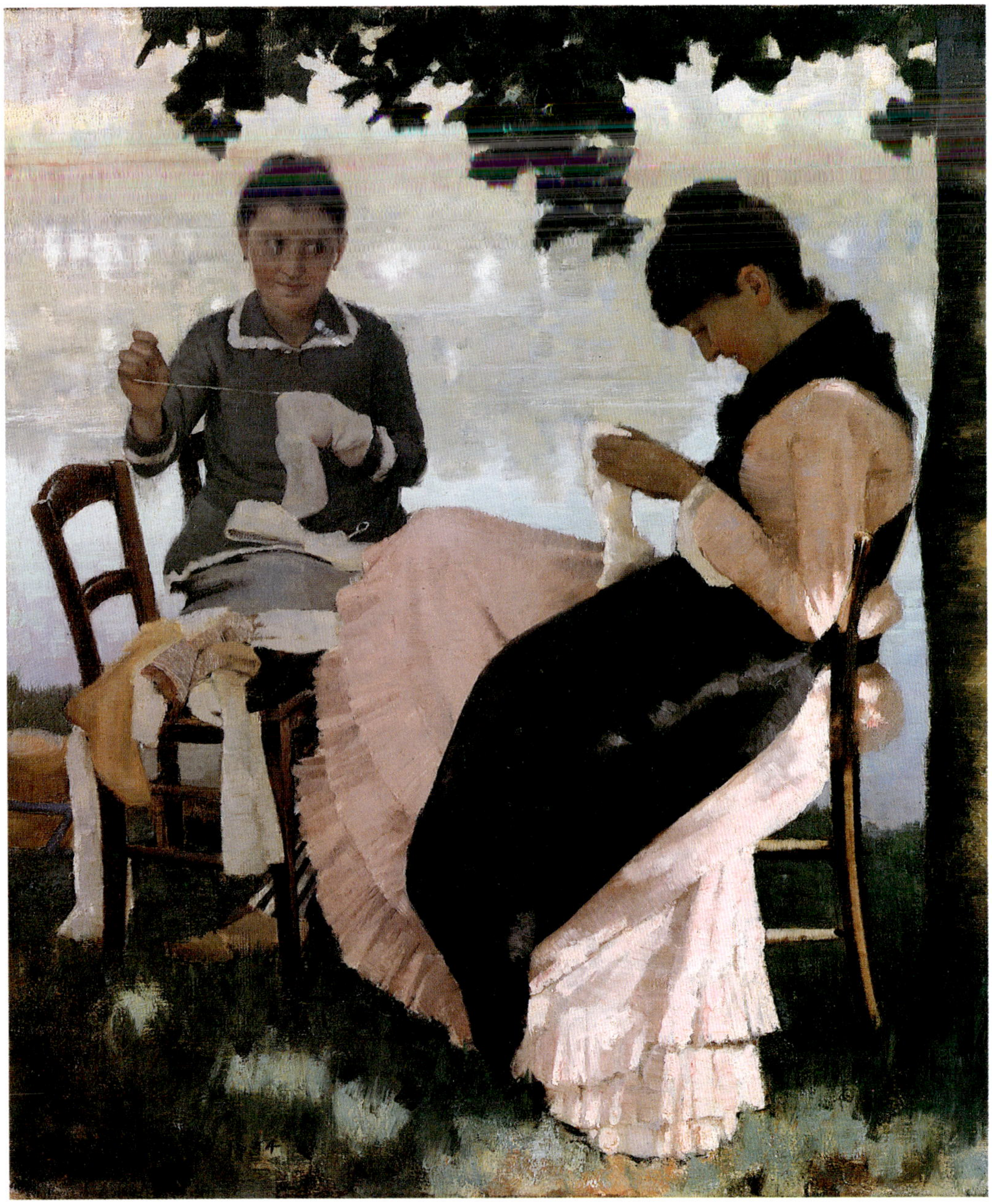

32 *Sewing in the Shade*, 1884, 22 × 18¼ (private collection, photo, Pyms Gallery, London)

supply of motifs. His curiosity, as much as that of bystanders, was aroused by the sight of a colleague at work. Painting in the open air became a kind of side-show, a public performance or piece of street theatre which greatly appealed to someone who was so resoundingly convivial as John Lavery. The unidentified young woman who forms the subject of *A Day in Midsummer*, probably also posed for *The Hammock—Twilight* (Plate 36), the first working of what was to become yet another favourite motif. Here Lavery's debt may well have been to Tissot whose *The Hammock* had created a stir at the Grosvenor Gallery in 1878.[34] Despite the fact that Tissot had displayed an indecent amount of ankle and petticoat, his compositional strategy evidently appealed to the young Lavery. Again, as in *Sewing in the Shade* (see Plate 32), the placid waters of the river Loing provide an

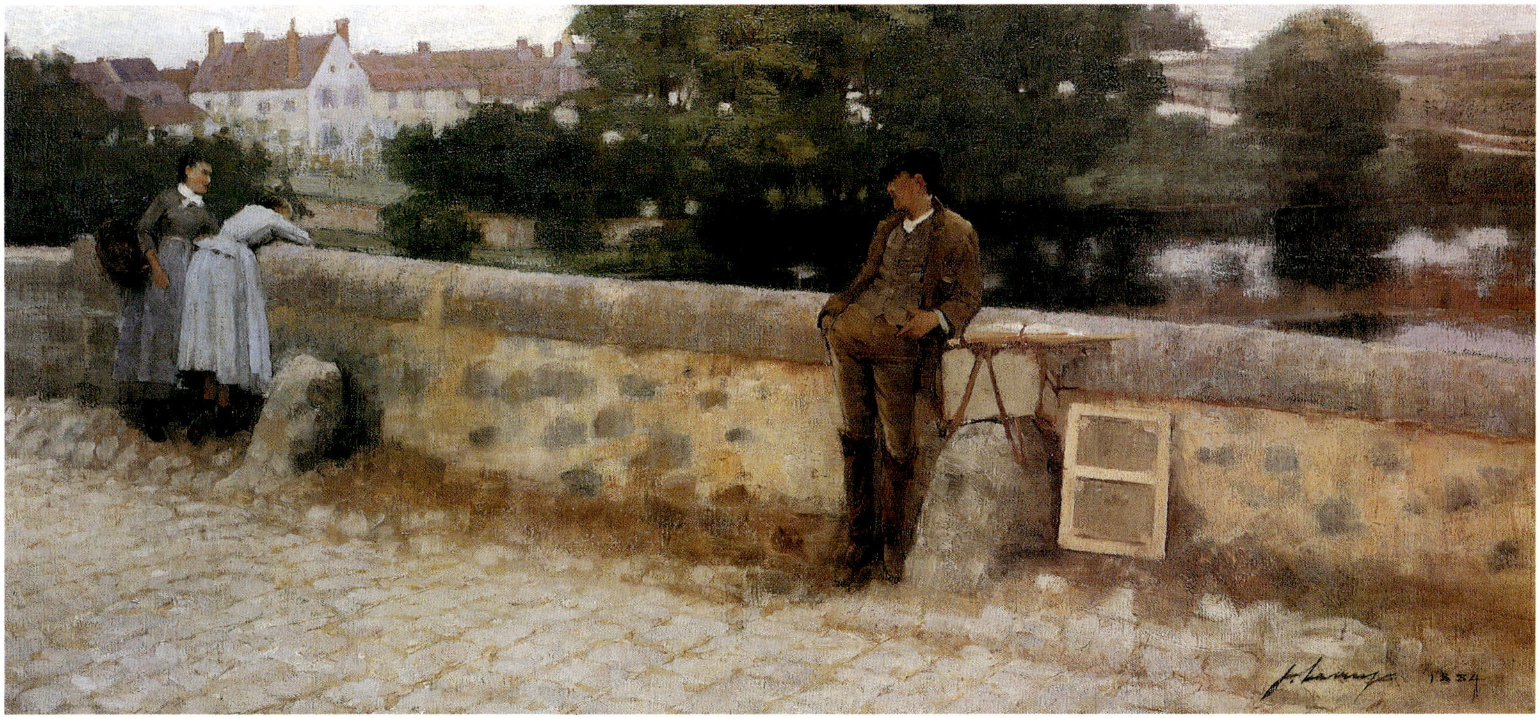

33 *On the Bridge at Grez*, 1884, $19\frac{1}{4} \times 39\frac{1}{2}$ (private collection, photo, Pyms Gallery, London)

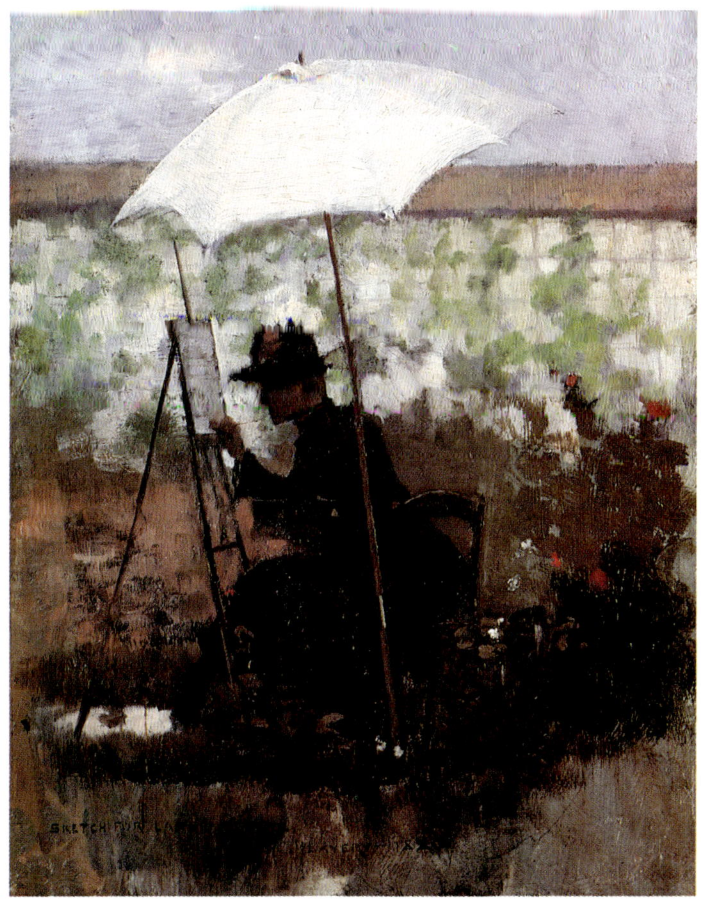

34 *Painting on a Summer's Day*, 1884, $9\frac{1}{2} \times 7\frac{1}{4}$ (private collection, courtesy Fine Art Society)

agreeable backdrop, while in the immediate foreground the space between the spectator and the young woman is defined by a stool. This symbolic separation is magnified by the deliberate obscuring of part of the face of the woman in the hammock. What we see is a dressed up middle-class version of the reclining nudes by Courbet and Manet. Clothing in this instance contributes to the allure of the sitter. The continuity of concern, of male describing and defining female beauty, established in works such as *After the Dance* is sustained.

It would be difficult to under-estimate the importance of these two eventful sojourns at what Lavery later described as, 'an inexpensive and delightful place'.[35] The village provided an escape from the claustrophobic atmosphere of the over-crowded ateliers. It was a provisional substitute for that essential relationship with subject-matter found in the specific *coin de terre*, which Bastien-Lepage commended to all of his young followers. To some extent this was enshrined in the patronage and policy of the French government which, during the early years of the Third Republic, favoured large naturalistic Salon paintings of provincial life. At the artists' colony, the congenial ambiance allowed Lavery to develop, whilst not being wholly committed to the French establishment's view of the artist's purpose. He discovered what were to become essential motifs, and at the same time, he acquired the confidence to work amidst all of the circumstantial distractions of painting in the open air. With this apprenticeship complete, he could return to Glasgow primed for ambitious projects.

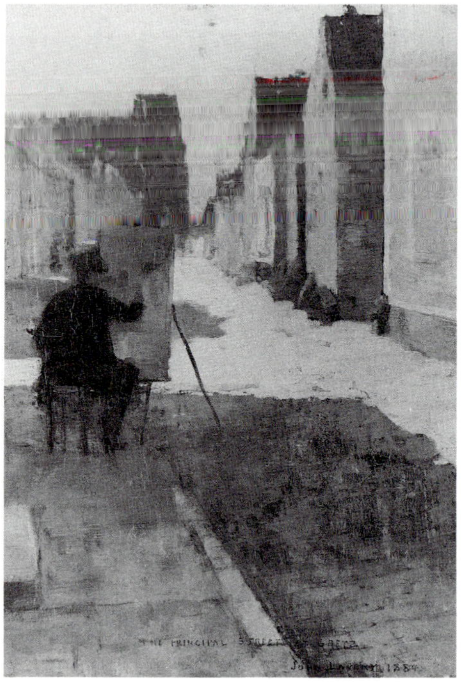

35 *The Principal Street at Grez*, 1884, $12\frac{3}{4} \times 9$ (private collection)

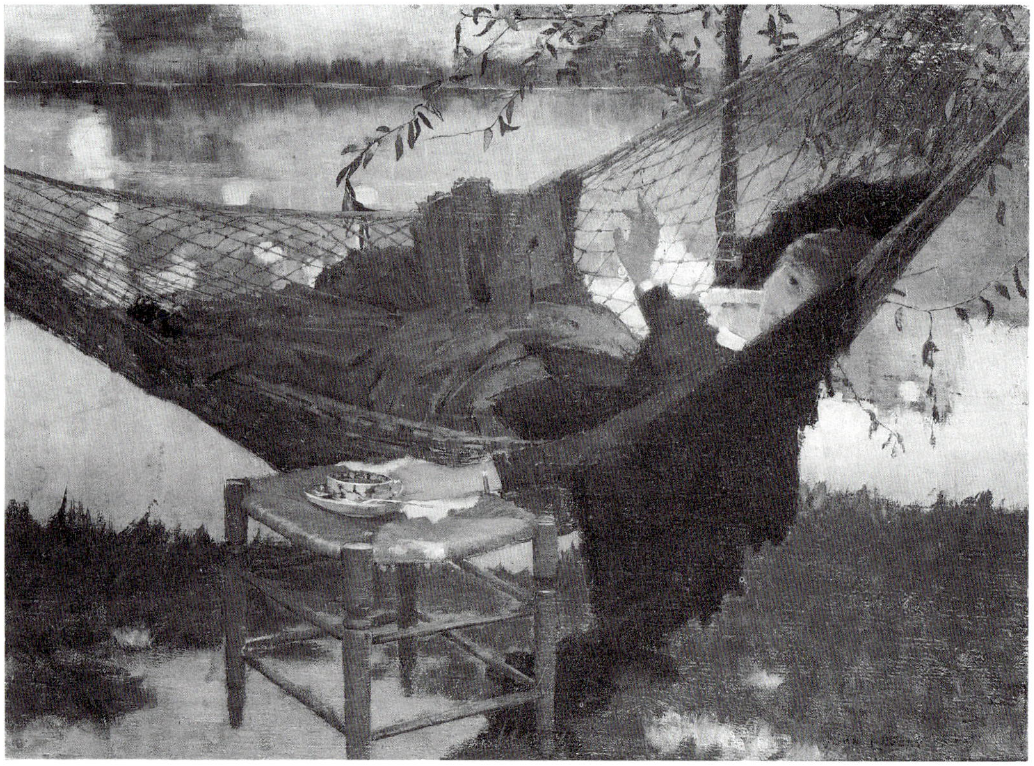

36 *The Hammock – Twilight*, 1884, 19 × 25 (private collection, courtesy Spink and Son)

4 The Glasgow Boy

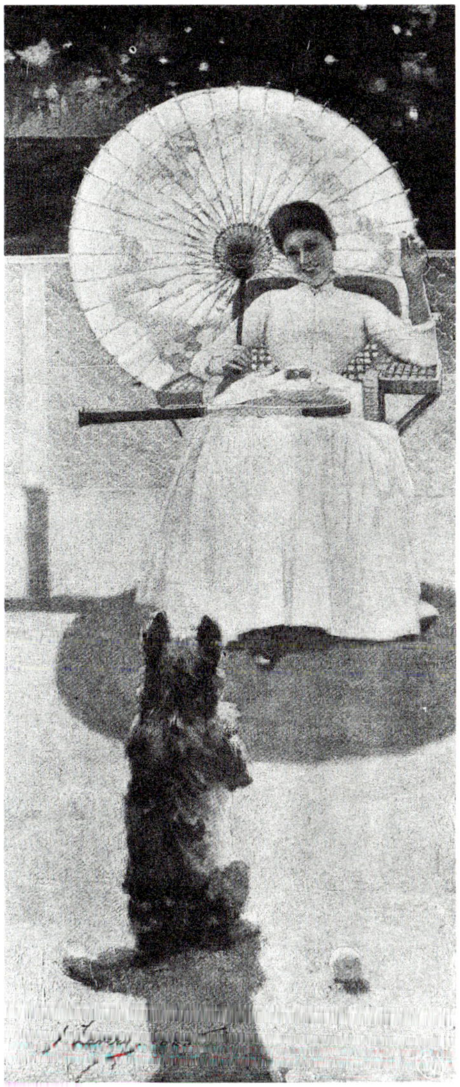

38 *Beg Sir!*, 1885, size unknown (present whereabouts unknown)

Four years after Lavery's return to Glasgow, *The Art Journal* noted that 'there is in Scotland, notably in Glasgow, a band of young painters who have broken from the traditions of the past and boldly struck into the road that is marked with the footprints of Bastien-Lepage.'[1] The occasion which provided the opportunity for this observation was the fine art display at the Glasgow International Exhibition. This huge multi-cultural festival, loosely modelled on the Great Exhibition, was staged on a parkland site at Kelvinside, under the shadow of Glasgow University. Following similar exhibitions at Edinburgh and Manchester in 1886 and 1887, the International Exhibition, partly motivated by rivalry, aimed to celebrate Glasgow's opulence as a trading and industrial centre.[2] Its industries were prominently featured. Its links with the outside world were implied in the great variety of foreign artefacts on show. The visitor, transported by Venetian gondola experienced the aroma of curry wafting from the Indian pavilion, mingling with that of coffee from the Dutch cocoa house.

The fine art exhibition within the International drew together important works by foreign artists, many of which, as a result of the activities of dealers like Cottier and Craibe Angus, were drawn from the newly formed collections of local industrialists. Many of these 'merchant princes' were also clients of the younger Glasgow-based painters to whom the writer in *The Art Journal* referred. Glasgow's distinctive modern style of painting was predominantly 'French' in character. Its painters, Lavery amongst them, had eschewed the 'gluepot' fakery of their predecessors. The *plein-air* naturalism of Bastien-Lepage had taken root.

When he returned to Glasgow at the end of 1884, Lavery realised that the peasant subject-matter, which had been such an important part of his work at Grez, could not be sustained. Two pictures of an old man and young girl, painted shortly after his return, sum up the French manner—almost as if they were demonstration pieces for the other Glasgow painters.[3] In *Youth and Age* (Plate 37) there is lifelike precision as well as strength and solidity in the modelling. The handling is in accord with the best atelier practice. The second version of these head studies, *Little Nell*, is deliberately 'ébauche'. From both these pictures, all contextual information has been removed. There is no setting and no clothing visible, only the unkempt beard of the old man betrays his lower class origins.

For all the attraction of painting Scottish, rather than French peasants, Lavery showed no inclination to plant his easel in the kailyard. Unlike some of his Glasgow contemporaries, he had no links with the lowland landscape and it would be artificial to manufacture them. He was already the most cosmopolitan of the Scottish artists and the life to which he aspired was that of the more leisurely middle-class conversation-piece. He admired the sophisticated urbanity of international painters such as Tissot, Heilbuth, De Nittis and Beraud, the social recorders of the Third Republic, and this is typified in works like *Beg Sir!* (Plate 38)

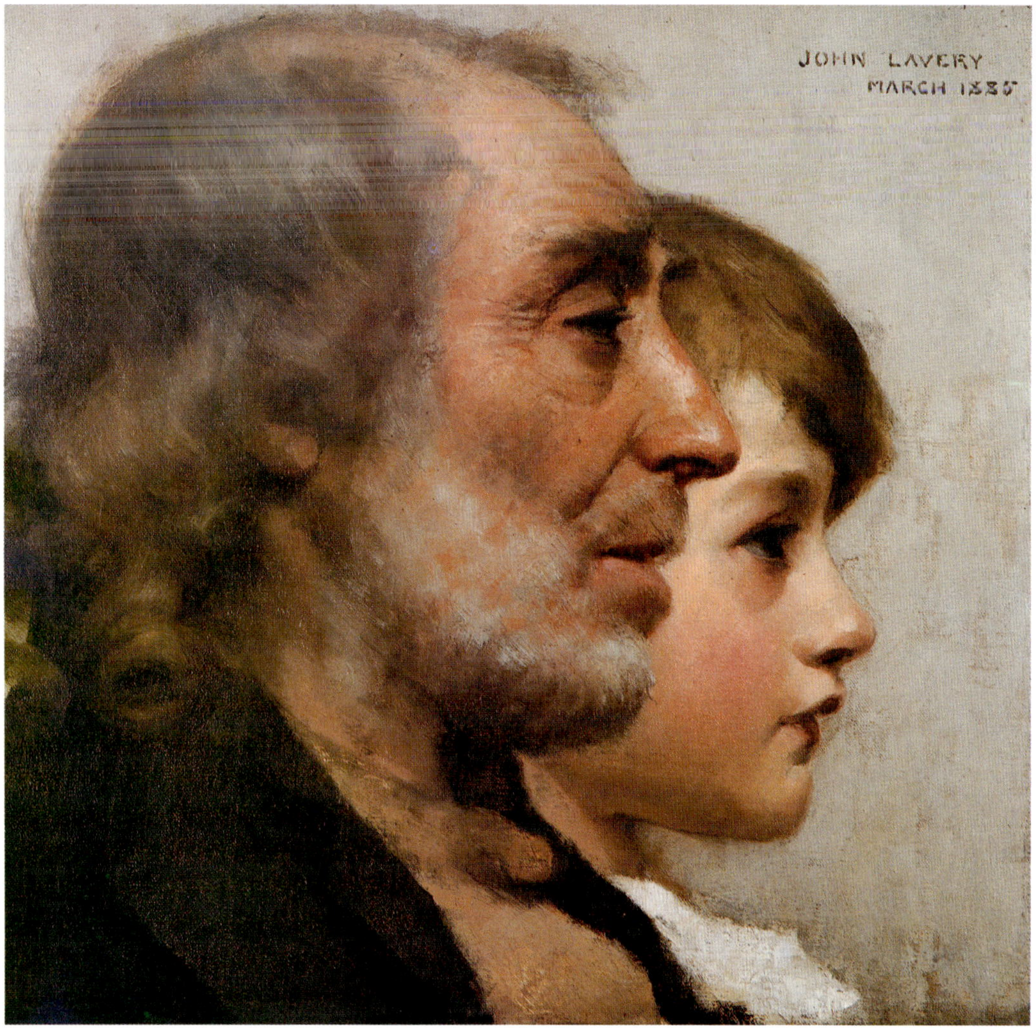

37 *Youth and Age*, 1885, 13 × 13 (Stonyhurst College)

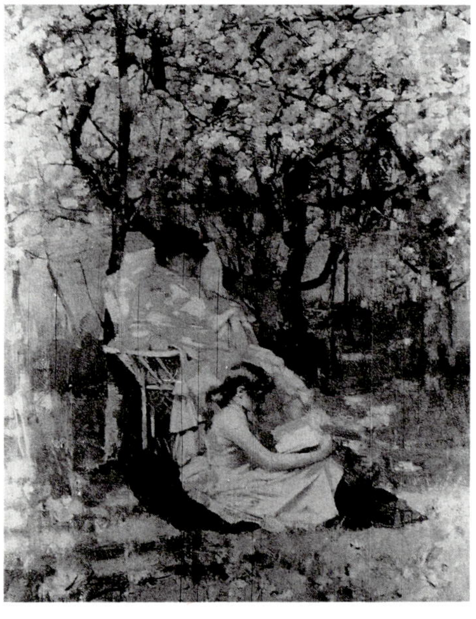

39 *Convalescence*, 1885, size unknown (private collection)

A second version of *The Hammock* painted around this time, reveals some of the difficulties of matching stylish technique with stylish subject-matter.[4] The broader square brush technique of his contemporaries might be suitable for portraying rustic retainers, but it must be adapted to the more refined sensibilities of the well-to-do. These patrons, their families and servants became Lavery's subject-matter. In *Convalescence* (Plate 39) for instance, Eva Fulton, the daughter of James Fulton, the wealthy Paisley wool and cotton manufacturer poses beside an ailing relative in a blossoming orchard. Lavery has reworked a subject which had been treated by Tissot, although the picture may reveal a broader knowledge of New English Art Club artists.[5] Clausen, for instance, was, at that moment painting orchard settings.[6] Lavery's picture, however, seems more genuinely impressionistic than those of his contemporaries, in that he draws fully upon the effects of sunlight falling through blossom.

Taken with the watercolours of 1885, *The Parasol* (Plate 40), *Lady on a Safety Tricycle* (Plate 41)[7] and *He Won't Bite You*, *Convalescence* forms a record of the leisurely life of the daughters of the Paisley industrialists. James Fulton, his

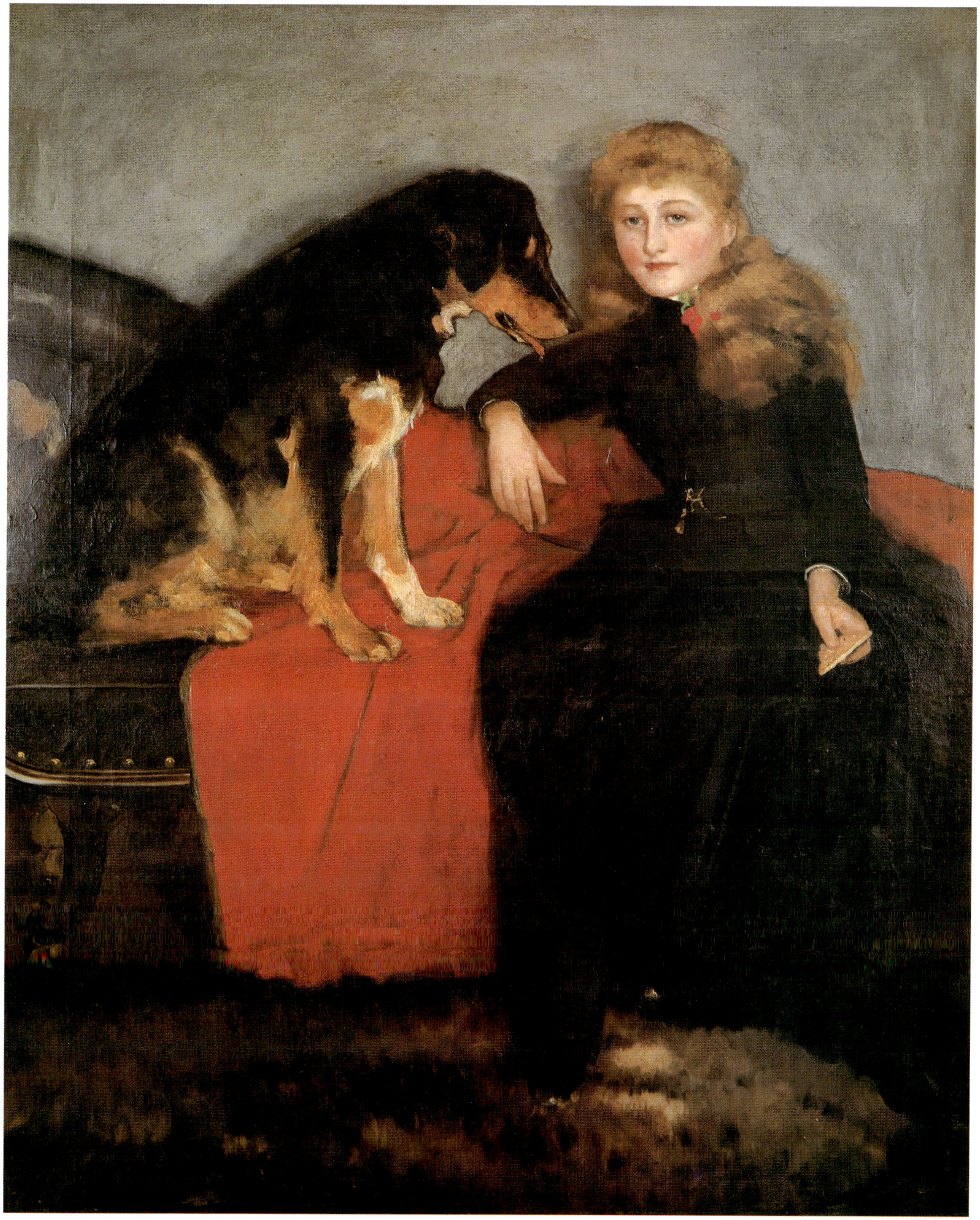

42 *Miss Eva Fulton*, 1886, $50\frac{1}{2} \times 40$
(Renfrew Museums and Art Gallery)

principal patron, was interested in art and was later to donate his important collection of French Realist and Barbizon painting to the Paisley Art Institute.[8] Lavery painted two very different portraits of his daughters. The first of these, a rather overwrought circular picture showing Alice Fulton in a white dress engulfed by white roses, is gruesomely claustrophobic and may have been done to Fulton's specification.[9] The portrait of Eva is altogether more daring since it recasts the theme of *Beg Sir!* (see Plate 38), but evokes Whistlerian propriety in the handling of tone. *Miss Eva Fulton* (Plate 42) goes beyond the impassivity of conventional portraits, and it is clear from it that the artist much preferred to construct a situation in which figures respond to one another.

Thus Lavery espoused a Baudelairian ideal of *la vie moderne*, which should concentrate upon well-mannered social exchange. There was no better setting for this than the ritualised combat of the newly popular game of lawn tennis. The social significance of this new sport can hardly be under-estimated. Along with cycling and roller-skating it was seen as a healthy pursuit for young people of both sexes, providing the opportunity for polite conversation between eligible partners under the supervision of their elders. The game and its attendant social rituals generated a suite of pictures. In *Beg Sir!* a young woman holding a parasol, sitting in a wicker chair with a racket on her lap, teases a dog.[10] The composition echoes Tissot's *Croquet*. In *The Tennis Match* (Plate 43), a male spectator casually chats to two women.[11] The courtly civilities of De Troy and the eighteenth century *petits-maîtres* are reshaped in contemporary terms.

Lavery also studied the more energetic aspects of the scene. The dynamic action of *A Rally* (Plate 44) challenged his powers of observation. A large instantaneous photograph, if it had been possible, would have been a useful aid, but it could not substitute for the concentration advocated by Bastien-Lepage. In their one encounter on the Pont des Arts, Lavery was advised to: 'Always carry a

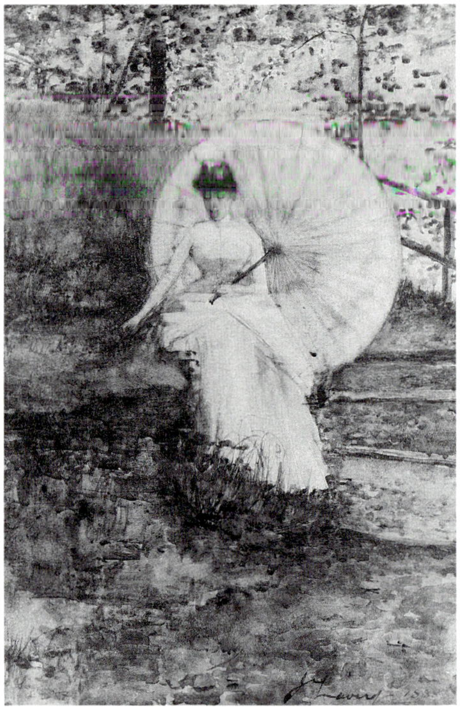

40 *The Parasol*, 1885, 20½ × 13¾, watercolour on paper (private collection, photo, Pyms Gallery, London)

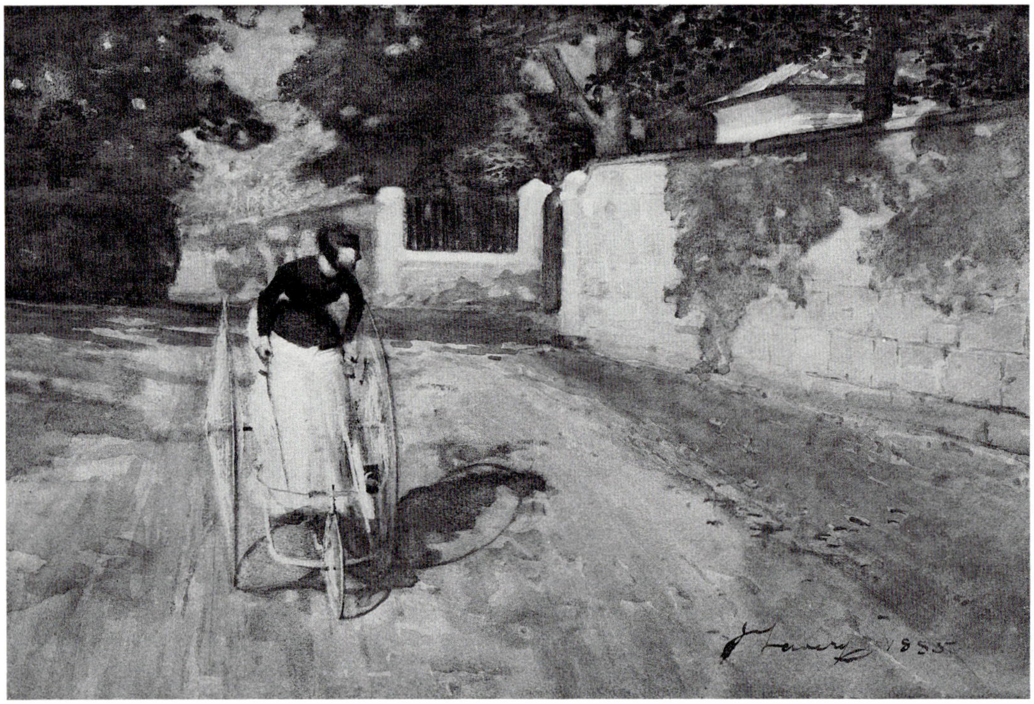

41 *Lady on a Safety Tricycle*, 1885, 13⅛ × 20½ (Government Art Collection)

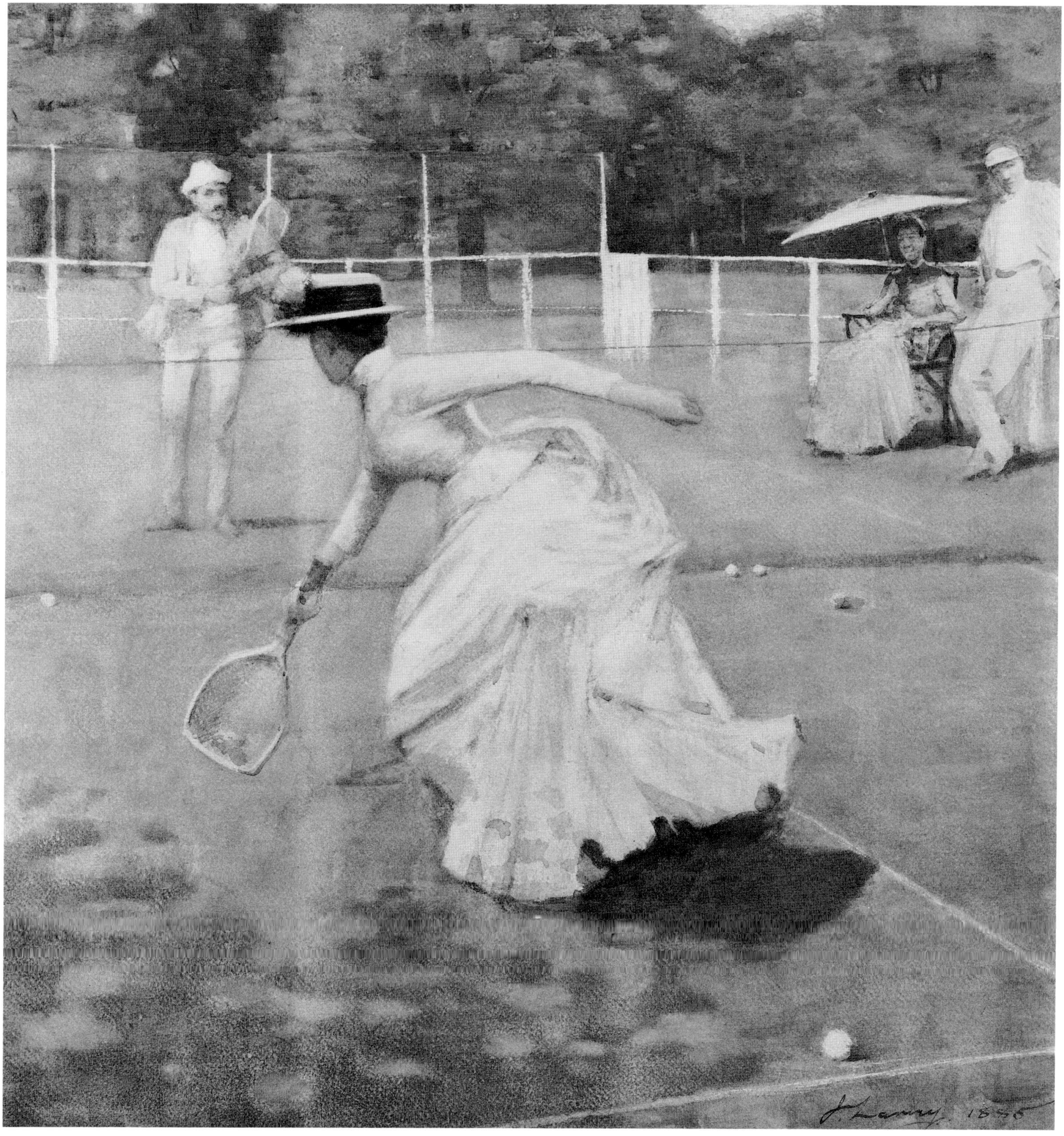

44 *A Rally*, 1885, 26 × 25, watercolour on paper (Glasgow Art Gallery and Museum)

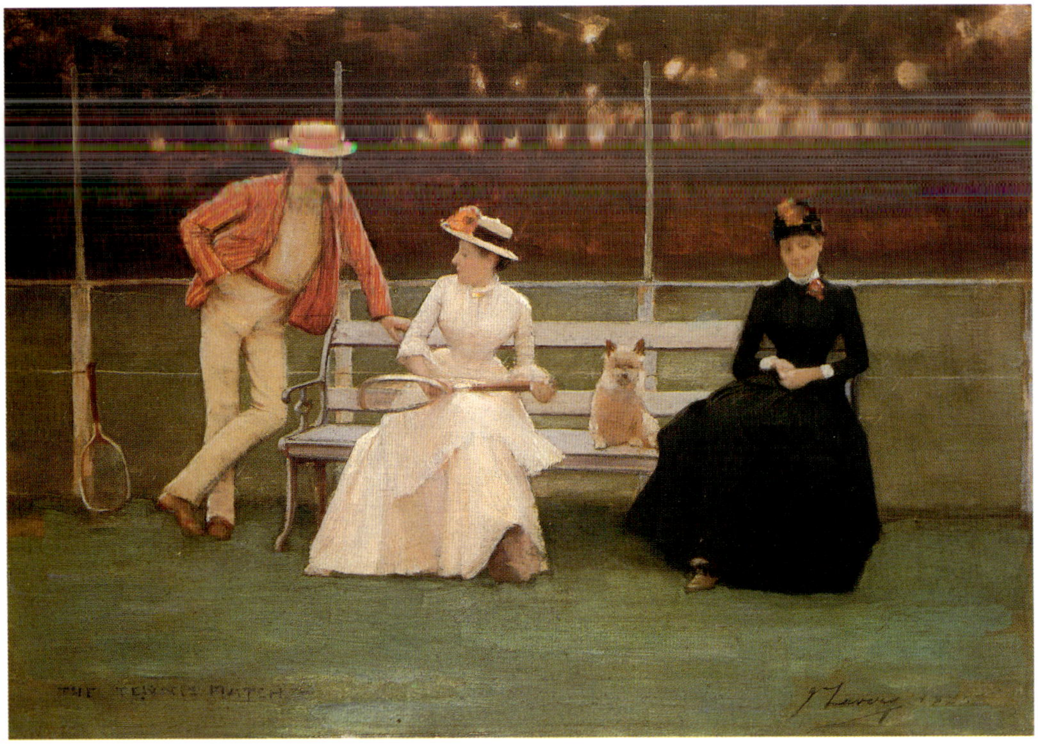

43 *The Tennis Match*, 1885, $11\frac{1}{2} \times 15\frac{3}{4}$
(Whitford and Hughes, London)

sketchbook. Select a person—watch him—then put down as much as you remember. Never look twice. At first you will remember very little, but continue and you will soon get complete action.'[12]

Alas the sketchbooks in which Lavery acquired this skill have not survived, but it was obviously fully developed by the time he painted *A Rally*. In this, the dynamic action of the female player's serve was recorded in watercolour, a medium which admitted no revisions or corrections. The result is something of a *tour de force*, comparable only to the large oil painting which became the definitive statement on the subject. Lavery's court was at Cartbank, Cathcart, near Paisley and his protagonists were the sons and daughters of the bourgeois, who, on a good summer's day came out to watch the game. It is they who form the select band of a dozen spectators in *The Tennis Party* (Plate 45), the definitive work in the series. Alix MacBride, one of its models, describes the painting as having been 'No special occasion but was just a composition in which at odd times my sister, a cousin and I posed for the principal figures—in those old tennis days we had a good number of friends coming about us and the other figures were taken from some of them.'[13]

Lavery was observed in his endeavours by more professional eyes. 'The help of critics was not wanting either. Arthur Melville, James Guthrie, Teddy Walton and others used to come to Cartbank in those days—and *The Tennis Party* underwent many changes before it resulted in the very fine picture it is today.'[14] It is likely, therefore, that what was to become Lavery's most universally applauded work was avidly discussed by the whole Glasgow community of artists. The extent of the changes in its progression may be gauged from the close comparison

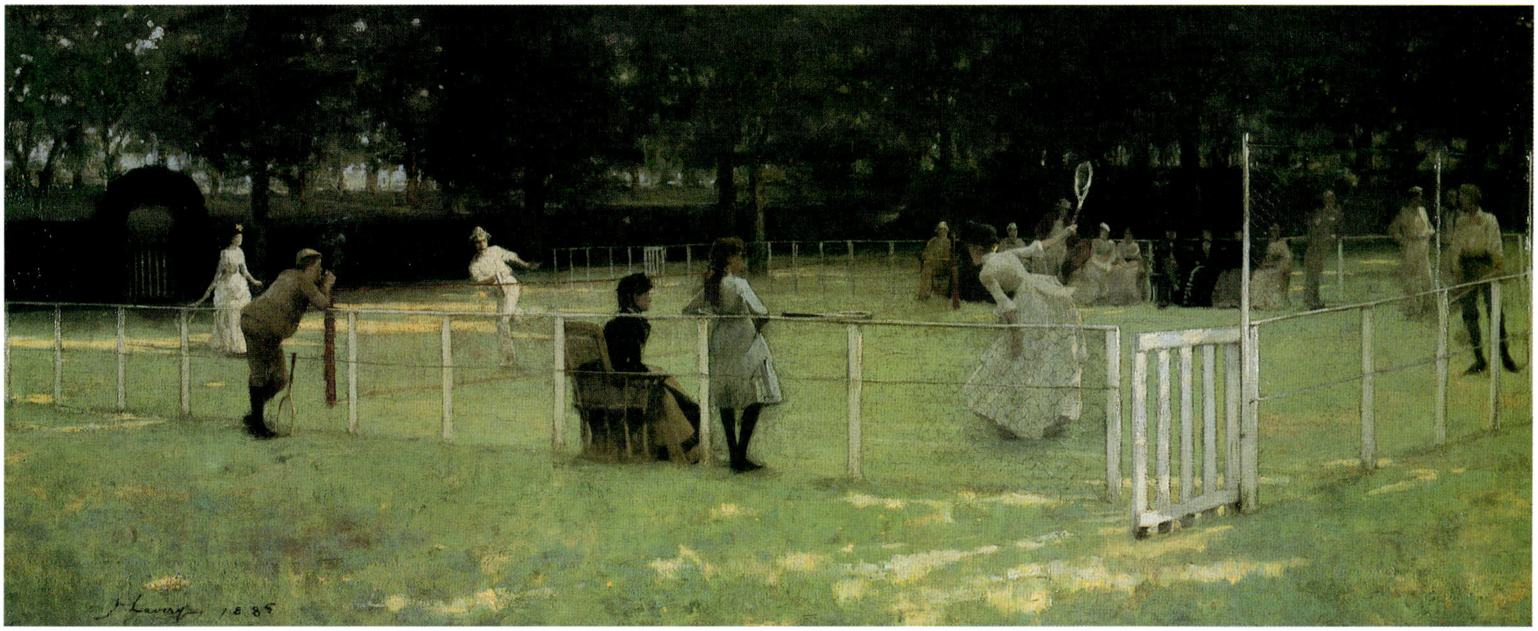

45 *The Tennis Party*, 1885, $30\frac{1}{4} \times 69\frac{1}{2}$
(Aberdeen Art Gallery)

of the finished picture with the small sketch (Plate 46).[15] This little painting vividly records Lavery's first thought for the pictorial arrangement. The gate and railings on the right formed the essential division of the canvas and in the first attempt, the action is contained on the left, by the white clad male player running to receive the shot. A solitary female figure in the now familiar basket chair, occupies the central foreground position as a counterpoint to the row of six spectators in the background. Lavery evidently felt that this disposition could be improved. He added a male spectator, casually puffing his pipe, on the left and the lady in the wicker chair obtained a young female companion. The number of background spectators was doubled and the positions of the two left-hand players reversed. It is easy to see that these additions contributed greatly to the strength of the composition, but they also distanced it from the spontaneous attack of

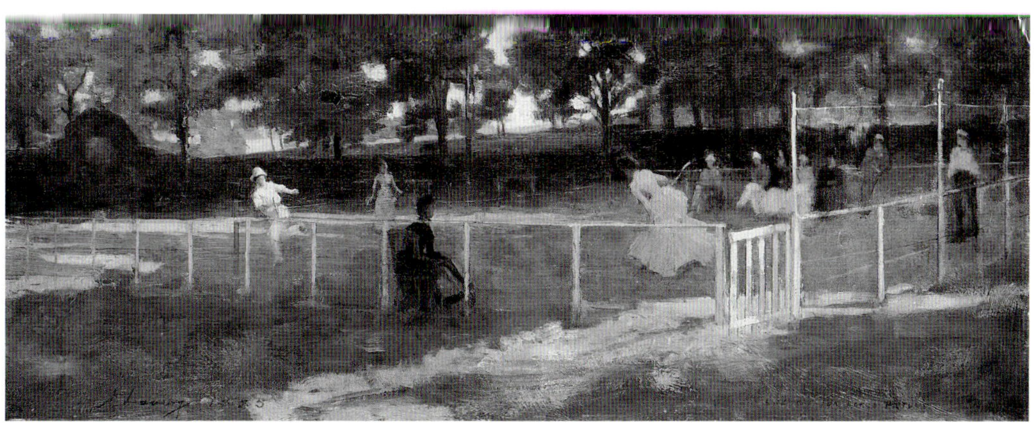

46 Sketch for *The Tennis Party*, 1885, $9\frac{1}{2} \times 23$ (Spink and Son, London)

Impressionism. Modern life, in Lavery's view, was not trivial; it could enlist all the serious academic ritual reserved for history painting, and yet at the same time, it should not appear stiff and posed. Artifice was essential to the most persuasive naturalism. Hence the cunning strategy of representing a complete view of the game, where action is mediated by the presence of spectators within the picture. The fact that the painting was regarded by one of its first reviewers as a 'first rate large sketch' illustrates the extent to which *The Tennis Party* departed from accepted standards of finish. It was nevertheless apparent that the 'effect' was 'very faithfully rendered . . . broad, pure and true in tint and tone'.[16]

Other reviewers commented upon the boldness and originality of the composition, and while it is certainly true that spectator sports had been painted before, Lavery's formulation was without precedent.[17] Elsewhere the picture was simply hailed as a 'lively work of the Impressionist School'.[18] Recognising perhaps that it caught some of the quality of Manet and Degas, George Moore applauded it in 1888 as '. . . a work of real talent'.[19]

Lavery decided to show *The Tennis Party* at the Royal Academy in London before sending it to the Glasgow Institute of Fine Arts. Even at this stage in his career his ambitions extended to the most prestigious arena. The picture, with *Beg Sir!* (see Plate 38) and *On the Bridge at Grez* (see Plate 33), formed a group of works of sufficient importance to introduce him to the London audience.[20] Right from the start of his Glasgow years, success south of the border was a priority, and if he was not exactly acclaimed by all critics, he did not go unnoticed either. Only Sir Frederic Leighton, President of the Royal Academy, failed to note *The Tennis Party* upon its first appearance. When two years later, it was shown at the Salon, he is reported to have remarked, 'now that's the kind of picture we should have for the Academy!'[21]

Lavery's appearance in London in 1886 was significant in itself. Many of the young artists of his generation felt, after their return from Paris, that the older academicians had closed ranks against them. Although some of their work was grudgingly admitted to the annual exhibitions, a great deal of hostility remained. In that very year, a breakaway exhibiting society, the New English Art Club was formed.[22] Its ambitions were unclear. Some members felt that it should be a rival organisation wresting power from the Academy, with democratically elected committees, imitating the Société des Artistes Français which had been formed to administer the Salon after the state withdrew at the end of 1880. Despite the heated discussion which took place over the winter months of 1886, the 'bigger movement', a democratised Academy, led by Holman Hunt, Walter Crane and George Clausen seemed destined to failure.[23] A writer in *The Art Journal*, thinking partly of Lavery's work in the 1886 Academy, protested that none of the followers of 'French Realism', '. . . can assert that they have not received their deserts at the hands of the Academy: there was not a room at the last exhibition which did not contain a dozen reflections of its tenets.'[24]

Alas in the diffusion of the attack, the Academy remained and the New English merely expanded its membership.

At the 1886 exhibition, *On The Bridge at Grez* (see Plate 33) had been compared with Frank Bramley's *Domino*, a picture which was also characteristically French in its handling. Not only were its 'real qualities of open air light' observed, but it was concluded, contrary to the views of conservative academicians, that Lavery and Bramley had both learned 'to handle paint in a good and sound school'.[25] The place for the graduates of this school was the New English Art Club into which Lavery was incorporated in 1887.[26] There were however, other attractions in London exhibiting. In 1886, Whistler had assumed presidency of the Society of British Artists and he set about encouraging young painters. Thus in the summer exhibition of 1887 Lavery's *Summertime* and *Convalescence* (see Plate 39), and two further pictures appeared at the winter exhibition.[27]. These works drew the praise of Frank O'Meara who wrote to Lavery from Etaples: 'I must compliment you on the work I saw of yours in London at Suffolk Street and Art Club. You have made a big stride of late and there is nothing like making progress, it quite makes life worth living.'[28]

By that year, Lavery would have encountered Whistler 'rather formally' as a result of his association with the society. Then one day by chance, 'at about four in the afternoon at Piccadilly Circus' he bumped into Whistler, 'Come', said Whistler, 'and have a cocktail', and they went to the Criterion and sat there for two or three hours. From there they went to Lavery's hotel and dined, and Whistler talked and talked and never left until four o'clock in the morning, fresh as ever, but leaving Lavery exhausted.[29]

We can only surmise the contents of this lengthy dialogue. It is likely that Whistler would have rehearsed his policies as president of the society with Lavery stressing the exclusivity of the club and the desire to create perfect viewing conditions for works of art. Whistler, for his part was savage in his exclusion of the work of older, more traditional members. 'He was', as Sidney Starr recorded, 'oblivious to every interest but the quality of the work shown', and his instruction to the 'Hanging Committee' was: 'If you are uncertain for a moment say "Out". We want clean spaces round our pictures. We want them to be seen. The British artists must cease to be a shop.'[30]

One innovation that Whistler introduced was the velarium, a muslin drape, suspended from the ceiling of the gallery, and so designed that it diffused the light evenly around the pictures.[31] We know that Lavery was very familiar with all the technicalities of this construction because he referred to it in some detail in a letter to the curator of the newly formed Belfast Museum and Art Gallery in 1927.[32]

In the course of this extended conversation, it is likely that Whistler would have taken the opportunity to expound his aesthetic doctrines—he may even have quoted chunks of the celebrated *Ten O'Clock Lecture* which he had delivered in London and Dieppe in 1885.[33] In this Whistler declared himself to be fervently against nature and the inch by inch fidelity to appearances which characterised Pre-Raphaelite painting. He wanted to rid art of all notions of morality, of narrative, of gratuitous detail. Nature, the world of appearances, seldom gave the artist sufficient impetus for a picture, and the artist drew from everyday experience those special circumstances worthy of a picture. This cultivated sensibility was seldom found on the walls of the Society of British Artists, and it could only be demonstrated by a policy of strict exclusivity. Thus the minor Victorian anecdotal painters were rejected in favour of younger talents like John Lavery. So successful was Whistler in pursuing this policy that by 1888, the society's total sales were less than £1000 and it was near to bankruptcy. The situation precipitated moves against Whistler by the more traditional 'British' artists. As he declared in leaving their ranks, 'the artists came out and the British remained!'[34]

Perhaps the most important aspect of this experience in Lavery's terms lay in the opportunity to get close to Whistler and his work. He would have studied and admired the paintings exhibited by the American master. Whistler's inaugural painting as president was of a large full-length classically draped figure, entitled *Harmony in Blue and Gold*.[35] In its use of a parasol and background balustrade, it could almost echo *Beg Sir!* (see Plate 38). Whistler clearly wished to revive classical subject-matter although this aspect of his work was most deeply problematic.[36] There is no mistaking its effect however upon the outer circle of Whistler followers. Theodore Roussel, Thomas Millie Dow and William Stott of Oldham all painted classical figures at this time. Stott's *Venus Rising from the Sea Foam* was perhaps the most controversial of these works in that he had the presumption to employ Whistler's model, Maud Franklin, to pose nude, and found himself being physically assaulted by Whistler as a result.[37] Lavery, at the same date produced several paintings on the theme of *Ariadne* (Plate 47), employing a model suspiciously similar to Maud. The artist, however, must have keenly felt the contradictions implicit in this kind of painting, and it is not surprising that in later years, *Ariadne* came to represent an impassé and an ideal. Like the work of the artist he was emulating, it was constantly scraped down and reworked.[38] The picture was planned as a back view female nude looking out to sea, her hair clasped in the manner fashionable at the time. In the two large versions, the model's long thick red hair was unclasped, making them even more comparable to Stott's *Venus*. It may be that this association prompted Lavery to refrain from exhibiting the picture until 1889 when it appeared at the Paris Salon. Thereafter, it was shown in Glasgow, Edinburgh and lastly in London at the painter's Goupil Gallery exhibition of 1891.[39] Critics recalled it throughout the next ten years as, 'his beautiful *Ariadne*', 'a lovely decoration'.[40]

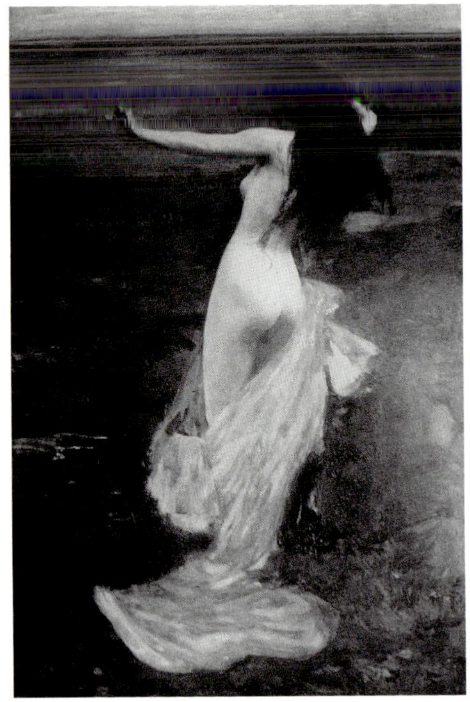

47 *Ariadne*, *c.*1887, size unknown (present whereabouts unknown)

There are a number of possible models for *Ariadne*. During 1887, Lavery painted several small portraits of girls with reddish brown hair. *A French Girl* (Plate 48) and *Girl with Ostrich Feather in her Hat* are two possible contenders for the role.[41] There were at least three girls in black painted that year, one of which may have been executed in Paris. This later picture reworks the motif of a woman with a pet dog surrounded by 'aesthetic' fans and screens and was given by Lavery to Doctor Sime four years later.[42] There is evidence to suggest that Lavery returned to Ireland in 1887, and again in 1890. The first of these expeditions was probably undertaken for the purpose of painting the untraced portrait of one of his relations, Mrs H. Morgan Byrne, shown at the Royal Hibernian Academy the following year.

Lavery clearly wished to keep all of his options open. Each of the important genres of painting was kept in play throughout the Eighties. He had committed himself to *la vie moderne* had made a brief foray into classical painting and with *The Fall of the Leaf* painted at the Glen, Paisley, he also produced a large Academy-scale landscape.[43] At this time he must have felt that one or two significant history

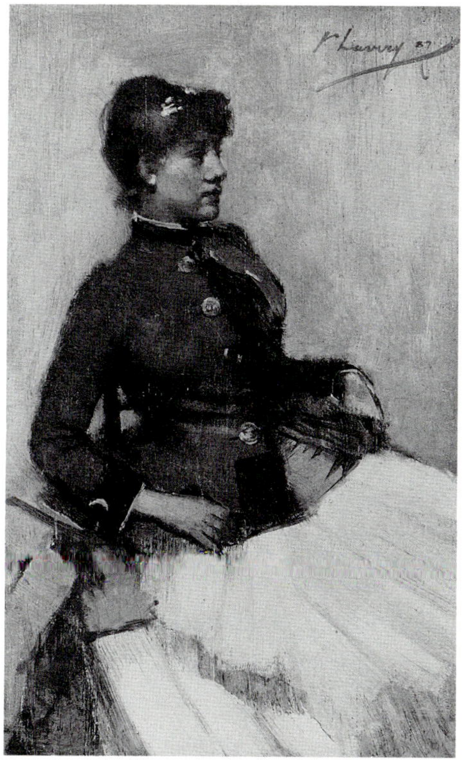

48 *A French Girl*, 1887, $7\frac{3}{8} \times 4\frac{3}{8}$ (private collection)

pictures would help to establish his reputation. It was not so much that he wanted to become a history painter *per se* as that the tragic story of Mary Queen of Scots attracted his attention.

His two renderings of Mary's flight after the Battle of Langside owed nothing to the earlier costume piece dramatists like William Powell Frith and Sir David Wilkie, both of whom had concentrated upon the religious conflict surrounding the catholic queen.[44] Lavery's idea of history painting was more up-to-date and drew upon his French training and background. During the years of the Second Empire and Third Republic, the range of history painting expanded considerably. Scenes of the Roman Empire supplanted those of mythology and painters expended great erudition upon episodes of medieval Gallic and Merovingian history.[45] Through these shone the power and superiority of Beaux Arts academicism. History was clothed in the atmospherics of contemporary experience.

Lavery seems to have first conceived the idea of painting Mary Queen of Scots around 1883, although he declared, 'I have seldom been inspired by the past . . . yet from the first day I held a paint brush my mind was made up to paint a great picture of the Scottish Queen and I spent some years reading up on the subject.'[46] The first of his two versions of the subject, *Dawn after the Battle of Langside* (Plate 49) was not completed until 1887.[47] It may have been the artist's attempt at an equivalent of Bastien-Lepage's *Joan of Arc Listening to the Voices* (see Plate 30), the by now legendary picture which had been shown at the Salon of 1880. Lavery's characterisation of the ill-fated Scots queen, however, carries none of the psychological penetration which was such a controversial aspect of Bastien's heroine.[48] With an unerring sense of the dramatic, Lavery selected the moment when the weary Mary Queen of Scots stares at defeat in the ashes of the overnight camp-fire in the woods of Rosneath. There is none of Jeanne d'Arc's disturbing other-worldliness about her expression, although it is evident that her mind turns upon the previous day's *débâcle*. There were nevertheless, some aspects of Bastien-Lepage's picture which were in Lavery's mind, as he tackled *Dawn after the Battle of Langside*. He later confessed, 'I concentrated on two scenes . . . when she attempted to reach Dumbarton Castle, accompanied by the faithful Lord Herries and a few other followers. I decided that this should be treated somewhat after the manner of Bastien Lepage, everything *en plein-air*.[49]

In terms of its spatial structure — the aerial effect of taking the spectator's gaze over the ashes of the camp-fire—the picture demonstrates Lavery's debt to the rustic naturalism of his mentor. Many of Bastien's British followers employed the same distancing devices. Principal figures were thus held back from close proximity and the space between them and the spectator was accentuated. With some irony, Lavery recounts that the model for Mary Stuart was an Irish girl named Bella Cullen. She was the daughter of an impoverished coal-miner who, although she had no education, had the bearing of a queen.[50] Alas, she apparently caught a chill while posing and died within six months of the completion of her sittings.

It is not possible to be certain how the realisation of Lavery's two Langside pictures progressed. By the beginning of 1886, the second, *Night after the Battle of*

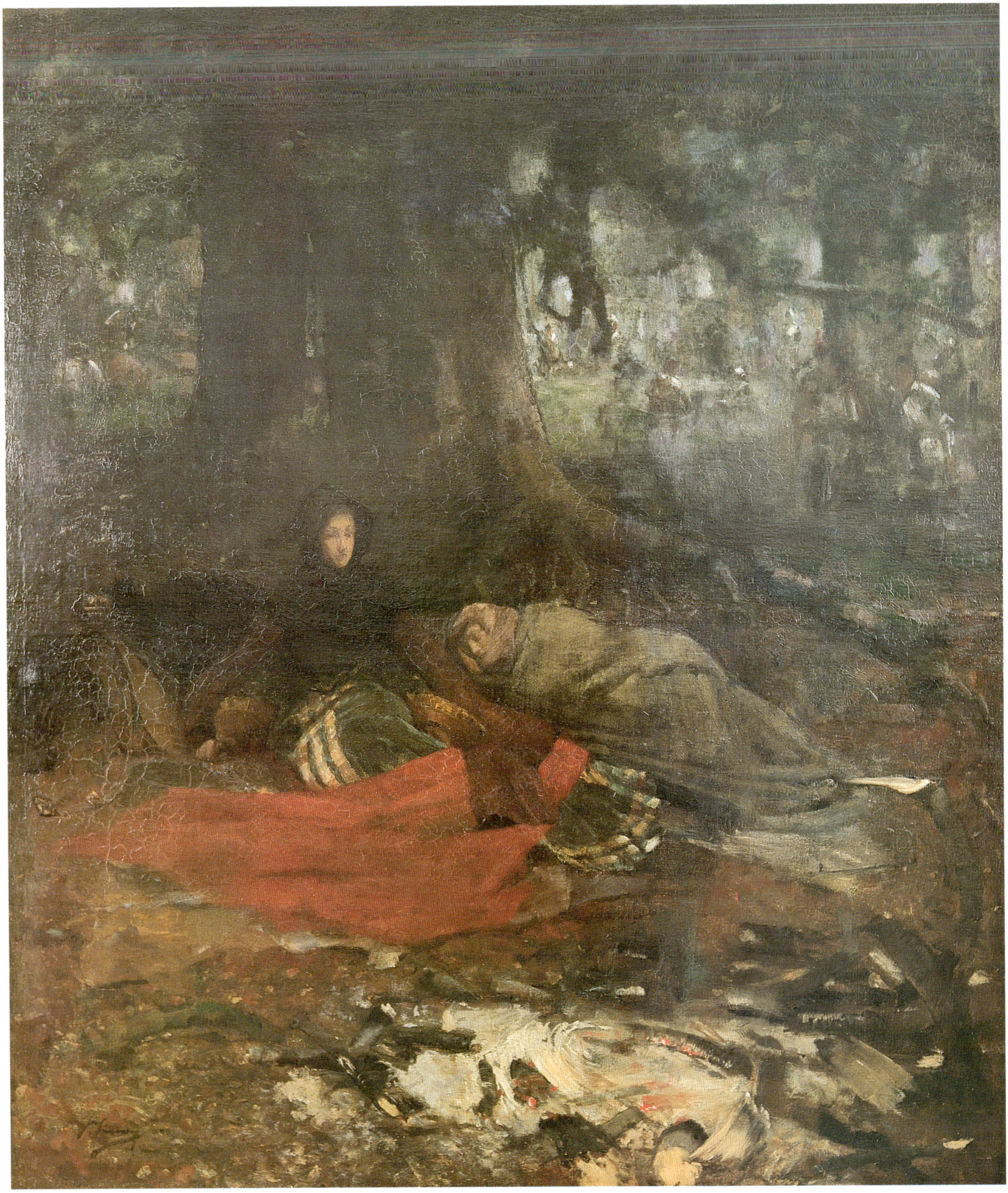

49 *Dawn after the Battle of Langside, 14 May 1568*, 1883–7, 50 × 42 (private collection)

Langside (Plate 50) had been begun. In May of that year, the artist wrote to Joseph Stevenson the authority on Mary Queen of Scots, in an effort to make his picture as historically accurate as possible. Stevenson informed Lavery that the queen had borrowed 'some clothes and a hood' from the Laird of Lochinvar and that her male attendants would still be in armour as they fled from the battle.[51] Lavery had great difficulty in obtaining genuine period armour which was, in the end, too small for the 'idle, good-for-nothing fisherman' who posed on horseback for Lord Herries.[52] He recounts that 'late on a summer evening' his model fainted and 'fell over with a rattle' on account of the tightness of his breast plate and helmet![53]

The mood of defeat which permeates *Night after the Battle of Langside*, echoes Meissonier's celebrated *1812 (The Retreat from Moscow)*, 1864, now in the Louvre. In the French picture, the figures are ranged to the right edge of the canvas, isolating the emperor astride a white horse, and followed at a distance by his retinue. The two pictures are nevetheless comparable. Lavery could not fail to have been familiar with Meissonier's painting as a student, despite the fact that by then it had a popular, rather than avant-garde reputation. There were serious problems in the realisation of this second Langside picture. According to Shaw Sparrow, the painting was revised over a ten-year period, before its eventual purchase by the Musée Royale des Beaux Arts, Brussels.[54] At one point, Lavery wanted to exhibit it at the Royal Academy, but was dissuaded from doing so by MacAulay Stevenson, who leapt onto the train beside him and throughout the journey argued that the picture was '"the soul of Scotland" and should not be exhibited south of the border'.[55] There may be some confusion in this tale, because the picture was, apparently, first exhibited in the artist's one-man exhibition at the Goupil Gallery, London in 1891. There, it was regarded as 'an historical picture of

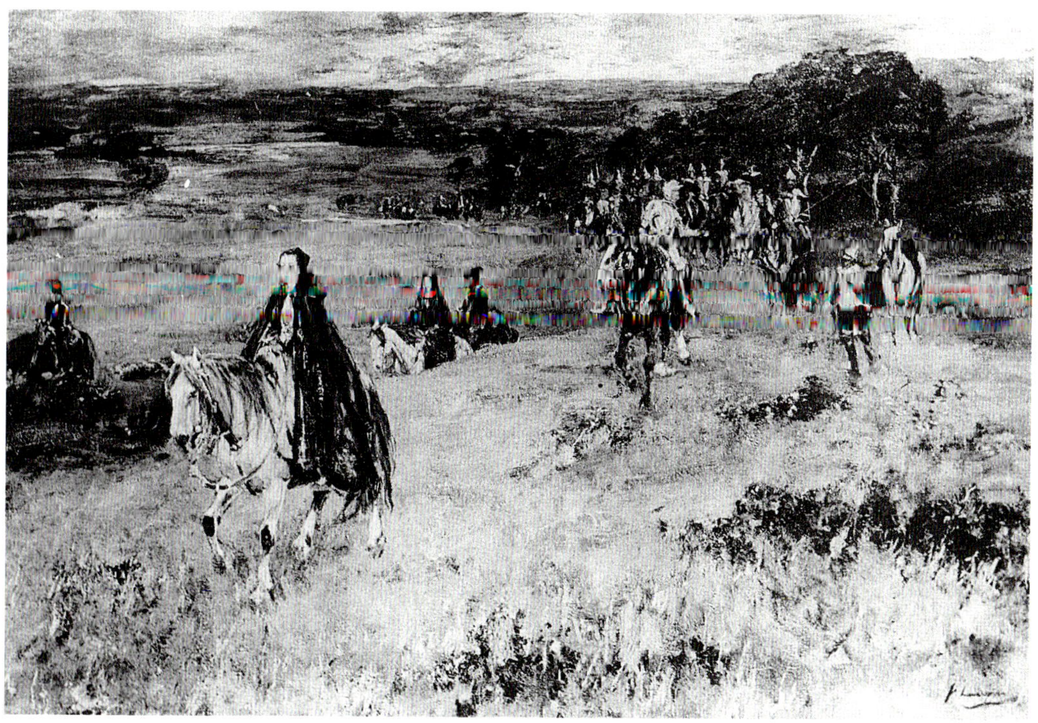

50 *Night after the Battle of Langside*, *c.*1887, size unknown (Musée Royale des Beaux Arts, Brussels)

remarkable pathos'.[56] Despite the objections raised concerning its London airing, the painting was not well received in Glasgow the following year. There it was hung too high to be seen at the institute and the painter withdrew it.[57]

By contrast, *Dawn after the Battle of Langside* was more quickly resolved and more universally acclaimed. It made its debut in the Fine Art Section of the Glasgow International Exhibition of 1888 and in the catalogue, Lavery printed an extract from a letter by Mary Stuart to the Cardinal of Lorraine: 'I have suffered injuries, calumnies, captivity, hunger, cold, heat, flying, without knowing whither, four score and twelve miles across the country, without once pausing to alight, and then lay on hard ground, having only sour milk to drink and oatmeal to eat, without bread, passing three nights with the owls.'[58]

The topicality of the work was increased by the collection of Mary Stuart's relics on display elsewhere in the International Exhibition and by the fact that all the waitresses at its cafes and kiosks were dressed in Mary Stuart costume.[59] However, in spite of the wealth of historical evidence on show, *Dawn after the Battle of Langside* was praised for neglecting the 'laboured learning that pleases the antiquarian'. *The Scottish Art Review* stated that, 'The traditions which have stifled the presentment of historical painting are here entirely abandoned; the subject is treated with a keen perception of the real conditions of the episode . . . details are not insisted upon; but in that weary dawn we feel this is how the poor Queen looked and felt.[60]

Two years later, *The Spectator* simply observed that in Lavery's painting 'history routs dimly in the background'.[61] It was left to foreign and more objective eyes to see that although the painter had been under French influence, this picture was 'entirely Scotch in colour as in spirit'.[62] An unidentified Hungarian artist whose review of the Munich Glaspalast Exhibition of 1891 was translated for the *Glasgow Evening Citizen* spelt out in full the degree to which Lavery had expanded the genre of history painting.

> Until now we have been pretty well accustomed to find in such pictures a tendency to theatrical effects and pathos carried to the furthest extent—exaggerated poses, straining eyes, contorted faces etc. etc. The Glasgow School knows nothing of these 'aids' and that a true artist can create a great work without them was fully and gloriously proved by Lavery in his great historical painting, *Queen Mary After the Battle of Langside*. This work of art is a contrast to all historical paintings hitherto seen. There is no striving after unnatural effects or pathos, and yet, in its simplicity, it expresses the tragic moment with more depth than any adventitious aid of pathetic 'properties' could have done.[63]

It is not surprising to find that elsewhere Lavery came to be considered the 'poet' of the Glasgow School and *Dawn after the Battle of Langside* was regarded as its most evocative image.[64]

The rise of the Glasgow School of painters was first appreciated at the International Exhibition of 1888. There, a series of pictures by younger artists, demonstrated for the first time that the city was not just a smoky industrial warren. Indeed *The Scottish Art Review* took a crusading role on behalf of the younger

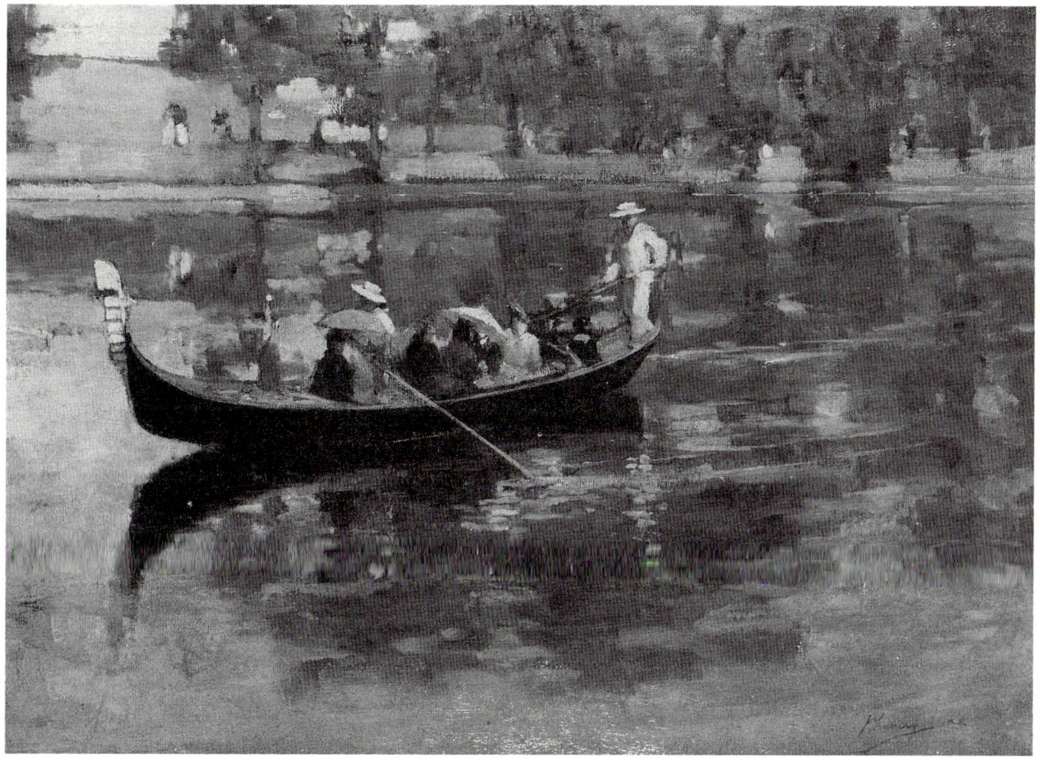

51 *The Gondola on the Kelvin*, 1888, $17\frac{1}{2} \times 23\frac{1}{2}$ (present whereabouts unknown, photo, Sotheby's)

artists.[65] Its unidentified critic considered pictures like Guthrie's *To Pastures New*, Roche's *Shepherdess* and Millie Dow's *Hudson River* before turning to Lavery's *Langside*. This group was sufficiently distinctive to stand apart from the acknowledged masterpieces by Corot, Millet, Diaz, Jacque, Wilkie and Chalmers which were also on display. The common character of the new painting was obvious from south of the border where *The Art Journal* noted that, 'There is in Scotland, and notably in Glasgow, a band of young painters who have broken from the traditions of the past and boldly struck into the road that is marked with the footprints of Bastien-Lepage . . .'.[66]

Such a phenomenon would instantly be recognisable for its accord with the general trend of French-inspired rustic naturalism most frequently seen in the work of Newlyn School. Its appearance was timely in that it coincided with the city of Glasgow's desire to achieve widespread recognition as a centre of trade and industry. In the fine arts, the exhibition set out to surpass those at Manchester and Edinburgh in the preceding years. Civic pride demanded that painters like Lavery, Henry, Guthrie and Walton be commissioned to execute allegorical representations of science, industry, art and agriculture for the interior of the 150-feet-high dome of the Grand Hall of the exhibition.[67] It quickly became the city's proud boast that this building, designed by James Sellars, was the largest of its kind since the Great Exhibition in London in 1862. Its design—in Sellar's words, 'oriental in character' suggesting 'the Alhambra and the Great Pavilion of Caliphat'—must have made the roundels by Lavery and the others seem incongruous. However, Kelvingrove also contained a reconstructed Dutch Cocoa House, a Medieval Bishop's Palace and numerous kiosks, bandstands and cafeterias.[68] Queen

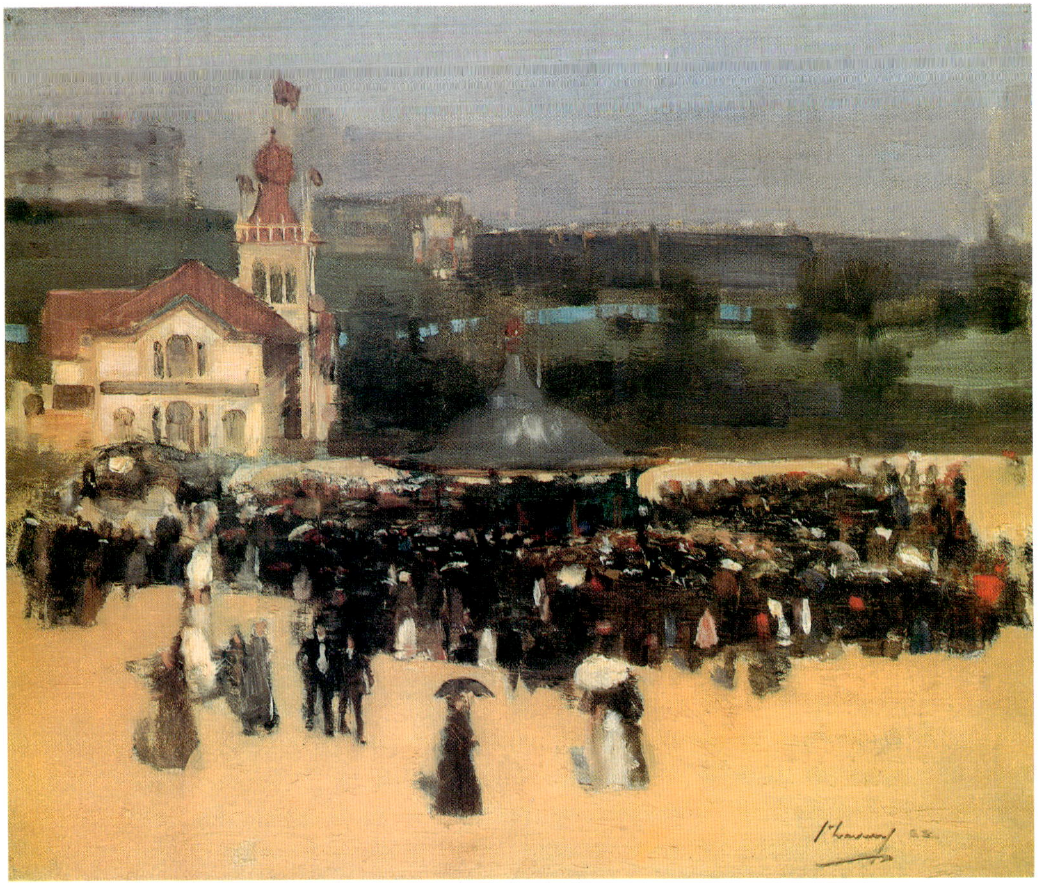

54 *The Blue Hungarians*, 1888, 12 × 14 (Andrew McIntosh Patrick Esq.)

Victoria consented to act as patron of the exhibition and the Prince of Wales, its honorary president, performed the opening ceremony on the 8 May 1888.[69]

Lavery became a sort of artist-in-residence at the exhibition, painting all aspects of its daily life. General views complimented the recording of specific incidents or particular characters. In each instance, Lavery would follow the Whistlerian precept of seizing upon the chief point of interest, locating it strategically within the rectangle and then elaborating the details. In this way, not only would a half-finished picture appear finished if it had to be abandoned for some reason; but the viewer, on the other hand would always have a focal point with which to identify.[70] The sheer diversity of the exhibition, its variety and incongruity was Lavery's chief challenge. A Venetian gondola sailed between the 'Moorish Palace' and the 'Gothic College', and this was depicted in at least two different studies (*The Gondola on the Kelvin*, Plate 51 and *A View from the Canal*, Plate 52).[71] Other general views showed the bustling crowds, often seen from above. This is the case in *The Glasgow International Exhibition, 1888* (Plate 53), a twilight scene larger than many other works in the series.[72] Here, as elsewhere in his international studies, Lavery reveals his debt to Whistler. Not only do the lights and lanterns recall Whistler's Cremorne nocturnes, but the wide foreground space dotted with figures, owes something to his *Nocturne in Blue and Gold, Valparaiso* which Lavery had had the opportunity to study at the Society of British Artists exhibition the previous year.[73] Lavery had observed how Whistler would mass the composition and then

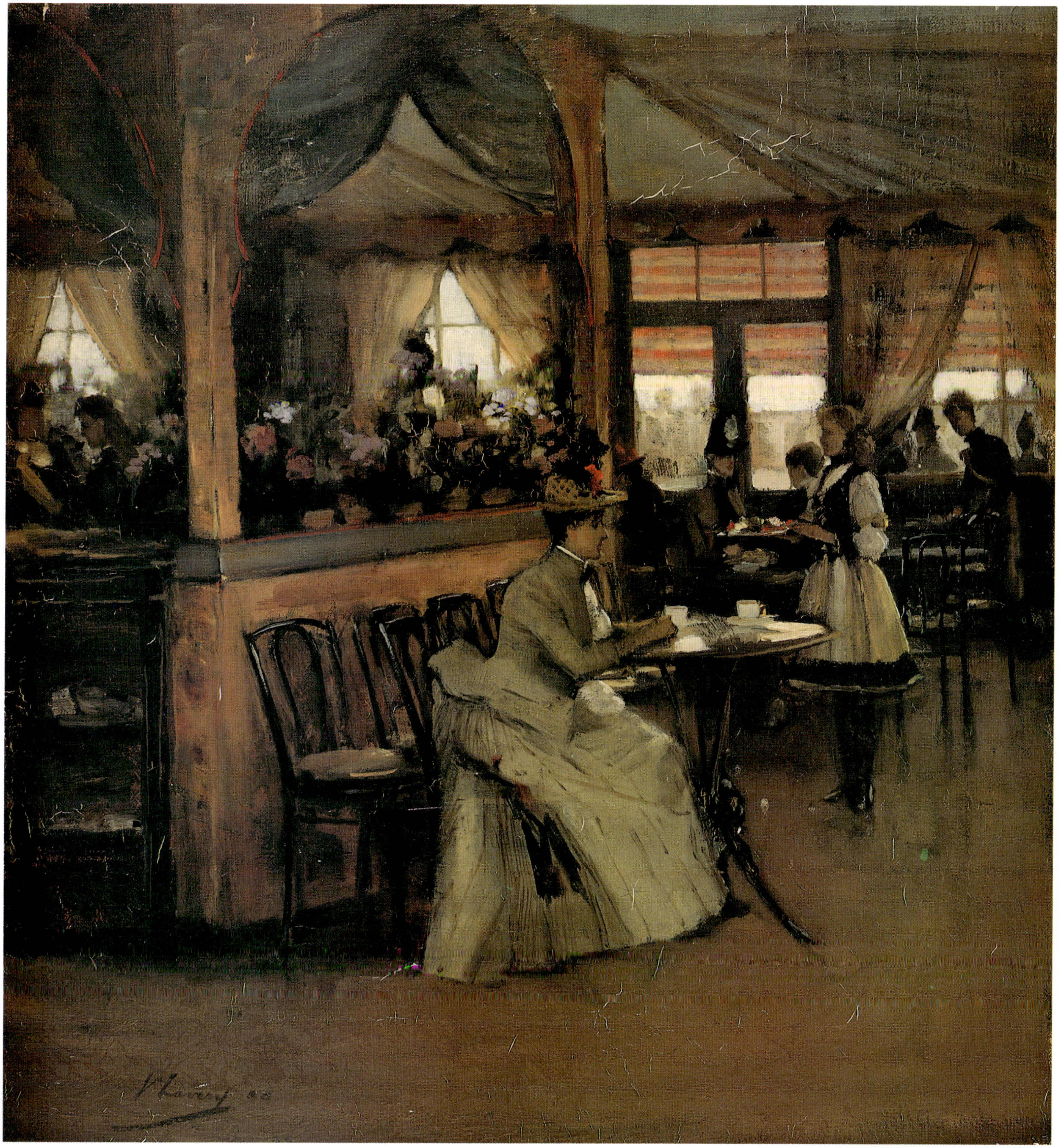

56 *A Cup of Chocolate*, 1888, 20 × 18
(formerly Whitford and Hughes, London)

would proceed to touch in the details. This method of exploiting the spontaneity of his attack became one of the essential features of Lavery's style, and it is evident in other works of the sequence, like *The Indian Pavilion* and *The Blue Hungarians* (Plate 54).[74] These two later paintings were reproduced in *The Scottish Art Review* beside a mock medieval 'ballade' wryly celebrating the exhibition as a 'mighty maze without a plan' whose secret purpose was as a

> . . . bait to make home coffers grow,
> And elevate other brother man
> With music (Blue Hungarian),
> The arts from Tay to Timbuctoo,
> The good and gods from Hindustan.[75]

After the closure of the exhibition and accounts were settled, it became known that it had made £40,000 profit. To portray the arts of the Orient, Lavery entered the pavilion where, in a reconstructed Indian street, there were cookery and pottery demonstrations. An Indian potter posed for an impromptu portrait (Plate 55). A British woman decorating pots provided a companion-piece, as did Welsh weavers, a cigar seller and various waitresses.[76] General views of the interior of the Dutch Cocoa House and several other cafés were executed (Plate 56). An event such as the Military Tattoo was recorded in a small vivid study of *The Musical Ride of the 15th Hussars* (Plate 57).[77]

However, the most important single occurrence during the entire exhibition was the queen's visit. Lavery was chosen by Glasgow Corporation to depict this event and was offered £600 for doing so.[78] On 22 August, therefore, he found himself high up on a platform peeping through a hole in a curtain as the elderly monarch 'wearing a widow's bonnet and looking rather severe' was wheeled into the exhibition in a bath-chair. Even though he was concealed from view, the artist recalled his trepidation in her presence: 'A movement of the curtain caused her to look in my direction, it seemed to penetrate the dark and expose me and my paint-box. For the moment, disconcerted, my hand trembled, but I managed to jot down a few notes of value.'[79]

Hesitation, if it was felt, is not obvious in Lavery's sketch of *The State Visit of Queen Victoria to the International Exhibition, Glasgow, 1888* (Plate 58).[80] Indeed the picture demonstrates his superb ability as a reporter and his spontaneous aesthetic judgement. It was later considered by James Stanley Little as 'more valuable than the finished work from the artistic, though obviously not from the narrative or historical point of view.'[81] These 'notes of value' contained in the rapid sketch were to be of enormous importance, as the event was obviously never to be re-staged for the artist's convenience. The visitors dispersed and the wooden exhibition buildings were dismantled, as Lavery endeavoured, over the next two years, to reconstruct his hasty impressions.

Before embarking upon this task, he staged an exhibition of fifty selected canvases, presenting his record of the sights of the International, at the Craibe Angus and Son Gallery, Glasgow, in October 1888. This show was a critical success, and the artist was warmly praised for the richness and variety of his studies, each was a 'completed picture'.[82] The oil sketching style which Lavery

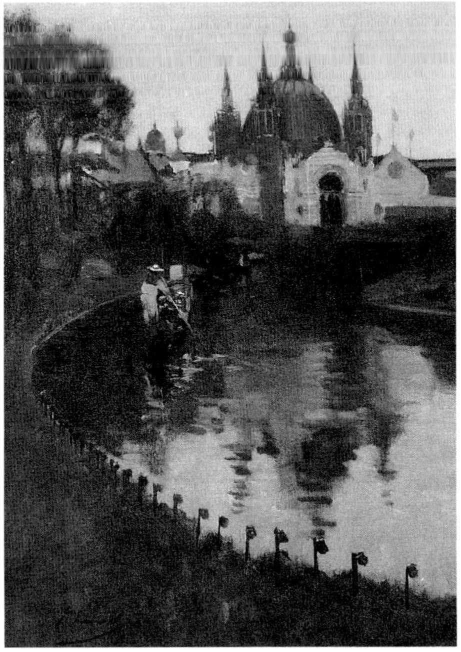

52 *A View from the Canal, Kelvingrove, of the Industrial Hall, at The First Glasgow International Exhibition, 1888*, 14 × 9⅝, (Cecil Higgins Art Gallery, Bedford)

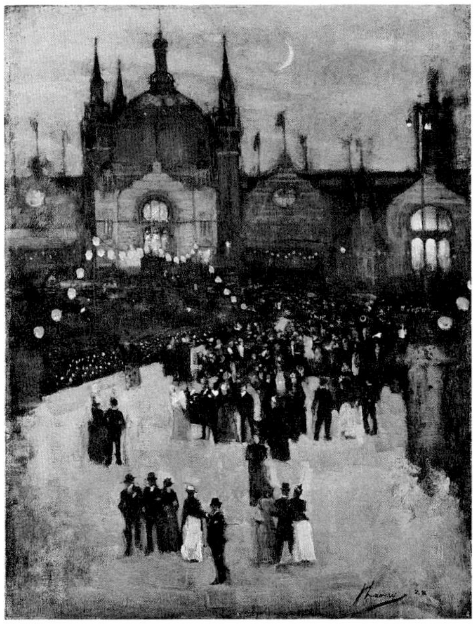

53 *The Glasgow International Exhibition, 1888*, 24 × 18 (Glasgow Art Gallery and Museum)

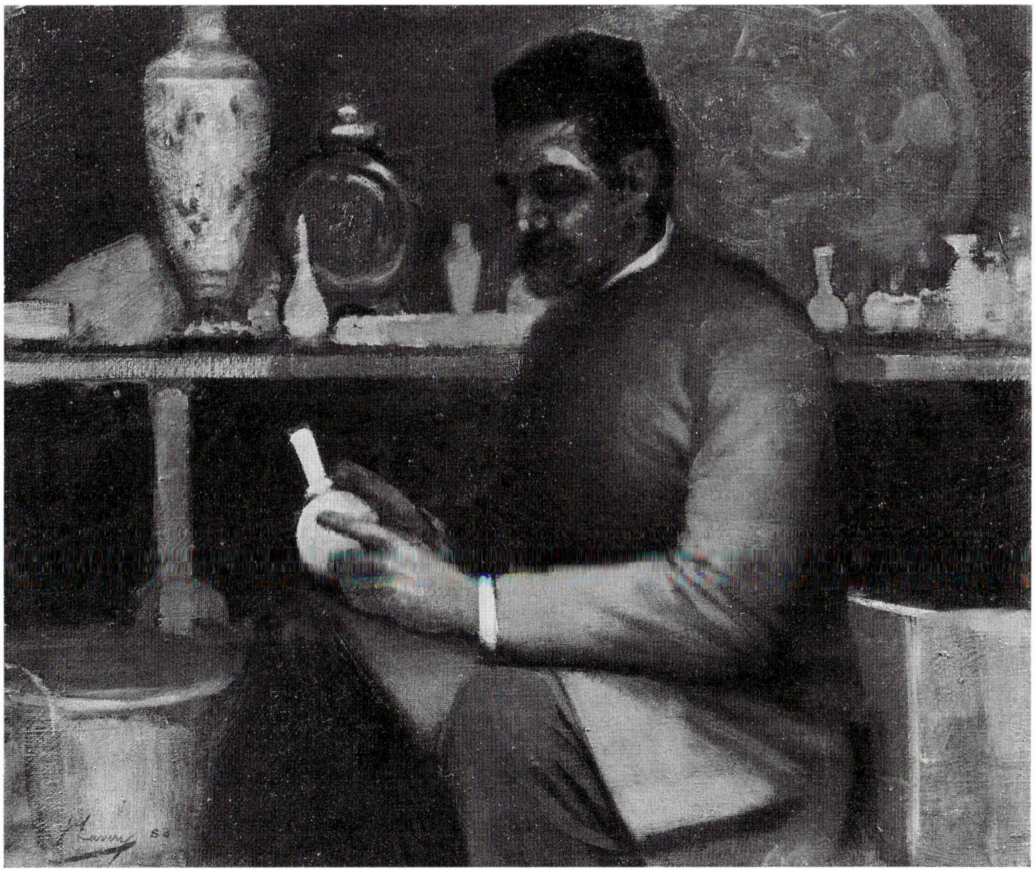

55 *Potter at Work*, 1888, 15 × 18 (Glasgow Art Gallery and Museum)

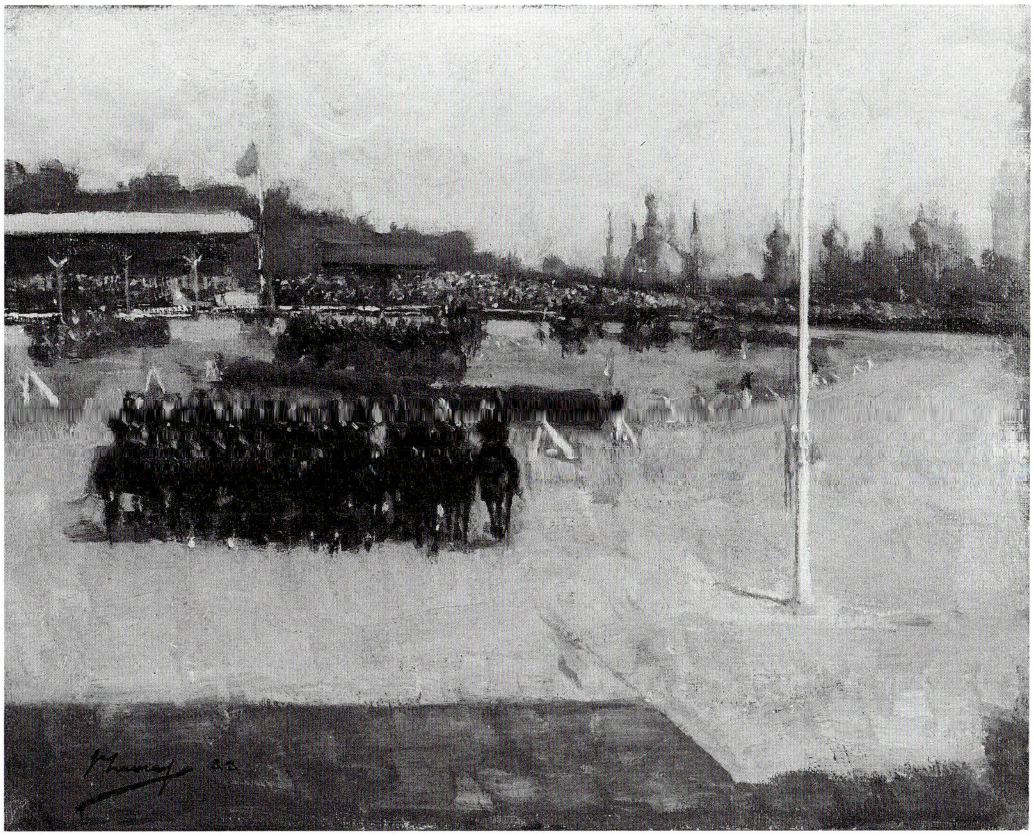

57 *The Musical Ride of the 15th Hussars during the Military Tournament, Glasgow Exhibition*, 1888, 12 × 15 (Dundee Art Gallery)

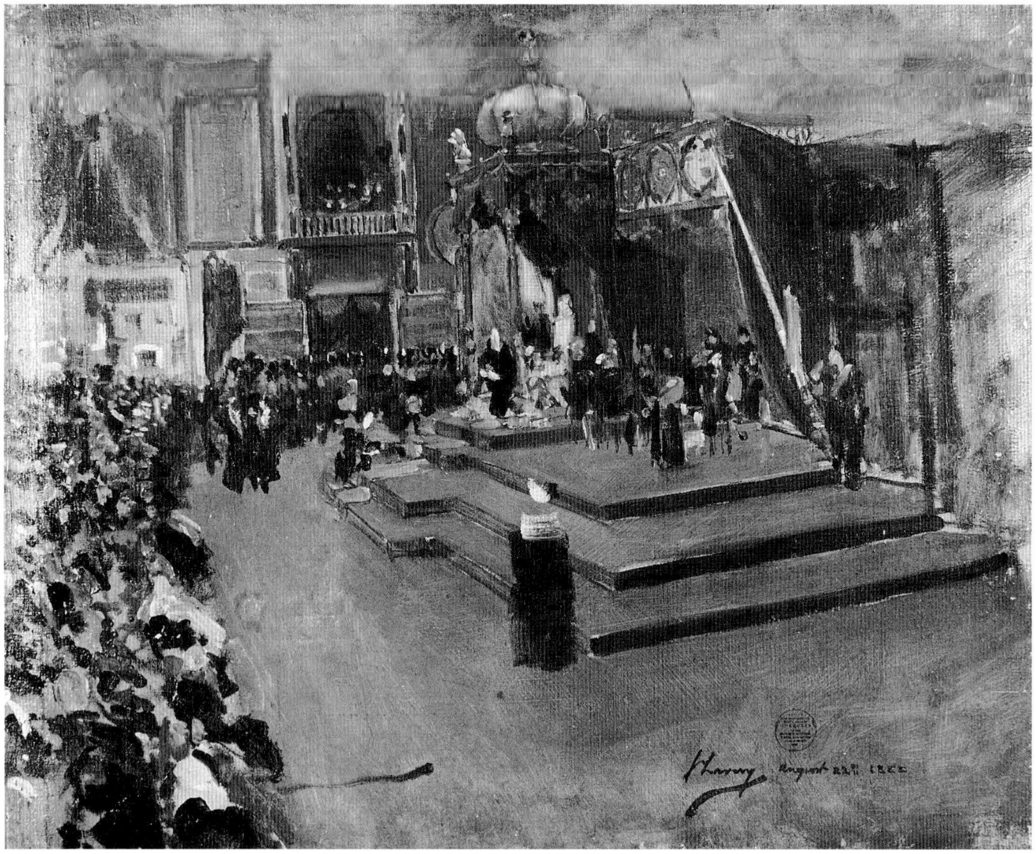

58 *The State Visit of Queen Victoria to The International Exhibition, Glasgow 1888*, 25 × 30 (Aberdeen Art Gallery)

evolved in these works—lightly indicating the main motif with the tip of a sable brush—was the basic drawing technique adopted for the numerous studies which followed *The State Visit* . . . There had been some 253 persons present on the occasion, and Lavery set about the Herculean job of making rapid portraits of all of them. Some could visit his Glasgow studio where they were photographed and a small study on panel was painted (Plates 59, 60 and 61). He encountered greatest difficulty, however, in obtaining the queen's consent for a sitting. Not only did he try to exert influence through her private secretary, Sir Henry Ponsonby, but he also sought the good offices of the Duchess of Buccleuch and Lady Southampton. Eventually, when he had reconciled himself to using a photograph, Prince Henry of Battenburg offered to intercede. As Lavery recalled, 'the Queen could refuse him nothing' and at the conclusion of his sitting, he arranged for the monarch and the painter to meet that afternoon at two o'clock. For this brief session, the queen wore the bonnet which she had worn at Glasgow and she stood in such a position as to give him the right profile view, '. . . at the same time looking me up and down . . .'[83] Lavery recalled that the topic of conversation between the queen and her ladies-in-waiting was flannel underclothing, but he was so concentrated upon the task in hand that he felt no embarrassment. Then, '. . . before I could complete my study she indicated that she had had enough, about twenty minutes it appeared to me, and turned and left the room without showing any interest in what I had done.'[84]

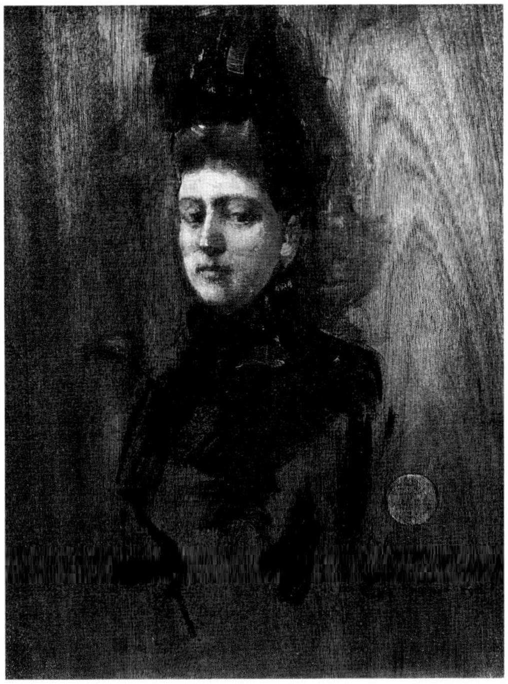

60 *Her Royal Highness, Princess Henry of Battenburg*, *c.*1889, 16 × 11¾ (Glasgow Art Gallery and Museum)

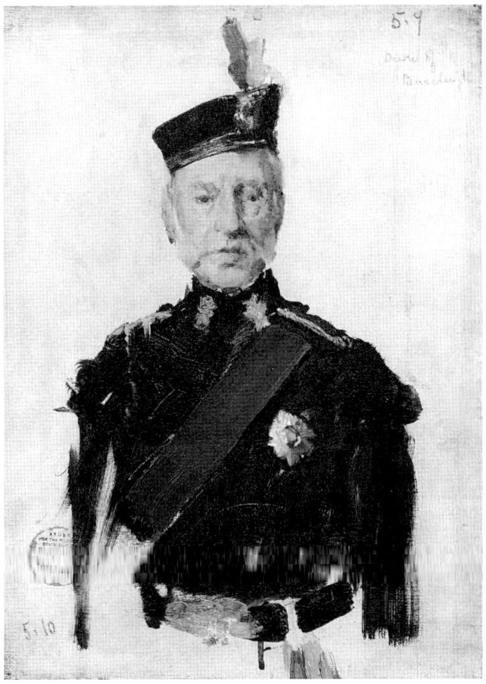

61 *The Duke of Buccleuch. c.*1889, 14 × 10 (Glasgow Art Gallery and Museum)

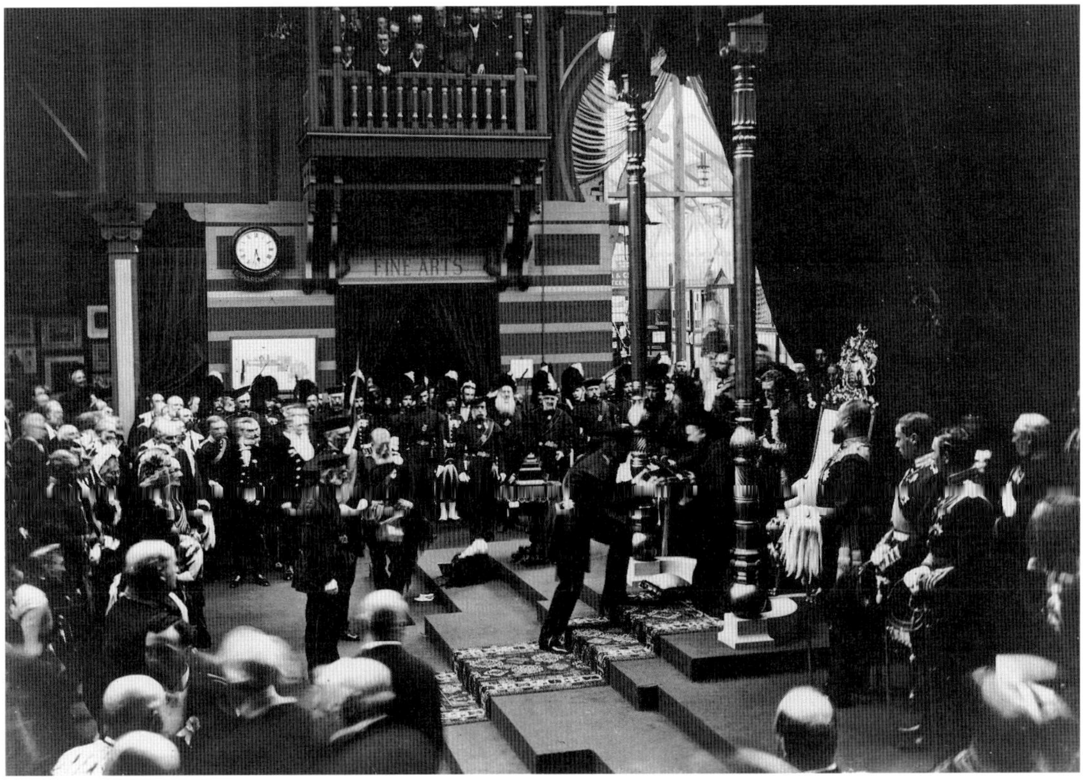

59 Photograph of The State Visit of Queen Victoria to The International Exhition, Glasgow 1888 (Glasgow Art Club, photo, Glasgow University)

When it became known that the queen had granted him a sitting, the artist had no difficulty in persuading the other important personages to comply. His efforts to reconstitute *The State Visit* . . . took him as far afield as Darmstadt where he painted the Grand Duke and Princess Alice of Hesse. This latter study bewitched the painter. She hypnotised me by the strange sadness in her eyes, 'like one on the verge of insanity yet sane enough to realise it'.[85] The profile of Princess Alice was shown at the Grosvenor Gallery in 1889.[86] Lavery was impressed by the gracious treatment he received in Germany, and although he was asked to return to paint a life-sized portrait of the princess, he never followed up the invitation.

Throughout 1889 he worked solidly in London and Glasgow towards the completion of *The State Visit*. . . (Plate 62) and in the first week of December 1890 the 8 feet × 10 feet canvas was erected in St George's Hall, Windsor Castle so that the last few figures could be added. All were reported to be very pleased with the results. While he was working on the portrait of Sir Henry Ponsonby, the queen came into the room and apart from observing that her head was too big for her body, said that she did not recognise Prince Henry and Princess Beatrice. Lavery had worked on these from photographs. Accordingly sittings were arranged for the next day.[87] The princess considered that there was too much foreground red carpet, but Lavery assured her that other ways of breaking up the space had not been successful.[88] Apart from these reservations, it was held to be successful. He noted that on 6 December 1890 the queen and princess had again inspected the work and pronounced their portraits 'very good'.[89] The picture was then brought back to Glasgow to go on exhibition by special arrangement with the Glasgow entrepreneur, Walter Wilson, at the Colosseum Warehouse. In the following spring the painting, with a complete set of preparatory portraits was displayed at McLean's Gallery in the Haymarket, London, where it received mixed reviews.[89]

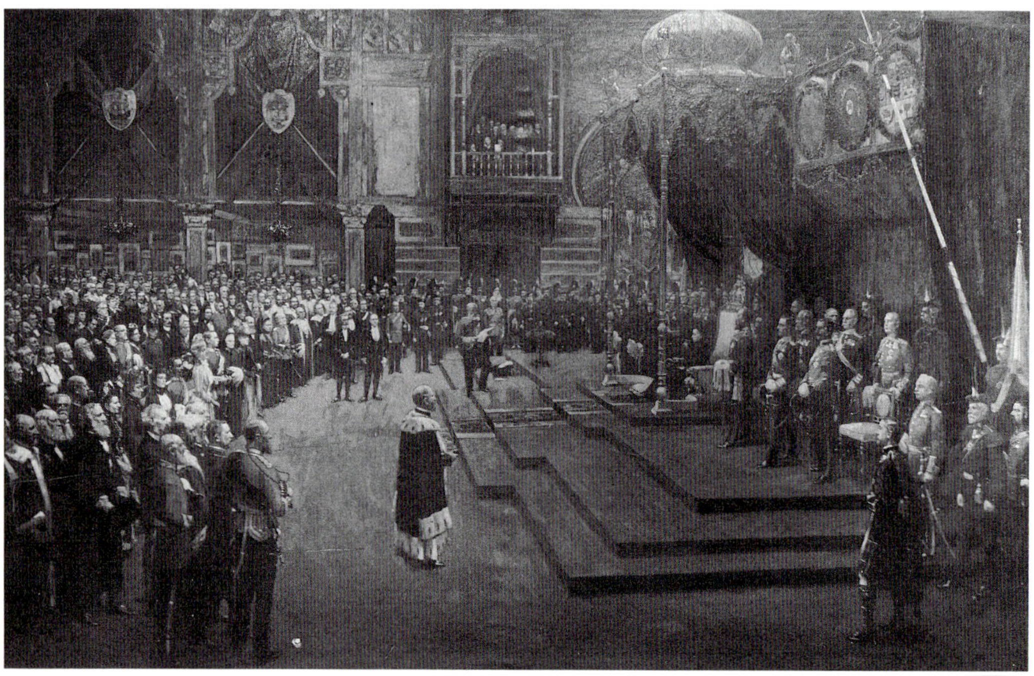

62 *The State Visit of Queen Victoria to The International Exhibition, Glasgow 1888*, 101 × 160 (Glasgow Art Gallery and Museum)

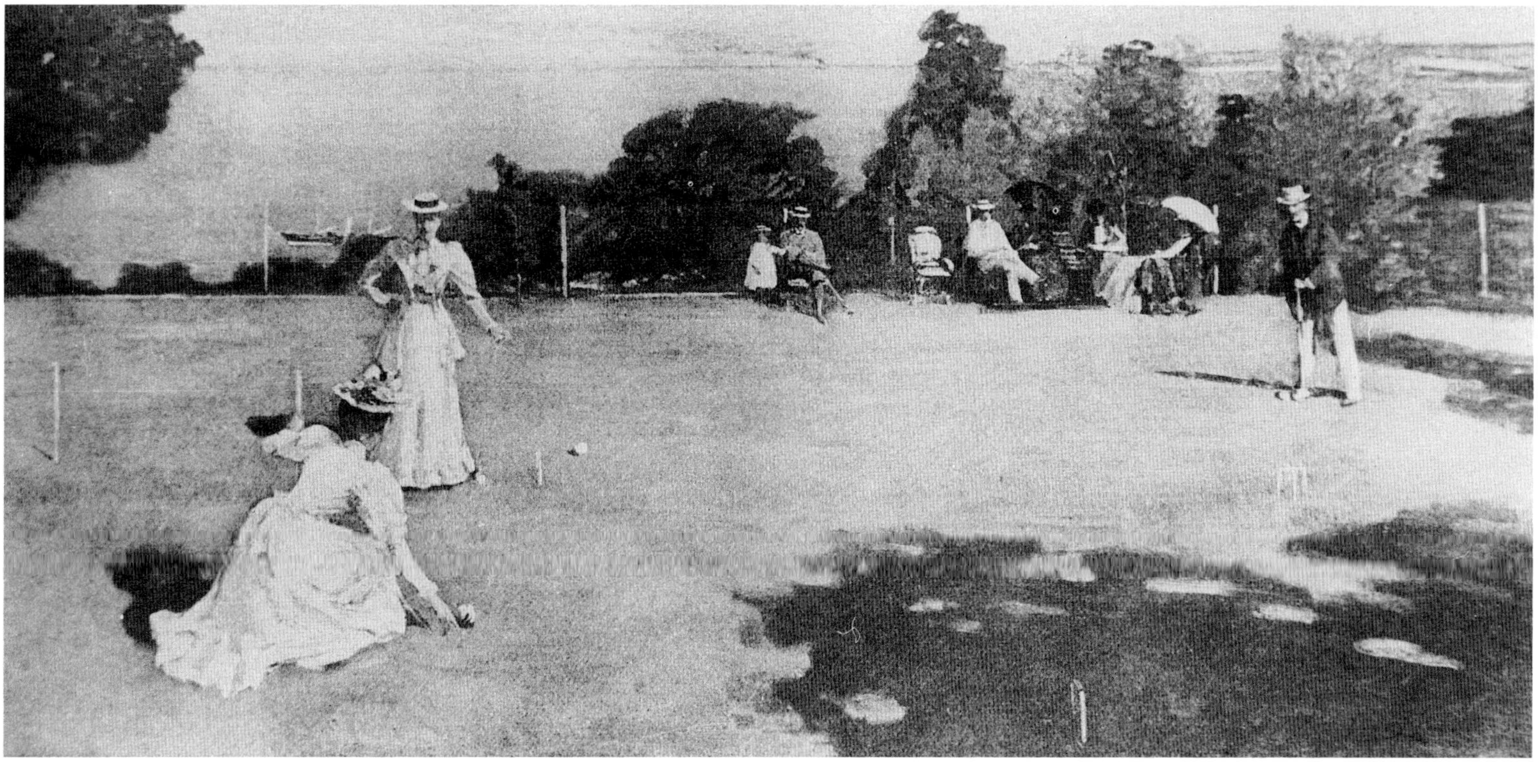

63 *Croquet – A Portrait Group*, 1890, size unknown (present whereabouts unknown)

Little, writing in 1902, felt that though 'by no means a mere machine' it could 'not be taken as representing Lavery at his best'.[91] *The Times* critic succinctly summed up the various demands of such a daunting labour: 'It is scarcely possible that such pictures should have an artistic interest equal to their historical or topical interest; and Mr Lavery has done more than paint creditably and cleverly a scene he would never have chosen to paint for himself.'[92]

Whilst it is true that Lavery would never have found much artistic interest in such an event before tackling it, it is also the case that in later life he returned on more than one occasion to just such commemorative tasks. Although he found the demand for large scale legibility—over 200 recognisable portraits in a single canvas—unconducive to the current Whistlerian ideal of evocation, he became fascinated by the sheer complexity of such events. There were of course, many notable precedents for scenes of this kind. In 1863 for instance, W. P. Frith had been commissioned to celebrate *The Marriage of the Prince of Wales and the Princess Alexandra of Denmark*, while nearer to Lavery's own time, *The Imperial Assemblage Held at Delhi on the 1st January 1877*, painted by V. C. Prinsep had been exhibited.[93] Perhaps the lacklustre reception of Lavery's work was due to the fact that there had been numerous pictures of this type in recent years. W. E. Lockhart's *The Queen's Jubilee Celebration* for instance, had been shown the previous year and was widely regarded as a failure. Nevertheless the illustrated weekly papers habitually recorded royal comings and goings and Lavery, like a newspaper reporter, treated the job as an exercise in documentation.[94] All of his studies were stamped and signed, giving additional authentication, and so that they would be instantly recognised as part of the grand jig-saw. Photographs were used, but not permitted to distort the effect. The reporter had to recreate each detail from life and then submerge it in the ensemble. Inevitably this effort helped to underwrite Lavery's future career as a portraitist. Many of his sitters of the 1890s had had some connection with the International Exhibition.

Although these years were dominated by the after-effects of the International, Lavery took opportunities for more recreational activities as they arose. He painted the Glen Concert staged at the estate of William Fulton in 1888 and produced a picture of *Paisley Lawn Tennis Club* in June 1889.[95] In a similar vein, he also painted *Croquet—A Portrait Group* (Plate 63) in 1890. The format of this work, a horizontal double square, suggested comparison with *The Tennis Party* but the picture was less tightly organised. In the background, Lavery painted a sweeping vista of sea and sky probably taken from the Firth of Clyde.[96] The effect of warm whites, vivid greens and brilliant ultramarines which caught the attention of contemporary writers, raises questions about Lavery's relationship to painters like Monet and Sargent, both of whom had recently been engaged upon hot summer-day *plein-air* pictures. *Croquet* was also believed by later writers, to be based upon Manet's picture of the same subject painted in 1873, however it is unlikely that the artist would have known of this earlier work.[97] He had, nevertheless, spent much of the previous year in London and probably would have participated in some of the debates about Impressionism. He may well have seen the exhibition of twenty paintings by Monet at the Goupil Gallery in April, and at the same time, have studied 'Impressionist' Sargents like *St Martin's Summer* and *A Morning Walk*, both of which were painted under Monet's influence.[98] En route to Darmstadt, he might also have visited the Exposition Universelle and other Paris shows, so that by the time he came to paint *Croquet* his ideas had been brought up to date. This is obvious from smaller works of 1890 like *On The Clyde: A Study of Lady Glen Coats* (Plate 64). The dramatic *contre-jour* effect of the figure under a sun umbrella seen against a bright cloudless sky recalls similar works by Monet, Sargent and Helleu. Further studies of *Hunter's Quay* (Plate 65) and *Yacht Racing on the Clyde* reveal a new freedom in the manipulation of paint that recalls the earlier seascapes of Monet. A picture of this type was admired by Little when he saw it hanging in the Cromwell Place studio in 1902, 'Grey it is; but the vessels move; we feel the wind driving their sails, and the greyness has a certain sparkle about it; it is in fact a living, in contradistinction to a dead-greyness, and is entirely in the sentiment of the subject.'[99]

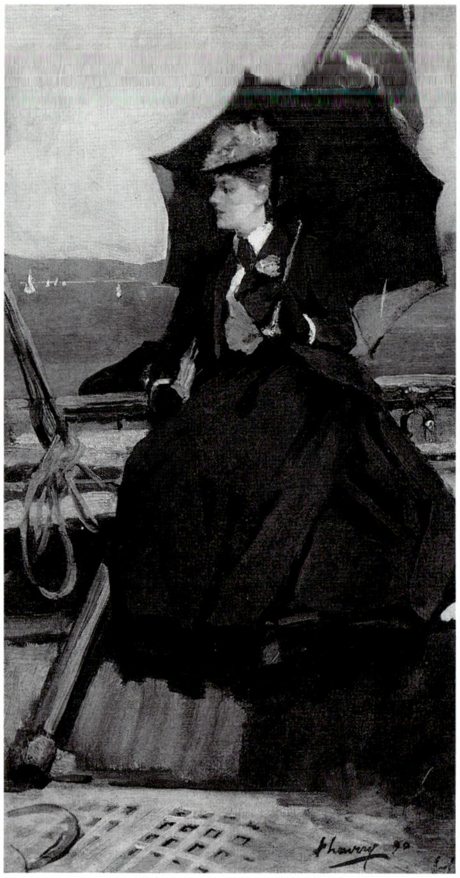

64 *On the Clyde – A Study of Lady Glen Coats*, 1890, 16 × 8 (present whereabouts unknown)

Lavery fully participated in the recreational activities of the Glasgow Art Club around this time. During the decade, the club had been the focus of friendly debate amongst the Glasgow Boys, and he had shown regularly at its informal exhibitions of members' work. On 29 November 1889, the club staged a Grand Costume Ball at St Andrews Hall in aid of the Scottish Artists' Benevolent Fund.[100] Lavery painted a canvas advertising the event, in the style of French music hall posters. It could possibly have been executed at an open meeting as the members decided upon the order of events. The dance menu listed on the palette above the piano has been deleted and then reworked.[101] The ball was an enormous success; 967 of the most prominent west of Scotland citizens attended. The guest list identifies most of Lavery's important patrons—Mr and Mrs Lawrie, the Glen

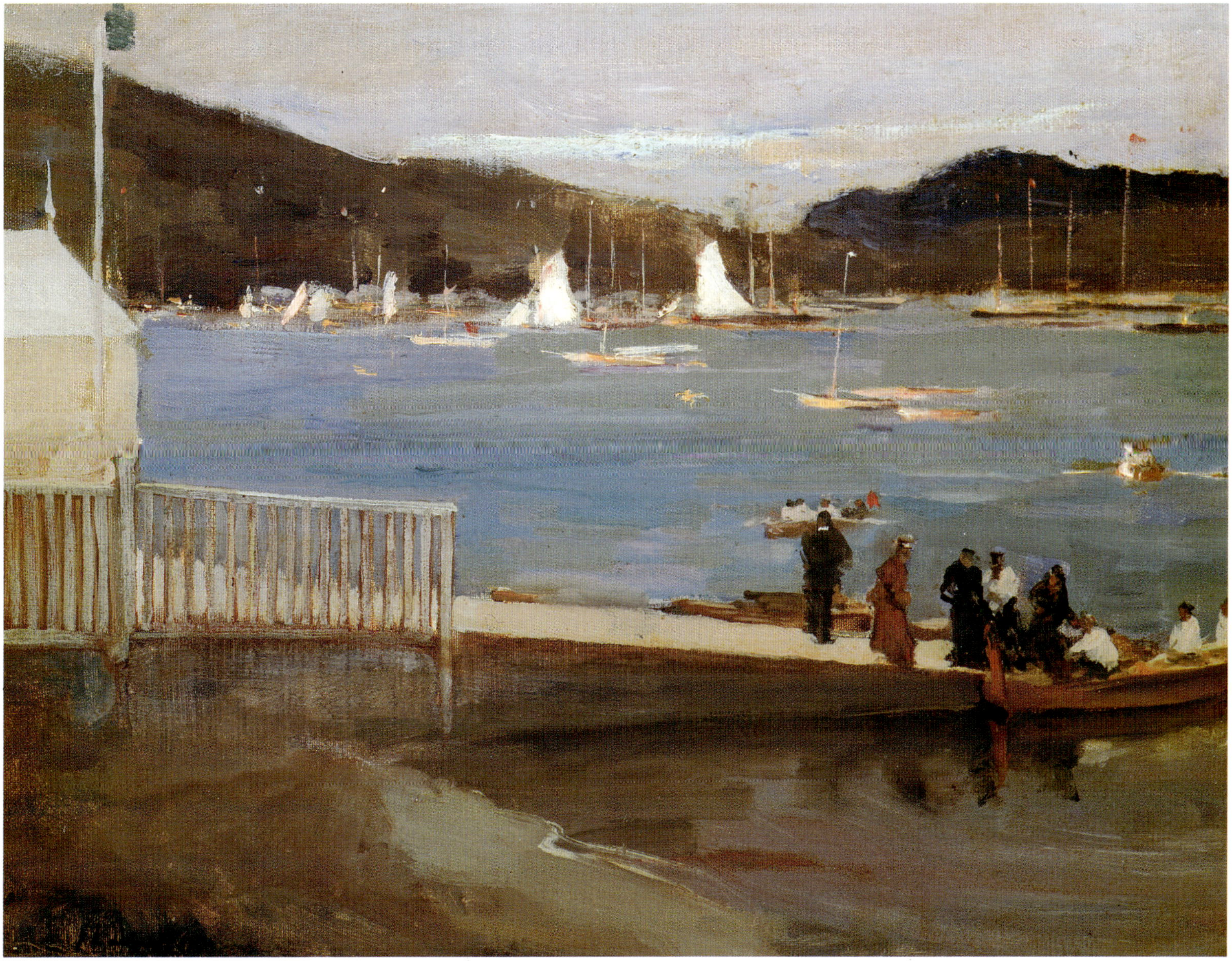

65 *Sailing Boats on the Clyde, Hunter's Quay*, 1890, 14 × 18 (Ewan Mundy Fine Art)

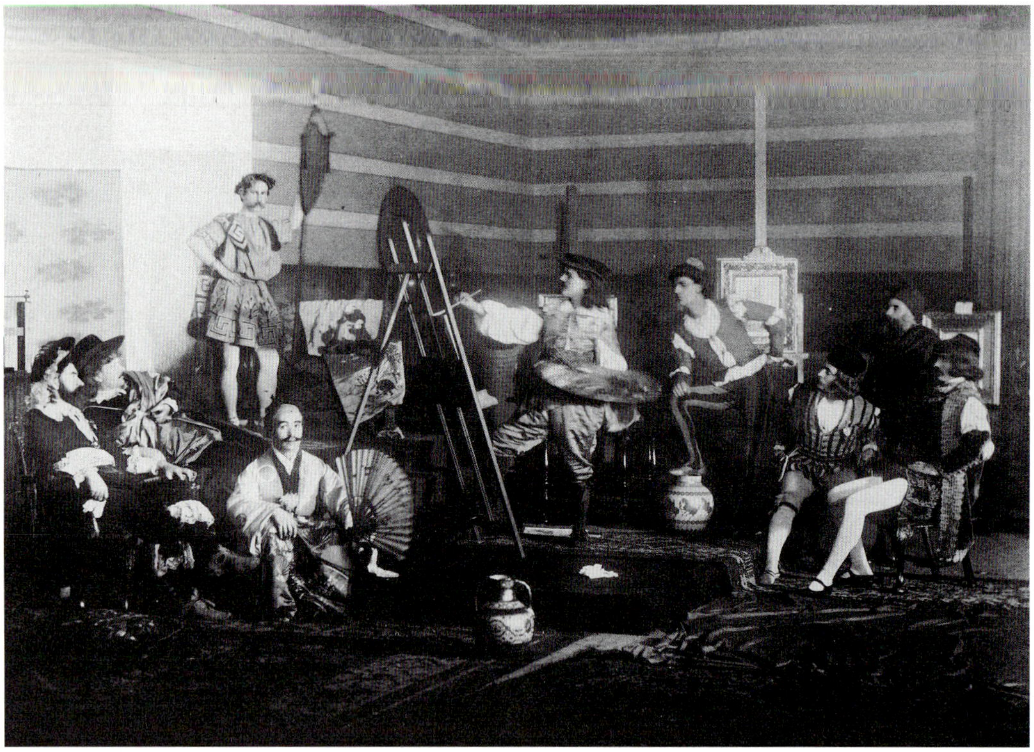

67 The Modern Artist's Studio, photograph, 1889, Lavery stands centre stage (photo, Mitchell Library, Glasgow)

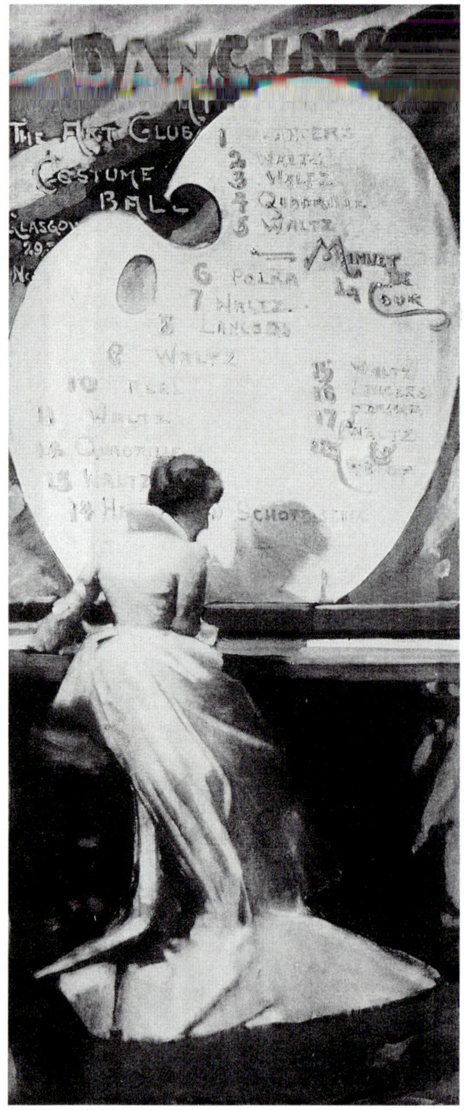

66 *Dancing at The Art Club*, 1889, size unknown (Glasgow Art Club)

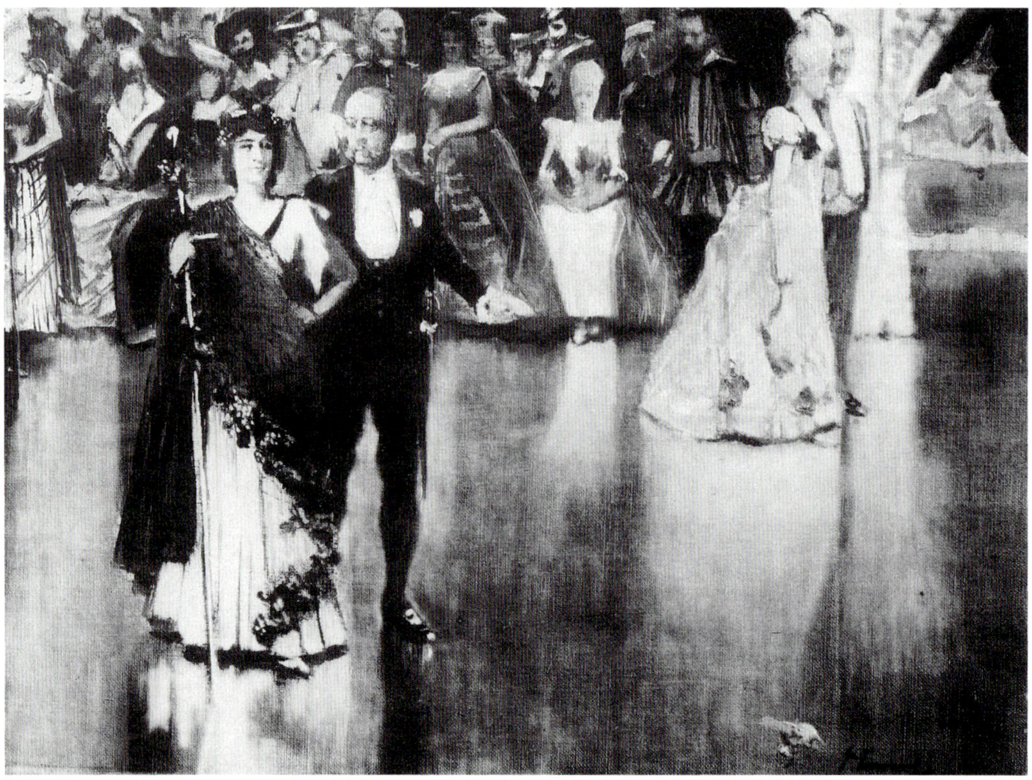

69 *A Corner of the Ballroom*, 1889, size unknown (present whereabouts unknown)

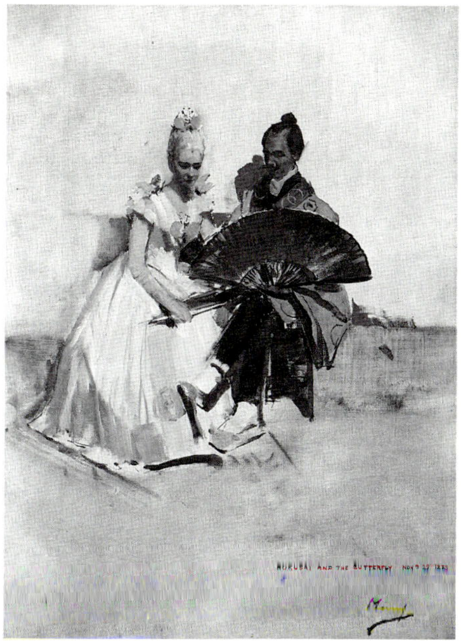

68 *Hokusai and The Butterfly*, 1889, 24 × 18 (National Gallery of Scotland, Edinburgh)

Coats . . . James Fulton went in Moorish costume with his daughter, Eva, as a waterlily. Lavery attended the ball, dressed in satin doublet and knickerbockers as Rembrandt. During the proceedings, a tableau based upon Delaroche's Hemicycle of the Arts was staged and Guthrie occupied a central role as the great classical painter, Apelles.[102] An additional side show was held in a room adjacent to the Octagon Hall which was furnished as a modern artist's studio painted in blue and gold. 'Here during the evening, Messrs Lavery, MacGregor Wilson, A. S. Boyd, Paterson, William Kennedy and Hamilton were at work taking sketches in accordance with an intimation displayed at the door by an artist's lay figure in these terms: "A fresh old master at work every half hour."'[103]

One of Lavery's half-hour efforts recorded the betrothal of Hokusai, played by E. A. Walton, to 'the golden butterfly', played by his girlfriend, Helen Law (see Plate 68).[104] The result, similar in style to the portrait sketches for the International Exhibition illustrates the artist's capacity, in this most social of situations to exclude all surrounding hubbub. In another untraced work, Lavery went even further and braved the dance floor to give a unique record of the progress of the pageant (see Plate 69).

With all this activity, Lavery can hardly have been aware of the rapid growth in the prestige of the Glasgow School. Following the success of the group at the Fine Art Section of the International Exhibition, the painter George Clausen suggested to Sir Coutts Lindsay that they be invited to exhibit in London in what was to be the last of the Grosvenor Gallery exhibitions.[105] Guthrie's *In the Orchard*, Henry and Hornel's *The Druids* and Lavery's *Dawn after the Battle of Langside* (see Plate 49) created a sensation in London that in the unbridled enthusiasm of one critic 'romped' in the fresh air, and united itself to live artistic qualities.[106] Then, by chance, two German artists, Herr Paulus and Herr Firle, visiting London, requested that the group of Glasgow pictures be shipped to Munich for the forthcoming Glaspalast Exhibition. Again the 'indescribable versatility' of the Glasgow Boys was applauded and from henceforth they were assured a place in the annals of modern painting.[107] It was this display which prompted the German art historian, Richard Muther, to give substantial coverage to the Glasgow School in his monumental three volume *History of Modern Painting*. He wrote, 'the powerful effect' which was made when the Scotch Gallery was open in the summer of 1890 at the annual exhibition in Munich was to be remembered for years to come.[108] Thereafter, Lavery had little difficulty in placing his work in the major European Salons. Only in London at the Royal Academy was he to encounter opposition, although in 1890, here too he was well represented with *The Bridge at Grez* (see Plate 28).[109]

By the beginning of 1891, Lavery was well established. He had finished *The State Visit . . .* (see Plate 62) he was bound for Morocco and he had a one-man exhibition in London planned for the following spring.[110] The loose federation of the Glasgow Boys facilitated his desire for experimentation and his leading role as one of the foremost young painters of his generation was openly acknowledged.

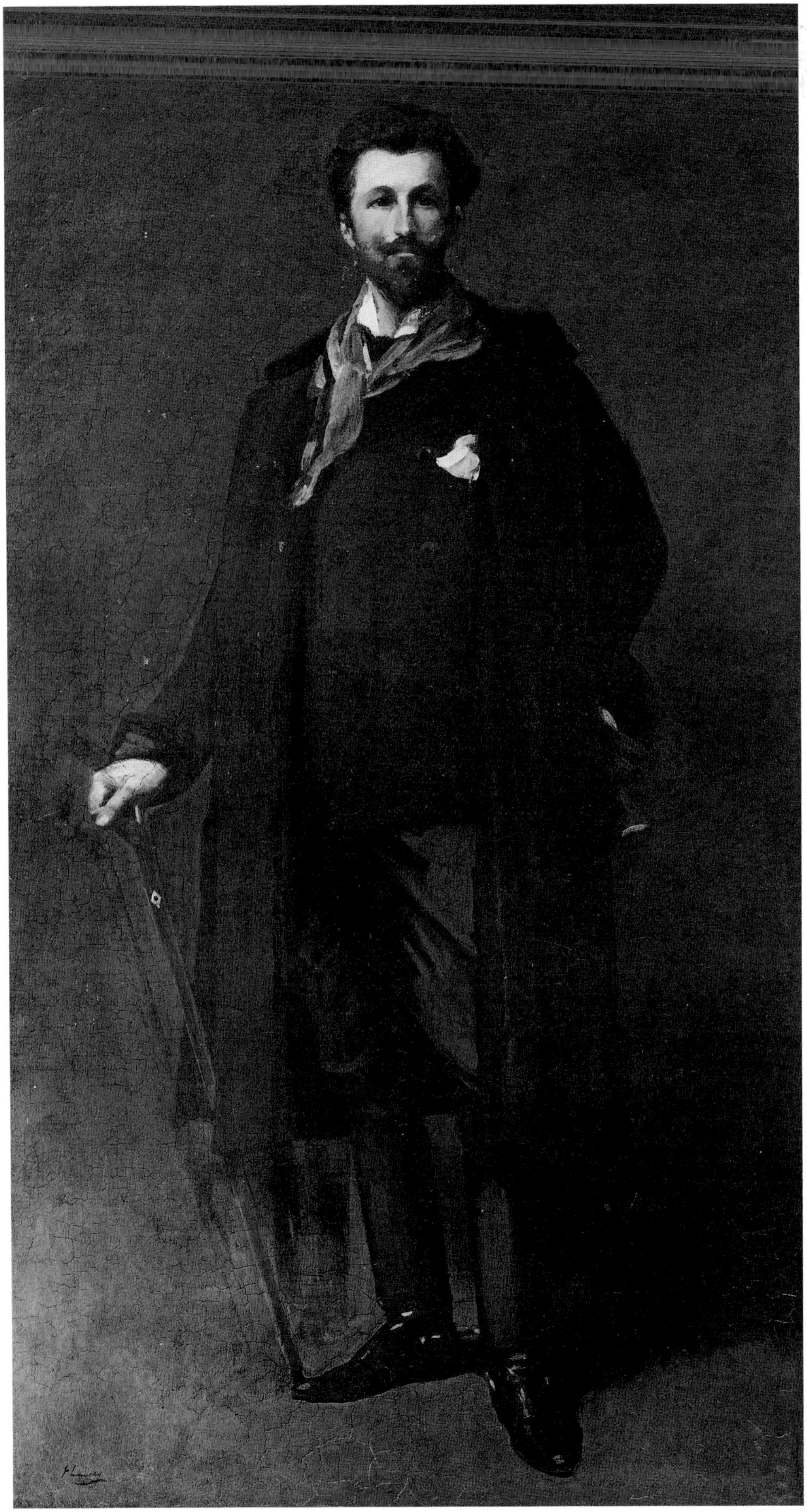

71 *Portrait of* R. B. *Cunninghame Graham*, 1893, 81 × 43⅛ (Glasgow Art Gallery and Museum)

5 Lavery and Whistler

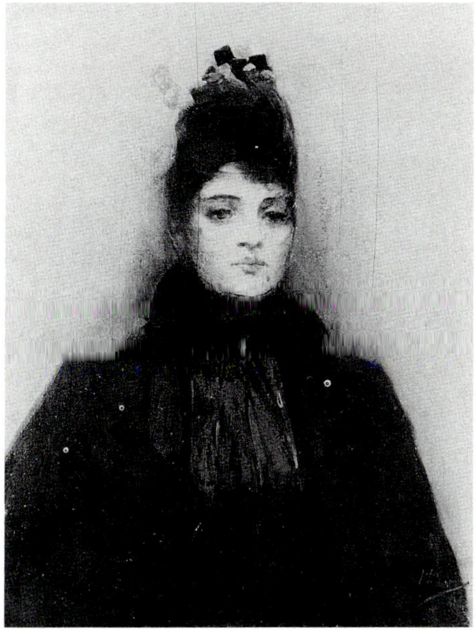

70 *An Irish Girl*, 1890, 27 × 21¼ (private collection)

One day in 1889 as he was leaving an artist's colour merchant's shop in Regent Street, Lavery caught sight of a beautiful flower girl in a red shawl and navy dress, named Kathleen MacDermott. He asked her to come to William Patrick Whyte's studio the following day. Both artists were 'bowled over' by her and Lavery asked her to return to Glasgow with him as his model.[1] Within a year however, she developed pulmonary tuberculosis and though he sent her to her married sister in Wales to escape the worst of the winter she took the first opportunity to rejoin him. They were married in March 1890 with Whyte and Joseph Crawhall as witnesses. After the birth of their daughter Eileen, Kathleen Lavery's health began quickly to deteriorate, so that by August 1891, the artist was in constant consultation with doctors.[2] Whyte took the ailing Kathleen from one health resort to another, finally coming to rest in a furnished villa at Kilmalcolm near Glasgow. There, she would sit in a sheltered garden, until it became too cold and the winter months began to draw in. Then, one Sunday morning, the artist recalled, he heard 'Whyte on the stair saying in a strained voice, "come quickly", She was being held up breathing with difficulty, her large eyes staring straight out . . . I tried to whisper a prayer in her ear. I could just hear "Goodbye", a gasp, and her head fell forward.'[3]

Lavery later discovered that Kathleen was only seventeen years of age when they met, and not eighteen as she had told him. She was not Irish, but Welsh and her real name was Annie Evans. As an old man, he vividly recalled their first encounter and asked his granddaughters in turn to don the red shawl and pose for him in remembrance of her.[4] Her facial type, with high cheekbones and strong jaw line, guided his selection of models throughout the Nineties.

Lavery painted Kathleen MacDermott's portrait on a number of occasions, the most important of which was as *An Irish Girl* (Plate 70).[5] This picture appeared in his exhibition at the Goupil Gallery in London in 1891, where it was grudgingly complimented by one critic for its 'tawdry beauty'. It was only in retrospect, that the picture began to assume significance as the first in a 'long series . . . in which he showed those qualities of pictorial taste and artistic finesse which have given him a distinctive position as a painter of women.'[6] These qualities were to distinguish Lavery from the other Glasgow Boys. A comparable work, *The Fur Boa* by William Kennedy employs more strident colour and incorporates a Japanese print in the background.[7] With *An Irish Girl*, Lavery moved much closer to the low-toned portraiture of Whistler. He probably visited Whistler in his studio around this time and observed the conscious contrivance of full-length portraits like *Rose et Argent: La Jolie Mutine*.[8] He would have noticed that the American painter hung muslin curtains on the studio windows to diffuse the light evenly around the figure and eliminate dramatic light and shade. Whistler would control the monochrome backdrop as the basis of his pictorial harmony. He would concern himself with placing the figure and with manipulating the abstract shapes thus created. In order to see the portrait as it emerged, he worked with long handled brushes that permitted the entire figure from head to foot, to be swept onto the canvas. In Sickert's words, 'he would pit himself against the unsleeping mobility of life itself'.[9] Lavery was deeply influenced by Whistler's approach. The regular contact between the two artists was to be sustained until Whistler's death in 1903. It matured over a decade in which Lavery witnessed the restless search for formal perfection in portraiture. This tenacity, this desire to seize the figure from life's continuum and fix it upon canvas, is most evident in Lavery's *Portrait of R. B. Cunninghame Graham* (Plate 71). Here the artist addresses directly the sources admired by Whistler in Velasquez' portraits. At first, he had been disappointed by the Spanish Master, but it was only when he tried to copy several of his works in the Prado, that their secrets began to unfold. As he later told Shaw Sparrow,

> I was at it (a copy of Don Carlos on horseback) only a few days when the graver qualities of Donna Maria of Austria imposed themselves upon me, and I hurried the copying of Don Carlos so that I might begin Maria of Austria. Scale in portraiture, you know, is among the most subtle difficulties that a painter has to contend against; it is one that Whistler took great trouble with. So, as women's portraits were my objective, I was anxious to get with exact truth all the measurements in my Velasquez.[10]

This process of realisation of the hidden character of Velasquez' work took more than one visit to complete. R. A. M. Stevenson recorded that the painter had, '. . . not found six months of study and careful copying sufficient to settle his opinions on the pictures of Velasquez. Upon his return in the following year, he found unexpected beauties in some canvases, he looked at others as if he had never seen them before, while the copy that in Scotland had been to him and to other painters the very interpretation of Velasquez now seemed lacking the essential spirit of the Master.'[11]

Lavery is likely to have reported his observations directly to Whistler in his studio in the rue du Bac. Whistler had moved to Paris around the time of his successful London exhibition, 'Nocturnes, Marines and Chevalet Pieces' at the Goupil Gallery in March and April 1892. Not only would Lavery have seen this exhibition, but he was one of the principal advocates in recommending Whistler's masterpiece, *Arrangement in Grey and Black No.2, Thomas Carlyle* for purchase by Glasgow Art Gallery.[12] But more than the other Glasgow painters, Lavery shared the Whistlerian aesthetic of colour harmony, tonal measurement and the control of texture. He responded to the desire to achieve a true abstract relationship between the figure's shape and the rectangle in which it was placed, in the *Portrait of R. B. Cunninghame Graham.*

Close examination of the paint surface of this picture reveals the tireless efforts of the painter to achieve his ideal abstraction. The right hand of the figure has been repositioned, as have both his legs. Extensive cracking in the paint surface around the shoulders, also indicates that there has been extensive revision. The artist later confessed that he had painted Cunninghame Graham, 'frankly in the manner of Velasquez, full-length and life-size, a harmony in brown. . .'[13] The picture closely

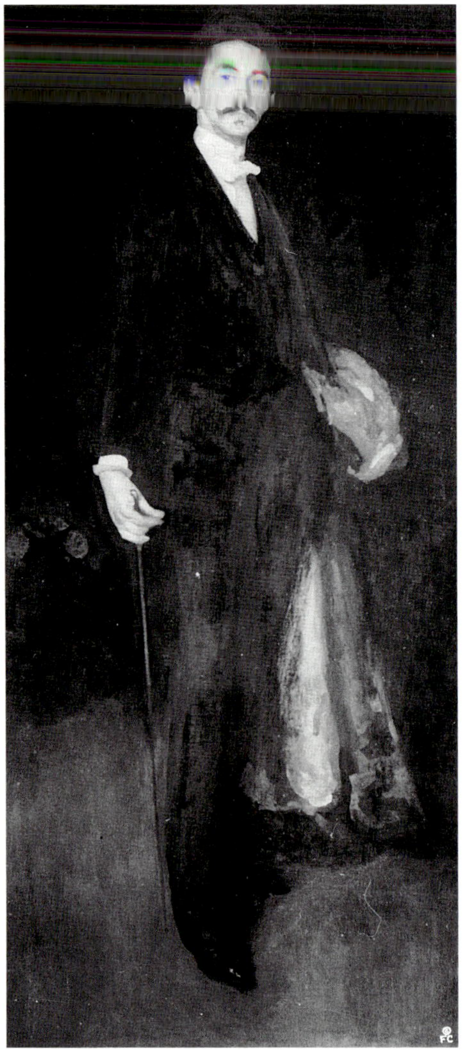

72 James McNeill Whistler, *Arrangement in Black and Gold: Comte Robert de Montesquiou*, 1893, 82 × 36 (Frick Collection New York)

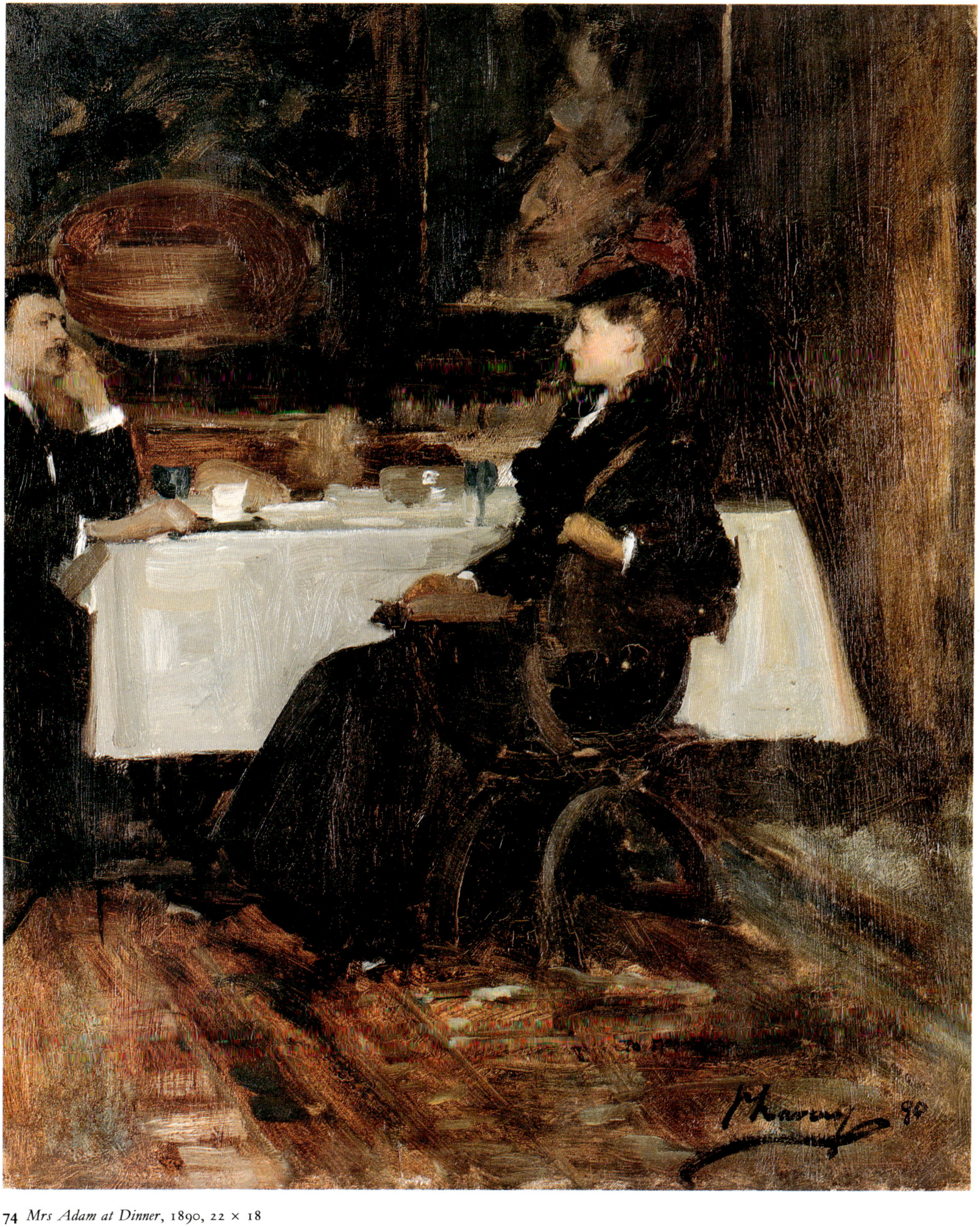

74 *Mrs Adam at Dinner*, 1890, 22 × 18
(photo, courtesy Sotheby's)

compares to Whistler's portrait of an effete French aristocrat, the celebrated *Arrangement in Black and Gold: Comte Robert de Montesquiou* (Plate 74) which had been begun in 1891. This too had numerous reworkings before it achieved its final perfection and exhibition alongside *Cunninghame Graham* at the Salon of 1894.[14]

Lavery's extrovert adventurer laird was anything but effete. Robert Bontine Cunninghame Graham was one of the most extraordinary characters of his age.[15] He was descended from the Earls of Glencairn and Menteith on his father's side and his mother was half Spanish. At the age of seventeen, he set off for Argentina to establish a ranch, but when this failed, he led the life of a gaucho, breaking-in mustangs and acquiring the skills of the bolas and the lasso. He returned to Europe in 1878, met and married the apparently Chilean-born, Gabrielle de la Balmondière and went back briefly to Gartmore, his family estate. However, finding life in Scotland boring, he and his wife set off for Texas to buy and sell cotton. Sadly this venture also failed and he was obliged to recoup his losses by working in a fencing academy in Mexico City as Professor Bontini! In 1883, Don Roberto, as he was known to his friends, returned home after his father's death to settle debts of £100,000. In 1886 he entered parliament and instantly acquired a reputation as an *enfant terrible*. He and Lavery may have met as early as 1888 when, as a Liberal Member of Parliament, his portrait was painted by George Percy Jacomb Hood, one of Lavery's student friends.[16] The artist records their having met when he was invited to Gartmore sometime after the latter's release from Pentonville prison. Graham served six months for his part in the Free Speech Riots in Trafalgar Square in 1888.[17] The two men established a more direct rapport on Graham's visit to Tangier in 1893 when, according to him, he stopped Lavery's runaway horse. The painter apparently introduced himself with the words, 'thanks, my preserver; my name is Lavery', and with that they sauntered back to town together talking of politics, women, horses and art. Graham only adds that he, being more practised, did most of the talking![18]

The portrait which resulted from these encounters reveals Cunninghame Graham's commanding character. At first, the artist familiarised himself with the features of his subject in a head and shoulders study that conveys something of the aristocratic impatience of the sitter (see Plate 73). He was larger than life, and he seems so in Lavery's rendition. Waxing lyrical, Shaw Sparrow enumerates his qualities as 'the man of action, and the student, and the man of fashion . . .' and concludes that 'to convey so much in a picture without losing the atmosphere of art, the non-assertion of good design, is, surely, a masterstroke.'[19] Lavery's visualisation inspired George Bernard Shaw's character of Captain Brassbound, and it is evident that the author saw Cunninghame Graham through the medium of his portrait. 'He is,' Shaw declares, 'a Spanish hidalgo, hence the superbity of his portrait by Lavery (Velasquez being no longer available).'[20] The image inspired other painters as well. In 1896, the young William Rothenstein submitted *The Swordsman* to the New English Art Club, and this work almost caricatures Lavery's portrait.[21]

The painter himself did not forsake his sitter. In 1898, he painted a large equestrian portrait of *Cunninghame Graham on Pampa*, and this too was based on a smaller sketch.[22] Don Roberto remained a firm friend until his death in 1936, and

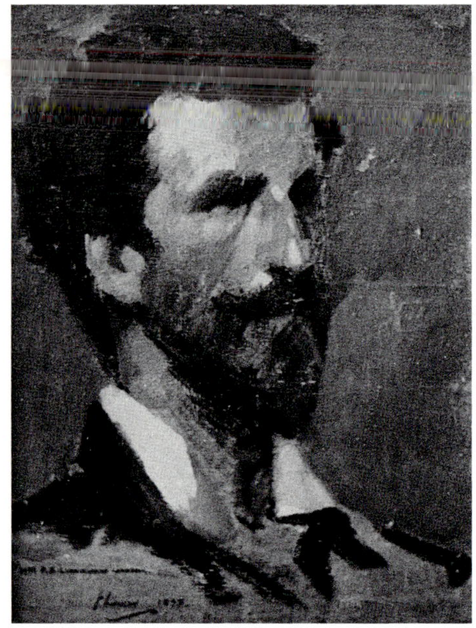

73 *Sketch of R. B. Cunninghame Graham*, 1893, size unknown (private collection)

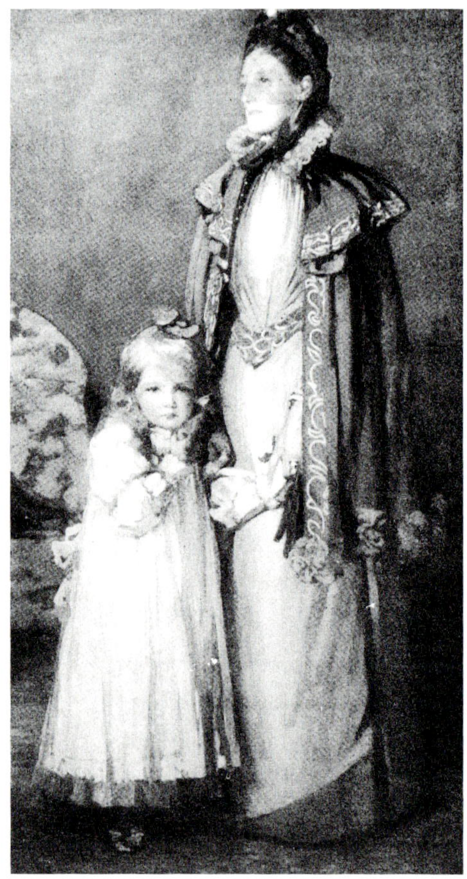

75 *Mrs J. J. Cowan and Laura*, 1892, size unknown (private collection)

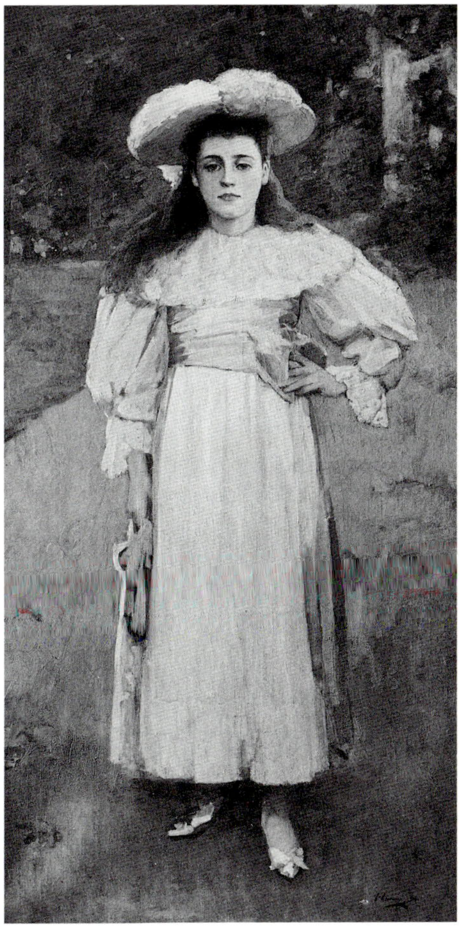

76 *Portrait of a Girl in White*, 1894, 71½ × 36 (Perth Art Gallery)

his biographer, A. F. Tschiffely records visiting Glasgow Art Gallery with him sometime in the Thirties for the purpose of studying the Lavery full-length.[23]

The qualities of design were if anything, more apparent in Lavery's female portraits of the period. In 1892, he showed about twenty such pictures at the Lawrie Gallery, Glasgow, in an exhibition which borrowed its title from Tennyson—'A Dream of Fair Women'. He also experimented with different formats and figure positions. *Mother and Son: Mrs Lawrie and Edwin*,[24] presents the two figures with simple frontality while *Katherine and Esther, daughters of Lord McLaren*,[25] combines a dramatic foregound side view portrait of Esther with her sister in the background, leaning against a table. This second picture attempts to convey something of the relaxed ambiance of the upper-class drawing room. Both pictures refer back to the sketch-like *Mrs Adam at Dinner* (Plate 74), a work which, like the tennis pictures, attempts to create the ambiance of social exchange.

Possibly because he had admired *Mrs Lawrie and Edwin* at the Glasgow Institute in 1892, John James Cowan of Edinburgh asked Lavery to paint the portraits of his wife and daughter. The full-length standing double portrait (Plate 75) was quite different in format from either earlier work. It showed Mrs Cowan's face, half veiled, in the fashion of the day. Lavery's lightly veiled *Irish Girl* (see Plate 70) would probably have been already familiar to Cowan, but in further exploration of the effect, the artist painted a low-toned head and shoulders study of a model wearing a face veil covering her eyes and nose.[26] This supporting study enabled him to execute the large canvas in only ten sittings of a couple of hours each.[27] The result was regarded by Cowan as one of the best Laverys ever painted. He recounts that his views were not shared by his five-year-old daughter, Laura. When the painter delivered his work, '. . . we were all admiring it when Laura herself appeared. Lavery said to her, "what do you think of it?" and for once he got a candid criticism, "I think it is just disgustin'"'[28]

The Magazine of Art, however, did not agree with the child's judgement. Admiring the pearl-greys in particular, it considered the painting to be one of the finest Laverys its critic had seen.[29] For his own portrait, J. J. Cowan sought Lavery's advice about obtaining sittings from Whistler. Lavery executed a small head study and sent it to Whistler, who, by December 1892 was well established in his studio at 110 rue du Bac, Paris.[30] Accordingly Cowan went to Paris the following summer in the vain hope of having his portrait painted. He believed, naively, that since the novice Lavery had painted his wife in ten sittings, Whistler, 'a master of his art', would do it in less. Alas this was not to be and sittings continued intermittently for the next seven years. Lavery recalled the difficulty which Whistler found in this commission. After the first two weeks he asked Whistler how he liked 'the Scotsman', only to be told that he was 'very difficult'. 'You knew what you were doing when you put him off on to me', Whistler remarked. Lavery had thought that he was doing Whistler a good turn and was surprised, years later, to see how little work had apparently been done on the canvas.[31]

It was, however, in the single figure full-length portraits that Lavery obtained his most satisfactory abstractions. At face value it would be easy to regard *Portrait of a Girl in White* (Plate 76) as an infanta inspired by a recent visit to the Prado.[32]

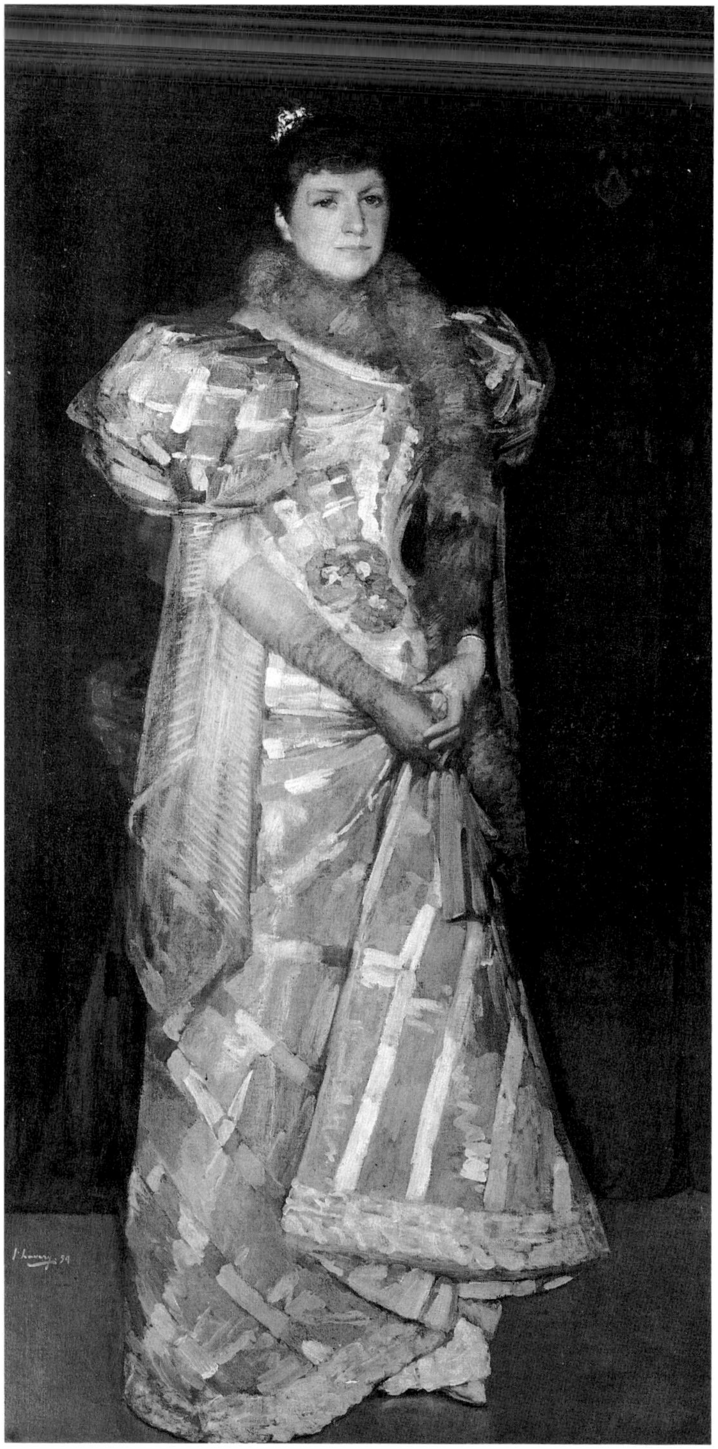

78 *Mrs Fitzroy Bell*, 1894, 72 × 36
(Glasgow Art Gallery and Museum)

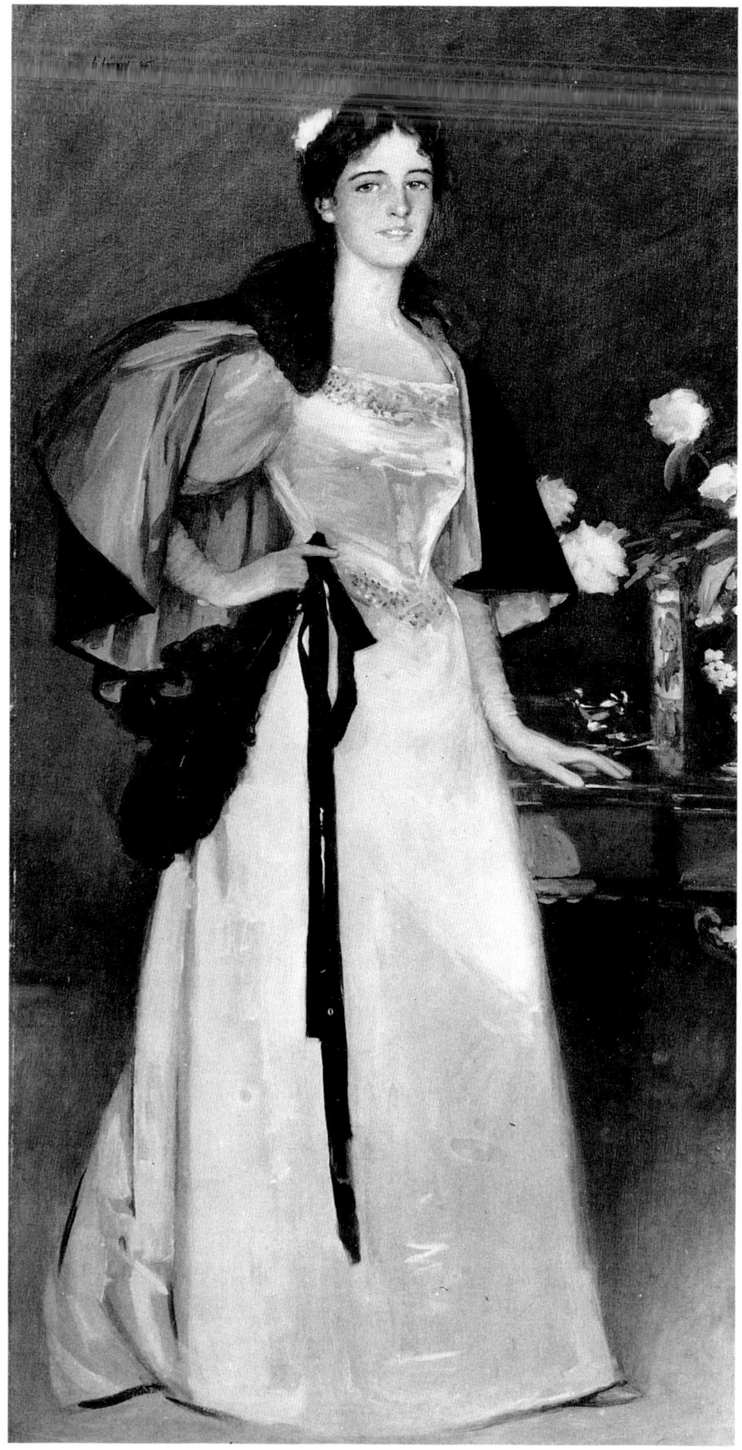

79 *Miss Mary Burrell*, 1895, 72 × 36
(Burrell Collection, Glasgow)

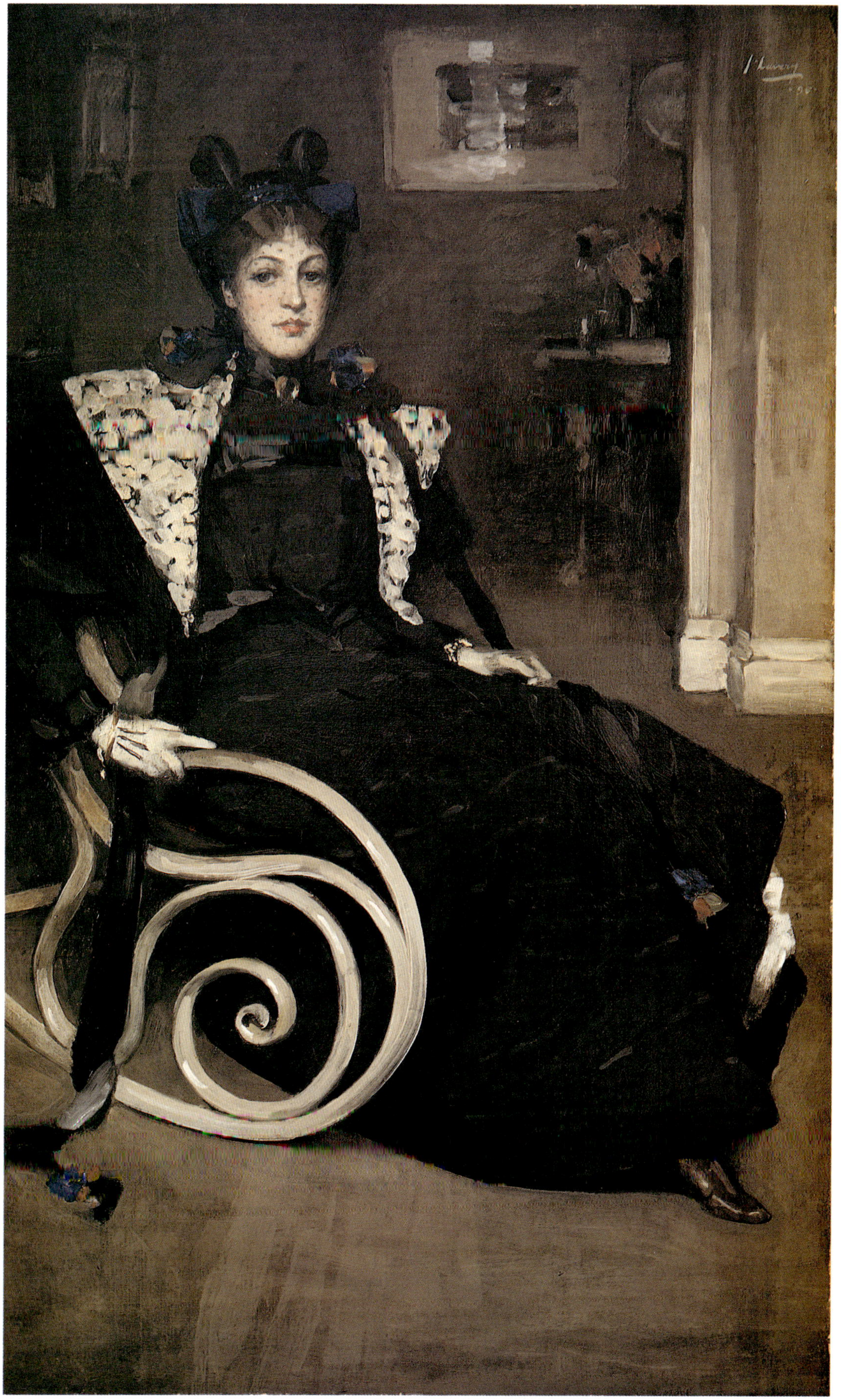

80 *The Rocking Chair*, 1895, 50 × 30
(Royal Scottish Academy, Edinburgh)

Her broad yellow sash and lacey cavalier sleeves have a distinctly seventeenth-century character, yet the lightly sketched trees in the background carry a suggestion of open-air that is not confirmed in the studio piece figure. This is one of a number of instances where the sketch, with its unresolved attempts at emphasising the halo of the picture hat, is much less laboured than the end product (Plate 77).[33] A similar model posed for the unlocated *Harmony in Brown* which was shown at the Royal Academy in 1894.[34]

Lavery moved even closer to Whistler in *Mrs Fitzroy Bell* (Plate 78),[35] a lady in a dazzling pink and mauve evening dress. Her hair is caught up in a chignon and upon the background screen, the artist has emblazoned a coat of arms, imitating the heraldic devices of ancient portraiture. But perhaps the closest evocation of court painting in these years, is the *Miss Mary Burrell* (Plate 79). Shaw Sparrow notes that this picture was painted immediately after a visit to Madrid,[36] but adds that the model's expression is gayer than those of Velasquez. Here the distinction between the exercise of style and the constraint of portraiture achieve a satisfying resolution. Like Whistler, Lavery demanded the right to take liberties with his sitter, demoting him or her to the rank of model. James Stanley Little, clarifying this point in 1902, recorded Lavery's views as follows;

> He holds that the artist has licence and prerogative to treat his sitter as he would treat a model, to this extent: he is entitled to seize upon and give prominence to those points which in form and colour suggest to him an attractive and interesting pictorial idea, and that, while the essential facts and characteristics which would enable a third person to recognise immediately the sitter in the picture must be preserved, the painter is entirely justified—further that no portrait can be a work of art otherwise—in treating his sitter subjectively, and infusing into his presentment his own artistic individuality.[37]

In this instance, Lavery achieved what Little referred to as, 'that happy equipoise'. The model's left hand rests gently upon a table as she turns to face the spectator just as Philip IV does in Velasquez' portraits. The paint surface is plain and contains no traces of the labour evident in *Mrs Fitzroy Bell* and the *Girl in White*. As if to emphasise the technical serenity of the picture, Lavery includes a blue and white Nankin vase on the table.

Miss Burrell's portrait indicates the growing prominence of Lavery's clientele. Having been elected to the Royal Scottish Academy in 1896, he submitted his diploma work, *The Rocking Chair* (Plate 80), a work that was recognised as a *tour de force*.[38] Again Lavery painted an elegant model wearing a light veil, through which her striking features are perceived. The dramatic design incorporates a side view of the bentwood rocking chair that has been painted without hesitation. A critic in 1914 commented upon this spontaneity, saying that it 'might have been finished yesterday, the paint is so fresh and glowing'.[39] As with *Mrs J. J. Cowan and Laura* (see Plate 75), the freshness of Lavery's characterisation of his sitters was sustained by his having found models with approximately similar features for intermediate head studies. One such is that of *Millie the Model* (Plate 81), who is presented with the same simple frontality as Mrs Christie Smith in *The Rocking Chair*.

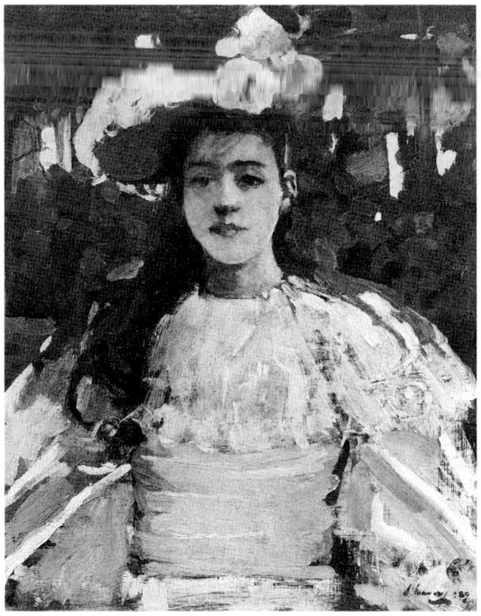

77 Study for *Portrait of a Girl in White*, 1894, size unknown (present whereabouts unknown, photo, Sotheby's)

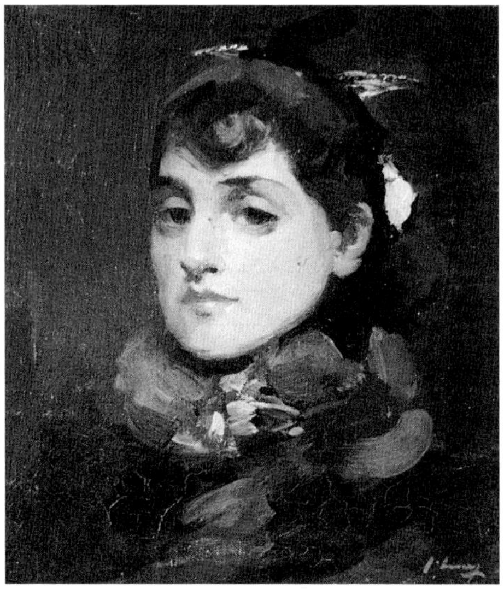

81 *Millie the Model*, *c.*1894, $13\frac{3}{4} \times 11\frac{5}{8}$ (private collection)

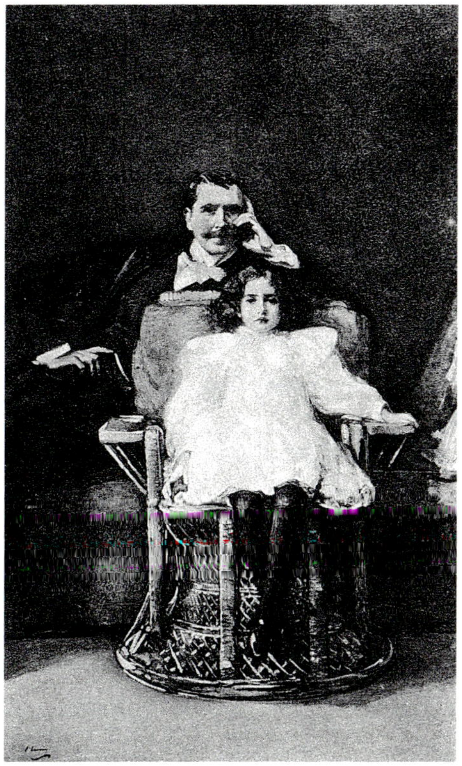

83 *Père et Fille*, 1898, 82 × 50 (Museé d'Orsay, Paris)

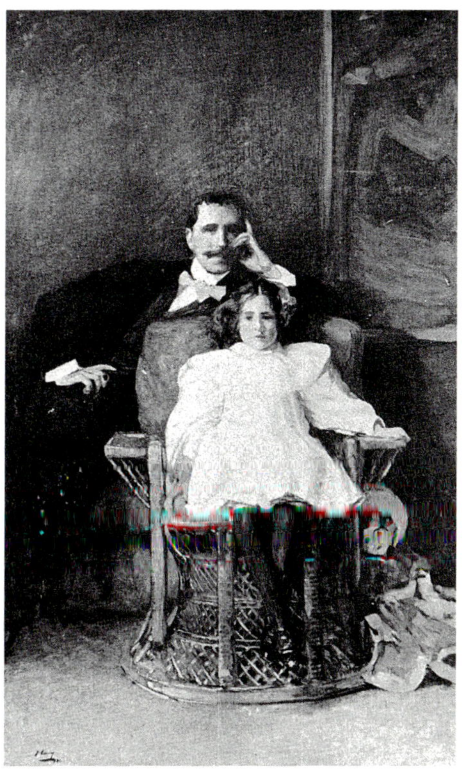

84 Père et Fille, unfinished state (photo, the author)

There were constant efforts at this time to portray Lavery as a mere camp follower of Whistler's. In the eyes of the critic of the Belgian periodical *l'Art Moderne*, he and Guthrie were both profoundly affected by Whisler but lacked his sense of 'immaterialité' and 'aristocratic distinction'.[40] Other critics felt that he had given his talent to the portrayal of mere accessories. At the same time his painting did not have the robustness of Academy portraitists like Fildes and Herkomer. He was striving for formal perfection and the more concentrated this became, the more tenuous it seemed. A picture could be so discrete that it failed to appear. This process had often led his mentor to destruction. Whistler had a reputation for wiping out the results of an entire sitting if it did not please him.[41] On one occasion in October 1902, when Lavery chanced upon him burning canvases, Whistler turned upon him and declared, 'to destroy is to exist you know'.[42] The conscious striving for understatement led to constant reworking and scraping down to such an extent that the end result was more of an evocation than a portrait. So subtle was *Nora* (Plate 82), for instance, that *The Art Journal* declined to reproduce it. It was a majestic picture singled out by Whistler: 'His well known portrait *Nora* is typical of his class but its extremely delicate nuances of tone forbid reproduction.Although it is to be seen that there is plenty of paint used in surface registration the result is so subtle and diaphanous that the effect seems as if colouring lay beneath the canvas. It is no secret that this portrait frequently won the admiration of Mr Whistler.'[43]

Nora was not the only Lavery painting for which Whistler expressed admiration. He recounts his bemusement when Whistler spotted his *Père et Fille* (Plate 83) set aside for repainting. At once Whistler declared, 'at last my dear Lavery, you have done it. It is beautiful. It is complete.'[44] Precisely when this event occurred and whether or not Lavery took Whistler's advice, remains a mystery. The evidence of the period reveals that the picture was reworked possibly after its showing at the first exhibition at the International Society of Sculptors, Painters and Gravers. Since Whistler and Lavery were president and vice-president respectively, it is likely that the painter was encouraged to exhibit his self-portrait with Eileen unfinished. There is almost acknowledgement of its unfinished status in *The Art Journal* critic's comment that it was '. . . already proving to be one of the best of the painter's portrait pictures . . .'[45] Lavery then tightened the features of the two figures and removed the doll lying on the floor beside the chair. The picture was re-exhibited at the Salon of 1906 and thereafter was acquired for the Musée du Luxembourg. In 1905 Camille Mauclair eulogised its agreeable naturalism finding in it a communion of spirit between father and daughter and a stable and protective relationship.[46] The picture's warmth and immediacy distances it from *Anne Montgomery Knox and her Father* (Plate 85), Lavery's Royal Academy exhibit of 1896.

Lavery's friendship with Whistler undoubtedly deepened as a result of their involvement with the International Society of Sculptors, Painters and Gravers. Relinquishing the New English Art Club, Lavery had begun to exhibit at the Society of Portrait Painters which was formed in 1891, and which despite its initial financial uncertainties, provided a regular venue for new work. His success at the Royal Academy up to this point, must have persuaded him that moving to

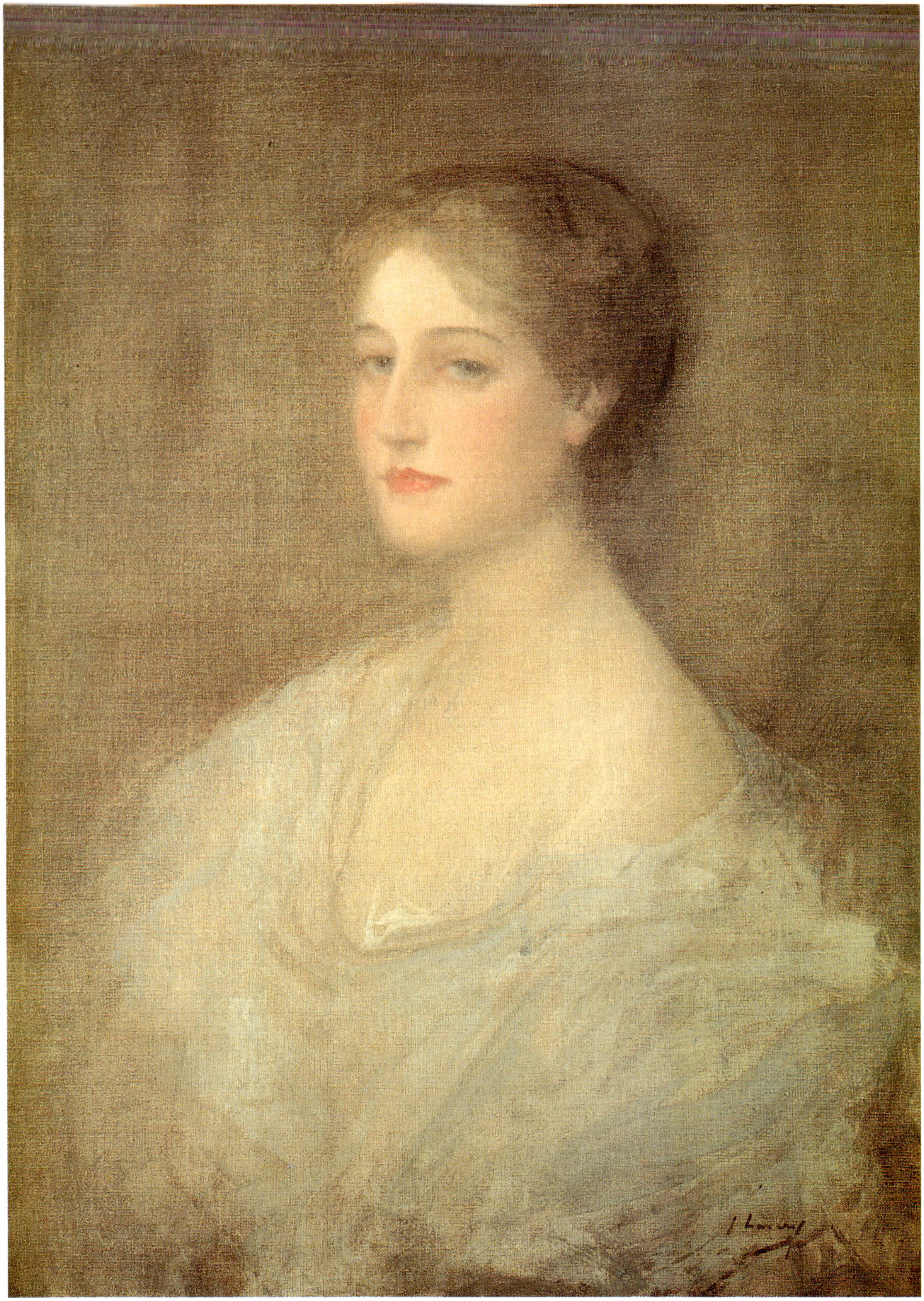

82 *Nora*, *c.*1896, 28 × 20 (private collection, photo, Pyms Gallery, London)

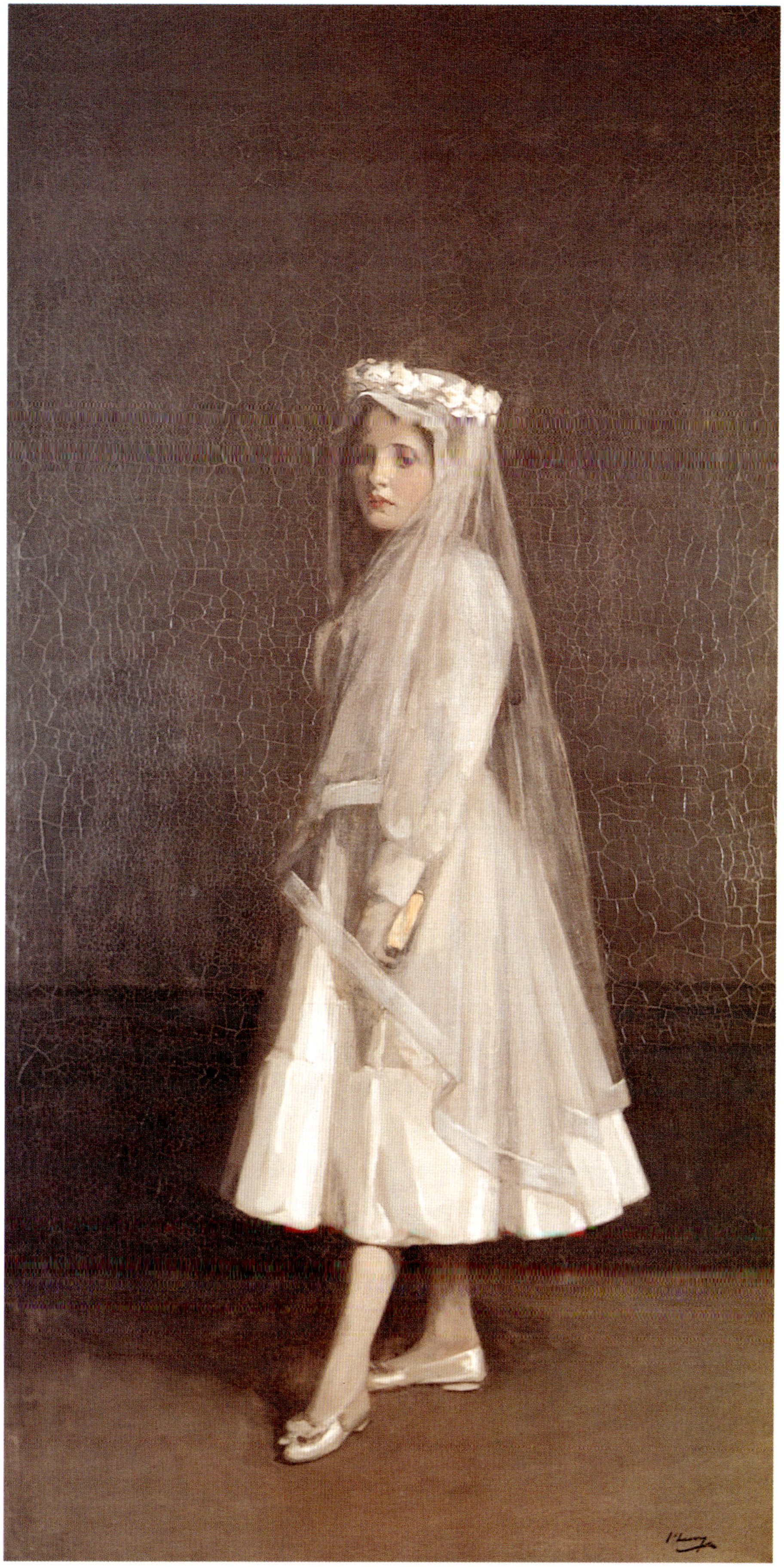

87 *Her First Communion*, 1902, $71\frac{1}{4}$ × 35 (private collection)

London would be in his interests. In 1896, therefore, he occupied a studio at 2 Spencer Street, Westminster, which had been lent to him by Alfred East.[47] However, he did not remain there for long. The following winter was spent in a rented studio in Rome, suffering from what was later described as 'Roman fever' in a vain attempt to gain a commission to paint Pope Leo X. By the beginning of 1898, he had purchased what was to be his home for the rest of his life, 5 Cromwell Place, South Kensington, the former residence of Sir Coutts Lindsay.

Ironically, in view of his removal from Glasgow, Lavery's canvases, following *Anne Montgomery Knox and her Father* were rejected at the Academy and henceforth he refused to exhibit there until he was elected Associate in 1911. During 1897, however, he was deeply involved in discussions to set up an international exhibiting society. These 'art congresses' were first suggested by the watercolourist, Francis Howard, and the idea was taken up with enthusiasm by the members of the Glasgow School now living in London. From the start, it was agreed that though he was now living in Paris, Whistler should be president of the new society. He and E. A. Walton approached the owners of the Grosvenor and Grafton Galleries in a failed attempt to secure a venue for the first exhibition to be held in 1898.[48] In the end, Howard's suggestion that they hold the show at Prince's Skating Rink, Knightsbridge owned by Admiral Maxse, was accepted.

On 23 December 1897, the first council meeting of the International Society was held. Lavery assumed the role of vice-president communicating the views of the members to Whistler and relaying Whistler's opinions to them.[49] There was much debate in the early meetings on the issue of whether only approved artists be invited to contribute. The president was insistent that only painters who were not affiliated to other academies or societies should be invited, and, following his recent treatment by the Royal Academy, Lavery is likely to have concurred. There were problems, however, in imposing this rule. J. J. Shannon, whose work was approved by Lavery and Whistler alike, was a regular Academy exhibitor. No decision was taken on the matter before the first exhibition and in the end it included paintings by more radical Academy regulars like Shannon and George Clausen. John Singer Sargent, now the darling of the Academy, violently objected to even being asked to contribute to the International. Lavery later recalled 'Whistler's agreeing that we should have a Sargent at our first international exhibition and I was deputed to see him. I shall never forget my surprise. He was quite affable till I told him the object of my visit when he suddenly became inarticulate with rage—he spluttered and fumed—I gathered that he would see the International dammed first including its Hon. Secretary and President.' It is unlikely that Sargent would have regarded Lavery as a rival and probable that his extraordinary response reflected his attitude to Whistler at that time.

Elsewhere, the organisers energetically enlisted support. Lavery confided to Whistler that 'Guthrie and Walton will beat up Scotland, Sauter Germany and London will be left to her own sweet will'.[50] A good deal of effort was expended in ensuring the support of prominent French painters like Lautrec, Puvis de Chavannes, Renoir, Monet and Degas. Loans were secured through dealers like Vollard, Durand-Ruel and Georges Petit.[51] Only Degas posed problems. He was angry when he discovered that he was being represented without his permission.

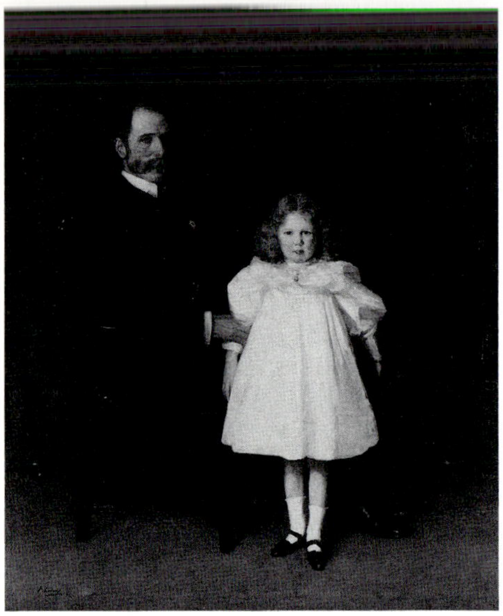

85 *Anne Montgomery Knox and her Father*, 1896, 72 × 59 (present whereabouts unknown, photo, Jones Photography, Gloucester)

Lavery desperately wrote to William Rothenstein in an effort to get him to use his influence: 'I am sure he need only know that the thing is an affair of the artist and not of the dealer or middle man, to give his consent.' With characteristic truculence, Degas advised Rothenstein to have nothing to do with the project. He told the young painter to show 'in colour shops, in restaurants—anywhere but at the brothels that picture shows are'.[52] Both artists were, however, represented in the exhibition. Beside these modern French painters, was hung the work of northern Europeans such as Zorn and Thaulow, alongside the Italians, Segantini and Costa. Belgian, Dutch and German art was also represented, but the dominant group by far were the Scots with forty of the 250 exhibitors.[53]

Lavery was closely involved in the installation and hanging of the exhibition and for this he and his committee received Whistler's seal of approval.[54] From Paris the following letter arrived, 'I have barely had more than time to perceive the rare appreciation and sympathy with which the plan of the walls has been carried out! The managing of the lighting, the placing of the "velum" as it is called here, about which I was so anxious, is most perfect. My compliments to the hangers whose labours must have been Herculean . . .'[55]

The exhibition was well received and even patronised by the Prince of Wales.[56] Following the Goupil Gallery retrospective, it was likely that now, at last, British critics were beginning to be receptive to the aesthetic principles of display associated with Whistler. This appreciation did not extend to the packers of exhibits who were employed at the end of the show to return Rodin's plaster cast sculptures. Their actions drew a stiff letter from Whistler,

> Monsieur Rodin has promised to put in writing his experience of the management of the 'International' at Knightsbridge. It is a matter of public noteriety that all his casts came back broken to bits!—and that, in one case, the ingenuity of the British packer (for whom the executive is responsible) was so unrestrained in its joyous impulses and inspiration, that without a moments hesitation, he summarily sawed off a *leg at the ankle!* and so brilliantly reduced the recalcitrant limb to immediate submission and *the fit of the box!*—so simple are the methods of genius! 'Ce sont les barbares!' said Monsieur Rodin. All comment would appear unnecessary.[57]

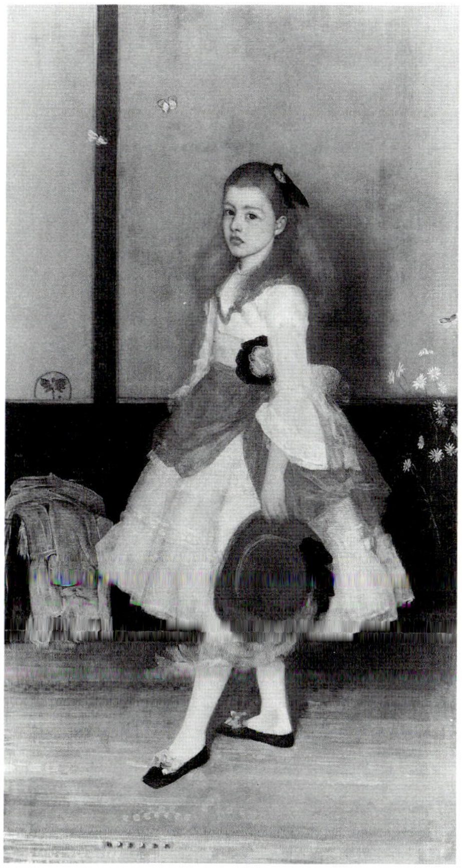

86 James McNeill Whistler, *Harmony in Grey and Green: Miss Cicely Alexander*, 1872–4, $74\frac{3}{4} \times 38\frac{1}{2}$ (Tate Gallery, London)

Despite the *débâcle*, Rodin did not withdraw from the second international society exhibition. Nevertheless, he was careful to send only bronzes to London on that occasion.[58] Lavery and Whistler were in close contact over the planning of this show. Lavery was in Paris in April 1899 to discuss the arrangements in person with Whistler and a few weeks later Whistler came to London and stayed at Cromwell Place in order to view the results. With the flair of a seasoned self-publicist, Whistler transcribed some of his more notorious reviews of *Harmony in Grey and Green: Miss Cicely Alexander* (Plate 86) which he wished to have reprinted in the catalogue. The finances of the society gave cause for concern to both artists, although the news of the £300 deficit from the first exhibition seems only to have sunk home with Whistler when he read in the papers that the second was being used as a place for public entertainment. He wrote to Lavery and the committee with some indignation: 'Gentlemen, I gather . . . that "string bands", "ice creams'', together with buttery teas and "other indecencies" pervade the Galleries "of an afternoon" . . .'[59]

Alas, Lavery's explanation, on behalf of the committee, does not survive, however, shortly after this letter was written, the affairs of the society were placed in the competent hands of the solicitor, William Webb.[60] Lavery's contributions to the second exhibition were not totally satisfactory; he showed four works, but the largest of these, *A Lady in Pink* and *A Lady in Purple* were totally repainted.[61]

Because there were numerous centennial exhibitions to be staged in 1900, the International Society did not reconvene until 1901 when the third show was held at The Galleries, 191 Piccadilly, a more central venue. Thereafter, its fortunes were more stable and it came to occupy a regular slot in the exhibition calender.

During the second half of the 1890s, Lavery's clientele widened considerably. Not only were his pictures admired at the Salon,[62] but their regular appearances at Munich Glaspalast brought him to the attention of German collectors. At this time, *The Tennis Party* (see Plate 45) was purchased by the Munich Pinakothek and Herr Steilhardt of Berlin purchased a picture known as *The White Duchess*. In April 1898, as a result of contacts established through the London-based German painter, Auguste Neven du Mont, Lavery went to Germany to paint the portraits of the Von Guilleaume family at Mulheim. Of these, *Frauline Bertha Von Guilleaume* was shown at the Society of Portrait Painters exhibition in 1901, and was recognised as a partial restatement of Whistler's *Harmony in Grey and Green, Miss Cicely Alexander*. At the same time, he was not forsaken by Glasgow. In 1899, he received a commission from the City Fathers to paint one of four sets of panels in the banqueting hall in the City Chambers. Walton wrote to him with a sketch of the proportions and dimensions for a preparatory oil study.[63] The general theme was to be the history and legend of the city, and while his three colleagues, Walton, Henry and Roche stuck to the brief, Lavery embarked upon an ambitious evocation of the city's modern industrial base. The subject he elected to portray was the activity at Fairfield Shipyard, Govan where a battleship for the Japanese navy was under construction.[64] Though the dramatic perspectives and bustle of activity somewhat conflict with the serene pilasters of the setting, Lavery's subject was rendered, for the most part, in a narrow range of greys and blues, recalling the early Thames pictures by Whistler and looking forward to the dockyard scenes of the Great War.[65]

However, the picture which acts as Lavery's homage to Whistler and which, at the same time, synthesises his own concerns of the 1890s is *Eileen—Her First Communion* (Plate 87).[66] Here again, he confronted the problem of painting a girl dressed in white in the manner of Whistler's celebrated infanta, *Miss Cicely Alexander*. This challenge was to be set by many of the artists of Lavery's generation. La Thangue, Clausen, Guthrie, Walton, Osborne, Orpen, Nicholson and others were directly influenced by it, and produced their own variations. Lavery was therefore challenging a common prototype, but his solution stripped away the artifice of Whistler, leaving out the dado and butterflies, but rediscovering, by contrast some of the frontal directness of Bastien-Lepage's *La Communiante*. It was the childish *ingénue* that Whistler particularly enjoyed, 'Staying with me for a few days at Cromwell Place, I saw a different Whistler from

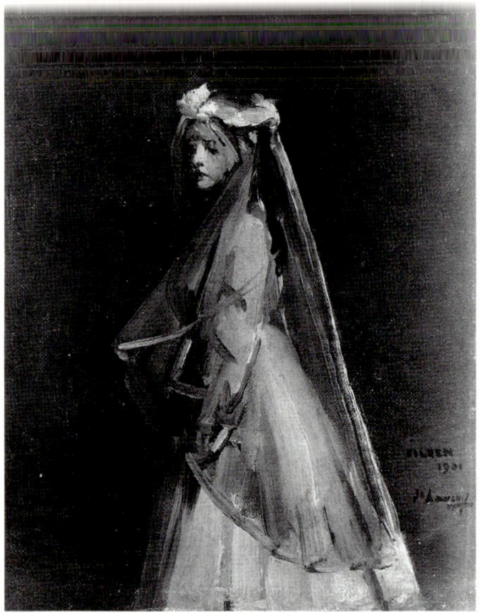

88 Sketch for *Her First Communion*, *c.*1902, 10 × $8\frac{1}{4}$ (Ulster Museum, Belfast)

the captious man I had known . . . My daughter, aged seven, was home from the Sacred Heart Convent, Roehampton; he called her the "Little Lady of the Holy Heart" and spent hours playing with her doll's house and teaching her amusing rhymes about "a tooter who tooted the flute" and so forth.'[67]

Whistler took a more serious interest in Lavery's painting. In 1924 Lavery recollected,

> I have sometimes been called a pupil of Whistler's. The only criticism or lesson I ever received from him was on a summer's evening about nine o'clock, he came to my studio and looking at a portrait of a little girl in white—certainly influenced by his *Miss Alexander* he remarked that the white frock was too high in key for the flesh tone and asking for some charcoal he rubbed it in the hollow of his hand, then rubbing his finger in this proceeded to tone the white paint on the picture in the most delicate manner possible conveying to me the impression that my work was too coarse and crude, and preventing me from painting with any vigour for nearly a year afterwards—possibly for many years."[68]

Despite the fact that he worked so close to Whistler, the consensus view was that Lavery was 'no mere imitator'—*Eileen, Her First Communion* had, in the words of the *Illustrated London News* been a 'trial of Mr Lavery's strength'. Despite his reservations, there seems no loss of vigour in Lavery's handling around 1900 when he was in continuous contact with Whistler. The rapport was sufficently close for regular visits to occur right up until the final months of Whistler's life. In October 1902, for instance, 'He had a bad turn while Lavery was with him and Lavery helped him to his bed—he could hardly get his breath. When he sat up again he drew his hand across his back and said, almost like a child, "I don't like this at all Lavery, not at all."'[69]

Further meetings occurred in December 1902 and January 1903.[70] Lavery was back in London in June 1903, painting W. E. A. Lecky's portrait, among other things, and the now very frail Whistler received his visits. There were disputes at the time between Pennell and Whistler, because, in Whistler's opinion, Pennell had failed to praise Lavery sufficiently in his reviews. Three days before his death, on 17 July 1903, Lavery went to see Whistler for the last time, but little could be said. He, Guthrie, Edwin Austin Abbey, Theodore Duret, Charles Lang Freer and George Vanderbilt were called upon to act as pall-bearers and convey the deceased master to his last resting place on 22 July 1903. It fell to Lavery on 15 December that year to pronounce the sad valediction upon the former first president of the International Society of Sculptors, Painters and Gravers. He declared,

> He was misunderstood and misrepresented, he who fought for the interests of his brother artists and the dignity of art. In his contention with Ruskin he demonstrated that painting and writing are separate independent arts, each with their own means of expression . . . of him as a friend I might speak feelingly, because I knew him intimately for a great many years. His

old world courtesy and kindly consideration were little understood but by those with whom he was in sympathy. In all my dealings with him, both as President and as friend, I found him full of the kindliest thoughtfulness.[71]

In 1905, Lavery, Guthrie, Walton and other members of the council of the International Society staged a large memorial exhibition for Whistler. Despite the fact that Rosalind Birnie Philip, Whistler's executrix, objected, London was added to Paris and Boston as one of the three venues. Miss Birnie Philip felt that because of his infamous handling by London critics, 'his express wish' was that there should be no exhibiting to commemorate his work in the British capital, However, in spite of her opposition, Lavery and his colleagues proceeded with the show and it occasioned a flurry of articles and other publications which added greatly to Whistler's renown.[72]

After Whistler's death, Lavery presided temporarily over the society, until, by general agreement of the council it was decided to invite Rodin to take up the office. Lavery was allotted the task of visiting Rodin's studio at Meudon to convey the invitation in person, and it must have seemed a difficult task in view of the general embarrassment felt at the damage to Rodin's casts several years before. Wisely Lavery took Albert Ludovici with him and the interview went well. During the next few years he continued to act as stage manager for the London shows and for Rodin's visits. The French sculptor, to everyone's satisfaction was lionised in London and he and Lavery swapped works.[73] Lavery also painted a definitive portrait of Rodin (Plate 89), and when he resigned from the office of vice-president after ten years of service, Rodin was understandably distressed.[74]

Reviewing the catalogues of the International Society during Lavery's term of office, it superficially seems as though its exhibitions defined the boundaries of Whistler's parish. Although there is no denying that Lavery reinforced the aesthetic ideas of which Whistler was the chief exponent, it must also be clear that the notion of a leader and followers is simplistic. Whistler, Lavery, Guthrie, Walton and others were all exploring a shared aesthetic. The tradition emanating from the seventeenth century and from Velasquez in particular, was commonly acknowledged. The presence of precedent increased the value of the work—only within strictly defined limitations could aesthetic principles be exposed. The decorative intensity and refinement of manner which Lavery sought, betrayed not only a genuine delight in appearances, it also embodied the serious belief that life itself should imitate the perfection of art. Lavery's work in the years which followed, abounded in subconscious echoes of Whistlerian motifs. The most obvious comparisons of similar subject are provided by the Tangier seascapes. In *The Studio*, Lavery succeeded to an ambition that Whistler left unrealised, that of painting a large studio interior, reworking the problems of *Las Meninas*. Finally, in 1934, as his second wife Hazel lay dying before him, the aged painter produced an image that is comparable to Whistler's last depictions of his beloved dying Beatrix. But it was faced with life, in representing the sitter as an eloquent abstraction, that Lavery achieved evocations comparable to those of Whistler and Velasquez.

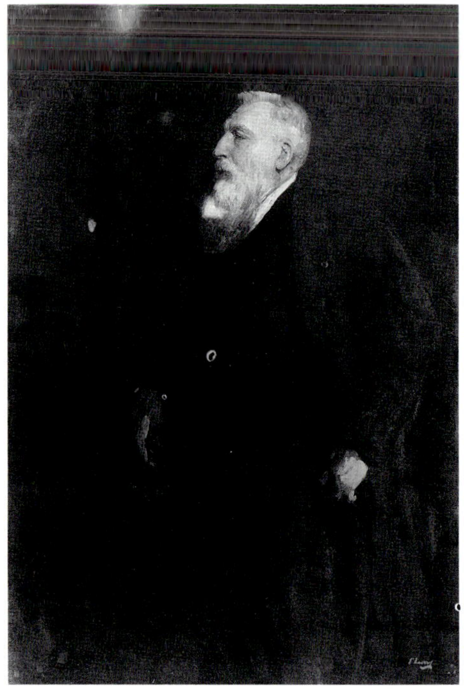

89 *Auguste Rodin*, 1904, $60\frac{1}{4} \times 40\frac{1}{4}$ (Tate Gallery, London)

6 The White City, Tangier and other Travels

> . . . the chief note of Tangier is its whiteness. White houses, sands like snow, and, above all, a dazzling white atmosphere.'[1]

These words were written by R. B. Cunninghame Graham in an article entitled, 'The Atmosphere of Morocco' in a *Studio* magazine yearbook in 1909. It was illustrated with twelve paintings by John Lavery. It was the third such essay to appear. The magazine had, in previous years, obtained the north African impressions of Frank Brangwyn and Norman Garstin. Both these artists were Lavery's contemporaries and he would have been familiar with their work.[2] Brangwyn and Lavery even exhibited pictures of similar Moroccan motifs in the 1890s.[3]

Throughout the nineteenth century north Africa had been a place of artistic pilgrimage. Delacroix and Delaroche had both painted in Morocco in the 1830s. Around the mid-century Gérôme, Lewis, and Holman Hunt preferred the eastern Mediterranean. In the 1880s, British artists rediscovered Tangier. By crossing the Straits of Gibraltar they found an instant Orient. Whereas earlier Orientalist painters concentrated upon narrating the eastern way of life, the rituals of the mosque and the harem, Lavery's contemporaries responded to this environment for its colour, light and for the abstract drama of shape which they found in its slab-like architecture. Describing this to a fellow painter in 1897 Norman Garstin wrote, 'that wall in front of you is homely whitewash, and steeped for a moment in a violet shade; a door opens and a rectangular slab of yellow white light from the opposite wall of the patio makes you blink, and deepens the violet of the near wall; purple patches of shade stain the patio's red tiles with silhouetted pictures of the fig leaves . . .'[4]

Here, in painter's terms, is an account of typical perceptions. The strong light, cloudless sky, white walls and bright colour of Arab dress created almost magic effects which swept aside the careful low-toned modulation of studio portraiture. After two years of intense preoccupation with *The State Visit* . . . (see Plate 62) Lavery needed the rejuvenation which his first experience of 'the White City' gave him. Two of his Glasgow School comrades, Arthur Melville and Joseph Crawhall had already visited north Africa and it is likely that their enthusiasm prompted his first expedition in the first few days of 1891. The circumstances of his swift departure were embroiled with the completion of *The State Visit of Queen Victoria* . . . In negotiating the contract for the picture Lavery had the option to exhibit it for a fixed period before consigning it to Glasgow.

Returning north, on the night express, he met a Glasgow retailer named Walter Wilson who offered him £1000 per month for six months for the right to exhibit the picture at the Colosseum Warehouse in Glasgow. After seeking advice, Lavery accepted this lucrative contract, only to be faced with the combined wrath of those who had originally placed the commission. 'The Baillies were shocked and the Lord Provost called a meeting of the Art Committee to find that according to the terms of the commission, I had the privelege of publicly exhibiting it for one year.'[5]

When he received a 'pre-emptory order' to withdraw the picture from such 'unseemly surroundings', Lavery hastened his departure for Tangier: 'To convey the idea that I had not received the letter I pinned a notice to my studio door stating "Out of town return in a few weeks", packed my bag got the night mail to London and sailed for Gibraltar from Tilbury next afternoon en route for Morocco.'[6]

Steaming south along the coast of Portugal Lavery may have recalled Melville's large watercolours which appeared regularly at the exhibitions of the 1880s. Melville accentuated that sense of abstraction, noted by Garstin, playing up the effects of strongly lit white walls against cloudless azure and ultramarine skies. Joseph Crawhall, Lavery's close friend, and later guardian of his daughter Eileen Lavery, appears to have first travelled to Spain and Morocco in 1884.[7] Crawhall

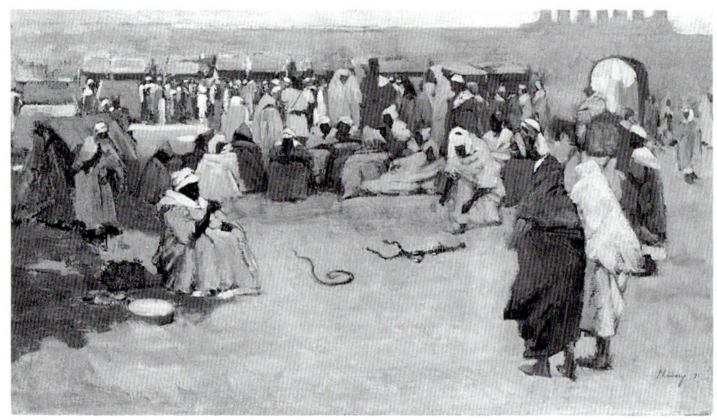

90 *The Snake Charmers*, 1891, 21 × 36½ (private collection)

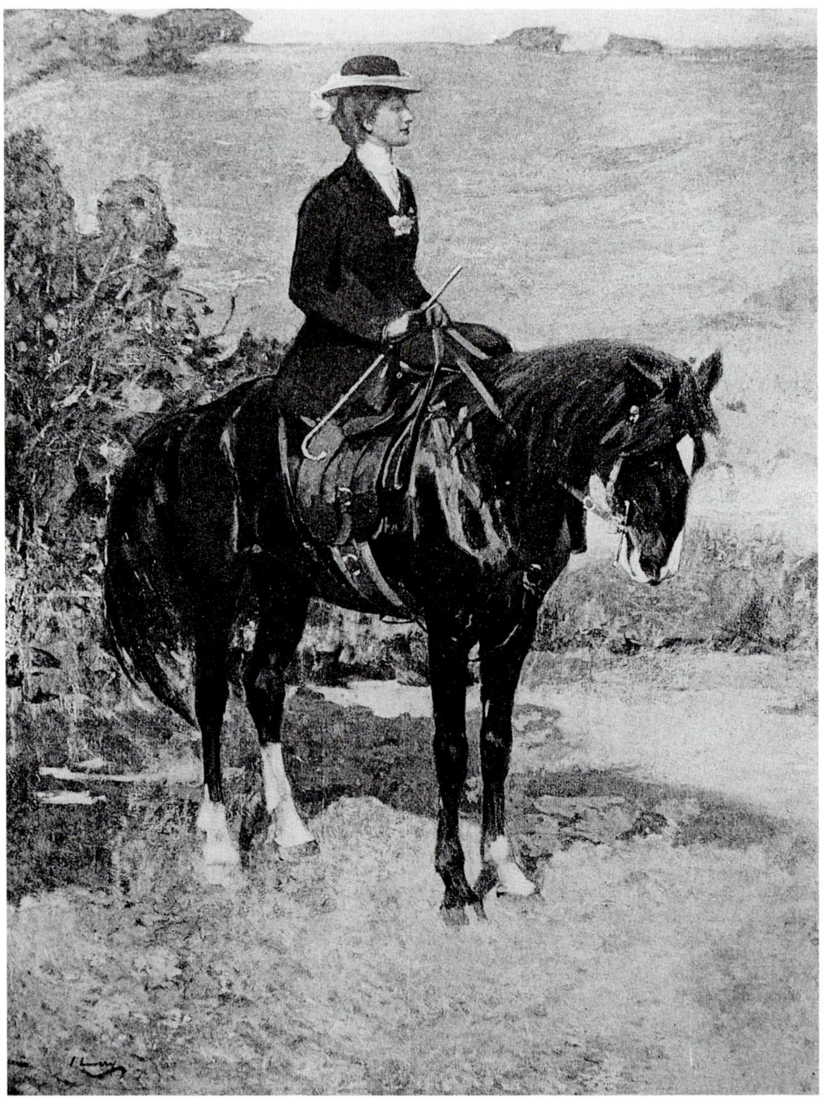

91 *An Equestrian Lady*, 1891, 96 × 72 (Glasgow Art Gallery and Museum)

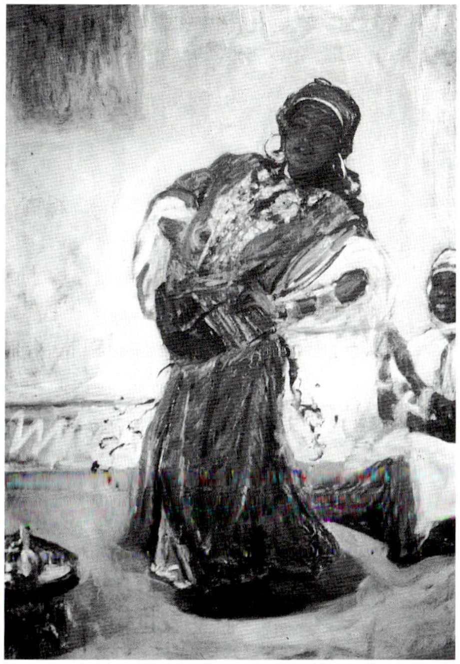

92 *A Moorish Dance*, 1892–1910, 50 × 30 (private collection)

returned to Tangier in 1887 to paint watercolours which played up the decorative aspects of the new photographic naturalism which would have greatly appealed to Lavery. Known in Tangier by the nickname 'Creeps', and for occasional bouts of heavy drinking, Crawhall fitted into the *émigré* community. He consorted with a notorious Spanish gambler, the Duke of Frias, and the weird and eccentric Bibi Carleton. It is easy to understand why Morocco became a source of fascination for Lavery, although his commitments forbade the excursion prior to 1891. Nevertheless he went there with a sense of mission. During his first winter on the north African coast, he produced a great variety of work. Almost half of the paintings shown at the Goupil Gallery in the spring of 1891 were produced in Morocco. There were views of the *casbah*, the *soko*, the mosque and the Jewish quarter. For one picture he ascended to the roof of the Hotel Continental and painted the first of many rooftop views of the city.[8] One of the largest and most impressive of the first sequence of Tangier paintings is *The Snake Charmers* (Plate 90).[9] In this, Lavery has depicted the *soko* or market place in the quiet of the afternoon. At this time, '. . . the place is empty except for the snake charmer and his audience, and the story teller and those who squat in a circle and listen with deep interest to his tales of love and adventure.'[10]

With the minimum of detail, Lavery set out the composition, stating the figures with broad painterly blocks. The desire for experiment led him to abandon the practice of light sable brush sketching. Spatial delineation is minimal, and is conveyed only by the scaling of figures and the elliptical shapes of the three serpents. Melville had treated such a scene in a large watercolour exhibited at the Glasgow Institute in 1889, but his composition was much more conventional and less atmospheric than Lavery's.

The most unusual of Lavery's Moroccan products to be shown in 1891 was *An Equestrian Lady* (Plate 91). As an upwardly mobile young artist, Lavery had been taking riding lessons in Glasgow in the previous year. Tangier provided the ideal community in which to exercise his new skill. In later years he was to become 'President' of the Tangier Hunt and with his daughter he would ride regularly along the beach. With *An Equestrian Lady*, he became a painter of horses and this was the first of his large equestrian portraits. It was criticised for the fact that '. . . we have a great deal of horse and very little of the lady . . .'[11] Despite the objection, the picture became one of Lavery's personal favourites, being reworked, retitled and extensively exhibited.[12] It has survived as *Idonia in Morocco*, named after its second model, Idonia la Primaudaye, a keen amateur painter who, along with her sister, Blanche, modelled for Lavery around 1901. A. C. R. Carter in 1904 reflected upon the originality of what had been transformed into a *tour de force*. Unlike the equestrian portraits of Velasquez in which horse and rider are seen against the sky, Lavery's receding hillside was conveyed with such 'subtle gradation' and such 'careful choice of pitch' that 'the complete suggestion of a living group set in real space and atmosphere is conveyed'.[13] Thus it seemed, in contrast to the seventeenth-century master, Lavery had engineered a naturalistic encounter rather than a formulaic regal portrait. Between its many exhibitions, the picture hung above the mantelpiece in the artist's studio in Cromwell Place.[14]

Following his first visit, Lavery was bitten by an enthusiasm for Tangier. At the beginning of the following year, he was back in the city, but on this occasion he concentrated upon studies for the major work which he intended to submit to the Royal Academy in 1893. To observe *A Moorish Dance* (Plate 92), Lavery placed himself in the *casbah* and carefully recorded the players of viols, tambourines and drums (see Plate 93). A number of studies (see Plate 94) for this picture were later inscribed with its title,[15] but others, more loosely related, are not. In *El Casbah* (Plate 95), for instance, Nubian and Arab musicians accompany an advancing female dancer. This arrangement of figures provided the essential disposition for the Academy painting, although the format was to be that of the full-length portrait. In concentrating the spectator's attention upon the foreground performer, Lavery obviously related his work to other important renditions of the same subject, from Delacroix's *Jewish Wedding*, 1837 to Gustave Moreau's notorious *Salomé*, 1876. Each of these earlier pictures lacked the immediacy of Lavery's swaying Arab girl, whose smiling facial expression might well have challenged public taste. She has none of the aloof objectivity of Sargent's full-length Javanese dancers painted at the Exposition Universelle three years earlier. In artistic terms, the work was not wholly satisfactory and the artist later removed the upper portion of the canvas. Around 1910, Lavery painted out some of the background musicians and entirely reworked the dancer from his Moorish maid, Aida, making her facial expression more passive. As it exists today, in mutilated form, this picture retains some of its original *éclat* in the slashing greens and reds of the Arab dress.[16]

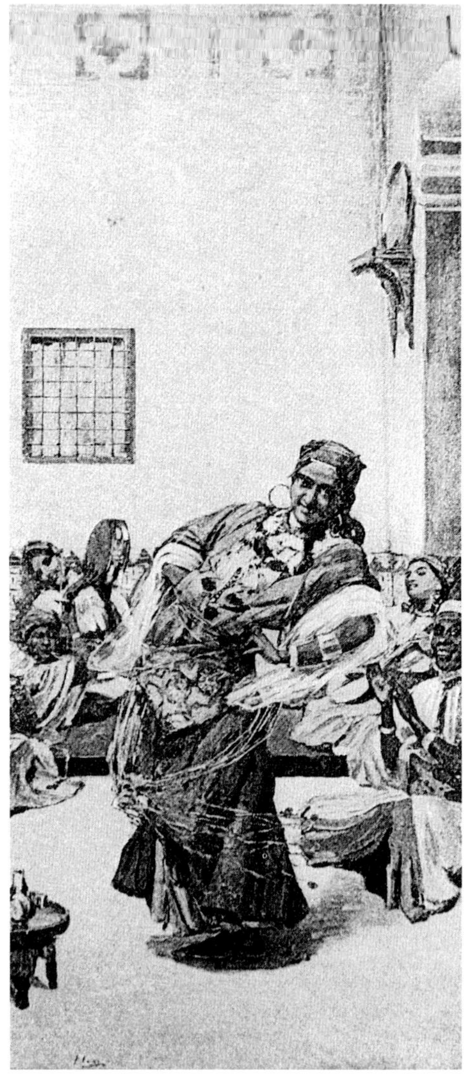

93 *A Moorish Dance*, 1892, 72 × 30, photo of original state (photo, the author)

These pictures must have been worked upon in the early months of 1892, because Lavery returned to Scotland via Seville in April of that year with Alexander Mann.[17] In a letter to his wife, who was remaining in Tangier, Mann relates that Lavery had made a little sketch of the bullring and though he caught a bad cold, he had also been sketching at the tobacco factory.[18] By 9 May both artists were in Madrid, and Lavery had again gone to make a sketch of a bullfight.[19] One of these is likely to be *Suerte de Capa* (Plate 96), a small picture which extends the technical experimentation of the Tangier paintings.[20] The translucent blacks formerly used for brief indication of the main features of the scene are here employed as smudgy shade, while the sunlit areas of the figures and the ring are noted in a bold mosaic of bright colour, reminiscent of Manet's treatments of similar scenes. Lavery was immune to the real horror of what he saw; only the passing spectacle attracted his eye. As he told Shaw Sparrow, 'I went to bullfights, and I painted them, or rather I painted something of them; for a curious thing happens when an artist sits down before his subject; material things vanish, only colour and its plots remain, and they look visionary. I have never seen a bullfight, though I have been present at twelve in Madrid and Seville. I don't think I *could watch* a bullfight, as I am very fond of horses; it is the moving colour that attracts me at this cruel sport.'[21]

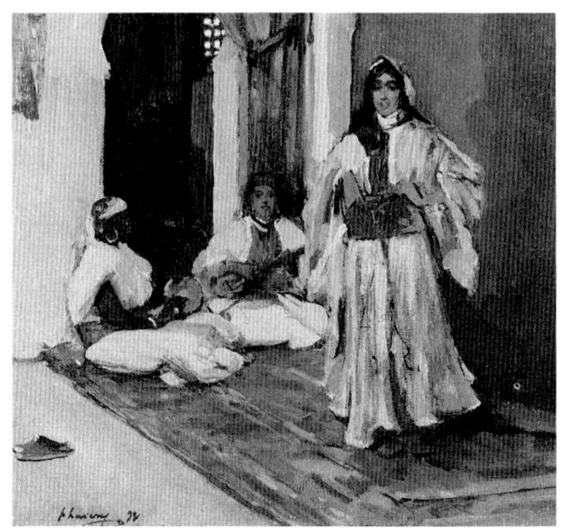

95 *El Casbah*, 1892, 10 × 11¼ (Allied Irish Banks PLC)

Not for the first time was Lavery to confess his indifference to what was actually going on under his eye as he painted it. So enthused was he by his Spanish trip, that he talked to Alexander Mann of returning the following year, however other travels intervened. Lavery lived in an age of tourism. He was an inveterate sight-seer and throughout his long career, he travelled widely. Whilst his various trips

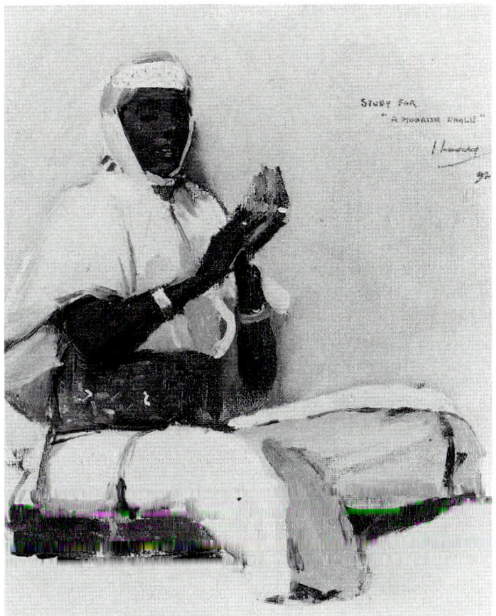

94 Study for *A Moorish Dance*, 1892, 9¾ × 8 (present whereabouts unknown, photo, Christie's)

to Tangier cannot be securely dated, many other expeditions remain unexplained. Often the only evidence for his having travelled to a particualr location exists in on-the-spot sketches. There are occasions when apparently documented trips are not confirmed by the existence of painted records. The itinerary of his travels in Germany, Holland, France and Italy, in 1892, in company with Alexander Roche and James Guthrie cannot be established, although references abound.[22] Two small oil sketches from the Riva dei Schiavoni suggest that Venice was seen for the first time. Visits to Spain and north Africa later in the 1890s may be assumed, but not precisely fixed.

In the early months of 1893, the time he would normally, in later years, be found in north Africa, he was busy painting portraits back in Glasgow. Nevertheless Lavery retained close contact with the artist community in Tangier, which was mostly comprised of Glasgow contemporaries who often travelled together.[23] Perhaps the most extraordinary character in the Scottish group was R. B. Cunninghame Graham, who, like Lavery, had an almost lifelong relationship with 'the White City'. For him, it was inextricably connected with Lavery's art and he came almost to see Tangier through paintings of it which he must have witnessed in production.[24] He provided the artist with instant theatre and his flamboyance frequently got him into scrapes with the Arabs. Lavery records that one afternoon in the *soko*, realising that the story teller held his audience spell-bound, Graham intervened to relive one of his House of Commons speeches in pidgeon-Arabic. As his audience began to examine their weapons, he was asked politely to withdraw.[25]

Holidays in north Africa compensated for business travel in the late 1890s. In 1898, for instance he made his first trip to the United States to act as a juror for the International Exhibition at the Carnegie Institute. The reasons behind his portrait sessions in Rome in the winter of 1896 and Berlin from the summer of 1898 remain initially obscure, although the German forays combined portrait commissions with the maintenance of his reputation in Munich, and his invitation to exhibit with the Berlin Secession. In the event, Lavery had three exhibitions at Schulte's Gallery, Berlin in 1899, 1902 and 1904 respectively.[26] These were followed by small shows in Munich and Dresden in 1905.[27] It is impossible to document his movements around these exhibitions, although the large number of portraits of German sitters which survive in illustration, suggest that Lavery must have spent extended periods of time there before the Great War.

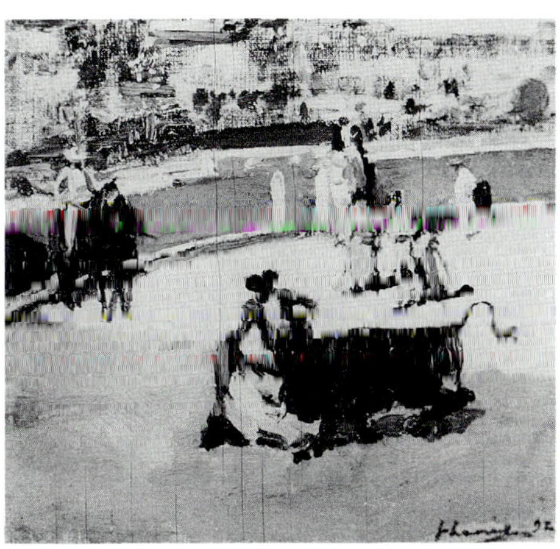

96 *Suerte de Capa*, 1892, 8 × 8½ (The Fine Art Society)

Around the turn of the century the painter was also recalled to rural France. He appears to have visited Grez and Marlotte in 1897 and 1900. Three notable pictures resulted from these trips and it is not possible to confidently ascribe the most important of these—a reworking of *The Bridge at Grez* (see Plate 28) to either expedition. On the first visit to the area in 1897, he spent some time with his and Guthrie's old friend, Arthur Heseltine (see Plate 97), now a resident of Marlotte. There, under the trees, by the river, he painted *A Garden in France* (Plate 98), one of his most impressionistic pictures to date.[28] Madame Heseltine and two other women acted as models for this mid-summer conversation piece. In a sketch (Plate 99) inscribed to her in 1900, the women are arranged differently from those in the final version. Lavery felt when he came to the larger canvas that the empty

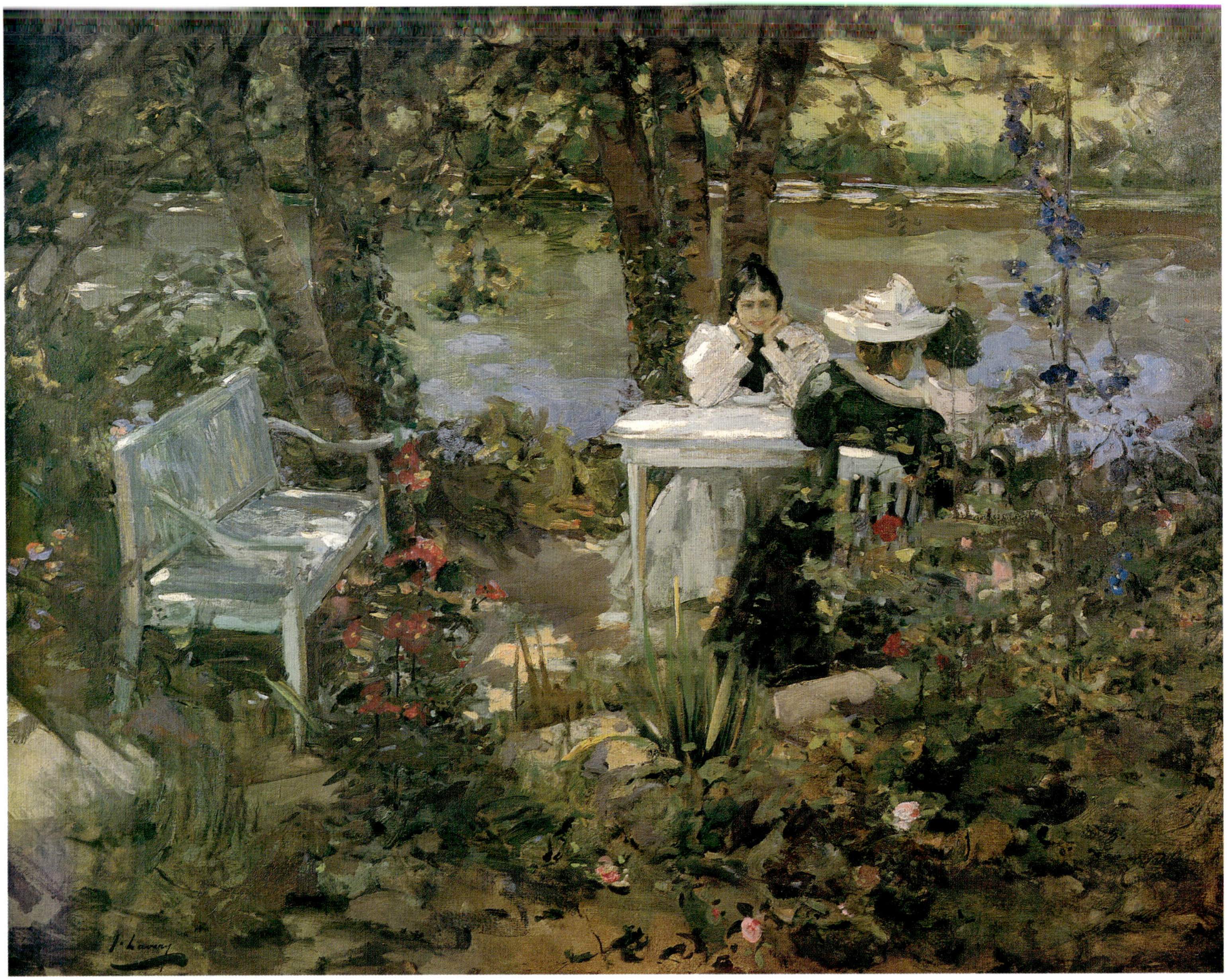

98 *A Garden in France*, 1898, $39\frac{3}{4} \times 50$ (private collection, photo, courtesy Pyms Gallery London)

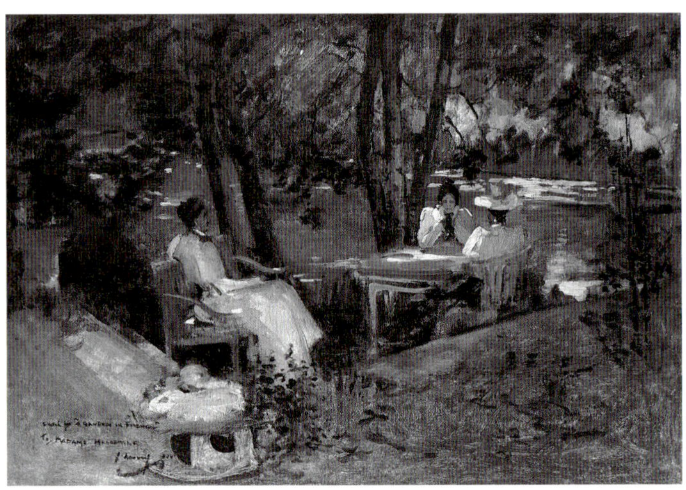

99 Sketch for *A Garden in France*, *c.*1898, $18\frac{3}{4} \times 26$ (private collection, photo, The Fine Art Society)

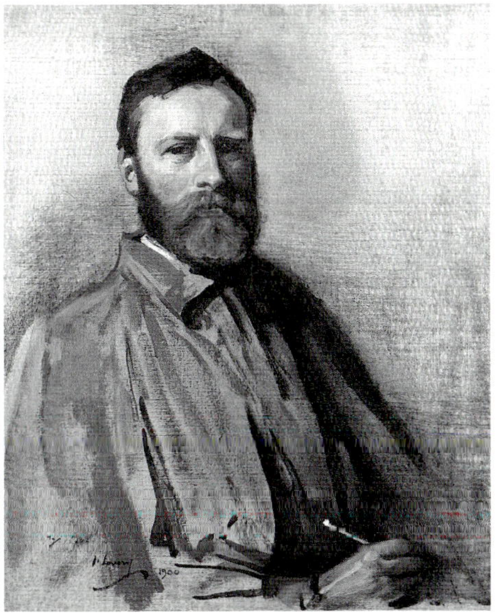

97 *Arthur Heseltine*, 1900, 18 × 14¼ (Castle Museum, Norwich)

bench on the left was worthy of study in itself. Thus, two women seated at the table are presented in back view, one almost obscured by tall hollyhocks. A third woman, possibly Madame Heseltine, her elbows resting on the table, retains her original pose from the sketch. With its dappled sunlight and dense foliage, the picture presents an idyllic view of French rural life which Lavery had savoured fourteen years earlier as a student. A just comparison for *A Garden in France*, might be Guthrie's *Midsummer*, 1892, glowingly described by George Moore as 'a bower of limpid green, here and there interwoven with red flowers'.[29] Although Guthrie later regarded this canvas as 'uncharacteristic', it, along with Lavery's *Croquet* (see Plate 63) and Clausen's *Evening Song*, 1892 achieved one of the high points of British Impressionist painting.[30] All these pictures were, to some extent, compared with Monet in the adoption of a warm green palette and complementary colour contrasts of strong yellow highlights with blue-purple shadows. *A Garden in France* is not quite so aggressive in its appropriation of Impressionist principle as these earlier works; the treatment of *sous-bois* dappled foliage is however reminiscent of Renoir.

Upon his return to Marlotte, in 1900, Lavery painted a souvenir portrait of Arthur Heseltine and an untraced picture entitled *A Lady Artist*.[31] However, perhaps the most important work executed on this visit was *The Bridge at Grez* (Plate 100).[32] The artist felt compelled to return to the exact location from which he had painted one of his most celebrated early pictures which had been recently

100 *The Bridge at Grez*, *c.*1900, 35¼ × 58½ (The Ulster Museum, Belfast)

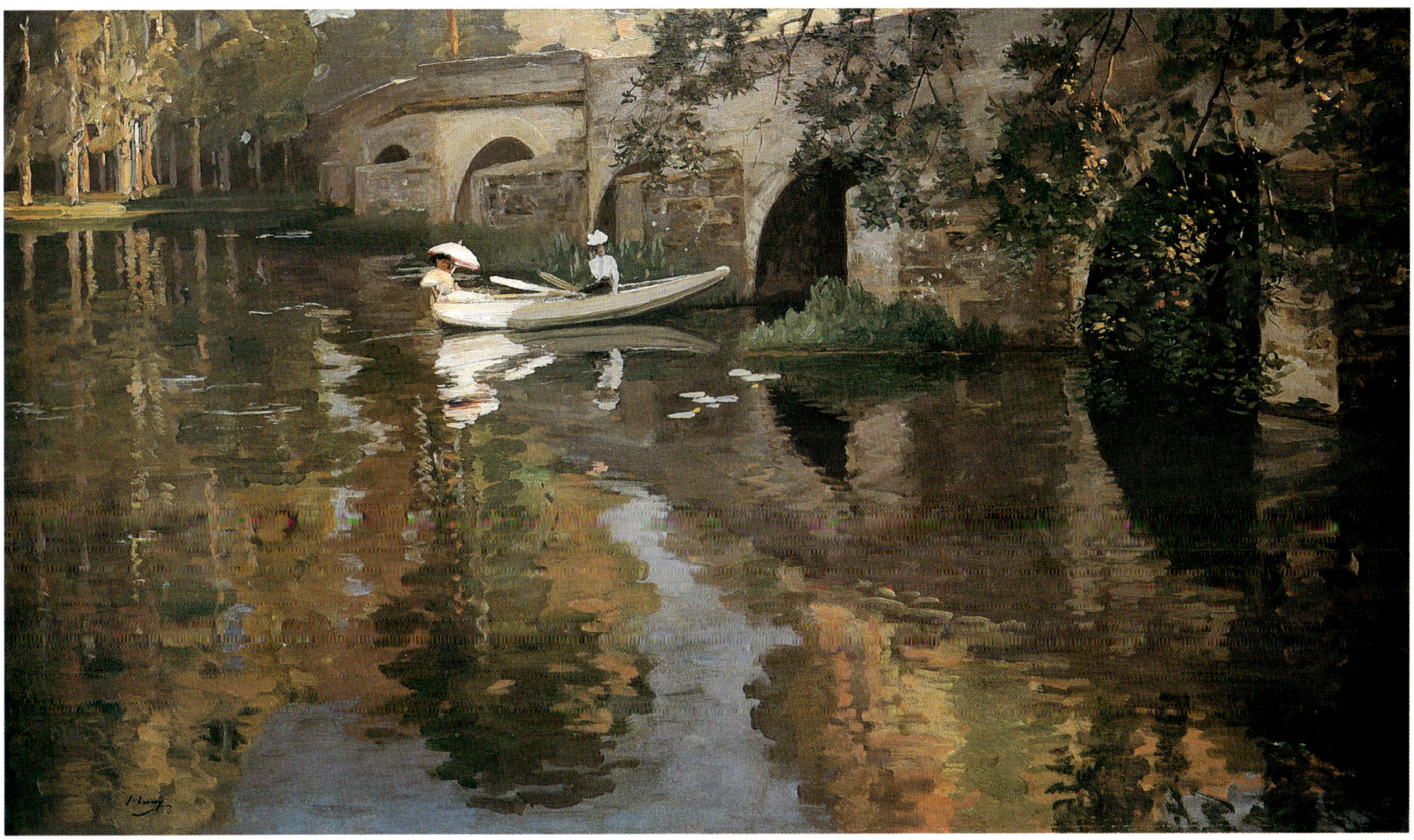

acquired by the Carnegie Institute, Pittsburgh. The second version differs in character from the first, avoiding its anecdotal interest. It gives the impression of having been painted from start to finish in a single session—'slick off' as A. C. R. Carter described it.[33] Percy Bate, comparing the picture with *Croquet* (see Plate 63) agreed that it was a *tour de force*.[34] This latter picture, recently re-exhibited, seemed much less startling than it had done ten years earlier, while *The Bridge at Grez* was '. . . indeed very remarkable, the skilful and free rendering of the limpid water and the masterly treatment of the transparent shadows, being as worthy of praise as the dexterous use of the chance gleam of sun-light on the overhanging trees and the beautiful placing on the canvas of the brilliant white of the parasol carried by the lady in the boat.'[35]

All the telling details observed by Bate help to evoke the atmosphere of the late summer afternoon. Like Monet's iridescent lily ponds, the river reflects the sky overhead as well as the dazzling detail of the sunlit boat.[36] The painting provides a visual counterpart for the verbal description of the River Loing at Grez by Birge Harrison, 'Such a river! A river to dream of: to read of in fairytales: a poem in reeds and water-lilies. Swathed deep in rushes, it idles down from mill to mill, now reflecting the open sky, and now lost in dusky lanes of foliage; with now a stretch of brightness struck by the wind, and now a glimpse of sunny meadow seen through the arches of the old bridge'.[37] Only Sargent, in pictures that were closer to Monet in inspiration, produced comparable images that convey the late Victorian summer paradise.

Lavery's supreme evocation of the luxury and tranquillity of the slow-moving stream was something that he later rejoined in works such as *Sutton Courtenay* (see Plate 154) and *The Thames at Maidenhead* (see Plate 153). The desire to relive the experience of youth, prompted possibly by the loss of the early version of *The Bridge at Grez* (see Plate 28) to Pittsburgh, seems to have motivated his French travels around 1900. Lavery clearly wished to gauge the distance between those early days and the now successful portrait painter. In 1903, for instance, he went to Concarneau and visited Alexander Harrison, Birge Harrison's brother. This was, in effect, a return to the era of Bastien-Lepage, and Harrison, Bastien's principal follower, was still adhering to the *plein-air* methods of the 1880s. No pictures from the expedition appear to have survived, save for a small canvas entitled *A Wet Day, Concarneau* (Plate 101).[38] It is therefore impossible to determine what he derived from this return to sources. However, the encounter was sufficient for Harrison to form his opinions of Lavery and these were communicated to Shaw Sparrow some years later. To him, the painter was like someone who 'talks with genuine enthusiasm about his real feelings, but who never thinks it necessary to raise his voice into a scream'. Lavery had 'style, not mere technical accomplishment'.[39] It must have been evident to the artist himself, as a result of this reunion that what had begun as the rustic naturalism of the 1880s had now matured into a manner which for all its personal characteristics bore significant relation to the mainstream Impressionism of the era.

Lavery returned to Brittany in the following year at the invitation of his old friend Joseph Milner Kite and stayed nearby at Beg-Meil. Mary Auras and an obscure Irish 'hanger-on' named Sheil were his travelling companions. He had the

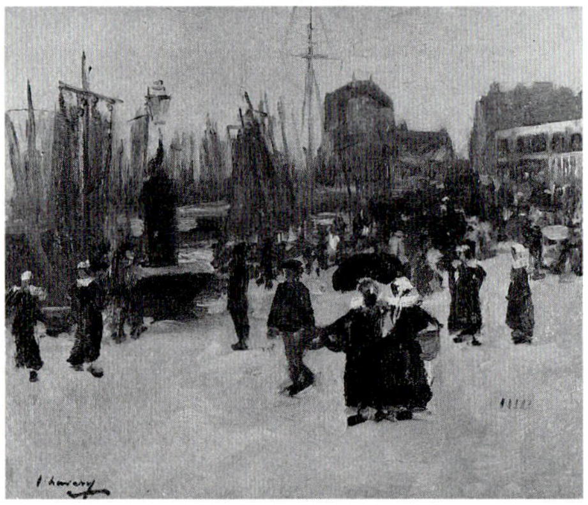

101 *A Wet Day, Concarneau*, 1904, 11 × 13 (present whereabouts unknown, photo, courtesy Christie's)

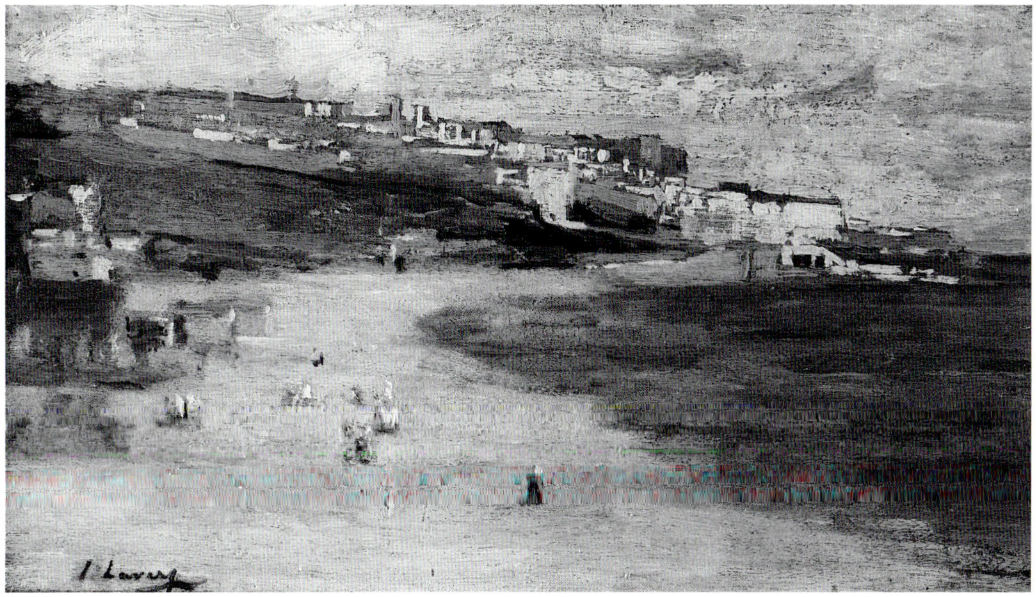

103 Study for *Tangier – The White City*, 1893, 5 × 8½ (photo, The Fine Art Society)

idea that he would paint a sequel to his earlier successful floral picture of Mary, *Printemps* (Plate 130).[40] *Summer*, a full-length of this favourite model under a large parasol, emerging from the sea, was later presented to the sculptor, Auguste Rodin. When he arrived, however, Lavery discovered that Milner Kite was engaged upon the portrait of the elder of two American sisters who were also staying there. Watched over by their mother, these were the daughters of Edward Jenner Martyn, a Chicago industrialist of Irish extraction. When Milner Kite got into difficulties with his portrait he called for his more experienced colleague's help. The result was that Lavery quickly came to be regarded as the master of the little group. Notwithstanding the good looks of Dorothy Jenner Martyn, Lavery was attracted to her younger sister, Hazel, who, as he later recalled, had the reputation of being the most brilliant and beautiful girl in the middle west.[41] Hazel was born in 1887 and had already exhibited drawings and etchings with some success. She had come to Brittany in order to experience life in an artists' colony at first hand—albeit under the strict supervision of her mother. Although he bashfully recalled that he could not understand what Hazel saw in him, their mutual attentions did not go unobserved. Mrs Jenner Martyn swiftly wrote to Edward Livingston Trudeau, the Canadian doctor to whom her daughter was engaged to be married, and asked him to come to the rescue. Although Trudeau married Hazel Jenner Martyn shortly after these events, she was just as swiftly widowed and left to bear Trudeau's daughter.[42] How the contact between Hazel and Lavery was renewed remains obscure—as does the detail of their courtship during the next few years. In 1905, for instance, he appears to have visited Laç Champex in Switzerland. A small canvas of two girls by a blossoming hedgerow records the visit.[43] On one occasion in 1907, Alexander Mann recorded bumping into Lavery on the channel packet to Boulogne and noting that he was meeting an unidentified lady friend and going to Paris with her.[44] Finally in July 1909, with her sister Dorothy as bridesmaid and Cunninghame Graham as best man, the couple were married at Brompton Oratory.

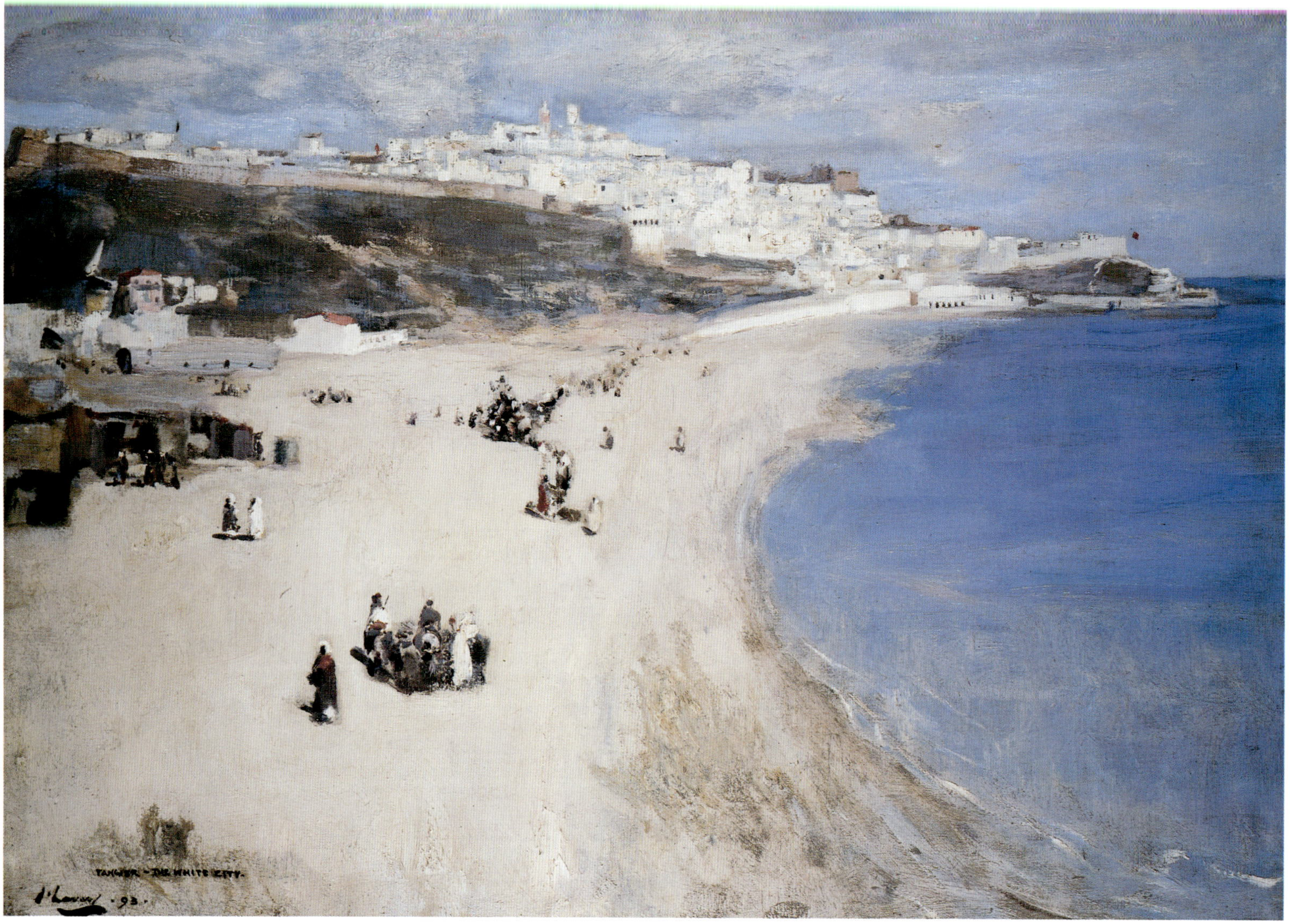

102 *Tangier – The White City*, 1893, $22\frac{3}{4} \times 31\frac{1}{4}$ (Ewan Mundy Fine Art, Glasgow)

Cunninghame Graham and Lavery had become close friends. He contributed the preface to the artist's one-man exhibition at the Leicester Galleries in November 1904. Despite the fact that only thirteen of the forty-nine pictures on show were obvious Tangier subjects, Graham took it upon himself to eulogise the white city. It is difficult to determine precisely which recent Tangier paintings were shown, but for the most part they seem to have been small landscapes. *Tangier—The White City* (Plate 102), for instance, painted eleven years earlier in 1893, takes a high viewpoint looking down upon the beach with the city itself in the distance (see also Plate 103). The emphasis upon the topography of the north African landscape is evident from the other works on display. They seem to illustrate expeditions and provide snapshot views rather than engaging with Arab life.[45] Many of them appear tentative and are atmospheric, almost Turner-like in their effects.

By the turn of the century Lavery was so familiar with the Arab way of life that he decided to establish a semi-permanent base at a little property on the hill outside Tangier. Known as Dar El Midfah, or 'the House of the Cannon'—because

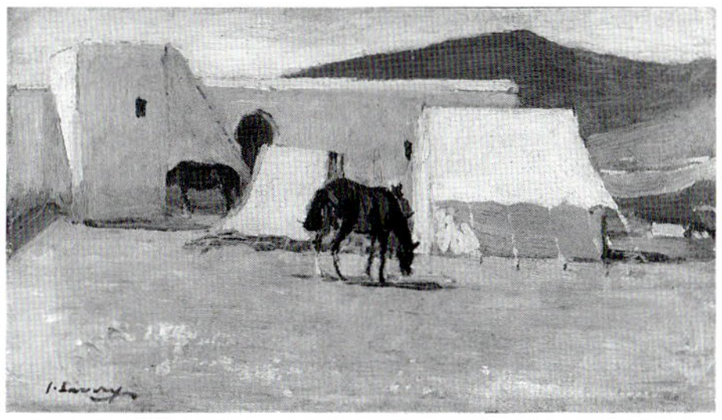

104 *Souvenir of Morocco*, *c*.1907, 5⅜ × 8⅝ (Glasgow Art Gallery and Museum)

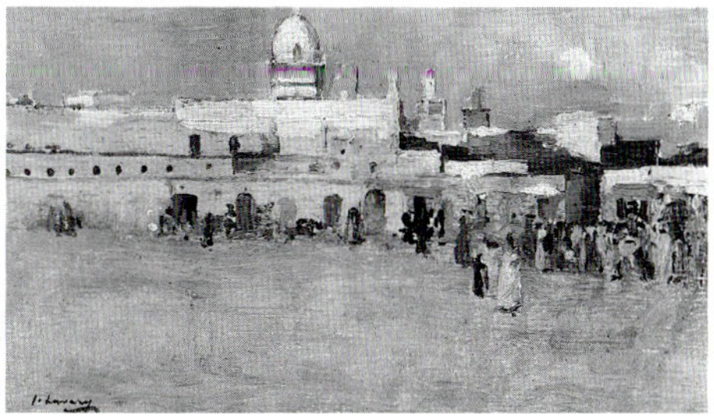

105 *The Market Place, Tetuan*, 1907, 5 × 8½ (private collection, photo, The Fine Art Society)

106 *The City of Fez*, 1907, 4¾ × 13⅞ (private collection, photo, courtesy Pyms Gallery, London)

apparently there was a half buried cannon in the garden—the house became a refuge in which future campaigns were planned.[46] From here, for instance, he made his eventful overland journey to Fez.[47] The journey to this famous city approximately 100 miles south-east of Tangier was made on horseback, in company with Walter Harris, *The Times* Morocco correspondent and Cunninghame Graham. The three men travelled down the coast to Tetuan and then struck inland to Fez via Arzila and Alcazar el Kebir. The journey can be reconstructed from Lavery's sketches (see Plate 104). Their camp outside the walls of Tetuan was commemorated in a swift sketch and the market place (Plate 105) in two further sketches. Arzila was represented by a street scene notable for its 'delightful Moorish gateway and tower'.[48] Alcazar was depicted in one view of the town and in one of the market place, described by Selwyn Brinton as a 'brilliant bit of colour'.[49] Other small panels were painted on this expedition but they are difficult to associate with specific locations.[50] Finally, Lavery painted a small panoramic landscape of the city of Fez (Plate 106) with the green and purple mountains in the distance, showing it to be a lush oasis lined with trees.

Despite the serenity of these tiny notes of colour, the journey was not without incident. On the second day, Lavery was trailing behind the other two and when he reached the brow of the hill to join them, he observed Harris and Graham surrounded by almost one hundred well-armed Moors. In the centre, '. . . their leader sat upon his horse, tall sinewy and brown, with a grey beard descending to his chest and mingling with his clothes'.[51] Harris, who was in deep negotiation with this chieftain, discovered that on the previous night they had been raided by a hostile tribe and were in hot pursuit. To extricate himself and his colleagues from a potentially murderous situation, Harris at first demanded payment of tribute money from the natives, but then in view of their misfortune, abruptly decided, to Lavery's great relief, not to insist upon this and to actually help them on their way by writing them a note of safe passage through the lands of the local brigand El Raisuli. All of this was probably meaningless, but it seemed to satisfy the tribesmen, and, heaving a sigh of relief the three explorers went on their way unharmed.

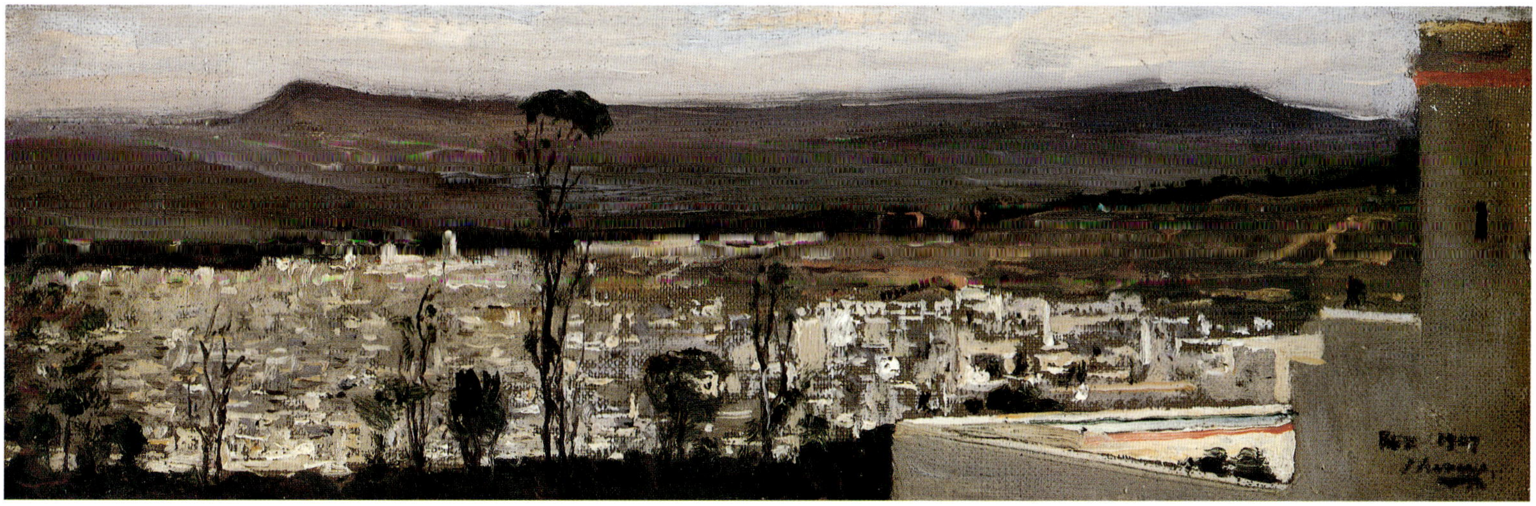

The remainder of their journey seems to have been positively idyllic. On one occasion they pitched their tents, as Cunninghame Graham described, '. . . close to an orange garden, from which came puffs of scented air, making one think, after a hard day's ride, that he had entered a terrestrial paradise. Frogs croaked, a water-wheel kept up a drowsy singing as it turned, the recent rains had clad the country all in flowers, myriads of marigolds—pink, white and yellow—. . . No needlework the hand of woman ever wrought, no blue beflounced crewel from either China or Japan, could equal them.'[52]

Lavery confirms the sense of magic he felt as the country unfolded before the travellers, and when they finally reached Fez, they arrived in a kind of paradise where they were entertained liberally by rich Moors. At Fez, Lavery was introduced by Walter Harris to Kaid MacLean, a fellow Scotsman who 'charmed the Sultan by the skirl of his bagpipes'. His daughter Nora made it possible for Lavery to obtain a view of the harem, and yet remain undetected. The artist recalled, I spent a week in a very uncomfortable and cramped position . . . most of the time the place was empty, and at no time did I see the women do anything other than lie about talking, singing, playing the gimbri and behaving in the orthodox manner in which I had been told they spent their lives. They were not more than fifty feet from where I was hidden, a deep pool dividing us . . .'[53] (Plate 107).

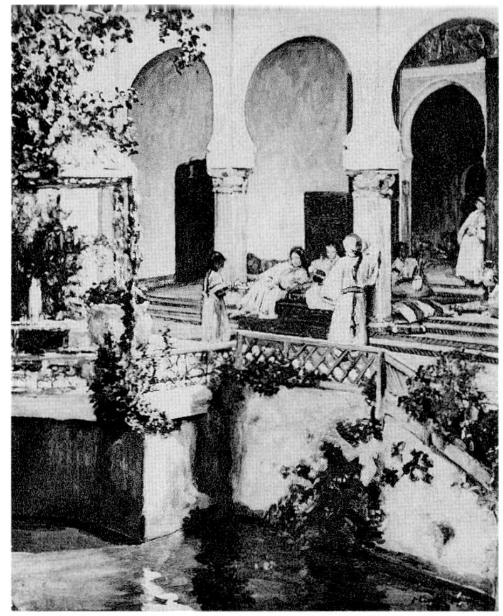

107 *A Moorish Harem*, 1907, size unknown (private collection)

Brinton noted the fact that the picture was of interest as a genuine harem scene—most others, of necessity, being studio products.[54] Lavery's picture, therefore, faithfully describes the lotus land of sunlit porticoes, trickling fountains and negro slaves, remote from western experience. Before exhibiting the painting at the Goupil Gallery in 1908, and despite the fact that a large frame had been made for it in Morocco, Lavery felt that he could only improve the composition by removing the upper and right-hand portions of the canvas. The central focus of attention—the group of women—remained intact.

Morocco dominated the 1908 exhibition. Over half the canvases on display had been painted there and to *The Studio* critic this opportunity to study another side of the portrait painter's talent should not be missed.[55] The most ambitious of Lavery's north African paintings was a large aerial view of *The Market Place, Tangier*. This showed a busy open space with crowds flooding through its gate, traders squatting in groups, a flock of sheep, horsemen and lame mules bringing goods for sale or barter. Beyond this enclave the city majestically topped the nearby hill and beyond that, stretched the blue seas of the Straits. Lavery's other ambitious Moroccan compositions included in the exhibition were *Under the Pergola* and *Evening, Tangier* (Plate 108).[56] The first of these remains unlocated, but it was regarded as 'Mr Lavery's dutiful answer to Turner's *Interior at Petworth*'.[57] The second, though it was viewed by one critic as 'hardly characteristic', is one of the artist's most typical Tangier paintings. The figure, in this instance, acts as a foil to the hilly landscape overlooking the Straits which provides a panoramic backdrop.

For many smaller paintings from the 1908 exhibition, Lavery positioned himself upon rooftops overlooking the city. Invariably the foreground was occupied by one or two Arab musicians sitting on or behind a parapet wall. As he discovered, the rooftops of Tangier generated their own form of life (see *The*

Housetops, Evening, Plate 109). Beyond them, the slab-like tower of the Green Mosque became a familiar landmark. Lavery's repeated engagement with this subject at different times of the day amounted almost to obsession.[58] His other enduring fascination was with the beach at Tangier. No less than six pictures in the 1908 exhibition depicted the stretch of sand at various times of the day and night. Some of these obviously recalled Whistler, but one, *The Seashore, Moonlight* in the opinion of Carter, '. . . does more than vindicate the strivings of Whistler. It is the first nocturn [sic] painted since Turner's'.[59] This painting was followed by numerous reworkings of Tangier Bay at night. *Moonlight, Tangier*, reproduced in colour by Shaw Sparrow is one example,[60] in which the blue blackness of the sea has been intensified and it appears to encroach remorselessly upon the land. To eyes schooled by the symbolist poetry of the period this 'mist wrapped land' was synonymous with mystery and imagination. Tangier was, after all, an ancient gateway to a lost civilisation.[61] To Shaw Sparrow, therefore, Lavery caught something of the magic of the North African night. Describing *Night: Tangier*, one of Lavery's Royal Academy exhibits of 1911, he talks of '. . . white Tangier at rest in a deep mystery of greyed blue and violet and lilac, the sea beyond, vague, darkling, potent; and near at hand across a terrace, the half glow from an artificial light gives a dull illumination, and some natives crouch under a low wall that looks spectral, like the town's population of roofs . . . This nocturne is not the moonlight of Turner nor the moonlight of Whister . . . it belongs partly to Tangier and partly to Lavery'.[62]

In each of these nocturnes, small foreground figures act as a foil to the immensity of space. Looking down at the beach, from high ground above, Lavery would often see white clad Arabs or darkly dressed Nubian figures walking along at the water's edge. In daylight versions of this theme, such as *A West Wind* (Plate 110), 1911, the figures are carefully placed against a backdrop of vivid cerulean and azure. The bright sandy foreground and humid sky convey the unmistakable atmosphere of the southern Mediterranean coast. Clearly Lavery was influenced by Whistler, one of whose beach scenes, *Blue and Silver, Trouville*, 1865, had been shown at the International Society in 1899, but in these later works the colour intensity which this coastline demanded in its freshness of hue, conveyed heat and humidity which Whistler never experienced.[63]

Lavery was now visiting Tangier regularly, taking with him his model, Mary Auras and his daughter, Eileen. He became an accepted figure amongst the British community, and in some ways, the extent of his acceptance by the Arabs was in his ability to obtain Moorish girls to act as models. In the early days at Tangier, the natives retreated shyly from him, believing that all painters possessed an 'evil eye'. By 1909, he had sufficiently overcome their inhibitions to enlist the services of several Moorish girls who posed as *Zachara and Hadeshia*, *Aida Ilbralme* and *Fatima Farghe* (Plate 111).[64] Perhaps the most alluring of these half-length portraits was *Zachra*, 1914.[65] Colourfully clad Nubian girls such as this became the painter's antidote to society ladies who habitually appeared in the studio dressed in black and grey. They demanded no posing or props and were unselfconscious. Such images would, inevitably appeal to Lavery's bourgeois clientèle.[66]

His reporting instinct, on occasion, led the artist to record newsworthy events

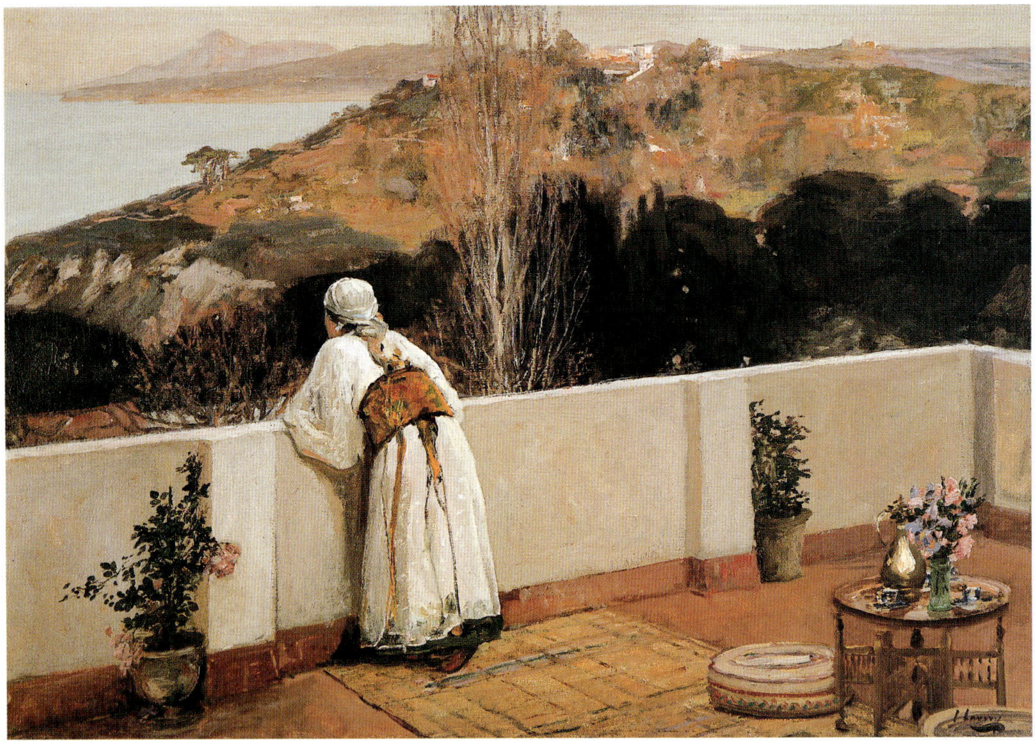

108 *Evening, Tangier*, 1907, 41½ × 29½ (Birmingham Art Gallery)

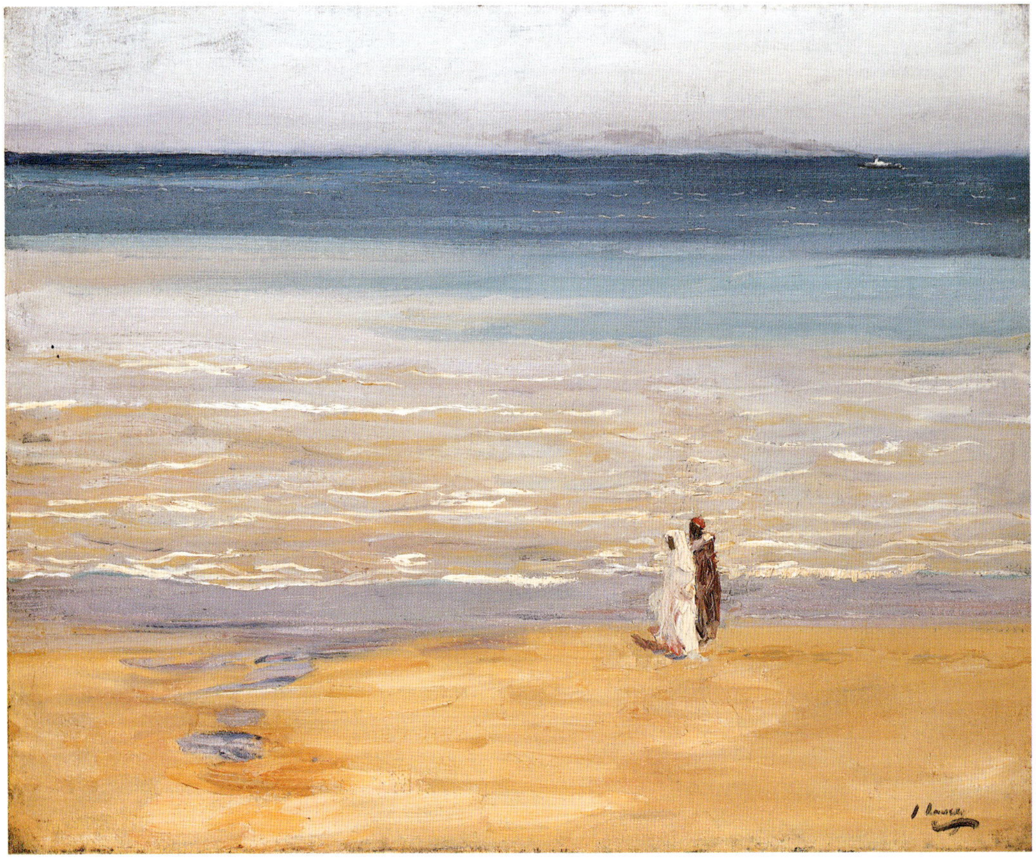

110 *A West Wind*, 1911, 25 × 30 (private collection, photo, Pyms Gallery, London)

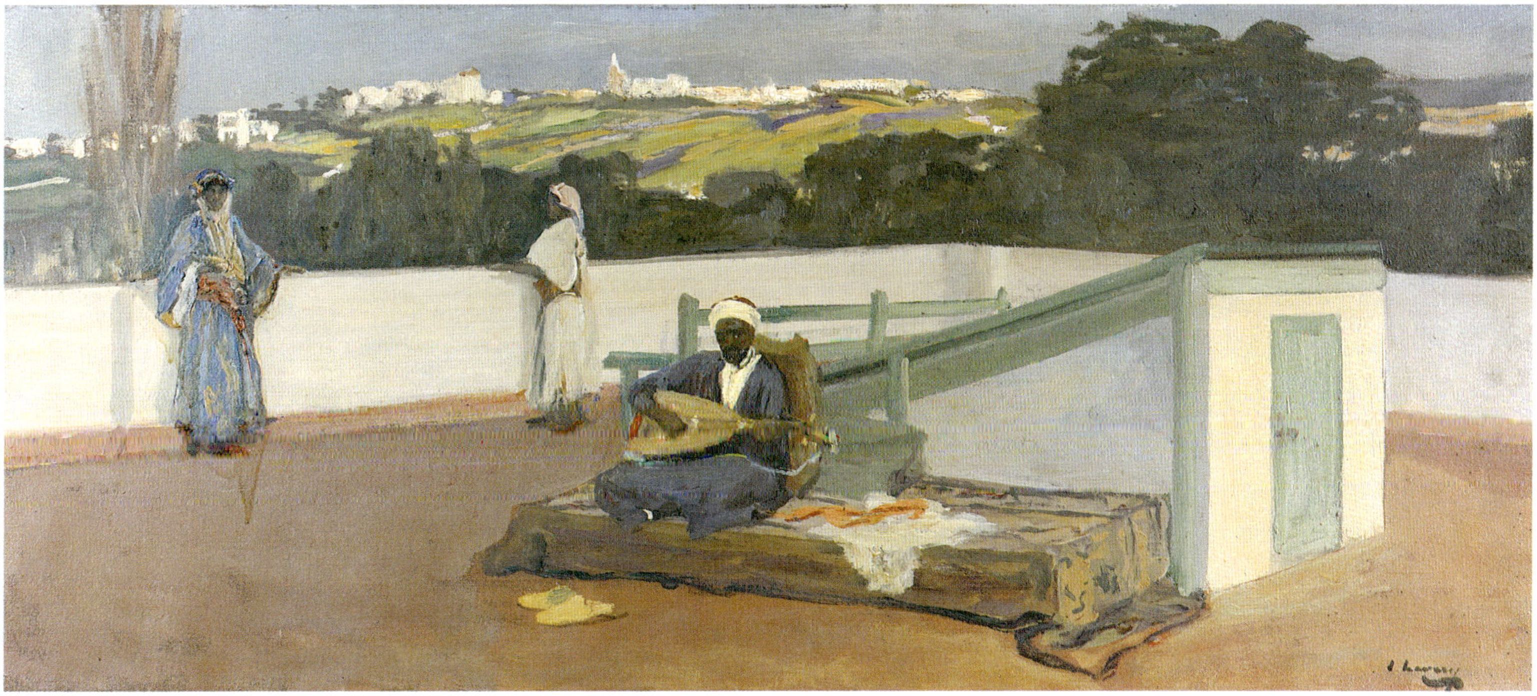

109 *The Housetops, Evening*, *c.*1907, 22 × 47 (private collection, photo, courtesy Phillips, London)

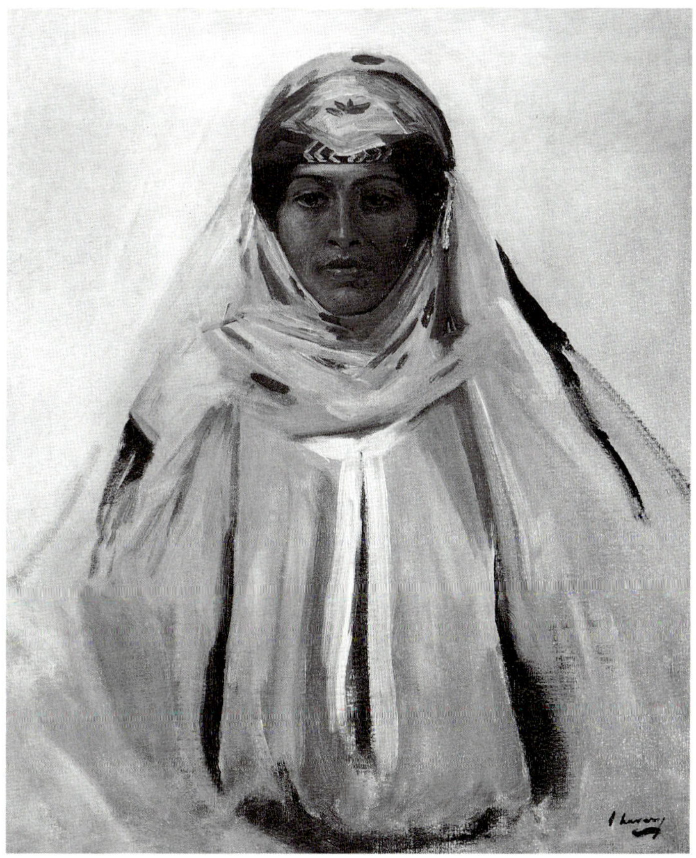

111 *Fatima Farghe*, *c.*1911, 30 × 25 (present whereabouts unknown, photo, courtesy Christie's)

which occurred during his Moroccan sojourns. Not only did he paint several religious festivals,but on one occasion he and Bibi Carleton rode out to witness a bloody battle between rival bands of tribesmen.[67] When, in December 1911, he heard that the P & O Liner *Delhi* had foundered a couple of miles from Cap Spartel, with members of the royal family and a consignment of gold bullion on board, Lavery hastened along the coast to paint the beached vessel (see Plate 112).[68]

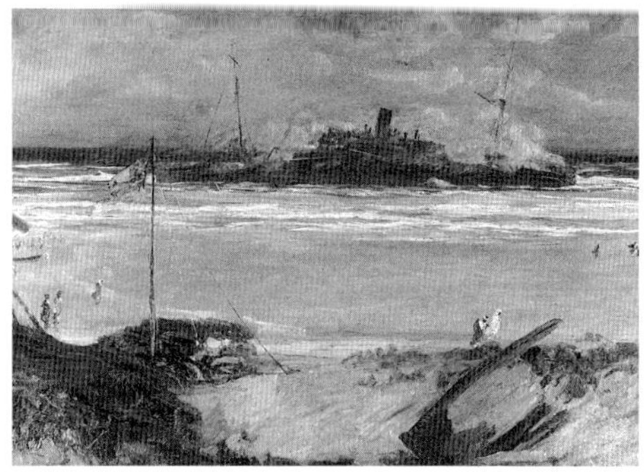

112 CSS *Delhi, Sidi Cassim, Morocco*, 1911, $32\frac{5}{8} \times 45\frac{3}{4}$ (present whereabouts unknown, photo, Christie's)

Lavery and his daughter, Eileen contributed greatly to the social life of the British settlement and they became close friends with Sir Reginald Lister, British envoy in Tangier. Recognising the weakness of the sultan and the desirability of controlling the Straits of Gibraltar, the British Legation at Tangier ensured the community in the immediate vicinity of the city of stability. As Envoy Extraordinary and Minister Plenipotentiary, Lister led a relaxed existence, riding on the beach with Lavery and Eileen or staging fancy-dress parties for the British expatriates.[69] He figures prominently in two of Lavery's most important interiors, *The Grey Drawing Room* (Plate 113) and *The Greyhound* (Plate 114).[70] Both pictures show the nonchalant Lister in conversation with Eileen Lavery, now a keen horsewoman. Dressed in riding habit she leans against a white marble fireplace, in both pictures. Lavery thus translates the idiom of Whistler's *Symphony in White No.2, the Little White Girl* into a conversation piece. Lavery's format was revisited with less obvious reliance upon Whistler by William Rothenstein in *Eric Gill and the Artist's Wife*, a double portrait painted three years later.[71] Critics observed the sensitivity of Lavery's manipulation of tone in *The Grey Drawing Room*.[72] With great subtlety the artist balances muted reds, ochres and greys in this tasteful interior. Only the mirror's reflection indicates the outside greenery of the garden. The formula is carried further in *The Greyhound*, where notes of shrill colour expose the occasional brashness of the Edwardian decor.[73] These pictures are a foretaste of the portrait interiors of the 1920s, and they demanded a flexibility of style in responding to and harmonising the accumulation of detail. They provide formal fixed perspectives on the fashionable interior; they refer to social tensions and codes of behaviour which attempt to recreate Edwardian morés in a colonised culture.

The two interiors were complimented by outdoor conversation pieces, some of which illustrate the daily life at Dar el Midfah. *The Windowsill*, for instance, shown in the 1908 Goupil exhibition, illustrates a young woman seated on a verandah windowsill talking to a man in the room beyond.[74] Lavery would often repair to the garden of Walter Harris's house where, on one occasion a moorish maid was painted sitting by the pond.[75] In 1905 the artist had painted a big picture, *A Windy Day* (Plate 115), showing two girls seated upon a parapet overlooking the sea. This bright Impressionist painting was later acclaimed at the Venice Biennale in 1907 and reshown at the International Society in 1910.[76] It paved the way for a series of terrace and verandah pictures around 1912. Tangier also enabled the artist to execute a number of sunlit portraits,the most important of which was a picture of Mary Auras and Eileen Lavery walking along the beach, entitled *Girls in Sunlight*.[77]

All of these pictures indicated Lavery's desire to extend the range and

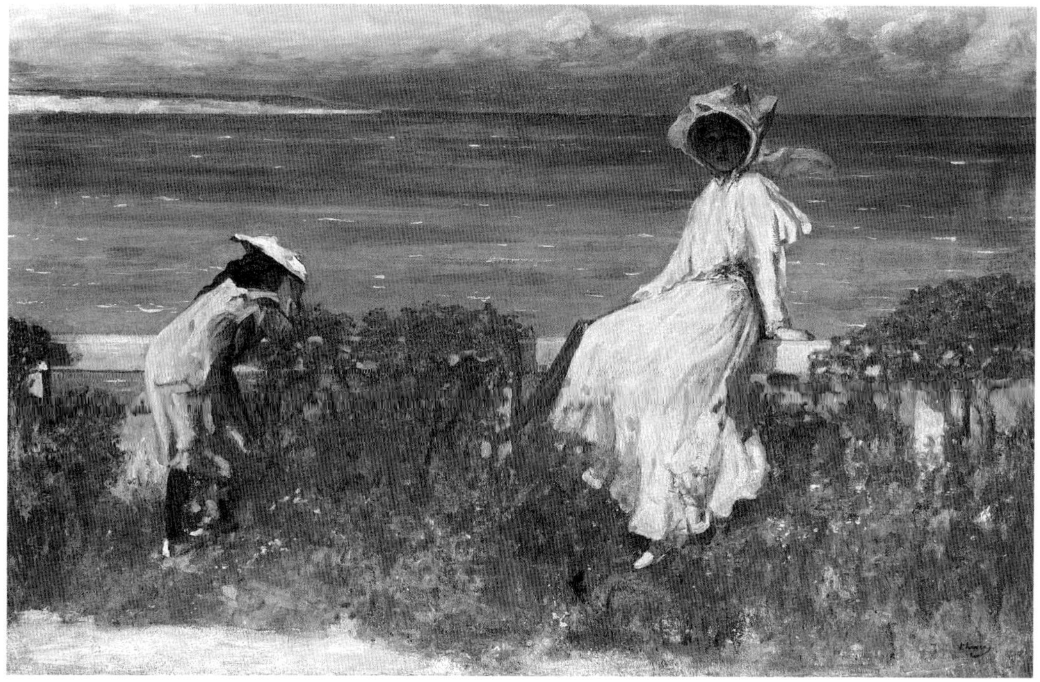

115 *A Windy Day*, *c.*1905, 47¼ × 73 (private collection, photo, Christie's)

possibilities of his work in Tangier. He remained undaunted by any task, but like the Impressionists before him, he was dissatisfied with his incapacity to produce more monumental and symbolic compositions. Having worked upon mural decorations and seen the efforts of painters like Clausen to scale up their rustic subjects, Lavery clearly sought large important commissions which would take him beyond the limitations of full-length portraiture. The equestrian portrait which he had tackled twice before, reclaimed his attention and he began to produce numerous sketches of Eileen in riding habit. One of these, *The Equestrienne* was shown at the Goupil Gallery in 1908.[78] At the same time, he painted many sketches for a large horseback portrait to be known as *The Amazon* (see Plates 116 and 117). The rider and her mount were to be seen upon a hilltop against the sky. This grand composition was one of the artist's most carefully planned works.

There were different riding habits and different horses; the horse was seen walking and the lance was carried in various ways, before the final sentinel pose was arrived at. With the aid of his numerous observations, Lavery painted the life-size canvas, nine feet by ten feet, in his studio at Tangier. When it was shown at the Royal Academy in 1911, *The Amazon* was regarded by critics as a *tour de force* and 'extremely effective' whether viewed from a distance or at close quarters.[79] It was a convenient punctuation point for Shaw Sparrow who, simulataneously was completing his monograph on Lavery and who saw it as a 'tribute to the *plein-air* movement'.[80] Lavery evidently wished *The Amazon* to assume emblematic proportions, by accentuating its statuesque qualities. The figure was intended to be a remote symbol of power, aloof, motionless, moved only by the breeze which chases the horse's tail and mane. Impassively *The Amazon* observes the distant horizon.

After his marriage, Hazel and her daughter, Alice, joined Lavery and Eileen at

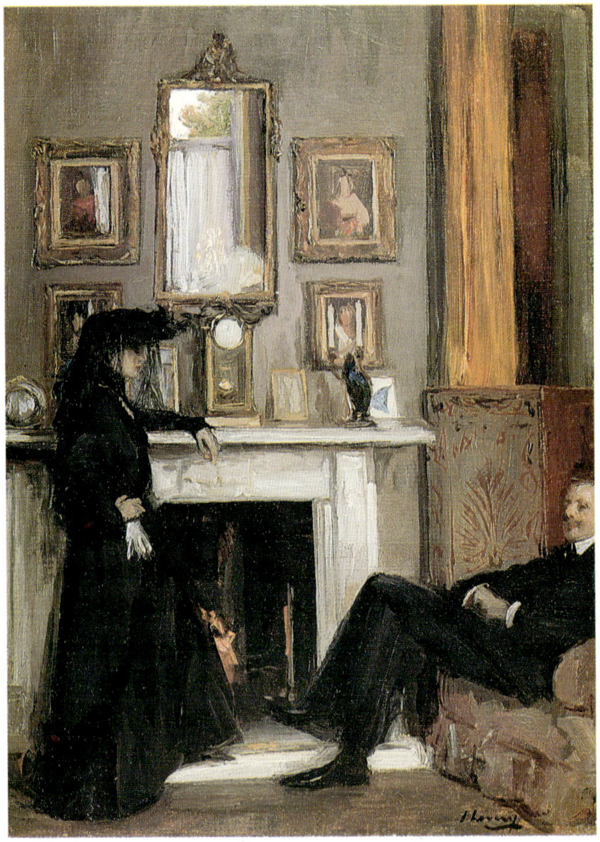

113 *The Grey Drawing Room*, 1910, 14 × 10 (private collection)

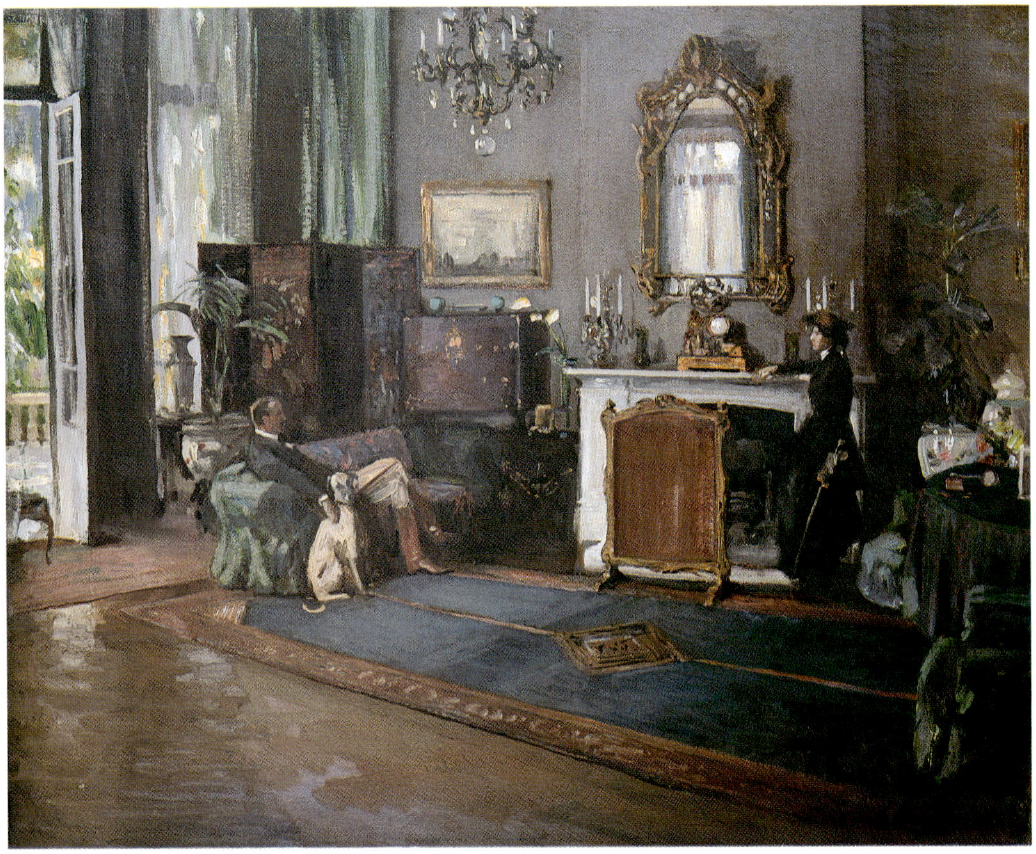

114 *The Greyhound*, 1910, 25 × 30¼ (The Ulster Museum, Belfast)

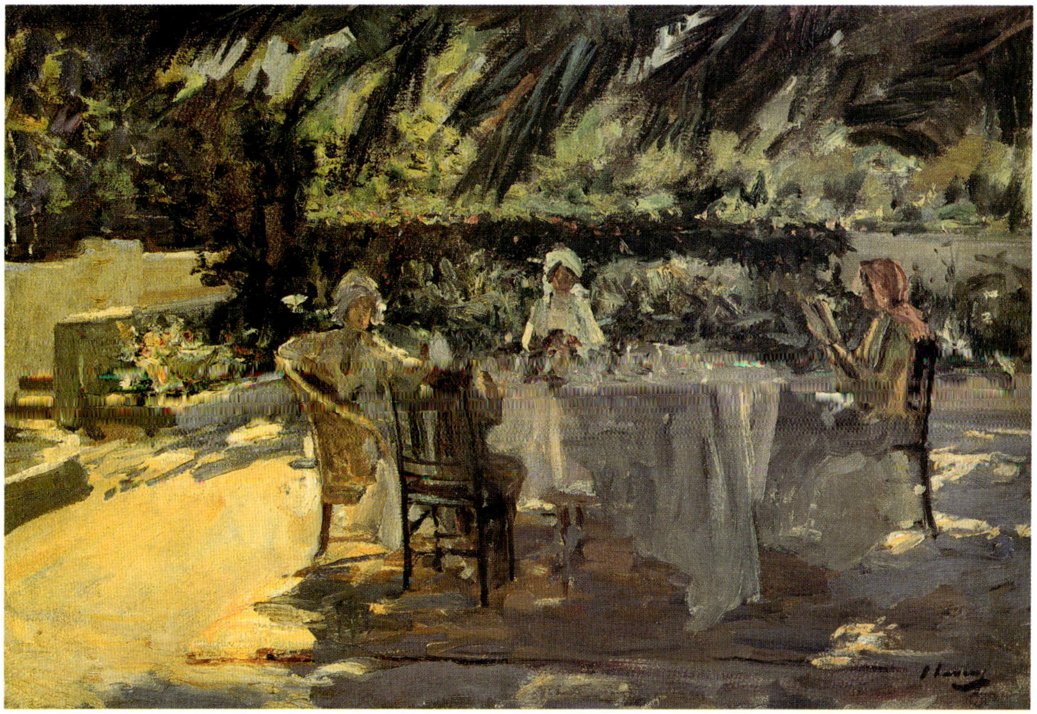

119 *Under the Palm Tree*, 1912, 18 × 24 (private collection)

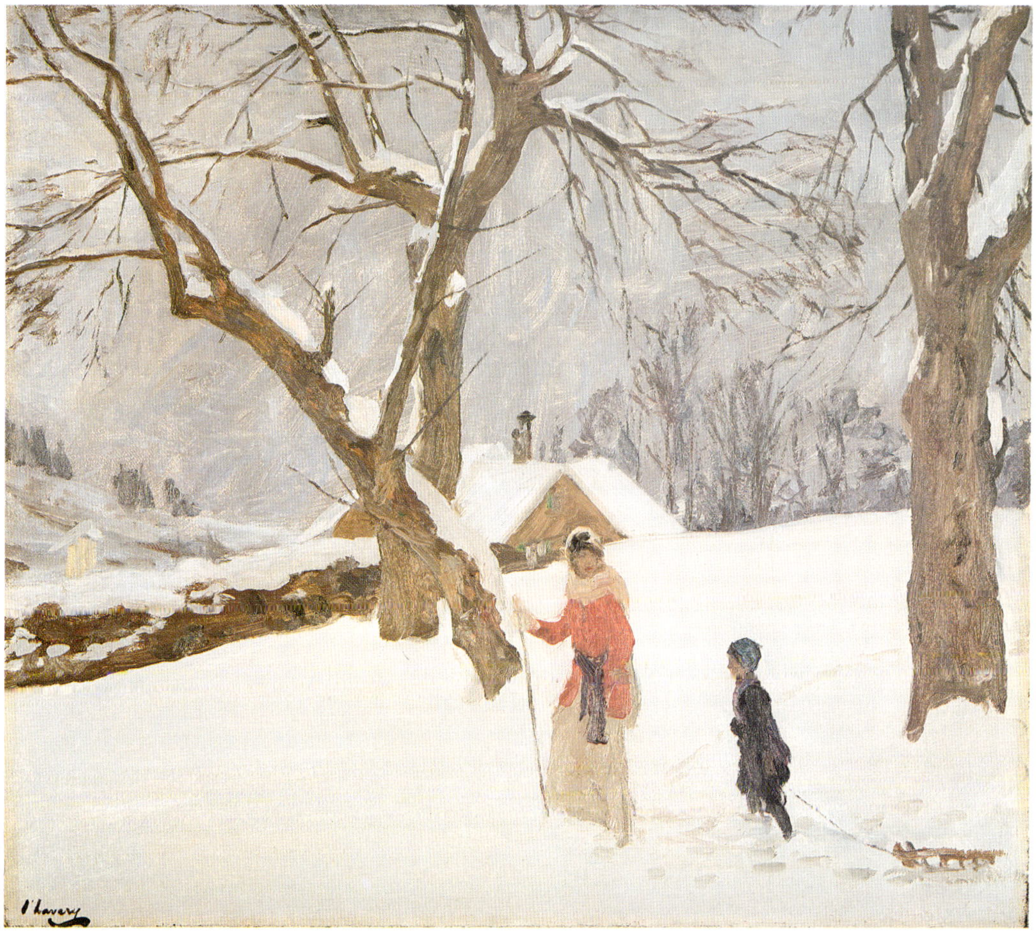

120 *A Winter Afternoon*, 1912, 25 × 27 (private collection)

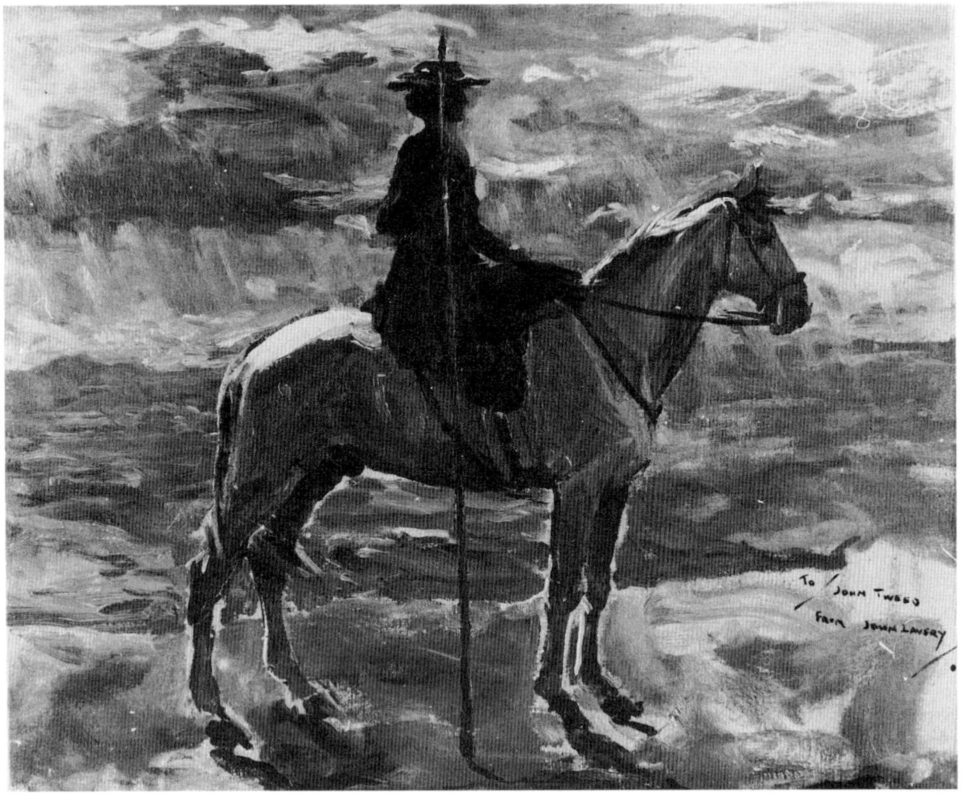

116 Study for *The Amazon*, *c.*1909
(photo, Fine Art Society)

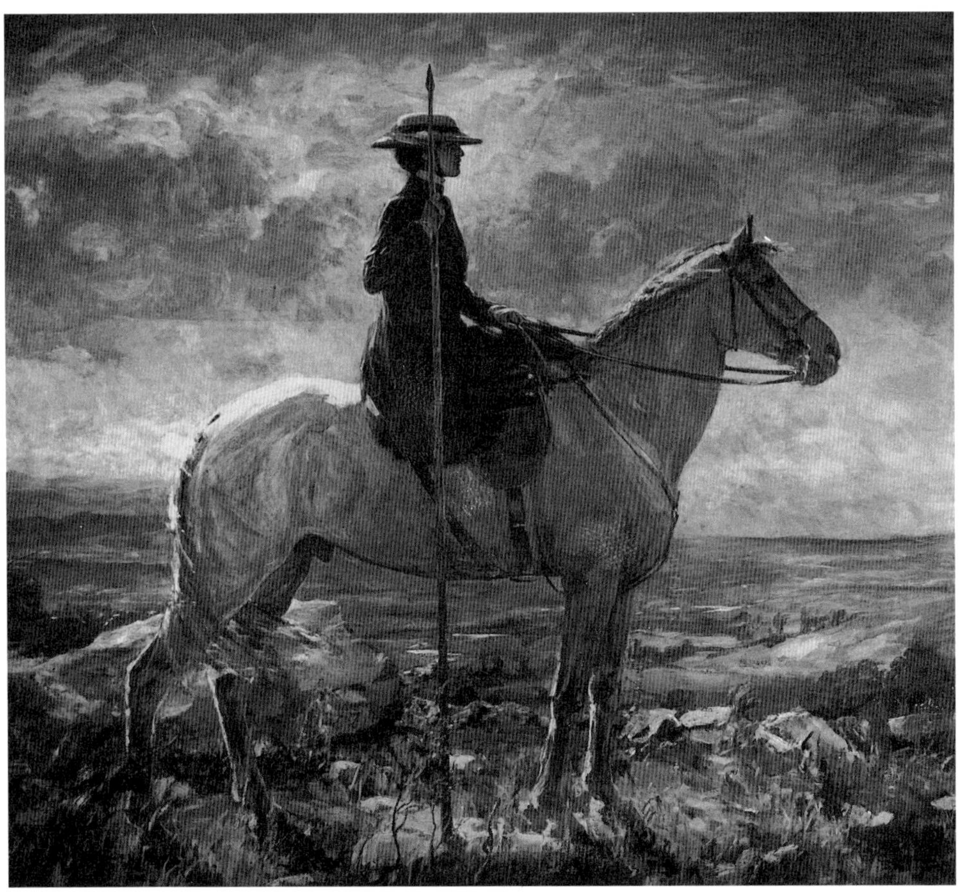

117 *The Amazon*, 1910, 106 × 119
(The Ulster Museum, Belfast)

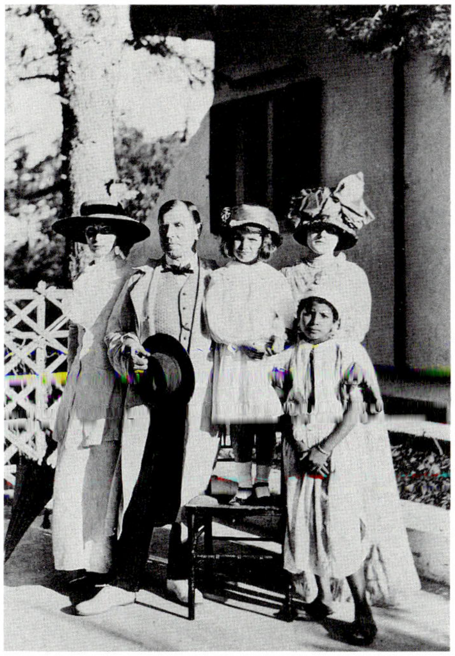

118 Hazel, John, Alice Eileen and Aida at Tangier, photo *c.*1910 (photo, Ulster Museum, Belfast)

Dar-el-Midfah. Family snapshots record the happy ménage (Plate 118). Small sketches were painted of breakfast groups on the verandah (Plate 119).[81] A larger study entitled *In Morocco*, 1912, shows Alice astride an Arab horse named Lily-Beau, being restrained by her anxious mother.[82] That year they took a winter holiday at Wengen in Switzerland. Snap-shots show the painter, Hazel and Alice ice skating. Two important canvases, *Japanese Switzerland* and *A Winter Afternoon* (Plate 120) were painted of Hazel and Alice in the snow.[83] Lavery records the frustration he caused through not being able to paint quickly enough for his models: 'On our last day at Wengen, I had to finish my *Japanese Switzerland*—Hazel and Alice in the snow—and they were very patient; but as time went on and Alice saw how little time would be left for a run on her luge, I overheard her say to her mother, "Isn't it a pity muffie, that we married an artist?"'[84]

The resulting canvases give no indication of haste. With the self-possession of an oriental draughtsman, Lavery took a brush loaded with paint and placed the dark shapes of his figures against the white snowy background, taking evident delight in the visual drama. On this holiday, Lavery was also attracted to the grandeur of the Alpine landscape. He painted at least four upright views of the Jungfrau and its surrounding peaks (see Plate 121).[85] To create a sense of distance, the foreground of these pictures often contain tiny skiing parties. Lavery may have been joined on this holiday by his friend and fellow International Society exhibitor, George Sauter.[86]

The hectic year 1912 also included a visit to Chicago, possibly to meet Hazel Lavery's family. Whilst there Lavery had his first experience of movie-making when he witnessed the unintended mauling by a panther of the heroine of a dubious melodrama called *Lost in the Jungle*.[87] No paintings appear to have survived from this voyage, though, as in other cases, it is inconceivable that the painting kit was not packed.

Even at home during these years prior to the Great War the Laverys spent a good deal of time away from Cromwell Place. There were visits to Ireland and Scotland, the latter being recorded in a fine landscape, *Loch Katrine* (Plate 122), an anticipation of the later moody scenes of Monte Carlo and Glendaloch.[88] They were invited by Lord Derby to visit Newmarket in the autumn of 1913. Before they set off, Hazel spirited the painter round to Harrods for a velour hat and coat, so that he would not look out of place in the horse-racing fraternity. Thus attired he set about painting scenes of the meeting, only to be interrupted by two policemen who thought he was a bookmaker erecting his blackboard. Only when they had received assurances from Lord Derby himself would the officers accept Lavery's presence and 'after that I could not see the course for police protection'.[89] Lavery delighted in recounting stories of this kind. Held back from close observation of the animals and their riders, he concentrated upon the totality of the spectacle.[90]

In these pre-war years a number of trips to Venice were made. In 1910 he received the signal honour of a retrospective exhibition of fifty-three of his most important works at the Venice Biennale.[91] In April that year Lavery visited the city in order to supervise the hanging and display of his paintings, and it was on this occasion that he probably painted *The Lido*.[92] Here, the positions of

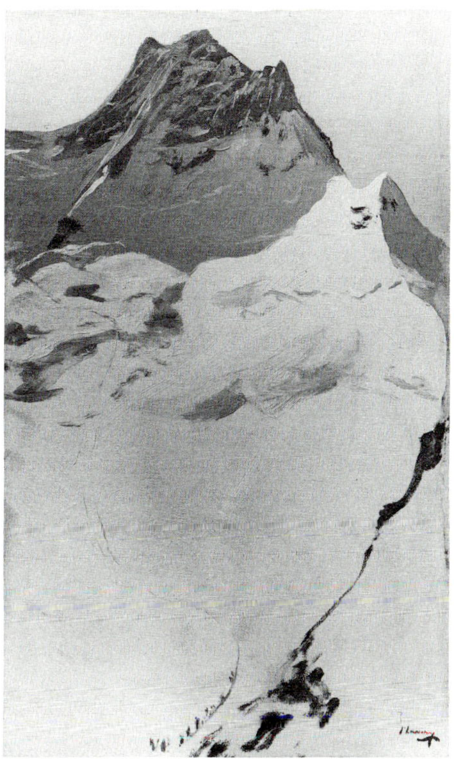

121 *The Summit of the Jungfrau*, 1912, 25 × 15½ (The Fine Art Society)

deckchairs and bathers extend the formal concerns of his Tangier beach scenes. It was in horizontal 25 × 30 inch canvases that Lavery produced an essential formula, susceptible to wide variation. Bands of limpid pigment swept across the canvas, subtly alternating in colour were to convey the coast at North Berwick and St Jean de Luz, the headland at Monte Carlo and the moody lake at Glendaloch.

The essential features of this approach however, had been established at Tangier in the early years of the century. The city itself was revisited for the last extended sojourn of 1920, and thereafter its magic remained vividly in the painter's memory. In 1933, he and Hazel passed through the Straits of Gibraltar for the last time, and he wrote nostalgically to Cunninghame Graham, 'We have just returned from a Mediterranean pleasure cruise passing Tangier in the twilight. I felt quite sad recalling the past. Bebe, Creeps, Frias and the rest. I suppose we ought to be grateful and believe in what you once described as that misleading statement "God is Love".'[93]

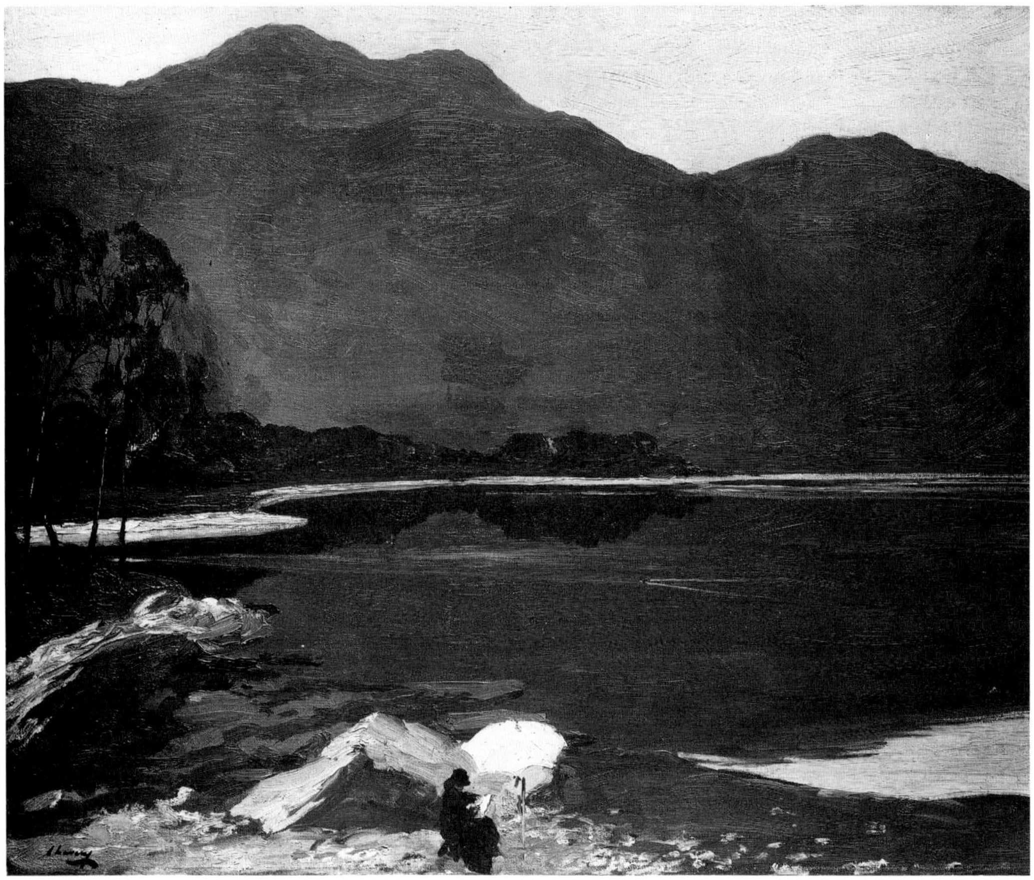

122 *Loch Katrine*, 1913, 25 × 30 (National Gallery of Scotland, Edinburgh)

7 Society Portraitist

The flowering of society portraiture in the 1890s eloquently attested to the wealth, confidence and ascendency of European culture. In England, late eighteenth-century traditions of grand manner portraiture were revived. The art journals up to the Great War frequently ran articles on Van Dyck, Lely, Reynolds, Gainsborough and Lawrence. New magazines like *The Connoisseur* and *The Burlington* emphasised the authority of a scholarship based upon notions of taste and quality. The eminent Edwardian wanted to be compared to his ancestors. In calling for his family portrait from Sargent in 1905, the Duke of Marlborough wanted something that would hang opposite Reynolds' celebrated picture of his predecessors at Blenheim.[1] Even when these notable forebears did not exist a portraitists job was often to suggest that they did. The portrait's success depended as much upon style and handling, as it did upon accessories. The painter's manner should call to mind the court styles of the seventeenth and eighteenth centuries. Oval portraits and full-lengths became popular again and leading society painters frequently worked in borrowed studios at fashionable spas or coastal resorts following the peripatetic existence of their clientele. How robust was Whistlerian abstraction in coming to terms with these demands?

Lavery energetically pursued this existence, but unlike Sargent or Boldini, he chose to work as much from models as on commission. As in the age of Gainsborough, there was an increasing market for fancy pictures of pretty models. Lavery's portraits aimed to be decorative in the Whistlerian sense and he continued the practice of constant revision. There are many instances of works being amended after their return from exhibition. This often meant the removal or addition of accessories, with such unsatisfactory results that it invariably led to the work being totally repainted. Shaw Sparrow was the first to record what he regarded as 'moods of vandalism' which led the artist to destroy some of his finest products: 'Several of Lavery's pictures now lie underneath other paintings and I reap regrets whenever I think of this fact.'[2] Shaw Sparrow could not understand Lavery's willingness to delete what he had already exhibited and regarded as finished. Pictures could as easily be wrecked in revision as improved, but the artist did not shy away from the challenge. The progress of many satisfactorily reworked pictures can be logged. *The Lady in Black No.2* for instance began life in 1896 as a portrait of Thalia Treadwell. Two years, and exhibitions in London, Paris, Munich and Edinburgh later, it was repainted from Mrs Swinnerton. The result was a severe commanding profile, which was as incisively naturalistic as Bastien-Lepage's *Portrait of Sarah Bernhardt*, 1879. In the winter of 1896, Lavery began a *Lady in Pink* in a borrowed studio in Rome. Unhappy with the result, he reworked the painting after his return, possibly from Nora Johnson and exhibited it at the International Society in 1899.[3] Several years later, he attacked the canvas with soap and benzol, removed most of the paint and reworked the idea from a young American, Miss Mary Delmar Morgan. The result with its suggestion of *décolletage* is much more rakish. It was shown at the International Society in 1904 and admired for its 'superb directness'.[4] Critics were evidently unaware of having seen the canvas before.

The upgrading and extensive revision of *A Lady in Pink* is symptomatic of larger changes of attitude in the increasingly successful painter. The softer lines and more diaphanous tiers of early twentieth-century *couture* gave a greater sense of movement—a sense of a body living within its clothes. The first version with its broad gilded chaise cutting the edges of the canvas, seems rather more static than the final product. Mary Delmar Morgan perches uneasily on a Queen Anne-style chair, resting her foot on an ornamental footstool. The animation of the figure was one of the principal indications of a new sensibility which turn-of-the-century critics found difficult to describe.

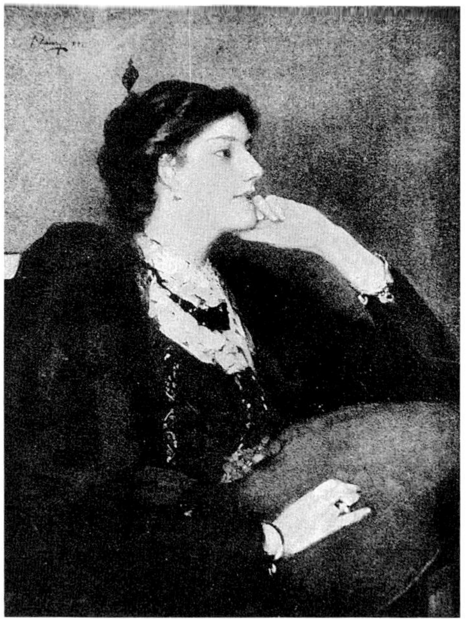

123 *A Lady in Black* *c.*1898 size unknown, (present whereabouts unknown)

When Lavery's *A Lady in Black* (Plate 123),[5] a portrait of Esther McLaren was exhibited, Frederick Wedmore toyed with the conventional comparisons with Whistler and Guthrie using terms like 'artistic feeling' to describe what he found impossible to express. He drew the conclusion that with all three artists, 'if a portrait is not in every case a likeness, it is at all events a picture—it is not only an attitude'.[6] Wedmore was grappling with the general Whistlerian principals which dominated Lavery's portraiture, namely that the image should be static and discreet. The artist was challenged with oversensitivity in this respect. He was also felt to be less concerned with character and personality than with decorative effect. When *Mrs Christie Smith* was exhibited at the Society of Portrait Painters in 1895, for instance, D. S. MacColl used the occasion to mount a general attack upon Lavery's desire to confect a striking colour harmony—'When he paints a pretty woman, he seizes upon one or two obvious points of likeness, fixes the general allure of the figure, and makes a striking assertion of the *éclat* of fair flesh . . . A painter who can imagine the beautiful harmony of colour in the draperies of one of those portraits, and whose appreciation of the principles of picture making is evidently so high, owes it to his talent to try for other virtues.'[7]

Irrespective of what these other virtues might be, Lavery had clearly used the occasion for colour experiment. Reading between the lines of other reviewers of the same exhibition, it sounds as if *Mrs. Christie Smith* was in competition with her large hat![8] MacColl evidently required greater naturalism and less striving for effect. It is important to realise, however, that the trend was against MacColl's puritan values. The growing taste of sitters in turn-of-the-century paintings was for some form of dramatisation in their effigies. The society hostess whose life was given over to self-projection, cared little for aesthetic discretion.

During these years, Sargent was an increasingly powerful presence in London exhibitions. After the success of his *Lady Agnew* in 1893, he had risen rapidly in the estimation of critics and clients alike, so that within eighteen months of the showing of Mrs Christie Smith's portrait, Sargent's *Mrs Carl Meyer and her Children* was hailed as 'unquestionably' 'the dominating picture' of the Royal Academy of 1897.[9] Lavery's portrait of *Mrs Colquhoun Reade* was unaccountably rejected at this same exhibition and thereafter he, like Whistler, refused to submit to its erratic selection process.[10] He was however conscious of the need to establish new goals in portraiture, to profit from his absorption of Whistler and move on.

There is a foretaste of new directions in works like *La Violoniste* (Plate 124) in which the sitter takes command of her surroundings. *La Dame aux Perles* (Plate 125), the portrait of the Austrian baronness, Marguerite von Hollrigl, confirms Lavery's new direction. In a dazzling virtuoso display of pearl greys and pinks, this picture bore direct comparison with *Lady Agnew*, yet it avoided Sargent's synthetic colour. 'The brushwork' in Shaw Sparrow's words seemed 'more evidently adept and alert than we are accustomed to see in the modest excellence of other good Lavery portraits'.[11] Here more than any previous portraits, the artist caught the sense of negligent alertness that Sargent often conveyed in his sitters. Although the model was 'in respose' she is 'like an actress who listens with patience and yet prepares for instant movement'.[12] This sense of latent energy is partly conveyed in the modulation of the silver dress and the painting of the hands which fall languidly over the sides of the wicker chair. For all her impassivity, *La Dame aux Perles* transmits considerable charisma.

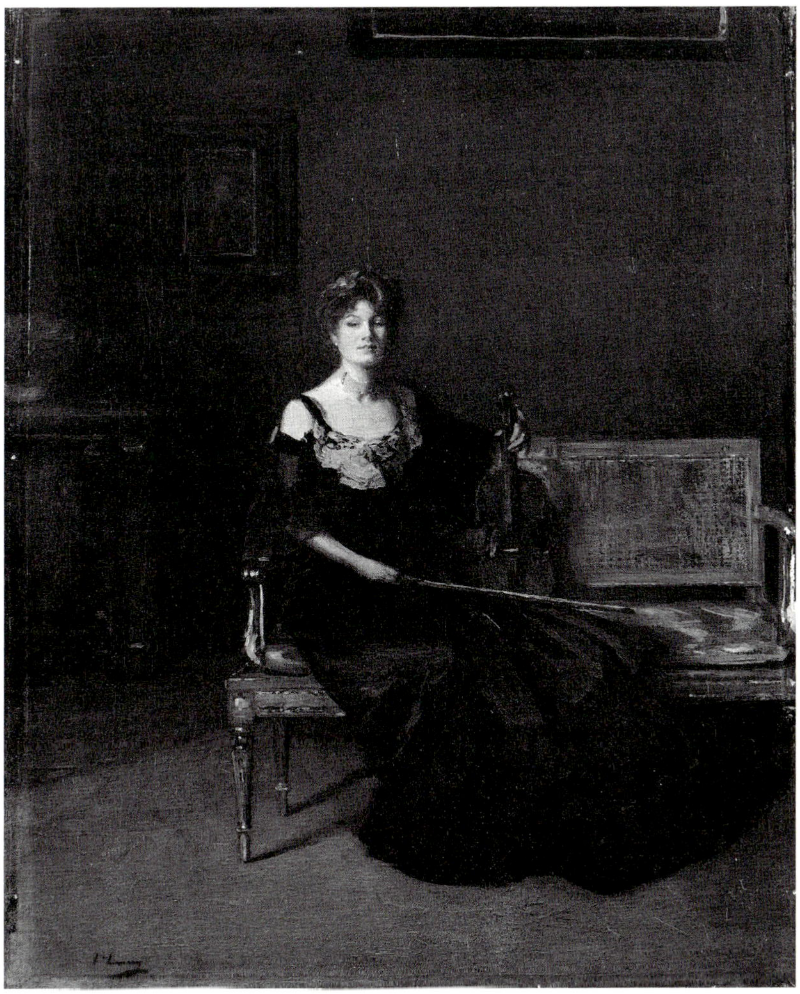

124 *La Violoniste*, c.1900, 22¾ × 17½ (private collection)

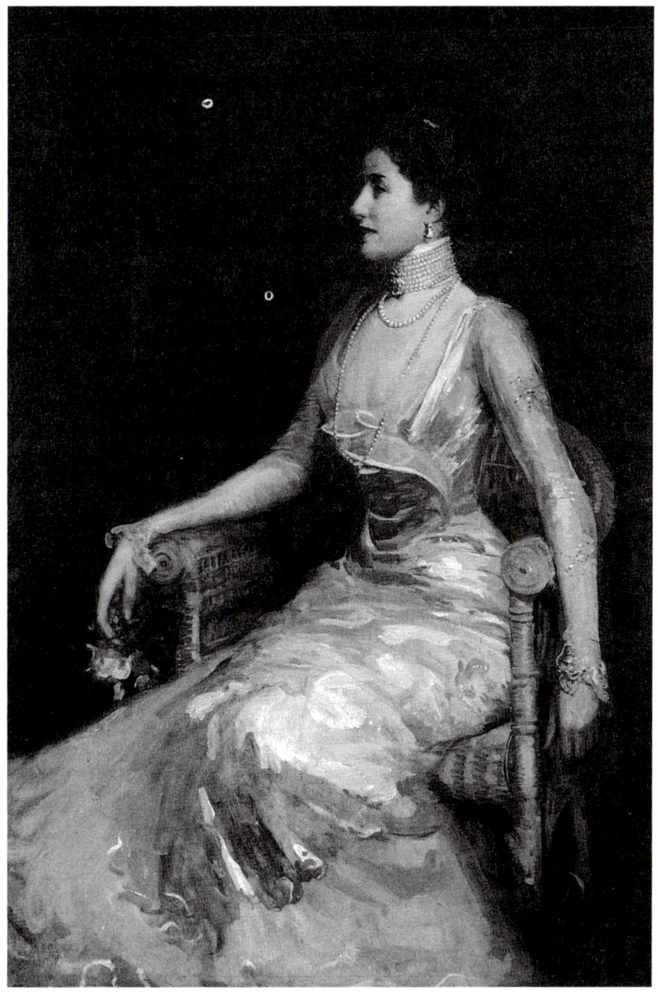

125 *La Dame aux Perles*, 1901, 54 × 40 (Hugh Lane Municipal Art Gallery, Dublin)

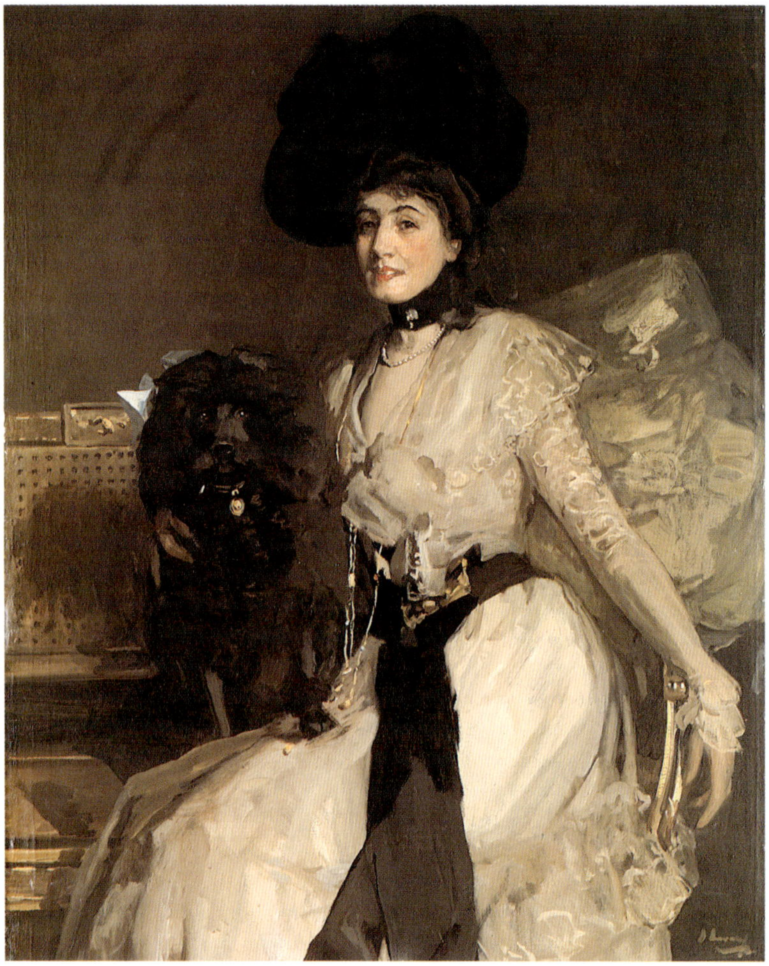

126 *The Black Poodle*, 1905, 50½ × 41 (present whereabouts unknown, photo, courtesy Sotheby's)

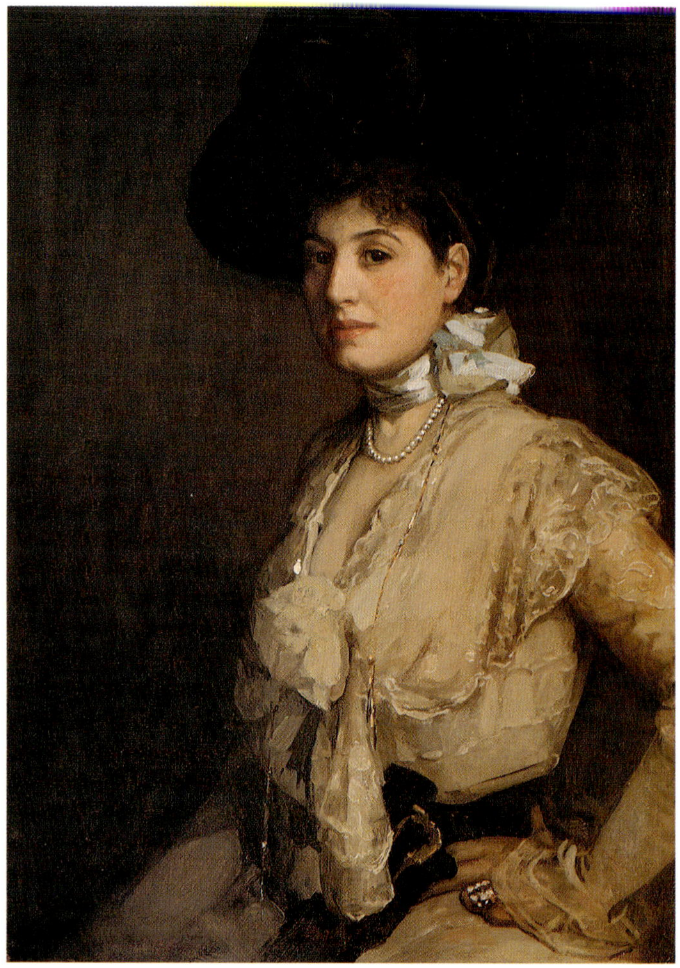

127 *Mrs Arthur Franklin*, *c*.1903, 33 × 23½ (present whereabouts unknown, photo, courtesy Sotheby's)

Alert aloofness characterises many of Lavery's portrayals of fashionable women in the Edwardian years. Mrs Arthur Franklin's portrait (Plate 126), reworked as *The Black Poodle* (Plate 127), conveys some of the independent attitudes of the Edwardian woman, expressed in dress codes. The addition of cocades, rosettes and sashes revive pompadour courtliness which was seen to great effect in the images of Gwendoline Churchill and the Hely-Hutchinson sisters.

Equally attractive, but less mature than the Austrian baronness, was Mary Auras. From around 1902, Fraulein Auras became Lavery's favourite model. They were introduced by the painter Auguste Neven du Mont at Unter den Linden. Mary was sixteen when they met and for about five years she was a regular member of Lavery's entourage, acting as a companion for Eileen.[13] The artist described her an 'an inspiration' and painted her portrait many times. This one model was portrayed in all his current formats—full-length, half-length, profile and oval. An oval portrait *Mary with Roses* (Plate 128), 1902 is one of his first portrayals of her.[14] Lavery had attempted a work of this kind, with much less

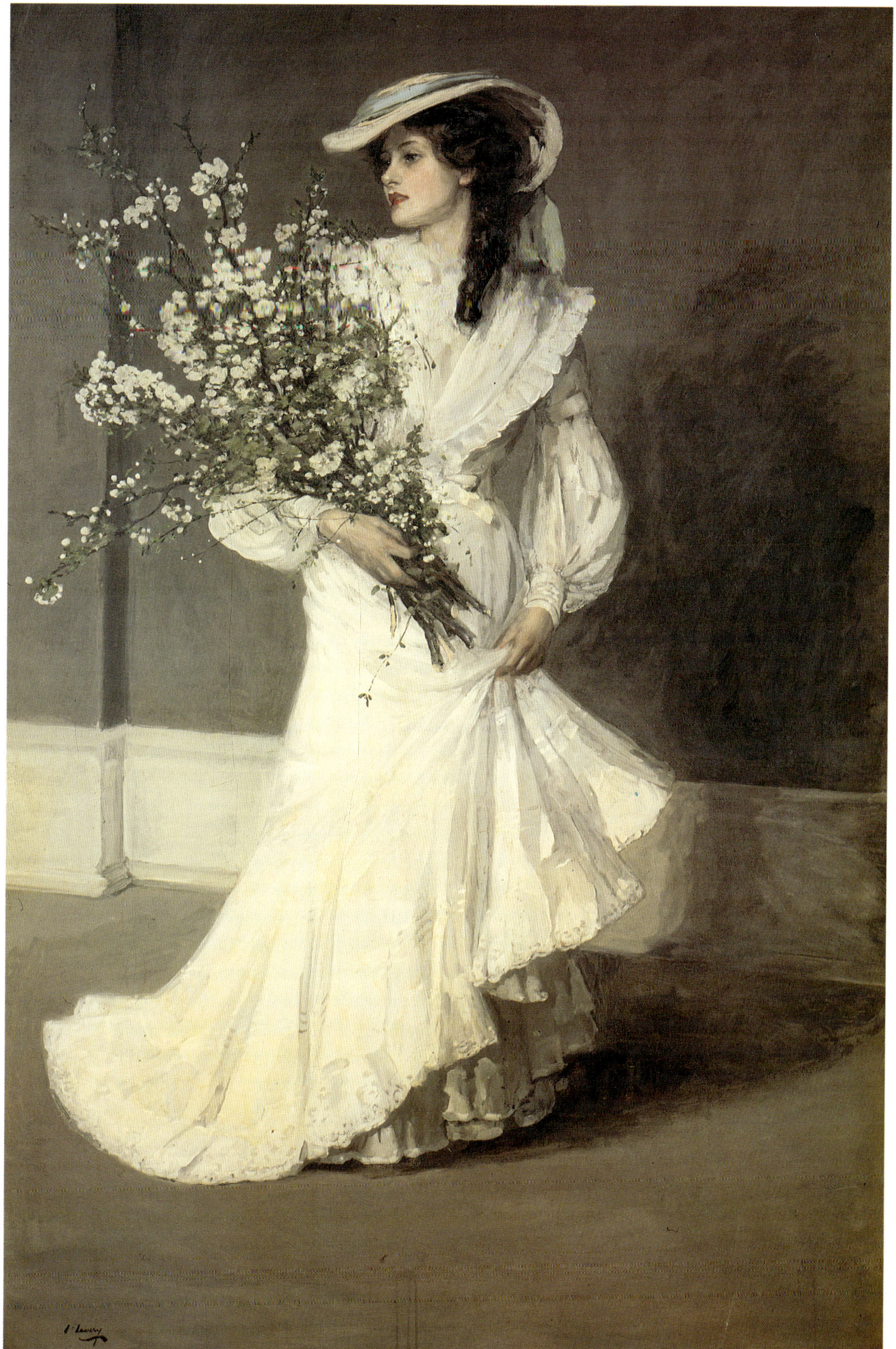

130 *Printemps*, 1903, 76 × 50
(Musée d'Orsay, Paris)

success in the *Portrait of Alice Fulton* in 1886. However in the earlier work, the flowers almost embalm the sitter, while here they naturally symbolise her youth and beauty. Lavery elaborated this idea in two notable full-lengths of 1903, A *Girl in White* (Plate 129) and *Printemps* (Plate 130).[15] The first of these is almost a preparation for the second, though it was possibly painted after. A. C. R. Carter nevertheless rhapsodised its qualities. 'Here' he said, 'is *une expression naive*—a gentle shyness—all that seems to conjure up a vision of English sweetness. In the painting of the soft textures of the muslin gown, Mr Lavery has contrived to give just values to the many varying surfaces in a masterly technique . . . The low, flat straw of the hat gives a soft shadow to the features; the coquettish curl, the bunched flowers complete an ensemble of charm.'[16]

Lavery took the model in the same attire and repainted her holding a large bunch of May flowers for *Printemps*. The wider format gave a greater sense of space around the figure and meant that its shape could be articulated to create a dramatic series of 'S' curves that cut an almost flamboyant silhouette against the plain monochrome wall. For Shaw Sparrow the ravishing qualities of the picture were summed up in a single sentence '. . . to love this portrait is to make a new friendship for the rest of one's life'.[17] The writer's avowal of the picture's greatness was perhaps, confirmed by its having been purchased for the Musée du Luxembourg in 1904. By that time, the painting had been extravagantly praised by French critics. Camille Mauclair, like Carter before him, tried in the overwritten manner of critics of the time, to convey its eighteenth-century English qualities. He commented upon the figure's lack of adornment. She wore a simple *bergère* hat and was not bejewelled or bedecked with ribbons and feathers, her head was 'languorously tilted', exposing her neck which was 'dove-like'. Her smile revealed a 'totally English charm'. Mauclair tried to express the derivation of Lavery's art: 'It has, in this work, the grace of Greuze, transposed into the recollections of the English School and, at the same time, the sultry look of a Rossetti'.[18] The critic went on to extol the handling of figure movement, of catching the model in a half-turn. He concluded that in the presence of this perfect portrait of a woman *rose et dorée* the viewer experiences rejuvenation. Leaving aside these *belles lettres*, the picture does stretch and expand our contemporary understanding of the sensibility of the period. Mary's costume was that of the late eighteenth century shepherdess, modified by contemporary *couture*. Her youth, her red hair hanging in ringlets, her spring flowers, presented an idyllic vision that was identified with an arcadian past. It is not surprising that this should have appealed more to French eyes than to the English. French art nouveau in these years was dominated by the notion of a revival of the style of the *ancien régime*. The Goncourts, whose study of the art of Watteau, Boucher and Greuze had been published in the 1860s, still commanded French aestheticism. The sublime sensual delight of the idyllic world of Cythera continued to function as an ideal. The fact that the work contained an 'English charm' only added to the pleasure it gave. Mauclair was obviously ignorant of the fact that the model was German!

The question remains as to Lavery's involvement in striking this deep chord in the French sensibility. He obviously intended to make *Printemps* look the way it does. Yet the concept which the picture embodies only appears extraordinary

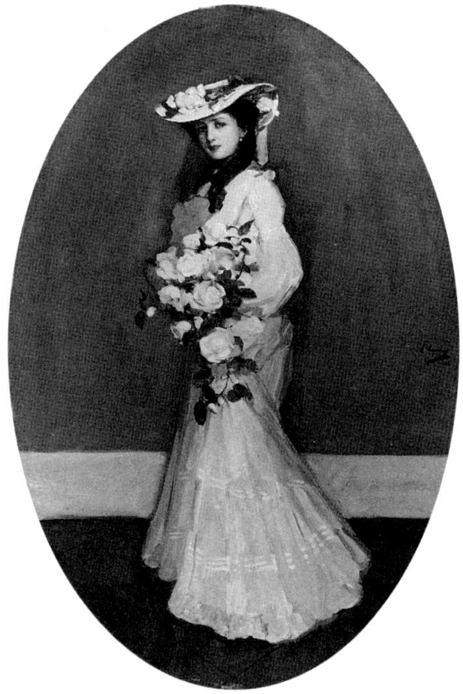

128 *Mary with Roses*, *c.*1902, oval, $40\frac{1}{4} \times 26\frac{1}{4}$ (Johannesburg Art Gallery)

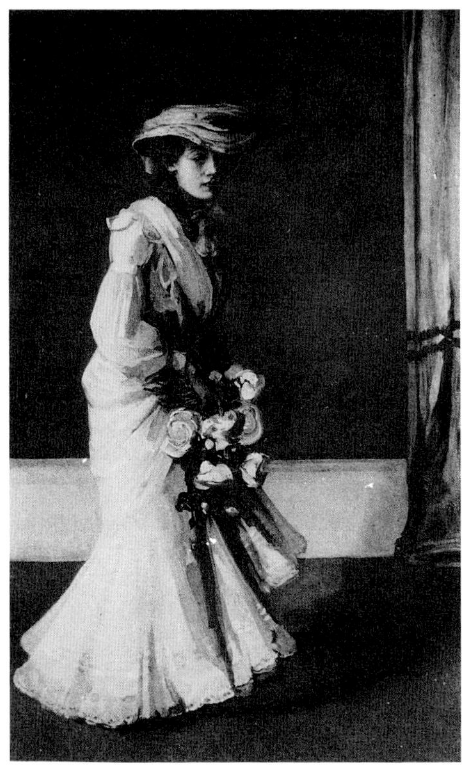

129 *A Girl in White*, *c.*1903, size unknown (present whereabouts unknown)

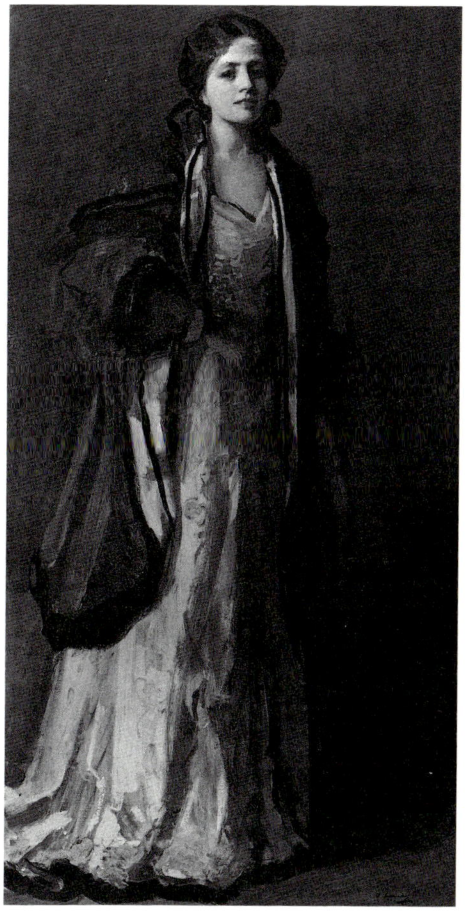

131 *Lady in a Green Coat*, *c.*1903, 72½ × 36¼ (Bradford Museums and Art Galleries)

when viewed in isolation. The artist's intentions were inevitably mediated by contemporary taste and by the portraiture of others. By 1904, he was sufficiently cosmopolitan to create a work of profound cultural significance which exposed some of the latent longings of the age. He could not have calculated the full effect of this upon others. British critics failed to grasp the significance of the purchase of *Printemps* by the French government. MacFall, writing in *The Academy*, regarded the event as 'strangely significant' and while he politely complimented the Musée du Luxembourg selectors, he felt bound to take the artist to task for all the reasons first adumbrated by D. S. MacColl. 'Mr Lavery's craftsmanship is virile and beautiful and forceful; his decorative sense is very great; his colour statement is fascinating; but when it comes to the essential statement to which all else should be subordinate, he is often content, for instance, with the mere statement of the beauty of the woman, when he should be telling us what that woman really is behind that exquisite screen of the lure of her sweet face.'[19]

MacFall was obviously conscious of the fact that while very little modern British painting was collected in France, the French state now possessed two of the best Laverys. Psychological penetration was not the aim of pictures like *Printemps*. It was not that Lavery, having developed the capacity for incisive character study in works like *Père et Fille*, had abandonded it for a more superficial exercise. MacFall was aware of Lavery's intention to summon a vision of female beauty; nevertheless, like many of his contemporaries he was inclined to moralise upon the adequacy of this. It was wrong to consider *Printemps* as a portrait when it was intended to be something other than that. The American critic, Christian Brinton wrote of these works that they were both portraits and pictures, 'They linger submissively on the dividing line between the exact and the undefined . . . In the precise turn of head, in veil lightly brushed aside, or in the soft gleam of ring, broach or bracelet, you have not only individuality but the secret of . . . feminine charm . . .'[20]

Such statements now appear dated. What is interesting is that to paint a portrait, in the early years of the century, was to create something more than a recognisable effigy. Not only did the sitter wish to collude with the manner of representation, she would also submit to adopting the role of model in an expression of the stylistic preference of the age. The degree to which this was self-consciously intended in *Printemps* can only he fully appraised by comparison with more orthodox portraits of Fraulein Auras. *Mary in Green* and *Lady in a Green Coat* (Plate 131) have none of the obvious fancy of *Printemps*. The first of these was praised for the technical qualities of 'beautiful drawing' and 'true values',[21] while the second drew Stodart Walker's attention because it illustrated the fact that Lavery was, '. . . ever obsessed by the colour possibilities of his models. He sees the colour métier of his sitters at a glance and weaves them into a harmony of paint with unerring skill.'[22]

Lavery painted many sketches and smaller portraits of Mary Auras, at least three of which were profiles.[23] Since *The Lady in Black No.2*, the artist had produced a number of profile portraits, the most important of which was *Mrs Brown Potter* shown at the International Society in 1901.[24] Carter reproduces a very different profile of Mary dated 1902. This was deliberately unfinished and in the loose indications of the hair and shoulders, the concentration of contour relaxes into soft cadenzas of paint, reminiscent of the unfinished head studies of Lawrence. These sketches were distilled into *Miss Auras—The Red Book* (Plate 132) which was compared with Romney's *Parson's Daughter* and which revealed to *The Studio* critic that '. . . the tradition has not left us which the eighteenth century transmitted to English art'.[25]

Despite the constant identification with past traditions Lavery remained outside the Royal Academy. Contemporary comparisons for his work, apart from Whistler and Sargent, were provided by the international group of society painters. Showing regularly in Berlin, Munich, Paris and Venice as well as at the International Society and the Society of Portrait Painters in London, Lavery was set apart from the artistic establishment associated with the Royal Academy. In

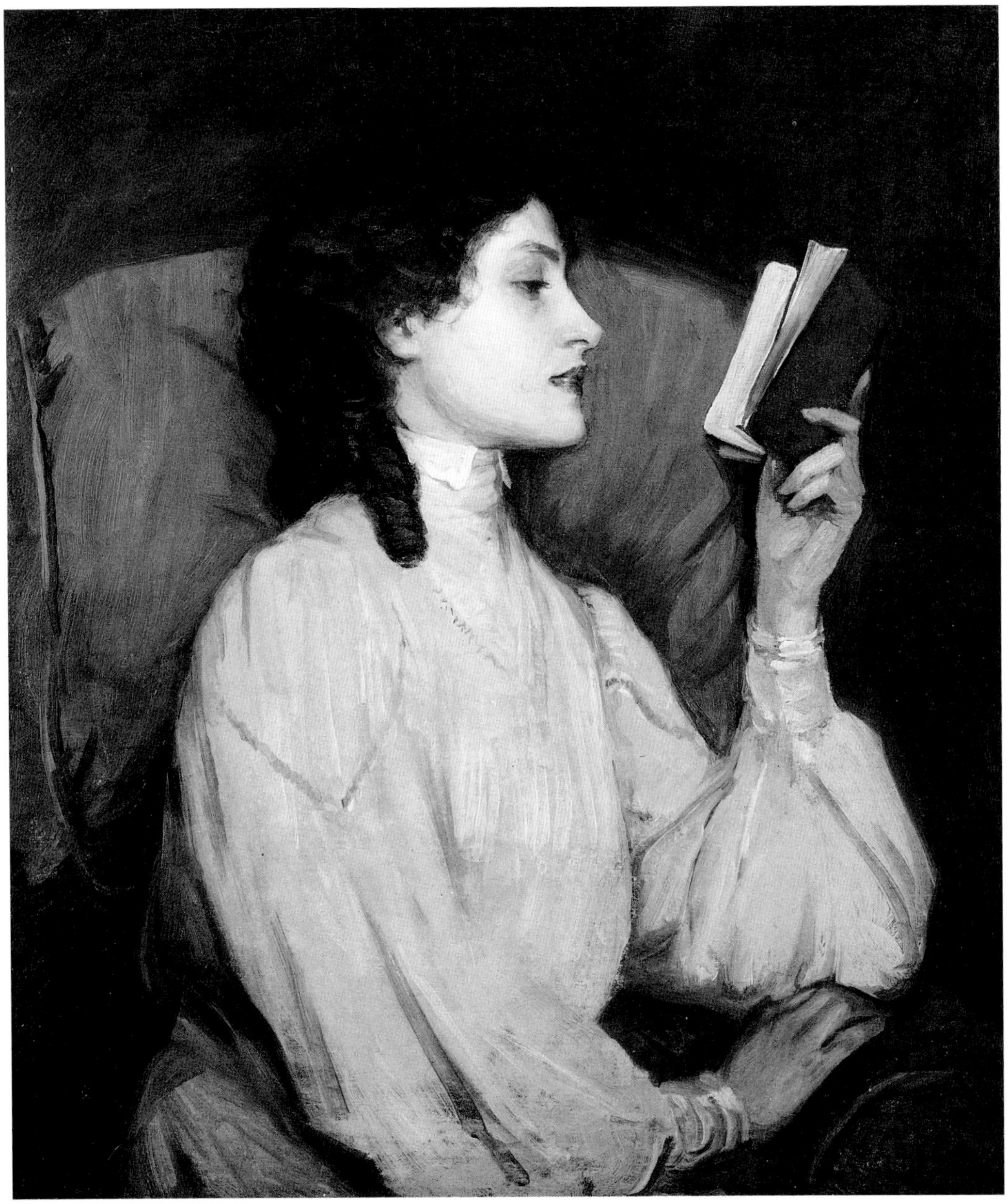

132 *Miss Auras – The Red Book*, *c.*1905, 30 × 25 (private collection, photo, Pyms Gallery, London)

1902 he painted a universally acclaimed portrait, *Le Chou Bleu* sometimes known as *The Blonde*. The elegant unidentified model, wearing a grey dress and a brown tunic, created an ensemble that attracted praise from one Salon critic who declared that it was, '. . . as confident as an Alexander, as erudite as a La Gandara, as serene as a Boldini, as stylish as a Zorn, as sensitively pulsating as a Whistler.'[26]

Alexander and Whistler were American, La Gandara was Spanish, Boldini, Italian and Zorn, Swedish. The picture was thus, firmly located in the international arena among painters who, like Lavery himself, were powerfully individual and whose reputations extended beyond their countries of origin. Each had initially made his name in Paris, although significantly, none was French.

It is difficult now to reconstitute the language of qualities which these pictures elicited. It would be easy to jump to the conclusion that international portraiture was fickle, fashion-conscious and had for its goal the mere celebration of contemporary chic. Floral full-lengths like *Polyhymnia* (Plate 133) and *Printemps* (Plate 130) were considered to be poetic abstractions in their time. However the appeal to poetry is difficult now to accept. It seems absurd, from the perspective of late twentieth-century cynicism that such notions were seriously regarded—as seriously, for instance, as Reynolds' *Mrs Siddons as a Tragic Muse* was taken in its day. Shaw Sparrow grappled inappropriately with *Polyhymnia* trying to invest it with grander meaning. Was she 'the muse of lyric poetry' or 'wisdom arrayed in a black which is not mourning' or did she merely represent 'much in the psychology of social butterflies?'[27] In the end such futile speculations are more interesting for the fact that they exercised the mind of the author, rather than because they provided a real clue to the painting's role and purpose.

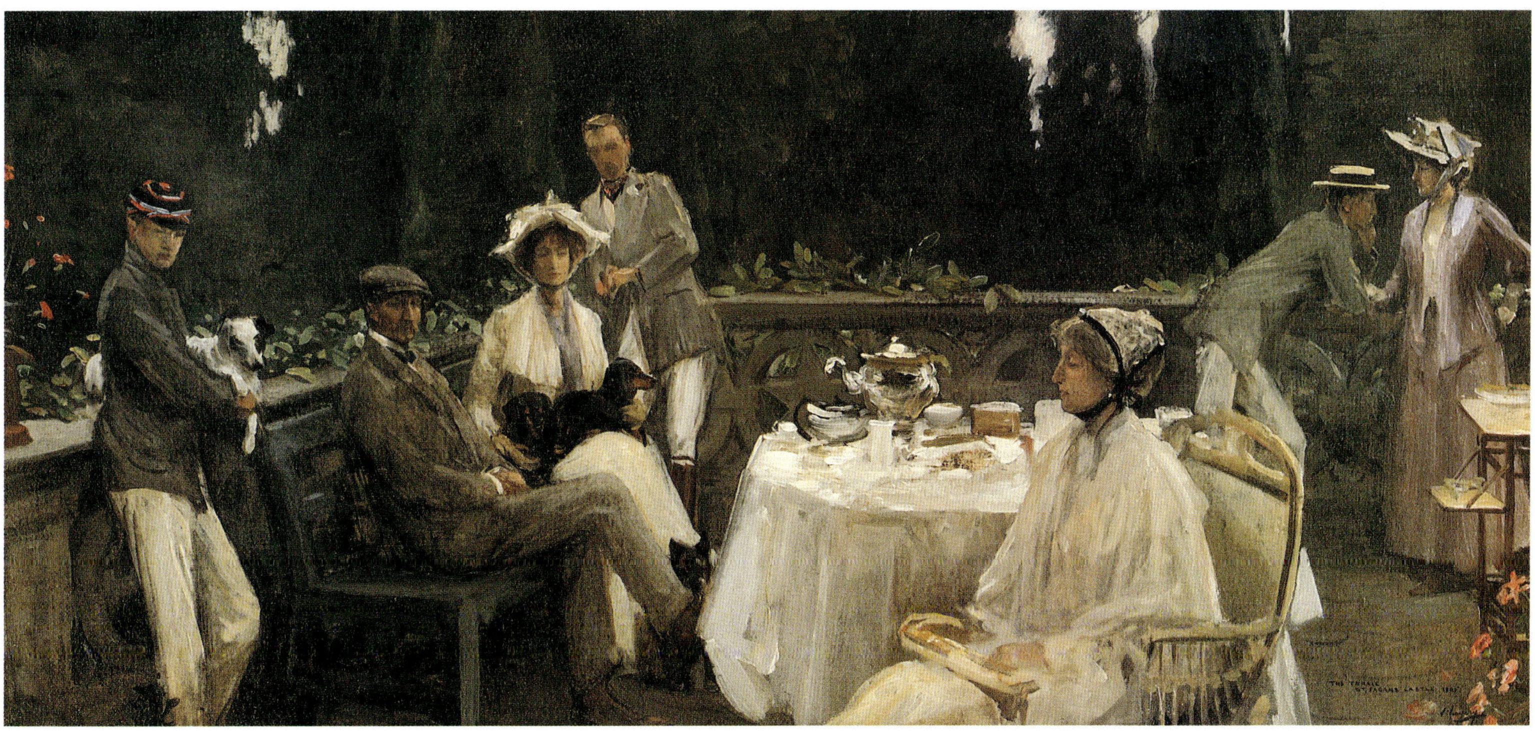

136 *A Family Group at St Fagans*, 1905, 22 × 46 (private collection, photo, John Bethel)

In 1904 Lavery was called upon by the Earl of Donoughmore to paint the portraits of *The Ladies Norah and Evelyn Hely-Hutchinson* (Plate 134). Not only were they represented together in a picture sometimes known as *The Sisters*, but they were also painted separately over the next two years as *Lady Norah Brassey* and *Lady Evelyn Farquhar* (Plate 135). James L. Caw admired *The Sisters* and declared that it was a picture which 'anyone might have been proud to sign'.[28] In 1908, Carter described Lady Evelyn's portrait as 'a shimmering vision' and 'the very coherence of portraiture'.[29] The obvious comparison which suggests itself for the double portrait is Sargent's *Ena and Betty Wertheimer*, however Lavery avoids the extrovert arrogance which became a fatal trap for the society portraitist. By this time, Sargent was being eclipsed by Boldini in the sheer bravura brilliance of his style. Sickert, for instance, described Boldini as the 'nonpareil parent of the wriggle and chiffon school'.[30] His figures seemed to collide on canvas, and to have been painted in a single burst of nervous energy. For Sickert, none of the portraitists of the period had 'lifted the fashionable flic-flac to the *nth* with the same ringmaster's flourish of the lash as has the wizard of Ferrara and the Boulevard Berthier.' Lavery avoided the eager competitiveness of the international set and flattered the aesthetic sensibility of his sitters. Thus *The Sisters* were praised by *The Times* as a 'charming group', in which 'nothing could be more effective than the colour scheme . . . with its juxtaposition of dark and light blue and many shades of white . . .'.[31]

Not all critics were favourably disposed to Lavery's stylish portrayal of elegant women. A cool and potentially hostile observer was the rather pedestrian face-painter, the Hon. John Collier. Collier criticised Lavery for losing character in favour of 'delicate tones and harmonies'. In researching his *The Art of Portrait Painting* in 1905 he contacted one of Lavery's female sitters and was furnished with an excellent account of the studio procedure. 'He has great consideration,' she declared,

> for the sitter—he arranges a large mirror which reflects him at work on the canvas so that the sitter may be interested. He spends a great deal of time and trouble to find a pose that in its simplicity is dignified and in its originality surprises and refreshes the eye. Two days I spent in the studio trying to take an unaffected pose. Mr. Lavery did sketch after sketch of me, till he found what he wanted.
>
> Then discarding the sketches he takes a canvas the size he requires, and within two hours he has the entire canvas covered—the texture of the frock, and the drawing of the features and pose of the figure almost complete; the following day the greater part of this paint is removed from the canvas and the picture again gone over from head to toe. This was repeated every day for almost two weeks, each afternoon the picture looking more complete, until finally he decides that he has reached his limit. Nearly all his drawing is done with the brush. He uses charcoal merely to map out or space his composition. His palette is very simple, the primaries, black, white, and burnt sienna—in all six pigments.[32]

Collier alludes to the similarity of Lavery's working method to that of Whistler.

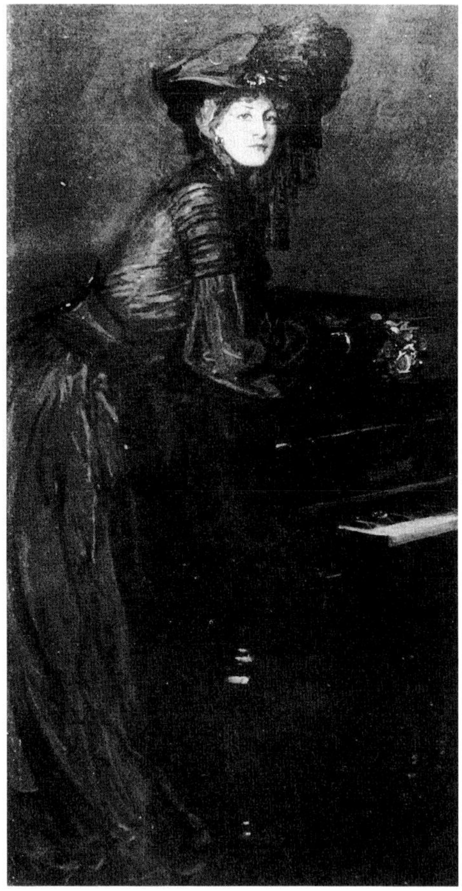

133 *Polyhymnia*, 1903, 72 × 36 (Galleria Nationale, Rome)

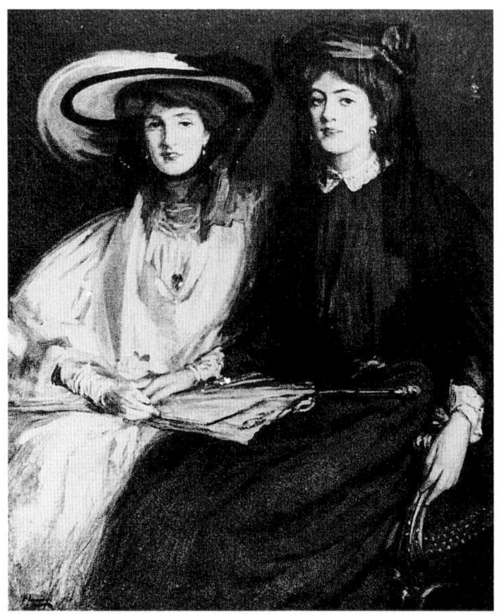

134 *The Ladies Nora and Evelyn Hely-Hutchinson*, 1904, 50 × 40 (private collection)

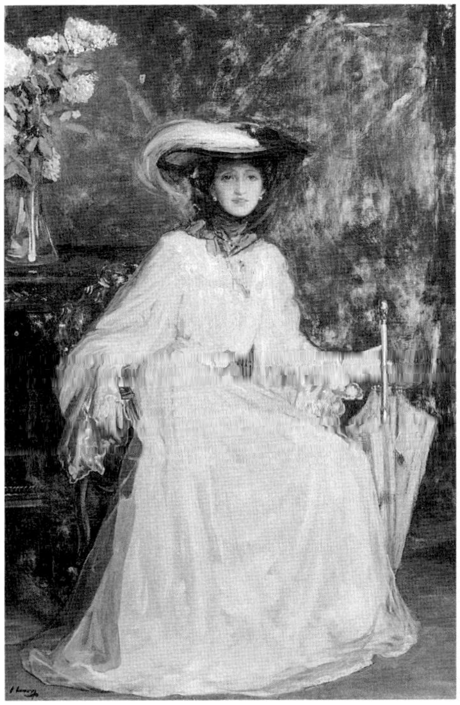

135 *Lady Evelyn Farquhar*, 1906, 71 × 47 (present whereabouts unknown, photo, Christie's)

While he worked over the whole canvas at each sitting he did not entirely repaint it. The fatal lowering of tone to which Sickert referred in his criticism of Whistler was a familiar danger which Lavery faced. Constant reworking also led to uneven drying and the consequent cracking and 'cupping' of paint surfaces, although this was less apparent the more he was drawn back to on-the-spot sketching.

Apart from the Donoughmore suite of portraits, Lavery's other important task in 1905 was to paint the Earl of Plymouth, Robert Windsor-Clive and his family at St Fagans Castle (Plate 136).[33] Whereas, the Hely-Hutchinson sisters were posed and painted at close quarters without much surrounding detail, the Windsor Clives were presented in a sketchy style, around the terrace tea-table. The work to some extent recreates the ambiance of other pictures of social gatherings such as *The Tennis Party* (Plate 45) and *Croquet* (Plate 63), however, its sketchiness more convincingly conveys a moment in time. The figures are mere indications rather than fully realised portraits. In this sense, Lavery appealed more directly to continental trends. It is likely also that the newly created earl, with his knowledge and appreciation of art, had requested an informal group, perhaps thinking of precedents in the work of Monet and Bazille.[34]

Discerning connoisseurs often knew precisely what they wanted in a portrait. Around this time, Mr Justice Darling, the notable collector, wrote to Lavery asking him to paint a small portrait of his daughter. In the letter he was quite specific about the effects he wished Lavery to achieve: 'What I should like would he an impression, or sketch—such as Vandyke (sic) and others some times made as preliminary to a portrait and I should like it small . . . I don't want a highly finished work but should prefer a study.'[35]

Judge Darling's taste was impeccable and be had done much to support young Scottish talent. His son Clive had been painted by William James Yule.[36] George Henry's dutiful portrait of him had been painted in 1898.[37] He was obviously aware of the current fashion for unfinished sketches and was anxious to acquire something that would be richly suggestive, rather than highly wrought. Accordingly, in 1906, a portrait, 14 × 12 inches, was delivered and the result must have been sufficiently satisfying for Sir Charles to request his own portrait as *The Black Cap*, an eerie picture of the death sentence being delivered. This was humorously dedicated by the artist to 'all Hanging Committees unfriendly to good work!'.[38] Despite the fact that he was described as a 'symphonist' and a painter of nocturnes, Lavery never employed these Whistlerian terms to entitle or describe his work. The great debt to Whistler remains evident in *The Green Sofa* (Plate 137), a picture in which colour and composition are most carefully controlled. The homage to Whistler's *Symphony in White No.3* is obvious, even though Carter felt that the 'cunning weft of blue and green and pale saffron' had been conceived with 'Dutch thoroughness.'[39] The inference was clearly that Lavery had successfully avoided slavish imitation of the currently fashionable pyrotechnics of Boldini and Sargent. Two salient examples of the restraining influence of past allegiances are *The Lady in Black, Mrs Trevor* (Plate 138) and *Mrs Vulliamy* (Plate 139), both of which display 'great freshness and spontaneity.'[40] In her portrait, Mrs Vulliamy adopted a pose frequently seen in full-lengths by Reynolds. She was painted directly upon an unprimed canvas, without revision,

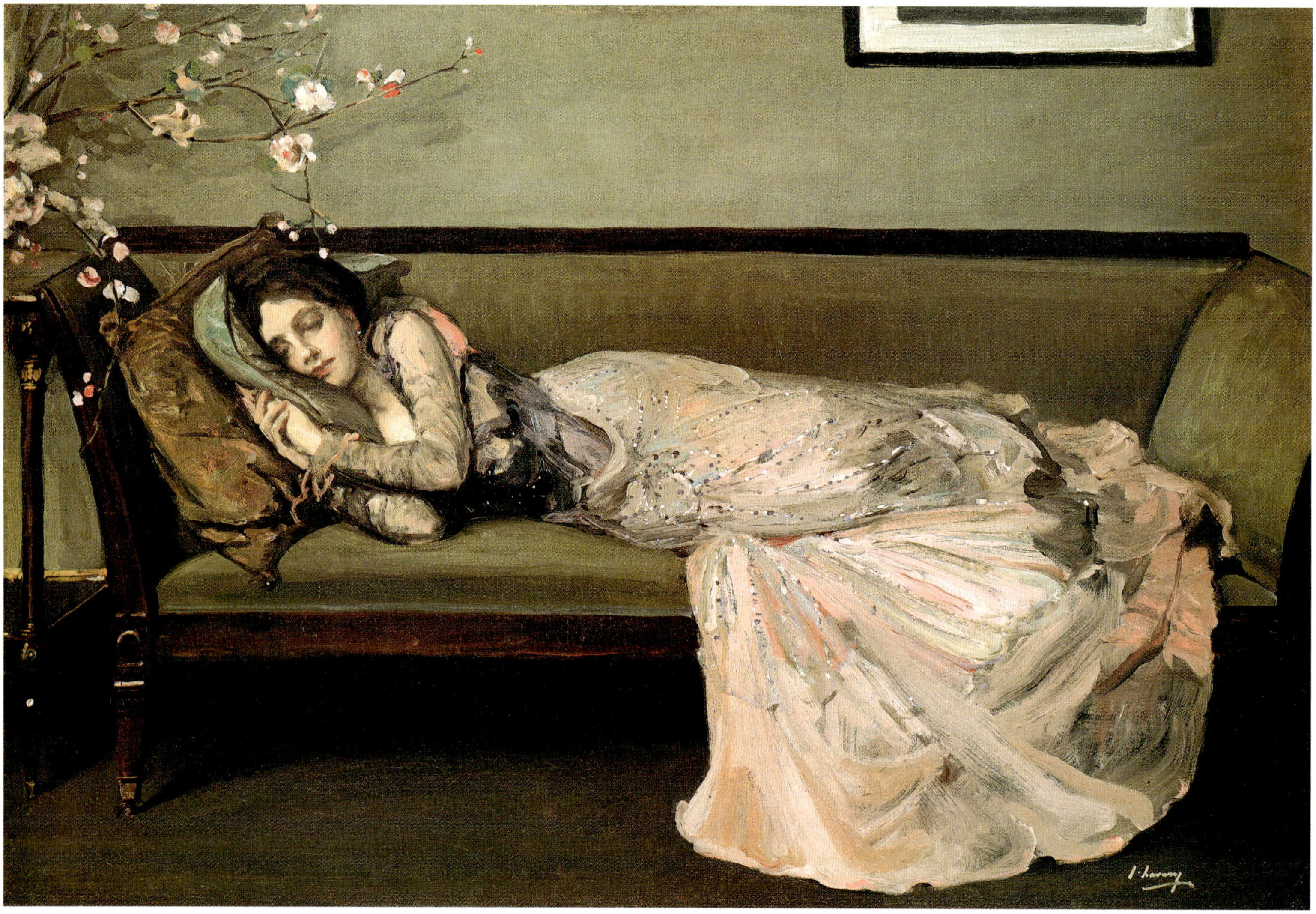

137 *The Green Sofa*, *c.*1904, 26 × 38 (private collection, photo, Hazlitt, Gooden and Fox, London)

and *alla prima*. It was an ultimate test of the painter's self-possession. Not only should he portray character, he should seize it instantaneously and interpret its reflection in contemporary costume and manners. This was not without its own problems as the artist himself admitted, '. . . the greatest difficulty the portrait painter has to deal with is dress . . . the artist who can so depict the fashion of its day that it shall be of his day, and yet for all time, and the picture be a thing of beauty, has solved the problem.'[41] Lavery continued to tackle these difficulties in the years up to and immediately after the Great War. His attitude to the problem was sharpened when in July 1909 he married a fashion-conscious woman.

The painting *Mrs Lavery and Alice (Mother and Child)* (Plate 140), represents the new family which the artist had acquired.[42] While it complements *Père et Fille* (see Plate 83), the picture echoes the format of the earlier *Mrs Lawrie and Edwin*. The dark and mysterious Hazel and the primly posed Alice, her hands sunk in a fur muff, stare out impassively at the spectator, and for the first time we see the features that were to haunt Lavery's work for the next twenty-five years. Hazel Lavery had already assumed the character of a *grande dame* when she was painted in

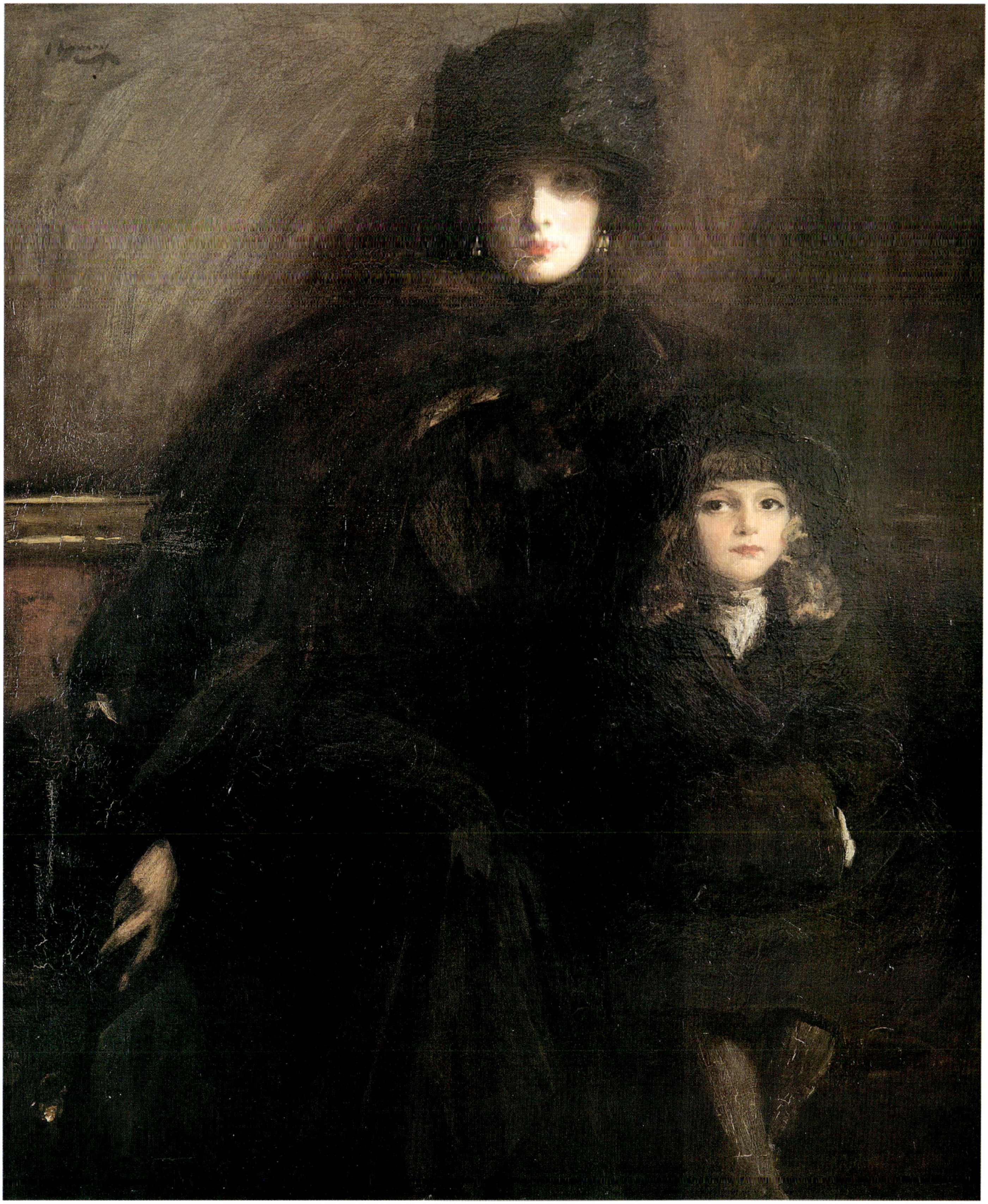

140 *Mrs Lavery and Alice (Mother and Child)*, *c.*1910, 50 × 40, (Hugh Lane Municipal Art Gallery, Dublin)

the majesterial *Silver Turban* (Plate 141) in 1911.[43] When it was exhibited there was great speculation on the identity of the sitter. Lavery's ability as a master of colour and tone struck new depths in the portrait. The heavy umbers of Hazel's fur-lined robe and the tonality of the background are lightened by a subtly conceived array of ochres, mauves and grey-blues which gave the effect of silver. Throughout the picture, the crumbly pigment, a product of considerable reworking, reaches almost Rembrandtesque intensity. For many years the painting hung prominently in the drawing-room at 5 Cromwell Place as clear proof of the maturity of Lavery's art.[44]

In the year following his marriage to Hazel, Lavery was honoured with a retrospective exhibition of fifty-three canvases at the Venice Biennale.[45] This was followed at the beginning of 1911 by his election to associateship of the Royal Academy.[46] The event was greeted as a 'sensation which exceeds even that of the Post-Impressionists', since Lavery had not exhibited at the academy since 1896. 'Admirable wisdom but somewhat belated' was the verdict of one paper.[47] It was clear in the height of the furore over Roger Fry's controversial exhibition 'Manet and the Post-Impressionists', that the beleaguered academy could not longer ignore the painter's European status. It needed his involvement in its exhibitions. As one journalist wryly commented, '. . . one might have thought that the lead of Paris, Berlin, Munich, Vienna, Madrid, Rome, Dublin, Philadelphia, Mannheim, Venice, Leipzig and New South Wales, not to mention the provincial capitals of England would before this have stirred the Burlington Bumpledom into paying this tribute to one of the greatest portrait painters of this or any other age.'[48]

At the same time, Lavery retained his loyalty to the International Society, exhibiting his more avant-garde compositions there. In the year of his election, for instance, the International received his large *Anna Pavlova as a Bacchante* (Plate 142).[49] The idea of painting the celebrated Russian dancer who was appearing in London for the first time in the summer of 1910, came from the editor of *The Illustrated London News*. A head and shoulders sketch was used by the paper as a full-page colour illustration to herald Pavlova's second season at The Palace Theatre in April 1911.[50] Lavery made a precondition of the commission that he be given 'a reasonable number of sittings and some kind of undertaking that appointments would be kept'.[51]

In the event, he need not have been so apprehensive. During her three months engagement, Pavlova came regularly to the studio and enacted the *Dance Bacchanal* in slow motion to assist the painter in obtaining the pose.[52] Lavery painted two full-length versions, endeavouring to capture the abandon of the dance and thus recreate the section from Pepita's ballet, *The Seasons*, which had caused a sensation on the first night of Pavlova's first London season. The artist took great pains to achieve the desired theatrical effect and saw the opportunity to portray synthetic lighting. He was clearly fired by the challenge of painting the likeness in a characteristic movement, rather than in facial features. Pavlova's head was thrown back and almost lost in a profusion of artificial pinks, greens and pale blues which were disassociated from the form. The effort, therefore, was not to freeze an instant within the dance, as in a photograph, but to convey its life and motion.

When it was exhibited at the International Society in 1911, *Anna Pavlova as a*

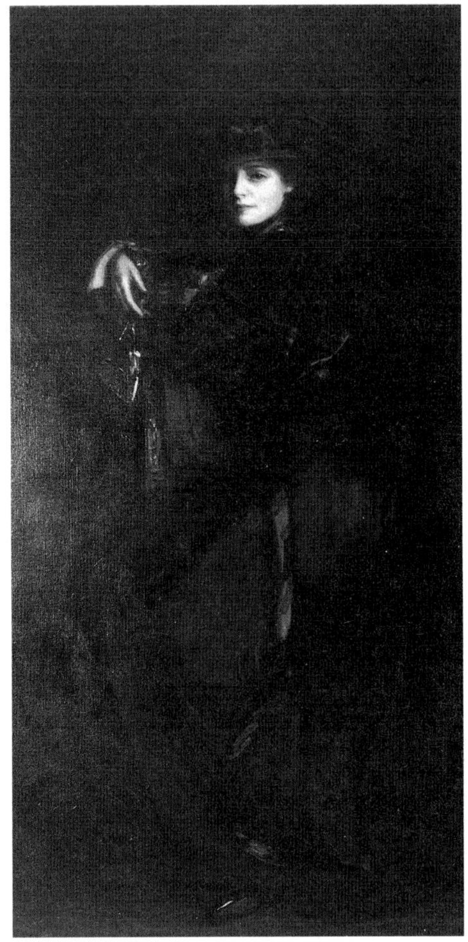

138 *The Lady in Black, Mrs Trevor*, 1909, 75 × 36 (The Ulster Museum, Belfast)

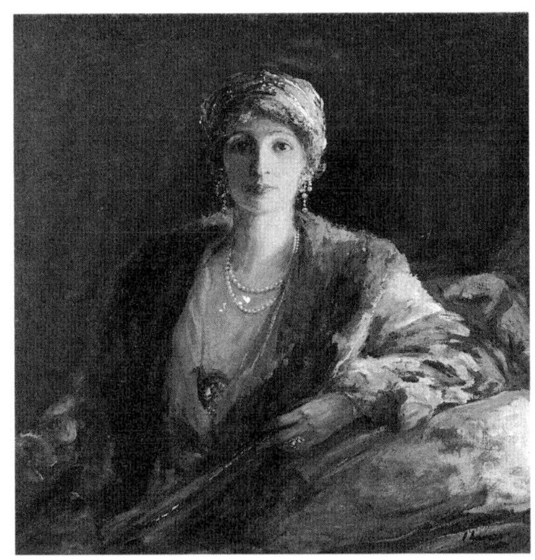

141 *The Silver Turban*, 1911, $33\frac{1}{2} \times 31\frac{1}{2}$ (The Fine Art Society)

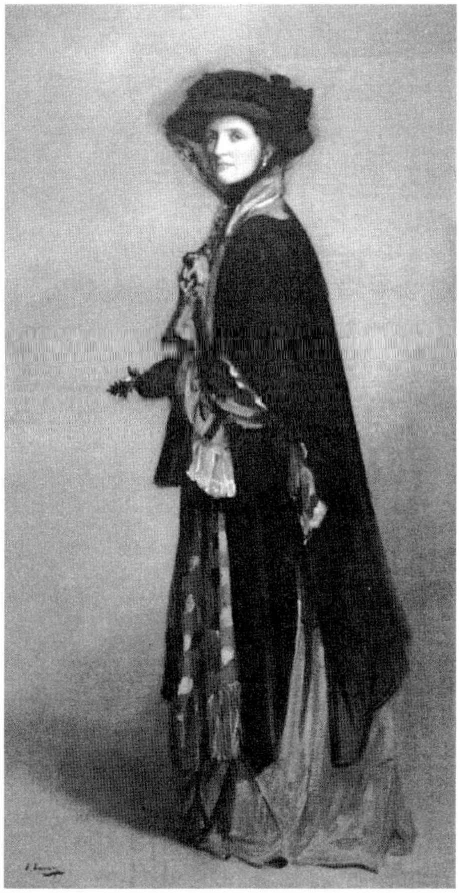

139 *Mrs Vulliamy*, 1905, 75 × 36 (Shipley Art Gallery, Gateshead)

Bacchante attracted as much virulent criticism as Fry's exhibition had done. *The Spectator*, for instance, saw it as 'an abrupt descent from the high level he often attains' and 'as uncompromising as a study by Degas'.[53] No one need contemplate the horror of Post-Impressionism when they could see Lavery's Pavlova. There were of course notable precedents for dancing figures apart from those of Degas. Lavery must have absorbed some of Rodin's obsession with figure movement and he might have seen Whistler and Toulouse Lautrec's depictions of the dancer Loie Fuller. Yet in the year of his election to the Royal Academy, far from conforming to the conventional stereotype, Lavery deliberately [illegible] the dancer's wild and untamed qualities. He attempted to convey the assault upon conventional sensibilities which her performances at the Palace Theatre had brought, and which, in turn, paved the way for the excesses of the Russian Ballet. He selected the *divertissement* from her programme for a second composition to be sent to the Royal Academy in 1912.[54] Perhaps because of the pressure of the dancer's bookings—she left London for a provincial tour in November 1911—*La Mort du Cygne* (Plate 144) was completed with sittings for the costume given by Hazel. Though he confessed that they were very different at close quarters, Lavery felt that Hazel, in stage makeup, could pass for the Russian dancer.[55] In addition, he used at least two head studies of Pavlova in the pose of the dying swan as *aides memoires*. While it excited less controversy than the earlier work, *La Mort du Cygne* received a lukewarm reception when it was shown in 1912. One critic declared that it was 'daring' and 'unbeautiful'.[56]

The following year, Lavery showed a more conventional full-length portrait of *Lady Gwendoline Spencer Churchill* at the Royal Academy.[57] This side-view figure, looking over her shoulder in the direction of the spectator is similar to the portrait of *Lady Young* 1898, which had been shown at the Exposition Universelle in Paris

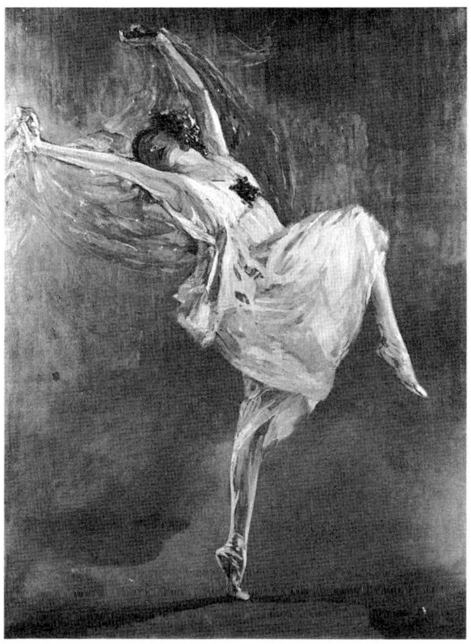

142 *Anna Pavlova as a Bacchante*, 1911, 78 × 57 (Glasgow Art Gallery and Museum)

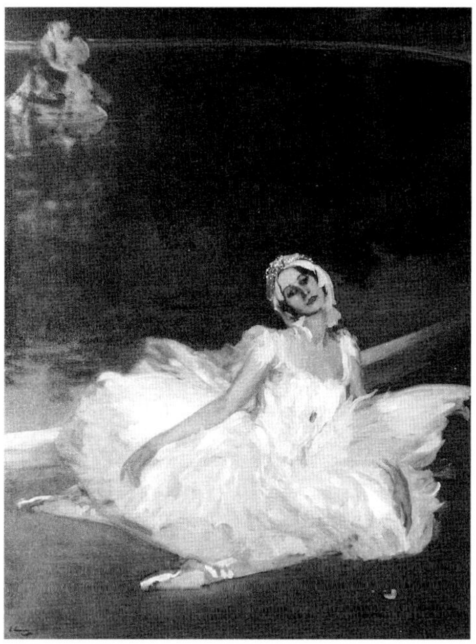

143 *La Mort du Cygne*, 1912, 78 × 57¾ (Tate Gallery, London)

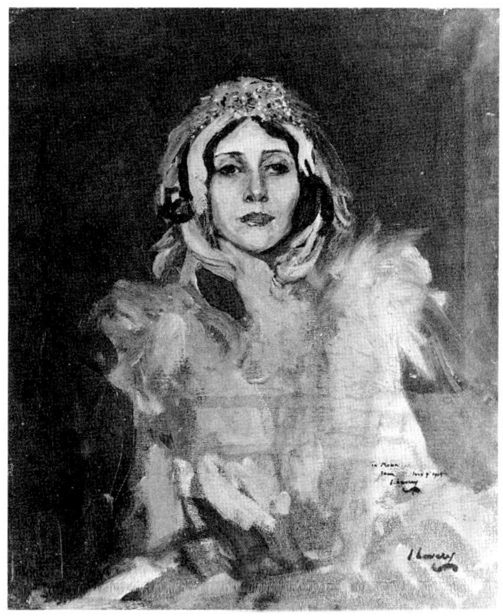

144 Study for *La Mort du Cygne*, *c.*1912, size unknown (present whereabouts unknown, photo, Sotheby's)

in 1900. In this instance however, the blackground, which originally contained a gilt Queen Anne chair, remained problematic and the picture was cut down to a three-quarter length and substantially reworked.[58] These difficulties were not encountered in the portrait of *Lady Diana Manners* which was executed in a single sitting in 1913. Stodart Walker was moved to use the term 'miraculous' in front of this canvas.[59]

The directness of these studies prepared Lavery to face thc challenge of *The Artist's Studio* (Plate 145).[60] This huge homage to Velasquez was begun around 1910. As originally conceived, it showed the artist, standing brush in hand, on the left, in exactly the position occupied by Velasquez in *Las Meninas*. After being exhibited in Rome, the picture was extensively reworked removing three supplementary figures, consigning the artist to a background mirror reflection

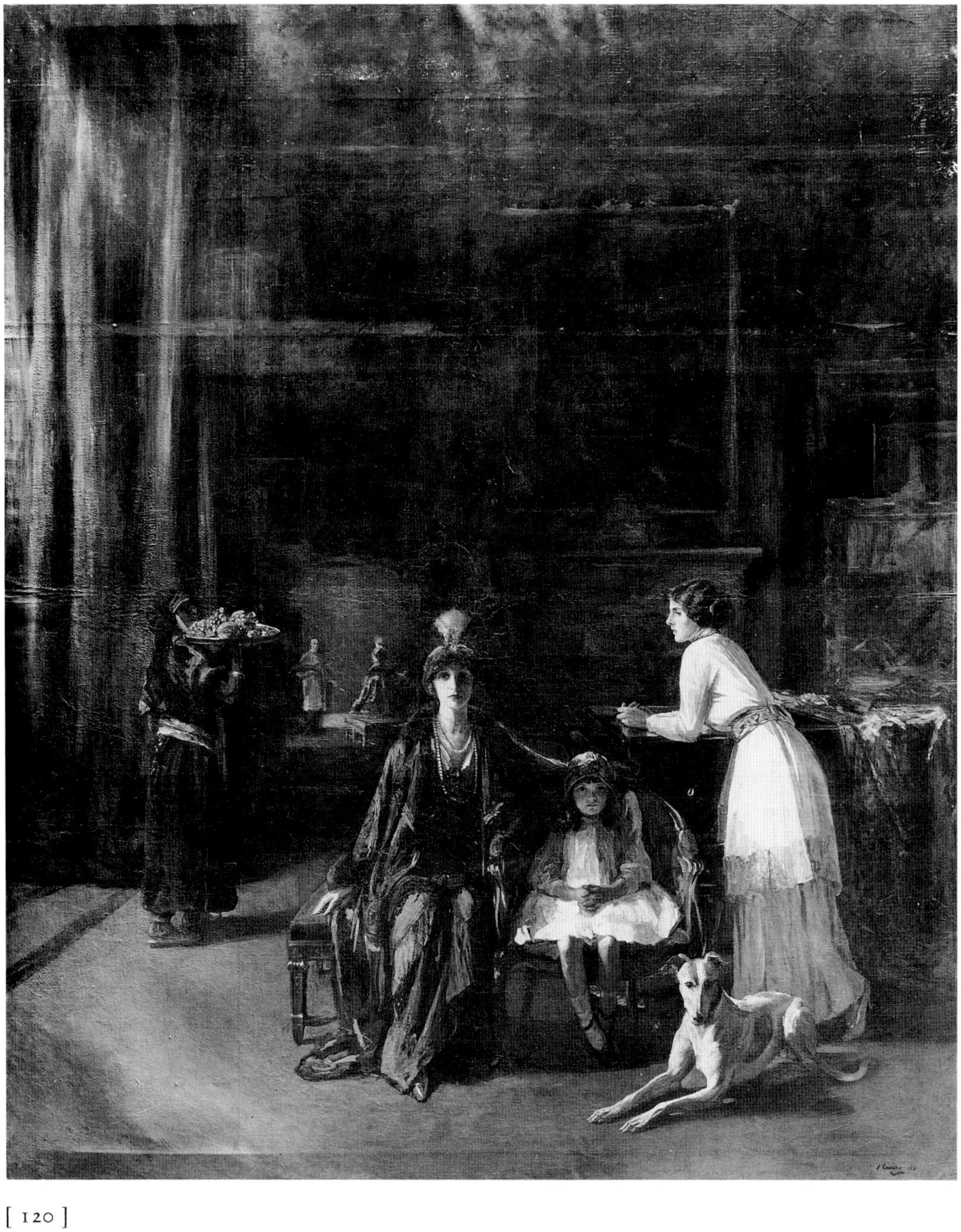

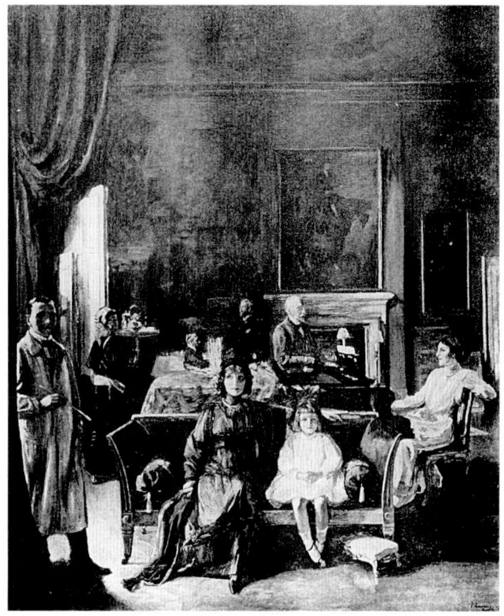

145 *The Artist's Studio*, *c.*1910 (photo, the author)

147 *The Artist's Studio*, 1910–11, $135\frac{1}{4} \times 107\frac{1}{8}$ (National Gallery of Ireland, Dublin)

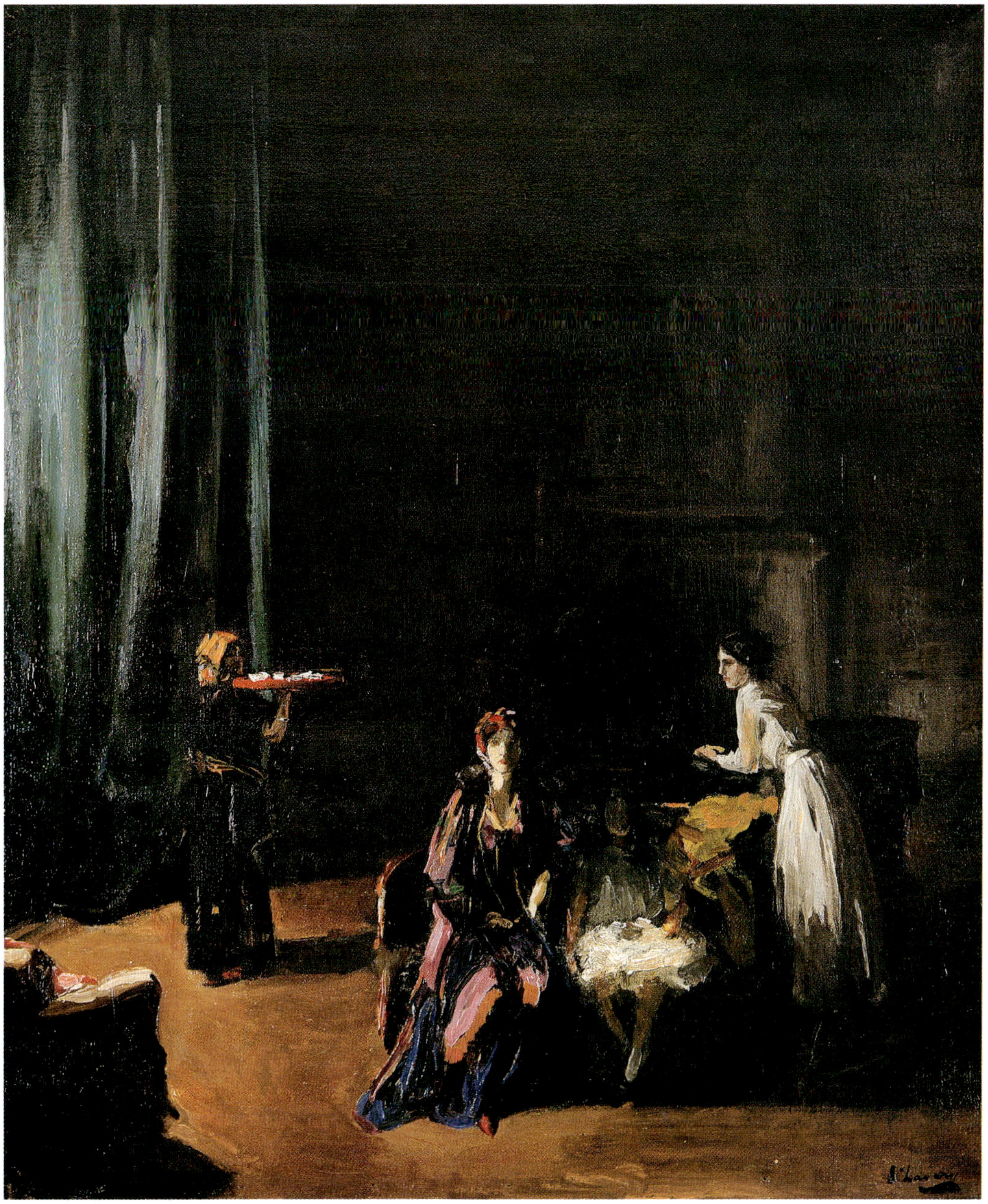

146 *The Studio*, 1911, 30 × 25 (private collection)

and repositioning the artist's daughter Eileen.[61] To establish the new grouping firmly in his mind, Lavery painted a small oil sketch in which the essential motif of his wife and stepdaughter, similar to *Mrs Lavery and Alice* (see Plate 140) was repeated, but this time framed by Eileen on one side and the Moroccan maid, Aida, on the other (see Plates 146 and 147). The final significant addition which brings Velasquez back into the forefront of the spectator's mind is the insertion of the mastiff named Rodney Stone, after the popular Conan Doyle hero. The shadowy background shows the familiar Cromwell Place setting. Above the mantelpiece hangs *Idonia in Morocco* and to the right, upon an easel, is the bust of Queen Mary, revealing that another important commission was in progress.

In 1912, Lavery was approached by the publisher, Hugh Spottiswoode with a commission to paint the royal family for a fee of £2000.[62] This was potentially an even more daunting task. After he had completed *The King, The Queen, The Prince of Wales and The Princess Mary, Buckingham Palace, 1913* (Plate 148), the painter would have the right to exhibit it before it was presented to the nation. Consonant with previous practice, the painter married separate head studies to the setting. These were executed at Lavery's studio during February and March 1913 (see Plates 151 and 152). On one of these occasions, the king asked to be introduced to the artist's wife and stepdaughter. Alice apparently told the king that she attended the same dancing master as the princess royal. This was a childish fabrication, and she later confessed that she had wished to make conversation to put the king at his ease![63] With these studies and a number of sketches of the White Drawing Room at Buckingham Palace, Lavery produced two oil sketches of the figure groupings for the queen's approval (see Plates 149 and 150).[64]

Then the large canvas was commenced. It was completed in time for the Royal Academy of 1913 and was regarded by *The Times* as 'a considerable success', notwithstanding 'the immense difficulties of the task'.[65] Stodart Walker greatly approved of its 'subtle blending of colour in the atmosphere'.[66] What was perhaps more satisfying for the painter was that the king and queen, when they visited Cromwell Place to view the picture, also approved of it. With pride, Lavery recounted, 'They were so pleased that the King said he would like to have a hand in it and thinking that royal blue might be an appropriate colour, I mixed it on the palette, and taking a brush he applied it to the Garter ribbon—the Queen, not to be outdone, following his example. It is recorded that when Velasquez completed *Las Meninas*, King Philip asked for a brush and colour and painted the Red Cross of the Knights of Calatrava on the breast of the painter in the picture.'[67]

Alas, there was no self-portrait ingeniously incorporated into the royal group to be so decorated. However, Lavery's own *Las Meninas*, was undergoing radical overhaul in the same studio amd must have been seen by the king and queen. Painting these large airy interiors simultaneously can only have been mutually beneficial for both canvases. With some confidence, Lavery could move principal figures around in order to establish satisfactory relationships. Thus the Prince of Wales was moved from the extreme right of the *Second Study* into a more central position in the main picture, just as the figure of Eileen had been repositioned in *The Artist's Studio*.[68]

The famous Velasquez of the Prado inspired both pictures as it had influenced Lavery's predecessors, Courbet and Whistler. Lavery's *Studio* has none of the bombastic egotism of Courbet's *l'Atelier du Peintre*. It was not painted to demonstrate command of critical and intellectual opinion. It did not contain a secret programme of social regeneration. These ideas of the realist had been recast by Whistler in terms of an aesthetic elitism in which Lavery acquiesced. Significantly, Whistler never realised his ambition to paint a large studio interior. Lavery approached him shortly before his death with a view to obtaining a painting for the proposed Gallery of Modern Art, Dublin. Within months of Whistler's death, Hugh Lane acquired one of the two versions of Whistler's *The Artist's Studio*, for the new Dublin Gallery. If he did not actually advise upon its acquisition, Lavery must have been very familiar with this painting and could only have approved of the choice.[69]

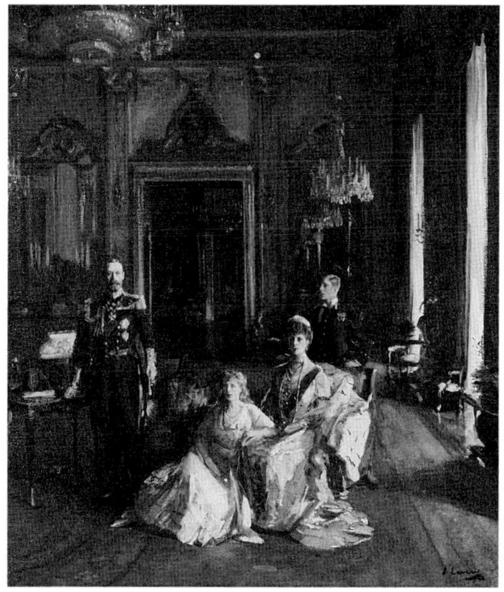

149 First study for *The King, The Queen, The Prince of Wales, The Princess Mary, Buckingham Palace, 1913*, 30 × 25 (reproduced by gracious permission of Her Majesty The Queen)

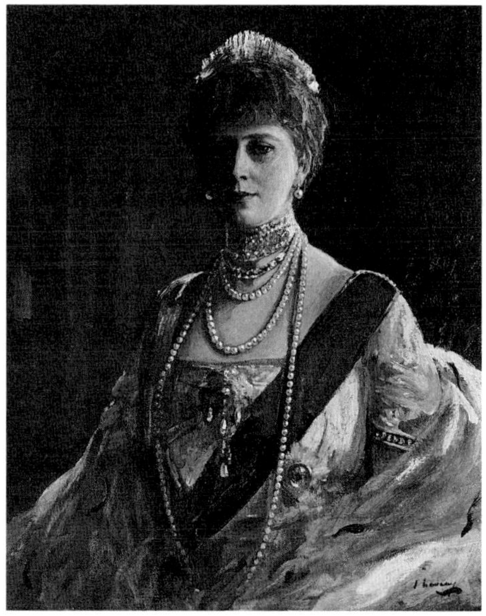

151 *Queen Mary*, 1913, 34 × 27 (reproduced by gracious permission of Her Majesty The Queen)

148 *The King, The Queen, The Prince of Wales, The Princess Mary, Buckingham Palace, 1913*, 134 × 107 (National Portrait Gallery, London)

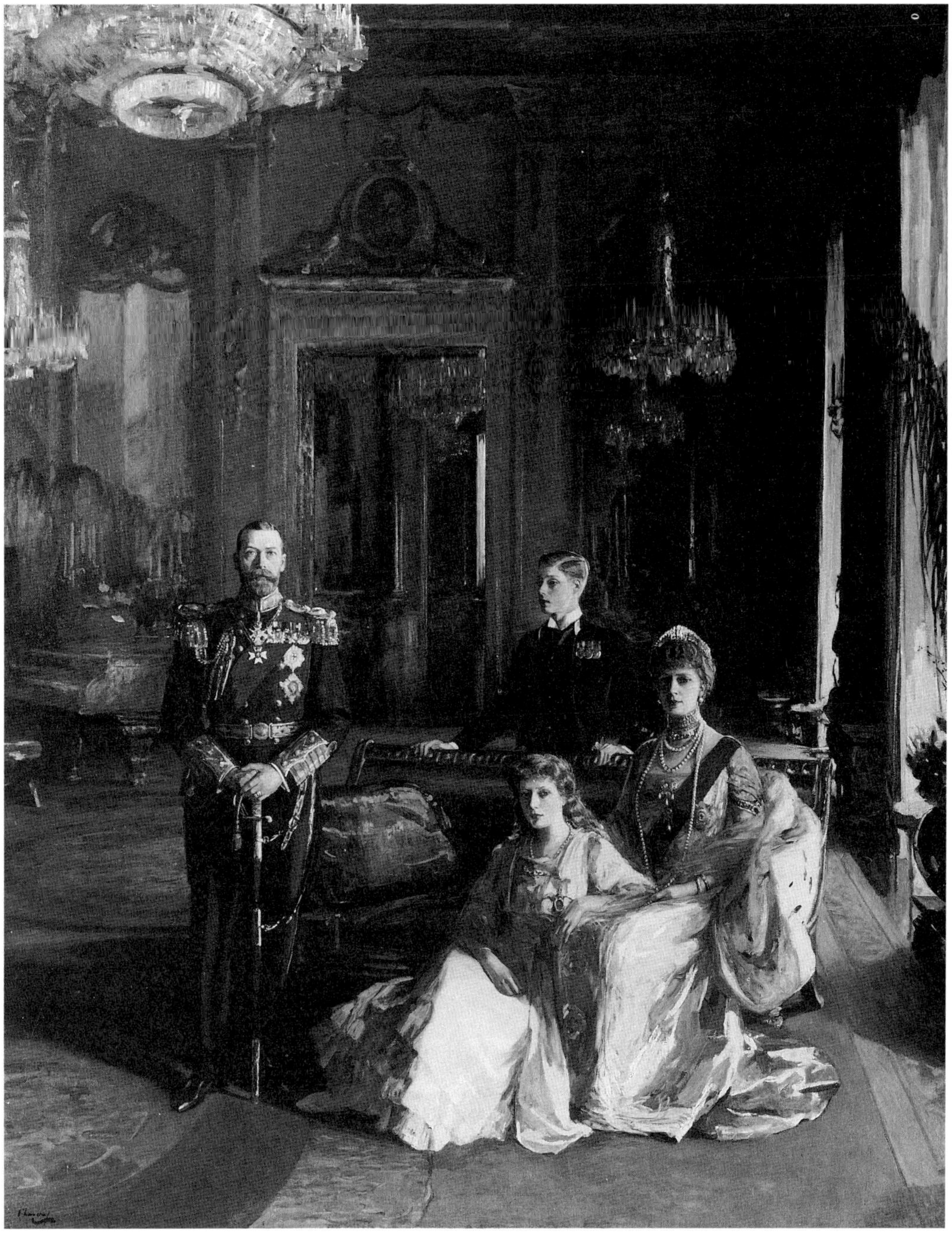

Whistler's picture, however, contains none of the dramatic chiaroscuro of Lavery's. Using the light from side windows, screened from the rest of the room by a heavy curtain, the artist isolates his foreground 'maids of honour'—the members of his immediate household. Only the mirror placed in the far corner articulates the darkened studio. Above the figures, the air contains the gloomy rectangles of favourite canvases, dimly perceived. The figures themselves assume positions already familiar from earlier works. The picture does, therefore, recount, as much as Courbet's, the painter's sentimental education. After it was shown at the Royal Academy in 1914, at the Royal Scottish Academy in 1916 and

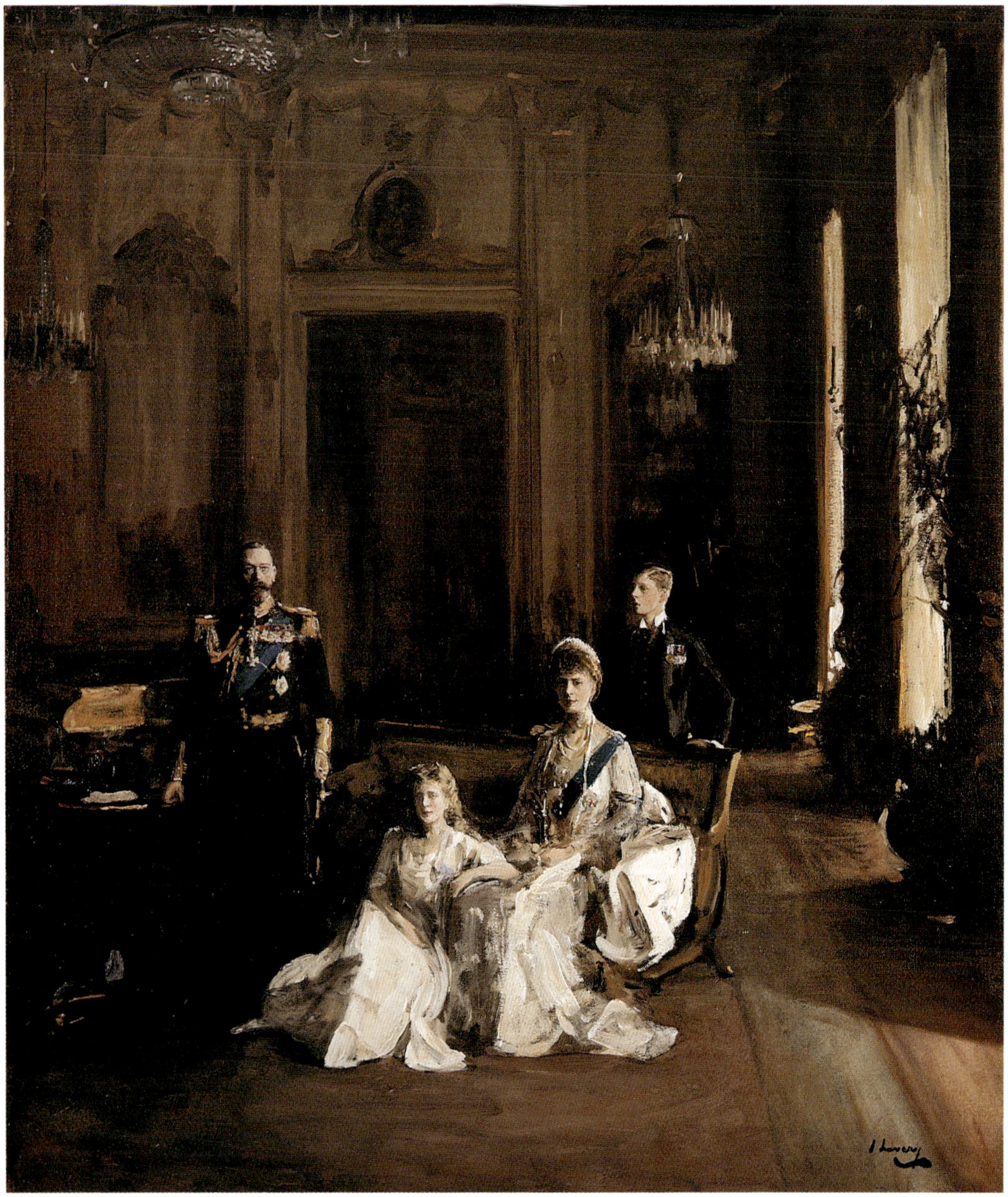

150 Second study for *The King, The Queen, The Prince of Wales, The Princess Mary, Buckingham Palace, 1913*, 30 × 25 (Ulster Museum, Belfast)

the Royal Glasgow Institute of Fine Arts in 1918, it was installed in the great library at Dunecht, the Aberdeenshire home of its purchaser Lord Cowdray.[70]

At the time of its first exhibition, Lavery staged an important retrospective of 150 pictures at the Grosvenor Gallery.[71] In turning to this painter, who had been the subject of a biography,[72] and 'numberless criticisms and appreciations'—Stodart Walker contented himself by arriving at the inexpressible individuality of Lavery's art—'a Lavery portrait is a Lavery'.[73] *The Times* reiterated Camille Mauclair in 1905 by dubbing him simply a 'painter of women'.[74]

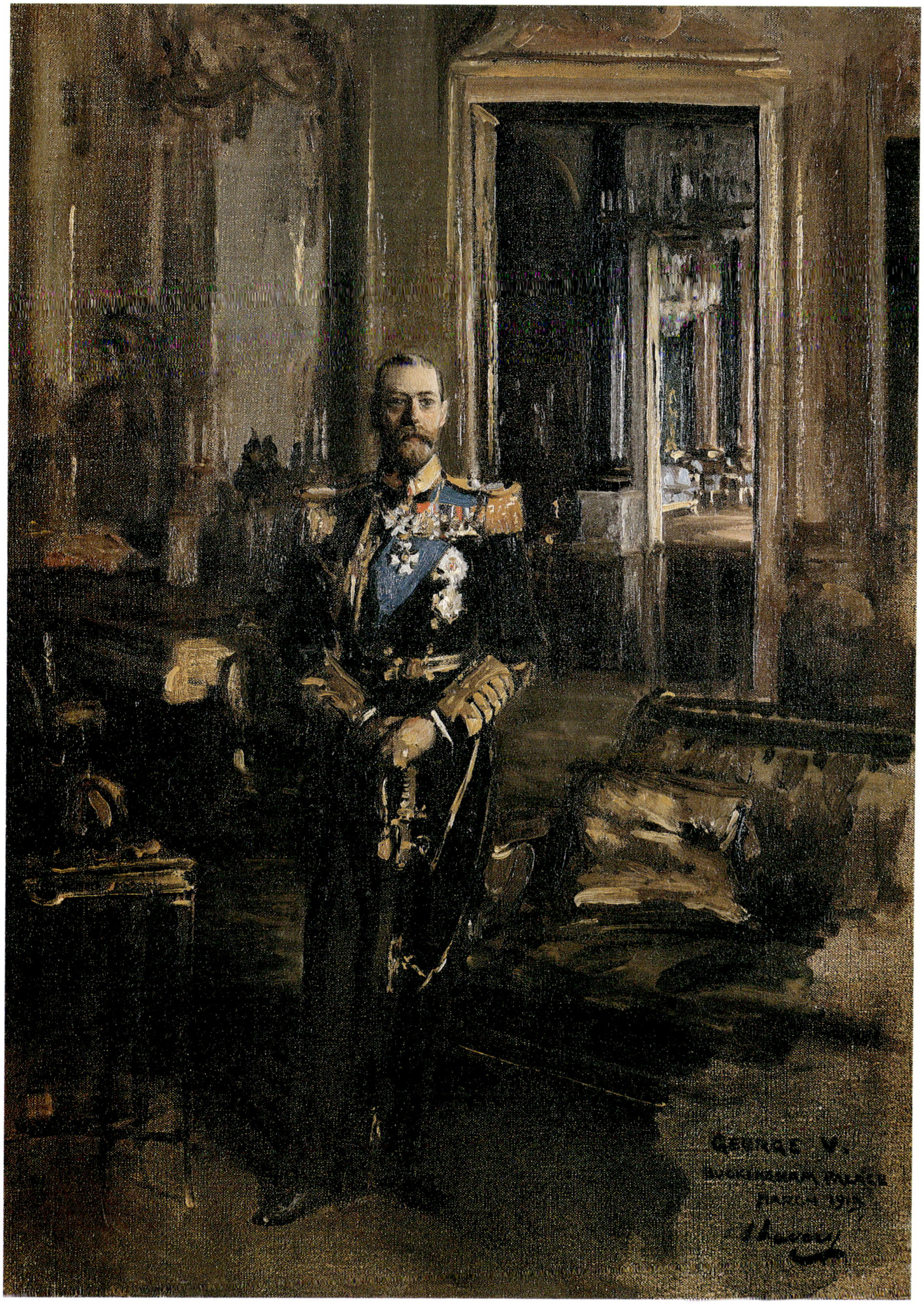

152 *George V, Buckingham Palace, March 1913*, 30 × 21 (private collection, photo, courtesy Pyms Gallery, London)

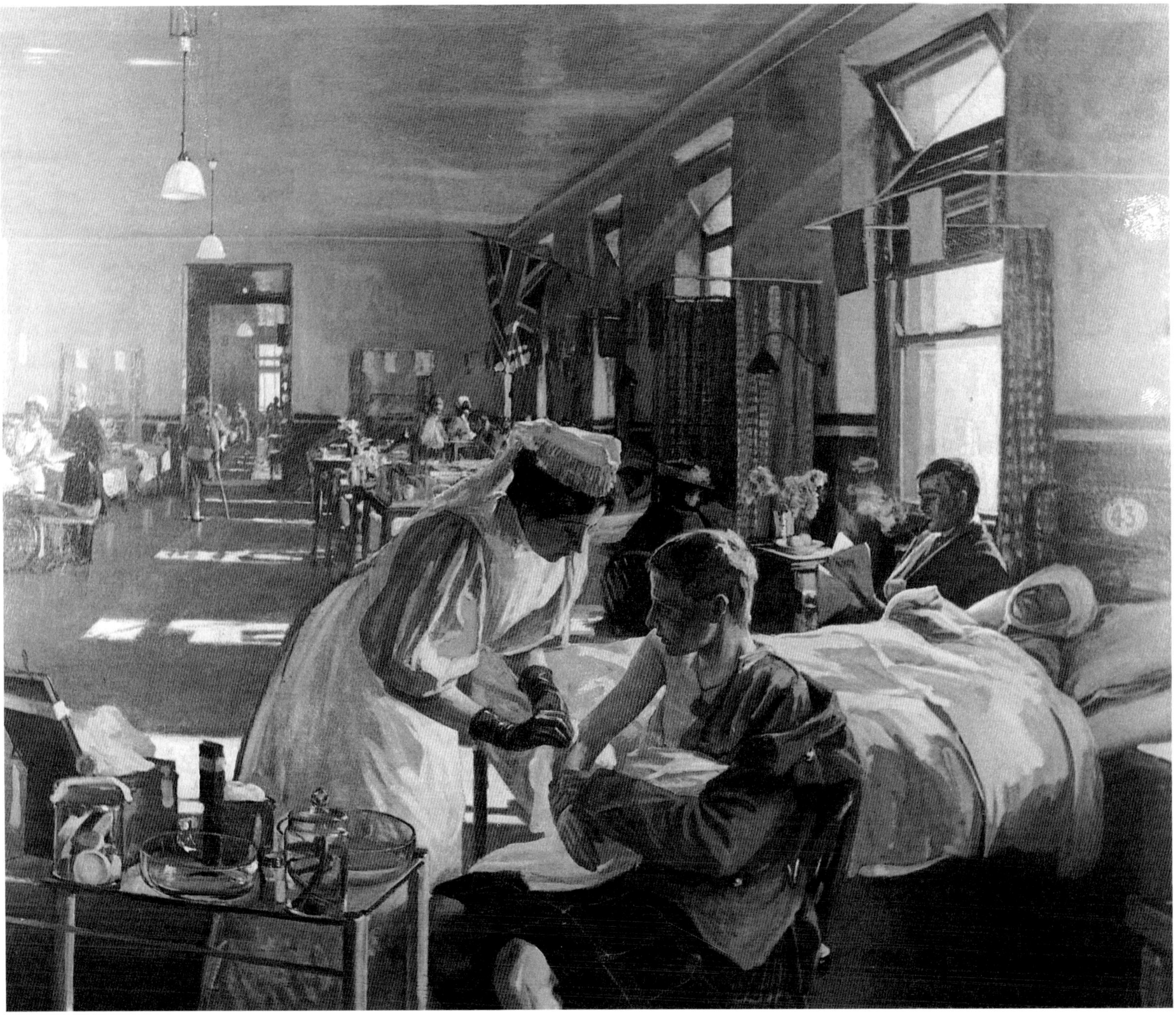

155 *The First Wounded at London Hospital*, August 1914, 69⅛ × 79 (Dundee Museums and Galleries)

8 The War Years

Lavery's keen visual curiosity drew him into recording the preparations for war. Although he readily admitted that its most horrific scenes were kept from him, his art was not hermetic and its spontaneous methods were well suited to portraying the visual pageant. His work therefore provides a unique record of war manufacture, of departures and returns and of caring for the wounded. As an official war artist, attached to the navy, he saw the war at sea, at first-hand. He also witnessed war in the air as one of the first painters to work from an airship. He did not experience the carnage of the trenches, or the monstrous suffering in overcrowded field hospitals. However, he did understand his role in the scheme of things and where visual beauty appeared, as in the departure of the fleet from Scapa Flow or in the kite balloons at Roehampton, or the cemetery at Etaples, his eye and hand responded with memorable results. As an established and well connected society painter, he was given a great deal of latitude. His life and commissions went on and the energetic activities of Hazel Lavery involved him in charity work. Society was reluctant to shed its frivolity and faddishness in the face of grim reality.

At first, therefore, the Edwardian summer was reluctant to end, and it continued on into the first years of the Great War. *The Thames at Maidenhead* (Plate 153), if the artist's dating is to be accepted, is an extraordinary celebration of the hedonism of the age.[1] A reworking of one of his earliest Grez motifs, it brilliantly contrasts the firey orange parasol with the blue-greys and dark greens of the river and its reflections, achieving a Japanese simplicity of composition. In the Twenties, Lavery returned to Maidenhead to paint busy scenes of the regatta, whilst in this view of the river, calmness and serenity reign supreme. The occupants of the punt remain unidentified, although the female figure remarkably resembles Hazel. A newspaper photograph published in connection with the Lavery exhibition of 1921 shows her looking on with extraordinary interest while the painter applies a final coat of varnish. Significant changes have occurred between the charming study for the picture and the finished version.[2]

The picture was the prototype of another large river scene, depicting Elizabeth Asquith and Lady Violet Bonham Carter, which was executed in the summer of 1917 and which, after several changes of title, became known as *Sutton Courtenay* (Plate 154).[3] This delightful idyll, painted at the height of the Great War, when the first London air raids were taking place, turns its back upon the reports of carnage. It also rejects the upheavals of contemporary art. It and its predecessor coincide respectively with the beginning and the end of the furore of Vorticism and they reveal none of the contemporary debate about abstraction which animated young painters. Lavery constantly sought stimulus for new beauties of design in the world around him, and in these Thames paintings, he produced a lush synthesis which combined ingredients of Impressionism with an open celebration of mental

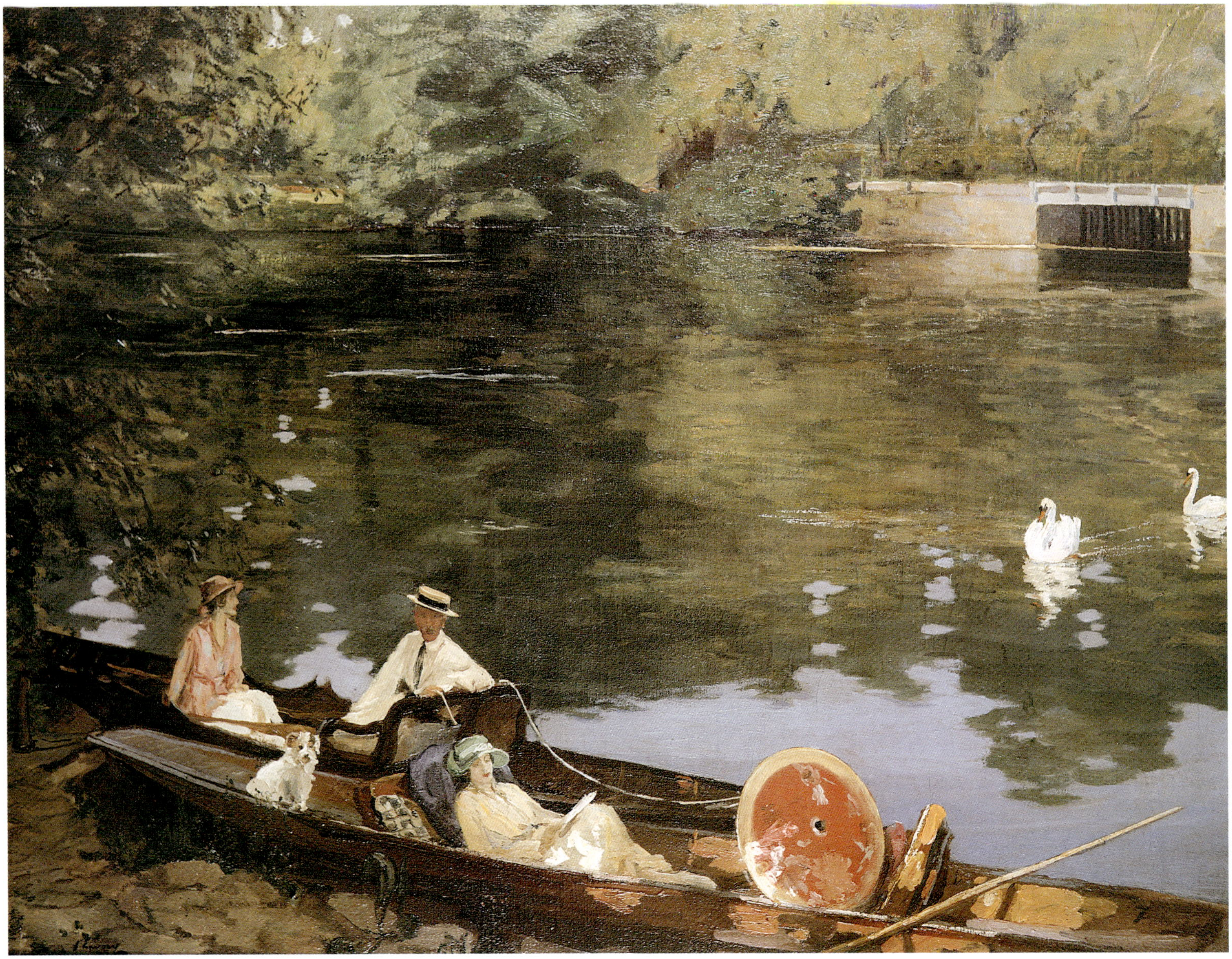

154 *Sutton Courtenay*, 1917, 40 × 50 (Hugh Lane Municipal Art Gallery, Dublin)

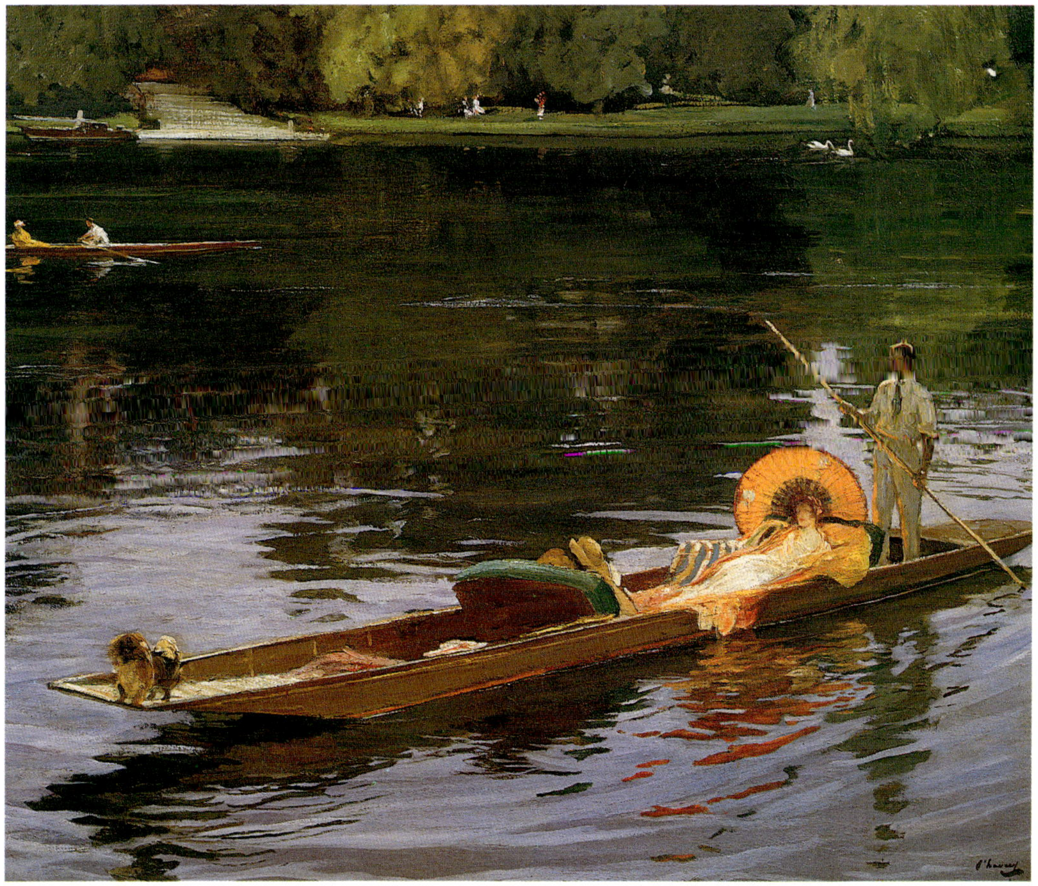

153 *The Thames at Maidenhead*, *c*.1913, 40 × 50 (private collection, photo, Whitford and Hughes, London)

and physical luxury. These pictures were Lavery's *Cythera*, his eighteenth-century lotus land of light, calm and voluptuousness. Despite the fact that he so willingly gave himself to depicting these pleasures, Lavery did not shy away from the war. He and Hazel were in Dublin on 4 August 1914, about to commence a two-week motor touring holiday. Later that day, in county Wicklow, he found himself on the fringes of a roadside meeting in which a young man was eloquently exhorting his listeners to fight, although it was unclear whether the enemy was England or Germany. The rest of the holiday passed without mention of the war, save for a heated discussion in Portrush when the names of British politicans, like Churchill and Asquith were linked to suitable uncomplimentary adjectives. The Laverys returned to find London 'in an uproar'.[4] The intrepid painter records that St James's Park and Green Park were quickly transformed into an army camp and his sketch of the scene, with Hazel and Alice on the side, observing the action, was one of the first images of war preparation.[5] At the same time, Lavery was on hand to portray the arrival of the first wounded at London Hospital (see Plate 155). In this instance, at least three sketches were produced as preparatory works. In two of these, a nurse is seen attending a wounded soldier,[6] who, by the time the large version was started had become a Highlander. In this instance, the artist was commended for his willingness to face up to stark reality. As he walked around Burlington House, in May 1915, the reviewer of *The Studio* felt that he could indict the Academicians for their ostrich-like insularity. 'Certainly there is no hint given by the show,' he declared, 'that this country is going through an experience almost without precedent in its history, and is engaged in what is actually a struggle for existence.'[7] Lavery was therefore a notable exception whose painting was to be commended as 'the most remarkable achievement in the exhibition.'[8] Though he felt the ambiguity of his position as a Belfast-born painter who had been honoured with important commissions in Germany, Lavery attached himself to the Artists Rifles, a company described as 'a scrubby lot of painters, sculptors, actors, musicians, hairdressers, scene shifters, etc., of all ages'.[9] He was at first contacted by a song writer named Raymond Rose and invited to Earls Court where drilling sessions were planned. Lavery arrived late and stood in the bemused and incredulous crowd. So irregular were the volunteers that a woman standing beside him thought that they must be German prisoners. He did not, however, last long with this motley crew and after the second or third route march, took the advice of his doctor, that he would do more for his country with his brush than with his rifle![10] In May 1915, he reported to Cunninghame Graham that he had had 'to fall out. The doctor won't pass me so I shall have to content myself by weilding the brush.'[11] At this early stage, Lavery had the impractical idea of loading his painting gear into a motor van and driving to the Western Front and 'if possible make records first hand'. However, he was forced to confide to his old friend, '. . . Hazel is agin it. She is in terror of the zeppelin and feels that if there is to be any masking up in the family it ought to be on a comprehensive scale, that is to say we ought all to be at home at the time.'[12]

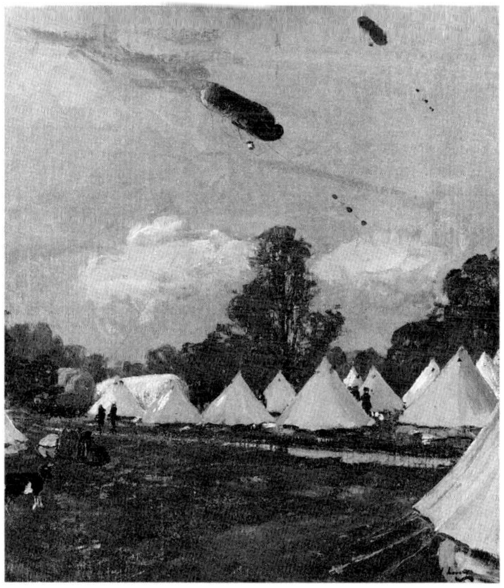

157 *Kite Balloons, Roehampton*, 1915, 30 × 25 (Imperial War Museum, London)

Hazel Lavery's apprehensiveness became in itself the subject for a painting (Plate 156). On 7 July 1917, twenty-one German Gotha biplanes attempted the second aerial bombing raid on London. Their engagement with aircraft of the Royal Naval Air Service and the Royal Air Force was clearly visible from the studio window at Cromwell Place and the attack was repulsed. Hazel Lavery in the resulting canvas was shown in back view, kneeling before a statuette of the Madonna as the battle raged in the skies above. Elsewhere, the room was cluttered with tubs of brushes and bottles of turpentine. Before he donated the painting to Belfast in 1929, Lavery painted out the statuette and with it, all reference to his wife's fretfulness.[13]

Nevertheless the picture remains one of his most arresting interiors. Only at a second glance, does the spectator realise the full importance of the battle raging beyond the security of the studio. Back in 1915 however, Hazel's fears were unfounded. Her life was threatened by a more random occurrence than any connected with the war. In July of that year, she and her husband were involved in a taxi crash in Park Lane and she was taken, unconscious, to St George's Hospital.[14] Lavery records that the after-effects of this collision, resulting in what must have been some sort of nervous breakdown, confined him to base for almost a year.[15] He suffered only delayed shock in the form of temporary amnesia and insomnia. But he was told by his doctor that if he persisted in his desire to get to the Front at all costs, he would only hasten his wife's death.[16]

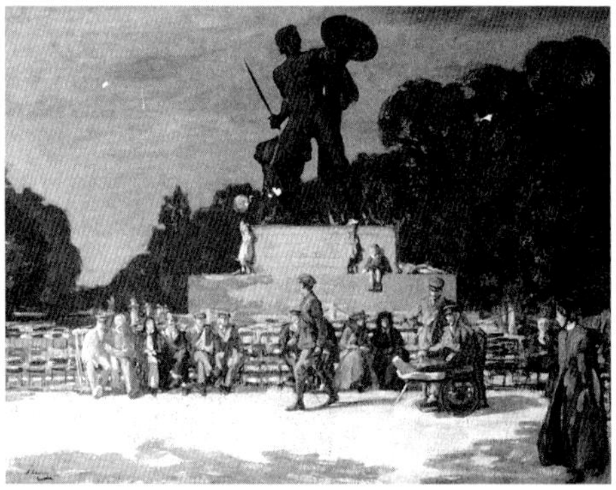

158 *The Heel of Achilles, Hyde Park*, 1916, 40 × 50 (private collection)

During 1915 and 1916, therefore, the artist made occasional visits to military camps in the London area. *Kite Balloons, Roehampton* (Plate 157) is one of the products of these foraging expeditions,[17] and is at the same time one of the first

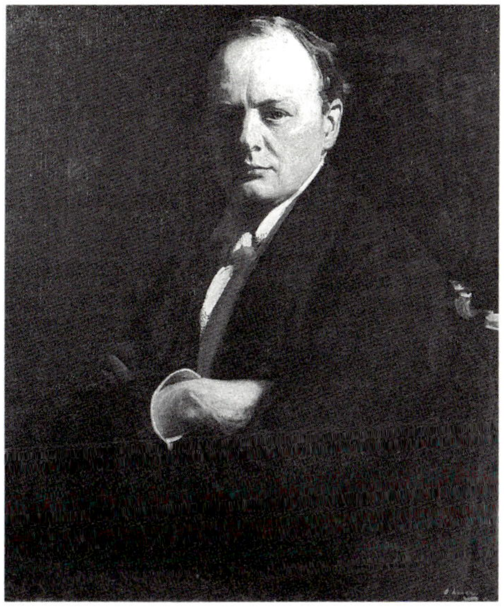

159 *The Rt Hon. Winston S. Churchill, OM, MP*, 1915. 30 × 25 (Hugh Lane Municipal Art Gallery, Dublin)

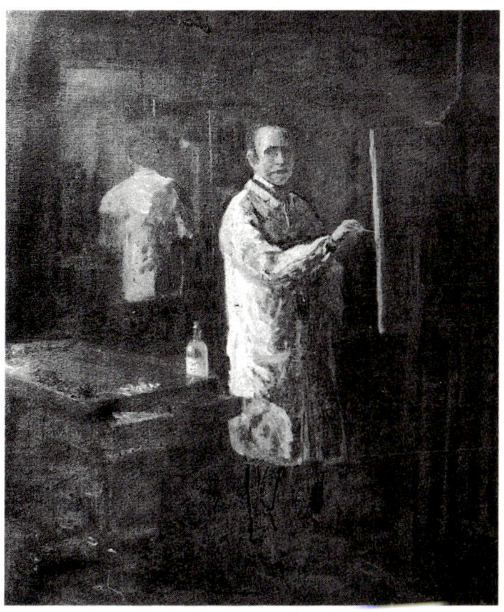

160 Winston S. Churchill, *Lavery Painting*, c.1915, size unknown (private collection, photo, Ian Kilpatrick)

representations of the dangerous activities associated with the observer corps. In 1916, Lavery attended the naval review at Crystal Palace, Sydenham, and executed several canvases.[18] These are unique records, not just of the display, but of the large exhibition structure, which itself had been commissioned in the service of war. Finally in 1916, Lavery painted a large canvas of the war wounded resting in the sun, under the large statue of Achilles at Hyde Park Corner.[19] Implicit in what came to be known as *The Heel of Achilles, Hyde Park* (Plate 158) was a latent symbolism. A snap-shot of the artist working upon a smaller version of the subject, shows him surrounded by onlookers, amongst whom are some of the wounded represented in the picture.[20]

Through these works, Lavery established an easy familiarity with military life and being well connected in aristocratic circles, he was able to make his way through some of the security screens which the war created. In 1915, he had one important pupil in Winston Spencer Churchill (see Plate 159). Having painted a full-length portrait of *Lady Gwendoline Spencer Churchill* for the Royal Academy exhibition of 1913, Lavery was already familiar with the Churchills. Winston, as First Lord of the Admiralty from 1911 to 1914, came to live around the corner from the Laverys, at 41 Cromwell Road. He and his wife Clementine, became regular visitors at the studio.[21] Finding himself out of office and therefore with time to spare, Churchill posed for no less than four portraits, while his wife and daughter sat for at least one.[22] It was probably as a result of seeing Lavery at work, that Churchill's own artistic impulses were stimulated (see Plate 160). In July 1915, the Laverys visited him at Hoe Farm in Sussex and both advised him on his new pastime.[23] While attending the studio in the month of May, Churchill had painted Lavery's portrait in a singular 'sitter's eye view' of the artist. No other painting reveals the working procedure of the fashionable portrait painter so clearly. Beside him stands the table-palette, a substantial purpose-built piece of furniture that in addition to providing a mixing surface, had drawers and compartments for spare tubes and brushes. This was apparently Lavery's own invention and was something that he was proud of.[24] Behind him, positioned on another easel, is a large mirror, placed so as to reveal the progress of his or her image to the sitter, and in the centre of Churchill's picture, stands the artist himself, clad in his white painting coat, with brush in hand. He stares out attentively at the spectator. This was the Lavery revealed to society women who provided portrait commissions during the Great War. One of these was Lady Victoria Primrose, the youngest daughter of the great racing patron, the Earl of Derby, who had invited the Laverys to Newmarket in 1913.[25] Others included the Dowager Lady Smiley, Miss Elizabeth Asquith, The Hon. Mrs Morrison-Bell and Mrs Walter Samuel.[26]

However, Lavery's most popular model during the Great War was undoubtedly his wife, Hazel. Despite the fact that she was nervous and apprehensive throughout the winter following the collison in Park Lane, Lavery executed the splendid, *Hazel in Black and Gold*.[27] As with all the major portraits, a sketch (Plate 161) preceded the full-length version and this established the main lines of the composition, playing up the strong light on the right edge of the stoll, the sashes and the shako.[28] The finished version (Plate 162) became the subject of extensive

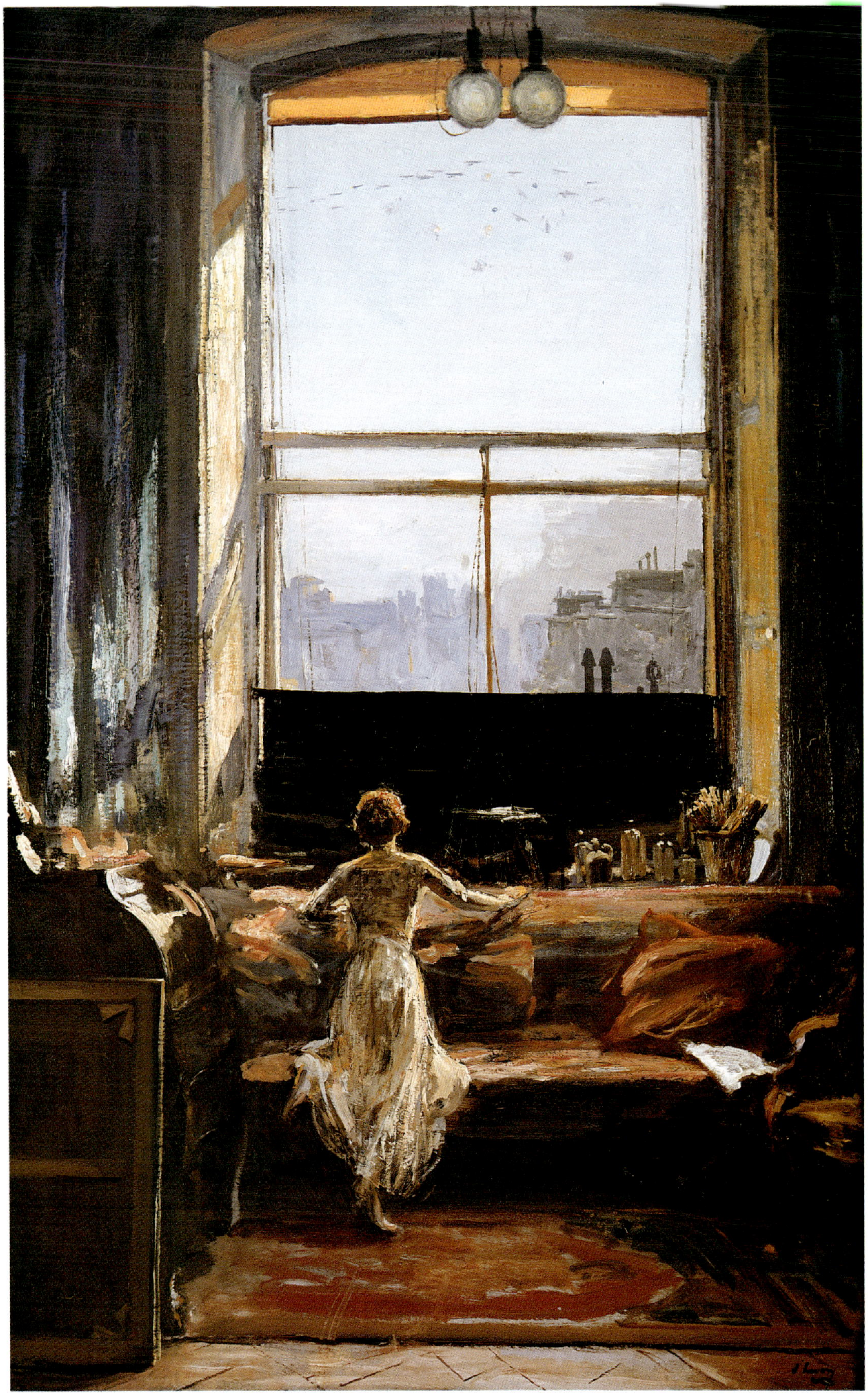

156 *The Studio Window, 7 July 1917*, $55\frac{3}{4} \times 35\frac{1}{2}$
(The Ulster Museum, Belfast)

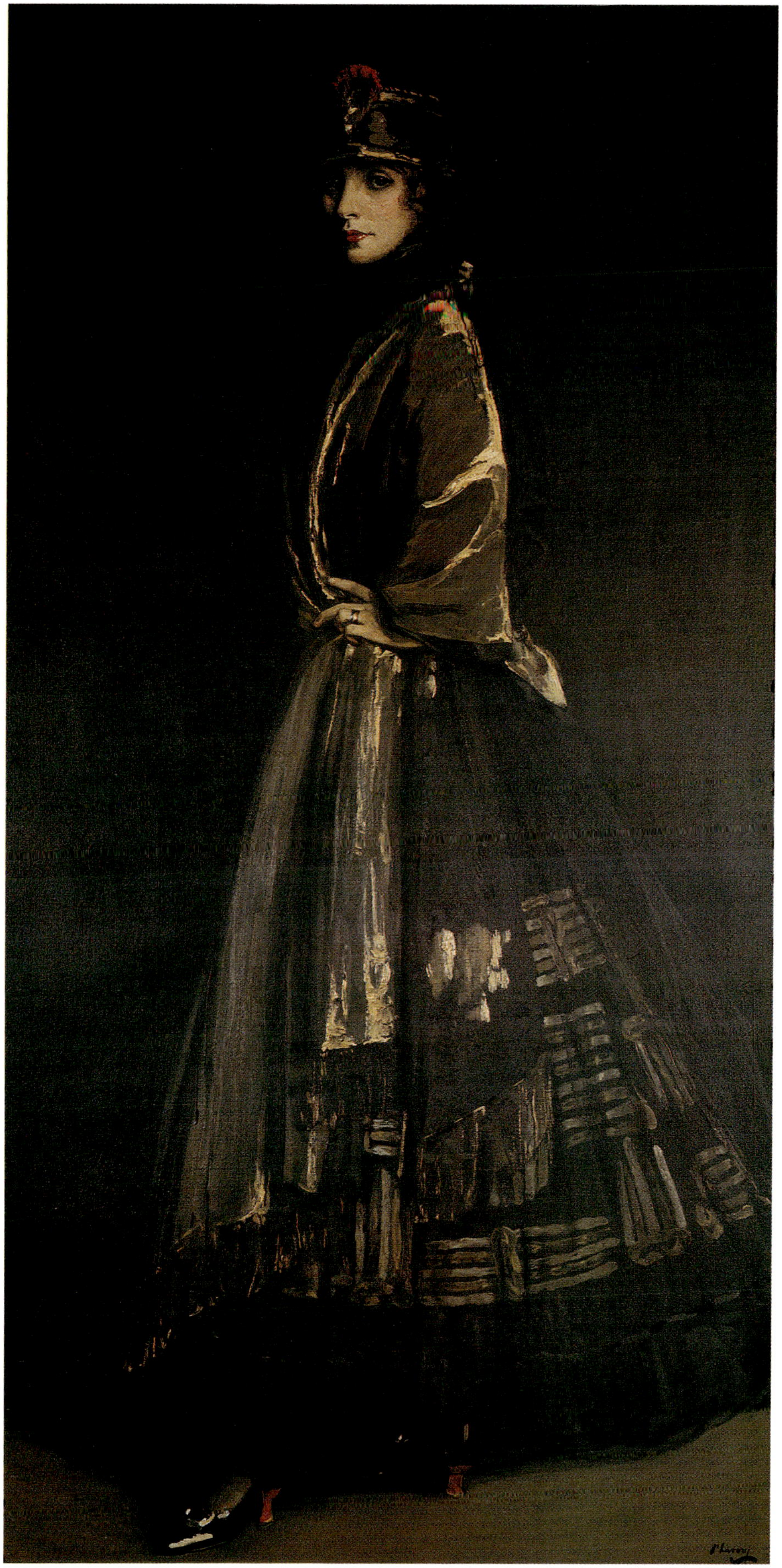

162 *Hazel in Black and Gold*, 1916, $72\frac{1}{4} \times 36\frac{1}{2}$
(Laing Art Gallery, Newcastle Upon Tyne)

comment in the social columns. Mrs Lavery was spotted at the private view, wearing a black satin highwayman's cloak, in company with Mrs Winston Churchill, and both were studying the portrait. It was variously described by contemporary journalists as a 'brilliant success' and a 'graceful harmony of colour'.[29] Fashion commentators were particularly captivated by the red-heeled shoes. One could not predict whether '. . . the coloured heels are going to have a universal vogue, but they are certainly very cute and chic when worn by women who have small feet. Mrs Lavery wears them successfully as you may note from her picture in the Academy.'[30]

Other reviewers found that the colour harmony 'inevitably recalled Velasquez' while one writer accentuated the full old masterish quality of the work. He declared, 'It is impossible to help thinking that in some distant future this portrait will only have gained by lapse of time, and that it will be regarded as one of the world's pictures. It has not very much colour, but as much as many of the old masters' portraits which have gained renown.'[31]

By the middle of 1916, Hazel was increasingly caught up in war charity work. Her involvement in concert tableaux began in June 1914, when, in company with other society ladies of American extraction, she personified 'Illinois' at the American Peace Ball at the Albert Hall. Social events such as this, were given a more pointed purpose as the horror of the war unfolded. The full history of war charity matinees and 'Masques' remains to be written. Hazel Lavery was a leading light in these activities, being an active member of the organising committee of the Italian Red Cross Matinee at the Savoy in December 1916. In this, Lady Diana Manners appeared for the first time as a sixteenth-century Madonna, a role which she later immortalised in Max Reinhardt's *The Miracle*. Hazel acted as a fifteenth-century Madonna in a triptych (Plate 163) designed by Lavery himself. Accompanying her were the Hon. Irene Lawley as St Katherine and Miss Phyllis Boyd as St Michael. When she reappeared in this guise in later years, one writer was moved to exclaim, 'What a picture Titian could have painted of Lady Lavery! What a wonderful expression of beauty of outline and of colour it would have been, with the red dress and the blue mantle and gracefully draped white veil on her head. Van Dyck too would have made a perfect Madonna portrait of her . . .'.[32]

By the time these words were written, Lavery had risen to the challenge by painting his own triptych, *The Madonna of the Lakes* (Plate 164), a work donated to St Patrick's in Belfast, the church in which he had been christened. On other occasions, Hazel Lavery posed as the Madonna in a reconstruction of Bouguereau's *Vierge Consolatrix* (see Plate 165), the favourite picture of Lavery's youth. One effusive society journalist described the event, '. . . the Virgin Mary seated, in dark blue mantle, across her knees a broken hearted girl having flung herself for consolation. You know the picture. Can you imagine how satisfying for this exquisitely human picture was the rapt ideal face of Mrs Lavery, surrounded by a halo of dull gold, her virgin-blue mantle falling in close folds, her hands outstretched. . . it really was one of the most perfect tableaux I have ever seen, so restrained and so true to the spirit of the picture.'[33]

Later tableaux featured Hazel as the Angel in a restaging of Rembrandt's *Vision of Daniel* (see Plate 166) at the Palace Theatre in aid of the British Women's

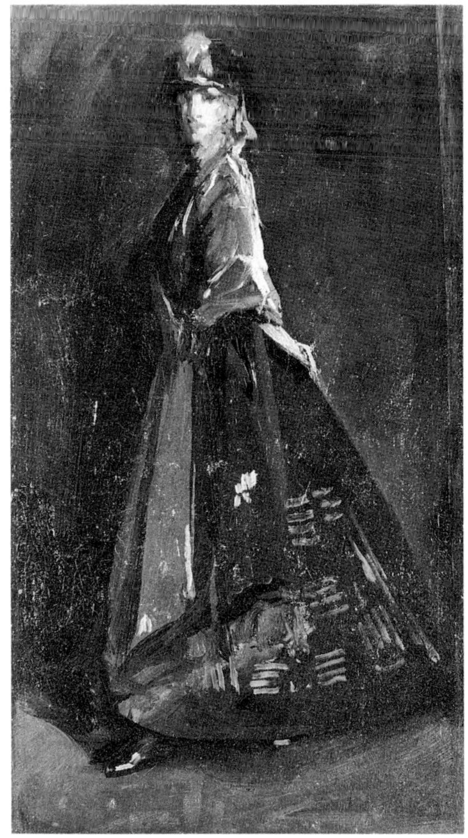

161 Sketch for *Hazel in Black and Gold*, 1916, 24¼ × 13¼ (Brighton Art Gallery)

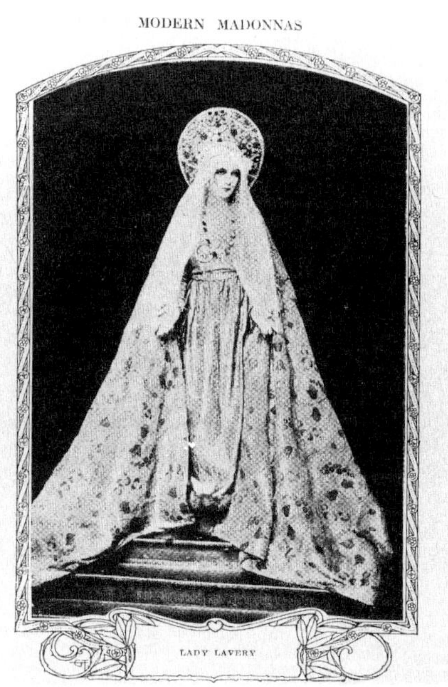

163 Hazel Lavery as 'A Modern Madonna' (photo source unknown)

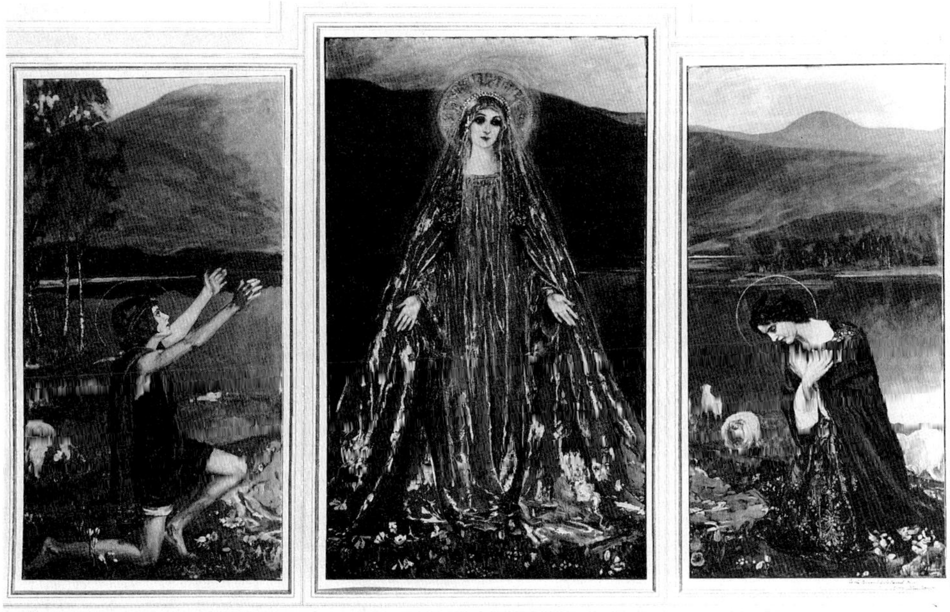

164 *The Madonna of the Lakes*, 1917, size unknown (St Patricks Church, Belfast)

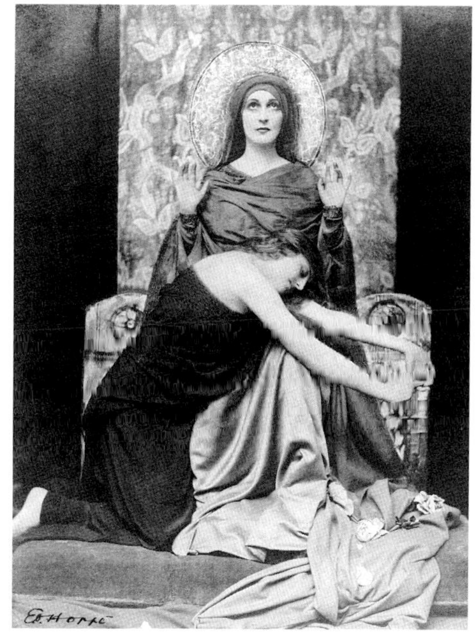

165 E. O. Hoppé, *Hazel Lavery Posing as Bourguereau's 'Vierge Consolatrix'* (photo, Ulster Museum, Belfast)

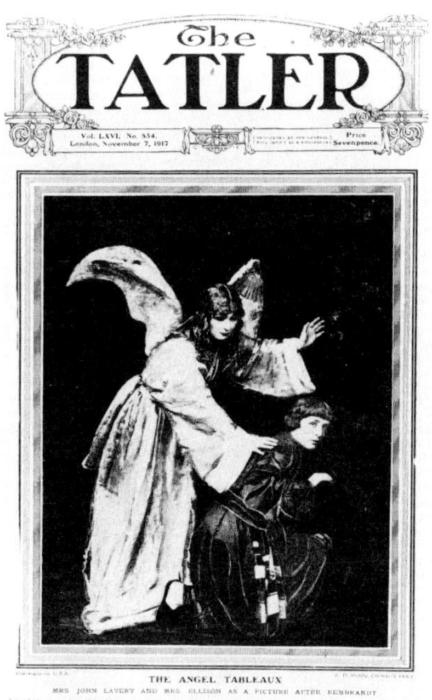

166 E. O. Hoppé, *Hazel Lavery Posing as The Angel in Rembrandt's 'Vision of Daniel'* (photo, Ulster Museum, Belfast)

Hospital and as *Our Lady of Pity* designed by Glyn Philpot in aid of the funds for the Sisters of Mercy Homes for Working Women at the Vaudeville Theatre.[34] In a more secular vein, she appeared as Beatrice, as a Carpaccio musician and in the pose of Joanna Heffernan in a reconstruction of Whistler's *Symphony in White No.3*. This latter event was staged at the Palace Theatre by the 'Concerts for the Front' Fund of the Ladies Auxiliary Committee of the YWCA, upon which Hazel sat. It raised £2,250. One waggish commentator around this time, even composed a celebratory doggerel.

> One thing, as we gaze
> In raptured amaze,
> We cannot refrain from enquiring—
> Is she ever tired
> Of being admired?
> For we're never tired of admiring![35]

Hazel's energetic cultivation of her social role during the war years matched her husband's diligent pursuit of new challenges. These led him to more direct involvement with the war effort. Before doing so, he, Alice and Hazel received an invitation from the Duke of Westminster to stay at his shooting lodge at Landes in the early months of 1917. Tangier had been out of bounds since the start of the hostilities, and so the Laverys were keen to accept the offer. At first they travelled to Paris where, sadly, the atmosphere of the *belle époque* had been swept away, 'everyone looked sad' and in the Quartier Latin '. . . it was as if a deadly plague had swept the place—scarcely a living thing to be seen'.[36] They called upon Lavery's old friend, the portraitist, Jacques-Emile Blanche, but he merely reflected the deathly atmosphere of the city. His studio had a 'stand still look' and when Lavery cheerfully tried to engage him in conversation, he received a forlorn reply, 'Ah, you English do not know what we French are going through. It is hell. There is no Salon. No one paints.'[37]

The Laverys hastened south, staying en route at the small chateau at Mimizan. In April, they were lodged at the Grand Hotel d'Angleterre at St Jean de Luz and here they were able, temporarily, to forget the conflict. Snapshots show the artist sketching in the town square. He painted at least five views of the harbour, logging the movement of the small steamers.[38] While they obviously recall the many coastal scenes painted at Tangier, these canvases bear the shrill solid blues of the *côte de l'Atlantique*. *Twilight, St Jean de Luz* (Plate 167) and *The Sands* both incorporate tiny foreground figures in order to give a sense of scale. In their fast flowing rivulets of paint, swept across the canvas, the St Jean de Luz canvases faintly echo the Valparaiso harbour paintings of Whistler. While he was staying so close to the Spanish border, Lavery took the opportunity to paint the Good Friday processions at Fuenterrabia. One large oil study shows the colourful provincial festival with its crowds and banners, seen from a high balcony.[39]

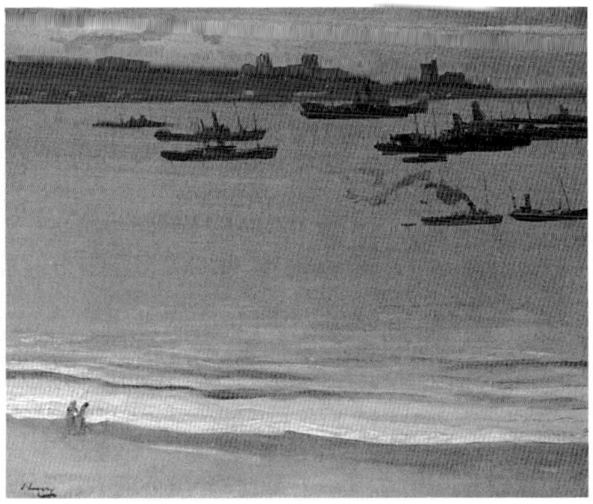

167 *Twilight, St Jean de Luz*, 1917, 25 × 30 (private collection)

While he was staying in France, Lavery wrote to Lord Derby in an attempt to revive the notion of taking a motor van loaded with painting materials to the Western Front. He proposed to stay on in France for six weeks, at his own expense under the care of General Rawlinson. The products of this expedition would be made available for war propaganda.[40]

Lavery may not have known that the official war artists scheme was about to be extended to painters, since its initial appointees, Bone, Dodd and McBey were primarily draughtsmen. Charles Masterman, Director of Propaganda at Wellington House already realised the need for images of war in colour at the time when Lord Derby started lobbying on Lavery's behalf. It was decided however, to restrict the painter to the Home Front giving him a Special Joint Naval and Military Permit, which, as Merrion and Susie Harries point out, was carefully worded to exclude much of what he might wish to paint. The permit was, in effect, a letter of introduction, issued on 3 August 1917 and to be presented at each installation for further permissions to be obtained.[41]

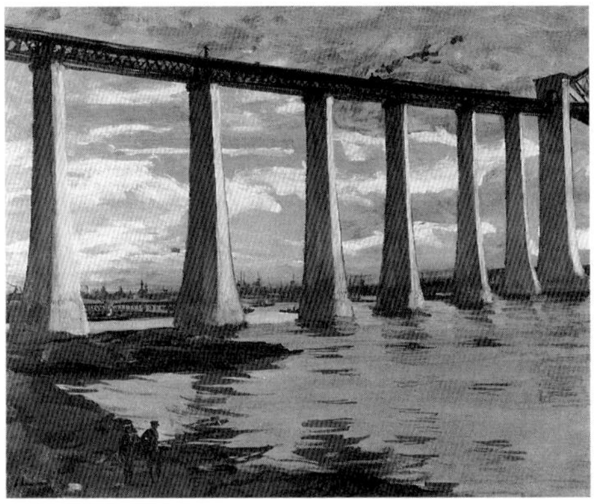

168 *The Piers, Forth Bridge, Kite Balloon and Grand Fleet in the Distance*, 1917, 25 × 30 (photo Christie's)

Undaunted, Lavery set off to paint the fleet at anchor in the Firth of Forth (see Plate 168). He had no sooner established himself when he was stopped by the police and marched off to headquarters. Thereafter, it seemed that everyone in uniform wanted to see his permit and it became especially irksome when the local children, on the alert for spies, started calling him 'the German spy painting oor brig (the Forth Bridge) and throwing stones'.[42] In spite of these difficulties, Lavery painted a number of standard sized, 25 × 30 inch canvases in the vicinity. These show different aspects of the bridge, either looking out to sea or with Granton Naval Base in the background.[43] Several views were painted of the base itself, of Leith, of Edinburgh from the castle and of ships at anchor in the Firth of Forth.[44] En route to or from Edinburgh, Lavery visited Newcastle upon Tyne and painted two canvases at the munitions factories at Elswick (see Plate 169). These provide a vivid record of the labour-intensive activity of supplying the war. Their sketchiness was well suited to the feverish activity represented. On Tyneside,

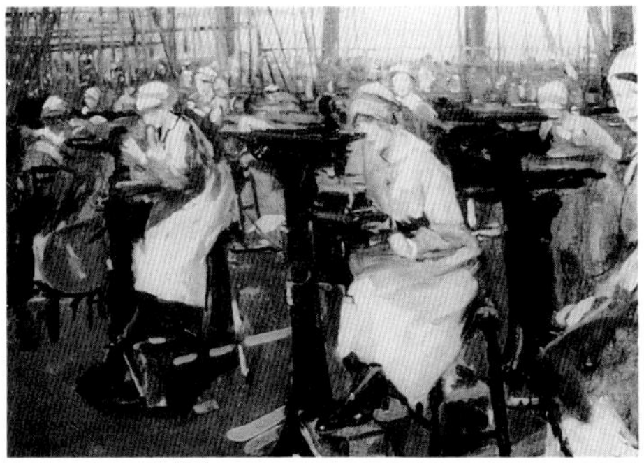

169 *Elswick*, 1917, 25 × 30 (Imperial War Museum, London)

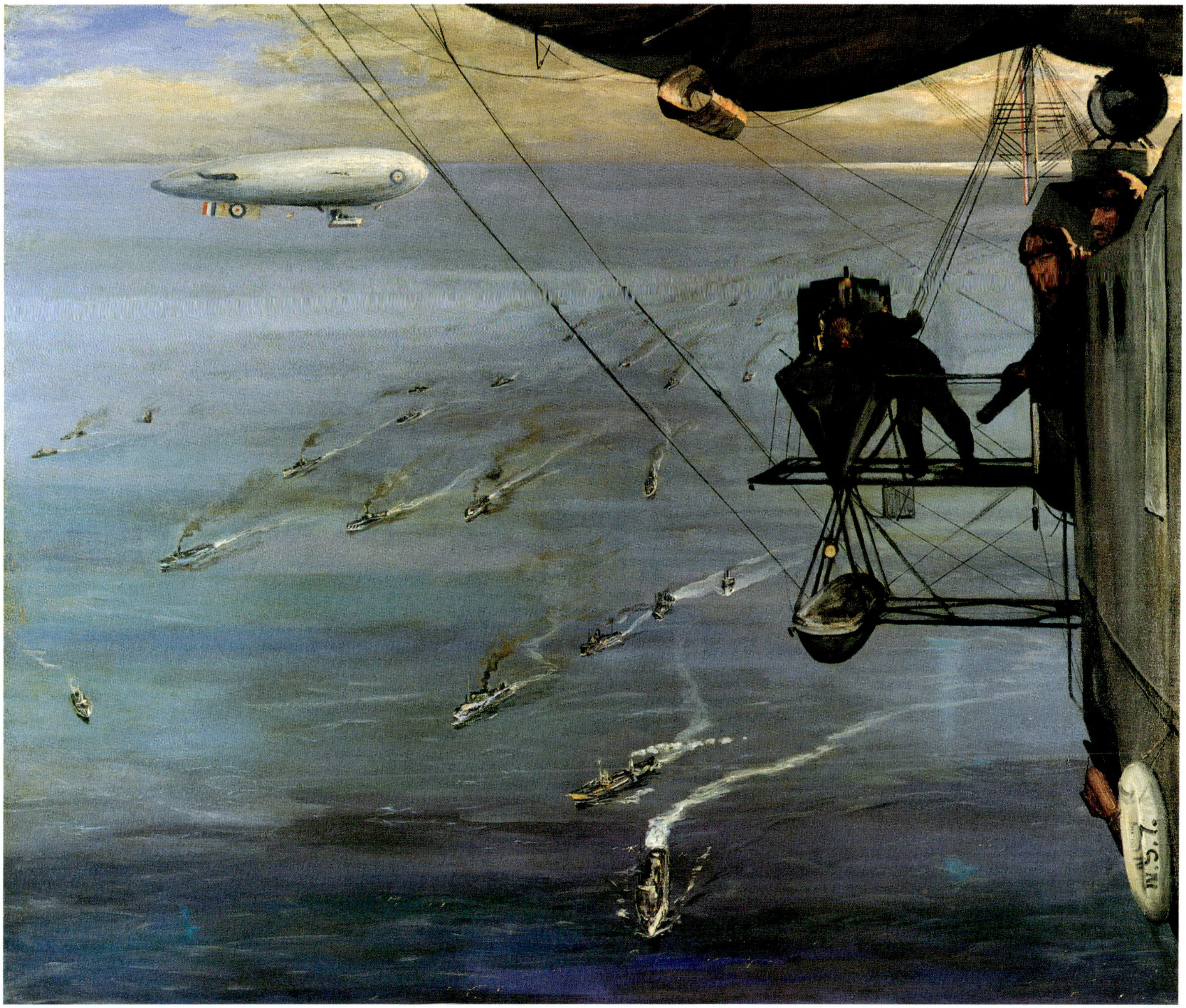

172 *A Convoy, North Sea, 1918, From NS7*,
68 × 78 (Imperial War Museum, London)

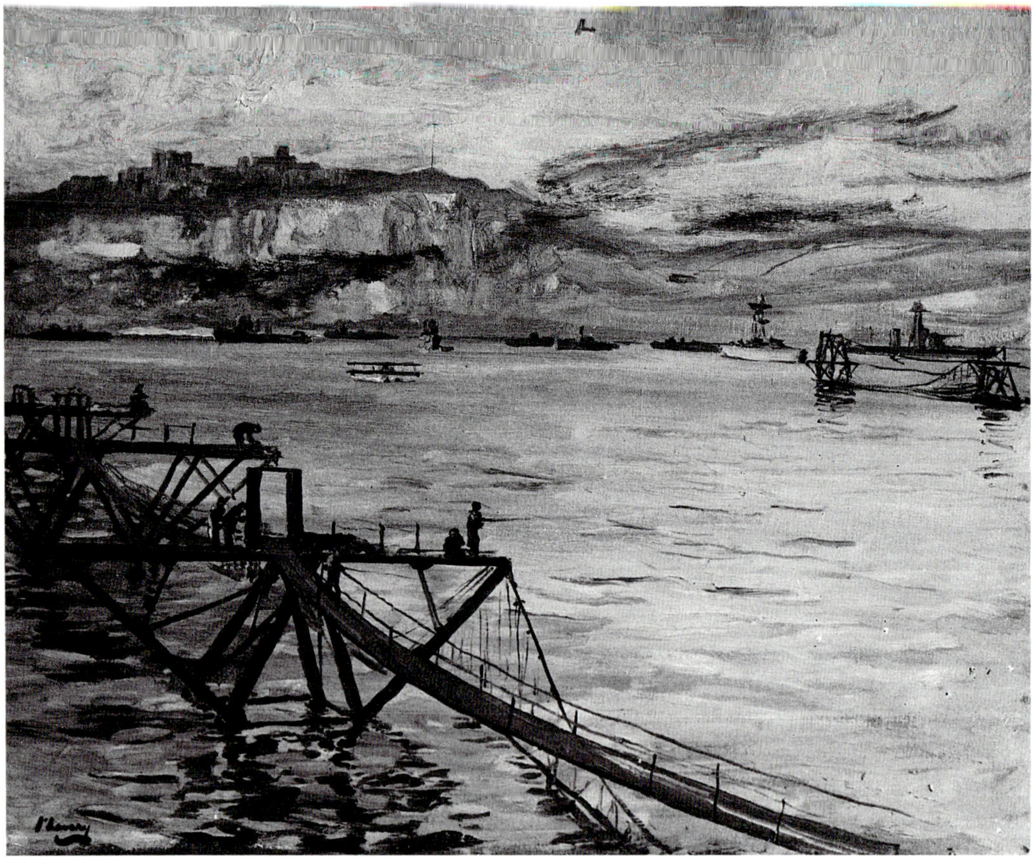

170 *The Entrance, Dover Harbour*, 1918, 25 × 30 (Imperial War Museum, London)

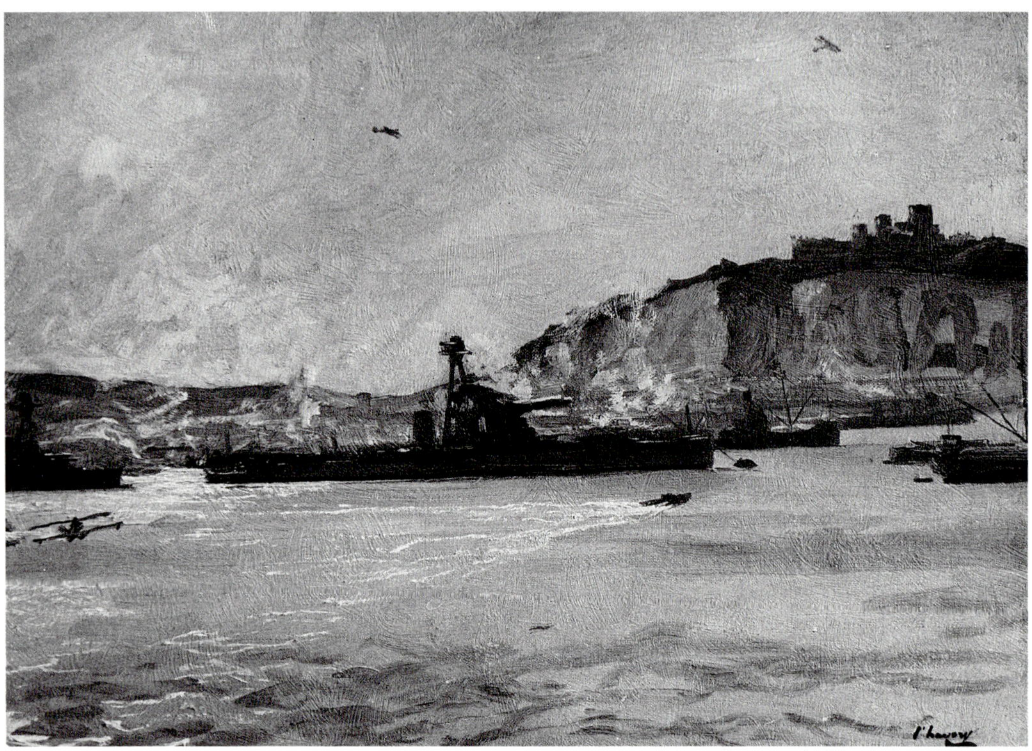

171 *The Monitors, Dover Harbour*, 1918, 25 × 30 (Imperial War Museum, London)

173 *The End, 1918*, 87 × 109
(Imperial War Museum, London)

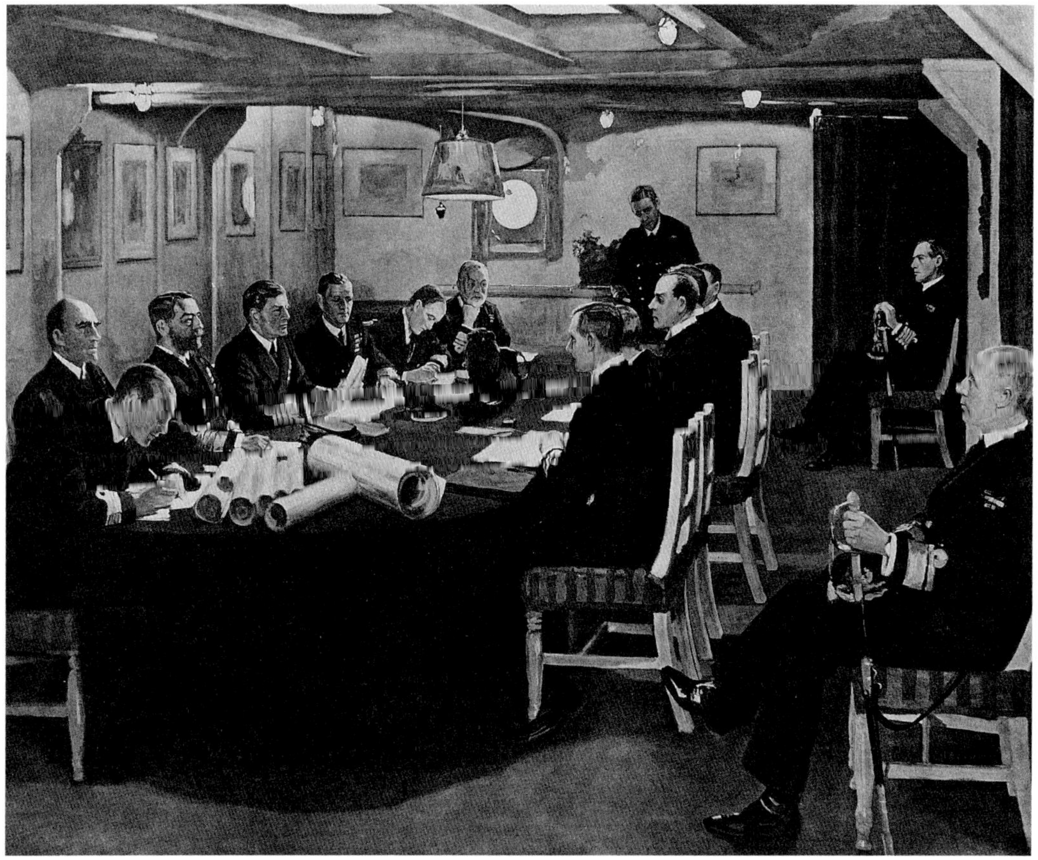

Lavery also painted *A Coast Defence*, a splendid nocturne showing an eighteen pounder anti-aircraft gun in action, as well as *The Breaking up of the HMS Illustrious*, a venerable battleship now being salvaged for war materials.[45]

Visits to Richborough and Harwich followed during that winter and it was probably because of his commitment to naval subjects that Lavery was selected in December 1917 before the Admiralty sub-committee of the Imperial War Museum and given a clearer brief.[46] As one of eight artists picked to represent 'every branch of the British Navy', Lavery was again dispatched to the north. His harshest war experiences came from painting on the impacted ice and in the biting winds at 'Hell's Gate' in the Orkneys. Despite the transient beauty of the sparkling sun over Scapa, Lavery quickly realised that, though well togged in an electrified suit taken from a German airman, 'nothing could live out of doors on those bare rocks . . . there was no standing against the wind'.[47] He did, however, bring back some arresting, if swiftly executed, sketches.[48]

In the early spring, Lavery painted troops embarking for the Front at Southampton,[49] and worked at the aerodrome at Hendon.[50] Two notable canvases, showing aspects of coastal defence were painted at Dover in May 1918. *The Entrance, Dover Harbour* (Plate 170) is elaborately protected by ranges of anti submarine netting that recalls the chain pier at Brighton painted by Constable and Turner. *The Monitors* (Plate 171) records the activities of the small reconnaissance and anti-submarine vessels of the Dover Patrol.[51] Lavery was to paint his first airborne studies at East Fortune in August 1918. These were conflated into a large picture entitled, *A Convoy, North Sea, 1918, From NS 7* (Plate 172).[52] He was, therefore, at the age of sixty-two, one of the first artists to work in the air, with memorable results.

Lavery's final war-time duty was to return to Scotland to Rosyth to depict the surrender of the German Navy in November 1918. The artist recalled that due to 'fog, mutiny and coal shortage' the German delegates did not arrive on the Quarter Deck of HMS *Queen Elizabeth* until late afternoon, when 'fog and darkness blotted out the detail'.[53] Lavery then proceeded to record the scene in the forecabin (see Plate 173), disguised in a post-captain's discarded uniform.

> I got a fairly good impression of the arrival on the quarter-deck and rushed down to the forecabin after them, but not in time to see their reception by the British Admirals, which did not take long. They were already seated when I took up my position, the door was closed and the proceedings began. Most people would have been all ears, but I was all eyes and heard very little, only once or twice when the German Admiral, who spoke perfect English, corrected an interpreter on some idiomatic point. Not to embarrass the delegates, I chose a place behind them where what I was doing could not be seen, even if they should turn round, which the Zeppelin Commander occasionally did, being nearest to me. He was a young man of the Prussian type, with closely cropped hair and flat back to his head. He . . . was ill at ease. The Admiral, whose profile I could see at times . . . was dignified, but one could tell by his voice the strain under which he was labouring . . .[54]

Negotiations were resumed the following day, and Lavery again concentrated upon the German delegates, knowing that it would be possible to obtain sittings from the British officers after the event.[55] From these various sketches, the large commemorative work, 87 × 109 inches, was painted. It was completed during 1919 and shown at the Royal Academy in 1920.[56]

As he was finishing this task, Lavery received his last commission connected with the war. This was for twelve paintings for the Women's Work collection at the Imperial War Museum. For these he was given specific instructions as to what should be represented—the army bakery at Dieppe, the Red Cross Hostel, Rouen, the Women's Emergency Canteen at the Gare du Nord, Paris and so on.[57] As images produced after the event, these canvases contributed to the view of Sir John Lavery as a safe Home Front artist. There is evidence that Lavery felt that they lacked the urgency of the war work of some of his younger Western Front colleagues. He stated openly that his painting of *The Surrender of the German Delegates* . . . was a poor production by comparison to Orpen's Peace Conference records. Clearly the circumstances, the cramped forecabin of a battleship did not compare with the monumental interiors of the Palace of Versailles, to which Orpen was dispatched.

Throughout the war, Lavery consistently promoted the cause of younger artists and their involvement with war work. He particularly commended Eric Kennington.[58] He was alive to the virtues of Nevinson, Nash, and Connard and attended Orpen's popular exhibition at Agnews in May 1918.[59] These experiences

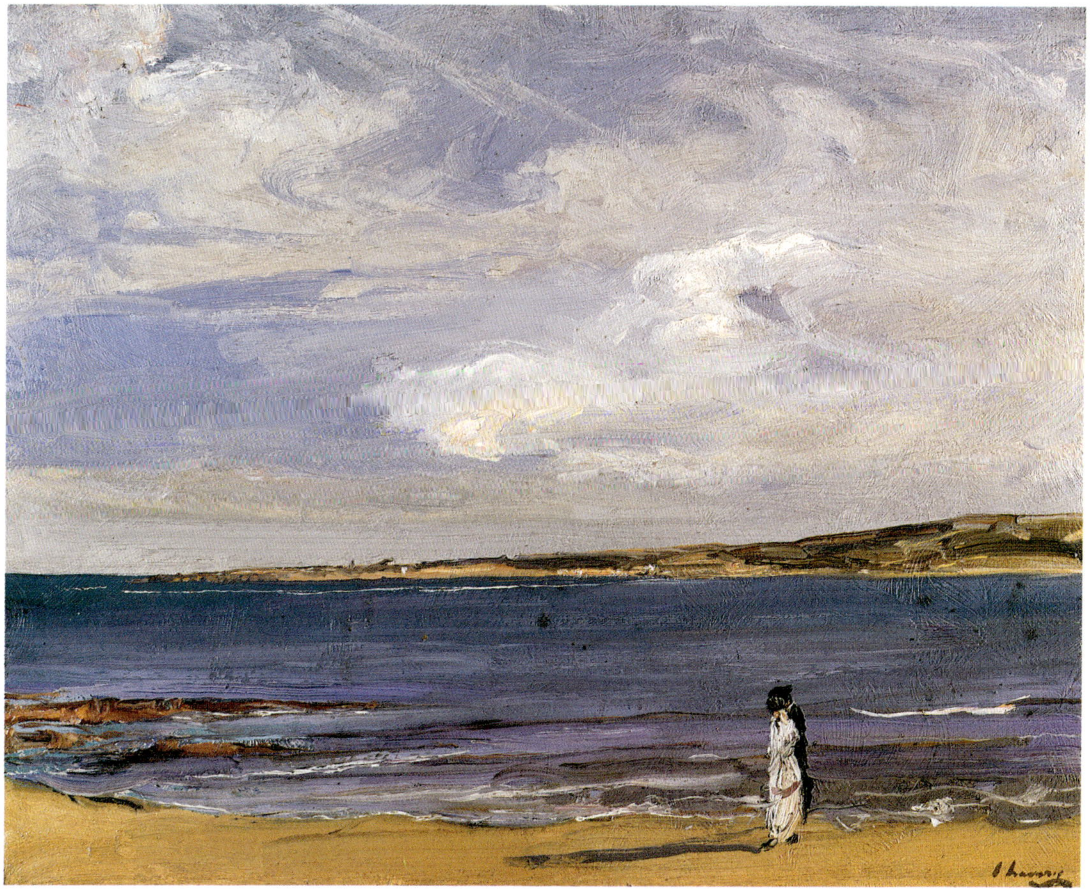

180 *Dunbar from Tyninghame*, 1919, 25 × 30 (photo courtesy Sotheby's)

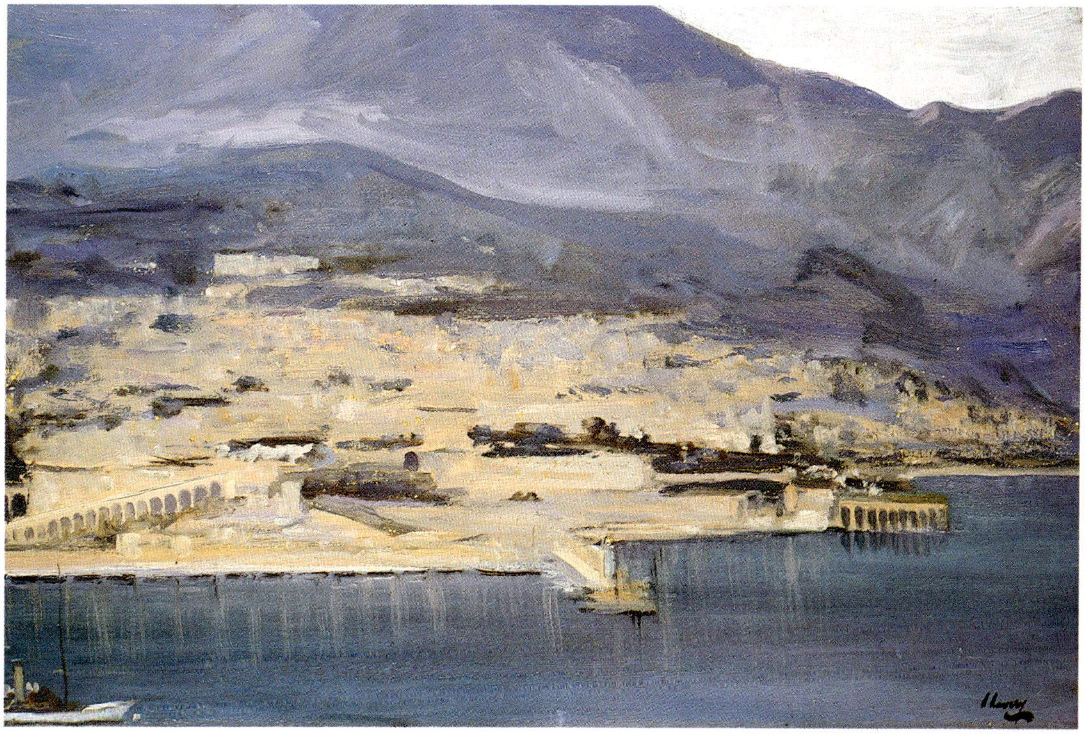

183 *Monte Carlo – Twilight*, 1921, 25 × 30 (private collection, photo, Pyms Gallery, London)

led him to downgrade his own efforts and dub them superficial: 'Escorting convoys in the North Sea and painting from "blimps" or numbered NS's, I felt nothing of the stark reality, losing sight of my fellow men being blown to pieces in submarines or slowly choking to death in mud. I saw only new beauties of colour and design. . .'.[60]

Despite the denigration of his own painting, Lavery added an important dimension to the imagery of the Great War. There was little overt emotionalism about his work; it did not portray the lunar landscape into which northern France had been transformed. His pictures did, however, aptly convey those chance moments when, for instance, to the rear of the NS 7 airship, a seering silver light breaks through on the horizon, as the pilots prepare to bomb what was thought to be an enemy submarine, but which turned out to be only a whale. Lavery alone could seize the novel designs made by the *British Mine-laying Submarines, Harwich* (Plate 174), 1917 and the haunting ranks of crosses in the *Cemetery, Etaples*, 1919.[61] There are few more arresting war paintings than *'The Silver Queen', Wormwood Scrubs, 1915, one of the original 'Blimps' or 'Rigids' at Pulham, 1918,* R *23 Type* (Plate 175) and ultimately these arouse the curiosity of the spectator just as much as the scenes of 'grim harshness and horror' which Lavery thought that he should have represented. There could have been no better pictorial dramatist of the Home Front and his images of the fleet recall the prose pictures of Churchill. The tremulous line of warships sailing off from Parkestone or the Firth of Forth, excited his imagination in the same way as the great naval review at Portland in 1914 was vividly recalled by his celebrated pupil.[62]

Lavery's knighthood in the New Year's Honours List in 1918, was received with universal approval. Telegrams of congratulation arrived at Cromwell Place from old friends like Lord Donoughmore and Lord Wimborne, and now more than ever the Laverys became the focus of public attention.[63] Their home was photographed for *Vogue* and *Lady's Pictorial* and Hazel's Regency taste in decor was eulogised. One piece of furniture, a cream and gold glass cupboard was apparently made from pieces of George IV's state coach. Elsewhere, in the dining room, white striped walls and Adam furniture were balanced by a black satin table cloth.[64] Lady Lavery excelled in fashion and as the hostess of numerous luncheons and suppers involving the great and the famous. Interviewed at the time of her joint exhibition with Sir John in 1921, a society reporter tried to encompass the many aspects of her life style.

> As hostess, Lady Lavery more often sets the pace in originality than follows, and she even finds time to take a hand at moulding feminine fashions. Her gowns invariably bear the mark of her own artistic personality. She was the first to wear a wreath of golden leaves in her hair which London greedily copied, and her experiments in rose-pink and in rose-red evening gowns were eagerly adopted by fashionable dress makers. In furnishing her home, she leads the prevailing modes, and new touches often find their way from within her walls to the rest of the world.[65]

Thus the Laverys' sense of style made them leaders of contemporary taste. Hazel's explorations of chic modishness, her 'experiments in rose-pink and rose-red' were

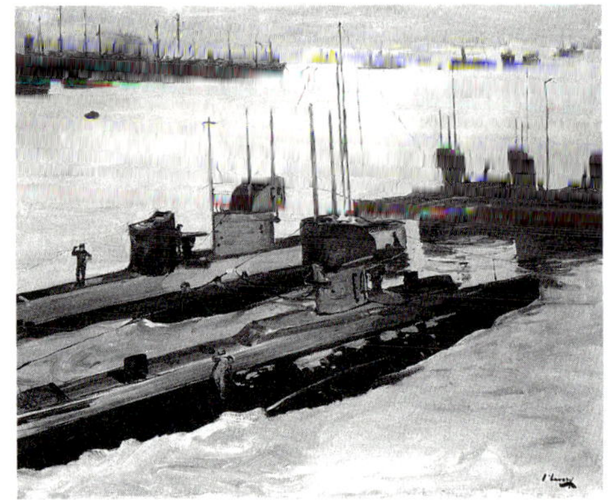

174 *British Mine-laying Submarines, Harwich*, 1917, 25 × 30 (Imperial War Museum, London)

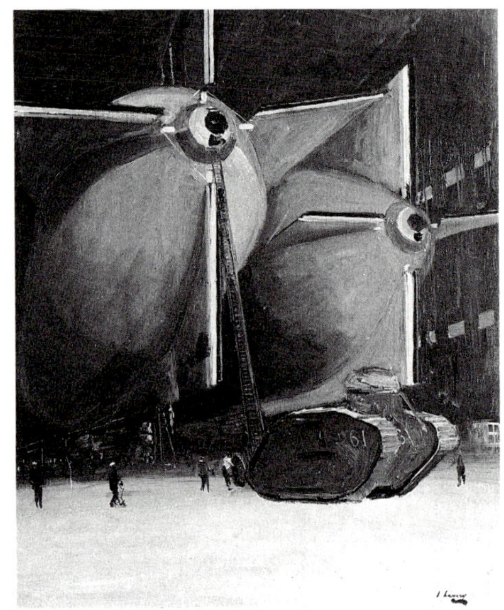

175 *'Rigids' at Pulham 1918, R23 Type*, 30 × 25 (Imperial War Museum, London)

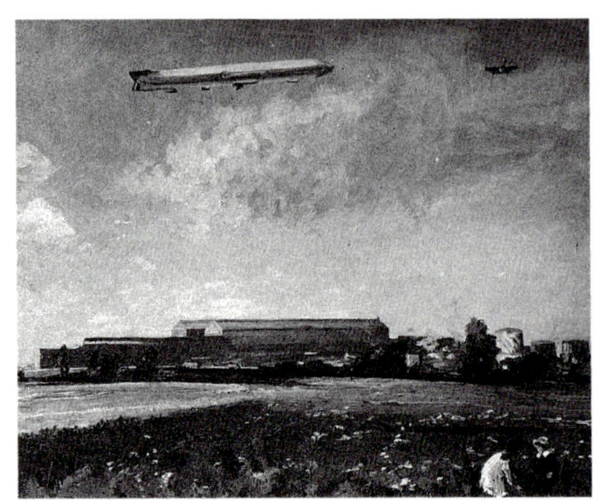

176 *Pulham, 1918*, 25 × 30 (private collection, photo, Ian Kilpatrick)

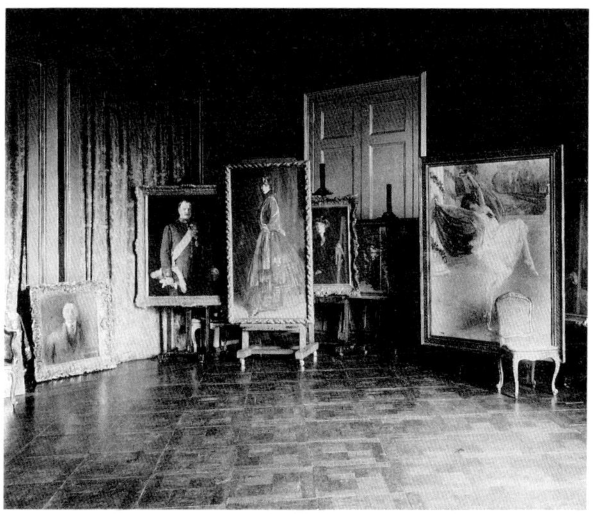

177 The Artist's Studio, photo *c.*1916
(source unknown)

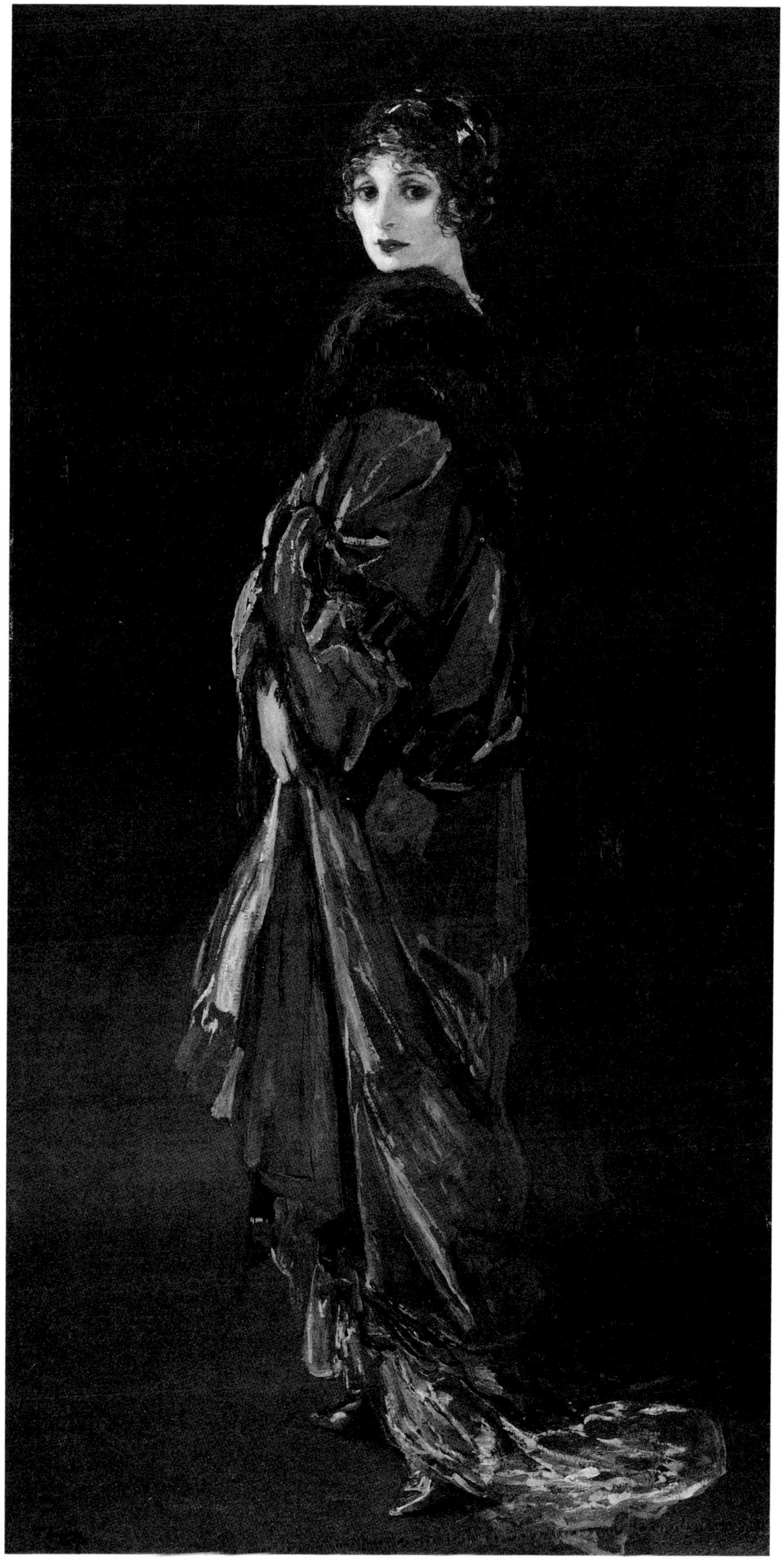

178 *Hazel in Rose and Gold*, 1918, 79 × 39
(Walker Art Gallery, Liverpool)

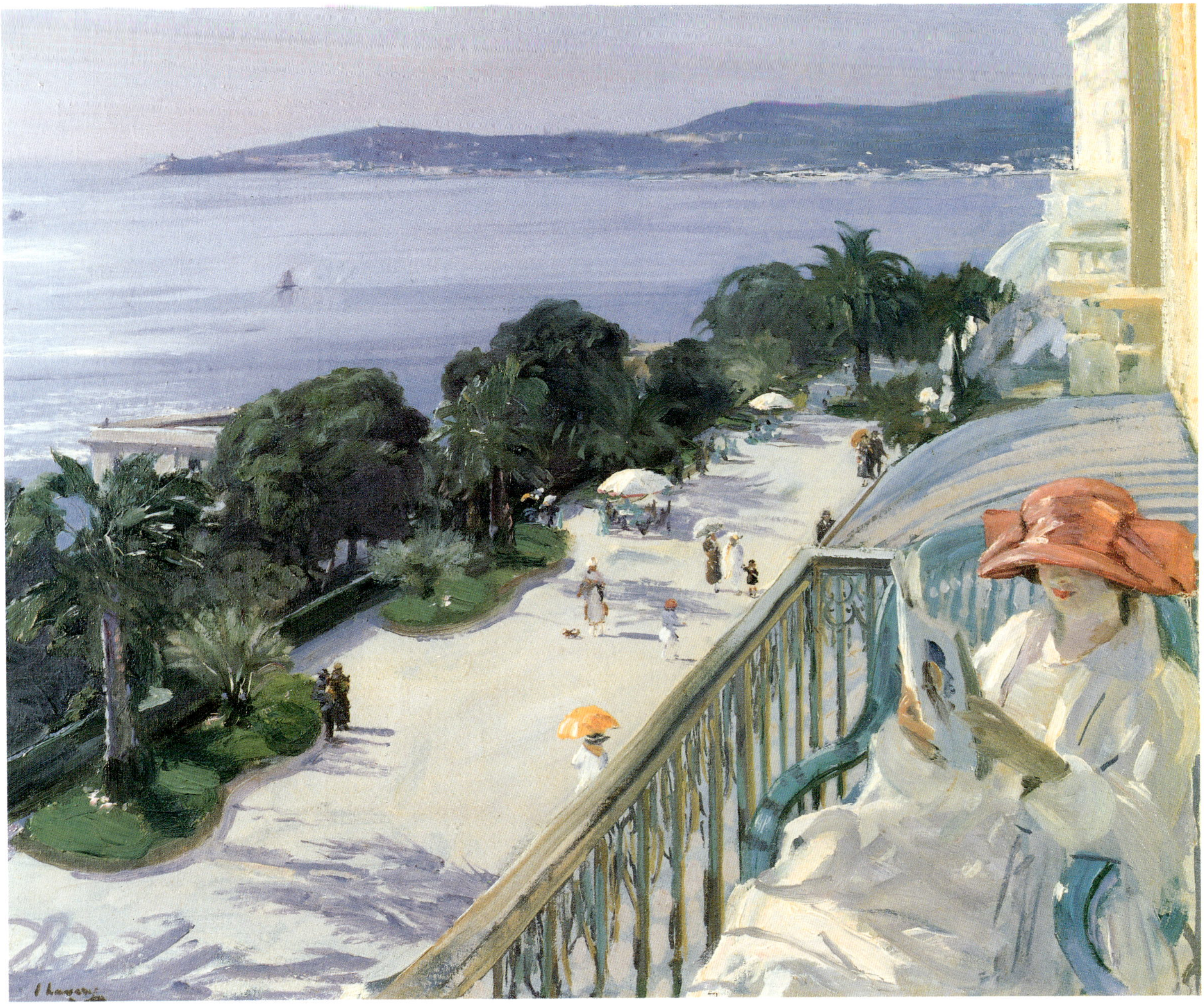

184 *The Terrace, Cap d'Ail*, 1921,
25 × 30 (private collection, photo,
courtesy Phillips, London)

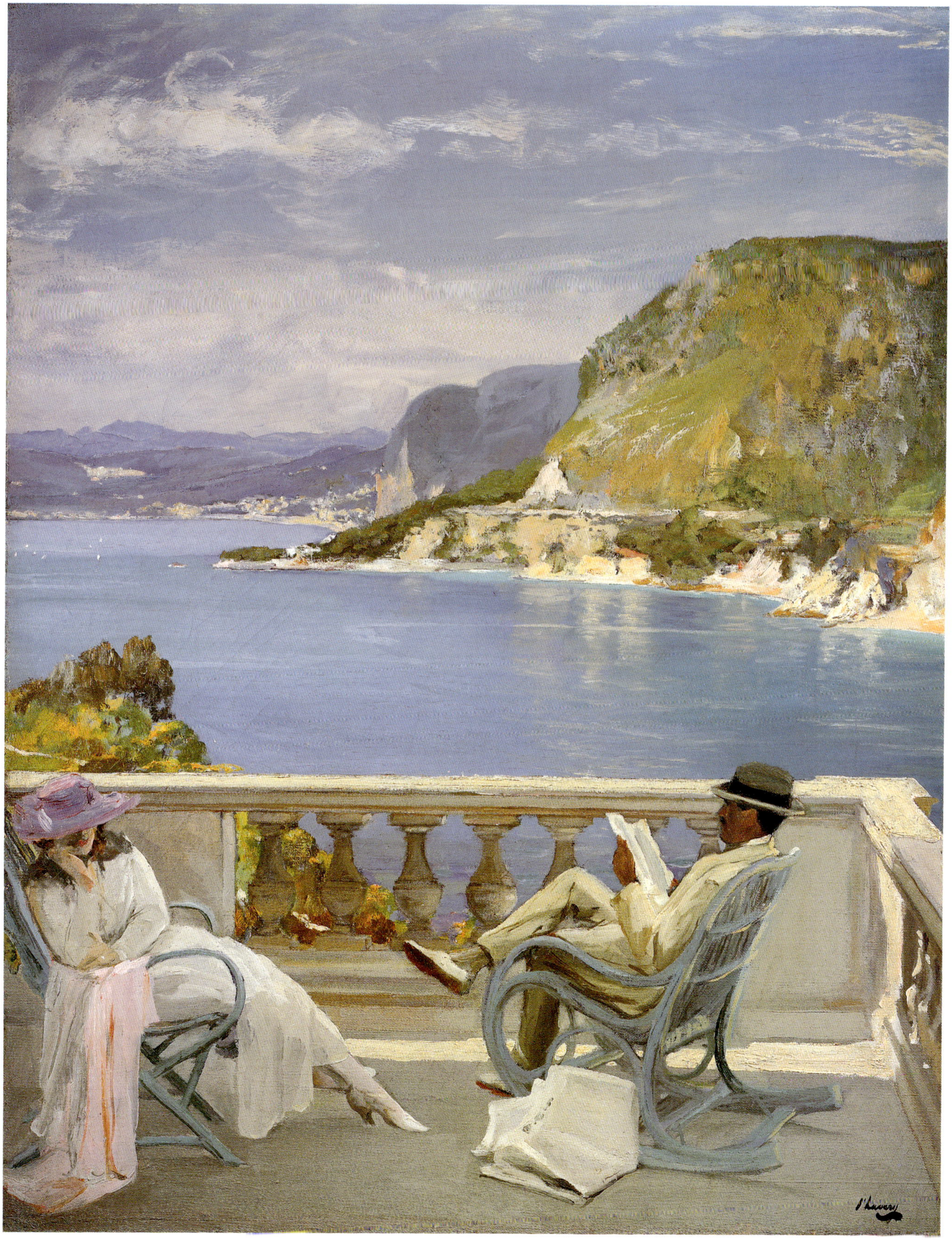

185 *The Honeymoon*, 1921,
36½ × 28 (private collection,
photo, courtesy David Messum)

the by-product of the formal and colouristic 'arrangements' that preoccupied the painter. The early Twenties saw such works as *Hazel in Rose and Grey, (Portrait in a Mirror)* (Plate 224), *The Red Rose* and *The Red Book*, but in 1918, in the midst of completing his war commissions, he painted the prelude to these 'arrangements' in the full-length portrait, *Hazel in Rose and Gold* (Plate 178).[66]

His affection for Lady Lavery's rose-coloured wrap was noted by one reviewer in a picture that combined delicate touches of purple, brown and gold. It was regarded as 'one of the most successful portraits he has ever done', when it appeared at the International Society in 1918, and its gracefulness was admired at the Salon d'Automne, the following year.[67] The painting was obviously more than a large fashion plate. It underscored the cult of personality that surrounded both artist and muse at this time. It represented them in a unified statement, and therein lay its power and appeal. Hazel's face, instantly recognisable from contemporary Hoppé photographs, from the portraits of Sargent, Birley, McEvoy and Praga, as well as from the elegant renditions of her husband, was already an icon.

In 1919, the social round recommenced amidst victory parades and celebrations. A war artist's pass secured a good vantage point for painting the military parade passing through Admiralty Arch. Watching the fireworks on the evening of the festivities Diana Manners fell through the skylight of of a house in Green Street and broke her leg. Her convalescence in the family home in Arlington Street became the subject of a brilliant study which was shown at the Royal

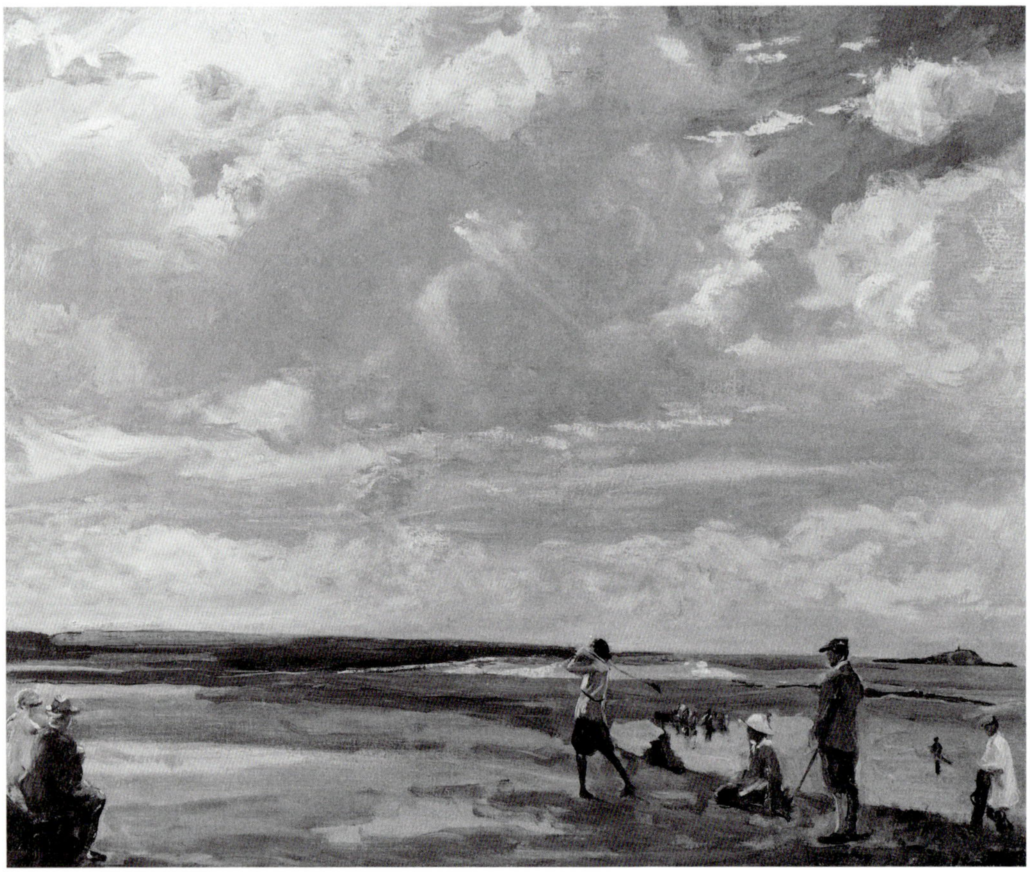

179 *Lady Astor playing golf at North Berwick*, 1919, 24½ × 29½ (present whereabouts unknown, photo, courtesy Christie's)

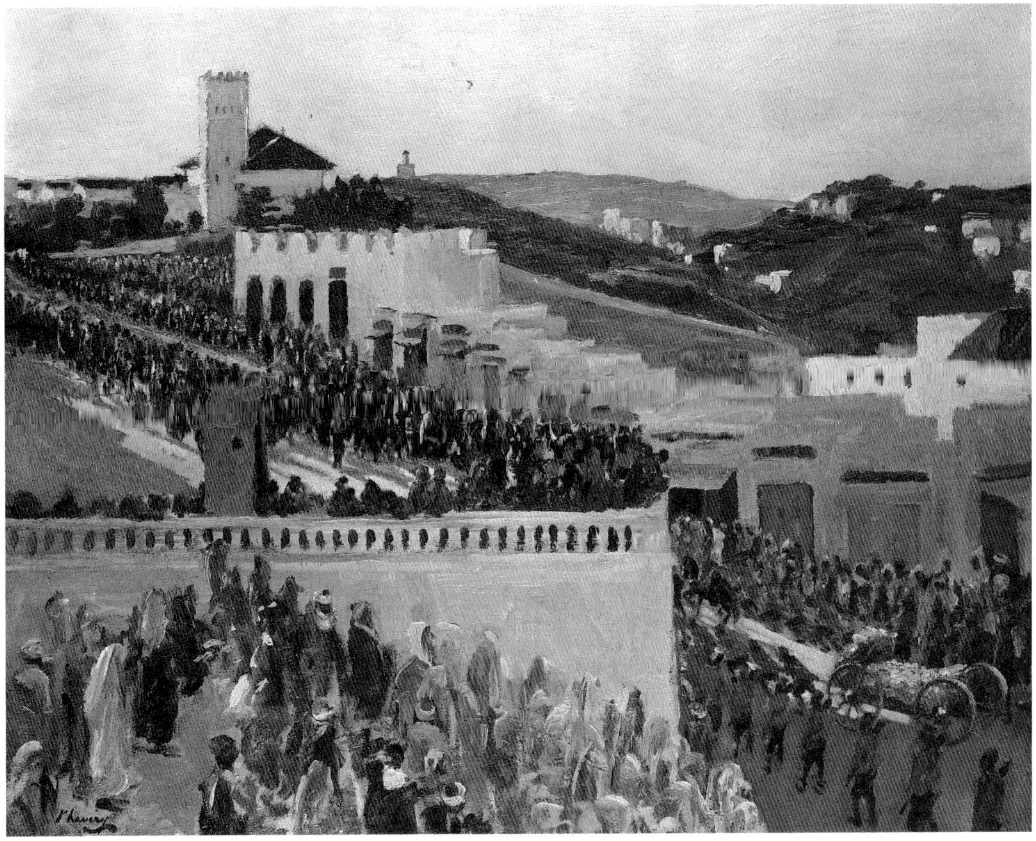

181 *The Funeral Procession of Kaid MacLean at Tangier*, 1920, 25 × 30, (private collection, photo, The Fine Art Society)

Academy in 1920 and later purchased by the Carnegie Institute in Pittsburgh. At the same time weekend parties, temporarily curtailed by the war, began again. Between 1919 and 1924 the Laverys frequently returned to Westerdunes in North Berwick, the home of Sir Patrick Ford, one of the artist's staunchest patrons. Being no more than an average golfer—an Irish caddie told him 'Ah, sir, there are very few who can play like you,'—Lavery painted landscapes of the links at North Berwick on many occasions (see Plate 179).[68] There were also vigorous scenes of windswept northern beaches such as *Dunbar from Tyninghame* (Plate 180) and *Rain in the Distance, the Beach, North Berwick*.[69] Ford's house also had its attractions. A Japanese garden had been created there and it too became the subject of several colourful compositions. These more relaxing circumstances may well have prompted a long sojourn in north Africa that winter. On this occasion, the Laverys cruised round the coast as far as Rabat and east as far as Tunis, where they stayed at the Arab Palace at Sidi-bu-Said.[70] Naturally, they used Tangier as a base and during their sojourn Lavery fulfilled the sad duty of painting the funeral cortège of his old friend, Kaid MacLean (see Plate 181).[71] The wide variety of subjects selected, including Arab processions, dervish dances and pictures of Tangier bay, indicates the relief he must have felt at escaping the war and being back in his old stamping grounds. He even journeyed inland to paint *The Walls of Marrakesh* (Plate 182) in a high-key palette that aptly expresses his renewed pleasure in the bright colour and strong light of Morocco. The first forays into the South of France were also made as part of this holiday, with views of the garden at

Villa Sylvia and other Riviera landscapes. Among the finest of these, was the nocturne of the promontory known as '*tête de chien*', *Monte Carlo – Twilight* (Plate 183). The saturation of brilliant ultramarines, intensified by sparkling lights creates a shimmering dream-like effect that was particularly admired by Churchill. In other examples, painted at Beaulieu, Cap Martin or Cap d'Ail, the clear light, heat and dazzling colour of the scene affected the artist as powerfully as it had Monet and Matisse. As if to underscore this mood of '*luxe, calme et volupte*' Lavery included figures lounging, reading or casually conversing in pictures such as *The Bay, Monte Carlo* and *The Terrace, Cap d'Ail* (Plate 184), ignoring, for the most part, their lush surroundings.[72] The most imposing of these pictures, one which sums up the entire experience with impressive scale is *The Honeymoon* (Plate 185), a possible celebration of the recent marriage of Lavery's former model, Mary Auras, to another of his Tangier acquaintances, Nigel d'Albini Black Hawkins. The couple, marooned on their terrace are alas, already oblivious to one another, as well as to the majestic sweep of the *cote d'azure* which surrounds them.[73]

The products of these expeditions were collected for a show at the Alpine Club Gallery in October 1921. The catalogue contained a rakish photograph of Hazel and John Lavery by Hoppé and in the exhibition, Sir John's pictures of Morocco, the Riviera and other scenes were accompanied by his wife's portrait and child studies. The 'Foreword' to the catalogue by Winston Churchill contained a fine appreciation of the mature style which Lavery had evolved. His power of concentration and ability to cope with the vicissitudes of nature and weather was warmly praised by someone who had first-hand experience of seeing the artist at work. As a consequence, Churchill noted, in these pictures 'we are presented with the true integrity of effect. And this flash is expressed in brilliant and beautiful colour with long ease of mastery.'[74]

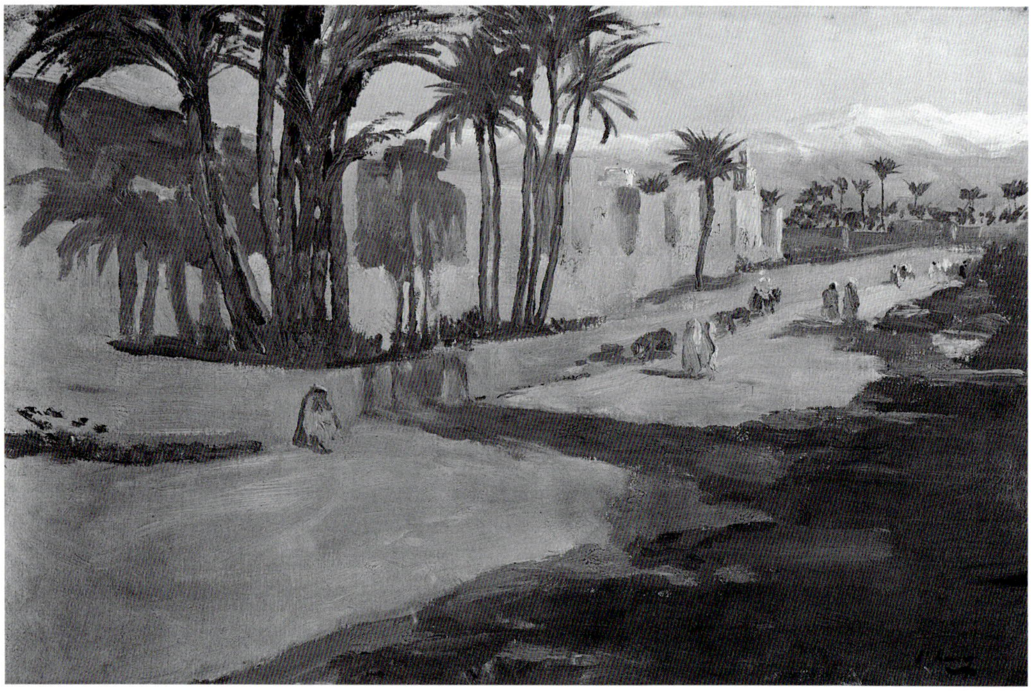

182 *The Walls of Marrakesh*, 1920, 20 × 30 (The Ulster Museum, Belfast)

9 An Irish Expatriate

Lavery was Irish by avocation as much as by birth. He lived through the stirring times in which cultural renaissance burgeoned into nationhood. At first unaware of his political role in these events, he was reclaimed by his native land as it sought to define the identity of its culture. His much lauded portrait of Kathleen MacDermott as *An Irish Girl* (see Plate 70) was one of the first modern images of Irish female beauty.[1] Its supremely sensitive notation of the ebbing life of its model set a compositional formula and a colour code which was later resumed by William Orpen with more overt symbolic intent in works like *Young Ireland*, *The Colleen* and *Bridgit, a picture of Miss Elvery*. However, although *An Irish Girl* was highly praised as a 'graceful study' the extent of its embodiment of nationality was left to the beholder.[2] To the early writers on the Glasgow School, Lavery's country of origin was only of incidental significance, to be quickly qualified by the fact that he had 'long since been resident in Scotland'.[3] To the young artist seeking fame and fortune, a sense of belonging to a particular place and people was unnecessarily constricting. Nevertheless, as the probable writer of Frank O'Meara's obituary for *The Scottish Art Review*, Lavery called attention to the question of nationality. Remarking that 'art conditions are at such a low ebb in Ireland', the writer confirmed that O'Meara's unfulfilled intention had been to return to his country of origin and improve the situation.[4] Whilst there is no evidence to confirm that Lavery was the author of these words, it seems not unlikely that he would have shared the expatriate painter's ambition to create a new Irish school. However, in the 1880s and 1890s he had to be ready to go where commissions took him. Even when he migrated from Glasgow for London, in company with other members of the Glasgow School, it was not to claim a London reputation so much as an international one. He must scarcely have been aware of the formation of the Gaelic League by Douglas Hyde in 1893, and only from 1901 did he begin to exhibit regularly at the Royal Hibernian Academy. Coincidentally, it was at that time that efforts were made to define an Irish sensibility in the visual arts. On 8 June 1903, Lavery received a letter from Hugh Lane, a man he had not met up to this point. It was written,

> . . . for the purpose of enlisting your sympathy in a matter which will I believe enormously add to the prosperity, prestige and happiness of our Country. It is that of obtaining for Dublin (what every provincial town in England possesses) a permanent collection of works by modern masters. As you probably know—Ireland at present cannot boast of even a single *private collection* of modern pictures so that our students—not rich enough to travel—have no opportunities of studying and assimilating the best productions of modern art. It is not only the artists that will benefit but the publick [sic] will have an opportunity of refining its taste—and the rich

> man will no doubt commence to collect. With a fund to purchase the best works painted by Irish painters more particularly—every year we will in time encourage and I hope produce a great school of painting in our midst as our best painters (in England) are either quite Irish like yourself or Irish Americans! If I might be allowed to talk over the possibilities of this scheme with you, I will esteem it a great favour, as your advice will be invaluable in this matter.[5]

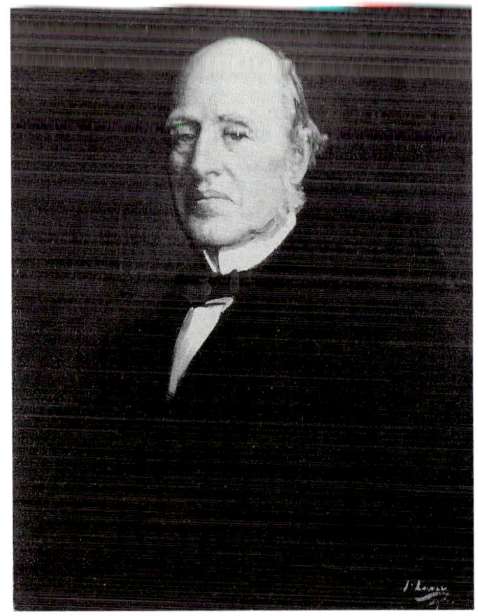

186 *William Edward Hartpole Lecky*, 1903, 25 × 18¾ (National Gallery of Ireland, Dublin)

Obviously anxious to profit from Lavery's extensive experience as an exhibition organiser, Lane's letter adopts a conspiratorial tone. In July, he wrote back to Lavery enclosing a report of House of Commons proceedings on the issue and, expressing his sadness at the death of Whistler, he sought Lavery's assistance in getting his executors to present a painting to Dublin in his memory.[6]

The first struggling attempt to present an Irish sensibility, however, was made by Lane. In 1904, when the group of Irish pictures assembled for the St Louis International Exhibition was refused insurance by the relevant Civil Service Department,[7] Lane negotiated its exhibition at the Guildhall Art Gallery, London. In some respects, the turn of events which led to eighteen of Lavery's best works, including the portrait of the great historian of eighteenth-century Ireland, *William Edward Hartpole Lecky* (Plate 186), being shown at the Guildhall was fortuitous.[8] Lavery was, along with Osborne, one of the best represented

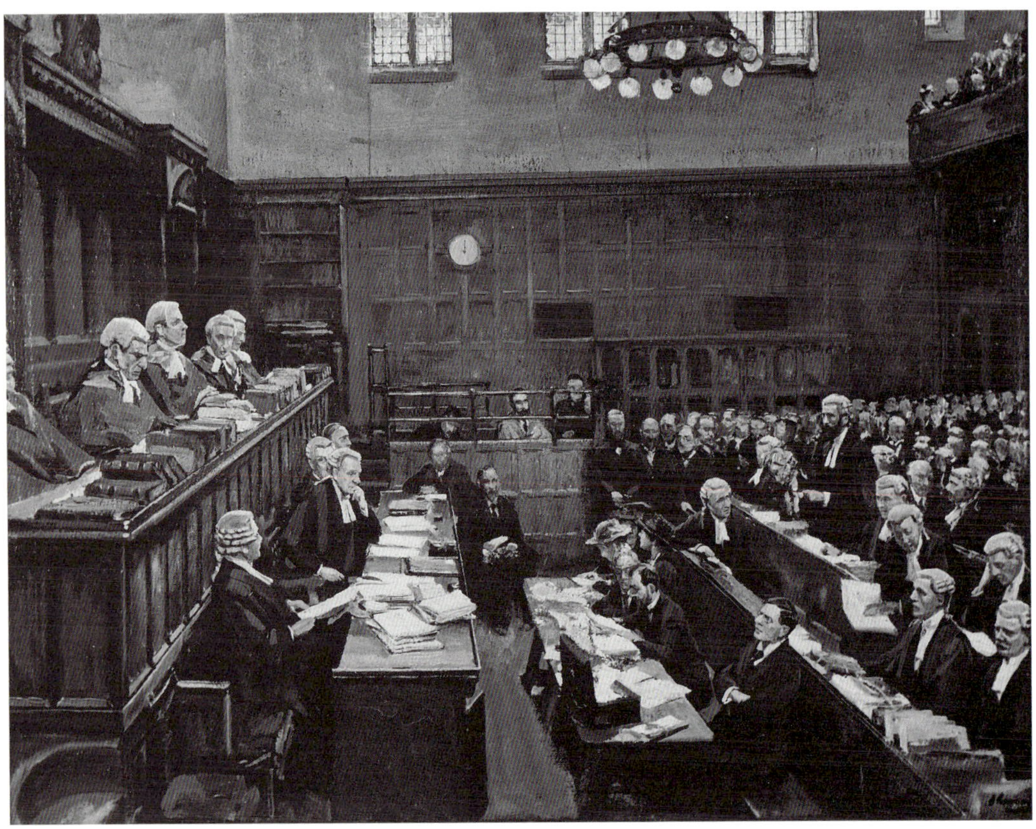

188 Study for *The Court of Criminal Appeal*, 1916, 25 × 30 (Hugh Lane Municipal Gallery, Dublin)

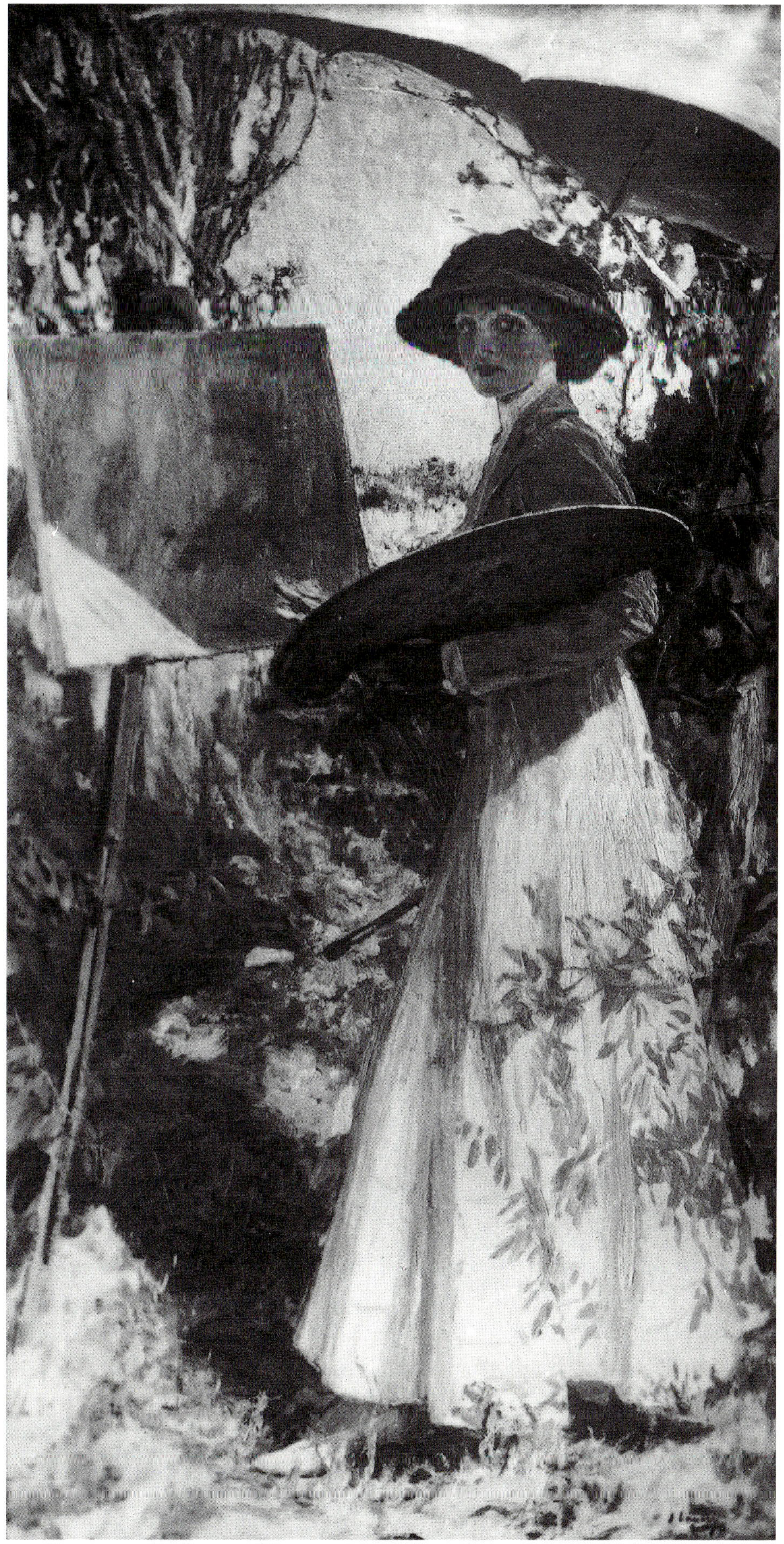

187 *Mrs Lavery Sketching*, 1910, 80 × 39 (Hugh Lane Municipal Gallery, Dublin)

modern Irish painters. *The Times*, however commented with incredulity upon his being placed amongst other painters of Irish origin. Its critic declared that, 'Mr Lavery is so identified with Scotland, that one scarcely looks for him in an Irish exhibition'.[9]

Lavery worked closely with Lane and as an afficionado of modern French painting, he would undoubtedly have supported the collector's taste in the work of the Impressionists. However, the general consensus was that such a heterogeneous display as was mounted at the Guildhall, did not indicate the national sensibility, for which Lane was striving. Referring to his appropriation of artists of the Glasgow School, Lavery chiefly, but also Henry and Roche, *The Art Journal* ruefully concluded that; 'Interesting as is this exhibition by "Irish painters"—it would be instructive to examine the claims of some represented to the title—it demonstrates that there is today no Irish School of pictorial art, no distinct national movement.'[10]

Lane's remedy for this situation was to exhort the city of Dublin to form a collection of modern painting in order to educate the public and young Irish artists. Lavery's positive support for this endeavour was expressed in the donation of *La Dame aux Perles* (see Plate 125), one of his best portraits, to the municipal collection in 1907. He must have closely followed Lane's battle to establish the collection in anything more than a temporary base.[11] His gift to Dublin was followed in 1910 by the city's purchase of *Mrs Lavery Sketching* (Plate 187), a fulsome Impressionist picture selected by Lane. The painter's act of generosity to the city of Dublin and this subsequent purchase must have been contributory factors in the decision of the burghers of Belfast to purchase *The Lady in Black* (see Plate 138) in 1913.[12] However, none of these pictures was overtly Irish in style or subject matter.

It was only on the prompting of his wife, Hazel, that Lavery began to ponder more deeply the question of national allegiance. Although she came from Chicago, Hazel Lavery was proud of her Galway ancestors. Perhaps initiated by Dublin's acquisition of one of her husband's first and most important portraits of her, her passion for Ireland grew. The Laverys began to visit Ireland regularly after 1913 and to occupy a niche in Dublin society.[13] Although they supported the cause for Irish nationhood, they did not involve themselves directly as more than spectators until after the Easter Uprising and the Casement trial. This latter event drew the artist directly into Irish affairs.

Having spent two futile years in Germany, trying to raise support for the Republican cause, Sir Roger Casement returned to Ireland, landing at Tralee Bay in April 1916, three days before the uprising.[14] Shortly after his disastrous disembarkation, Casement was arrested and brought to London for trial at the Old Bailey, charged with high treason. His defender, the inappropriate Sergeant Sullivan refused to accept Casement's plea of guilty, and his wish not to recognise the court. During the trial, Sullivan was submitted to persistent hectoring from the Attorney General and he broke down and had to leave the court. Partly for these reasons, it was he who advised upon an appeal which was held in July 1916. However, because he insisted upon refusing to bring up the wider issues of nationalism, the appeal was predictably futile.[15] Lavery was invited by the Lord

189 *The Madonna of the Lakes, the Lakes of Killarney*, 1913, 16 × 30 (present whereabouts unknown, photo, courtesy Christie's)

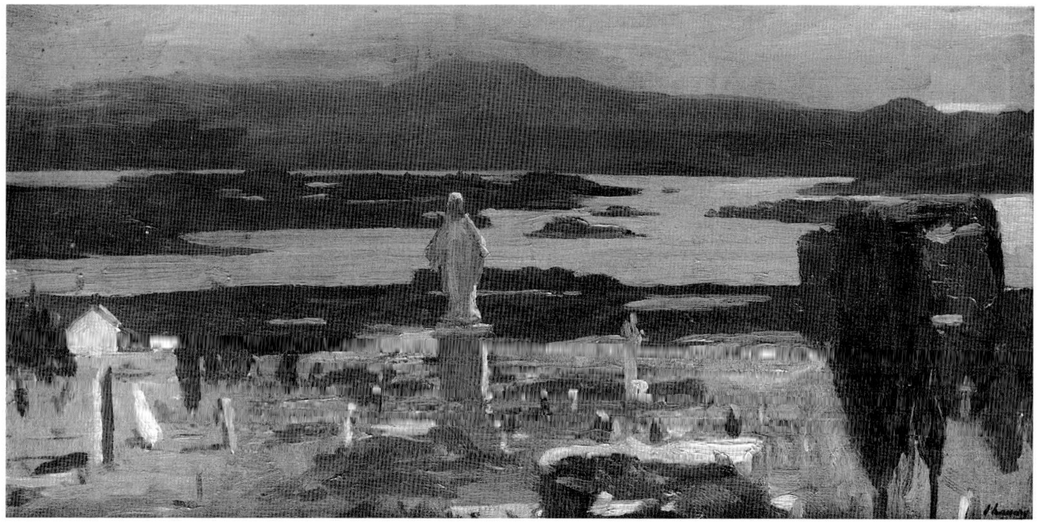

Chief Justice, Sir Charles Darling to record this controversial event and to do so he was placed in the jury box surveying the packed courtroom, but with his painting kit on the seat beside him, well out of sight (see Plate 188). The mood of concentration was such that Lavery's activities were detected only by the prisoner who sat in the dock facing him. During his last days in the condemned cell, Casement wrote to his sister inquiring 'who was the painter in the Jury box?' and who was the 'beautiful' and 'sad-faced' lady who sat near him?[16] Lavery followed the now familiar practice of making a sketch of the scene and then progressed to the final version which was presented by Darling to the law courts. Reflecting upon what had passed before his eyes, the artist declared that, 'It was difficult to realise that a man's life was at stake in the drowsy monotony of the talk that went on for two days, or even at the end when Justice Darling, in the most casual manner, said "the Appeal is dismissed". Casement stood up and looked round the Court, waved to someone in the gallery, turned his back and disappeared down the stairs that would lead to the scaffold.'[17]

In a letter to Lavery, Casement's sister expressed her gratitude that 'it is an Irishman who is painting the picture'. The whole tragic event must have served to underline Lavery's growing commitment to his native land.[18]

Inspired by his wife's success in tableaux vivant, staged in aid of war charities, Lavery painted Hazel as *The Madonna of the Lakes* (Plate 189) for the Royal Academy of 1917.[19] For this triptych, Eileen Lavery posed as St Brigid and Alice as the young St Patrick against a backdrop of what was intended to portray the Kerry lakes. A small study painted in a graveyard overlooking the lakes may have given the painter his vision of a picture which would allude as much to myth as to religion. The frame was specially designed by Sir Edwin Lutyens using celtic spiral motifs and the whole ensemble was intended as a focus for Irish catholic piety.

It must be seen alongside such allegorical works as *The Holy Well*, being painted concurrently by William Orpen. Such images, intended to establish an Irish cultural identity were generally misunderstood by sceptical English eyes. Lavery's

Madonna . . . was savaged by critics in 1917, although it found a sympathetic home in St Patrick's church, Belfast, where the artist had been christened as a baby. The picture was greatly admired by its recipients as an 'outstanding example of ecclesiastical decorative art', which combined the ethereal vision of Our Lady with the more material and human qualities of St Patrick and St Brigid.[20] Lavery followed this act of generosity by donating a celtic cross carved in Irish oak by the Belfast sculptor, R. May, at the beginning of 1920.[21] However, not to cause offence to the protestant population of his native city, he simultaneously presented a study for *The King, The Queen The Prince of Wales, The Princess Mary* (see Plate 148) . . . to Belfast Corporation—'to show the other side that I was not a bigot'.[22]

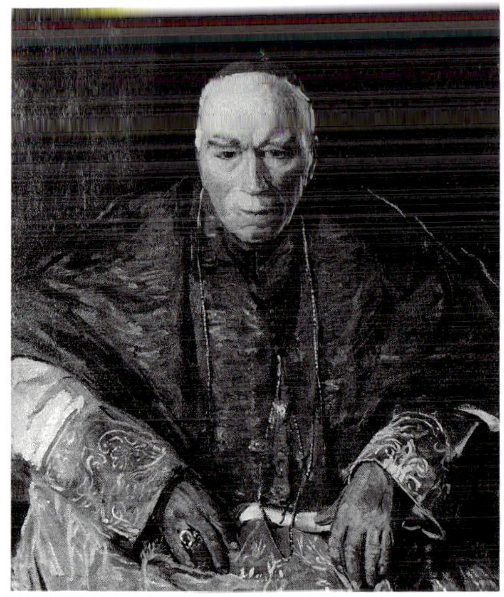

190 *His Eminence Cardinal Logue*, 1920, 31 × 25¼ (The Ulster Museum, Belfast)

In 1919, Lavery painted his first portrait of the Marquis of Londonderry and a close friendship blossomed between the two men, in spite of the painter's avowed republicanism and the sitter's staunch unionism.[23] Through Londonderry's good offices Lavery was able to arrange sittings with churchmen and political leaders. In October 1920, Hazel and he went to Armagh where he painted the portrait of Michael Logue, Primate of all Ireland. Lavery recollected the ancient city with its two cathedrals, catholic and protestant, facing one another upon opposite hills.[24] His impression of *His Eminence Cardinal Logue* (Plate 190), 'a little old man with round shoulders and his head shot forward, with beetling brows and long upper lip . . .' was even more vivid.[25] Unable to see the colour of the primate's eyes, Lavery asked him to look up. When he noted that they were 'Irish grey', the sitter insisted that they were black, but had perhaps 'become grey with the years'.[26] Cardinal Logue was eighty years old when his portrait was painted. Born at Carrigart, County Donegal, he had been educated at Maynooth and had become Professor of Dogmatic Theology at the Irish College in Paris in 1866. He ascended to the archbishopric of Armagh in 1888 and was created cardinal in 1893. An Irish speaker, he was a keen supporter of the Gaelic League and it was due to his enthusiasm that the funds for the completion of Armagh Cathedral were raised. At the time of Lavery's visit, he was however, 'a lonely old man', with 'something simian' about his appearance. Lavery felt that the cardinal might not be pleased with the end result of his labour but in the way he looked at the portrait and the compliments which he paid to the artist and his wife, it was clear that age had reconciled him to his rather ugly features. Indeed he often recalled that one of his parishoners had once referred to him as '. . . the ugliest man God ever made'.[27] Lavery's rendering of the primate is, nevertheless one of his most formidable later works. Not only does it beg comparison with Velasquez' *Pope Innocent X* (Galleria Nationale, Rome) as an image, but it reveals the extent to which, at a deeper level Lavery had absorbed the lessons of the Old Masters. The fluid drawing of the lace and the sketchy handling of the hands, shows us an intimate appreciation of the work of seventeenth-century cavalier painters. These peripheral effects serve to concentrate the spectator's attention upon the cardinal's face and character with an intensity comparable to that which commanded the artist. The result, in the opinion of one distinguished contemporary observer suggests a battle of personalities between painter and sitter.[28] So significant was this portrait, that it spawned a series of paintings of clerics later in the decade which included, *Cardinal Hayes, Archbishop of New York, Bishop Grierson* and *Archbishop MacRory* none of

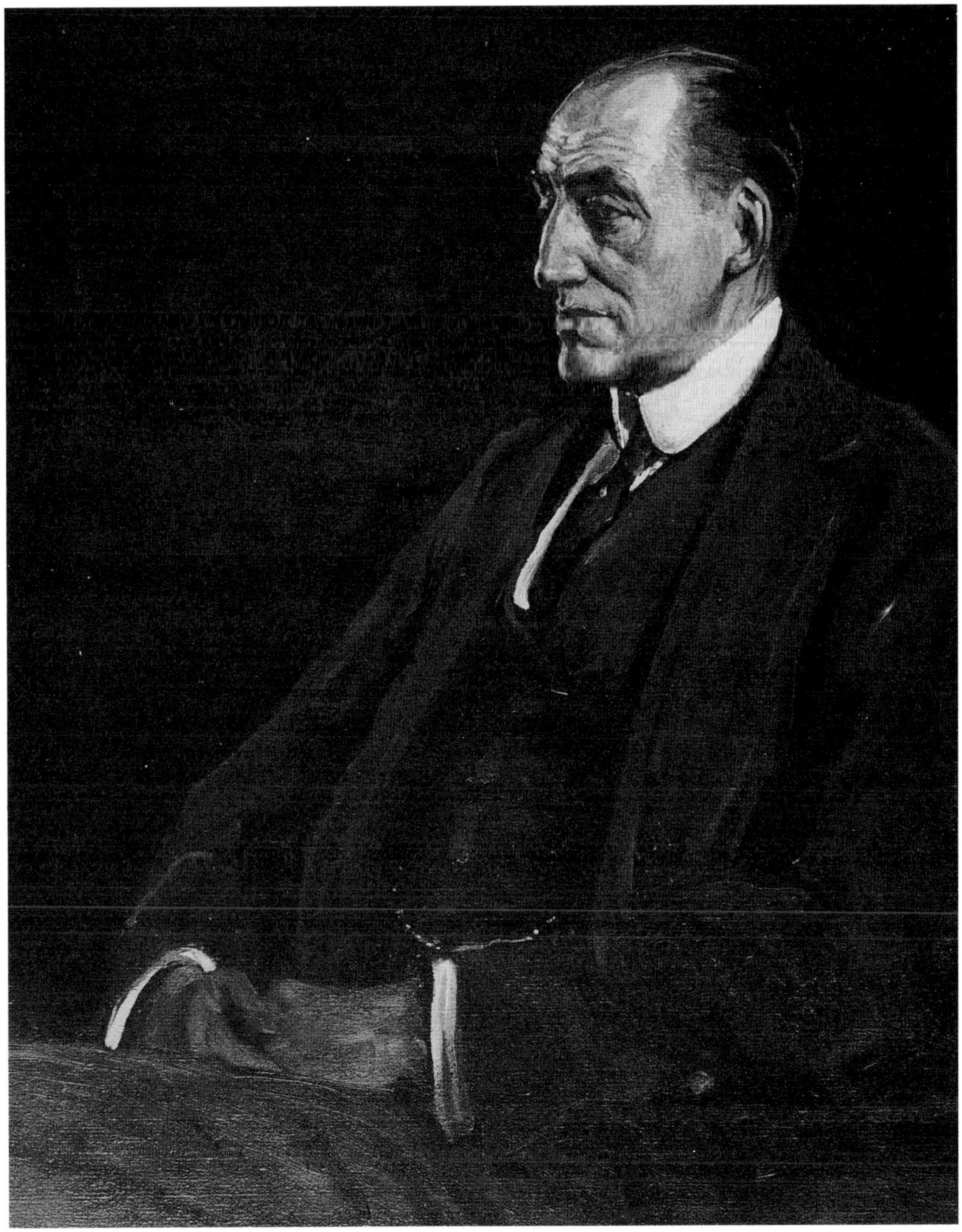

191 *Lord Carson of Duncairn*, 1921–2, 25 × 30 (The Ulster Museum, Belfast)

whom possessed the commanding presence of Michael Logue. Lavery took no regard for the sectarian origins of Northern Irish clerics, painting portraits of both catholic and protestant churchmen. When he was half-way through the portrait of the *Most Reverend Charles Frederick d'Arcy*, the Church of Ireland Archbishop of Armagh, in June 1928 at Mount Stewart, the home of the Londonderrys, Lavery received an anomymous letter threatening his life. He took the incident philosophically and when he showed the letter to his wife, she simply remarked, 'never mind, carry on'.[29]

As a portraitist, Lavery trod the tightrope of Irish politics with some success, believing that in art the warring factions ought to discover a common cultural heritage. He scrupulously avoided partiality during his lifetime and only at the time of writing his biography did he publish a letter to Churchill signed jointly by Hazel and he, declaring that, '. . . the removal of the "Castle" and all its works, leaving Irishmen to settle their own affairs, is the only solution left.'[30]

There was an inkling of this conviction in the perceptive response of one sitter. In 1916, Lavery had painted the portrait of Sir Edward Carson, former Solicitor General for Ireland, Member of Parliament for Dublin University and now closely associated with the Unionist cause. Realising that the painter hailed from Belfast and was a catholic, Carson, comparing his portrait with that of his opponent, John Redmond, remarked to the painter, 'Ah it's easy to see which side you're on'.[31]

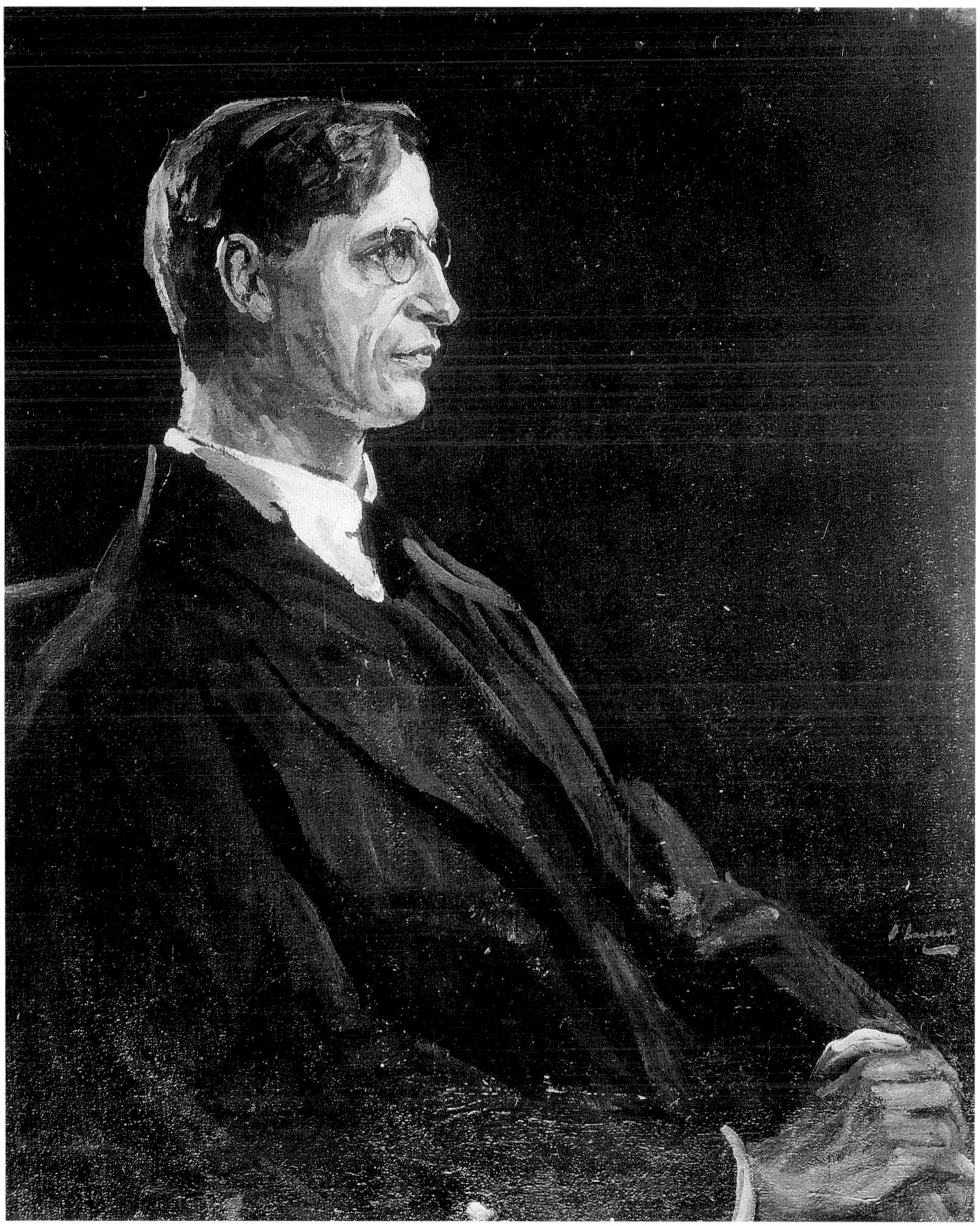

192 *Eamon de Valera, 1921*, 25 × 30 (Hugh Lane Municipal Art Gallery, Dublin)

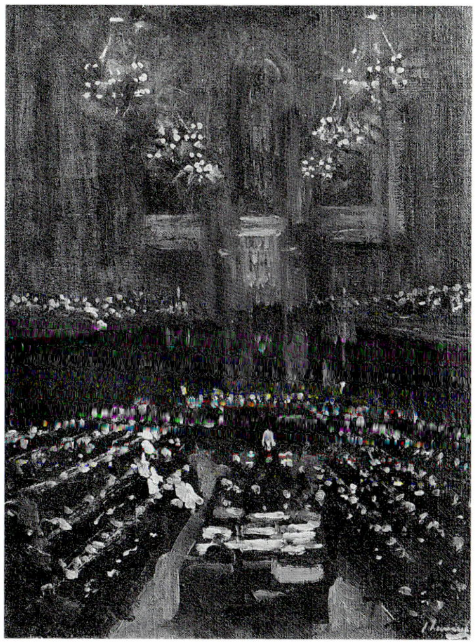

193 *The Ratification of the Irish Treaty in the English House of Lords, 1921*, 14¼ × 10¼ (National Gallery of Ireland, Dublin)

Carson's likeness, despite the coarse features of the sitter, is one of the most imposing of Lavery's political portraits. When he painted Carson a second time, in February 1922, for presentation to the city of Belfast, Lavery records that his sitter again fell into reverie in front of his picture, only this time he dubbed it, 'Edward Carson after the surrender'.[32] (see Plate 191).

The 'surrender' referred to was, of course, the Irish Treaty which had been passed through the House of Lords in December 1921. Up to that point, Lavery had keenly involved himself in Irish affairs. When in October 1920, Terence McSwiney, the Lord Mayor of Cork, died on hunger strike in Brixton jail, Lavery attended his funeral at Southwark Cathedral and recorded the event. The following autumn saw him busily engaged in a sequence of paintings of Irish leaders carried out in London during the period of safe conduct arranged during the treaty negotiations. Erskine Childers, secretary of the Irish delegation, wrote to Lavery in October 1921 conveying the warm thanks of his colleagues and offering to arrange sittings 'as soon as possible', though Childers himself could not be induced into the Cromwell Place studio.[33] By that stage, de Valera's portrait (see Plate 192) had already been painted—his short mission to London in July 1921 having failed. Lavery regretted that in this instance, he was given merely a single sitting of a couple of hours and could produce no more than a simple record of appearances.[34] The other pictures which followed were those of Robert Barton, Gavin Duffy, Arthur Griffith and Michael Collins and it was clearly the charisma of the latter to which Lavery most warmly responded. Within a short time, Collins and Lady Lavery became close friends and in later years, the artist was to claim that due to Hazel's intervention, both sides in the Irish dispute achieved the necessary compromise. There was no doubt in the minds of jealous contemporaries like Shane Leslie, that a special chemistry existed between Hazel Lavery and Michael Collins. It has been sufficient to fuel continual unsubstantiated speculation of an affair. By the beginning of December 1921, an agreement was ready for hasty debate in the House of Lords (see Plate 193), where it was proposed by Earl Morley (see Plate 194). Here again, Lavery took up his observation point in the spectators' gallery and in a swift sketch, later transformed into a large commemorative oil, he recorded the scene.[35] The resulting picture, exhibited at the Royal Academy in 1922 was praised by James L. Caw for its 'purely pictorial' qualities. It was 'rich and mellow in colour, the effect of the ensemble being . . . beautiful in its dark clearness'.[36]

The terms which were ratified in the House of Lords on 16 December 1921 made it possible for any Irish county to secede from the newly proposed dominion. As expected, six of the Ulster counties had already opted to remain as part of Great Britain. In addition, Ireland's new leaders were in bitter disagreement on the terms of the treaty. Feuding within Irish Republican Army factions continued and Collins came to feel that by signing the treaty he had, in effect, signed his own death warrant. Bitter internecine struggles between the newly formed Free State Army and the anti-treaty IRA ensued to the point where within twelve months the major signatories were dead. In August 1922, Arthur Griffith died of a heart attack and within weeks of this sad event, Collins himself was dead (see Plate 195).

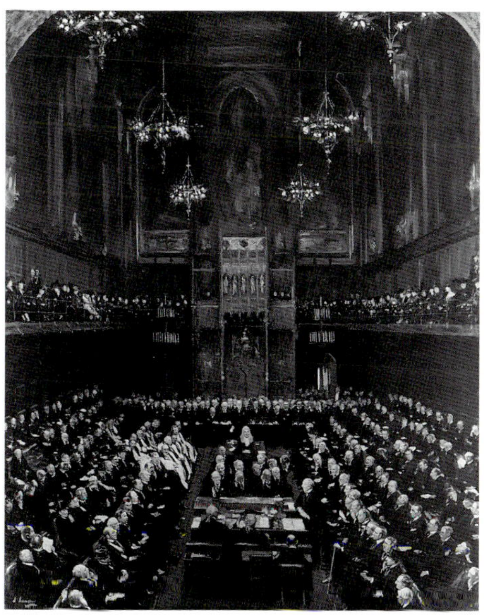

194 *Earl Morley Addressing the House of Lords, 1921*, 50 × 40 (Glasgow Art Gallery and Museum)

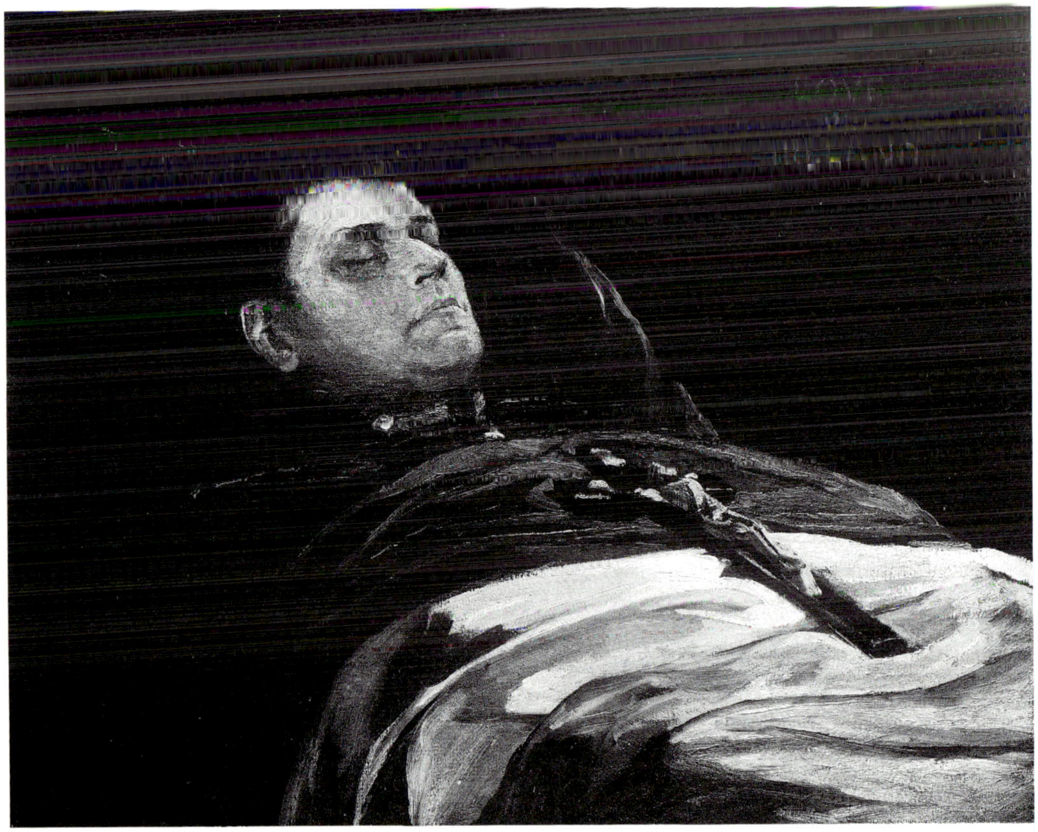

195 *Michael Collins ('Love of Ireland')*, 1922, [illegible] (Hugh Lane Municipal Art Gallery, Dublin)

Lavery recounts that Hazel and he went to Dublin after the treaty was signed. It was there he realised the hostility that awaited Collins. On one occasion, after they had lunched together at the Gresham Hotel, O'Connell Street, Collins was held up at gun point by a youth who he later disarmed. On another occasion at Kingstown Hotel, Hazel apparently saved his life by sitting between him and the window. After dinner, the Irish leader and Lady Lavery went to visit Horace Plunkett and on the way back, their car was caught in a hail of bullets. Both escaped without injury and as Lavery records, '. . . Collins made light of it, but complained of a pain in his side that he thought might possibly be his appendix. After much persuasion he accepted my hot-water bottle, and placing it under his tunic he smilingly said that the pain had gone. With a "God bless you both" he jumped into his car with Emmet Dalton and Joe Riley, dashing off into the night. That was the last I saw of him alive.'[37]

Thereafter, Hazel Lavery was full of premonitions and found it difficult to sleep. The next ambush, outside the town of Macroom, found its target. On the morning of 23 August 1922, Lady Lavery's 'very English' maid coolly reported, 'they have shot Mr Collins, my Lady'.[38]

Lavery's depiction of the *Requiem Mass for Michael Collins* (Plate 196) follows the format of that of Terence McSwiney, two years earlier. However, the occasion provided the opportunity for a more intimate *envoi* to a personal friend. He painted a portrait of Collins in death which he described in *The Life of a Painter* as follows,

> Any grossness in his features, even the peculiar little dent near the point of his nose, had disappeared. He might have been Napoleon in marble as he lay in his uniform, covered by the Free State Flag, with a crucifix on his breast. Four soldiers stood round the bier. The stillness was broken at long intervals by someone entering the Chapel on tiptoe, kissing the brow, and then slipping to the door where I could hear a burst of suppressed grief. One woman kissed the dead lips, making it hard for me to continue my work. All day I strove to record the mystery that seemed to play about that mouth, the lips appearing to move at times.[39]

When he returned to Kingstown that evening, Lavery showed his canvas to the night porter who laconically remarked, 'well now, that is the last of Mike; the next one will get the same.'[40]

Having closely identified with Collins, the artist could not understand the tone of this enigmatic remark. Its grim portent, however, must have been confirmed when, a few months later, Lavery heard that Kevin O'Higgins had been assassinated on his way to Mass. With him went the ambition that the Laverys should occupy Vice-Regal Lodge as the last Imperial Envoys in the Free State. By the time of O'Higgins' demise, this was already an impossibility, if it was ever really possible. Lavery himself regarded the notion as an 'absurdity' and 'told Kevin so', but he was hurt for his wife whose ambitions were greater in that direction. Hazel had already seen the Lodge and was delighted by its eighteenth-century character. However, as Lavery realised, her Celtic Revival view of Ireland was unsuited to the harsh realities of sectarian strife. 'Hazel's Ireland', in Lavery's words, 'was as unreal as a mirage in the desert'.[41] She was, however, seriously engaged in Irish politics and in his last letter to her, Kevin O'Higgins set out his views on all the various factions now at war, as well as expressing the clear duty to carry on and endeavour 'to save Michael's achievements for the Country from destruction'.[42]

It was undoubtedly for this reason that the Laverys spent so much time in Ireland during and immediately after the declaration of the Free State. Although he was often in Dublin, Lavery did not neglect his native city. Having been received as an Honorary Member of Belfast Art Society in 1904, he showed regularly with the society and was elected its president in 1919. In that year, Hazel and he visited Belfast to attend the opening of the annual exhibition and to preside over an afternoon tea at the Midland Hotel.[43] Two years later, in June 1921, when King George V and Queen Mary visited the province to open the Northern Ireland Parliament at Stormont, Lavery, on behalf of the society pledged his loyalty to the throne and with it the hope that the king's visit would 'bring a new era of peace throughout this land'.[44]

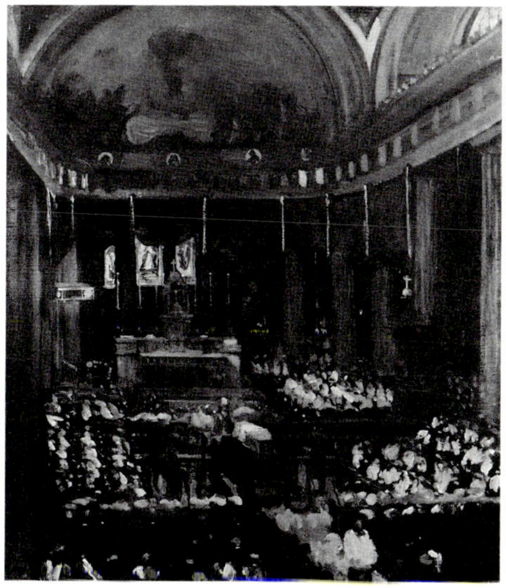

196 *Requiem Mass for Michael Collins*, 1922, size unknown (present whereabouts unknown, photo, Christie's)

During these years, the Belfast press took great interest in Lavery's work. Back in 1914, at the time of his Grosvenor Gallery retrospective, the *Evening Telegraph* had published an extensive article pointing out that 'the artist whose name is on everybody's lips—prince's and peasant's—is assuredly Belfast born'.[45] Throughout the ten years up to the end of his term of office as the Art Society's president, Lavery was regarded as Ulster's most distinguished painter. In October 1924, he

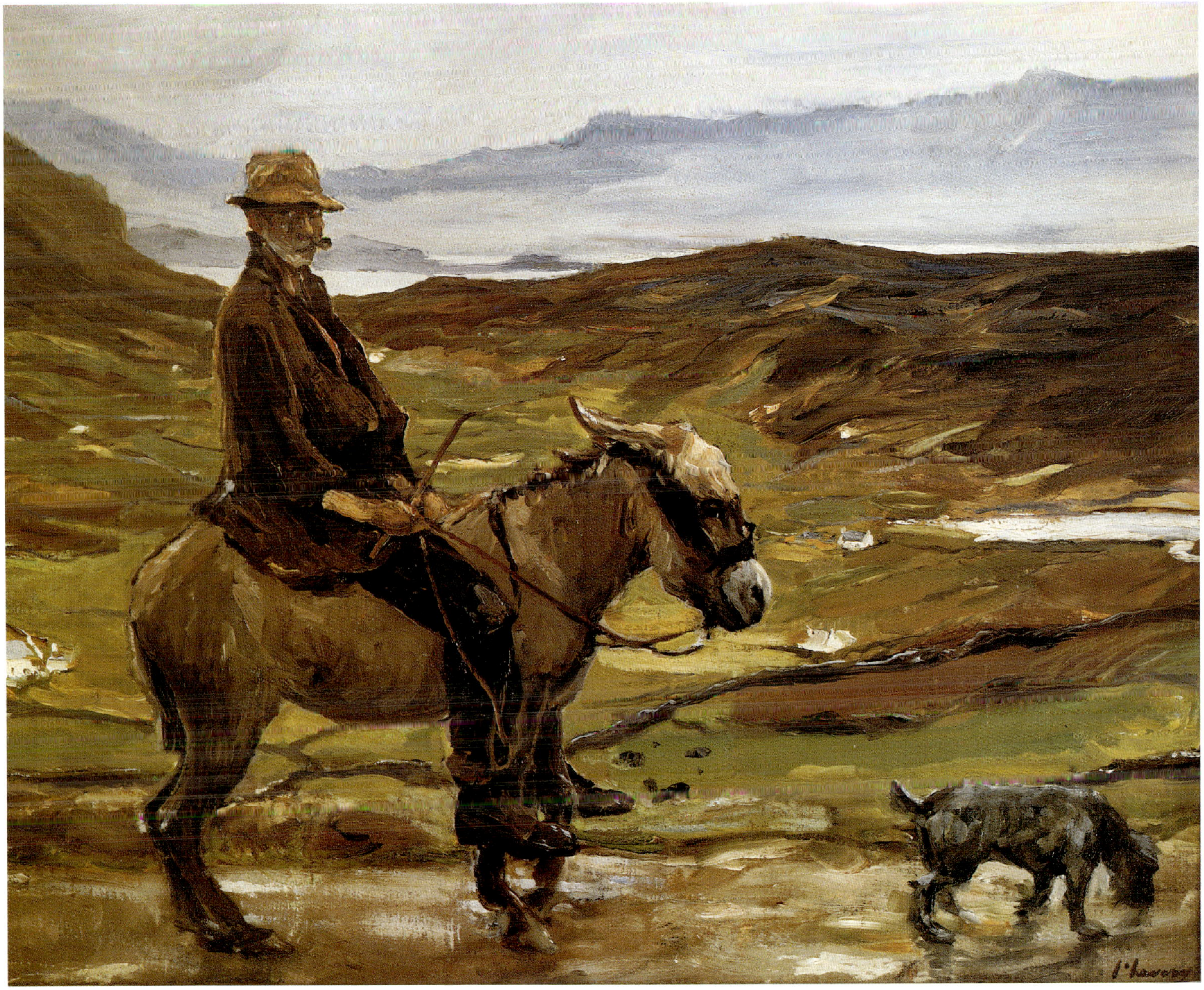

198 *The Kingdom of Kerry*, *c.*1925,
20 × 24 (private collection)

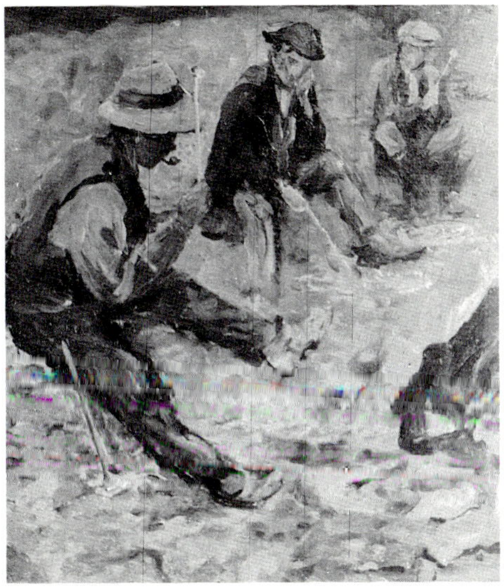

197 *The Stonebreakers*, *c.*1925, 14 × 18 (private collection, photo, Ian Kilpatrick)

showed a portrait of his successor in the office, Lord Londonderry, and with due deference, the *Belfast News Letter* critic wrote, 'Comment on Sir John's work would be superfluous, if not presumptuous, for his fame is world wide, and anything from his brush commands universal attention. Suffice it to say that the picture of the noble Marquis in black and gold robes of the Chancellor of Queens University is a speaking likeness, even to the half-cynical, half-humourous set of the mouth, the poise of the head and the earnest thoughtful expression of the eyes.'[46]

Earlier in that year, the Laverys had visited southern Ireland and the painter briefly returned to peasant subject-matter. At Tramore he painted *The O'Sullivan Family*; an itinerant with a penny whistle who became known as *Phil, the Flutor* and *The Stonebreakers* (Plate 197).[47]

In May 1927, Lavery showed some of these works at an exhibition of paintings by Irish artists at the Fine Art Society. Perhaps his most significant exhibit was *The Kingdom of Kerry* (Plate 198), a painting of an old white bearded peasant riding a donkey, on a high road in the Kerry hills. Comparison with work of the younger Irish painters of the Twenties would seem appropriate, given Lavery's admiration for the work of Sean Keating. However, the lack of caricature in what became in the hands of others a common Irish peasant stereotype, redeems the picture from sterile repetition. All these pictures catch something of the way of life of the rural poor of Ireland and contribute an additional aspect to the canon of emblematic Irish images.

When, in 1926 the Free State was establishing an airforce, it purchased a few biplanes from the British government and these were painted in Irish colours before being flown to Dublin. Lavery was on hand to dash off a swift sketch of the

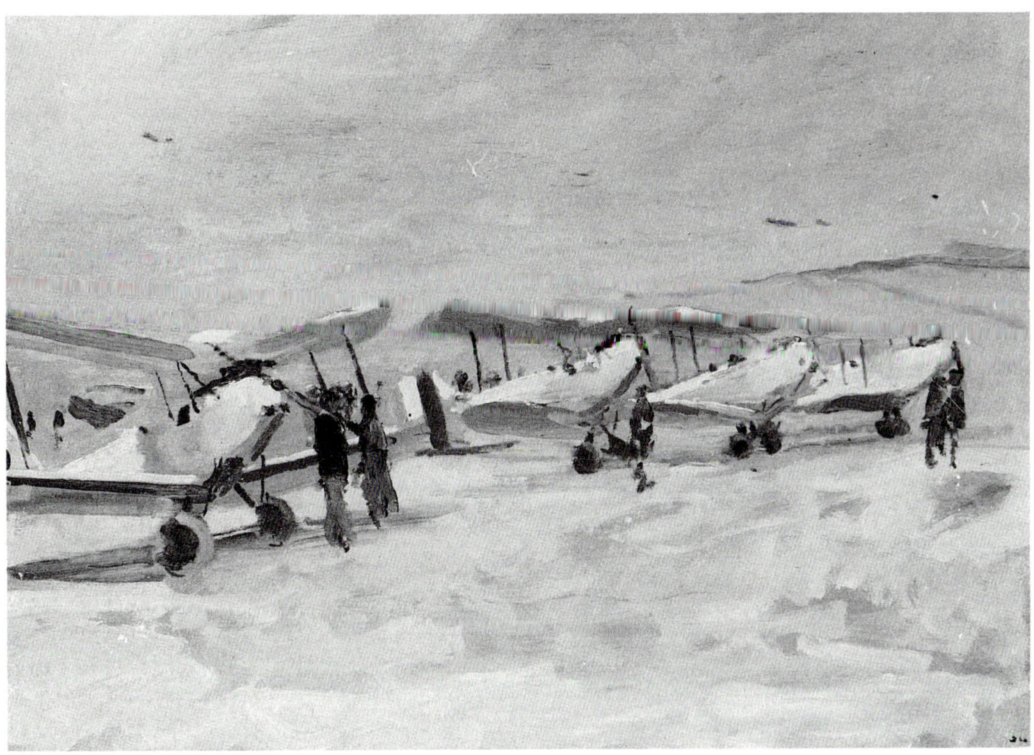

199 *The First Flight to Dublin*, *c.*1925, 18 × 24 (private collection, photo, Ian Kilpatrick)

scene before their departure. *The First Flight to Dublin* (Plate 199) was apparently flown by Lavery's daughter, Eileen and his son-in-law, the Master of Sempill, and it was Eileen who later posed for the painter in flying gear as *The First Irish Airwoman*.

Around the time of the Irish troubles, Lavery re-established contact with his cousins at Soldierstown. He was later to promote the artistic career of a nephew of the Cleneghan family, the offspring of Henry Lavery's daughter. He occasionally visited the family during the late Twenties.[48] It was on such a visit in the summer of 1928 that he painted the Orange parade at nearby Portadown. Lavery later reflected a great deal upon this experience. He recalled, for instance, that as a child growing up in what later became Northern Ireland, it was thought unwise for a 'Papisher' to be about when the processions were passing. In 1928, at the age of seventy-two he was witnessing his first Orange parade. He was moved to record in an unpublished diary, 'I have seen many processions and exhibitions of intense feeling but nothing to quite equal the austere passion of the Twelfth in Portadown (see Plate 200). The colour was more beautiful than anything I have seen in Morocco, black and orange predominating with every other colour except green adding to its beauty and the dozens of big drums beaten with canes by drummers whose lives seemed to depend on the noise they were able to make, their coats off, their shirt sleeves rolled up, their rists [sic] bleeding and a look in the eye that boded ill for any interference . . .'[49]

From a high vantage point in the main street, he watched the procession of

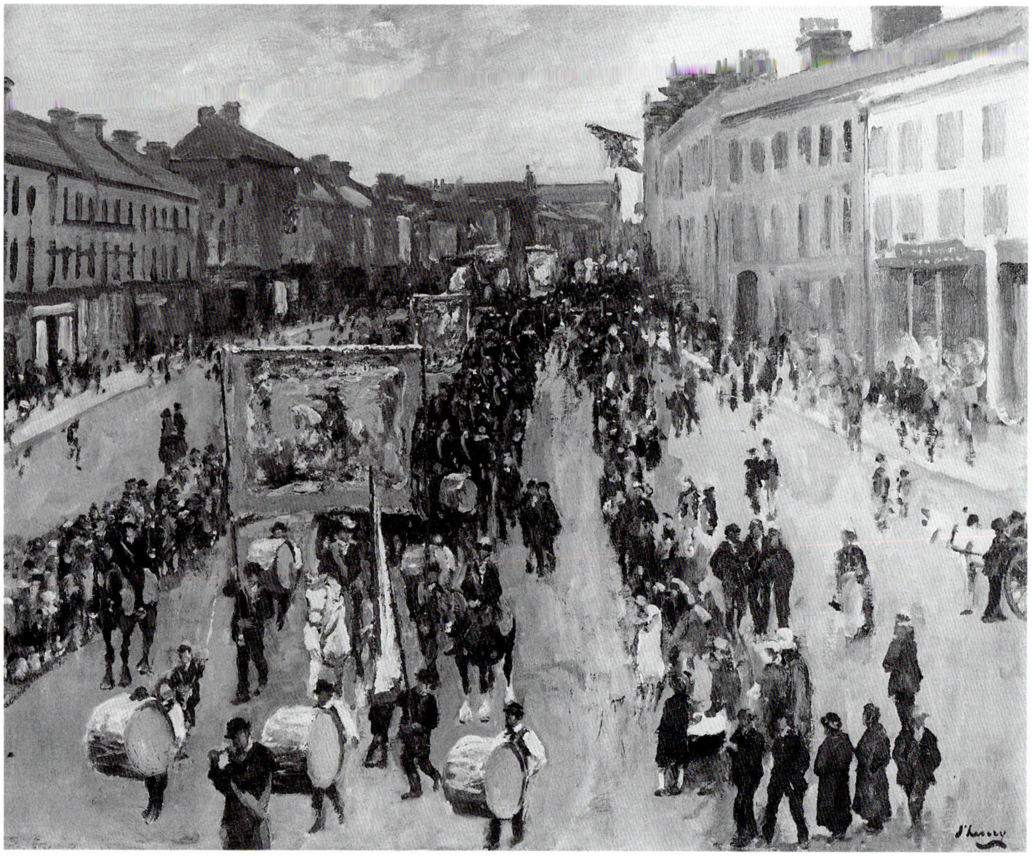

200 *Twelfth of July, Portadown*, 1928, 25 × 30 (The Ulster Museum, Belfast)

banners and flute bands and swiftly depicted the swaying 'Lambeg' drummers with amazing acuity. After completing the picture, he was whisked off to a weekend party with the Rothschilds at Waddesdon Manor in Buckinghamshire. Even Hazel was staggered at his tenacity when, immediately upon arrival, he set to work. She confided to Thomas Bodkin, 'I have never known such sweltering heat and John painted the proceedings having arrived that morning from Belfast! He is a marvel for he had painted a picture at Portadown, the preceeding day of the 12th celebrations! Such a beautiful little picture and it goes to the Belfast collection I regret to say.'[50]

By the time this letter was written, Lavery was already in negotiation to donate two evenly balanced collections of his work to Dublin and Belfast. Having decided upon this course of action in 1927, his work programme for the following year, in addition to *The Twelfth of July, Portadown* included portraits of the Grand Masters of the Orange Lodge . . . *Sir Joseph Davison MP* and the *Rt Hon. Sir Edward M. Archdale, DL, MP.* These were probably executed in order to complement the portraits of the Uprising leaders to be presented simultaneously to Dublin. Lavery was consulted upon the installation of the Belfast collection and in January 1928, he wrote to advise its curator, Arthur Deane on the question of lighting in the galleries. With the aid of sketch diagrams, Lavery described Whistler's designs for the Society of British Artists in which a skylight in the centre of the ceiling, aided by a suspended velarium, created an even diffusion of illumination.[51] In the end this advice was disregarded by the architect, James Cumming Wynnes, and when Lavery visited the gallery, he found the result, despite claims to the contrary not wholly successful. He wrote to Bodkin that, 'the scheme . . . made the side wall fully lit and the end walls, "places of honour" in half light'.[52]

Nevertheless, by the beginning of 1929, around thirty pictures were earmarked for Belfast, and those not already in the province were dispatched from Lavery's studio in March 1929.[53] Wishing to catalogue the collection, Arthur Deane wrote to the artist to query matters of dating. The reply he received from Lady Lavery indicated that some of the Belfast pictures had had interesting metamorphoses. *The Mother*, for instance, dated by Shaw Sparrow to 1907, and originally a profile portrait of Mary Auras had been transformed in 1924 with a new model in the person of Eileen Lavery.[54] *Summer* was painted from a 'Scottish lady' in 1907 and repainted from Lady Lavery herself in 1926. 'All artists', Lady Lavery explained, 'take liberties with wives and daughters and we all have had amputations of arms, legs and hands which are attached to other bodies in John's pictures. But it is really confusing to be decapitated and without permission . . . There are in fact in the collections, portraits of all the family masquerading as "Summer" or "Spring" or "Ladies in Black", "Green" or "Rose"! For John never hesitates to cry "off with a head" and "on with yours" if it suits his mood. Hence I think the dates in the catalogue should be treated with a certain elasticity don't you?'[55]

The Belfast collection was favourably reported in the local press and was so popular that at the beginning of the following year, the aldermen conferred upon the artist the Freedom of the City.[56] In his speech of acceptance on 22 April 1930, Lavery expressed the hope that Belfast would become a great international art centre.[57]

If Belfast lionised Sir John Lavery in 1930, Dublin was also laying claim to him. The sequence of events north of the border, had been sparked by the impetus to donate equal collections to both sides. At the end of August 1927, Lavery had written in confidence to Thomas Bodkin indicating his wish to give thirty paintings to Dublin.[58] The proposal was, however, overtaken later that year by an invitation from the 'Note Committee' of the Free State, 'that I should design a head for them, preferably I take it, one from my wife', to be used for reproduction on the new Irish currency.[59] For her part, Lady Lavery was extremely flattered by the suggestion, though she expressed reservations. In an effusive letter to Bodkin, who probably originated the idea, she gave voice to these fears: 'I really feel that you are too kind and generous when you suggest that my humble head should figure on the note, and you know I said from the first that I thought it wildly *improbable*, *unlikely*, *impracticable*, *unpopular*, *impossible* that any committee would fall in with such a suggestion. Indeed apart from anything else I think a classic head, some Queen of Ireland, Maeve, perhaps would be best, someone more robust and noble and fitted for coinage reproduction. . .'[60]

These objections were, however, put to one side as Lavery worked over the Christmas period upon a half-length oval representation of Kathleen ni Houlihan (see Plate 201), the legendary heroine mythologised by Yeats. Unhappy with his first version, he reworked the head and by the end of February, it was in such a state that Hazel Lavery was able to report to Bodkin, '. . . John *greatly* improved the "note" head and altered the size by reducing the drapery around the head and making it less clumsy about the chin: he also accentuated certain things about the face, and had it rephotographed. They received instructions from him to use their latest photograph and to reproduce the alterations he had made in their final design. . .'.[61]

The resulting canvas is unusual in Lavery's oeuvre, in that it lacks the active paint surface which characterises the immediacy of his style. Its colours are dull and muted and in general terms, the work has something of the mural-like quality of the paintings of Puvis de Chavannes, being more self-consciously drawn than painted. These stylistic devices obviously made it easier for the work to be photographed and then engraved (see Plate 102), but they also relate to the community of images which Lavery himself had initiated with *An Irish Girl* (see Plate 70). Upon this foundation, a formidable corpus of pictures had been built in the first decade of the century and the notion of the symbolic embodiment of Ireland had been extended into the Twenties by the younger generation of Irish painters like, Sean Keating, Patrick Tuohy and Charles Lamb in a modern classical style derived from an amalgam of Puvis and Augustus John.[62] The 'Note' head was nevertheless, Lavery's most significant contribution to this imagery and arguably it was the most important symbolic representation of Erin ever produced. The case here rests upon its constant usage—up to 1975—in Free State currency. Hazel Lavery's dark eyes and wistful looks became an embodiment of the land and people which she identified as her spiritual home and family. The potency of the symbol transcended both model and artist, to be recognised in more universal terms by future generations of Irishmen as the embodiment of their nationality.

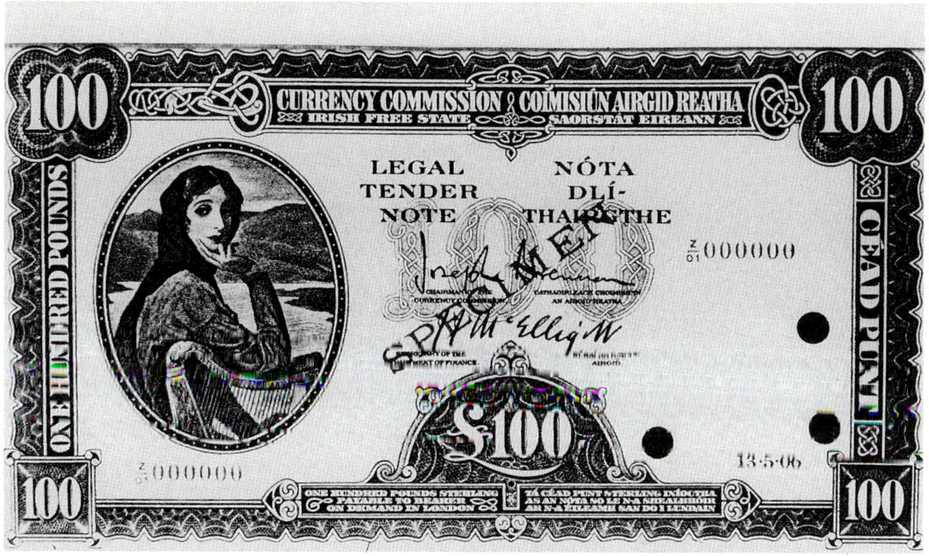

202 Irish Currency, 1928–75

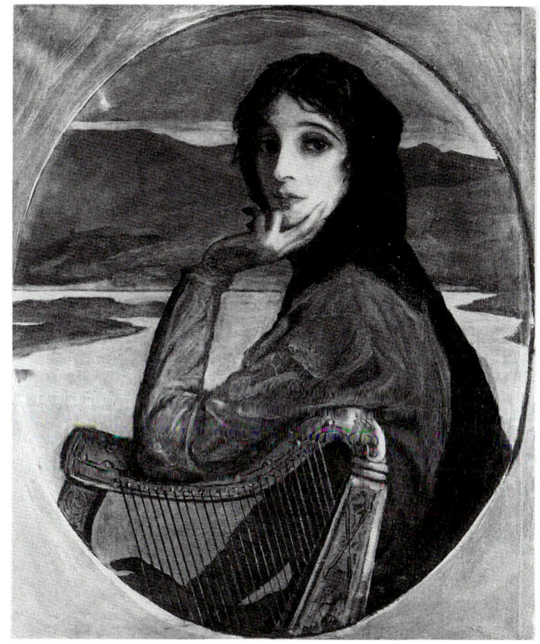

201 *Lady Lavery as Kathleen ni Houlihan*, 1927, 30 × 25 (Central Bank of Ireland, Dublin)

Throughout these years, the Laverys visited Ireland on numerous occasions, often two or three times a year. Contacts were maintained with artists and writers on both sides of the border.[63] Even when wintering at Mougins, Hazel Lavery could confess to Bodkin in confidence, that she greatly missed the country of her adoption. 'I feel lonely here. Everyone is disgustingly rich and callous, not intelligent, and worst of all, very often inclined to be "arty" . . . I feel very far away from Ireland, the place I love best, and read *The Times* [Irish] and even that awful *Independent* from page to page . . . .[64]

Lavery exorcised his feelings in other ways, and on one notable occasion, the irony of painting an Irish subject from the vantage point of Cannes greatly appealed to his sense of humour. In August 1929, Lavery went to Lough Derg to paint the ancient Irish pilgrimage known as St Patrick's Purgatory.[65] He asked Shane Leslie to supply him with some details of the history of this extraordinary place. These are recounted in his autobiography (see Plate 203).[66] Before he set off, he wrote to the prior stating his proposal. He records, 'Not being a pilgrim in the strict sense of the word, I was allowed to keep my boots on, a privilege also extended to the Prior who welcomed me on landing and helped me with my painting outfit to a cold grey stone building, where he gave me, so far as I could see, the only furnished room in it. I discovered afterwards that it was his own bedroom, and that the three or four nights when I occupied it he had slept in another part of the building on the floor.'[67]

Lavery was perturbed to discover that, contrary to his expectations, the pilgrims were not picturesque peasants but 'everyday types one would see in the streets of Belfast or Dublin'.[68] Also, to his amazement, the weather was unpredictably good, and while he was on his way back to London, he was obliged to admit to Bodkin, 'I am on my way home from St Patrick's Purgatory where I wanted to paint the pilgrims in their devotions and above all plodding through the mud and rain but alas the rain has come after I have left and my pictures, I fear, will look like a crowded summer resort making Purgatory a thing to long for . . .'.[69]

At least two preparatory sketches for *St Patrick's Purgatory* are known.[70] Both of these show that the painter distanced himself from the drama of the scene in order to give a panoramic view of the numerous pilgrims quietly encircling the stoney shrines of the saints. Presiding over their devotions was the bell tower of the modern basilica, beyond which stretched the silver lough and the moody southern uplands of Donegal. Lavery was affected by the experience. He recounts the tale of a pilgrim who found spiritual peace in an annual trip to Lough Derg. This man turned out to be a university professor from England. He prompted Lavery to reflect, 'I could not help thinking that perhaps there was something to it, and that I might paint better if I took my head out of the paint pot for a moment and thought of other things than trying to paint pictures. The mood did not last. I was no sooner back and had turned out my studies than the problem of picture making banished everything else. I excused myself on the ground that I had a purgatory of my own. . .'.[71]

This purgatory must have been easier to bear at Cannes than in Donegal, because it was at the Hotel Beau Site that Lavery resumed his Lough Derg studies for the large painting exhibited at the Royal Academy in 1930. He complained to Bodkin, 'We are basking in sunshine . . . while I paint from studies made at Lough Derg . . . the Saint would appear to be somewhat nomadic, it is said he cleared out all the Vipers on St Marguerite an Island I can see from my studio window.'[72]

St Patrick's Purgatory gives no evidence of the eccentric circumstances of its creation. Unlike nineteenth-century paintings of rustic devotions, like those, for instance, of Alphonse Legros, its movements are oddly uncoordinated. The pilgrims are scattered at random amongst the circular shrines and are a mixture of shawl-clad provincials and city folk. Two young women, fashionably dressed deftly pick their way, barefoot amongst the stones and puddles, whilst others kneel to pray. The picture therefore expresses something of the incongruity of modern religious belief that was apparent to its painter. At the same time it unquestionably summed up the rawness of the western landscape.

Despite Bodkin's support, Dublin procrastinated over the terms of Lavery's gift, and the Attorney General, Hugh Nihill Kennedy raised 'secret' legal difficulties. It seemed to observers that some Dublin officials were peeved at the thought that Belfast should receive equal recognition at the same time.[73] Yet since both gifts were unsolicited, there ought to have been no delay in their acceptance. It was only with the suggestion that the collection be presented as a memorial to Lady Lavery after her death, that in the summer months of 1935 the Dublin gift was finally accepted.[74] In response to his generosity, Dublin also conferred upon him the Freedom of the City and his investiture on 17 September 1935 was greeted by cheering crowds. In his speech of welcome, President Cosgrave made the point that Lavery must be the only person alive to enjoy the freedom of both Irish capitals and that the portraits which he had given to them illustrated the makers of recent Irish history.[75] Lavery was deeply moved by the occasion—perhaps the

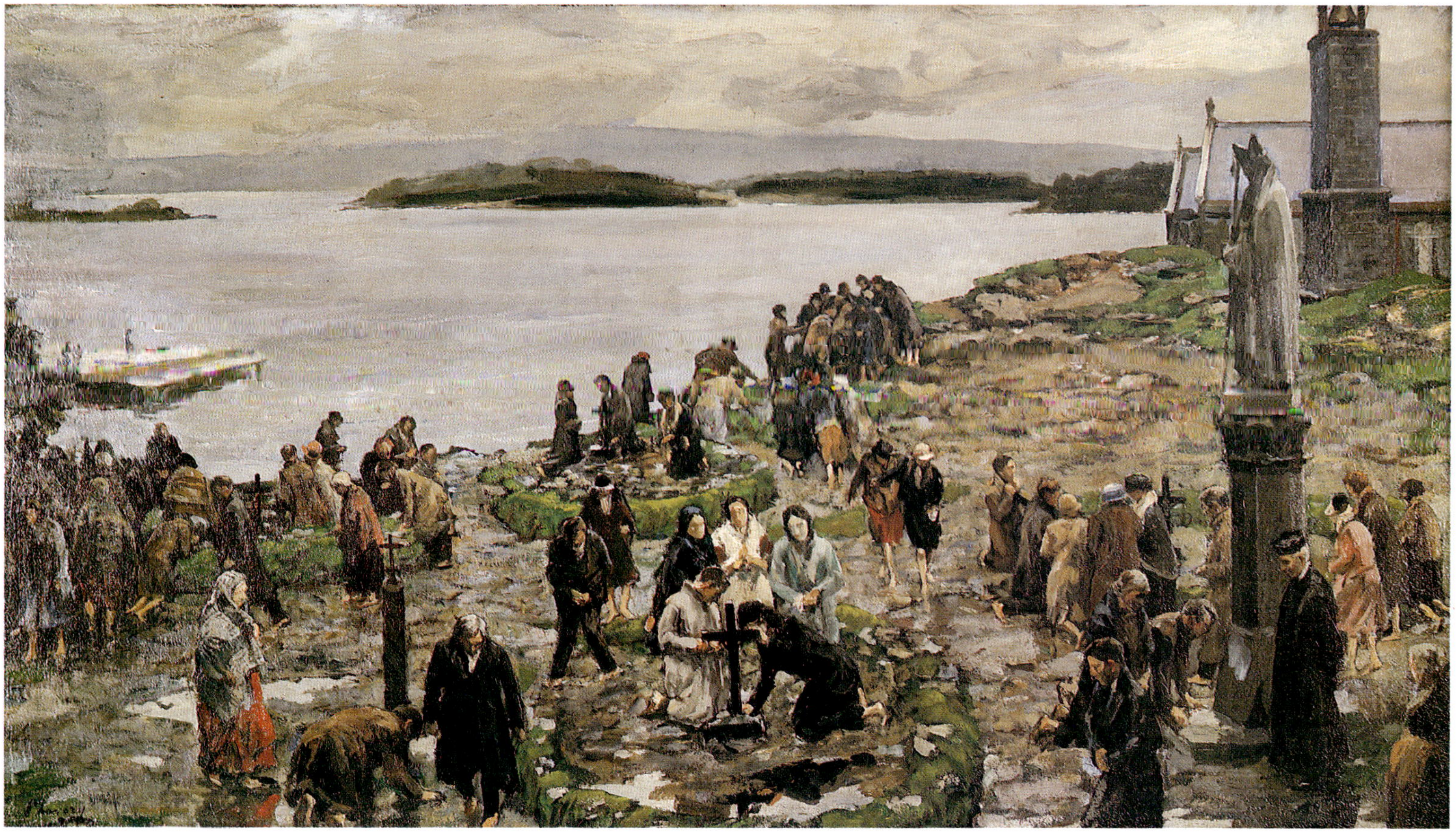

203 *St Patrick's Purgatory*, 1929–30, 23 × 42 (Hugh Lane Municipal Art Gallery, Dublin)

more so because his old friend, Count John McCormack was present and he too had donated a Lavery painting to the Dublin collection in memory of Hazel.[76]

These belated tributes, coupled with the fact that his step-daughter, Alice was now firmly rooted and child-rearing in Kilkenny, cemented Lavery's attachment to Ireland. He was to die there at the beginning of 1941. It should be recognised however, that while his native land provided him with comfort and honour in his old age, Lavery was not waylaid by public applause. He lived long enough to recognise, at the time of writing his autobiography, that 'every horror is committed in the name of nationalism'.[77] He could not accept the excesses of civil war, and although there was no mistaking his sympathies, he was loyal to his artist friends north of the border. Throughout the 1930s he acted as the first President of the Ulster Academy of Arts.[78] Lavery therefore avoided identification with the factions; he was not a painter on the barricades, but rather hesitatingly entertained 'vague thoughts of Velasquez as Ambassador for Philip IV, Vandyke [sic] and other artists in diplomatic positions . . .' at the same time recognising the absurdity of these thoughts.[79]

His Irish subject-matter of the inter-war period is, nevertheless, of considerable importance, demonstrating as it does, a commitment to Irish cultural regeneration. His reporting instinct was to the fore in splendid evocations of Irish life and landscape and these pictures find a place amongst those of a much younger generation of self-consciously 'Irish' painters. Lavery did not share their allegiance to an exclusively Irish imagery, but it is the measure of his distinction that he was able to provide a resumé of recent developments in Irish art and create, in the 'note' head, a symbol as well as a synthesis. His close-up portrayal of the dead Collins, in its stark simplicity and lack of rhetoric must have provided an inspirational talisman. Equally his portraits, in a stirring cavalcade, gave vivid perceptions of the makers of modern Ireland. Their donation to Dublin and Belfast were the final payment of the debt which Lane's letter had made him aware of, back in 1903.

In August 1937, William Butler Yeats visited the Municipal Gallery in Dublin, for the first time after a long absence. The sight of the collected portraits of his 'fellow-workers' and the reminder of the 'events' of Ireland's recent past left him 'overwhelmed with emotion'.[80] The poem which resulted from this experience, recalls a number of the Lavery paintings which were then hanging in the gallery. He wrote,

> Around me the images of thirty years:
> An ambush; pilgrims at the water side;
> Casement upon trial, half hidden by bars,
> Guarded; Griffith staring in hysterical pride;
> Kevin O'Higgins' countenance that wears
> A gentle questioning look that cannot hide
> A soul incapable of remorse or rest;
> A revolutionary soldier kneeling to be blessed;
>
> An Abbot or Archbishop with an upraised hand
> Blessing the Tricolour. 'This is not', I say,
> 'The dead Ireland of my youth, but an Ireland
> The poets have imagined, terrible and gay.'
> Before a woman's portrait suddenly I stand,
> Beautiful and gentle in her Venetian way.
> I met her all but fifty years ago
> For twenty minutes in some studio.
>
> Heart-smitten with emotion I sink down,
> My heart recovering with covered eyes;
> Wherever I had looked I had looked upon
> My permanent or impermanent images:
> Augusta Gregory's son; her sister's son,
> Hugh Lane, 'onlie begetter' of all these;
> Hazel Lavery living and dying, that tale
> As though some ballad-singer had sung it all;

The references here are obvious, and with them Lavery took his place beside an heroic generation.[81]

10 Portrait Interiors

> Here we have Sir R. A. etc. etc. Lavery among us, but I have not seen him, or for a long while noted at what hotel he is advertised to be stopping—but he has no use for mere artists—especially the rest of the imported crowd Sir [?] Lazlo [sic] and Harrington Mann and a lot more. He may have come off socially, but artistically *nup*. Still his idea of doing the millionaires surrounded by their millions was not bad.[1]

These words written by the aged Joseph Pennell in 1926, go beyond professional rivalry. Twenty years earlier, Pennell had been envious of Lavery's relationship with Whistler and now he was prepared to imply that Lavery had forsaken his fellow artists and was in league with money. Unlike other society portraitists, Lavery had the good idea of 'doing the millionaires surrounded by their millions'. Pennell was obviously referring to Lavery's recent exhibition of 'Portraits, Interiors and Landscapes' which had been staged at Duveen Galleries, New York and which was, at the time of his writing on display in Boston. The exhibition was an expanded form of the show of twenty-three 'Portrait Interiors' at the Leicester Galleries, London in 1925. At its original venue, this collection of paintings had attracted favourable comment. Writing in *Apollo*, Desmond MacCarthy compared the works to contemporary French portrait photography and declared that they were important as, '. . . records of our times and significant commentaries upon that reckless changing thing called "good taste" . . . But . . . let us remember the intention of the artist: however characteristic the pose and aspect of the figures in these pictures may be, his own interest has been distributed over the whole picture. He shows himself in this little exhibition . . . as a painter of interiors.'[2]

Duveen in transposing the exhibition to Fifth Avenue, New York, was proud of his entrepreneurial skill in promoting British art.[3] Neither he nor the artist would have been aware of Pennell's carping criticism, which would only have been totally fair if the works had been commissioned or were part of some elaborate self-promotion on the part of the sitter. While this was not the case, it would be equally untrue to suppose that Lavery was motivated exclusively by the formal concerns of representation. These works function in the same way as photographs of the rich and famous in a glossy magazine. They are extensions of the artist's identity as a documentarist, like the late portraits of Vuillard. Country house interiors like *A Bedroom at the Wharf, Sutton Courtenay* (Plate 204), and *The Dining Room at Lennoxlove* (Plate 205) asserted the superiority of European aristocratic culture, just as Walter Gay's views of empty rooms in French *chateaux* fed upon the new world fascination for the *ancien régime*.[4]

Pennell's venom was directed at pictures which Lavery had been producing for the last four or five years augmented by earlier notable images.[5] Arguably, the recent work had a long lineage stretching back to *Her Portrait* (see Plate 12) in

1882. *The Artist's Studio* (see Plate [illegible]), the painting of George V and his family (see Plate 148) and *The First Wounded* (see Plate [illegible]) had been monumental interiors, with figure groups acting as the central focus. The new interiors, like *The Greyhound* (see Plate 114), and *The Grey Drawing Room* (see Plate 113) subordinated figure to setting. The spatial structure was often elucidated by sunlight streaming in from side windows. An element of Impressionism was permitted and this was particularly evident in *The Dining Room at Lennoxlove*. In even conditions of lighting, the spontaneity of approach worked less well and on occasion, the artist was compelled to resort to carefully ruled perspective grids. He was clearly excited by the challenge of these diverse situations. He was captivated by the loss and rediscovery of contour, by the use of highlights and by

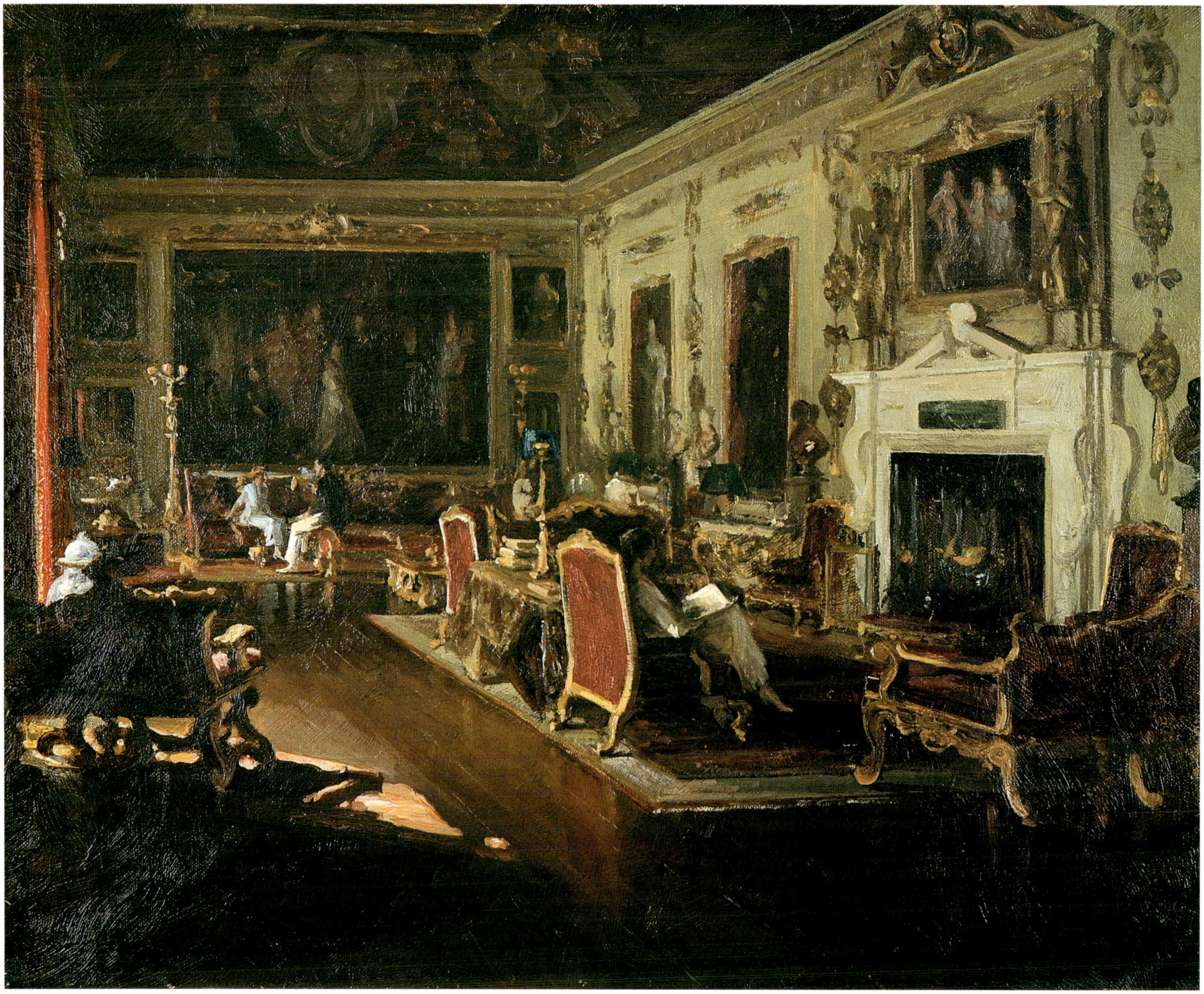

207 *The Van Dyck Room, Wilton*, 1921, 25 × 30 (The Royal Academy of Arts, London)

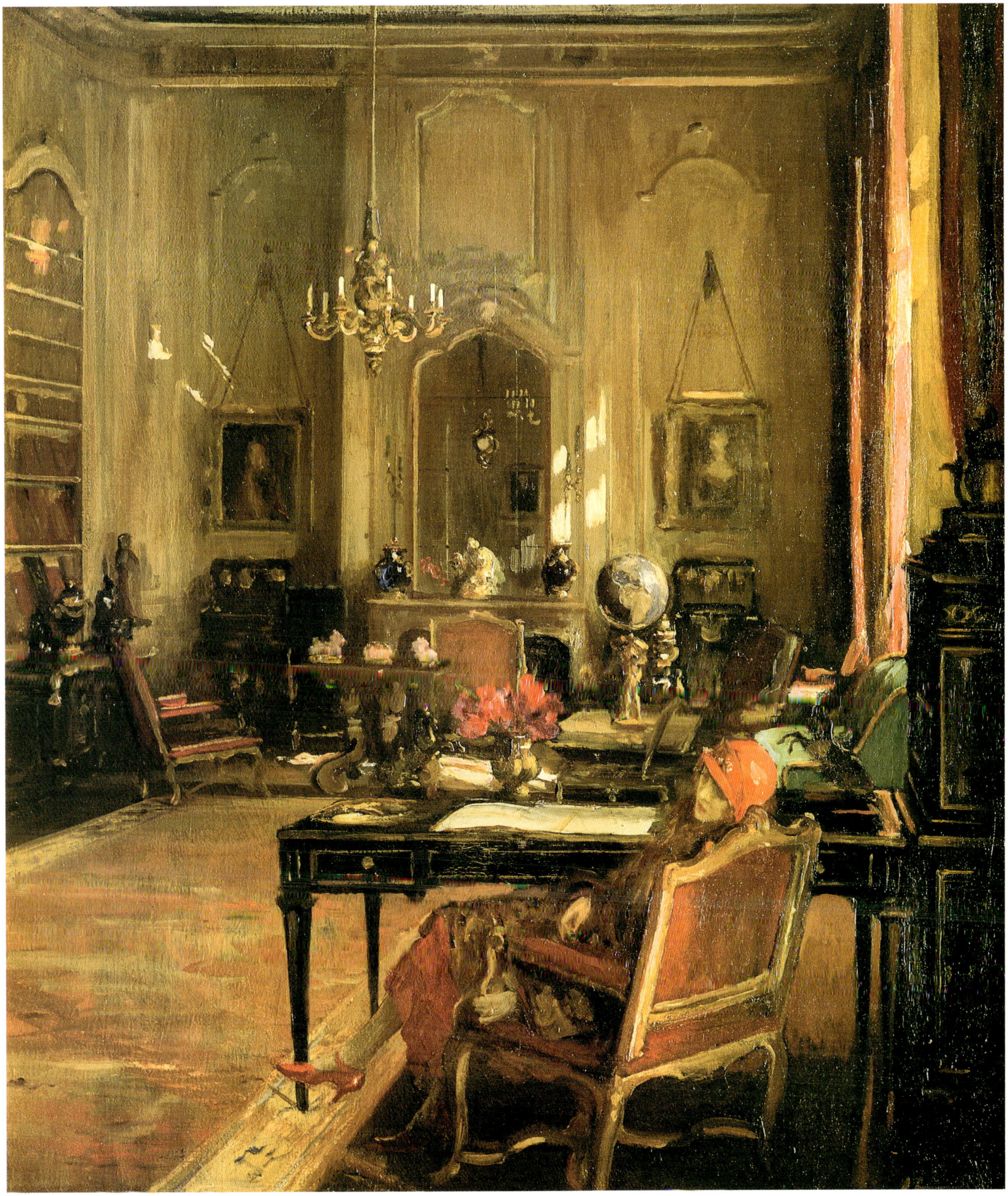

206 *The Red Hat, A Mayfair Drawing Room,* 1925, 30 × 25 (present whereabouts unknown, photo, courtesy Christie's)

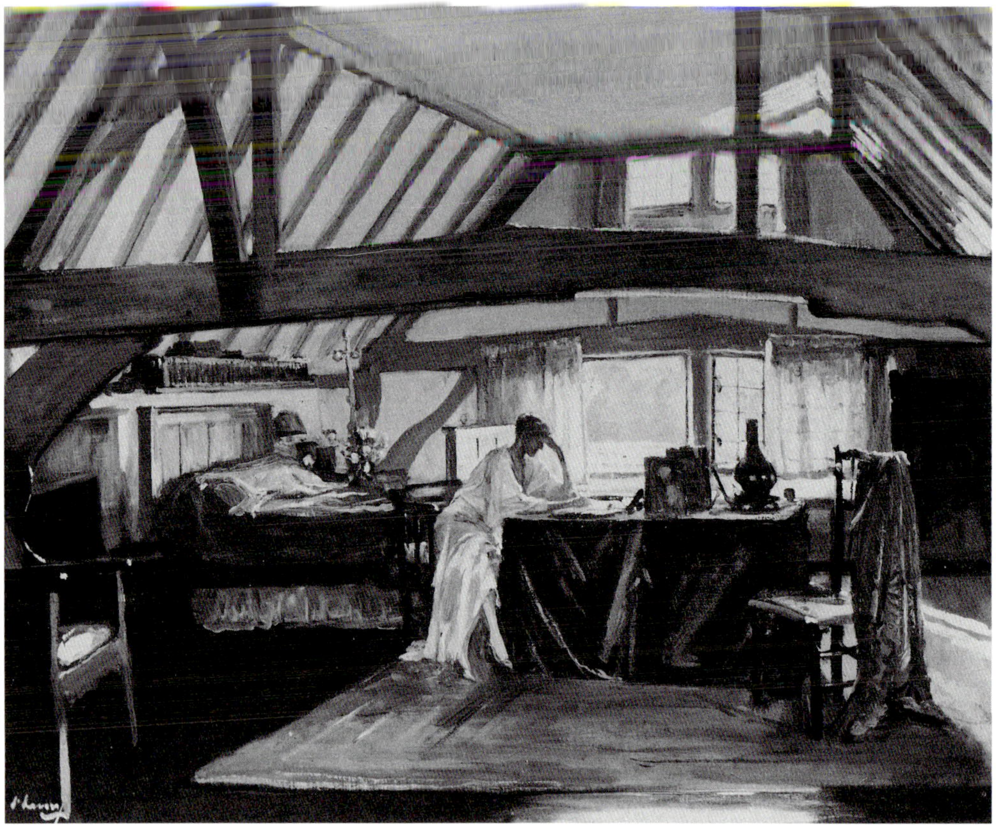

204 *A Bedroom at The Wharf, Sutton Courtenay*, *c*.1922, 25 × 30 (present whereabouts unknown, photo, The Fine Art Society)

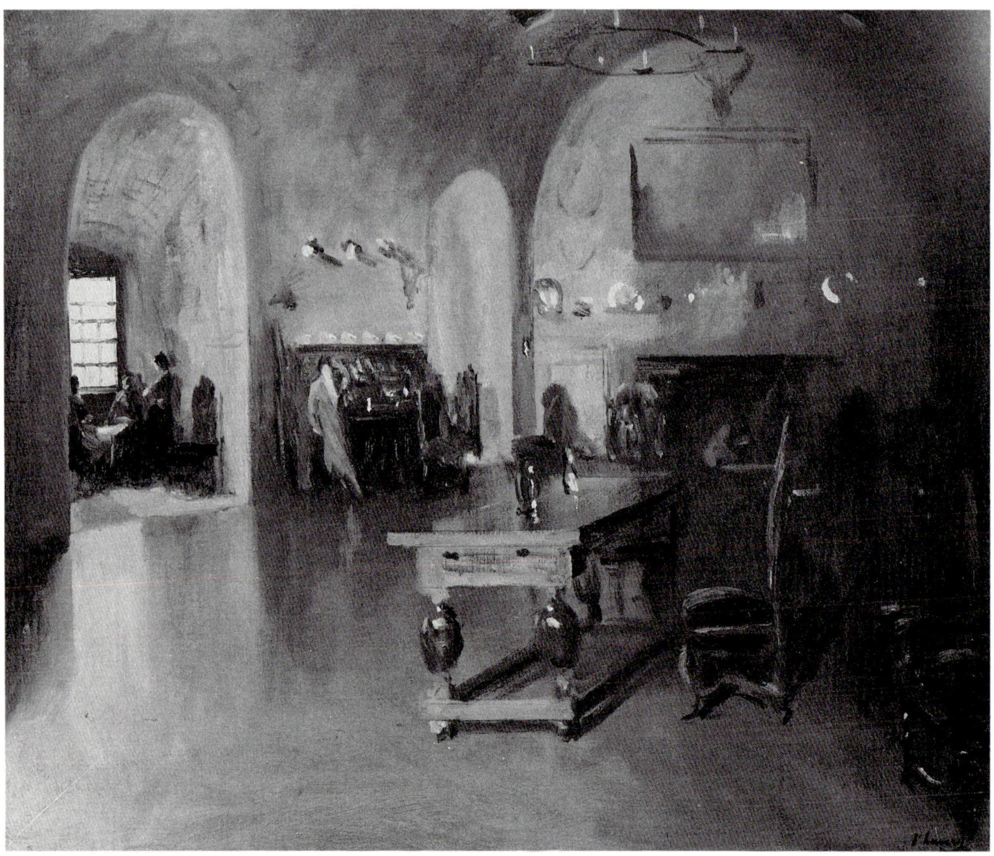

205 *The Dining Room at Lennoxlove*, *c*.1922, 25 × 30 (present whereabouts unknown)

the distribution of colour. In *The Red Hat*, *A Mayfair Drawing Room* (Plate 206) and *Lady Juliet Trevor at Coombe Court* the occupants of the room are submerged in its contents. Bric-a-brac, chinoiserie candelabra and giltwood furniture glitter in the *clair-obscure* of an English afternoon. These unique qualities, this physiognomy of place, enticed him, as the character of an interesting sitter had done formerly. It was more important now to observe how his personnages occupy the rooms they inhabit, than to fix their features immutably. The Herbert family are incidental to the Double Cube Room at Wilton (see Plate 207). The woman reading by the fire is an almost accidental presence, like the woman in *A Grey Summer's Day, Grez*. At the far end of the room, a couple sit chatting, but they are colour notes, highlit like the candelabra and the chinoiserie. Not for the first time, Lavery was applauded as the master of apparent casualness.[6] James L. Caw described this first of the new phase of portrait interiors, presented to the Royal Academy as the artist's diploma work as 'a delightful abstraction . . . rich toned yet sparkling.'[7] Other works of this sort followed. Several rooms at The Wharf, the home of Lord Oxford, were painted. Mrs McLaren is shown in what was described as a 'magnificent' drawing room in South Street, while Lady Cunard is shown sunk in a settee chatting to George Moore, in *A Salon* at the Ritz.[8] Mary Borden casually smokes a cigarette, seated facing an oriel window in Bisham Abbey. One of the most interesting of this series, since it enshrined an enduring relationship was *Count John McCormack and his Family* (Plate 208) at Esher Place.[9] We do not know in what circumstance Lavery first met the great Irish tenor, but their admiration was mutual. His room

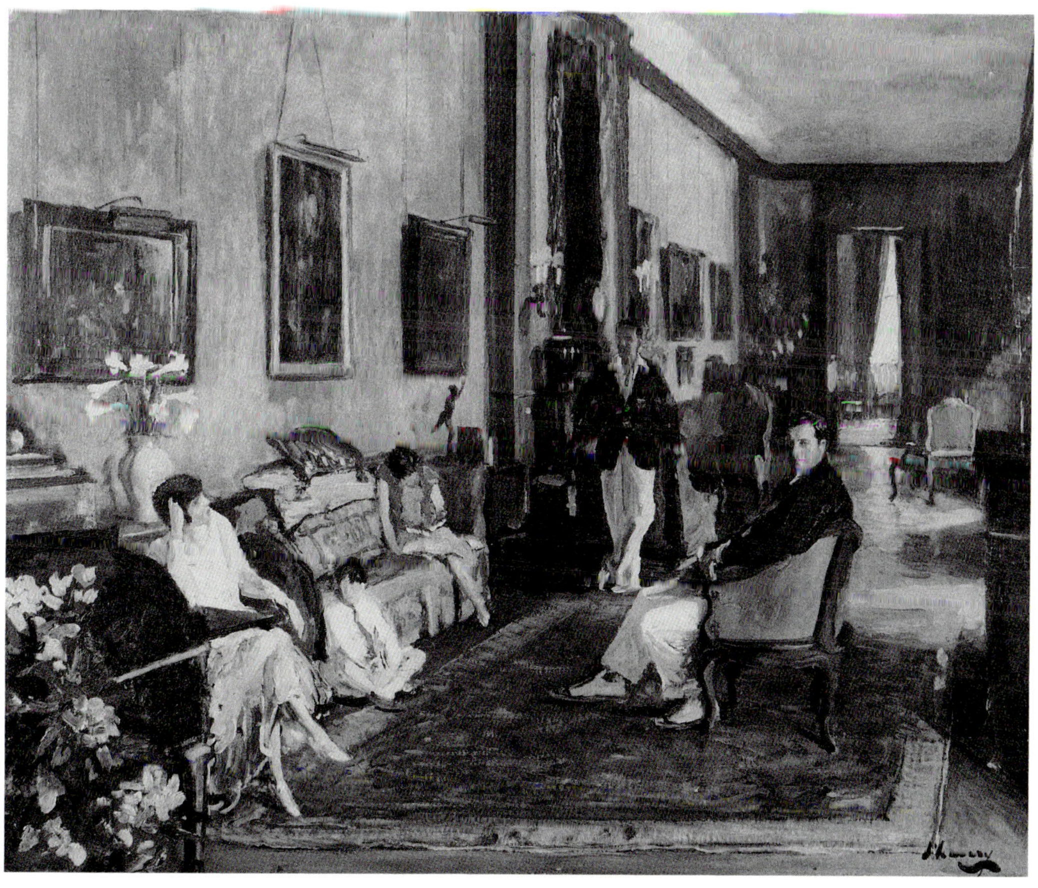

208 *Count John McCormack and his Family*, *c.*1925, 20 × 27 (Hugh Lane Municipal Art Gallery, Dublin)

shows the familiar mixture of modern fittings — spot lights above the paintings for instance — with eighteenth century style furniture. Here too, the occupants are portrayed with studied casualness. The girl reading and the boy squatting on the floor display brilliant economy.

Seeing the portrait interiors *en masse* in 1925, Desmond MacCarthy felt 'the pervasive influence of fashion in decoration borne in on us'. While the pursuit of style was regarded as superficial, for him 'there is something more in fashion—and something odder.' It was as if Lavery's exhibition had elucidated 'a phase of taste'.[10] It had expressed something more profound than the glittering spectacle of appearances. Lavery directly alluded to the innovative eclecticism of contemporary decor by painting its taste leaders. *The Hall, Argyll House—A Summer Day*, (Plate 209) 1925, for instance, depicts part of the home of Sir Arthur and Lady Colefax, founders of the decorating firm of Colefax and Fowler. In this case the ambiance is understated and precedence is given to the balance which is struck between the stairway conversation and the expectant pekinese.

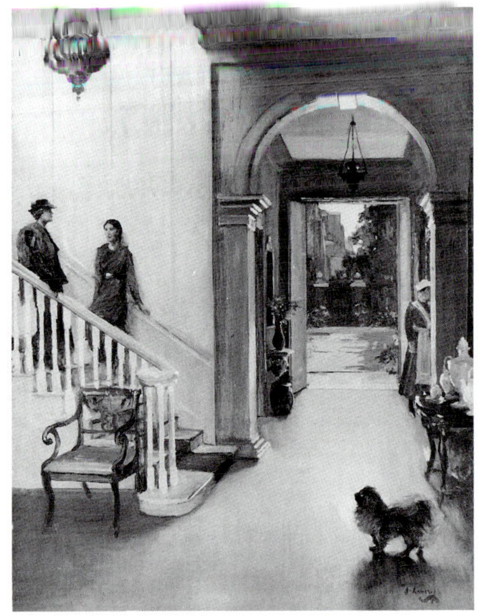

209 *The Hall, Argyll House – A Summer Day*, 1925, 23½ × 17¾ (present whereabouts unknown, photo, courtesy Sotheby's)

These points were more meaningful in the American context, and MacCarthy's article was extracted for *The American Magazine of Art* in February 1926.[11] Following the fine review of the portrait interiors in the New York paper *The Art News*, the scene was set for Lavery's success in the new world. In October 1925, the paper had informed its readers that the painter already had a number of portrait commissions arranged prior to his anticipated arrival late in November.[12] Then, in a review of the London exhibition, its readers were informed about the 'charmingly intimate little paintings' which Lavery intended to show at Duveen's: 'These small works evince an unusual dexterity in the suggestion of atmosphere and are painted with the insight of one who comes to them, not as an outsider, but as one who, having an entrée to them, understands to the full, their essential character. . . He can paint fine furniture and *objets de vertu* with as excellent an appreciation of their points as any one living, and . . . can weld them into one decorative whole . . .'.[13]

The American audience was therefore acutely aware of Lavery's social cachet. He could not afford to slip into a cheap hotel in New York and expect to go unnoticed. 'You must appear as though money were no object', a friend told him on arrival, and accordingly he was promptly rehoused in the Ambassador overlooking Central Park.[14] From its lofty windows, several views of the park were painted (see Plate 210). Apart from these, Lavery seems to have executed mainly portraits. His *Cardinal Hayes*, though for obvious reasons, it might be compared with *Cardinal Logue* (see Plate 190), is a salient example of the more conventional style demanded by American clients. The few interiors that date from the winter of 1925, like *The Library, 58 East 68th Street*, remain unlocated.[15]

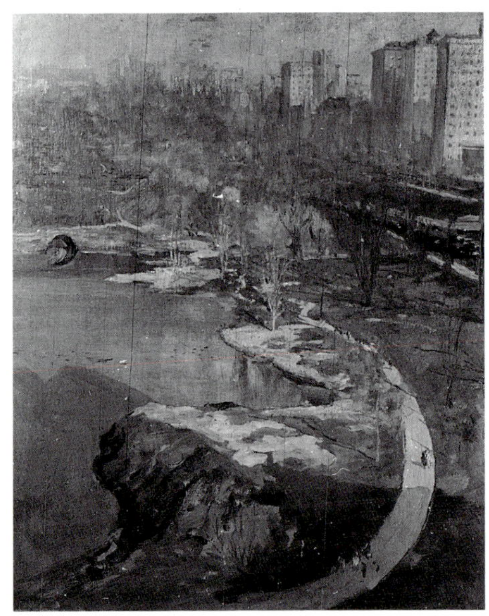

210 *Central Park from the Ambassador*, 1926, 25 × 30 (private collection, photo, Ian Kilpatrick)

The exhibition at Duveen's Gallery toured to Boston, Chicago, Pittsburgh and Harrisburg during the early months of 1926 and was so successful that a further show was organised at Whitehall, Palm Beach, Florida at the end of the following year. Again, the Laverys accompanied the exhibition, although in a letter to Bodkin, Hazel confessed that she was '. . . never happy in America, altho' John is very successful there and this time especially . . .'.[16] The warm climate in Florida provided Lavery with many more opportunities to pursue non-commissioned work than New York had done. He returned to pictures of recreational activity. Several swimming parties were painted and at least one sketch of a tennis match containing a woman reading in the foreground, probably modelled by Hazel.[17] The air of exuberance, in these pictures was condensed into more finite statements on subsequent winter holidays at Cannes.

When not engaged in such pursuits, Lavery looked for ways to scale up the general concept of the portrait interior into a type of group portraiture that retained some element of informality. In the early 1920s, he had painted at Ascot, Sandown and Newmarket.[18] A view of *The Jockey's Dressing Room at Ascot* (Plate 211) was shown at the Royal Academy in 1924.[19] The artist records some of his adventures in obtaining good racing scenes, on one occasion painting Ascot in the rain, which resulted in him having to spend the following two weeks in bed. In artistic terms these occasions were not so disastrous in that the on-the-spot sketches were worked up into more substantial results. In *Ascot* (Plate 212), for instance, the vivid notation of the crowd in the small study was replicated on a large scale in staccato strokes.[20] However, the dressing rooms and weighing rooms at Ascot, Epsom and Hurst Park gave opportunities for the artist to extend his preoccupation with portrait interiors. The shed-like buildings themselves were not particularly interesting, but Lavery enjoyed the animated chatter of the jockeys. A sketch (see Plate 213) of *The Weighing Room, Hurst Park* (Plate 214)[21] provided the basis for a larger group portrait incorporating thirteen of the most famous jockeys of the day dressed in the most important racing colours.[22] The picture was reproduced with numbered codes identifying the figures.[23] It seems almost as if the unresolved impression in the sketch has come together in a

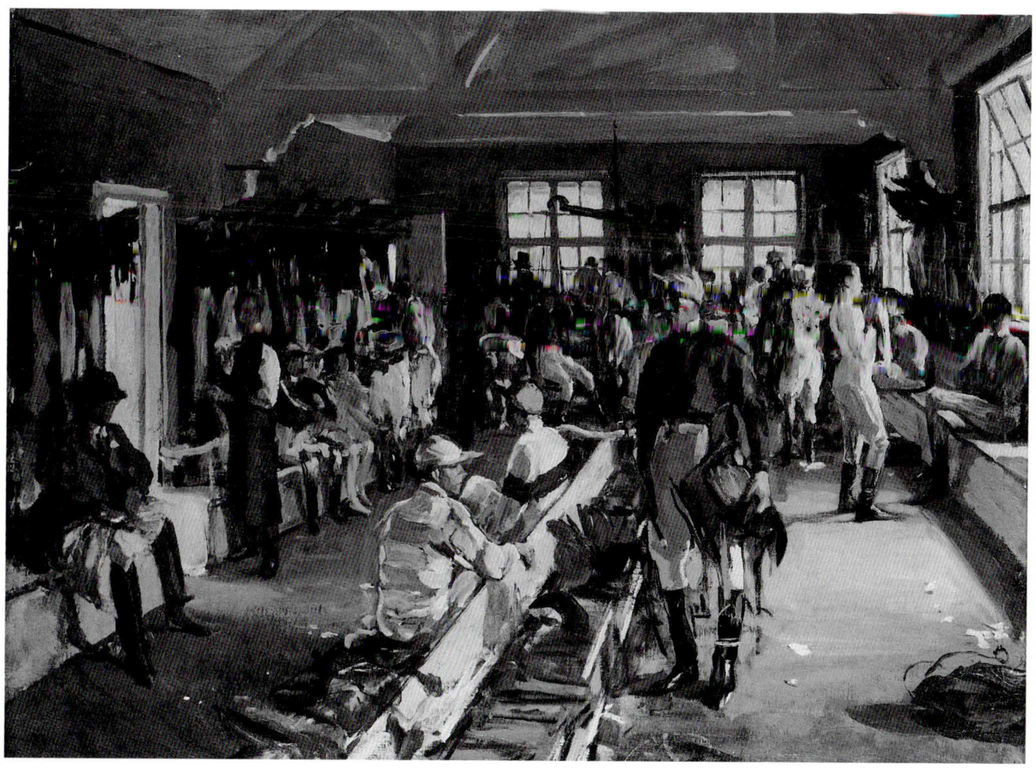

211 *The Jockey's Dressing Room at Ascot*, 1923, 25 × 32 (Tate Gallery, London)

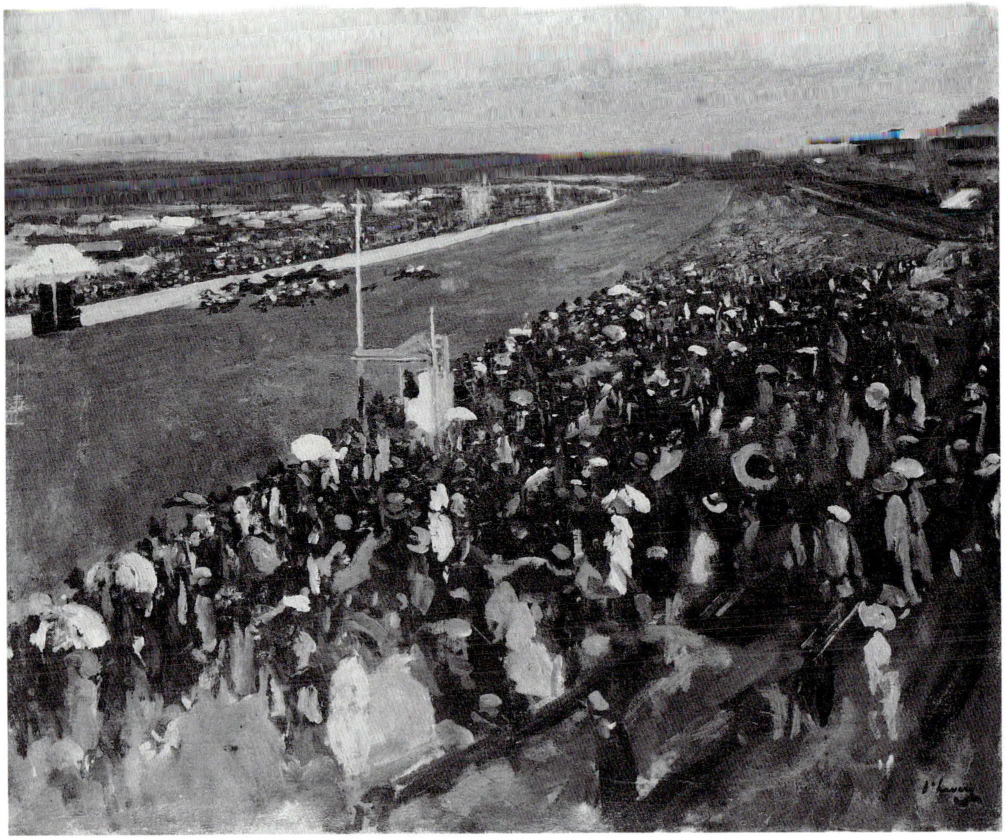

212 *Ascot*, 1923, 25 × 30 (private collection, photo, courtesy Richard Green)

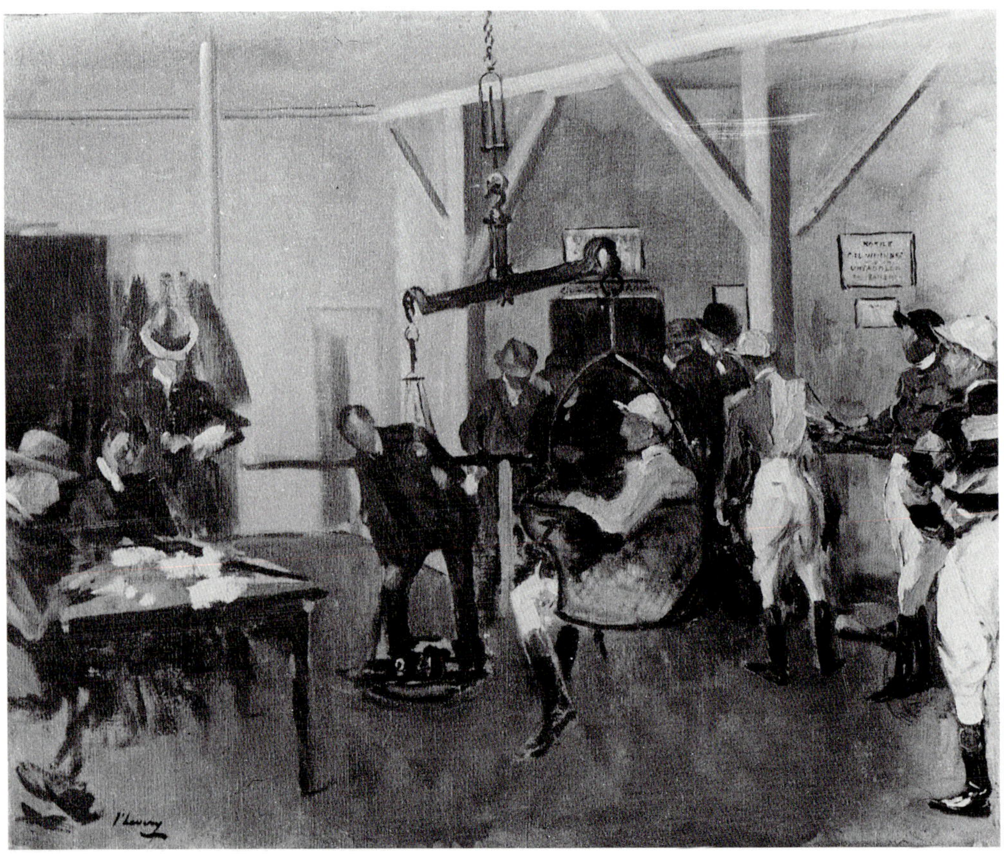

213 Sketch of *The Weighing Room, Hurst Park*, 1924, 20 × 24 (The Ulster Museum, Belfast)

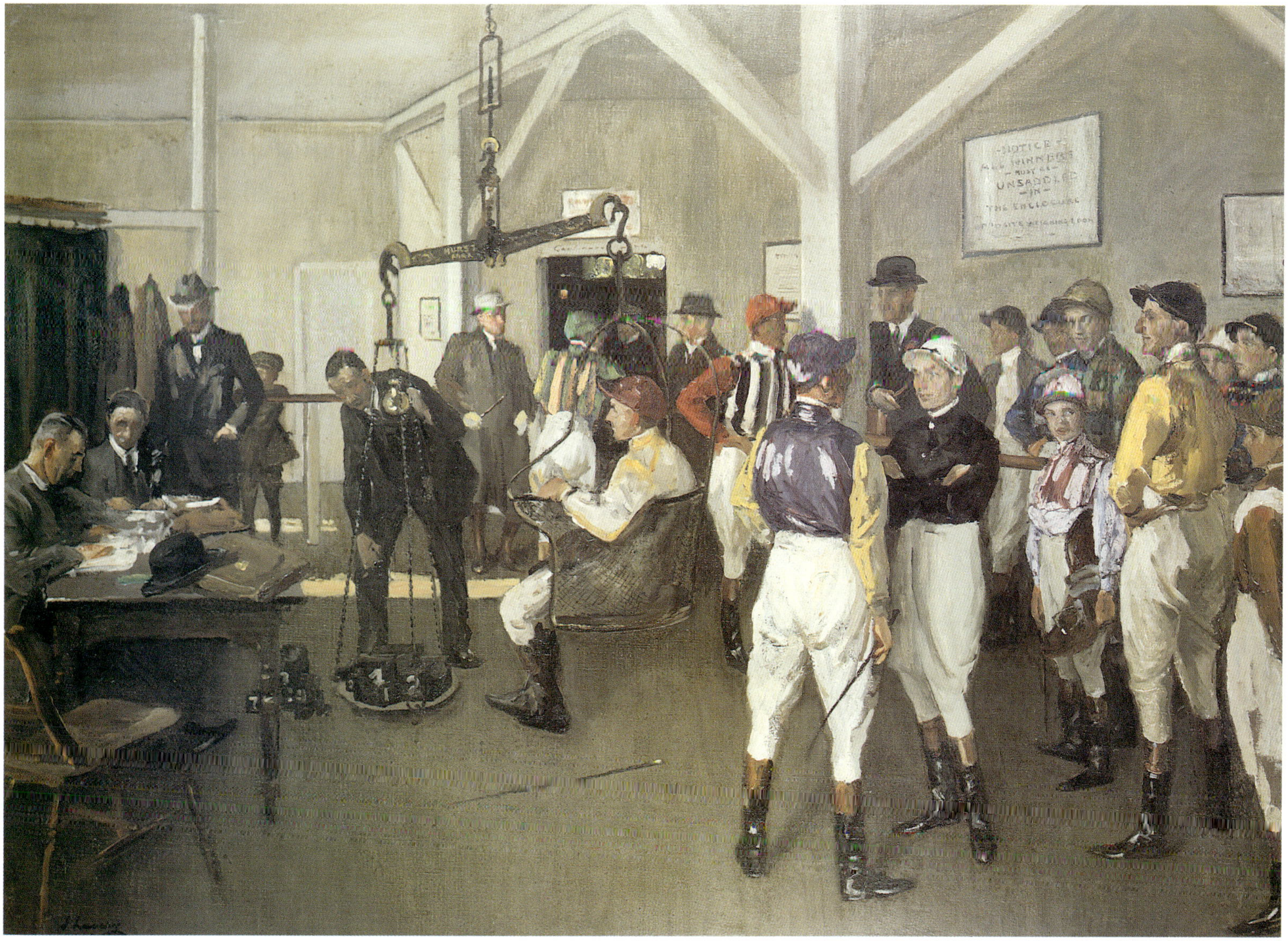

214 *The Weighing Room, Hurst Park*, 1924, 30 × 40 (private collection, photo, Pyms Gallery, London)

spontaneously successful image. The jockey in the scales, the central motif of the sketch, has been demoted in the finished picture in order to extend the composition and make a stronger asymmetry. Such details as the whip thrown to the floor, and the strong sunlight falling into the room from the right, add an undeniable air of authenticity. Lavery recalled that he induced a jockey—in this case Donoghue—to pose in the scales on the assurance that he would win the race, in this instance thought to be the Lincoln Handicap. When to his amazement, this actually happened, all the other jockeys, from that day onward, would touch Lavery's shoulder for good luck before leaving for the paddock.[24]

More orthodox portrait interiors that attracted attention for their inhabitants, rather than for their setting, are those which incorporate J. M. Barrie and George Bernard Shaw. Two portraits of the author of *Peter Pan* were painted around 1925 (see Plate 215). One entitled, *A Garret in the Adelphi*, exhibited in the London exhibition, shows Barrie, 'stretched in reverie upon a dark settle'.[25] It reveals

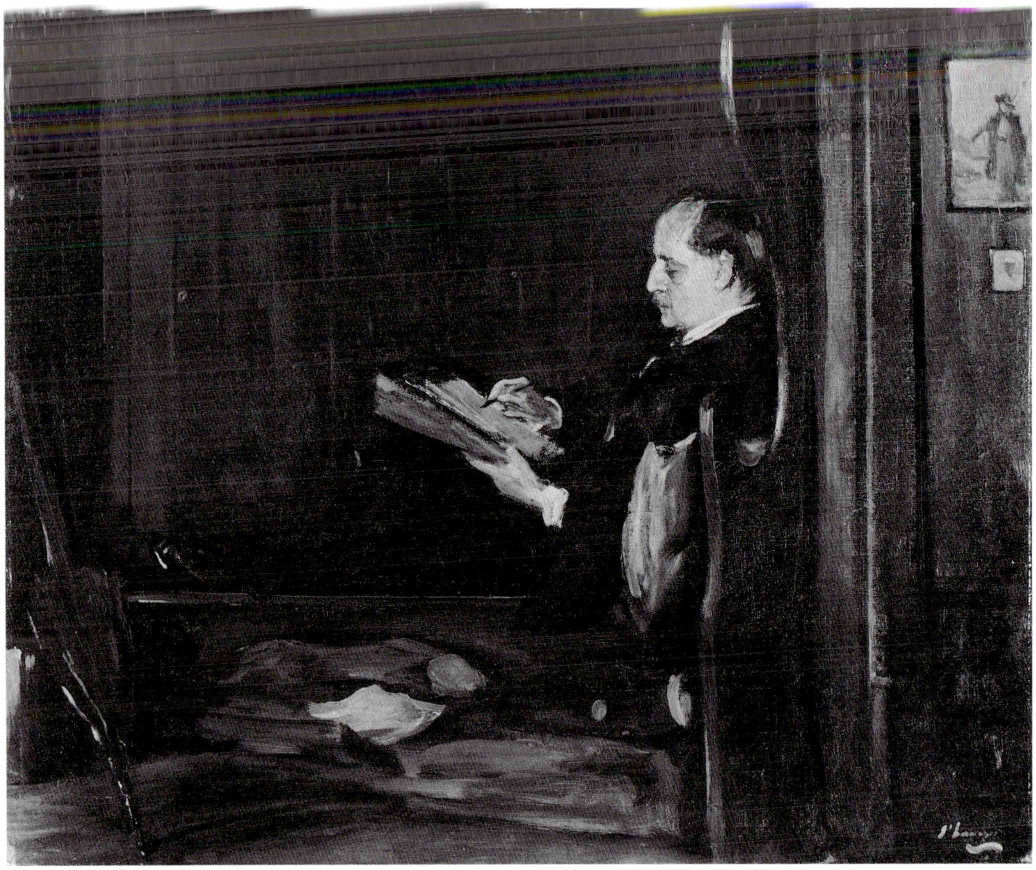

215 *J. M. Barrie*, *c.*1925, 25 × 30 (Scottish National Portrait Gallery, Edinburgh)

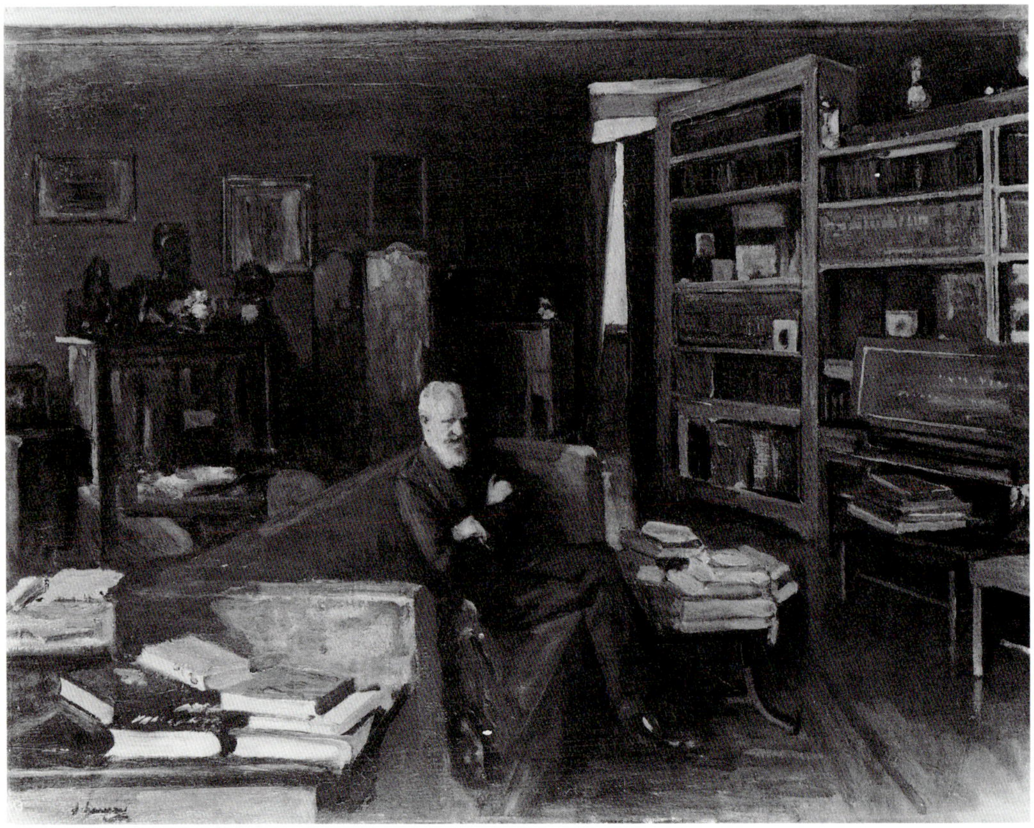

216 *George Bernard Shaw, Adelphi Terrace*, 1927, 24 × 30 (Hugh Lane Municipal Art Gallery, Dublin)

much of the writer's paraphernalia and piles of books. A more intimate second portrait was however, Barrie's preferred image. Being sensitive about his height, his legs were, in this second version, lost mostly in shadow.[26] The profile head is certainly one of the most sensitive of Lavery's late portraits, delicately drawing the pallid features of the ageing author. Two years before his death, Barrie wrote to Lavery complimenting him upon what he considered 'a charming picture', but adding the self-deprecating remark that 'no doubt some other head might be more interesting on the shoulders of the sitter'.[27]

In 1925, Lavery had the opportunity to paint another famous inhabitant of Adelphi Terrace.[28] On this occasion the distinguished sitter agreed to pose for his wife Hazel, rather than for Lavery himself.[29] Undaunted, the artist prevailed upon George Bernard Shaw to let him paint alongside Hazel. However, while she produced a creditable likeness, Lavery's was less than satisfactory and eventually he painted over it.[30] Two years later, a second opportunity presented itself when he went to paint Shaw in his flat (see Plate 216). Lavery records that he wanted to show the playwright and his wife, Charlotte, but she, being superstitious, could not be induced to participate. For this reason, Shaw appears alone on the sofa, and looking, in Lavery's words, 'somewhat dejected'.[31] Shaw's study is slightly jumbled and lacks the symmetry and sophistication of Mayfair drawing rooms. In the Thirties Lavery's marked preference was for work-rooms and more private spaces. Ramsay MacDonald was painted *en retraite* at Lossiemouth and John Masefield admitted the painter to his study as one of a very privileged few.

These were, however, late additions to the canon of portrait interiors. On more ceremonial occasions Lavery was still in demand. He was, for example, invited to record *The Opening of the Modern Foreign and Sargent Galleries* (Plate 217) at the Tate

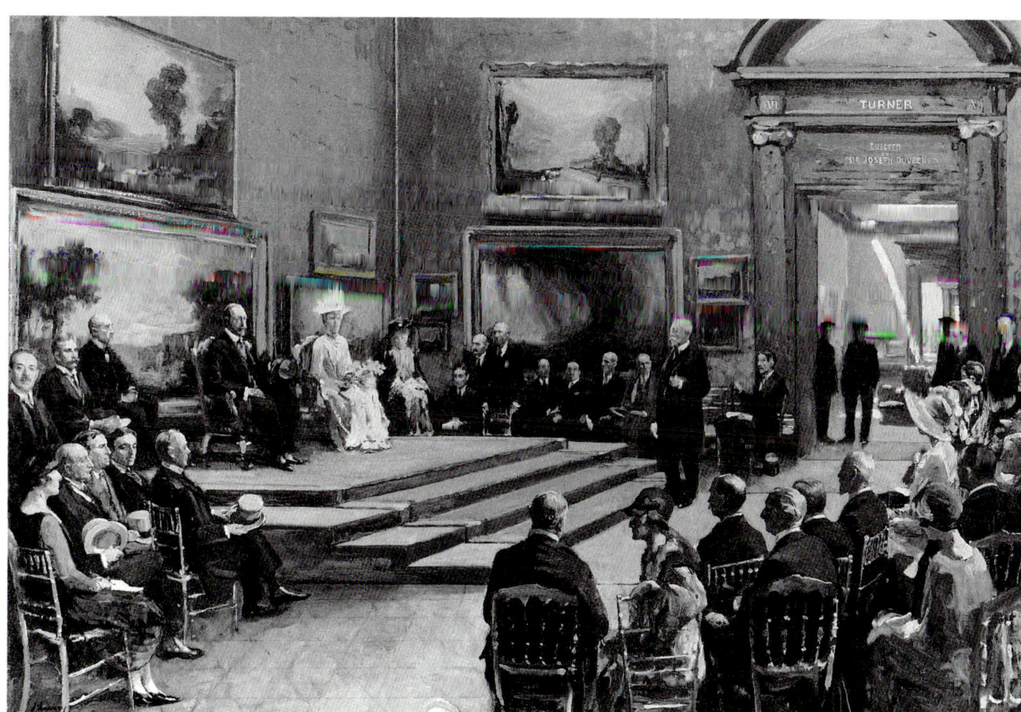

217 *The Opening of the Modern Foreign and Sargent Galleries at the Tate Gallery*, 1926, 33¾ × 46 (Tate Gallery, London)

Gallery in 1926. Joseph Duveen, who commissioned the work as well as the new galleries, saw their installation as a monument to his promotion of British art. Although this was a royal occasion, it did not pose the huge problem of painting a crowd in which everyone must be recognisable. Apart from the royal entourage, the audience comprised, museum staff and invited guests, many of whom Lavery already knew.[32] When it was finished, this commemorative work was dispatched to the Royal Academy of 1929 in the company of a very different group portrait interior. Capitalising upon the popular interest in the lives of the rich, Lavery decided to paint *Les Salons Privés, Monte Carlo*. The artist had visited Monte Carlo on his Mediterranean cruise of 1920 and returned to the south of France for winter holidays at the end of the decade staying at L'Enchantment at Mougins or at the Hotel Beau Site at Cannes.

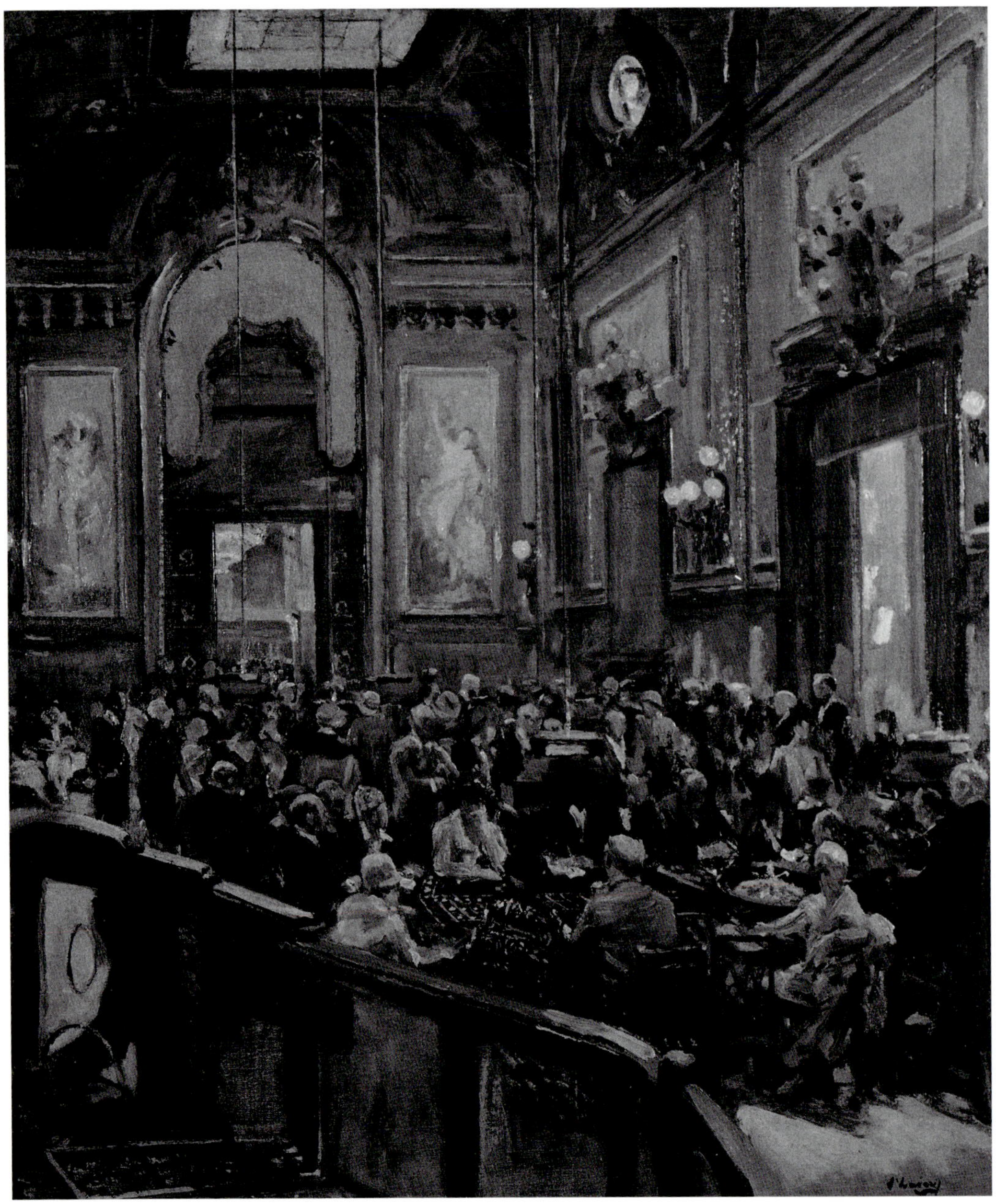

218 *Monte Carlo, Afternoon*, 1929, $24\frac{1}{4} \times 20\frac{3}{8}$ (Southampton Art Gallery)

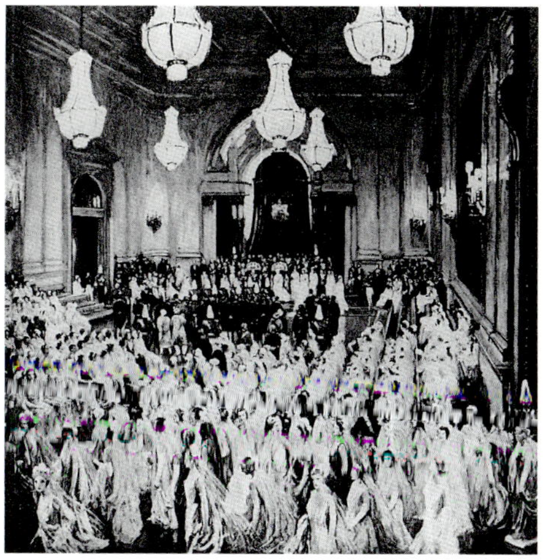

219 *Their Majesties' Court, Buckingham Palace*, 1931, size unknown (present whereabouts unknown)

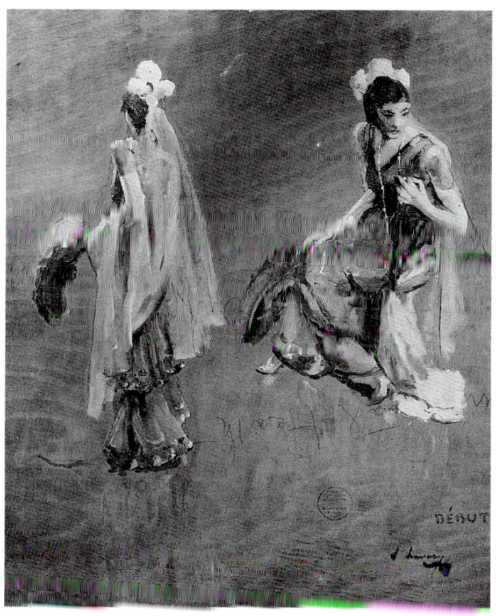

220 *The Debutantes*, 1931, 18 × 14½ (private collection, photo, Pyms Gallery, London)

In February 1929, Hazel reported in a letter to Thomas Bodkin that her husband was, '. . . painting such a beautiful interior of the Salle Prince at the Casino, like his House of Lords picture, quite his best manner . . .'[33] The prospect of depicting a recognisable gaming room clearly attracted the artist, as it had his Victorian predecessor, W. P. Frith. Without resorting to the moralising overtones of Frith's *Salon d'Or, Homburg*, Lavery responded to the bustle of the scene, and using small disconnected studies on a single canvas, he recorded the poses of the principal identifiable players (see Plate 218). From his vantage point above the cashier's desk, the artist had an uninterrupted view of the entire Salon with its riotous Second Empire decor. The sheer vulgarity of the colour offended more delicate temperaments. One critic declared that, 'There is an inevitable gaudiness of colour, especially in the bright pink carpet, which is calculated to jar on the sensitive mind.'[34]

Lavery's undoubted ability as a recorder of the social scene, suited him exactly to grand events. In the following two years, he received important commissions to paint royal receptions. Both of these, *Their Majesties' Court, Buckingham Palace 1931* (Plate 219) and *HRH The Prince of Wales receiving from the Lord Mayor, Letters Patent . . . granting Livery to the Honourable Company of Master Mariners . . . 1932*, followed the now familiar formula of individual portrait sketches combined with a sketch of the ensemble to make a large and imposing group portrait.[35] Jottings like *The Debutantes* (Plate 220) bear out *The Art News* critic's observation of Lavery's 'talent for suggesting personality with the most economical means'.[36] Here again, Lavery faced the familiar problem of resuscitating the liveliness of his sketches in the final composition. He was not regarded as having been unsuccessful in this. *The National Graphic*, for instance, reflected upon *Their Majesties' Court* . . . as the picture which 'caused a stir at this year's Royal Academy and . . . won unstinted praise from the critics . . .' It provided 'ample evidence of the skill that has made Sir John the most sought after Court and Society portraitist of our time.'[37] Such praise undoubtedly led to Lavery being selected by Lord Wakefield for *The Master Mariners* . . . group portrait, but in this instance, the result appears undeniably stiff.[38]

Lavery returned to more informal interiors with *The Prime Minister at Lossiemouth* and *War Memories*. The first of these, a painting of Ramsay MacDonald, was highly acclaimed and was reproduced on the front cover of *The Illustrated London News*,[39] while the second showed David Lloyd George dictating his memoirs.[40] In each, however, the interior is less interesting for itself than for the personality it contains. In the case of both sitters, more formal portraits were being painted simultaneously and the interior was merely a form of limbering up to the task.

Lavery continued throughout the inter-war period to produce formal portraits and the Royal Academy visitor saw them pass by in regular succession. A number of these are of special interest for the characters they encapsulate. In 1924, for instance, the sensitivity of *The Marquis of Londonderry, KG. Chancellor of Queen's University, Belfast* makes it directly comparable to Sargent's *Philip Sassoon*.[41] In 1930, Lavery was commissioned to paint *Hugh Cecil Lowther, Fifth Earl of Lonsdale* (Plate 221) by the city of Doncaster. Lavery records that this noted sportsman, remembered today because of the Lonsdale belts, was one of the 'best dressed' and 'most paintable' Englishmen he knew.[42] Hugh Cecil Lowther was a national personality, larger than life, and habitually clad in pale grey suits, decorated with a gardenia buttonhole. His features, blemished by years in the boxing ring, were of great interest to the portraitist, but alas, although he prepared the way with a preliminary sketch,[43] Lavery's portrait in garter robes, pleased neither sitter nor painter. To make up for its inadequacy, the artist produced a portrait in everyday costume which more satisfactorily conveys Lonsdale's formidable personality.[44]

During these years, Lavery had equally numerous female sitters. His daughter Eileen, now happily married to her second husband, the Master of Sempill, was less available to him. Sempill, a distinguished aviator, was a genial companion who induced the painter to take to the air for flights to and from his country cousins at Moira. Of his three granddaughters, Diana, the only child from Eileen's first marriage to James Dickinson, became a frequent sitter in the early Thirties. Two portraits of her were shown at the Royal Academy in 1931 and 1934.[45] *Diana on Hampstead Heath* (see *Hampstead Heath*, Plate 222), combines a number of paintings of the Heath executed around 1930 with a profile study of Diana astride a fine piebald pony. The figure is seen silhouetted against the sky and the simple contrasts of low-lying green landscape traversed by sandy paths, create a sense of abstract patterning. *The Portrait of Diana Dickinson*,[46] three years later, provides a more immediate reaction to a rakish personality (see Plate 223). By the time it was painted, the sitter had acquired the reputation of a tear-away, involving herself with the show-biz cowboy, Goldie Buttner and later taking small parts in Hollywood movies. In her portrait, she has become the striking debutante, losing the vulnerability of the brilliant oil sketch.

However the best way to monitor the development of Lavery's formal portraiture during the period, is to consider the images of Lady Lavery. In 1922, her portrait was purchased by Lady Cunard and offered as a gift to the Tate Gallery. To everyone's amazement, the gift was declined, but it was promptly accepted by the Guildhall Art Gallery.[47] Usually known as *Hazel in Rose and Grey* (Plate 224), referred to by the artist as *Hazel: Portrait in a Mirror*, this picture resumes many of the qualities first seen in *La Dame aux Perles* (see Plate 125), although in this instance there is a greater sense of theatre. Hazel's right hand falls limply across the arm of the chair while she twirls a long string of pearls in her left. Plucked and pencilled eyebrows, hennaed hair, caught at the neck with a white rose, reveal the bearing of a leader of contemporary fashion. A similar affectation is found in *The Red Rose* and *The Red Book* of 1923, though in these the tones are less ethereal.[48] The resplendent *Green Coat* (Plate 225), shown at the Royal Academy in 1925, is instantly less affected.[49] Originally the picture was simply entitled, *Lady Lavery* and there was almost a suggestion of *déshabillé* in the bare arms and shoulders. When it came back from the exhibition, the artist elaborated the composition, inserting the shimmering green coat. The model's gaze in this portrait is much less coquettish and the full waxen beauty of her features is revealed.

In its original form the painting was used as an advertisement for Pond's Cream (see Plate 226), a product Lady Lavery endorsed.[50] She also approved the

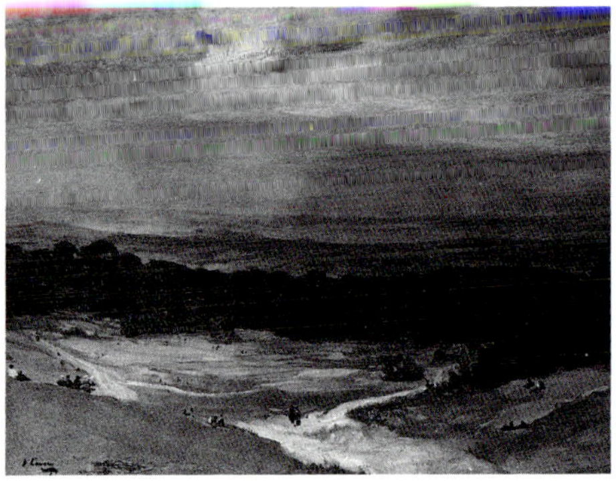

222 *Hampstead Heath*, *c.*1930, 24 × 32 (private collection, photo, Ian Kilpatrick)

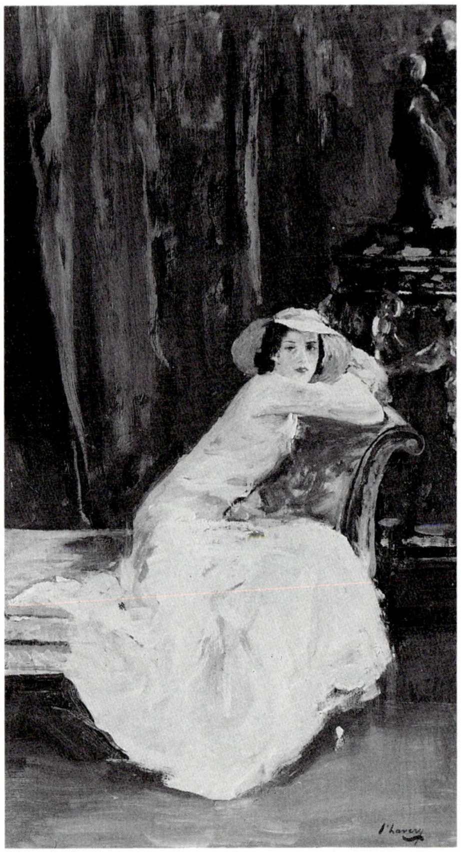

223 Sketch for *Portrait of Diana Dickinson*, 1934, 23¾ × 12½ (private collection, photo, Pyms Gallery, London)

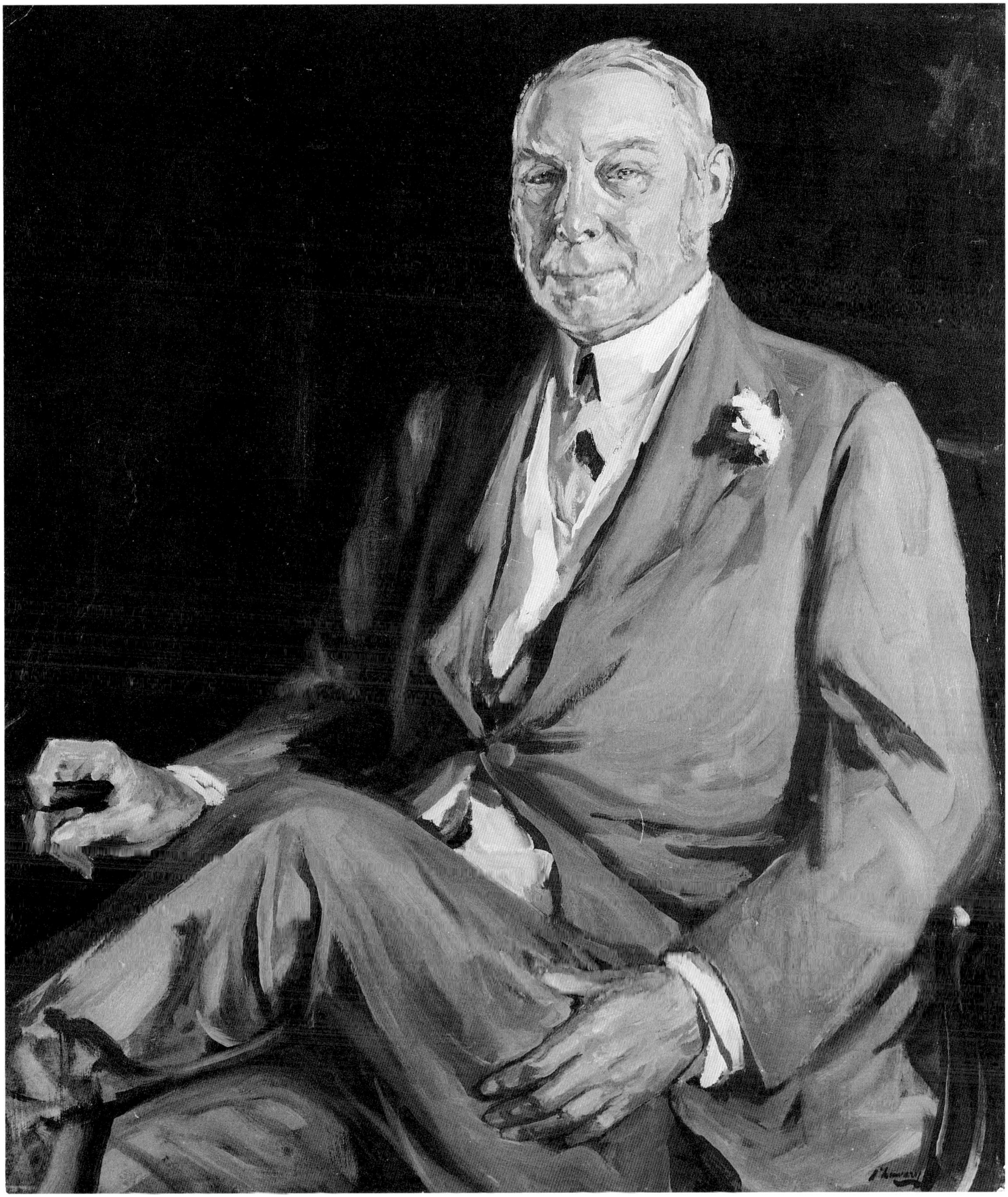

221 *Hugh Cecil Lowther, Fifth Earl of Lonsdale*,
1930, $37\frac{1}{4} \times 31\frac{1}{4}$ (private collection)

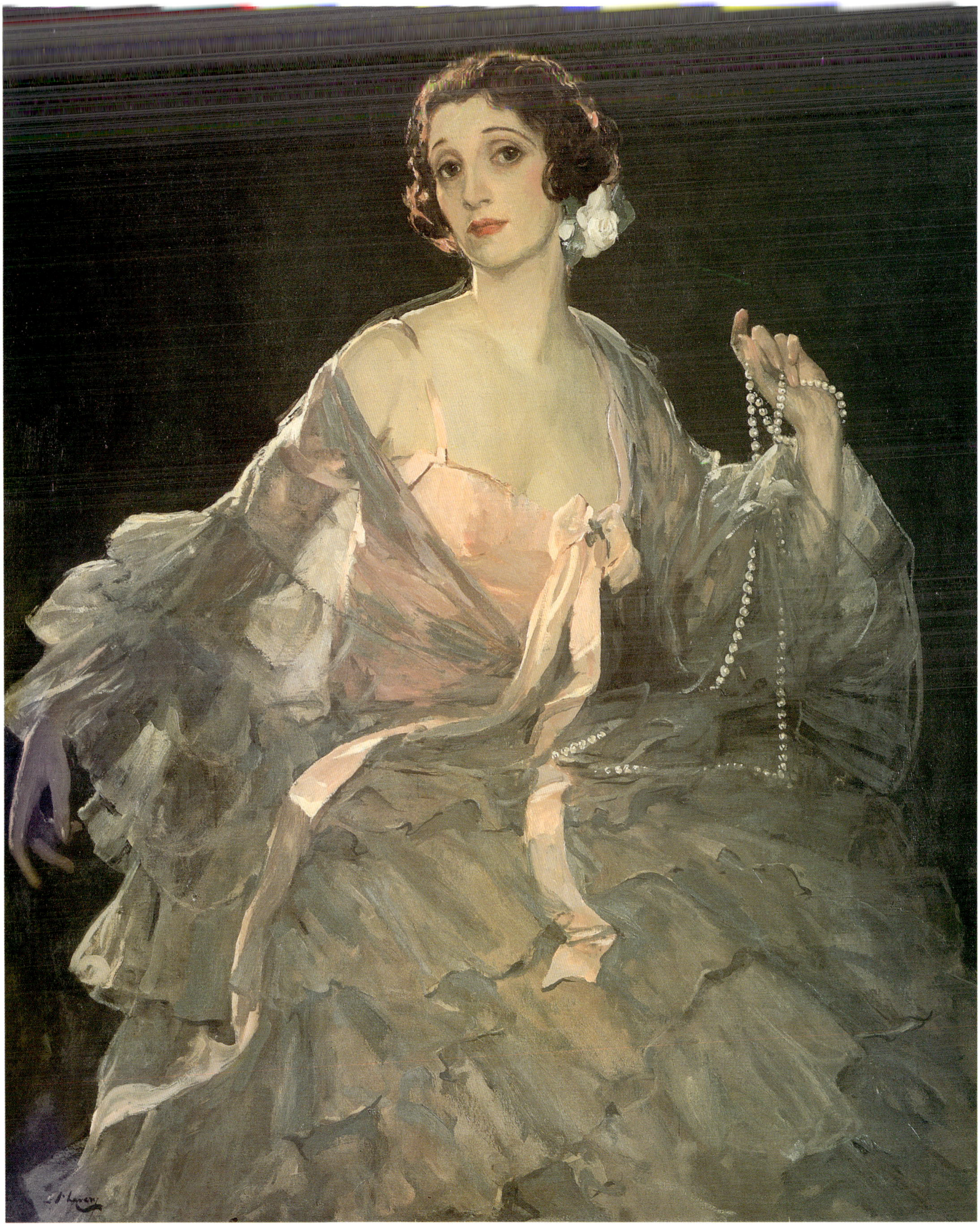

224 *Hazel in Rose and Grey*, *c.*1920, 50 × 40
(Barbican Art Gallery, London)

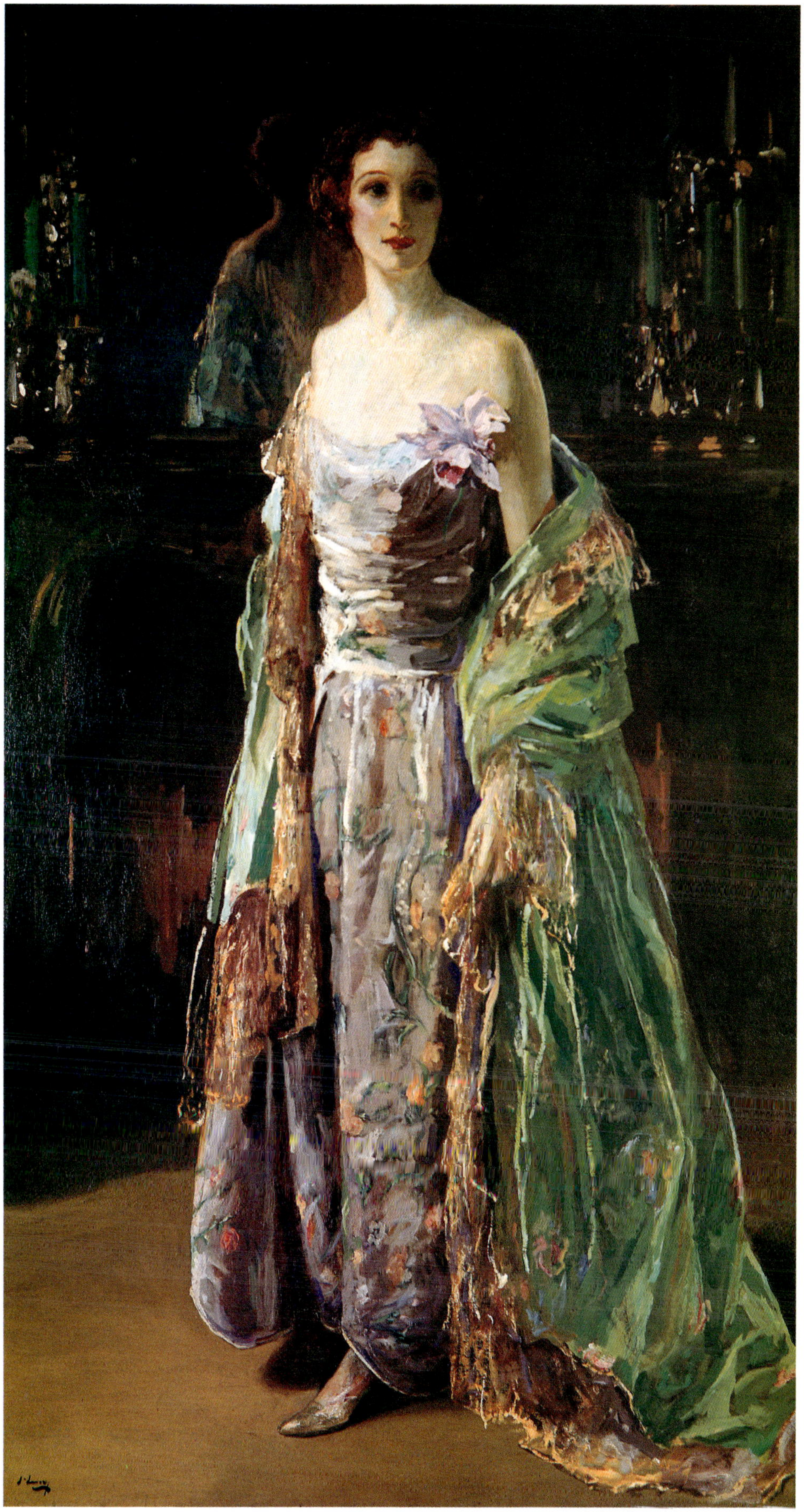

225 *The Green Coat*, 1925, 78 × 42¼
(Ulster Museum, Belfast)

alterations made to the picture, and its eventual destination. In May 1929 she wrote to Arthur Deane of Belfast Art Gallery, 'I am really delighted to say that John is sending a very good full-length portrait of me called *Hazel in Green and Mauve* [to Belfast]. It is to my thinking the best one of me he has ever painted and I prefer it to the head he originally selected I hope you will approve the change as I like to have the best of his work to be seen in Belfast, his own native land and city'.[51]

With a frequent and familiar model, Lavery achieved some of his most penetrating results. This is the case with *The Gold Turban* (Plate 227), 1929.[52] A belated companion to the highly regarded early painting, *The Silver Turban*[53] it has resonant, almost Rembrandtesque candour. Unlike the work of 1911, a new urgency had entered the handling of the paint. It is as if the picture contains a premonition of its subject's demise. Hazel is swathed in fur and as she flicks her head nervously to the right, light sparkles upon the surface of the turban.

During the early 1930s, Hazel Lavery appears often in the artist's work, but she is seen mostly in back view as she waits for tennis matches and swimming sessions to finish. 'I am forever watching Alice playing tennis', she confessed to Bodkin in 1930.[54] The definitive work of this type was *Les Orangers du Beau Site de Cannes (Tennis under the Orange Trees, Cannes)* (Plate 228), exhibited at the Royal Academy of 1929, although the vivid sketch given to his secretary, Charles Robert Chisman, has a lightness of touch which belies the age and experience of its maker. Not only had Lavery laid the ground work for this composition in Florida in the winter of 1927, he had also sketched a tennis match at Trent Park, the home of Sir Philip Sassoon in May 1928.[55] The subject was brought back into contemporary currency by the fact that, having been de-accessioned from the Munich Pinakothek, the celebrated early *Tennis Party* was purchased by Sir James Murray and presented to the City of Aberdeen. It was exhibited at the French Gallery in the winter of 1926–7 and was hailed as one of the most interesting pieces exhibited in London at the time.[56] It seems inevitable that the painter should have gone to study his own early work. His renewed interest in tennis as a subject was also the result of Alice's skill. At Cannes the Laverys were friendly with Lyttleton Rogers, the Irish International tennis player and with his help, Alice's game improved to the extent that she reached the finals of the Cannes Handicap in 1930.[57] During their stay, in March 1930, Alice married a well-to-do Irish farmer, Peter Mc Enery.[58] In these later pictures, Lavery selected a more aerial viewpoint than for the original *Tennis Party* (see Plate 45), thus creating a layered composition, with a screen of spectators interposing between the viewer and the game. This effect is carried to even more radical ends in *Woman in a Red Dress reading by a swimming pool*.[59] During the late 1920s, Lavery was as keenly interested in painting public baths as he was in painting tennis matches. Not only did he represent pools in Florida and Cannes, but when in London he depicted the nearby *Chiswick Baths* on at least two occasions.[60] *Woman in a Red Dress . . .* upstages the activities of the pool however, and draws the viewer to the brilliant vermillion of Hazel Lavery's dress.

The Laverys were back in Cannes in the early months of 1931, while Sir John recovered from a prostate operation.[61] No major works appear to have been painted during this sojourn. In 1933, Sir John and Lady Lavery went on an

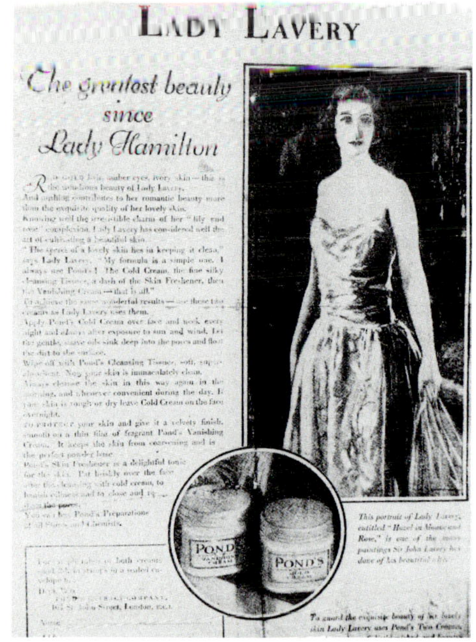

226 Advertisement for Pond's Cream (source unknown)

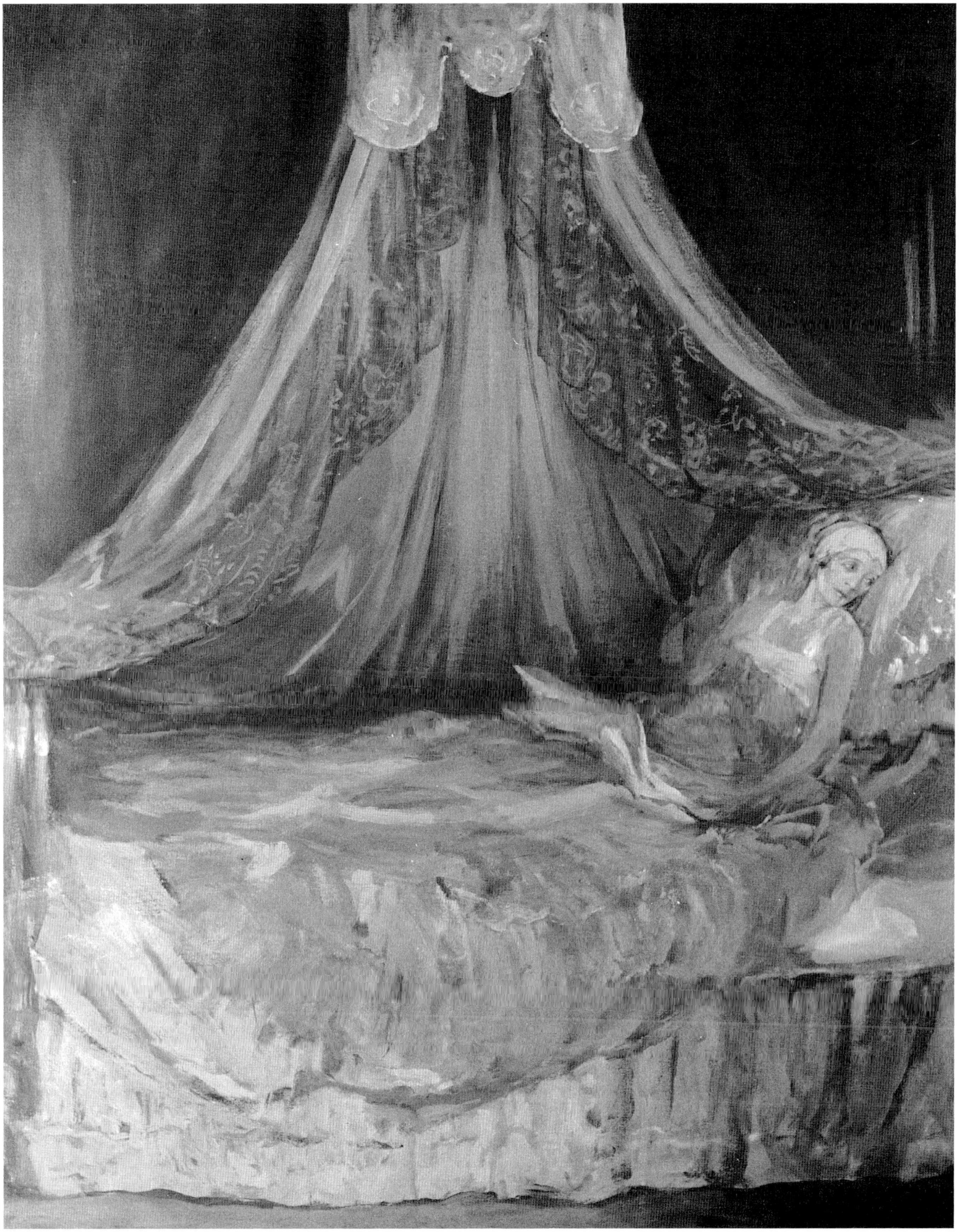

229 *The Unfinished Harmony*, 1934, 50 × 40
(Hugh Lane Municipal Art Gallery, Dublin)

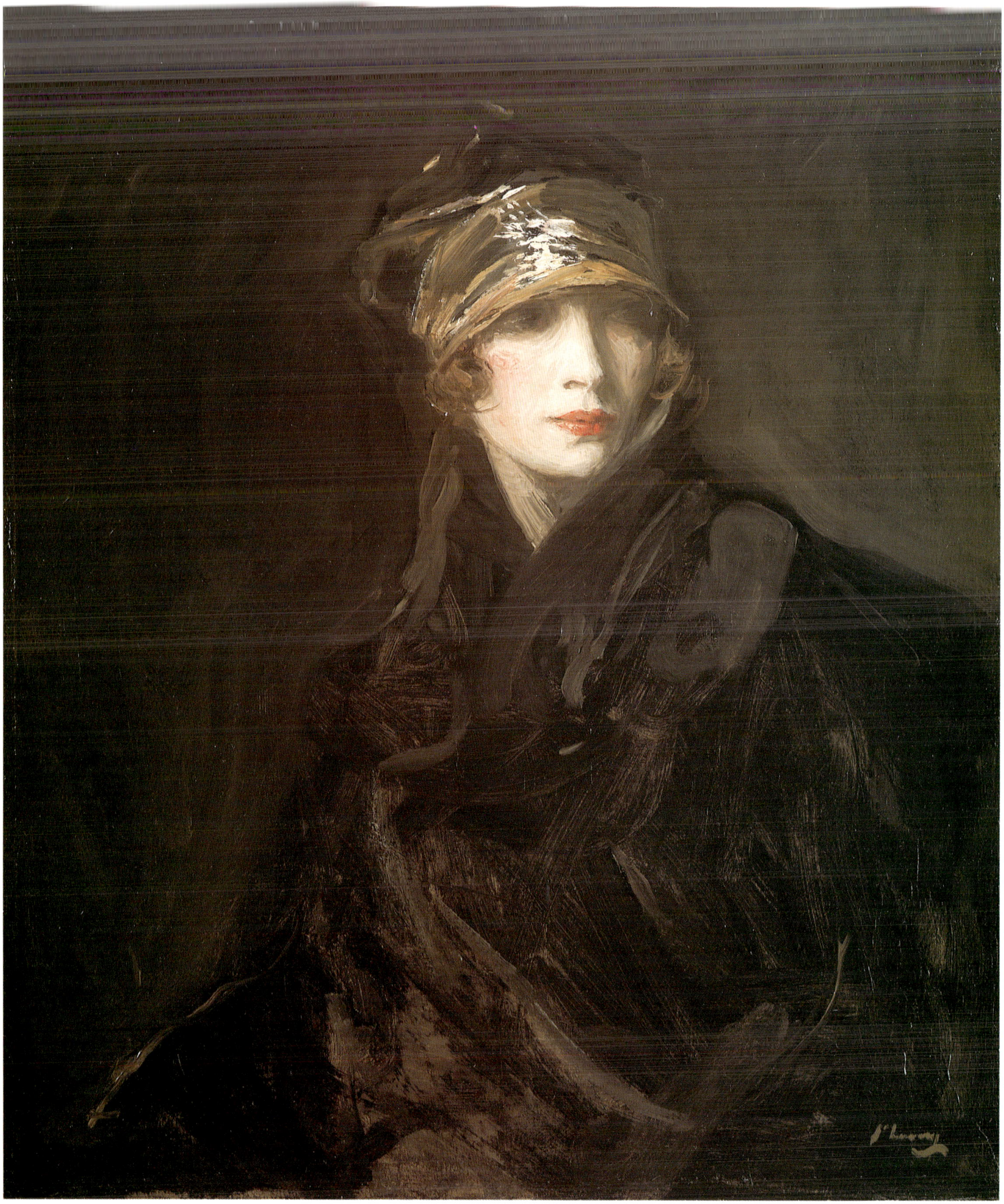

227 *The Gold Turban*, 1929, 30 × 25 (private collection, photo, Pyms Gallery, London)

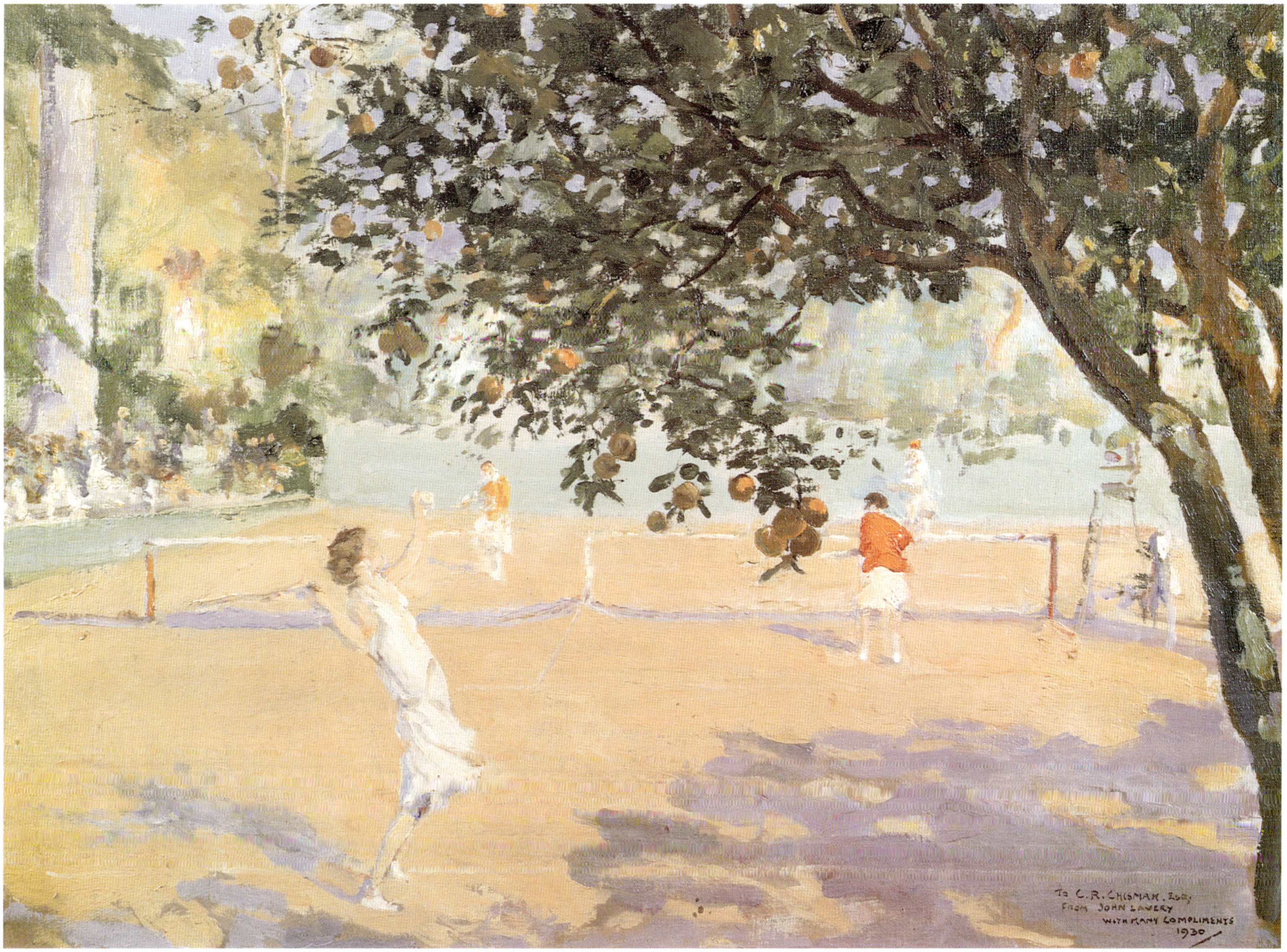

228 *Tennis under the Orange Trees, Cannes*, 1930, 18 × 24 (private collection, photo, courtesy Richard Green)

extended summer cruise through the Mediterranean, passing Tangier and stopping at Rome and Naples.[62] While in Rome, Lavery visited the Galeria Nationale and offered to repaint his early portrait of Mary Delmar Morgan, *Polyhymnia* (see Plate 155) because it had fallen into a state of disrepair.[63] By the end of that year, Hazel's health, which had never been strong, took a turn for the worse. Lavery later declared that her heart was weakened by the effects of an anaesthetic administered for the removal of a wisdom tooth, however, she had suffered intermittently from nephritis since Alice's birth.[64] The beginning of 1934, was spent in bed with pleurisy and double pneumonia and at the beginning of April she reported to Bodkin that she hoped to go to Brighton to convalesce.[65] This trip took place around Whitsun and as she rested, taking the sea air, Lavery painted sketches of Brighton Pier from the hotel window. Alas the trip did not produce the desired effect and Lady Lavery returned to her 'boudoir prison' in which she passed the remainder of the year. During that time, the painter worked upon *The Unfinished*

Harmony (Plate 229), a large picture of the bedridden Hazel, framed by pink awnings.[66] Hazel considered this a 'sad picture' and possibly for this reason, it remained unfinished at the time of her death. A friend disclosed its existence to the press and after his wife's death, the painter was asked about it. He stated to reporters,

> It is turned to the wall. I have not touched it since a month before she died. I know it would be useless to put my brush to that picture just now. It would bring back too many memories, happy memories and sad memories. They would crowd round me and I might spoil my picture. She never really wanted me to do that picture, but the colouring of the room appealed to me irresistably. The lovely canopy, her pale but oh! such beautiful features—and the rich colours of everything round her. Of course the picture had to be done. She was so patient with me and would lie perfectly still while I painted. She once said, 'I do not like leaving behind such a sad souvenir of myself.' But I could not believe that she would not recover. Then the day came when I had to lay aside the picture. But I will resume work on it some day.[67]

In some respects, as a portrait in death, the picture is comparable to Monet's and Whistler's images of similar scenes. Monet astonished himself with his seeming callousness in painting the dying Camille, his common-law wife, while Whistler in a late lithograph, similar in compositional format to *The Unfinished Harmony*, portrayed his wife Beatrix in her last illness. The poignancy of these scenes, separates them from the rest of the artists' oeuvre. In Lavery's case, the picture was too touchingly personal to be immediately completed after the event. However, he did take up the painting later in 1935, perhaps to exorcise the memory, and with a view to presenting it to the city of Dublin as a memorial to his wife. The question remains, however, as to whether such a work ever could be regarded as complete. Its macabre expressiveness, relying more on line than tonal contrast, places it in an extraordinary position, tangential to the main thrust of Lavery's art.

Hazel Lavery died on Thursday, 3 January 1935. Numerous tributes flooded into Cromwell Place. *The Times* obituary two days later, as well as describing her social accomplishment as the entertainer of writers, painters and politicians, referred to her 'perfectly simple and natural loving-kindness'.[68] It went on to speculate, 'Lady Lavery's artistic monument will not be her husband's career. This is not to take anything away from Sir John Lavery's great talents but only to suggest the value in the "production" of such talents, of a beautiful, popular, socially gifted and devoted wife, particularly when their possessor is a modest and retiring man.'[69]

There is no doubt that Lavery derived valuable support from Hazel. He profited greatly from her central position in London society and in his generosity he attributed much of his success to her, even though he had attained pre-eminence as a painter before their marriage. 'She made sitters talk to her, which set them at their ease while I was painting them', he later recalled.[70] Hazel also brought him back to his native land and, as an exacting critic, stimulated him to new subject-matter. Her ability in this respect was the result of her own artistic talent. In the words of Cecil Beaton, '. . . she drew expertly but never concentrated long enough on her work . . . She was a charming, feminine amateur.'[71] In his diary, the photographer paid eloquent tribute to the assistance Hazel had given him early in his career.

> Not only has one of my first and favoured stars ceased to shine, but I have lost a true and sympathetic friend. When I started my career, Hazel was one of the first to overwhelm me with encouragement and kindness. She sent notes, drawings, criticisms and suggestions. She sympathised with my despairs. And now, poor Hazel has been laid in her coffin and taken to Kensal Rise Cemetery. A living spirit has become a thing of the past. Those who loved her will perhaps make a legend of her, decorating her memory with the tuberoses, orchids and crimson roses that she surrounded herself within life. But soon and inevitably, even these dearest friends will be busy going out to lunch with someone else.[72]

These sentiments were echoed by the numerous socialites and literati who had decorated Lady Lavery's luncheon tables.[73] Close friends remained loyal to her memory and continued to miss her as time passed.[74] A requiem mass attended by a large number of the aristocracy, government ministers and ambassadors was held at Brompton Oratory on 7 January and this too was widely reported.[75] Two days prior to this, Lavery paid his own final tribute by sketching Hazel's coffin as it lay

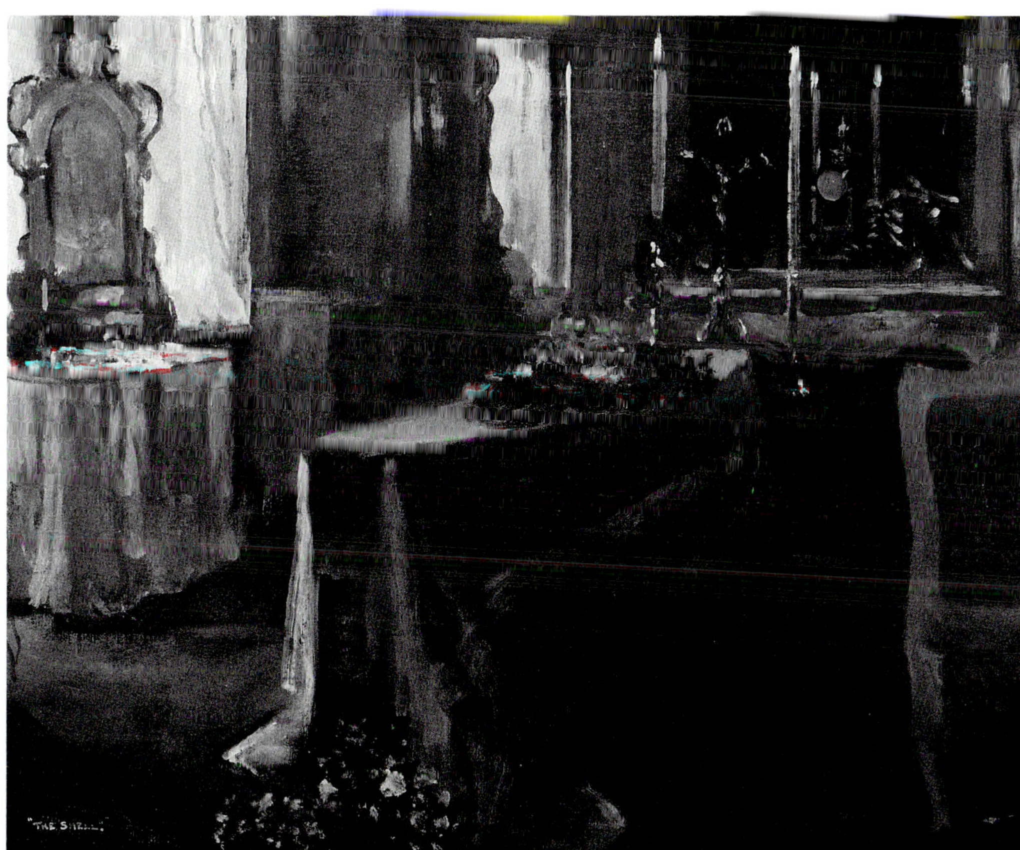

230 *'It is Finished' 5th January 1935*, 19½ × 23½ (Hugh Lane Municipal Art Gallery, Dublin)

draped with flowers in her small bedroom. The painting entitled '*It is Finished' 5th January 1935* (Plate 230) is a touching record of the dim light of the death chamber, an oddly intimate still-life flanked by tall tapers and a crucifix, that functions as a sad and inadequate valediction. 'Neither in paint nor in words', Lavery wrote, 'do I feel I could ever do justice to Hazel . . . Her rare beauty of face and character must have been known personally to be believed, and so upon the things nearest to me I will write least.'[76]

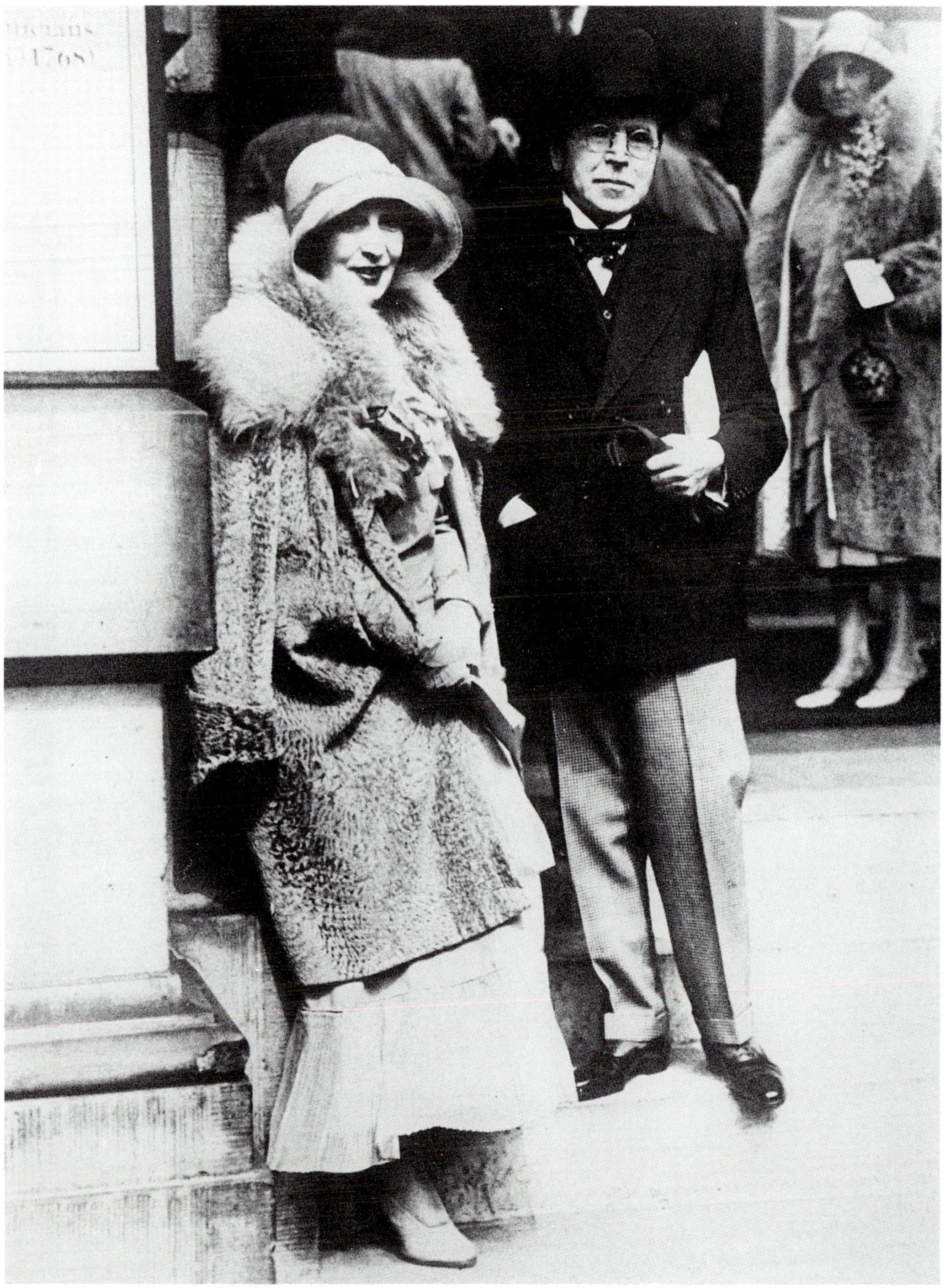

231 Sir John and Lady Lavery at a Royal Academy Private View, photograph *c.*1930 (photo, the author)

11 'A Newer World'

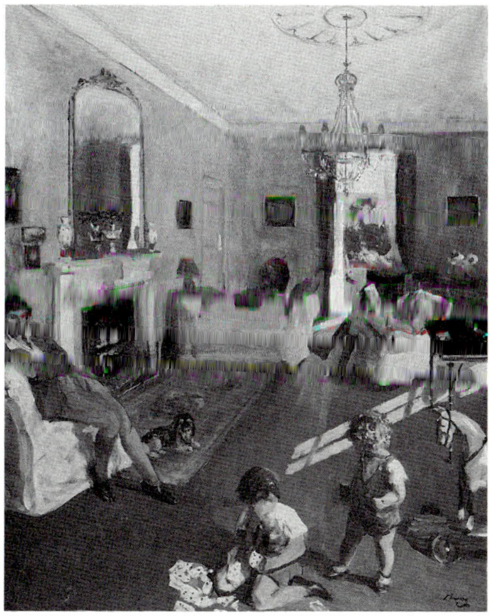

232 *Mrs McEnery and her Family at Rosenarra*, 1935, 36 × 28 (private collection)

This grim year dealt Lavery a second blow. For several years Eileen had endured bouts of tuberculosis. During the early months of the year she took to Hazel's sick-bed in Cromwell Place. When the weather improved she moved to her small house at the Lizard in Cornwall, where she was nursed by a former school friend of Alice's, Katherine Fitz Gerald. Alas, her condition did not improve and she died in her father's presence in July 1935. The deaths of Hazel and Eileen left Lavery depleted. He immersed himself in the treadmill activity of painting. Katherine Fitz Gerald, who had been acting as his secretary for a number of years, came to live at Cromwell Place. Ann Forbes Sempill, the second of his granddaughters, joined her the following year. Initially, Lavery cut a sad and lonely figure in society. In his diary, 'Chips' Channon gives a glimpse of the bereaved artist at a supper party thrown by the Londonderrys in March 1935. 'In the evening to Londonderry House where we found half political and social London at the Londonderry's old fashioned, distinguished "do". We supped with Mrs. Keppel, Lady Oxford and poor Sir John Lavery, nearly eighty and recently a widower . . .'.[1]

Clementine Churchill's belief that Lavery 'would not last long' after Hazel's death was, however, misplaced.[2] Gradually he found a new *modus vivendi* and when he had stopped working on *The Unfinished Harmony* (see Plate 229), his painting returned to more optimistic themes. To some extent, this was the result of being looked after by attractive young women who brought their own society to Cromwell Place and whose bubbling conversation often centred upon the latest movie star heart-throbs.

The memory of Hazel and Eileen was exorcised by events in Dublin in September 1935 when he received the Freedom of the City. At a celebratory luncheon, Lavery paid affectionate tribute to his wife and openly declared that the idea for the gift had been hers in the first place. John McCormack, who spoke at the luncheon, took the opportunity to present *Sutton Courtenay* (see Plate 154) to the city in memory of Hazel. Much was made in the congratulatory speeches of Lavery's Irish parentage and the fact that 'in days of anxiety and tribulation this country had faithful loyal adherents in the Lavery household in London'.[3] A visit to Alice's home at Rosenarra House, Kilkenny, was incorporated into this trip and Lavery took the opportunity to paint *Mrs McEnery and her Family at Rosenarra* (Plate 232), a picture which resumes many of the qualities of the earlier portrait interiors, but which is more insistently domestic.[4] Alice and her husband, clad in jodhpurs and puttees, are shown having just returned from a ride and their relaxed postures recall the similar relationship of Eileen and Sir Reginald Lister in *The Greyhound* (Plate 114).[5]

During these months, Lavery returned to a theme which had been consistently treated throughout his long career. At Ranelagh he produced many small oil sketches (see Plate 233) for a large picture of Lilian Millar reading in a hammock

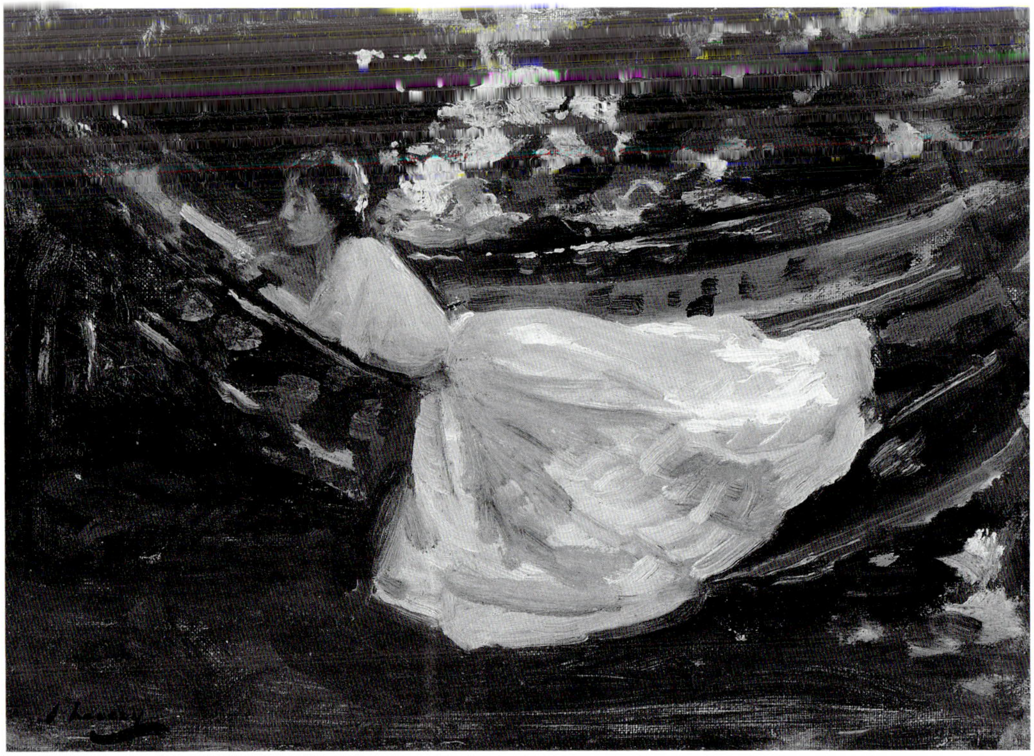

233 Study for *Summer*, *c.*1910, size unknown (private collection)

imitating earlier studies of Mary Auras in the original version painted around 1905. The work was exhibited at the Royal Academy in 1936, entitled *Summer*.[6] Lavery may have been encouraged to a radical rethink of this subject because in 1935 his attention was drawn to the fact that *The Red Hammock* (Plate 234) was in a state of serious deterioration. The painting had been originally executed in 1907 and was donated to Belfast after it was repainted in the mid-Twenties using Hazel as a model (see Plate 235). Realising the difficulty of repair, Lavery embarked upon a replacement replica using a new canvas.[7] The Edwardian rococo flavour of the original must have been difficult to recreate at a time when the memory of the model was still fresh. As a result, the handling of the figure lacks authority. The more modern version of the subject, *Summer* was more successful in its sketches than in its finished form. Its large-scale fantasy, reminiscent of Fragonard, seems far removed from the world of the automobile and aeroplane. Its celebration of youth and sensuality coincided with Hitler's annexation of the Rhineland. To some extent, the painting must embody Lavery's search for lost illusions, but he did not linger in nostalgia. The following year at Palm Springs, he took out 'piles of organdie and muslin dresses', but disgarded them and ended up painting Lilian and his grand-daughter, Diana, sunbathing.[8]

In sharp contrast to *Summer* Lavery showed his portrait of *Grey Owl* (Plate 236) in 1936.[9] The Red Indian chief had toured Britain in the previous twelve months. The son of a government scout and an Apache mother, Grey Owl had wandered from his birth-place on the Mexican border as far north as Canada. He had fought as a sniper in the Great War and returned to live in the wild in the untamed regions of Northern Ontario. His extraordinary story entitled *Pilgrims of the Wild*

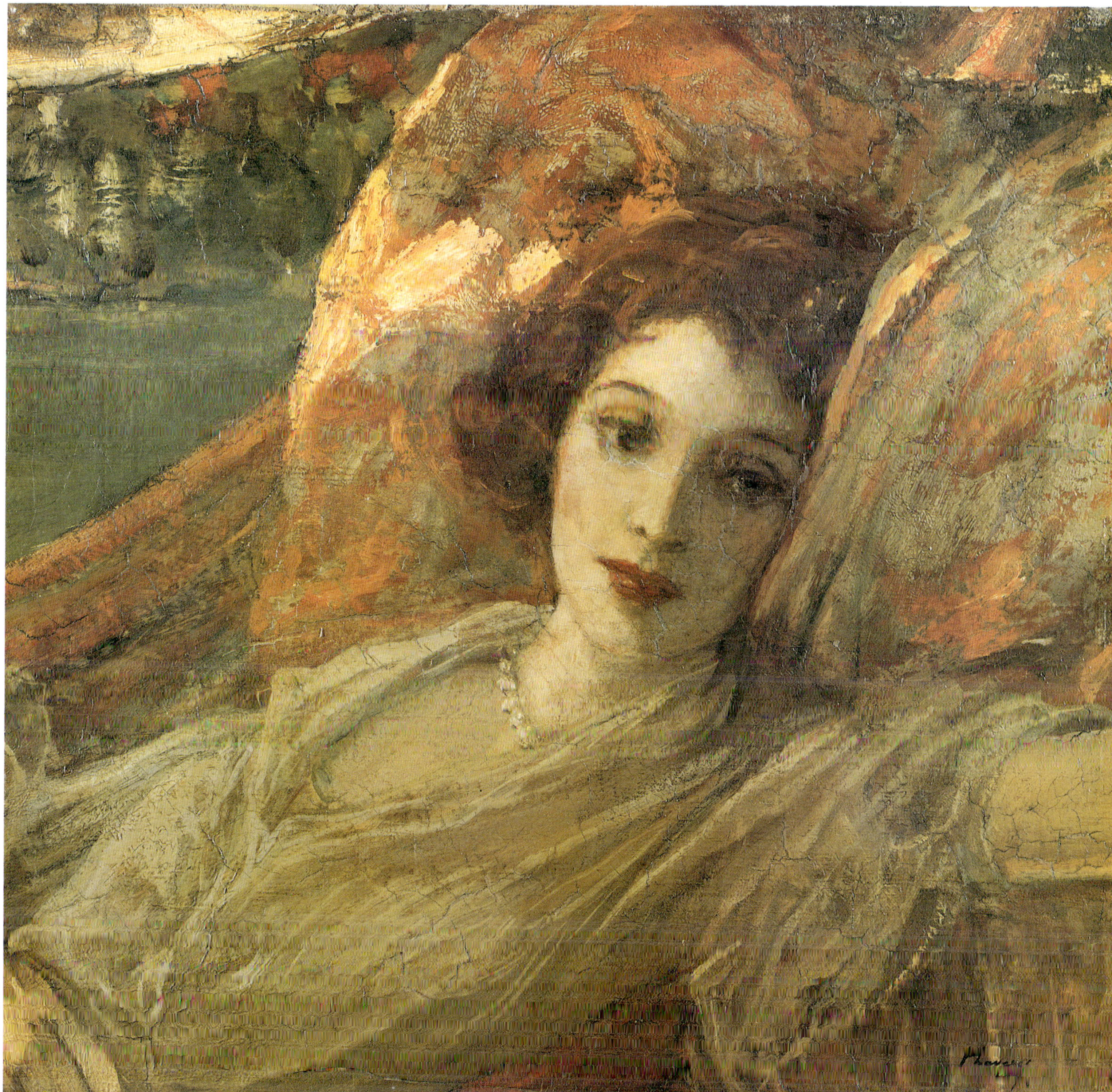

235 Hazel in *The Red Hammock*, *c.*1923,
22 × 22, (private collection, photo, courtesy
Phillips, London)

captivated audiences and made him a public celebrity. For Lavery, he was not the first Red Indian sitter. As far back as 1898, on his first visit to New York, he had painted *Thunder Cloud* in full headdress, but in this instance, the simple unpretentiousness of the noble savage was well conveyed in a direct and faithful likeness.[10]

Thunder Cloud was one of forty-eight canvases included in a small retrospective exhibition at the Victoria Art Galleries, Dundee organised by John Robertson. The 'Foreword' to the catalogue was written by Sir Patrick Ford, who also lent eight works to the show. Ford saw Lavery as 'a singularly fresh and engaging personality', and reiterating Cunninghame Graham he declared, 'No new subject daunts him, and some of his most successful achievements have resulted from adventures into fresh woods and pastures new.'[11]

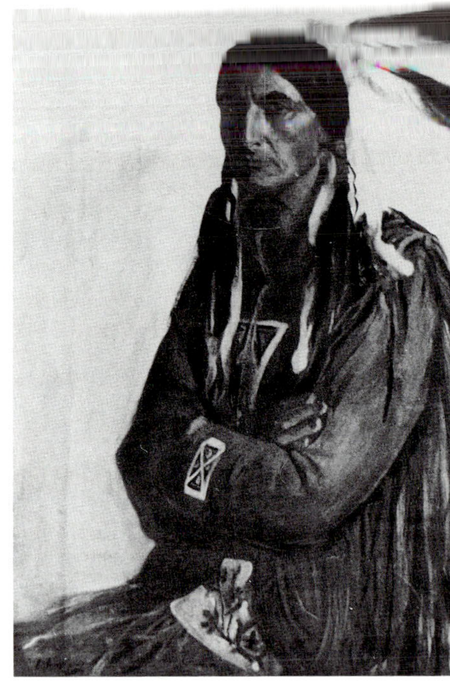

236 *Grey Owl*, *c*.1936, size unknown (present whereabouts unknown)

In 1936, Lavery himself set off for the new frontier, and inspired by his grand-daughter's conversations, went to Hollywood to paint portraits of the stars. Before Hazel's death, he recalled being dazzled by a fully lit location shot at Buckingham Palace, and he felt that in the artificial world of the movies, almost any of the conditions he sought could be recreated. At first it seemed as if he was right. At MGM studios there was 'part of a ballroom, a street, a lake, real cypress trees with their tops cut, half a stairway, a balcony . . .'.[12] He must have faced the same diversity at Paramount, where shortly after his arrival, he was invited to luncheon by Alison Skipworth, a woman whom he had painted forty-eight years earlier as an artwork demonstrator on the Doulton stall at the Glasgow International Exhibition. Through this fortuitous contact, he was introduced to Marlene Dietrich and several other stars. It was agreed that Miss Dietrich's portrait would be painted on the set between 'takes'. However, although a space was cleared for his easel, Lavery soon ran into difficulties.

> . . . after the first morning at Paramount Studios I saw there were new problems to solve that I had not prepared for. The awful confusion, Directors, Producers, scenario-writers, the dozens of camera-men, sound-recorders, scene-shifters, not to speak of actors and actresses, stand-ins and extras. Lights on, lights off—'cut! cut!' repeated in a loud voice until one wondered if there would be anything left . . . suddenly the Director's voice raised above it all—'silence please!' then you might hear a pin drop, afraid to breathe or move while voices were being recorded. I would stand paralysed until relief came. Then Marlene would rush in and take up her pose in front of her make-up glass. After a couple of mornings I gave it up . . . .[13]

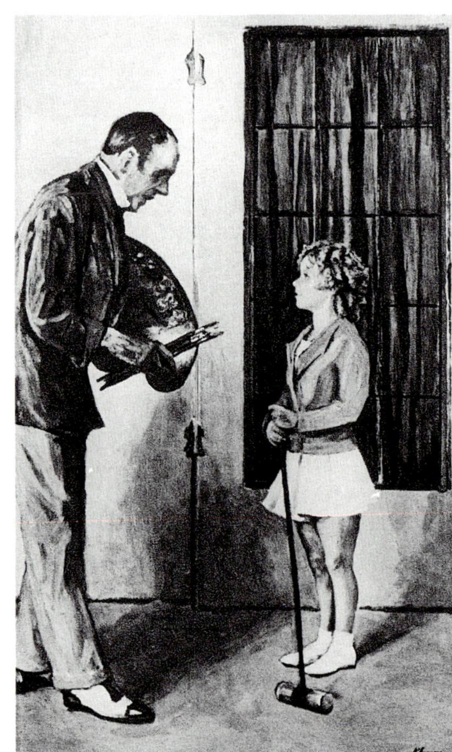

237 *Shirley Temple and the Painter*, 1937, size unknown (present whereabouts unknown)

Lavery got further with Maureen O'Sullivan and Loretta Young, who were painted as *Stars in Sunlight*, a work exhibited at the Royal Hibernian Academy in 1937.[14] His real success, however, was with Shirley Temple, an intelligent child 'with the most perfect manners.'[15] Family snap-shots indicate the Lavery spent some considerable time with the child star, sketching her by the pool with Katherine Fitz Gerald and lounging in a deckchair. At the same time, he embarked upon a full-length double portrait *Shirley Temple and the Painter* (Plate 237). In this, the eighty-year-old artist, fashionably clad in two-tone shoes, bends forward to speak to the child. Echoes of *Père et Fille* (see Plate 83) were unintentional. The

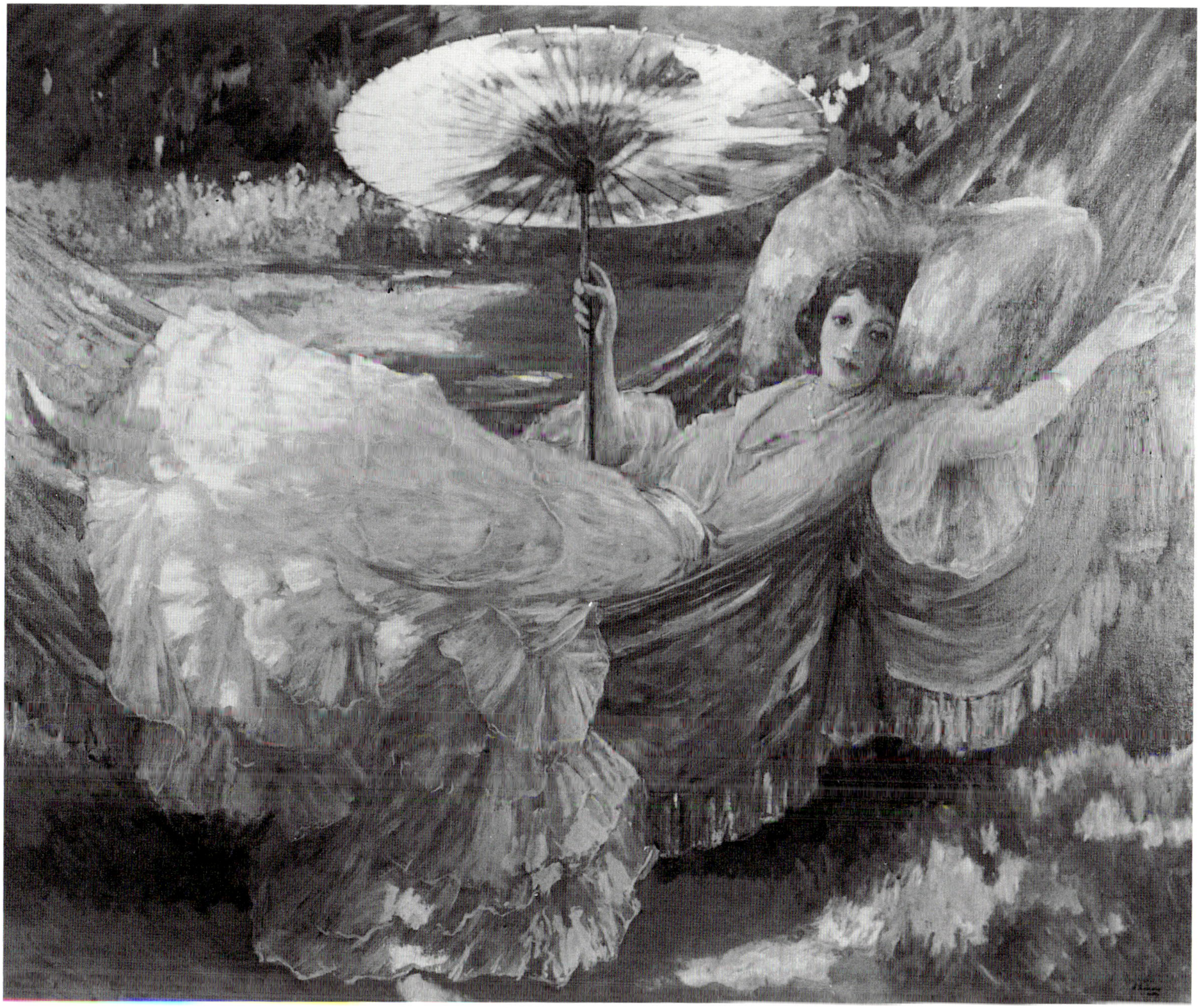

211 *The Red Hammock* c.1925, 68 × 89
(The Ulster Museum, Belfast)

picture was more of a commemoration of an encounter. In it the artist, palette in hand, crosses the footlights and enters his own stage. The engaging sitter invites him to neglect his utensils for a game of croquet.

When they were exhibited at the Society of Portrait Painters in November 1936, Lavery's paintings contained 'much interest for the public'. *Shirley Temple and the Painter* was hailed as an important work. The *Sunday Times* critic felt that, 'in all his long and honourable career I do not think Lavery has ever given us a picture of greater charm and finer technical suavity.'[16] These plaudits compensated for the time that was wasted on the set. Lavery expended a lot of energy to no avail preparing to paint various scenes from *Romeo and Juliet*, starring Leslie Howard, Oliver Messel and Norma Shearer. He spent two days sketching the square at Verona in preparation for the fight scene between the Capulets and Montagues, only to be told that the scene had been postponed indefinitely. The balcony scene was equally impossible because it required thirty-two electricians to light the set and none could be spared from other duties on the painter's behalf. Finally, he sketched the tomb scene, after persuading Norma Shearer to pose. At last it seemed that he might be able to finish one piece of work at least. Accordingly, he left his painting kit standing by the set in order to resume work the following day, only to discover that 'next morning the tomb, my painting outfit, and every vestige of the elaborate scene had been cleared away, leaving a great empty studio in semi-darkness . . .'[17] A sequence of oil sketches of these scenes testify to the abortive nature of Lavery's experiments.[18] Despite the fact that the director, George Cukor, won Lavery's admiration for his 'patience' and 'charming manner', no one seemed able to provide the essential information about 'what was going to take place and when'.[19] Upon reflection, Lavery felt that he had failed to respond to the situation in the right manner. The general effect rather than the particular detail should be sought. His methods had not been suited to his subject.

Lavery's hectic Hollywood tour in 1936, accompanied by Diana Dickinson and Lilian Millar, was tempered by a visit to Gordon Coutts who lived at Palm Springs. Coutts was the son of a boxer from Aberdeen and though he might well have followed in his father's footsteps, he had ambitions to become a portrait painter. He had admired Lavery for many years, though it is unclear under what circumstances they were first in contact. When Lavery reached Palm Springs, it was obvious that Coutts was dying and he found before him 'a poor weak invalid in a much-heated studio, unable to breathe anything but its vitiated air'.[20] The atmosphere must have been uncomfortable because Coutts' temper, placid and charming in public, was unleashed in private with his wife, Gertrude. It was from this unstable household that Lavery flew back to London in the winter of 1936.

On the outward or return trip, Lavery stopped in New York to paint a portrait interior of Lord and Lady Duveen and their daughter, in their Fifth Avenue apartment (see Plate 238).[21] Since they appear in the foreground of this carefully constructed modern 'period' interior, the picture has an undeniable staginess that is mediated only by the presence of two wire-haired fox terriers—the fashionable dogs of the day. Upon his return, Lavery was taken up by the Wimbornes and he painted their musical soirées.[22] In the resulting Royal Academy picture, Viscountess Wimbourne looks round apprehensively at the spectator as he enters

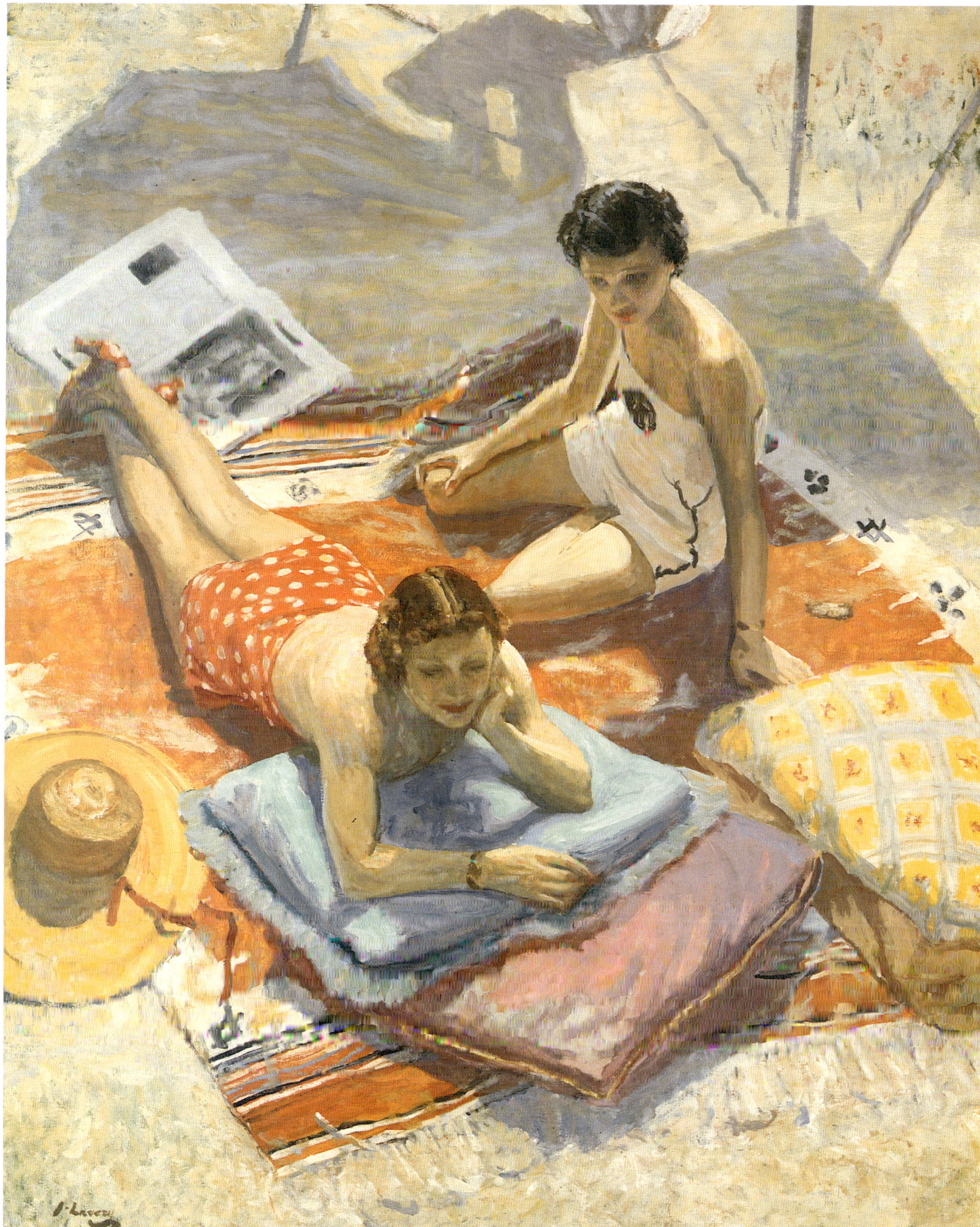

239 *Sunbathers*, 1937, $55\frac{1}{2} \times 43\frac{1}{2}$ (private collection, photo, courtesy Sotheby's)

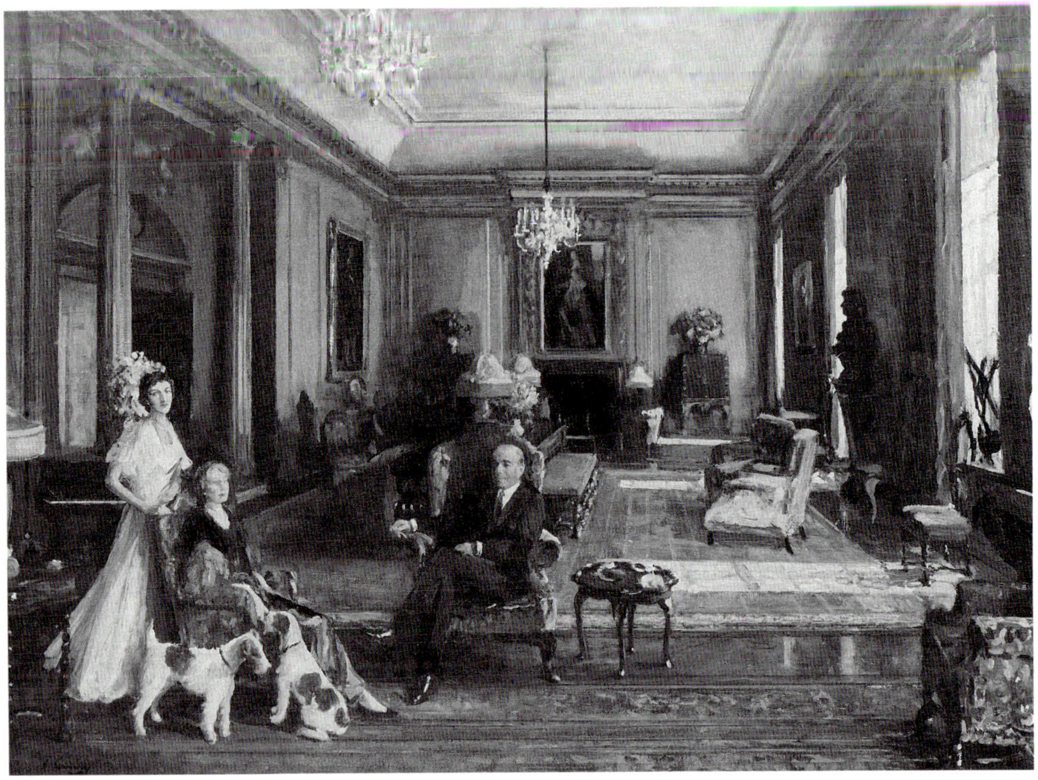

238 *Lord Duveen of Millbank at Home*, 1937, $30\frac{1}{2} \times 40\frac{1}{2}$ (Ferens Art Gallery, Kingston Upon Hull)

the grand salon in which her ensemble perform. The ornate decor of the room recalls something of the Second Empire excesses of the Salle Prince. These paintings, accompanied by *Sunbathers* (Plate 239), a Palm Springs work, made a strong representation at the Academy in 1937. There is evidence that the artist himself was particularly pleased with this sequence of paintings. In May he received a letter from Thomas Bodkin complimenting him on the works, 'especially one of yourself in red shirt with two bathing belles'. On 29 May, the artist wrote back thanking Bodkin 'a thousand times' for his words of encouragement and adding, 'For although I don't think either you or Kenneth Clark know anything about "painting" pictures I will admit you know a good one when you see it.'[23]

The praise may well have been a deciding factor in Lavery's decision to return to Palm Springs later in the year. The most important event, however, of the first half of 1937 which caught the popular imagination, was the Coronation of King George VI.[24] Lavery set out to record the procession as it passed down Piccadilly and to do so, he positioned himself up on a balcony overlooking the road (see Plate 240). He was surrounded by a bevy of young women. Snap-shots were taken to indicate their position (see Plate 241) and the painter executed numerous rapid sketches of guards and footmen in their processional regalia. Lavery had painted pageant history on many occasions and his first experience had taken him to a high balcony for a similar viewpoint to record *The State Visit of Queen Victoria to the Glasgow International Exhibition*. On that occasion, he had concealed himself behind a curtain and now, he was part of an oblivious cheering crowd. The ceremonial cast his mind back to the incident recalling Velasquez, when as a

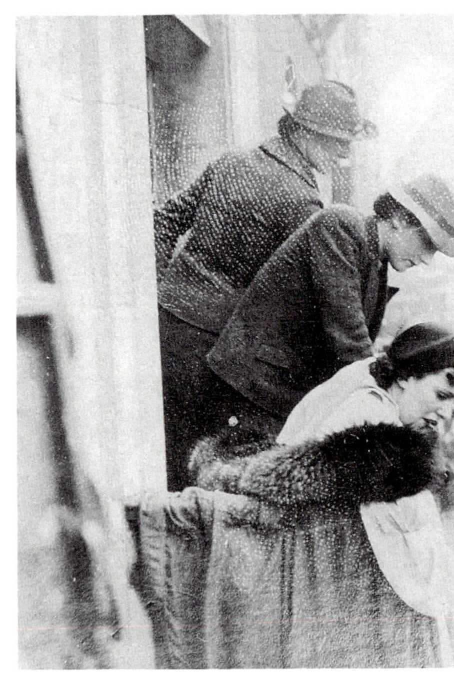

241 Katherine FitzGerald, Diana Dickinson and Ann Forbes-Sempill at the Coronation, 1937, (photo, the author)

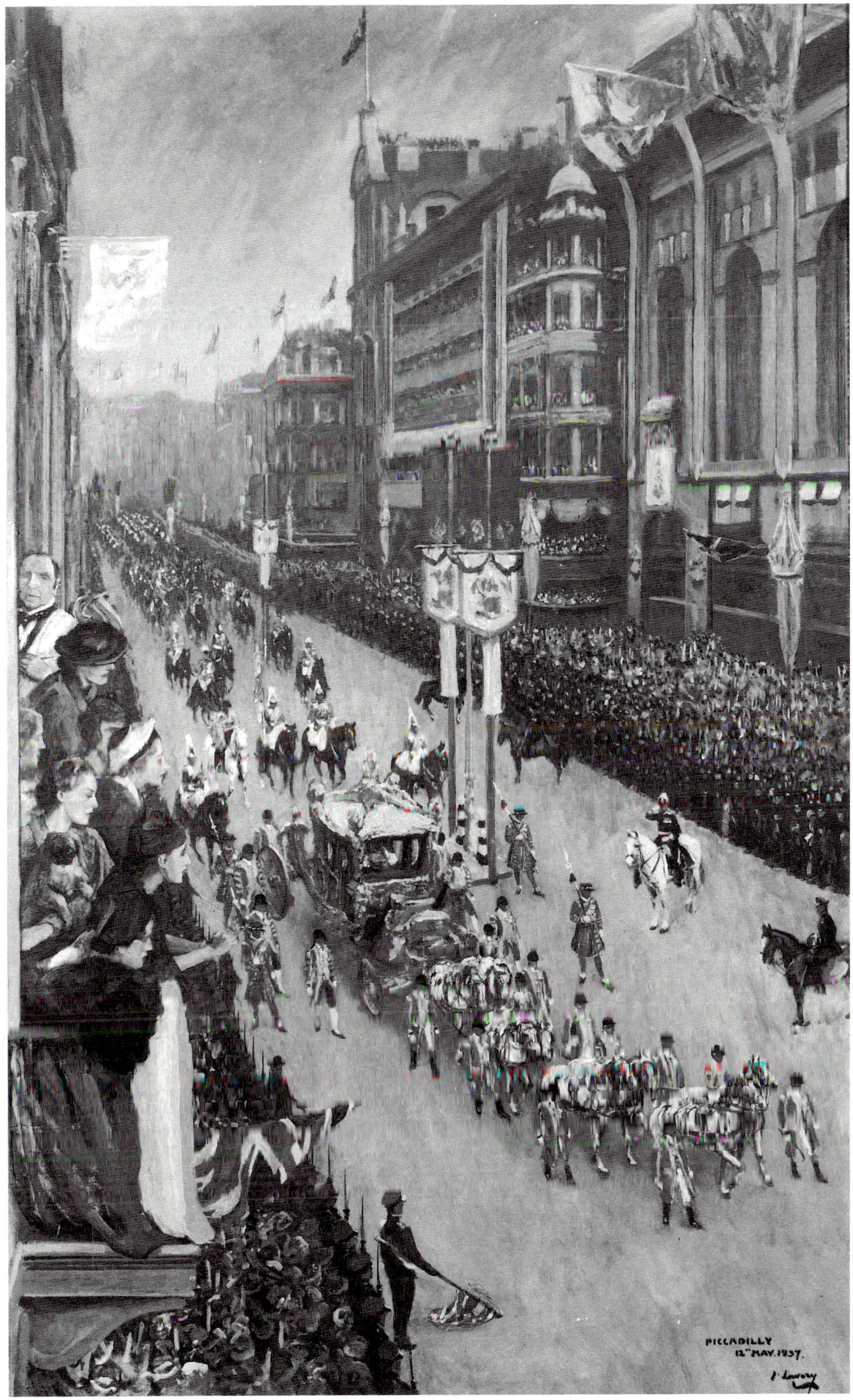

240 *Piccadilly, 12 May 1937*,
(The London Museum)

younger man, he had painted this new king's father. Thus, on the balcony, on the extreme left, surrounded by his maids of honour, he included his own self portrait. To Edward Knoblock this virtuoso display was simply 'brilliant'.[25]

Around this time Lavery received news of Gordon Coutts' death, and with it an insistent call from his wife, Gertrude, that he should return to Palm Springs (see Plate 242). With some candour the artist described his state of mind upon receipt of this invitation—and *cri de coeur*, 'It is true that to a certain extent, the sufferings of others reach me, so that when Eileen and Hazel, for some reason known to the Divine Power, were made to suffer many months in agony I had an acute form of remorse afterwards. This caused me to bury myself in my painting until I was aroused by the fact that I was alone and being slowly led into a new life . . . I was prepared to throw up everything and return to the happiest days of my existence—the life of an irresponsible bohemian . . .[26]

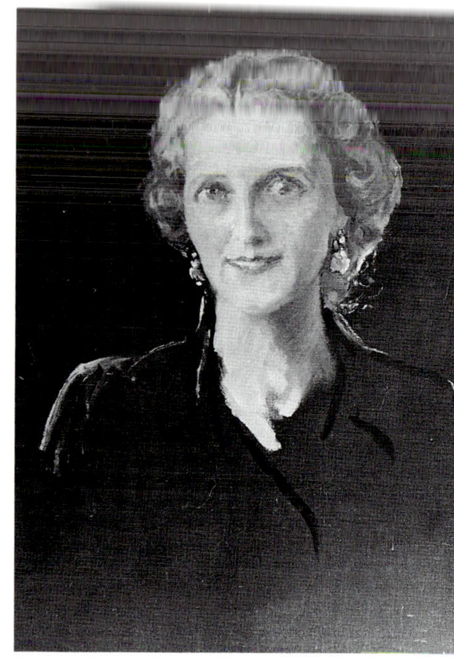

242 *Mrs Gordon Coutts*, 24 × 20 (private collection, photo, Ian Kilpatrick)

He felt that there was little left for him at Cromwell Place and wished to 'strike out anew . . . I would end as I began—in freedom'.[27] Taking Ann and Katherine with him, he flew to New Orleans where they were met by Gertrude Coutts, who had driven 3000 miles from Palm Springs to join them. The years of strain which led to her husband's death, had lifted and she too seemed reborn. Alas, her new exuberance was tragically quenched. On Sunday, 19 December 1937, she and an artist friend called Jack Schurch, took Lavery, Ann and Katherine to supper at a desert restaurant known as Green Shack. Returning at about 11 p.m., Lavery records that Gertrude, who had been a trained opera singer, broke into a loud rendition of *Ave Maria*. Then the car came to a halt with a flat tyre. Lavery and Katherine promptly got out to examine the wheel and as they stood by the vehicle, it was suddenly struck by another car. Mrs Coutts, in the back seat at the time of impact, was so severely injured that she died in hospital the next day.[28]

The artist was undoubtedly shaken by this eerie and unnerving event but he stayed on in Palm Springs until the new year. The incident was the last one to be recounted in *The Life of a Painter* and it did, no doubt, enforce the idea of mortality upon his mind and make him see the vanity of his recent ambitions to throw off over fifty years of successful professionalism.

At some point early in 1938, he set off for Florida and there he painted Lady Castlerosse as she posed on a diving board in swimming costume. Numerous sketches supported the composition which was intended for submission to the Royal Academy of that year. The adventure in taking the large finished version from Miami to New York involved a long car journey in which Katherine Fitz Gerald and Ann Forbes-Sempill were obliged to use the canvas as a makeshift mattress. At one point, driving through torrential rain, a bridge and part of the road were swept away in front of them and they were marooned. When they were rescued, having spent a full night in the car, the canvas was flown to New York and from thence to London to be consigned to the Academy undamaged.[29]

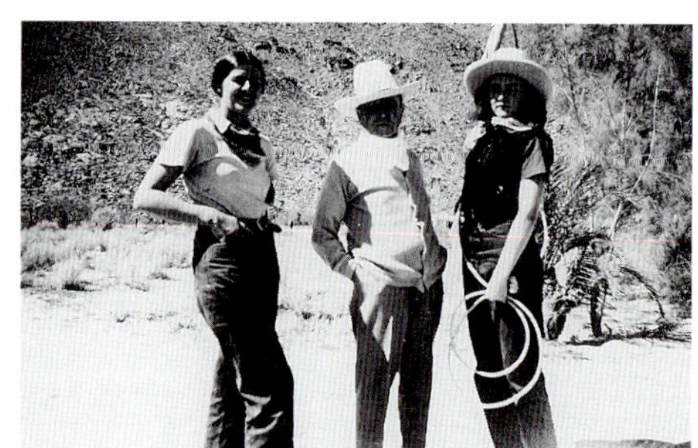

243 Katherine Fitz Gerald, Lavery and Ann Forbes-Sempill at Palm Springs, snapshot 1937 (photo, the author)

Returning to England on the liner *Bremen* in May 1938, Lavery's introspection led him to think in terms of setting down on paper some of the more extraordinary episodes from his long and eventful life. With the help of Alice, Ann, Katherine and John Stewart Collis, he began the task of writing his memoirs. When completed, the text was edited and improved by John Masefield, whose portrait

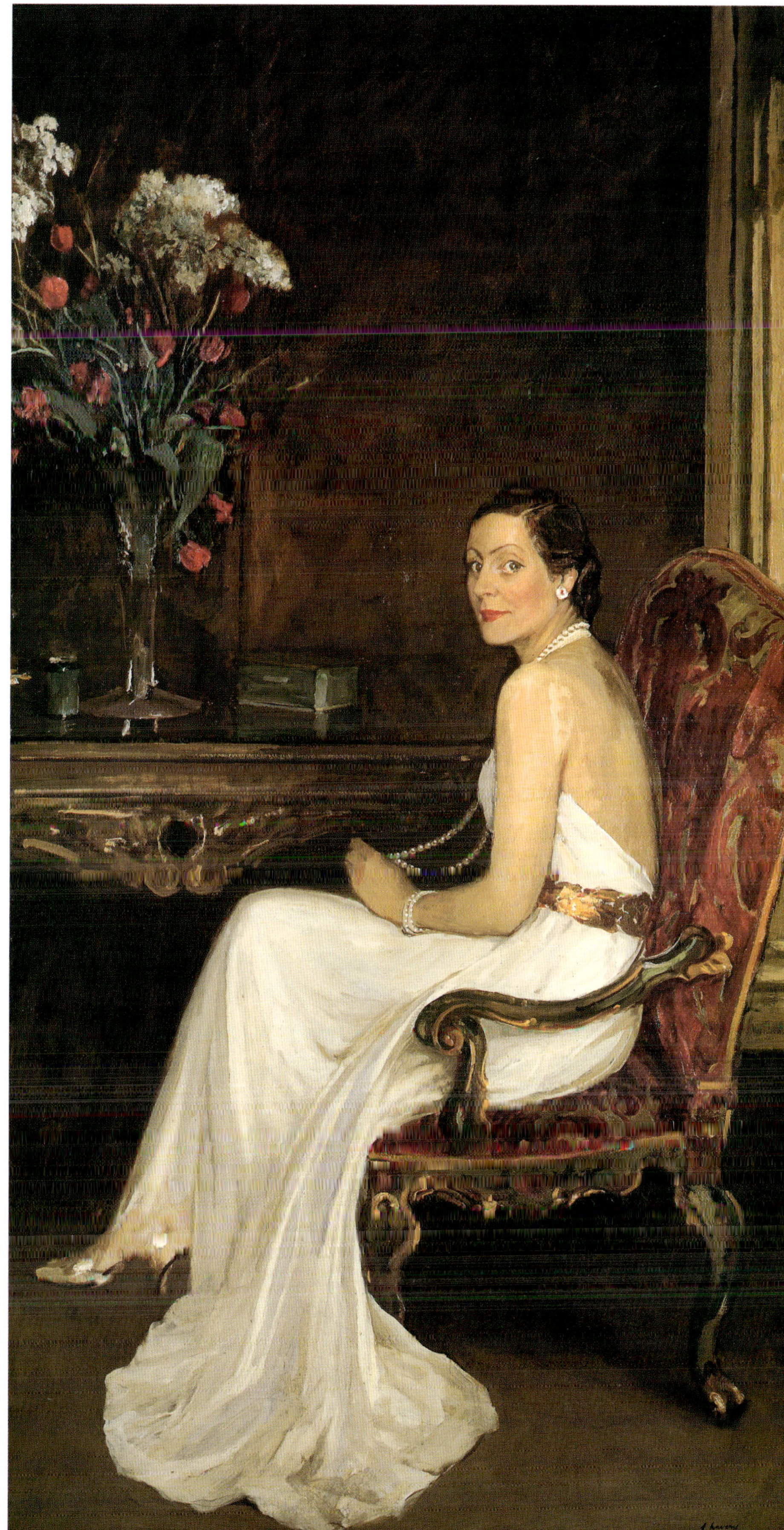

245 *Viscountess Wimborne*, 1937, 78 × 40 (present whereabouts unknown, photo, courtesy Colnaghi's)

had been commissioned by an American admirer. Lavery went to the Cotswolds to stay with the poet while he painted the picture. In order to get a true impression of his subject, he delicately negotiated access to Masefield's study—his 'Holy of Holies'.[30]

During these last years, it seemed important to Lavery to maintain contact with his provincial roots. From the Twenties onwards, he paid occasional visits to his relations at Soldierstown and Moira. His cousin Kate's son, Edward, took up sculpture and using his family connections came to London to study. Edward Cleneghan executed a fine bust of Lavery, and was introduced by him to William Rothenstein, the principal of the Royal College of Art. After some training at the Royal College and at the Slade School of Fine Art, Cleneghan returned to Ireland at the outbreak of war in 1939 to manage his family's public house.[31] The mood of reflection, of honouring old allegiances, in these years not only brought forth a verbal record of Lavery's early life, it also encouraged him to fill in the visual gaps. He painted a portrait of his sister, Jane, from a photograph of 1876 and produced a commemoration of his first wife, Kathleen MacDermott, in *Kathleen (The Flower Girl)* (Plate 244), a painting for which Ann and Diana modelled.[32] These sentimental images may have helped him to atone for the remorse he felt at the early tragic deaths of both women who ought to have meant more to him at the time.

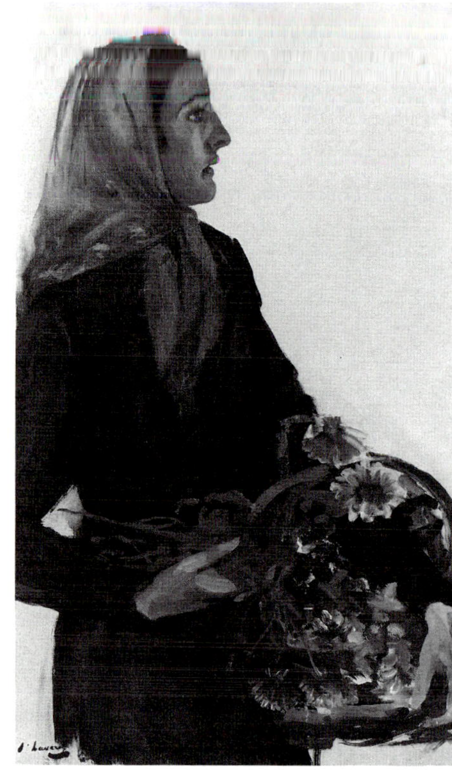

244 *Kathleen (The Flower Girl)*, *c.*1936, 36 × 22½ (private collection)

Lavery broke through to new insights in two superbly self-confident full-length portraits, his last important statements in the genre. The first of these was the portrait of *Viscountess Wimborne* (Plate 245) exhibited at the Royal Academy in 1939.[33] From an artist of Lavery's advanced years, this was a dazzling display, summoning methods and techniques which were deep-rooted in his art. What appears to be just another society portrait of a fashionable woman, in a sheer, backless evening dress, is in effect a summation of fifty years experience. The staccato shorthand of the white dress, the rapid notation of the gilded table and vase of tulips and lilac have undeniable echoes of Velasquez, particularly the seminal full-length portrait of *Philip IV* in the National Gallery, London. Like the great masters of the seventeenth century, Lavery's goal was to be able to recognise, in the objects he saw, the paint formula that would convey their existence. Visual appearances were seized immediately and pieced together from numerous small perceptions. Lavery's art had never been one of suppliant contemplation. It fed constantly upon new challenges and could only return to accepted modes, such as the full-length, when some renewal had taken place. The cycle of introspection and remorse, the Palm Springs interludes prepared the eighty-two-year old painter to depict *Viscountess Wimborne* with all her vamp-like allure.

In 1939, Lavery went on to paint the portrait of *Katherine Fitz Gerald* (Plate 246), a work of delicate psychological penetration.[34] Though it portrays the sitter in evening dress, the picture expresses the intimate friendship that had grown between the painter and his last secretary.[35] As with his earlier full-lengths, Lavery executed a reduced version of the arrangement before proceeding to the large canvas. The freedom of delivery in the handling of paint in this sketch is as fresh, vibrant and disciplined as that of his Glasgow International sketches of the 1880s.

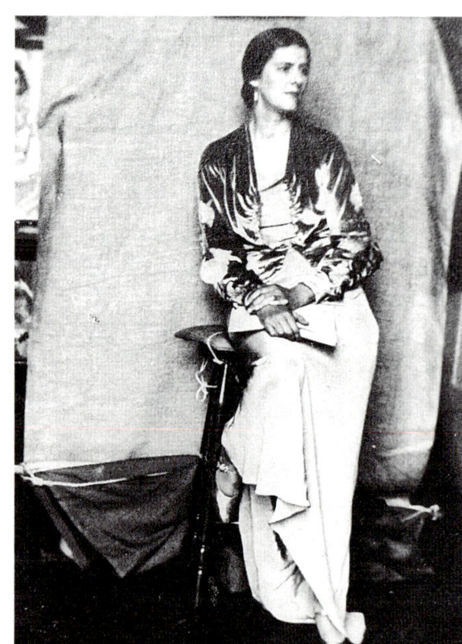

248 Katherine Fitz Gerald posing for her portrait. *c.*1939 (photo, the author)

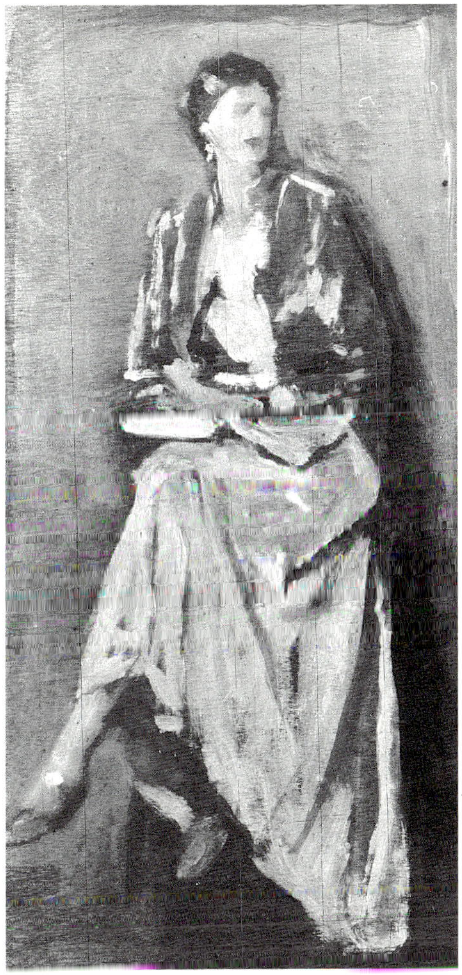

247 Study for *Katherine Fitz Gerald c.*1939, 16 × 8 (private collection, photo, Ian Kilpatrick)

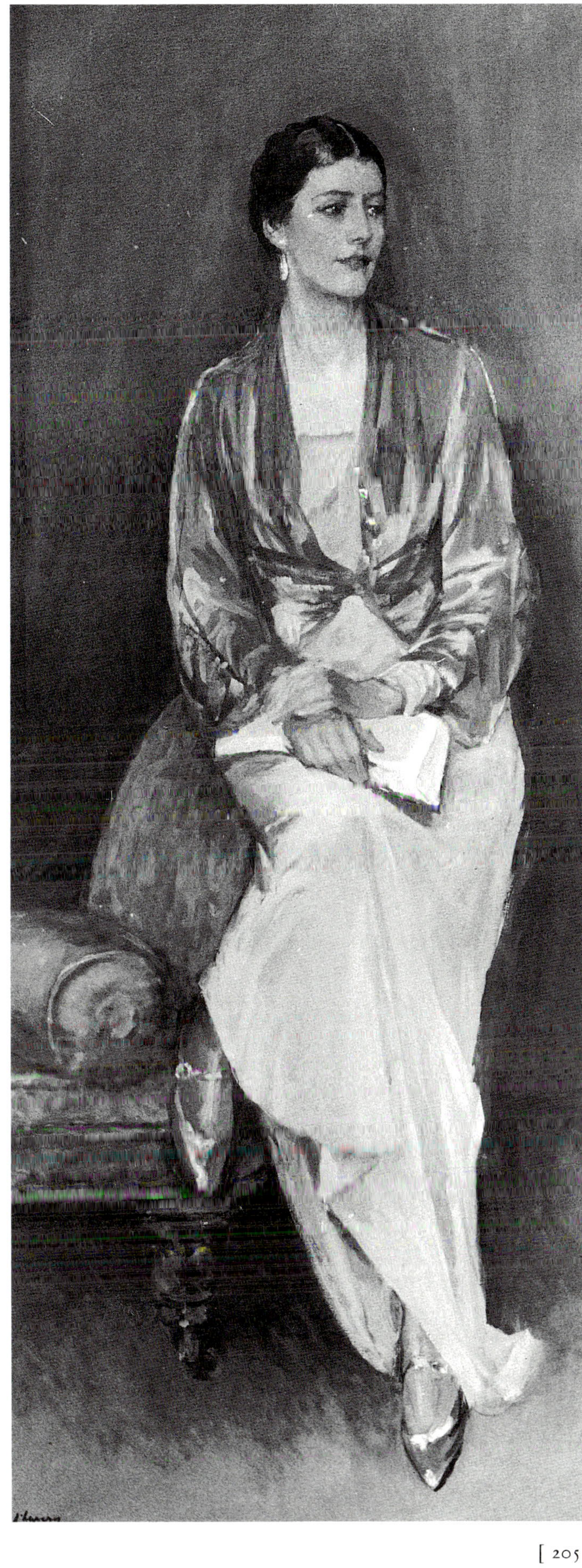

246 Katherine Fitz Gerald, *c.*1939, 73 × 30½ (private collection, photo, Ian Kilpatrick)

He also prepared the way for the large picture with a photograph of Katherine adopting the same pose. The authority of his [illegible] and sense of abstract composition were carried through to the exhibited work (see also Plates 247 and 248).

These pictures provoked little interest at the Royal Academy. They evoked aesthetic debates long since defunct, and now unrecognised by the younger generation. The taut rigour of line and the flashes of insight into human character now no more considerable than the flaccid academy impressionism of Lucy Kemp Welch and Dorothea Sharp, the stiff Orpen imitations of Reginald Eves and David Allison or the cool competence of Gerald Kelly and Sir Arthur S. Cope. If Lavery was, for the most part, ignored by critics at the academies of the late Thirties, he continued to provoke the incidental interest of the smart set, leaving the full richness of his late work to be discovered after his death.

He had seen more of Alice and her family in these last years and when, after the publication of the *Life of a Painter* at the beginning of 1940, he contemplated the bombing and destruction which was to come, neutral Ireland seemed like a haven. Accordingly he wrote to Alice inviting her to accept him as a superannuated evacuee, 'London is no place for the old or the young, we are only in the way, will you take me till it is over?'[36] Installed in Ireland, he painted his last ambitious canvas of a *Gipsy Encampment* (Plate 249) near Rosenarra House.[37] Alice later recalled with pleasure these last months: 'We all had a very happy Christmas that year, but it was his last one, he saw the new year in and was planning to paint a picture of the meet of the Hunt at our house, but it was not to be. He died . . . very peaceful, of bronchial trouble at our house, Rosenarra, Co. Kilkenny on January 10th.'[38]

Tributes, obituaries and souvenir recollections followed Lavery's death. The story of his life was retold frequently in the press. His honours were enumerated. A memorial exhibition of his work was staged at the Leicester Galleries in April 1941 containing fifty-three paintings from the studio, the earliest being a view of the Glasgow Exhibition. In the catalogue, Edward Knoblock paid tribute to Lavery's ruling passion for painting unencumbered by theory. The artist himself had declared that he was no theorist and felt that it 'may well be dangerous to know too clearly what one is doing'.[39] Untheorised passion coupled with a 'joy in everything beautiful' was Knoblock's way of crystallising Lavery's achievement as a painter.[40]

Undoubtedly, he came from a generation for whom the disparagement of theory was a common attitude. The artist depended upon well-honed impulses. Whistler's famous reliance upon 'the experience of a lifetime' could well have been added to Knoblock's checklist. Art had to be made before it could be criticised or theorised and the painters of Lavery's era regarded themselves as makers and were content to leave criticism and theory to others. Whistler was attacked during Lavery's lifetime for spending too much time composing his own defence. While absolution from responsibility for the meaning of his work might be claimed, it may not be so easily won. Lavery obviously did respond with 'joy in everything beautiful', but his idea of what constituted beauty was as subtly received and interpreted as was his 'passion' to paint. Lavery's idea of the beautiful grew in the

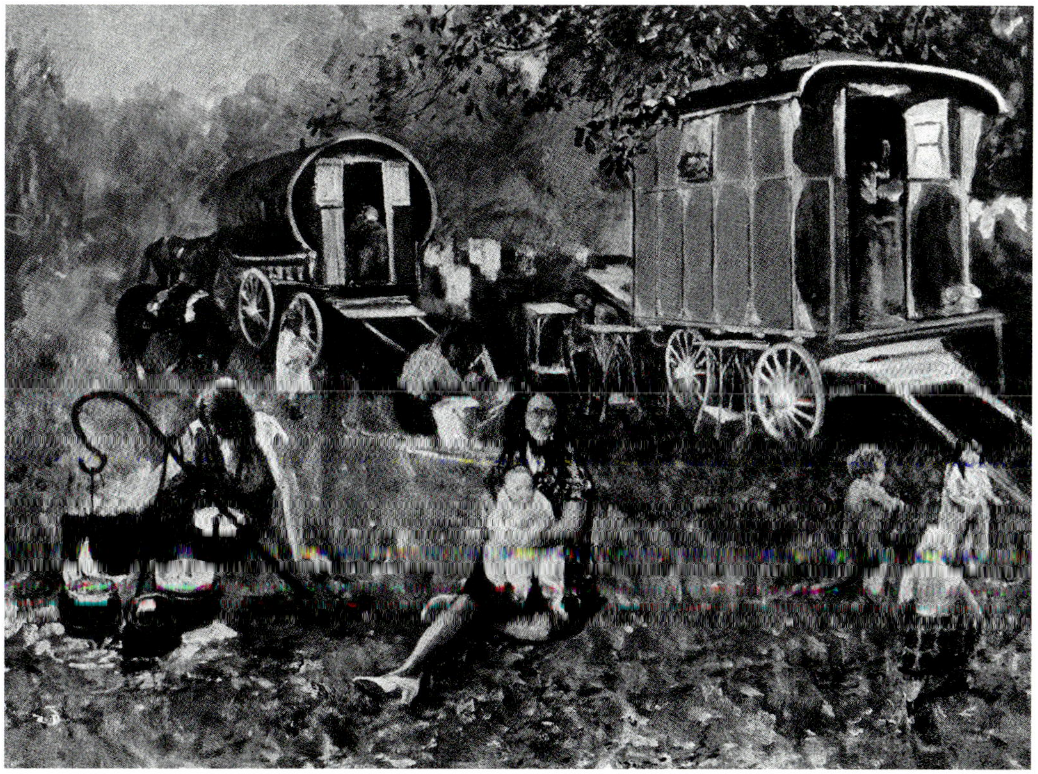

249 *Gipsy Encampment*, 1940, 40 × 50 (private collection)

shadow of Whistler's aesthetics. When he began to step out into his own limelight, he was, like any artist, directed by the circumstances in which he found himself, though these circumstances were not so much dictated by the whim of fortune as he often liked to pretend. He did consciously construct his life, taking decisions, regardless of his own safety, in order to place himself before a new challenge. His eye could search out new beauties of design, and in an industrial age, there were many new opportunities. His willingness in these circumstances separates him from those other Glasgow School and International Society painters who found their metier in portraiture and stuck to it. He was an artist-reporter in modern terms. Outgoing and gregarious, he could make a memorable picture out of the most unpromising material. This capacity brought him out beyond Whistler, as a less equivocal exemplar of the spirit of the seventeenth-century court painters. He enjoyed creating his own court, but was equally concerned that it should not subside into well-ordered atrophy, and his natural impatience led him at times to break with the familiar in order to more securely possess it. He enjoyed the role of being a 'kept-painter' in the society of the Fords, the Churchills, the Londonderrys . . . but the courtier's role was not his only ambition. It was rather the by-product of the daily pageant that would sustain his creative impulses. Evelyn Farquhar, Mary Auras, Diana Manners and many other maids of honour were part of this passing scene which Hazel Lavery came to dominate for most of the painter's life. All came under Lavery's brush and were seized from the continuum of existence, to be fixed with unerring concentration. It was such a vivid picture of the daily hubbub which Lavery's great friend R. B. Cunninghame Graham recorded,

> . . . his back turned to a mirror, and with his patient seated on the throne, Lavery . . . paints away. The person who is being painted chats with her friends; doors close and open; someone has just forgotten that she has left her husband sitting in a shop, and screeches down the telephone . . . scents, noise, confusion . . . and still the picture grows. Now he steps back, just missing treading on a lady's toes. She begs his pardon and he, courteously smiling, accepts the excuse . . . and before my eyes the picture has steadily advanced.[41]

Many eye witnesses attest to Lavery's formidable powers of concentration which rendered him oblivious to all around. Even Lady Lavery was at times astonished by his capacity to render on canvas subjects that were fast-moving and that demanded a snap-shot mentality. Her social binges were meditated by long periods sitting, reading in the car, while he painted something or other. It was Lavery's ability to transcend the literal and to seize something of the flash of personality in the scene before his eyes, that characterised his best portraits and his formidable records of pageant history.

After his death at Kilkenny on 10 January 1941, Sir John Lavery's body was temporarily interred in a lead-lined coffin which, after the Second World War, was transferred to Putney Vale, to lie beside that of Lady Lavery.

During the Thirties, and arguably for the entire inter-war period, Lavery's work might be regarded as having been eclipsed by the mainstream of Modernism. In a sense, it could not have been otherwise. Like George Clausen, Stanhope Forbes, Philip Wilson Steer and Walter Sickert, Lavery was a survivor from an earlier generation. Left to his own devices, in paintings like *Summer*, he regressed to Edwardian rococo. There was no inconsistency in this: it merely demonstrated the perceived relationship, in the early years of the century, between Impressionism and the painters of the *ancien régime*. This eclecticism, in the Thirties, was an old game. The young artists of that period were interested in Surrealism and the école de Paris, and only in the Euston Road School was there a return to ideals of legibility, comparable to those with which Lavery had begun his career. Generally his sense of modishness and his attraction to spectacle kept him in touch with the contemporary scene. He was the lone society portraitist at a time when the genre had all but disintegrated. This was noted by Richard Shone who remarked that in the last decade of his life, 'the full blooded portrait looked increasingly freakish though Lavery . . . kept pace with the Oxford bags, bare backs and lipstick'.[42] This resourcefulness, which involved no loss of integrity, saved him from joyless repetition. And when a broader view is taken, even the old man's paintings will seem resplendent with the energy of youth.

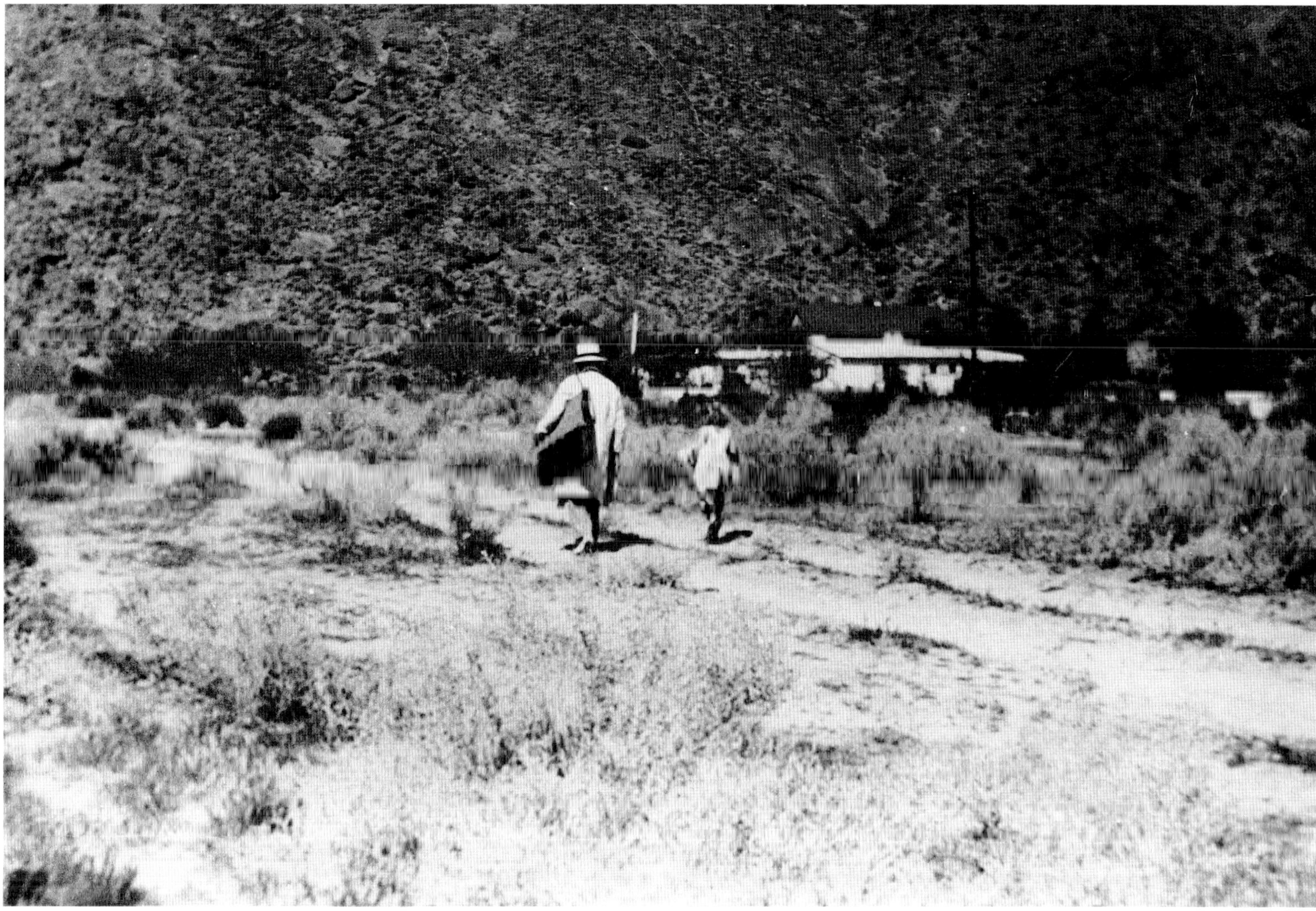

250 Sir John Lavery going out to paint at Palm Springs (photo, the author)

Notes

CHAPTER I

1. For reference to the Bann Laverys see, May Blair, *Once Upon the Lagan*, Belfast 1981, p. 103.
2. Sir John Lavery, *The Life of a Painter*, 1940, (herein *Life*), p. 15.
3. See for example Alfred Esmore, 'A Famous Ulster Artist', in *Lady of the House*, June 1913, *Belfast Evening Telegraph*, 17 June 1914 *et al* give 20 March 1856 as Lavery's date of birth. *The Belfast Telegraph*, 6 March 1933 produced a celebratory article for his 77th birthday. I am grateful to George McConkey for tracing these articles.
4. I am grateful to George McConkey and the staff of the Public Record Office, Belfast for checking these details on my behalf.
5. Since the disaster occurred so soon after departure it was assumed that it had happened off the Welsh rather than Irish coast. This mis-information is quoted in the Ulster Museum and the Fine Art Society, *Sir John Lavery RA, 1856—1941*, catalogue of an exhibition by Kenneth McConkey (herein *catalogue*), p. 9.
6. *The Times*, 6 May 1859, quoted by Walter Shaw Sparrow, *John Lavery and his Work*, 1911, (herein *Shaw Sparrow*), p. 14. An illustration of Lavery's father's public house in Belfast carries the name of his brother Richard (see 1). This suggests that the two brothers had, at some point been in partnership and that Henry ceded the business to his brother at the time of his departure for the United States.
7. *Life*, p. 15.
8. ibid., p. 16.
9. ibid., p. 18.
10. *Shaw Sparrow*, p. 22.
11. *Life*, p. 29.
12. ibid., p. 30.
13. *Shaw Sparrow*, p. 24.
14. ibid., p. 27.
15. ibid., p. 28.
16. *Life*, p. 39.
17. ibid., pp. 39—40.
18. This work was sold at Christie's, 12 June 1987, lot 97 (4).
19. *Shaw Sparrow*, p. 33; this ill-fated effort was rejected at the Royal Academy and at the Glasgow Institute before it eventually perished in a studio fire.
20. ibid., p. 22.
21. *Pious Reflections* remains untraced. It was in a private collection in Scotland *c.*1950; see Ulster Museum files. It was originally sold at the Glasgow Institute of Fine Arts for £10.
22. *Life*, p. 45.
23. *Catalogue*, no. 1(7)
24. *Catalogue*, no. 3(8)
25. *Mariana*, was exhibited at the Glasgow Institute of Fine Arts in 1881, no. 577 with the quotation from Tennyson, 'Is this the end?—to be left alone, to live forgotten and die forlorn'. Other works of the period such as *Charity* and the heavily retouched *Girl with a Tapestry* demonstrate Lavery's belief that solitary female subjects were a formula for commercial success.
26. This work is contained in a private collection in Scotland.
27. *Life*, p. 201.
28. In 1881 the Paisley Institute contained *On the Road to the Moss—Connemara*, no. 268, untraced. I am grateful to Dr Kelly of Belmullet for his efforts to locate evidence of the artist's early sojourn in the west of Ireland.
29. For reference to Paris as 'the capital of art' see Kenneth McConkey, 'From Grez to Glasgow, French Naturalist Influence in Scottish Painting', *Scottish Art Review*, vol. XV, no. 4, 1982, p. 16, quoting Albert Wolff, *La Capitale de L'Art*, Paris 1886. See also John Milner, The Studios of Paris, *The Capital of Art in the late Nineteenth Century*, 1988.

CHAPTER 2

1. *The Bailie*, 23, 30 Nov. 1881, and *Quiz*, 25 Nov. 1881, quoted in R. Billcliffe, *The Glasgow Boys*, 1985, p. 22.
2. *Life*, pp. 46—7. These events are also recounted in an unpublished ms. diary of 1924 in a private collection.
3. For reference to Bouguereau see Musée du Petit Palais, Paris, Montreal and Hartford, *William Bouguereau*, catalogue of an exhibition by Mark Steven Walker *et al*, 1984—5.
4. ibid., p. 63.
5. Shirley Fox, *An Art Student's reminiscences of Paris in Eighties*, 1909, pp. 53—4.
6. *Shaw Sparrow*, p. 38.
7. ibid., p. 39.
8. In 1881 he showed *Rehearsing*, *'Do you think so?'*, *A Maiden of the Last Century*, and *Forgotten*. In 1882, *A Remembrance of the Louvre*, *A Little Arab*, *Mistress Anne Page* and *Her Portrait (12)* were exhibited.
9. A possible companion piece, *His Portrait* was shown at the Glasgow Art Club in November 1882, see R. Billcliffe, *op. cit.*, p. 63. This untraced work was shown at a loan exhibition as the 'Gift of Sir Peter Coats' at Paisley in September 1882 (no. 139).
10. See Crawford Centre for the Arts, *John Lavery, The Early Career, 1880—1895*, catalogue of an exhibition by David Scruton, 1983, no. 3. The modern life *fusain* has not been studied as a genre, although it was practised by many artists. For another salient example by Leon Lhermitte, a frequent Glasgow exhibitor and 'Black and White' exhibition juror, see *Quartet—Musical Evening at Amaury Duval's* in G. P. Weisberg, *The Realist Tradition*, Cleveland 1980, no. 169, p. 194.
11. P. Jacomb Hood, *With Brush and Pencil*, 1925, p. 24.
12. *Catalogue*, no. 4; David Scruton, *op. cit.*, no. 3; R. Billcliffe, *op. cit.*, p. 53.
13. *Head of a Brigand* was sold by Sotheby's, Scone Palace, 13April 1981, lot 406.
14. Glasgow Institute of Fine Arts, 'Black and White Exhibition' 1882, no. 305.
15. The fact that his two early *plein-air* Salon pictures, *Les Deux Pecheurs* (1883, no. 1424) and *La Rentree des Chèvres* (1884, no. 1433) remain untraced makes it particularly difficult to assess the degree of Lavery's absorption of the contemporary idiom.
16. *Shaw Sparrow*, pp. 40—1.
17. Emile Zola, *Le Bon Combat, de Courbet aux Impressionistes*, Paris, 1975, pp. 206—7, quoted in Kenneth McConkey 'The Bouguereau of the Naturalists, Jules Bastien-Lepage and British Art', *Art History*, vol. 1, no. 3, 1978, p. 371.
18. See Kenneth McConkey, 'Listening to the Voices: A Study of Jules Bastien-Lepage's *Joan of Arc*', *Arts Magazine*, January 1982, pp. 154—60.
19. *Life*, p. 51; G. P. Weisberg, *op. cit.*, pp. 208—10 (entry by Kenneth McConkey).

20. For further reference to Bastien-Lepage's exhibitions in London, see Kenneth McConkey, *op. cit.*, 1978.
21. *Shaw Sparrow*, p. 48.
22. *Life*, p. 51.
23. *Shaw Sparrow*, p. 48.
24. A work of this title was exhibited at the Glasgow Institute of Fine Arts, 1883, no. 154, although the price given is £5, this suggests that it was a small variant rather than the present picture (15).
25. See David Scruton, *op. cit.*, no. 1; this work was probably exhibited at the Glasgow Institute of Fine Arts in 1883 as *A Heart for a Rose*, no. 516.
26. Glasgow Institute of Fine Arts, 188[illegible], no. 197.
27. For Lavery's early admiration for Frederick Leighton see *Shaw Sparrow*, p. [illegible].
28. This work remains untraced. First exhibited at Glasgow Institute of Fine Arts in 1883, no. 478, it was apparently sold at Sotheby's in the 1970s.
29. *Catalogue*, no. 6(18).
30. Whistler's *Arrangement in Grey and Black, No.1, The Artist's Mother* was shown at the Salon of 1883. Lavery is unlikely to have been familiar with it prior to this date.
31. *Catalogue*, no. 7(19).
32. D. S. MacColl, 'Professor Brown, Teacher and Painter', *The Magazine of Art*, 1893, p. 407.
33. George Moore, *Confessions of a Young Man*, 1888 (Digit Books ed., 1961), p. 114.
34. Salon 1883, no. 1424. See note 15 above.
35. *Shaw Sparrow*, p. 43.
36. Private collection, Scotland.

CHAPTER 3

1. *Life*, p. 53.
2. See G. P. Weisberg, ed., *Corot*, catalogue of an exhibition at Tokyo, Osaka and Yokohama, 198[illegible], no. 2[illegible]; for reference to Marlotte see Grand Palais, Paris and the Royal Academy of Arts, *The Hague School*, catalogue of an exhibition, ed. Ronald de Leeuw, John Sillevis and Charles Dumas, 1984, p. 204. For further reference to the Grez artist community see Kenneth McConkey, *op. cit.*, 1982; Julian Campbell, *The Irish Impressionists*, catalogue of an exhibition at the National Gallery of Ireland, Dublin, 1984; and *Frank O'Meara and his contemporaries*, at Dublin, Cork and Belfast, 1989. The Grez and Barbizon colonies are also considered in Michael Jacobs, *The Good and Simple Life*, Oxford, 1985, pp. 17—42.
3. W. H. Low, *A Chronicle of Friendships, 1873—1900*, New York, 1908.
4. R. L. Stevenson, 'Forest Notes', *Cornhill Magazine*, 1876, p. 552.
5. See McConkey, *op. cit.*, 1982, p. 24; Campbell, *op. cit.*, 1989, p. 38.
6. *The Magazine of Art*, 1884, p. 341.
7. See Jacobs, *op. cit.*, pp. 30—5.
8. *Shaw Sparrow*, p. 44. For further reference to Alexander Harrison and American 'tonalist' painting see the Dayton Art Institute, *American Expatriate Painters of the Late Nineteenth Century*, catalogue of an exhibition by Michael Quick, 197[illegible]; see also Annette Blaugrund, *Paris 1889, American Artists at the Universal Exposition*, catalogue of an exhibition at the Pennsylvania Academy of Fine Arts, 1989, pp. 160—1; G. P. Weisberg, *Beyond Impressionism, the Naturalist Impulse*, 1992, pp. 148—52.
9. Victor Champier, 'Le paysage et la mer', *L'Exposition des Beaux Arts (the Goupil Salon)*, Paris 1882, p. 222.
10. *Shaw Sparrow*, p. 47.
11. Leonce Benedite, *The Luxembourg Museum*, 1913, p. 50; see also Daniel Bernard, 'La peinture de genre', *L'Exposition des Beaux Arts (the Goupil Salon)*, 1881, p. 57. Louis Welden Hawkins (1849—1910) was born in Stuttgart of English parents but was naturalised as a French citizen in 1895. His later work revealed symbolist tendencies and he exhibited at the Salons of the Rose et Croix.
12. *Life*, pp. 54—5.
13. Will Low, *op. cit.*, p. 67; quoted by McConkey, *op. cit.*, 1982, p. 24.
14. An early photo of Lavery by James Craig Annan shows the artist posed in front of O'Meara's *The Widow*, see Scottish Arts Council, *Glasgow Portraits by J. Craig Annan (1864—1946) Photographer*, catalogue by George A. Oliver, 1967, p. 34. See also the letter contained in Tate Gallery Archives, 7245.228 dated 8 December 1887 from Etaples, Pas de Calais, quoted by Julian Campbell, *op. cit.*, p. 47.
15. *Shaw Sparrow*, p. 46.
16. ibid.
17. Paisley Art Institute, 1883, no. 342, as *A Passing Salute*; Royal Scottish Academy, Edinburgh, 1884, no. 766; Exposition Universelle, Paris, 1889; Royal Academy 1890, no. 679; Glasgow Institute of Fine Arts, 1891, no. 393. The picture was finally acquired by the Carnegie Institute, Pittsburgh, in 1898, was deaccessioned in the 1950s and appeared in the Fine Art Society *Sring Exhibition*, 1991, no. 34, from which it passed to a private collection (24). I am grateful to Suzanne Tise and Gabriel P. Weisberg for their efforts to try to locate this picture for me.
18. *Dundee Advertiser*, 8 January 1891.
19. Gleeson White, ed., *The Master Painters of Britain*, Birmingham 1910, p. 346.
20. *Life*, pp. 55—6.
21. *Catalogue*, no. 7(25).
22. Paisley, 1883, no. 73; Edinburgh, 1884, no. 801; Glasgow, 1885, no. 271.
23. R. L. Stevenson, *op. cit.*, 1876, p. 553.
24. *Catalogue*, no. 10(27), Glasgow Institute of Fine Arts, 1885, no. 697. See also G. R. Halkett, *Illustrated Notes on the Glasgow Institute of Fine Arts*, 1885, p. [illegible].
25. This work has been extensively discussed in recent years, see McConkey, *op. cit.*, 1982, p. 29; Kenneth McConkey, 'Rustic Naturalism in Britain', *The European Realist Tradition*, Indiana, 198[illegible], p. 221; Roger Billcliffe, *The Glasgow Boys*, 1985, pp. 92, 97, 99; Kenneth McConkey, *British Impressionism*, 1989, p. 34; G. P. Weisberg *op. cit.*, 1992, p. 144.
26. The general comparision of compositional format between these two works was first made in Kenneth McConkey, 'The Bouguereau of the Naturalists: Bastien-Lepage and British Art', *Art History*, vol. 1, no. 3, 1978, p. 373.
27. *Catalogue*, no. 12(31).
28. Careful examination of the picture surface reveals that the forearm and left hand edge of the girl and the barge pole have been altered to bring them into a more central position.
29. The listings of Lavery's early exhibits contain a number of possible alternative titles for the present work. The Paisley Art Institute exhibition, for instance, contained *It was about a lover* in its annual winter exhibition in 1884 (no. 19). It is not inconceivable that this was retitled and exhibited at the Royal Scottish Academy, Edinburgh in 1887 as *The Two Friends*. Kennedy's *Mlle Cunégonde*, painted at Grez, was shown at the Glasgow Institute of Fine Arts in 1885, no. 586 and was illustrated in Halkett's *Notes*, p. 43. For further reference see Newcastle upon Tyne Polytechnic Art Gallery, *Peasantries*, catalogue of an exhibition, ed., Kenneth McConkey, 1981, no. 54. For further reference see Roger Billcliffe, *op. cit.*, 1985, p. 102.
30. For a full discussion of this work see Pyms Gallery, *Impressions and Realities*, catalogue of an exhibition (entry by Kenneth McConkey), 1985, no. 9, pp. 28—31. For reference to O'Meara's profile in caricature, see Julian Campbell, *op. cit.*, fig. 8, p. 45.

31. For reference to this work see Kenneth McConkey, *op. cit.*, 1989, p. 31. *A Pupil of Mine* was exhibited at the Royal Scottish Academy in 1886, no. 440.
32. *Catalogue*, no. 9(35); Loudan's work was later exhibited as *A Village in the Gatinais*, at the Grosvenor Gallery 1885, no. 219.
33. For reference to *A Day in Midsummer*, see Arts Council, *Landscape in Britain, 1850—1950*, catalogue of an exhibition seleceted by Frances Spalding and Ian Jeffrey, 1983, no. 82.
34. Barbican Art Gallery, *James Tissot*, exhibition catalogue ed. Krystyna Matyjaszkiewicz, 1984, no. 123. The picture was re-exhibited at the Glasgow Institute in 1880.
35. *Life*, p. 53.

CHAPTER 4

1. *The Art Journal*, 1888, p. 276.
2. For further reference see Stanley K. Hunter, *Kelvingrove and the 1888 Exhibition*, privately printed, Glasgow, 1990; Perilla and Juliet Kinchin, *Glasgow's Great Exhibitions*, 1988.
3. *Catalogue*, nos 13 and 14 (37).
4. This unsigned version is contained in a private collection and, whilst similar in format to (36), has a more awkwardly posed figure.
5. Basket chairs and convalescents abound in Tissot's work, salient examples include, *A Convalescent*, 1876, Sheffield City Art Galleries and *Soir d'été*, *c.*1881, Musée d'Orsay, Paris.
6. See for instance, Tyne and Wear Museums, and Bradford Art Gallery and Museum *Sir George Clausen, RA 1852—1944*, catalogue of an exhibition by Kenneth McConkey, nos 38, 40, 41 and 42.
7. *Catalogue*, 18 and 19(40 and 41).
8. James Fulton (1848—1933) was the son of a manufacturer of fashionable shawls. He owned the 'Glen' estate at Paisley, where he staged annual concerts which Lavery attended, and, on at least one occasion, painted (Renfrew District Council Museums and Art Galleries). His collection of French pictures included works by Boudin, Diaz, Rousseau, Corot and Lhermitte.
9. Coll. Renfrew District Council Museums and Art Galleries; David Scruton, *John Lavery, the early career, 1880—1895*, catalogue of an exhibition at the Crawford Art Centre, St Andrews, 1983, no. 10.
10. *Catalogue*, p. 23, fig. 6; untraced, Royal Academy 1886, no. 687. *The Illustrated London News*, 22 May 1886, p. 525 in reviewing *Beg Sir!* at the Academy referred to the background of the picture incorporating a beach scene. This suggests that the painting was possibly reworked by Lavery before its eventual disappearance.
11. For further reference see *Moments et Folies de la Femme Fatale*, catalogue of an exhibition at Whitford and Hughes, London, 1985, no. 19.
12. *Life*, p. 57.
13. Letter dated 18 December 1943, Aberdeen Art Gallery files. The writer, Alix MacBride died in November 1955 at the age of 97.
14. ibid.
15. The sketch (46), having been sold by Spink and Son, *c.*1971, reappeared in Sotheby's, 22 Nov. 1983, lot 67. It was included in *Catalogue*, no. 16a.
16. *The Athenaeum*, 26 June 1886, p. 852.
17. *The Illustrated London News*, 22 May 1886, p. 525.
18. *The Builder*, 15 May 1886, p. 705. Roger Billcliffe in *The Glasgow Boys*, 1985, p. 185 quotes additional reviews from *Glasgow Evening News*, 28 January 1887, *North British Daily Mail*, 28 January 1887 and *Glasgow Herald*, 16 February 1887. For yet further references see *Catalogue*, no. 16.
19. *The Hawk*, 8 May 1887, p. 259; quoted by Anna Gruetzner in Royal Academy of Arts, *Post-Impressionism*, catalogue of an exhibition, 1979, no. 317.
20. *On the Bridge at Grez* as no. 52 in the exhibition was actually hung in Gallery I.
21. *Shaw Sparrow*, p. 48.
22. Tyne and Wear Museums, *op. cit.*, 1980, pp. 31—2.
23. ibid.
24. *The Art Journal*, 1886, p. 320.
25. *The Saturday Review*, 22 May 1886, p. 705.
26. Lavery exhibited *A White Rose*, no. 16 and *Portrait of a Girl in White*, no. 69; both pictures remain untraced.
27. *Summer Time* and *Convalescence* were exhibited as nos 117 and 173 respectively. *A Girl in Grey* and *Portrait of Master Hubert Stewart Smiley* appeared as nos 354 and 412 in the winter exhibition of 1887—8.
28. Letter dated December 1887, Tate Gallery Archives 7245.228.
29. E. R. and J. Pennell, *The Whistler Journal*, Philadelphia, 1921, p. 47.
30. E. R. and J. Pennell, *The Life of James McNeill Whistler*, 1908, vol. II, p. 62.
31. A watercolour drawing for the velarium is contained in Hunterian Art Gallery, University of Glasgow.
32. Letter dated 17 January 1928, Ulster Museum files.
33. Contained in James McNeill Whistler, *The Gentle Art of Making Enemies*, 1890, (1967 reprint), pp. 135—59.
34. E. R. and J. Pennell, *op. cit.*, 1908, vol. 2, p. 71. Lavery was of course one of the artists.
35. ibid., pp. 59, 63.
36. McLaren Young, MacDonald, Spencer and Miles, *The Paintings of James McNeill Whistler*, 1980, no. 79.
37. For further reference to the incident surrounding Stott of Oldham's *Venus Rising from the Sea Foam* (Oldham Art Gallery), see Stanley Weintraub, *Whistler, a Biography*, New York, 1974, pp. 324—6.
38. See J. S. Little, 'A Cosmopolitan Painter', *The Studio*, vol. XXVII, 1902, p. 115.
39. For further reference see *Catalogue*, no. 23(47). The picture was shown at the Goupil Gallery exhibition in 1891, no. 5.
40. E. R. Pennell, 'Art in Glasgow', *Harpers New Monthly Magazine*, February 1895.
41. Both of these pictures passed through the Fine Art Society in the 1970s.
42. This picture, inscribed verso 'Paris', appeared as no. 14 in *The Painted Lady*, an exhibition at Bourne Fine Art, Edinburgh, 1982.
43. Untraced; for further reference see *Shaw Sparrow*, p. 173.
44. William Powell Frith's *John Knox Reproving Mary, Queen of Scots*, Sheffield City Art Galleries; Sir David Wilkie's *John Knox Dispensing the Sacrament at Calder House*, National Gallery of Scotland, Edinburgh.
45. Not only had Sir Lawrence Alma Tadema painted such scenes in the 1860s, but a generation of Third Republic painters had revisited them in the 1880s. A salient example of work in this kind of subject-matter, which Lavery might have seen, was Luminais' *Les Enerves de Jumieges*, first shown at the Salon of 1880.
46. *Life*, pp. 57—8.
47. *Catalogue*, no. 8(49).
48. For further reference see Kenneth McConkey, *op. cit.*, *Arts Magazine*, 1982.
49. *Life*, p. 58.
50. ibid., p. 60.
51. Letter dated 14 May 1886, Tate Gallery Archives, 7245.189.
52. *Life*, p. 59.
53. ibid.
54. *Shaw Sparrow*, p. 70.
55. *Life*, p. 86.
56. *The Saturday Review*, 20 June 1891,

pp. 742—3.
57. *Shaw Sparrow*, p. 71.
58. *Dawn, 14 May 1568* was exhibited as no. 542. Lavery also showed *The White Rose*, no. 258, lent by James Fulton.
59. See *The Art Journal*, 1888, 'Supplement', p. 12.
60. *The Scottish Art Review*, 1888, vol. 1, p. 149.
61. *The Spectator*, 10 May 1890, p. 658.
62. Fritz von Ostini translated in *The Weekly News*, 20 September 1890.
63. *Glasgow Evening Citizen*, 3 March 1891.
64. *The Artist*, May 1891.
65. 'Art in the West of Scotland', *Scottish Art* [illegible]
66. *The Art Journal*, 1888, p. [illegible]
67. Lavery's canvas has not survived, and from contemporary illustrations it is difficult to discern its quality.
68. *The Art Journal*, 1888, 'Supplement', p. 3.
69. *The Illustrated London News*, 19 May 1888 and *The Graphic*, 12 May 1888 reported extensively on these events.
70. Mortimer Menpes, *Whistler as I Knew Him*, no date, p. 22 quotes Whistler adopting a similar compositional practice to that which he undoubtedly advocated to Lavery. 'I began first of all by seizing the chief point of interest. Perhaps it might have been the extreme distance . . . if so, I would begin drawing that distance in elaborately, and then would expand from it . . . in this way the picture must necessarily be a perfect thing from start to finish. Even if one were to be arrested in the middle of it, it would still be a fine and complete picture.'
71. *The Graphic*, 12 May 1888, p. 531, quoted in *Catalogue*, p. 37.
72. *Catalogue*, no. 26(53).
73. Whistler's *Nocturne in Blue and Gold, Valparaiso* was shown at the Society of British Artists in 1887, no. 156.
74. *Catalogue*, no. [illegible](14), and [illegible]. The *Blue Hungarians* were a popular band of Hungarian Hussars.
75. Martin Quern, 'The Ballade of Kelvin Hall', *Scottish Art Review*, vol. 1, 1888, p. 181.
76. *Catalogue*, nos 31 and 33.
77. *Catalogue*, no. 32(57).
78. Crawford Art Centre, *op. cit.*, pp. 33—5, *Catalogue*, pp. 38—40; the circumstances surrounding the receipt and delivery of this important commission remain slightly obscure. Lavery referred to it in random notes in extant diaries and these have been used below to reconstruct the sequence of events which led to its completion and eventual display.
79. *Life*, p. 60.
80. *Catalogue*, no. 34(58).
81. J. S. Little, *op. cit.*, 1902, pp. 118—19.
82. *Catalogue*, pp. 36—7 quoting *The Bailie*, 3 October 1888, p. 11 and *The Glasgow Herald*, 1 October 1888.
83. *Life*, p. 62.
84. ibid., p. 63.
85. ibid., p. 64.
86. Grosvenor Gallery, 1889, no. 119.
87. *Life*, p. 65.
88. ibid.
89. Unpublished ms. diary, private collection.
90. *The Athenaeum*, 13 June 1891, p. 773 and *The Saturday Review*, 20 June 1891, pp. 742—3.
91. J. S. Little, *op. cit.*, 1902, p. 118.
92. *The Times*, 9 June 1891.
93. For further reference see *Catalogue*, p. 40 and Crawford Art Centre, *op. cit.*, 1983, p. 35.
94. For Lockhart's picture see *Pall Mall Gazette* '*Extra*', 1890, pp. 4—5.
95. Crawford Art Centre, *op. cit.*, 1983, nos 11, 12 and 13.
96. For further reference see David Martin, *The Glasgow School of Painting*, 1897 (1976 reprint), p. 40 and J. S. Little, *op. cit.*, 1902, p. 115 where entitled *A Portrait Group*. See also *Shaw Sparrow*, p. 153.
97. Scottish Arts Council, *Glasgow Boys*, 1968, Part 2, p. 28.
98. *The Magazine of Art*, 1889, 'Art in May' p. xxix. For a discussion of Sargent's Impressionist works see W. H. Gerdts, 'The Arch-Apostle of the Dab-and-Spot School: John Singer Sargent as an Impressionist', in Patricia Hills, ed., *John Singer Sargent*, catalogue of an exhibition at the Whitney Museum of American Art, 1986.
99. J. S. Little, *op. cit.*, 1902, p. 10.
100. Scottish Arts Council, *op. cit.*, 1968, p. 44.
101. I am grateful to Roger Billcliffe for drawing my attention to this work.
102. There were two Apelles, the other being the Glasgow painter Corsan Morton.
103. Glasgow Art Club, *The Grand Costume Ball*, Glasgow 1890, p. 7. This publication, produced by the Art Club, acted as a souvenir and record of the event.
104. *Catalogue*, no. 44(68).
105. *Shaw Sparrow*, p. 61.
106. ibid.
107. *The Scotsman*, 10 September 1890 quoting from *Munchener Neueste Nachrichten*, a review by Fritz von Ostini.
108. Richard Muther, *The History of Modern Painting*, 1896, vol. 3, p. 688.
109. Royal Academy, 1890, no. 679, illustrated in *Pall Mall Gazette* '*Extra*', 1890, p. 69.
110. Lavery's one-man exhibition in London was to be held at the Goupil Gallery in June 1891, consisting of 35 works.

CHAPTER 5

1. *Life*, p. 66. William Patrick Whyte met Lavery when they were students together at the atelier Julian. He exhibited at the Glasgow Institute although, for the most [illegible] London, where he became almost a surrogate father to Eileen Lavery, the painter's daughter. Lady Sempill recalls visiting 'Uncle Whyte' as a child with her mother, in a flat near to Westminster Cathedral. He was addicted to Venice and the Loire Valley. A portrait of him by Lavery (illus. *Life*) shows one of his paintings of Venice in the background and a canvas of the Loire at Champtoceaux inscribed 'To Eileen' exists in a private collection.
2. Tate Gallery Archives, 7245.15, letter from James Guthrie dated 6 August 1891.
3. *Life*, p. 69.
4. *Catalogue*, no. [illegible]
5. *Catalogue*, no. 45(70). A profile of Kathleen MacDermott is contained in the collection of the artist's descendants.
6. James L. Caw, *Scottish Painting, Past and Present*, 1908, p. 378.
7. William Kennedy, *The Fur Boa*, *c.*1890—1, Glasgow Art Gallery and Museum.
8. Whistler's *Rose et Argent: La Jolie Mutine*, Hunterian Art Gallery, University of Glasgow. This picture was being painted at the time when Lavery visited Whistler after his installation at the rue du Bac. See *Catalogue*, p. 27, note [illegible]
9. Walter Sickert in *The Daily Telegraph*, 25 April 1925.
10. *Shaw Sparrow*, p. 96.
11. R. A. M. Stevenson, *Velasquez*, 1895, (reprint 1900), pp. 95—6
12. Robert Crawford, LLD, DL, 'How we bought the Whistler Carlyle', *Glasgow Evening News*, 23 March 1905; reproduced as Appendix in Glasgow Art Gallery, *Whistler: Arrangements in Grey and Black*, 1951, pp. 21—2; see *Catalogue*, p. 27, note 33.
13. *Life*, p. 89.
14. *Catalogue*, no. 49(71).
15. For the standard biography see A. F. Tschiffeley, *Don Roberto, Being the Account of the Life and Works of R. B. Cunninghame Graham, 1852—1936*, 1937.

16. [illegible] Gallery, 1888, no. [illegible]
17. For further reference see A. F. Tschiffeley, *op. cit.*
18. *Shaw Sparrow*, Preface, p. XVIII.
19. ibid., p. 137.
20. From the introduction to *Captain Brassbound's Confession*, quoted in *Life*, p. 89.
21. Untraced, illustrated, *Pall Mall Gazette 'Extra'*, 1896, p. 120.
22. Coll the sitter's descendants. I am grateful to Lady Polwarth for calling my attention to this work. *Cunninghame Graham on Pampa*, exhibited Salon, (Societé Nationale des Beaux Arts), 1898, no. 713, National Musuem of Fine Art, Buenos Aires, Argentina. For reference to Pampa see A.F. Tschiffeley, *op. cit.*, p. 181.
23. A. F. Tschiffeley, *op. cit.*, p. 410. Cunninghame Graham, besides writing the introduction to Shaw Sparrow's monograph, dedicated a collection of essays—*Charity*, London (Duckworth), 1912, 'To John Lavery A.R.A.'.
24. Modern Gallery, Venice.
25. Exhibited at the Royal Academy, 1892, no. 181, reproduced *Royal Academy Pictures*, 1892, p. 127.
26. Now known as *The Face Veil*, private collection.
27. Private Collection. J. J. Cowan, *From 1840 to 1932*, Edinburgh 1933, p. 168.
28. ibid., p. 156.
29. *The Magazine of Art*, 1893, p. 258.
30. Glasgow University Library, Whistler Papers, L.19, letter dated 2 December 1892; L.20, letter dated 29 December 1892.
31. J. J. Cowan, *op. cit.*, p. 168.
32. Perth Museum and Art Gallery. For further reference see Crawford Art Centre, *op. cit.*, no. 19.
33. Formerly Whitford and Hughes, London.
34. Royal Academy, 1894, no. 393, probably destroyed.
35. *Catalogue*, no. 50(78).
36. *Shaw Sparrow*, p. 142.
37. J. S. Little, *op. cit.*, p. 118.
38. *Catalogue*, no. 51(80).
39. A. Stodart Walker, 'The Art of John Lavery, RSA, ARA', *The Studio*, vol. LXII, 1914, pp. 3—4.
40. *L'Art Moderne*, Triezieme Année, no. 40, 1 October 1893, p. 314.
41. E. R. and J. Pennell, *The Life of James McNeill Whistler*, 1911, p. 364.
42. E. R. and J. Pennell, *The Whistler Journal*, Philadelphia, 1921, p. 258.
43. A. C. R. Carter, 'John Lavery, R.S.A.', *The Art Journal*, 1904, p. 10.
44. *Life*, p. 120.
45. *The Art Journal*, 1898, p. 253. The use of the phrase 'portrait picture' is noteworthy here. It underlines the distinction critics increasingly made between mere face painting and the higher pictorial and aesthetic intentions of the artist.
46. Camille Mauclair, 'John Lavery', *L'Art et Les Artistes*, Tome 2, 1905, p. 7.
47. *Shaw Sparrow*, p. 137.
48. E. R. and J. Pennell, *The Life of James McNeill Whistler*, 1908, vol. 2, p. 216.
49. Whistler's correspondence with Lavery during the period in which he held the Office of President of the International Society of Sculptors, Painters and Gravers is contained in the Tate Gallery Archives, 7245.258—7245.315. Nine letters from Lavery to Whistler are preserved in Glasgow University Library, Whistler Papers.
50. Glasgow University Library, I.28, letter dated 3 March 1898.
51. See Albert Ludovici, *An Artist's Life in London and Paris, 1870—1925*, 1926, pp. 124—33.
52. William Rothenstein, *Men and Memories, 1872—1900*, 1931, p. 336.
53. For further reference see Joy Newton and Margaret F. MacDonald, 'Whistler, Rodin and the International', *Gazette des Beaux Arts*, VIe Periode, Tome CIII, Mars 1984, pp. 115—23.
54. Albert Ludovici, *op. cit.*, p. 135.
55. Tate Gallery Archives, 7245.262, letter dated 18 May 1898.
56. ibid.
57. Tate Gallery Archives, 7245.266, letter dated 5 February 1899.
58. Rodin exhibited *Head of Bellona* (no. 37) and *Group* (no. 42) at the second exhibition of the International Society.
59. Tate Gallery Archives, 7245.284, letter dated 3 June 1899.
60. Tate Gallery Archives, 7245.283, letter dated 1899.
61. International Society, 1899, nos 90 and 218.
62. *Catalogue*, p. 25, note 24.
63. Tate Gallery Archives, 7245.193, letter dated 19 January 1899.
64. Information from an unidentified Press cutting, Eddie Cleneghan's scrapbook.
65. For further reference to this sequence of works see Scottish Arts Council, *The Glasgow Boys*, Part 2, 1968, p. 82; *The Magazine of Art*, 1901, pp. 123—5.
66. *Catalogue*, no. 55(87).
67. *Life*, p. 119.
68. Unpublished ms. Diary, 1924, private collection.
69. *The Illustrated London News*, 23 January 1904, p. 134.
70. E. R. and J. Pennell, *op. cit.*, 1921, p. 258.
71. ibid., pp. 270, 273—4.
72. *The Art Journal*, 1904, p. 37.
73. Tate Gallery Archives, [illegible] January [illegible]
74. Lavery presented *Summer*, *Eileen*, and *Idonia La Primaudye* to Rodin. Rodin presented Lavery with *Head of Gustave Geffroy*, (Bronze), *Fugit Amor*, (Marble), *Le Frère et La Soeur*, (Bronze), and *Le Bon Genie*, (Bronze).
75. *Shaw Sparrow*, p. 167 claims that the strain imposed by his position as Vice-President began to affect Lavery's health. His resignation was reported in *The Times*, 18 December 1907.

CHAPTER 6

1. R. B. Cunninghame Graham, 'The Atmosphere of Morocco' in *Sketching Grounds, Studio Special Number*, 1909, p. 145.
2. See for instance Norman Garstin, 'Tangier as a Sketching Ground', *The Studio*, vol. 11, 1897, pp. 177—82.
3. Brangwyn's *Oranges* was exhibited at the Royal Academy in 1894, see *Pall Mall Gazette 'Extra'*, 1894, p. 56.
4. Norman Garstin, *op. cit.*, p. 178.
5. Unpublished ms. Diary, 1924, private collection.
6. ibid.
7. For further reference to Arthur Melville see Dundee Museums and Art Galleries, *Arthur Melville 1855—1904*, catalogue by Gerald Deslandes, 1977. For reference to Joseph Crawhall and his expeditions to Tangier, see Vivien Hamilton, *Joseph Crawhall, 1861—1913, one of the Glasgow Boys*, 1990, p. 48; see also Adrian Bury, *Joseph Crawhall, The Man and The Artist*, 1958, p. 55. For further reference see R. B. Cunninghame Graham, 'Creeps', in *Writ in Sand*, 1932, p. 81—87, in which Cunninghame Graham quotes Lavery's assessment of Crawhall as 'the Great Silence'.
8. This picture was exhibited at the Goupil Gallery, London, *Pictures by John Lavery*, June 1891, no. 23. It was sold Christies, Scotland, 19 April 1984, lot 28.
9. *Catalogue*, no. 46(90).
10. *Life*, p. 98. Lavery may have been led to this subject by his having seen Melville's *The Snake Charmers*, a large watercolour formerly in the collection of Sir James Bell, Lord Provost of Glasgow. Melville's composition is, however, very different from Lavery's, being upright in format.
11. This picture was exhibited at the Goupil

Gallery, London, *Pictures by John Lavery*, June 1891, no. 12. *The Saturday Review*, 20 June 1891, pp. 742—3.

12. Reworking of this picture *c.*1901 was confirmed by J. S. Little in 1902 and he refers to *A Lady on Horseback* as one of the artist's 'quite recent productions' (*The Studio*, vol. XXVII, 1902—3, p. 118).
13. A. C. R. Carter, 'John Lavery R.S.A.', *The Art Journal*, 1904, p. 10.
14. The painting is dimly discernible hanging above the mantlepiece in *The Studio* (147). Contemporary photographs also indicate its prominent placing. After the artist's death, it was donated to Glasgow City Art Gallery and Museum by Francis Howard.
15. One study for *A Moorish Dance* was sold, [illegible]; another was sold in Christie's, London, [illegible] November 1985, lot 217.
16. Lavery also removed the upper portion of the canvas. The picture exists in this altered format and in an unfinished state in a private collection.
17. Alexander Mann's letters to his wife have survived in a private collection. I am grateful to Martin Hopkinson of the Hunterian Art Gallery, University of Glasgow, for drawing my attention to those containing direct reference to Lavery.
18. Letters dated 21 April, 24 April and 1 May 1892.
19. Letter dated 9 May 1892.
20. *Catalogue*, no. 48(96).
21. *Shaw Sparrow*, p. 98.
22. Letter from James Guthrie, undated, Tate Gallery Archives, 7245.12, stating that Guthrie hoped to catch Lavery before he set off for Tangier and asking to be remembered to 'Melville and friends' and also enquiring if Mrs Lawrie is going out.
23. See for instance the introduction to the catalogue of Lavery's exhibition at the Leicester Galleries, November 1904.
24. ibid.
25. *Life*, p. 98.
26. Fourteen works appeared in the first exhibition, eighteen in the second and twenty-five in the third.
27. At this time a laudatory article signed 'Von H. S.' appeared in *Die Kunst für alle*, vol. 24, 1909, pp. 417—22.
28. Julian Campbell, *op. cit.*, p. 192 considers the dating of the sketch, 1900, to be 'more likely' the date of the finished work. It must, however, be the case that the sketch was either painted after the Philadelphia version, or that it was post-dated. *A Garden in France* was exhibited at the International Society in 1898, no. 242 and at the Carnegie Institute, Pittsburgh, in 1898, no. 50.
29. Quoted by Ailsa Tanner in *Helensburgh and the Glasgow School*, catalogue of an exhibition at Helensburgh, 1972.
30. For further reference see Tyne and Wear and Bradford Museums, *op. cit.*, 1980, p. 55.
31. This work inscribed 'To Joe' is contained in Castle Musem, Norwich.
32. This picture is dated verso, 1901, see *Catalogue*, no. 52(100).
33. *The Art Journal*, 1904, p. 9.
34. Percy Bate, 'Some Recent Glasgow Painting', *The Magazine of Art*, [illegible] p. 309.
35. ibid.
36. Close examination of the picture surface reveals that originally the composition contained a diagonally placed boat which was obliterated as the painting progressed.
37. Lowell Birge Harrison, 'In search of Paradise with Camera and Palette', *Outing*, 1893, vol. 21, p. 310. I am grateful to William H. Gerdts for calling my attention to this article.
38. Sold Christie's, 14 Nov. 1986, lot 34(101).
39. *Shaw Sparrow*, p. 102.
40. *Life*, p. 128.
41. ibid., p. 129.
42. ibid., p. 130. Dr Trudeau came from a well-known French-Canadian medical family. His father directed a sanitorium outside Toronto at the turn of the century.
43. *A Swiss Chalet, Lac Champex*, private collection, Ireland.
44. A letter, date unknown, written by Alexander Mann from Lugano, mentions having seen Lavery on a cross-channel ferry. I am grateful to Martin Hopkinson for this reference.
45. A small panel, 5 × 8½ in., *The Beach at Tangier*, Fine Art Society (103) was painted from the same viewpoint and maybe a study for *Tangier, The White City* (102). For a full discussion of the types of work Lavery produced in Tangier see, Kenneth McConkey, 'The White City, Sir John Lavery in Tangier', *The GPA Irish Arts Review Yearbook*, 1989—90, pp. 55—[illegible]
46. *Life*, p. [illegible]
47. Selwyn Brinton in 'An English Artist in Morocco', *The Connoisseur*, 1907, pp. 34—41 states emphatically that the 'special subject' of his article was 'the visit of Mr. John Lavery to this country in the spring of last year [1906], when he penetrated inland as far as Fez'. Lavery's view of the city is, however, clearly inscribed 1907(106), see *Sketching Grounds, Special Number of The Studio*, 1909, reproduced opposite p. 148. Lavery in *Life*, p. 96 gives the month of their expedition as February.
48. Selwyn Brinton, *op. cit.*, p. 40.
49. ibid.
50. It is likely that *Souvenir of Morocco* (104) coll. Glasgow Art Gallery and Museum was painted on this trip.
51. Lavery quoted by Brinton, *op. cit.*, p. 39. Percy Jacomb Hood, *op. cit.*, 1925, p. 6, records his adventures with Walter Harris on a trip to Morocco around this time. Harris himself was a notorious character. Born in 1866, he began to write for *The Times* at the age of 21. He was captured by El Raisuli, the brigand leader and held prisoner for a time in [illegible]. A great lover of moorish art, he remained in Morocco until his death in 1933. Lavery painted his portrait ([illegible]) and a small view of the garden of the Villa Harris, reproduced *The Studio*, vol. XLV, 1908, p. 178, remains untraced. For further reference see *Tangier Gazette*, [illegible] April 1933.
52. Quoted by Selwyn Brinton, *op. cit.*, p. 40.
53. *Life*, p. 103.
54. Selwyn Brinton, *op. cit.*, p. 41. This picture was exhibited at the Goupil Gallery in 1908, no. 3, and it was hailed by A. C. R. Carter as a *tour de force*, challenging 'any of J. F. Lewis's experiments in this class of subject', *The Art Journal*, 1908, p. 234.
55. *The Studio*, vol. XLIV, 1908, p. 70.
56. These pictures were no. 37 and no. 59 in the Goupil Exhibition. For further reference to *Evening, Tangier*, see *Catalogue*, no. 60.
57. *The Art Journal*, 1907, p. 234.
58. See for instance *Catalogue*, no. 59. *The Housetops, Morning* and *The Housetops, Night* were nos 6 and 51 in the Goupil Gallery exhibition of 1908. Their general theme was one which was frequently treated by Orientalist painters such as Gérôme and Constant.
59. *The Art Journal*, 1907, p. [illegible]
60. *Shaw Sparrow*, reproduced facing p. 64.
61. Christian Brinton quoted in *Shaw Sparrow* p. 109.
62. *Shaw Sparrow*, p. 111.
63. Whistler's *Blue and Silver, Trouville*, was exhibited at the International Society of Sculptors, Painters and Gravers, 1899, no. [illegible].
64. Illustrated in Cunninghame Graham, *op. cit.*, 1909, p. 148.
65. Sold Christies and Edmistons, Edinburgh, 30 November 1982.
66. *Life*, pp. 104—5.
67. ibid., p. 101.
68. *Catalogue*, no. 65.
69. See photographs contained in Hazel Lavery's scrapbook, private collection.
70. Royal Academy, 1911, no. 647, *The Grey*

Drawing room (113) and for reference to *The Greyhound*, see *Catalogue*, no. 64.

71 Rothenstein's double portrait was sold by Sotheby's, 19 May 1982, lot 97.
72. *The Art Journal*, 1911, p. 166.
73. For discussion of this interior see Kenneth McConkey, 'Hazel in Black and Gold', *Irish Arts Review*, vol. 1, no. 3, p. 16.
74. This picture remains untraced. It was reproduced in *The Studio*, vol. XLI, 1908, p. 75.
75. A number of works might be cited to suit this description, see *An Arab Courtyard*, inscribed to Walter Harris, Sotheby's, 27 March 1991, lot 15; and *In the Garden, Tangier*, inscribed to Thomas Sinclair of Lisburn, Sotheby's, 13 May 1987, lot 59.
76. Reproduced in *The Studio*, vol. L, 1910, p. 25.
77. Reproduced as the frontispiece in *Shaw Sparrow*.
78. Reproduced in *The Studio*, vol. XLIV, 1908, p. 70, present whereabouts unknown.
79. *The Art Journal*, 1911, p. 167. Stodart Walker in 'The Art of John Lavery, RSA, ARA', *The Studio*, vol. LXII, 1914, p. 14, also praises the picture.
80. *Shaw Sparrow*, p. 154.
81. See *Shaw Sparrow*, opposite p. 44.
82. *In Morocco*, Adelaide Art Gallery; oil sketches for this picture exist in two private collections.
83. *Catalogue*, no. 68(120).
84. *Life*, p. 131.
85. *Catalogue*, nos 69 and 70, and works in private collections.
86. Sauter's *The Weisshorn*, a work similar in composition and format to Lavery's mountain-scapes, is contained in Leeds City Art Galleries.
87. *Life*, pp. 236—7.
88. *Catalogue*, no. 71(122).
89. *Life*, p. 175. This event must have occurred prior to the war, since it is recounted in an unidentified press cutting, Lady Lavery's scrapbook, private collection.
90. *Newmarket, Houghton Meeting* and *String out, Exercising Newmarket* were sold by Christie's, 30 October 1970, lots 195 and 196.
91. See *IX Esposizione Internazionale d'Arte della citta di Venezia, 1910, Catalogo;* Lavery's retrospective was staged in Sala 8 and consisted of 53 works with an introduction to the catalogue by A. C. R. Carter.
92. Reproduced *The Studio*, vol. LVII, 1912, as colour plate.
93. Card dated 8 September 1933, National Library of Scotland, Edinburgh. Bebe was obviously Bibi Carleton, 'Creeps' was Crawhall and Frias was the Duke of Frias whose wife's portrait was painted by Lavery around 1894.

CHAPTER 7

1. For a recent discussion of this picture see National Gallery of Art, Washington, *The Treasure Houses of Britain*, catalogue of an exhibition edited by Gervaise Jackson-Stops, 1985, no. 570 (entry by Richard Ormond and Gervaise Jackson-Stops). For further discussion on the portraiture of the period see Kenneth McConkey, *Edwardian Portraits, Images of an Age of Opulence*, Woodbridge, 1987; also, Kenneth McConkey, 'Well-bred Contortions', in Sir Roy Strong, ed., *The British Portrait, 1660—1960*, 1991.
2. *Shaw Sparrow*, p. 149.
3. ibid., pp. 93—4.
4. *The Studio*, vol. 32, 1904, p. 66.
5. This picture was perhaps the first in Lavery's erratic numbering system for his 'ladies in black'. Numerous pictures however, bear the title both before and after the portrait of Esther McLaren.
6. Frederick Wedmore, 'Some Portraits of this Season', *The Studio*, vol. 5, p. 123.
7. *The Spectator*, 23 November 1895, p. 725.
8. See for example *The Magazine of Art*, 1896, pp. 94—5. This particular portrait remains untraced.
9. Royal Academy 1897, no. 291, for further reference see Leeds Art Galleries, *John Singer Sargent and the Edwardian Age*, catalogue of an exhibition by James Lomax and Richard Ormond, 1979, no. 41.
10. *Shaw Sparrow*, p. 178.
11. ibid., p. 134.
12. ibid.
13. *Life*, pp. 76—7.
14. Coll. Johannesburg Art Gallery.
15. Reproduced in *The Art Journal*, 1904 as frontispiece. *A Girl in White* is presently untraced.
16. *The Art Journal*, 1904, p. 10.
17. *Shaw Sparrow*, p. 134.
18. Camille Mauclair, 'John Lavery', *L'Art et les Artistes*, 1905, vol. 2, p. 9.
19. Haldane MacFall, 'The Art of John Lavery', *The Academy*, 24 December 1904, p. 646.
20. Quoted by Selwyn Brinton in *The Studio*, vol. XLV, 1908, p. 174.
21. Camille Mauclair, *op. cit.*, p. 8.
22. A. Stodart Walker, 'The Art of John Lavery, RSA, ARA', *The Studio*, vol. LXII, 1914, p. 9.
23. Three portraits entitled, *Mary No. II*, *Mary No. III* and *Mary No. IV* were shown at the artist's exhibition at the Leicester Galleries in 1904.
24. International Society of Sculptors, Painters and Gravers, 1901, no. 48.
25. *The Studio*, vol. XLIII, 1908, p. 226, a review of the International Society's 'Fair Women' exhibition.
26. Quoted by *Shaw Sparrow*, p. 147.
27. ibid.
28. James L. Caw, *Scottish Painting, Past and Present*, 1908, p. 379.
29. *The Art Journal*, 1908, p. 234; see also *The Times*, 18 June 1908, p. 19.
30. Walter Sickert, *A Free House*, 1947, p. 83.
31. *The Times*, 8 January 1906, p. 7; see also *The Studio*, vol. XXXVII, 1906, p. 113.
32. Hon. John Collier, *The Art of Portrait Painting*, 1905, pp. 75—6.
33. For reference to this picture, see National Gallery of Art, Washington, *op. cit.*, 1985, no. 573 (entry by Kenneth McConkey).
34. Robert Windsor Clive, was keenly interested in art. A few years prior to having his portrait painted by Lavery, he had published a book on *Constable*. For further reference see Jane Abdy and Charlotte Gere, *The Souls*, 1984.
35. Undated letter *c.*1904, Tate Gallery Archives, 7245.204.
36. For further reference see Pyms Gallery, London, *William James Yule, 1867—1900*, catalogue of an exhibition by Annette Wilson, 1983.
37. International Society of Sculptors, Painters and Gravers, 1899, no. 129.
38. *Shaw Sparrow*, p. 188. The Darling family portraits remain untraced.
39. A. C. R. Carter, *op. cit.*, p. 234.
40. Selwyn Brinton, *op. cit.*, 1908, p. 176.
41. Quoted by Selwyn Brinton, *op. cit.*, 1908.
42. *Catalogue*, no. 63(140).
43. Royal Academy, 1912, no. 4; *Royal Academy Pictures*, 1912, p. 79.
44. See *Lady's Pictorial*, 13 December 1919, p. 779 and undated cutting from *Vogue* in Lady Lavery's scrapbook.
45. Reported in *The Times*, 13 April 1910, p. 5, see chapter 6, note 90.
46. Reported in *The Art Journal*, 1911, p. 70.
47. Unidentified source, Lady Lavery's scrapbook.
48. Unidentified cutting, Lady Lavery's scrapbook.
49. *Catalogue*, no. 67(142); exhibited at The International Society, 1911, no. 33.
50. For a chronology of performances see

Anna Pavlova 1882—1931, catalogue of an exhibition at the London Museum, 1956.
51. *Life*, p. 171.
52. ibid., p. 173.
53. *The Spectator*, 15 April 1911, p. 563.
54. Royal Academy, 1912, no. 415(143).
55. *Life*, p. 173. Sargent, who visited the studio one day when Hazel was posing, confirmed the likeness. However, Victor Dandre, the dancer's husband did not feel that *La Mort du Cygne* provided a good likeness and preferred *Anna Pavlova as a Bacchante*, see *Royal Opera House Retrospective 1732—1982*, catalogue of an exhibition at the Royal Academy, 1982, no. 89, p. 53.
56. Unidentified cutting, Lady Lavery's scrapbook.
57. Royal Academy 1913, no. 537, *Royal Academy Pictures*, 1913, p. 32.
58. The original size, 84 × 42 in. was reduced to 47 × 37 ins. by the time it was shown at the Grosvenor Gallery *Retrospective Exhibition of the Works of John Lavery 1880—1914*, no. 7. See also *The Studio*, vol. LXII, June 1914, reproduced p. 8, sold Phillips, 14 Nov. 1989, lot 36, as *A Lady in Black Velvet*.
59. *The Studio*, vol. LXII, 1914, p. 6.
60. *Catalogue*, no. 72(145, 146, 147).
61. While it is likely that Lavery overhauled *The Studio* as suggested and close study of the *pentimenti* tends to confirm this, it cannot be ruled out that the artist produced another quite separate version of the picture apart from the study.
62. *Catalogue*, no. 74(148).
63. Unidentified cutting, Lady Lavery's scrapbook.
64. *Life*, p. 159.
65. *The Times*, 8 June 1904, p. 56.
66. *The Studio*, vol. LXII, 1914, p. 12.
67. *Life*, p. 159. The Royal Collection contains a *Sketch for The Royal Family (First Study)*, (inventory no. [illegible]) and head studies for each of the protagonists (inventory nos [illegible]). The Ulster Museum contains a *Second Study* (see note 64 above). Variations between these two works suggest that the first was completed in more detail, specifically for presentation. In both, the king rests his hand upon a table, though in one it is a Louis XVI marble topped table, and in the other it is a circular Regency pedestal table. It has been suggested that this alteration may have been a suggestion of Queen Mary's, since she was a keen enthusiast for Regency furniture (I am grateful to Charles Noble for giving me access to catalogue notes on the Royal Collection). In the final picture, however, both tables were omitted, and since neither study shows the king in his final pose, it was assumed that the alteration was made upon the large picture. In January 1986, a full-length study (152), appeared at Pyms Gallery, London, inscribed Buckingham Palace, March 1913. This clearly shows His Majesty adopting the final pose, his hands resting upon his sword hilt. The National Portrait Gallery version was reproduced as a mezzotint by Richard Smythe, and published by Agnews, and Smythe is reported to have offered advice to the artist on the composition (I am grateful to Colin Smythe for bringing this information to my attention).
68. See note 61 above and *Catalogue*, no. 71.
69. MacLaren Young, MacDonald, Spencer and Miles, *The Paintings of James McNeill Whistler*, 1980, no. 62, p. 36.
70. The picture was ineffectively hung at the Royal Academy in 1914 (no. 718), see Stodart Walker, *op. cit.*, 1914, p. 12. It was subsequently shown at the Royal Scottish Academy, 1916, no. 196, and thereafter at the Glasgow Institute of Fine Arts 1918, no. 413.
71. Grosvenor Gallery London, *A Retrospective Exhibition of the Works of John Lavery 1880—1914*, 9 June to 31 July 1914.
72. Walter Shaw Sparrow, *John Lavery and his Work, with a preface by R. B. Cunninghame Graham*, Kegan Paul, Trench Trubner and Co., *c.*1911.
73. Stodart Walker, *op. cit.*, 1914, p. 6.
74. *The Times*, 8 June 1914.

CHAPTER 8

1. *The Thames at Maidenhead* (155) is clearly dated in the artist's hand on the reverse, 1913.
2. *Catalogue*, no. 95. The Pavilion and Boathouse have been removed and the swans on the right and the couple in the skiff added.
3. *Catalogue*, no. [illegible](154).
4. *Life*, p. 138.
5. Untraced; reproduced, Robert Ross and C. E. Montague, *British Artists at the Front, II, Sir John Lavery A.R.A.*, 1918, n.p., where dated December 1914.
6. One of these, untraced, was sold on behalf of the Jubilee Fund for Queen's District Nurses in Belfast in 1937. See *Belfast Telegraph*, 10 September 1937; I am grateful to George McConkey for drawing this reference to my attention. This may be the study presented by the artist to the Ulster Division Fete in 1917, presumably to commemorate the heavy losses sustained by the Division in the Battle of the Somme which reappeared in Christie's, 6 Nov. 1992, lot 53. A final study is contained in *Life*, plate 22.
7. *The Studio*, vol. 65, 1915, p. 25.
8. ibid.
9. *Life*, p. 139.
10. ibid.
11. National Library of Scotland, Edinburgh, letter dated 28 May 1915.
12. ibid.
13. *Catalogue*, no. 81(156), and oral information supplied by John Hewitt, Esq.
14. Reported in *The Tatler*, 21 July 1915.
15. *Life*, p. 140. The difficulties of establishing the correct sequence of events at this point are increased by Lavery's faltering memory as recorded in *Life*. S. and M. Harries in their chapter on Lavery in *The War Artists*, 1983, p. 34, misdate the car crash to 1917.
16. *Life*, p. 141.
17. *Catalogue*, no. 82(157).
18. *Catalogue*, no. 83, and at least two other works in private collections.
19. Private collection, Dublin(158).
20. Lady Lavery's scrapbook, private collection.
21. See Martin Gilbert, *Winston Spencer Churchill, Companion to Vol.V, Part 2, The Wilderness Years 1929—35*, 1981, letter dated 3 January 1935.
22. *Catalogue*, no. 77(159). *Mrs Winston Churchill with her daughter, Sarah* was sold by Christies, 4 March 1977, illustrated *Apollo*, May 1977, p. 398. This work was purchased by the National Portrait Gallery (5184).
23. See *Strand Magazine*, December 1921, the first publication of Churchill's essay 'Painting as a Pastime'. See also Martin Gilbert, *op. cit.*, vol. IV, Part 2, p. 1059, letter from Winston Spencer Churchill to his wife Clementine, dated 27 March 1920, 'how I wish Lavery were here to give me a few hints'. Lavery and Churchill painted together in 1921 at Cap Ferrat.
24. *Lady's Pictorial*, 13 December 1919. Table palettes were not unique to Lavery. His design is likely to have been a variant on Whistler's.
25. *Life*, p. 175. For reference to Lady Victoria Primrose's portrait see Colnaghi and Clarendon Galleries, *Society Portraits 1850 to 1950*, 1985, no. 48, catalogue by Christopher Newall. Lord Derby himself was painted at this time and his portrait exhibited, Royal Academy 1916, no. 466.
26. *The Dowager Lady Smiley*, Royal Academy 1915, no. 509; *Miss Elizabeth Asquith*,

Royal Academy 1916, no. 364; *The Hon. Mrs Morrison-Bell*, Royal Academy 1917, no. 122 and *Mrs Walter Samuel*, Royal Academy 1917, no. 370.

27. *Catalogue*, no. 75(162).
28. For an extended discussion of this picture, see Kenneth McConkey, 'Hazel in Black and Gold', *Irish Arts Review*, vol. 1, no. 3, pp. 12—17.
29. Unidentified press cuttings, Lady Lavery's scrapbook.
30. ibid.
31. ibid.
32. Unidentified cutting, *c.*1918, reproducing a photograph by E. O. Hoppe: Lady Lavery's scrapbook.
33. ibid. Unfortunately it has not been possible to date this event, restaged for a photograph by Hoppe.
34. These took place on 6 November 1917 and 4 January 1918 respectively. On each occasion photographs by Hoppe appeared in *The Tatler*.
35. Unidentified press cutting, Lady Lavery's scrapbook.
36. *Life*, p. 141.
37. ibid., p. 142.
38. *Catalogue*, nos 79 and 80.
39. Private collection, Dublin.
40. S. and M. Harries, *op. cit.*, 1983, p. 34. See also Kettle's Yard, Cambridge, *Artists at War 1914—18*, catalogue of an exhibition by Robert Cumming, 1974, p. 9. See also Newcastle upon Tyne Polytechnic Art Gallery, *Artists and the Great War*, catalogue of an exhibition by Kenneth McConkey, 1979.
41. ibid., p. 35.
42. *Life*, pp. 145—6; quoted by S. and M. Harries, *op. cit.*, 1983, p. 35.
43. See for instance Ross and Montague, *op. cit.*, 1918, plate VI, and *The Forth Bridge*, Christies, 4 March 1983, lot 233.
44. Various private collections and the Imperial War Museum. Lavery seems to have followed the policy of painting one view of the subject for the Ministry of Information, and one for himself. Many of these latter pictures remained in his studio at the time of his death.
45. Ross and Montague, *op. cit.*, 1918, plate IX; coll. Imperial War Museum. Other variants are contained in private collections, as is *The Breaking up of HMS Illustrious*.
46. S. and M. Harries, *op. cit.*, 1983, p. 130.
47. *Life*, p. 151.
48. Lavery's Admiralty Permit, dated 2 January 1918 is contained in Tate Gallery Archives, 7245.154. It is stamped Inverness 8 January 1918 and states that all pictures must be submitted for censorship.
49. Two versions of the picture of American troops embarking are known. One in the Imperial War Museum (1279) and the other in a private collection. A large work derived from these is also contained in the Imperial War Museum (2616).
50. Ross and Montague, *op. cit.*, 1918, plate XII; this work is presently in a private collection.
51. Imperial War Museum, (1261 and 1280).
52. Reproduced S. and M. Harries, *op. cit.*, 1983, following p. 134(172).
53. *Life*, p. 146; coll. Imperial War Museum (1265).
54. ibid., p. 147.
55. A study for Admiral Beatty reading the terms of the Armistice, coll. Imperial War Museum (2617).
56. Royal Academy 1920, no. 199(173).
57. For reference to this project, see S. and M. Harries, *op. cit.*, 1983, p. 144. These pictures are contained in the Imperial War Museum (2881—2892).
58. Lavery greatly admired Kennington's *The Kensingtons at Laventie* (Imperial War Museum) (*Life*, p. 144) and when approached by the young artist in a barber's shop, Lavery wrote to Masterman on his behalf. See Tate Gallery Archives 7245.16.
59. ibid., p. 142.
60. ibid., p. 148.
61. *Catalogue*, nos 85(174) and 88.
62. See Winston Spencer Churchill, *The World Crisis*, 1931, p. 86.
63. Cuttings and telegrams, Lady Lavery's scrapbook.
64. *Lady's Pictorial*, 13 December 1919.
65. Unidentified source, *c.*1921, Lady Lavery's scrapbook.
66. *Catalogue*, no. 91(178)
67. Unidentified source, Lady Lavery's scrapbook. A study for the picture exists in the National Gallery of Ireland (1251).
68. *Life*, p. 183. Numerous golf pictures exist in private collections. Many have passed through the salerooms in recent years. They were invariably painted at North Berwick, Westerdunes, being located opposite the ninth hole. I am grateful to Sheriff Harold Ford for information concerning Lavery's visits to Westerdunes.
69. *Rain in the Distance, North Berwick* was sold at Christie's 12 March 1993, lot 65.
70. *Life*, p. 104. See *Hazel at Sidi Bu Said, Tunis, 1919*, in the Belgrave Gallery, *British Post-Impressionists and Moderns*, 1985, no. 15.
71. Formerly Fine Art Society, Glasgow Institute of Arts, 1920, no. 445.
72. For further reference to *The Bay, Monte Carlo*, see Kenneth McConkey, *A Free Spirit, Irish Art, 1860—1960*, 1990, pp. 148—9; *The Terrace, Cap d'Ail*, was sold at Phillips, 16 June 1981, lot [illegible]. Various versions of pictures of the terrace and pergola at Villa Silvia and other gerdens exist in private collections. To these should be added *A Garden in France*, Richard Green, *Modern British Paintings*, 1987, no. 2.
73. Throughout the works of the 1920s, figures are used as a foil to the hedonistic celebration of the *côte d'azure*. *The Terrace at Cannes*, 1931 (Phillips, 5 Nov. 1991, lot 26) resumes the *ennui* evident in *The Honeymoon*.
74. Alpine Club Gallery, *Pictures of Morocco, The Riviera and other Scenes by Sir John Lavery RA; Portrait and Child Studies by Lady Lavery*, foreword by Winston S. Churchill, 1921, p. 4.

CHAPTER 9

1. See Chapter 5, note 5.
2. David Martin, *The Glasgow School of Painting*, 1897, (1976 reprint), p. 40.
3. ibid., p. 39.
4. *Scottish Art Review*, vol. 1, November 1888, pp. 156—7, quoted by Roger Billcliffe, *op. cit.*, p. 88.
5. Tate Gallery Archives, 7245.230.
6. Tate Gallery Archives, 7245.229.
7. Thomas Bodkin, *Hugh Lane and His Pictures*, Dublin 1956, pp. 8—10.
8. *Catalogue*, no. 57(186).
9. *The Times*, 30 May 1904, p. 12.
10. *The Art Journal*, 1904, p. 236.
11. See Thomas Bodkin, *op. cit.*, pp. 17—27.
12. *Catalogue*, no. 60(187).
13. Visits to Dublin are recorded in 1913 and 1914.
14. For a full account of these events see Brian Inglis, *Roger Casement*, 1973.
15. ibid., pp. 346—51.
16. *Life*, p. 190. Casement apparently wrote 'who was the painter in the jury-box painting a picture of the court? I should think he came dangerously near "aiding and comforting" if not indeed "compassing" from the way he eyed Mr. Justice Darling delivering judgement. Surely it is treason to take a Judge's head off on the bench!'
17. ibid., p. 190.
18. ibid.
19. Royal Academy 1917, no. 84(164).
20. *The Irish News*, 4 April 1919, Belfast City Library, cuttings book 13. I am grateful to George McConkey for obtaining this reference for me.
21. *Belfast Telegraph*, 27 January 1920, Belfast

City Library cuttings book 13.
22. *Life*, p. 208.
23. Reproduced *Life*, plate 26.
24. *Life*, p. 210.
25. *Catalogue*, no. 94(190).
26. *Life*, p. 209.
27. ibid.
28. The Ulster Museum, *Seamus Heaney, A Personal Selection*, catalogue of an exhibition, 1982, no. 8.
29. *Life*, p. 211.
30. ibid.
31. ibid., p. 208.
32. ibid., see also letter from Edward Carson dated [illegible] February 1922, Tate Gallery Archives, [illegible].
33. *Life*, p. 213. See also letter dated 21 [illegible], Tate Gallery Archives, 7245.220.
34. *Life*, p. 213.
35. *Catalogue*, no. 89 refers to the sketch in the collection of the National Gallery of Ireland.
36. *The Scotsman*, 29 April 1922.
37. *Life*, p. 216.
38. ibid., p. 217.
39. ibid.
40. ibid., p. 218.
41. ibid., p. 221.
42. ibid., p. 219.
43. Martyn Angelsea, *The Royal Ulster Academy of Arts*, Lisburn 1981, p. 56.
44. ibid., p. 62.
45. *Evening Telegraph*, 17 June 1914. I am grateful to George McConkey for locating this reference.
46. *Belfast Newsletter*, 8 October 1924, Belfast City Library, cuttings book 16. I am grateful to George McConkey for locating this reference.
47. These pictures are contained in the collections of the descendants of Lavery's legatees.
48. Verbal information from Mrs Claire Downing.
49. *Catalogue* no. 101(200).
50. Letter to Thomas Bodkin, dated 17 July 1928, no. 588, Trinity College Library, Dublin.
51. Letter dated [illegible] January 1928, Ulster Museum files.
52. Letter dated [illegible] October [illegible], no. [illegible], Trinity College Library, Dublin. Bodkin wrote back agreeing with Lavery's appraisal (see letter 553).
53. Information from Ulster Museum files.
54. Hazel Lavery to Arthur Deane, letter dated 8 May 1929, Ulster Museum files. Lady Lavery dates *The Mother* to 1908, though related works exist in private collections, one a study of 1907. Another is a larger more finished oil clearly dated 1900. All of these pictures appear at some point to have been based upon the familiar profile of Mary Auras.
55. ibid.
56. Articles describing the new collection are contained in the files of The Ulster Museum. The main descriptions are contained in 'Belfast's new art gallery', *The Irish News*, 11 July 1929 and 'Stately Structures', *Belfast Telegraph*, 9 July 1929. Interviewed after the event, the artist declared that he had made the donation 'for two reasons—one that I was born in Belfast, and the other that they had built a gallery there, but had no pictures to put in it', [illegible] December 1929.
57. Lavery was informed of the honour by Alfred S. Moore. He wrote to Moore that he was 'not over familiar with the history of art or with the lives of artists but I shall be surprised if such a unique compliment has been paid to art, considering existing conditions. It would be in the nature of things if Belfast, the last important city in the Empire to build an Art Gallery, became a great Art Centre and induced students from all parts to come to study …' Letter dated 15 January 1930 from the Hotel Beau Site, Cannes; Alfred S. Moore collection, L3, Belfast City Library. Lavery was, as *The Irish News* pointed out, the first catholic Freeman of Belfast and the first artist to be honoured with the title. In conferring the honour, the city was responding to pressure by Alderman James A. Doran, Chairman of the Libraries, Museums and Art Committee and also from *The Irish News*. At a civic reception held on 22 April 1930, Lavery's name was added to the Roll of 56 Belfast Burgesses. In replying to a speech of welcome, the artist again expressed his hope that Belfast would become a great international art centre and declared how flattered he was by the city's confidence in him, particularly that of the Fine Art Committee which had placed a gallery at his disposal in the new Art Gallery. 'When one considers the vagaries of gentlemen of my profession, it is difficult to realize the extent of the trustfulness and confidence this meant on the part of the Fine Art Committee, and coming from Belfast too, where we are said to be more cautious than the Scots themselves.' Reported in *Belfast Telegraph*, 22 April 1930, p. 4.
58. Lavery to Thomas Bodkin, 29 August 1927, letter 546, Trinity College Library, Dublin. Bodkin had been appointed Director of the National Gallery of Ireland the previous month. From the start of their negotations, the Laverys wished their gift to go to Dublin—but it is equally clear that they identified Bodkin as its curator. The initial wish therefore may have been that the pictures be housed in the National Gallery of Ireland.
59. Lavery to Thomas Bodkin, dated 30 December 1927, letter 547, Trinity College Library, Dublin.
60. Letter to Thomas Bodkin, dated St Stephen's Day 1927, no. 578, Trinity College Library, Dublin.
61. Letter dated 28 February 1928, no. 580, Trinity College Library, Dublin.
62. Lavery actually owned a painting by the young Irish artist Sean Keating entitled *Kathleen Ni Houlihan*. Reference to this work is contained in the inventory of the contents of the artist's studio at the time of his death. The picture remains untraced.
63. See for instance *catalogue* no. [illegible], *Dublin Horse Show*, a work of *c.*1928 inscribed to the playwright, Lennox Robinson.
64. Letter dated 2 December 1928, no. 595, Trinity College Library, Dublin.
65. *Catalogue*, nos 107(203) and 108.
66. *Life*, pp. 202—3.
67. ibid., p. 204.
68. ibid.
69. Lavery to Thomas Bodkin, dated 10 August 1929, letter 551, Trinity College Library, Dublin.
70. *Catalogue*, no. 108, and an upright version of the composition inscribed 'To Monsignor Vance, April 1929', formerly the Fine Art Society.
71. *Life*, p. 206.
72. Lavery to Thomas Bodkin, dated 12 January 1930, letter 556, Trinity College Library, Dublin.
73. For reference to this question, see Hazel Lavery to Thomas Bodkin, letter 580, dated 24 February 1928, Trinity College Library, Dublin.
74. For a full list of the collection donated to Dublin, see *Life*, pp. 256—7.
75. Unidentified press cutting, Eddie Cleneghan's scrapbook.
76. *Catalogue*, no. [illegible].
77. *Life*, p. 207.
78. For an account of his activities in this respect see Martyn Angelsea, *op. cit.*
79. *Life*, p. 221.
80. Quoted from a speech delivered at the Banquet of the Irish academy of Letters, 17 August 1937. For further reference see A. Norman Jeffares in *A Commentary on the Collected Poems of W. B. Yeats*, 1968, p. 482.
81. The first three stanzas of 'The Municipal Gallery Revisited' are quoted from *The Collected Poems of W. B. Yeats*, 1979 edn, p. 368. In 1912, Yeats had composed 'To a Wealthy Man who promised a second

Subscription to the Dublin Municipal Gallery if it were proved the People wanted Pictures', (published in *Responsibilities*, 1914), as a way of expressing his solidarity with the current attempts to establish the collection. The Lavery paintings referred to in 'The Municipal Gallery Revisited' are *St Patrick's Purgatory*, *Court of Criminal Appeal*, the portraits of *Arthur Griffith* and *Kevin O'Higgins*, *The Blessing of the Colours*, *Mrs Lavery sketching*, and *The Unfinished Harmony*.

CHAPTER 10

1. Elizabeth Robbins Pennell, *The Life and Letters of Joseph Pennell*, 1930, vol. II, p. 340, letter to Butler Wood dated 3 January 1926.
2. Desmond MacCarthy, 'Sir John Lavery's Portrait Interiors', *Apollo*, vol. 2, 1925, pp. 267—8.
3. Sir Joseph Duveen, *Thirty Years of British Art* (*Studio* special autumn number), 1930, p. 95.
4. For further reference see Grey Art Gallery and Study Centre, *Walter Gay: A Retrospective*, exhibition catalogue by Gary A. Reynolds, New York, 1980.
5. Lavery had been producing portrait interiors consistently since 1921 when *The Van Dyck Room, Wilton* was painted, see *Catalogue*, no. 93(207).
6. ibid.
7. *The Scotsman*, 24 June 1921.
8. MacCarthy, *op. cit.*, pp. 268—9.
9. *Catalogue*, no. 96(208). In 1924, Lavery gave John McCormack one of his arab sketches of 1920, entitled *Rue des femmes, Rabat*, see Sotheby's, 13 November 1985, lot 220.
10. MacCarthy, *op. cit.*, p. 273.
11. *The American Magazine of Art*, vol. XVII, February 1926, no. 2, pp. 55—64.
12. *The Art News*, 17 October 1925.
13. *The Art News*, 24 October 1925, p. 12.
14. *Life*, p. 225.
15. Royal Academy, 1926, no. 55. This picture showed the library of Harold Pratt. The home of Dr Alexander Hamilton Rice, the explorer, was another of the five interiors which were apparently completed during this first trip to New York. Upon his return to England in March 1926 Lavery was reported to have painted the portraits of 15 millionaires. In a newspaper interview, he declined to name them because 'they were just ordinary millionaires' and no one would know them if he did! He added that in America 'everyone is a millionaire ... and one needed to be a millionaire many times over before one counted there.' Unidentified cutting, Eddie Cleneghan's scrapbook.
16. Letter 576, 29 November 1927, Trinity College Library, Dublin.
17. The most important of these was entitled *Winter in Florida*, formerly Roy Miles Fine Paintings, London. Related studies are contained in two private collections.
18. For reference to Lavery's first encounters with the racing fraternity, see Chapter 6. He had visited Newmarket in 1913, and painted his first racing scenes In 1919 he had painted *The Derby in the Rain* (ex Fine Art Society). In 1923 he painted a similar racing picture at Ascot (Sotheby's, May 1986), while he was working on *The Jockey's Dressing Room* ...
19. Royal Academy 1924, no. 663.
20. *Life*, pp. 174—6.
21. *Catalogue*, no. 97(213).
22. Private collection, formerly Pyms Gallery, London (214).
23. See *The Illustrated London News*, 9 May 1925, p. 893 and *The Graphic*, 9 May 1925, p. 759.
24. *Life*, p. 174.
25. MacCarthy, *op. cit.*, p. 271. This picture was exhibited at the Leicester Galleries, *Portrait Interiors*, October 1925, no. 10.
26. *Life*, p. 164.
27. Letter dated 20 October, 1935, quoted in *Life*, p. 164.
28. *Life*, p. 161, Lavery apparently met Shaw in the 1890s and had painted his portrait around 1913.
29. Hazel Lavery's portrait is contained in Manchester City Art Gallery. In the opinion of the author, a version of Shaw's portrait offered for sale at Phillips, London 14 November 1983, lot 18, was also extensively worked upon by Hazel Lavery, although attributed to her husband.
30. *Life*, p. 162.
31. ibid.
32. Letter to D. S. MacColl, 8 July 1926, University of Glasgow Library, L61.
33. Letter 596, dated 19 February 1929, Trinity College Library, Dublin.
34. *Catalogue*, no. 102(218).
35. Royal Academy, 1932, no. 238; Royal Academy 1933, no. 217.
36. *The Art News*, 24 October 1925, p. 12. For reference to *The Debutantes*, see Pyms Gallery, *Impressions and Realities*, catalogue of an exhibition, 1985, no. 30(220).
37. *The National Graphic*, 2 June 1932, pp. 318—19.
38. Reproduced *Royal Academy Pictures*, 1933.
39. Royal Academy, 1934, no. 44.
40. *Catalogue*, no. 110. *Lloyd George's War Memories* was published in six volumes, 1935—6.
41. *The Marquis of Londonderry*, is illustrated in *Life*, plate 26. Sargent's portrait of Philip Sassoon is contained in the Tate Gallery.
42. *Life*, p. 176.
43. This sketch was originally exhibited at P. & D. Colnaghi, *Their Majesties' Court, Buckingham Palace, 1931, Portrait Studies and other sketches by Sir John Lavery RA*, 1932, no. 65. For further reference see *The Studio*, vol. 104, 1932, p. 271.
44. *Catalogue*, no. 103(221). The portrait in everyday costume was exhibited at the Salon in 1933, while the portrait in darker robes in its finished version was exhibited at the Royal Academy in 1931, no. 305, Doncaster Art Gallery. A study for this ceremonial work was sold at Christie's, 6 March 1986, lot 51.
45. These were exhibited at the Royal Academy 1931, no. 343 and the Royal Academy 1934, no. 179.
46. *Catalogue*, no. 109(223).
47. For further reference see Barbican Art Gallery, *The City's Pictures*, 1984, no. 53(224).
49. *Catalogue*, no. 98(225).
50. Unidentified press cutting, Eddie Cleneghan's scrapbook.
51. Hazel Lavery to Arthur Deane, letter dated 8 May 1929, Ulster Museum files.
52. *Catalogue*, no. 106(227).
53. Formerly The Fine Art Society(143), see Chapter 7, note 54.
54. Letter dated 20 February 1930, Trinity College Library, Dublin.
55. William Morris Art Gallery, Walthamstow.
56. W. Egerton Powell, 'Personality in Art', *Artwork*, vol. 2, no. 8, 1926—7, pp. 205—6.
57. Lady Lavery to Thomas Bodkin, letter dated 20 February 1930, Trinity College Library, Dublin, and unidentified press cutting, Eddie Cleneghan's scrapbook.
58. Card announcing the marriage, 4 March 1930, at Notre Dame d'Esperance, Cannes; Private Collection.
59. Richard Green, Fine Paintings, London.
60. *Catalogue*, no. 104.
61. Verbal information from Mrs Alice Gwynn.
62. Letter to Cunninghame Graham, dated 8 September 1933, National Library of Scotland, Edinburgh.
63. Letter to Cunninghame Graham, dated 29 August 1933, National Library of Scotland, Edinburgh.
64. Unidentified press cutting, Eddie

Cleneghan's scrapbook.
65. Hazel Lavery to Thomas Bodkin, letter dated 5 April 1934, no. 635, Trinity College Library, Dublin.
66. Some Press reports of the period quote the title of Lavery's last depiction of Hazel as *The Unfinished Symphony*.
67. Unidentified press cutting, Eddie Cleneghan's scrapbook.
68. *The Times*, 5 January 1935.
69. ibid.
70. *Life*, pp. 197—8.
71. Cecil Beaton, *The Wandering Years, Diaries* [illegible], 1961, pp. [illegible]
72. ibid.
73. See for instance an unidentified 'Woman friend' in *The Times*, 7 January 1935.
74. Undated letter from Lady Cunard, [illegible], Tate Gallery Archives.
75. *The Times*, 8 January 1935, lists those present.
76. *Life*, p. 198.

CHAPTER II

1. Quoted in Robert Rhodes James ed., *Chips, The Diaries of Sir Henry Channon, 1970* (1984 reprint), p. 40, entry for 27 March 1935. I am grateful to Hywel James for drawing my attention to this reference.
2. Martin Gilbert, *Winston Spencer Churchill, Companion Volume V, Part 2, The Wilderness Years, 1929 to 1935*, 1981, Clementine to Winston Spencer Churchill, letter dated 5 January 1935.
3. Unidentified press cutting, Eddie Cleneghan's scrapbook.
4. *Catalogue*, no. 112(232).
5. See *Catalogue* 64(114).
6. Royal Academy 1936, no. 229. Sketches for this picture exist in a private collection. It was reproduced in *Life as Lilian at Ranelagh*.
7. From information contained in Ulster Museum files.
8. *Life*, p. 246. The resulting work *Sunbathers* is illustrated in *Life*, plate 55. It was sold, Phillips, London 12 November 1985, lot 242A. A second, originally larger version of the subject was that shown at the Royal Academy in 1937, no. 320(239).
9. Royal Academy, 1936, no. 555, untraced.
10. Lavery's portrait was used as the cover for the souvenir programme for Grey Owl's second United Kingdom Tour in 1937. I am grateful to Brian Mills for bringing this programme to my attention.
11. Victoria Art Galleries, Dundee, *Paintings by Sir John Lavery, Kt, RA, RSA* catalogue introduction by Sir Patrick Ford, September 1936.
12. *Life*, p. 241.
13. ibid., p. 240.
14. Royal Hibernian Academy, 1937, no. 107, Limerick Art Gallery.
15. *Life*, p. 239.
16. *Sunday Times*, 22 November 1936.
17. *Life*, p. 244.
18. These sketches are contained in a private collection.
19. *Life*, p. 245.
20. ibid., p. 247.
21. *Catalogue*, no. 113(238).
22. Royal Academy 1937, no. 83.
23. Letters 567 and 568, dated 27 and 29 May 1937, Trinity College Library, Dublin.
24. This work was exhibited as *Piccadilly, 19 May 1937*, Royal Academy 1938, no. 250.
25. The Leicester Galleries, *Memorial Exhibition of the work of Sir John Lavery*, RA, introduction, p. 4.
26. *Life*, p. 249.
27. ibid., p. 250.
28. See *Palm Springs News*, 23 December 1937, pp. 1, 3, 4, 5, 6 and *The Limelight*, 25 December 1937, pp. 1, 13.
29. Unidentified press cutting, Eddie Cleneghan's scrapbook.
30. *Life*, p. 166.
31. ibid., p. 206, and verbal information from Mrs Claire Downing.
32. *Catalogue*, no. 114(244).
33. Royal Academy, 1939, no. 159. For further reference see Colnaghi and Clarendon Galleries, *Society Portraits*, catalogue of an exhibition by Christopher Newall, 1985, no. 49(245).
34. Royal Academy, 1940, no. 328(249).
35. Several smaller portraits of Katherine Fitz Gerald exist in collections of descendants of the sitter.
36. Letter from Mrs Alice Gwynn, dated 5 June 1971, Ulster Museum files.
37. Royal Academy, 1940, no. 252.
38. Letter from Mrs Alice Gwynn, dated 5 June 1971, Ulster Museum files.
39. The Leicester Galleries, *op. cit.*, introduction by Edward Knoblock, p. 2.
40. ibid., p. 3.
41. *Shaw Sparrow*, preface, 'His Life and Miracles' by R. B. Cunninghame Graham, pp. [illegible].
42. *The Burlington Magazine*, vol. CXXVIII, February 1986, p. 161.

List of Illustrations

Where known, sizes are given, height before width, in inches. Unless otherwise stated, the medium is assumed to be oil on canvas or panel.

221 *Hugh Cecil Lowther, Fifth Earl of Lonsdale*, 1930, $37\frac{1}{4} \times 31\frac{1}{4}$ (private collection).

222 *Hampstead Heath*, *c.*1930, 24 × 32 (private collection, photo, Ian Kilpatrick).

223 Sketch for *Portrait of Diana Dickinson*, 1934, $23\frac{3}{4} \times 12\frac{1}{2}$ (private collection, photo, Pyms Gallery, London).

224 *Hazel in Rose and Grey*, *c.*1920, 50 × 40 (Barbican Art Gallery, London).

225 *The Green Coat*, 1925, $78 \times 42\frac{1}{4}$ (Ulster Museum, Belfast).

226 Advertisement for Pond's Cream (source unknown).

227 *The Gold Turban*, 1929, 30 × 25 (private collection, photo, Pyms Gallery, London).

228 *Tennis under the Orange Trees, Cannes*, 1930, 18 × 24 (private collection, photo, courtesy Richard Green).

229 *The Unfinished Harmony*, 1934, 50 × 40 (Hugh Lane Municipal Art Gallery, Dublin).

230 *'It is Finished' 5th January 1935*, $19\frac{1}{2} \times 23\frac{1}{2}$ (Hugh Lane Municipal Art Gallery, Dublin).

231 Sir John and Lady Lavery at a Royal Academy Private View, photograph *c.*1930 (photo, the author).

232 *Mrs McEnery and her Family at Rosenarra*, 1935, 36 × 28 (private collection).

233 Study for *Summer*, *c.*1910, size unknown (private collection).

234 *The Red Hammock*, *c.*1923, 68 × 80 (The Ulster Museum, Belfast).

235 Hazel in *The Red Hammock*, *c.*19[illegible], [illegible] × 22, (private collection, photo, courtesy Phillips, London).

236 *Grey Owl*, *c.*1936, size unknown (present whereabouts unknown).

237 *Shirley Temple and the Painter*, 1937, size unknown (present whereabouts unknown).

238 *Lord Duveen of Millbank at Home*, 1937, $30\frac{1}{2} \times 40\frac{1}{2}$ (Ferens Art Gallery, Kingston Upon Hull)

239 *Sunbathers*, 1937, $55\frac{1}{2} \times 43\frac{1}{2}$ (private collection, photo, courtesy Sotheby's).

240 *Piccadilly, 12 May 1937*, (The London Museum).

241 Katherine FitzGerald, Diana Dickinson and Ann Forbes-Sempill at the Coronation, 1937, (photo, the author).

242 *Mrs Gordon Coutts*, 24 × 20 (private collection, photo, Ian Kilpatrick).

243 Katherine Fitz Gerald, Lavery and Ann Forbes-Sempill at Palm Springs, snapshot 1937 (photo, the author).

244 *Kathleen (The Flower Girl)*, *c.*1936, $36 \times 22\frac{1}{2}$ (private collection).

245 *Viscountess Wimborne*, 1937, 78 × 40 (present whereabouts unknown, photo, courtesy Colnaghi's).

246 Katherine Fitz Gerald, *c.*1939, $73 \times 30\frac{1}{2}$ (private collection, photo, Ian Kilpatrick).

247 Study for *Katherine Fitz Gerald* *c.*1939, 16 × 8 (private collection, photo, Ian Kilpatrick).

248 Katherine Fitz Gerald posing for her portrait. *c.*1939 (photo, the author).

249 *Gipsy Encampment*, 1940, 40 × 50 (private collection).

250 Sir John Lavery going out to paint at Palm Springs (photo, the author).

Bibliography

Baldwin Brown, G., *The Glasgow School of Painters*, Glasgow 1908.

Billcliffe, R., *The Glasgow Boys*, London 1985.

Caw, J. L., *Scottish Painting, Past and Present*, London 1908.

Crookshank, A., and The Knight of Glin, *The Painters of Ireland c.1660—1920*, London 1978.

Hardie, W. R., *Scottish Painting 1839—1939*, London 1976.

Harries, S. and M., *The War Artists*, London 1983.

Irwin, D. and F., *Scottish Painters at Home and Abroad*, London 1975.

Jacobs, M., *The Good and Simple Life, Artist Colonies in Europe and America*, Oxford, 1985.

Lavery, John, *The Life of a Painter*, London (Cassell), 1940, (herein *Life*).

MacMillan, D., *Scottish Art: 1460—1990*, Edinburgh 1990.

McConkey, K., *A Free Spirit—Irish Art 1860—1960*, Woodbridge, 1990.

McConkey, K., *British Impressionism*, Oxford, 1989.

McConkey, K., *Edwardian Portraits, Images of an Age of Opulence*, Woodbridge, 1987.

Martin, D., *The Glasgow School of Painting*, London 1897 (Edinburgh, reprint 1976).

Shaw Sparrow, Walter, *John Lavery and his Work*, London (Kegan Paul, Trench, Trubner and Co. Ltd), n.d. (1911), with a preface by R. B. Cunninghame Graham (herein *Shaw Sparrow*).

Shone, R., *A Century of Change, British Painting since 1900*, Oxford, 1977.

UNPUBLISHED SOURCES

Tate Gallery Archives, collection of letters, cuttings etc. donated by Lady Sempill, 1972.

Trinity College, Dublin, collection of letters from Sir John and Lady Lavery to Thomas Bodkin.

University of Glasgow Library, collection of letters from Lavery to Whistler and D. S. MacColl.

National Library of Scotland, Edinburgh, collection of letters from Lavery to R. B. Cunninghame Graham.

Mrs Jacqueline Donnelly, Lady Lavery's scrapbook and associated correspondence.

Mr Ivan Downing, Eddie Cleneghan's scrapbook, and correspondence between Lavery and his cousin Kate.

LAVERY EXHIBITIONS

London, Goupil Gallery, 'Pictures by John Lavery', June 1891 (35 works)

London, Leicester Galleries, 'Cabinet Pictures by John Lavery', with a prefatory note by R. B. Cunninghame Graham, November 1904 (49 works)

London, Goupil Gallery, 'John Lavery RSA, RHA', June—July 1908 (66 works)

Venice, Biennale, 1910 (53 works)

London, Grosvenor Gallery, 'A Retrospective Exhibition of the works of John Lavery 1880—1914', June—July 1914 (150 works)

London, Alpine Club Gallery, 'Pictures of Morocco, The Riviera, and other scenes by Sir John Lavery, RA: Portrait and Child Studies by Lady Lavery', 1921, with a foreword by The Rt Hon. Winston S. Churchill, PC, MP (26 works by Sir John Lavery and 28 by Lady Lavery)

London, Leicester Galleries, 'Portrait Interiors', October 1925 (23 works)

New York, Duveen Galleries, 'Portraits, Interiors and Landscapes by Sir John Lavery RA, RSA, RHA, LLD', November—December 1925 (35 works)

Boston, Robert C. Vose Galleries, 'Portraits and Landscapes of Sir John Lavery RA', December 1925 to January 1926 (34 works)

Pittsburgh, Carnegie Institute, 'Portraits, Interiors and Landscapes by Sir John Lavery', March—April 1926 (49 works)

London, P. & D. Colnaghi & Co., 'Their Majesties' Court, Buckingham Palace, 1931, Portrait Studies and Other Sketches by Sir John Lavery RA' 1932 (81 works)

Dundee, Victoria Art Galleries, 'Paintings by Sir John Lavery, Kt, RA, RSA', September 1936 (48 works)

London, Leicester Galleries, 'Memorial Exhibition of Paintings by the late Sir John Lavery RA', April 1941, with an introduction by Edward Knoblock (53 works)

Belfast, Museum and Art Gallery, 'Loan Exhibition of paintings by Sir John Lavery, RA, 1856—1941', June 1951 (35 works)

London, Spink & Son, 'Sir John Lavery, RA, 1856—1941', June—July 1971, with an introduction by Lady Sempill (70 works)

St Andrews, Crawford Art Centre, 'John Lavery, The Early Career', catalogue by David Scruton, 1983 (41 works)

Edinburgh and London, The Fine Art Society; Belfast, Ulster Museum; Dublin, National Gallery of Ireland, 'Sir John Lavery RA, 1856—1941', catalogue of an exhibition by Kenneth McConkey (115 works)

GENERAL EXHIBITIONS

Glasgow Art Gallery and Museum, 'The Glasgow Boys 1880—1900' organised by the Scottish Arts Council, 1968

London, Royal Academy of Arts, 'Bicentenary Exhibition', 1968

Helensburgh and District Art Club, 'Helensburgh and the Glasgow School', 1972

Glasgow Art Gallery and Museum, 'Scottish Painting 1880—1930', 1973

London, The Fine Art Society, 'The Glasgow School', 1970

Bradford, Cartwright Hall, 'Edwardian Reflections', 1975

Bradford and Hull, Cartwright Hall and Ferens Art Gallery, 'English Impressions', 1978

London, The Royal Academy of Arts, 'Post-Impressionism', 1979

Newcastle upon Tyne, Polytechnic Art Gallery, 'Artists and the Great War', 1979

Glasgow and London, The Fine Art Society, 'Guthrie and the Scottish Realists', 1981

London, Arts Council of Great Britain, 'Landscape in Britain, 1850—1950', 1983

Dublin, National Gallery of Ireland, 'The Irish Impressionists', 1984

London, Christie's, 'The New English Art Club Centenary Exhibition', 1986

London, Royal Academy of Arts, 'The Edwardians and After, the Royal Academy 1900—1950', 1988

Dublin, Hugh Lane Municipal Art Gallery, 'Frank O'Meara and his Contemporaries,' 1989

Nottingham, Castle Museum, 'British Impressionism', 1989

Cologne, Wallrat Richartz Museum, '*Landschaft im licht*, 1860—1910', 1990

London, Mall Galleries, 'Royal Society of Portrait Painters, Centenary Exhibition', 1991

London, Tate Gallery, 'The Swagger Portrait', 1992

Works by Lavery have regularly appeared in recent years in the catalogues of The Fine Art Society, Pyms Gallery, London, and Richard Green. Where relevant these have been cited in the text.

ARTICLES

Anon., 'Mr Lavery and Modern Art', *The Connoisseur*, 1914, pp. 273—4.

Brinton, Selwyn, MA, 'An English Artist in Morocco', *The Connoisseur*, 1907, pp. 34—41.

Brinton, Selwyn, MA, 'Some Recent Paintings by John Lavery, RSA, RHA,' *The Studio*, vol. XVI, 1908, pp. 171—80.

Carter, A. C. R., 'John Lavery RSA', *The Art Journal*, 1904, pp. 6—11.

Carter, A. C. R., 'Recent Work by Mr Lavery', *The Art Journal*, 1908, pp. 233—6.

Davis, Frank, 'Sir John Lavery, RA', *Octagon*, vol. VIII, Summer 1971, pp. 4—9

Little, James Stanley, 'A Cosmopolitan Painter: John Lavery', *The Studio*, vol. XXVII, 1902—3, pp. 3—13, 110—19.

MacCarthy, Desmond, 'Sir John Lavery's Portrait Interiors', *Apollo*, vol. 2, 1925, pp. 267—73

MacFall, Haldane, 'The Art of John Lavery', *The Academy*, December 1904, pp. 645—6.

McConkey, Kenneth, 'From Grez to Glasgow: French Naturalist Influence in Scottish Painting', *Scottish Art Review*, vol. XV, November 1982, pp. 16—34.

McConkey, Kenneth, 'Hazel in Black and Gold', *Irish Arts Review*, vol. 1, no. 3, pp. 12—17.

McConkey, Kenneth, 'The White City—Sir John Lavery in Tangier', *The GPA Irish Arts Review Yearbook, 1989—90*, pp. 55—62.

Mauclair, Camille, 'John Lavery', *L'Art et Les Artistes*, Tome 2, 1905, pp. 6—10.

Ross, Robert, and Montague, C. E., 'British Artists at the Front II, Sir John Lavery ARA', 1918.

Stodart Walker, A., 'The Art of John Lavery, RSA, ARA, etc.', *The Studio*, vol. LXII, 1914, pp. 3—16.

Von H. S., 'John Lavery', *Die Kunst fur alle*, vol. 24, 1908, pp. 417—22.

Index

Page numbers in italics refer to illustrations and captions.